THE ROUTLEDGE HANDBOOK OF
ACCOUNTING INFORMATION SYSTEMS

The Routledge Handbook of Accounting Information Systems is a prestige reference work offering a comprehensive overview of the state of current knowledge and emerging scholarship in the discipline of AIS.

The pace of technological-driven change is rapid, and this revised edition provides a deeper focus on the technical underpinnings and organisational consequences of accounting information systems. It has been updated to capture the changes in technology since the previous edition. It now includes chapters and scholarly thought on artificial intelligence, predictive analytics and data visualisation, among others. Contributions from an international cast of authors provide a balanced overview of established and developing themes, identifying issues and discussing relevant debates. The chapters are analytical and engaging. Many chapters include cases or examples, and some provide additional resources for readers. The chapters also provide a reflection on where the research agenda is likely to advance in the future.

This is a complete and indispensable guide for students and researchers in accounting and accounting information systems, academics and students seeking convenient access to an unfamiliar area, as well as established researchers seeking a single repository on the current debates and literature in the field.

Erik Strauss is Professor of Accounting and Control at Witten/Herdecke University, Witten, Germany.

Martin Quinn is Professor of Management Accounting and Accounting History at Queen's Management School, Queen's University Belfast, Northern Ireland.

'Brings together some key insights on the interface between accounting and information systems.'

— *Al Bhimani, London School of Economics, UK*

'This book provides a good introduction to AIS and the contemporary research that is being done on it. Given the growth and influence of AIS on our daily lives, as touched on within the chapters, it is timely that such a book be produced.'

— *Stephen Jollands, University of Exeter, UK*

'Finally a text that addresses the organizational aspects of AIS! Covering the most recent insights from multiple knowledge domains – change, integration, implementation, it is all there!'

— *Hanno Roberts, Norwegian Business School, Norway*

THE ROUTLEDGE HANDBOOK OF ACCOUNTING INFORMATION SYSTEMS

Second Edition

Edited by Erik Strauss and Martin Quinn

Routledge
Taylor & Francis Group

LONDON AND NEW YORK

Cover image: monsitj/Getty Images

Second edition published 2023
by Routledge
4 Park Square, Milton Park, Abingdon, Oxon, OX14 4RN

and by Routledge
605 Third Avenue, New York, NY 10158

Routledge is an imprint of the Taylor & Francis Group, an informa business

First edition published by Routledge 2017

British Library Cataloguing-in-Publication Data
A catalogue record for this book is available from the British Library

Library of Congress Cataloging-in-Publication Data
Names: Quinn, Martin, 1973– editor. | Strauss, Erik, 1982– editor.
Title: The Routledge handbook of accounting information systems /
edited by Martin Quinn and Erik Strauss.
Other titles: Routledge companion to accounting information systems.
Description: 2nd edition. | Abingdon, Oxon; New York, NY: Routledge,
2023. | Series: Routledge international handbooks | Earlier edition
published as: The Routledge companion to accounting information
systems. | Includes bibliographical references and index.
Identifiers: LCCN 2022022298 (print) | LCCN 2022022299 (ebook) |
ISBN 9780367678111 (hardback) | ISBN 9780367678135 (paperback) |
ISBN 9781003132943 (ebook)
Subjects: LCSH: Accounting—Data processing. | Management
information systems.
Classification: LCC HF5679 .R68 2023 (print) | LCC HF5679 (ebook) |
DDC 657.0285—dc23/eng/20220623
LC record available at https://lccn.loc.gov/2022022298
LC ebook record available at https://lccn.loc.gov/2022022299

ISBN: 978-0-367-67811-1 (hbk)
ISBN: 978-0-367-67813-5 (pbk)
ISBN: 978-1-003-13294-3 (ebk)

DOI: 10.4324/9781003132943

Typeset in Bembo
by codeMantra

CONTENTS

Contents

FIGURES

TABLES

CONTRIBUTORS

Benoit A. Aubert is a Professor at HEC Montreal (Canada) and a Fellow of the CIRANO (Center for Interuniversity Research and Analysis on Organizations). His previous roles include Director of the Rowe School of Business at Dalhousie University and Head of the School of Information Management at Victoria University of Wellington (New Zealand). His main research areas are risk management, innovation, outsourcing and business transformation.

Joan Ballantine is an accounting graduate and a Fellow of the Association of Chartered Certified Accountant (FCCA). After working in industry, she took up her first lecturing position at Queen's University Belfast and subsequently joined Warwick Business School, Warwick University. During her ten years at Warwick, Joan gained her doctorate and was actively engaged in delivering executive education/consultancy to a range of private- and public-sector organisations. She returned to Northern Ireland to take up the post of Senior Lecturer at Queen's University Belfast before being appointed to her current position as Professor in Accounting at Ulster University in 2008. She is an active researcher, has been published in IS and accounting journals (*EJIS, JIT, MAR, FAM, JOBE, SIHE, Accounting Forum, Accounting Education*), sits on a number of editorial board positions and has examined numerous doctorates. She has almost 3,500 citations to her name according to Google Scholar: https://scholar.google.com/citations?hl=en&user=VnGdN7cAAAAJ.

Jean-Grégoire Bernard is a Senior Lecturer at the Victoria School of Business and Government at Victoria University of Wellington in New Zealand. His research focuses on issues pertaining to digital innovation, online communities and online disinformation. His work has been published in *Social Media + Society, Information Technology for Development, Communications of the Association for Information Systems* and the International Conference on Information Systems.

Dr. Bibek Bhatta is a Lecturer in the areas of accounting and finance at Queen's University Belfast. Bibek worked in commercial banks for more than five years before completing his PhD in finance. His banking experience centres mainly around credit analysis and credit control. He has delivered lectures in finance in both developed and developing countries.

His research interests lie in international investments, corporate governance, corporate finance and fintech.

Sharlene Biswas is a Lecturer at the University of Auckland Business School. She teaches courses on management control systems, cost accounting, and performance measurement and evaluation and has research interests in innovation practices and family businesses.

Dr. Malcolm Brady is an Associate Professor at DCU Business School, Dublin City University, where he teaches business strategy to undergraduate, masters and executive students. He researches in the areas of business strategy, business processes and business models drawing on game and institutional theory. He has a particular interest in health and education sectors.

Krister Bredmar holds a position as Professor in Business Administration, School of Business and Economics at Linnaeus University in Sweden. He has, in over 30 years, interested himself in how information systems affect managers in different ways. His research has been published internationally both in articles and in books. His current research deals with digital transformation in SMEs.

Dr. Noel Carroll is a Lecturer in Business Information Systems at NUI Galway and Programme Director for the MSc in Information Systems Management (ISM). He is also a researcher with Lero – the Irish Software Research Centre. His research interests include seeking ways to support organisations in developing transformation strategies, for example, large-scale agile transformations, digital innovation and health informatics for multinationals, SMEs and start-ups. He enjoys exploring new (interdisciplinary) theoretical perspectives around managing and sustaining transformation processes. Noel has edited special issues, published, chaired and reviewed for leading international journals and conferences in his field.

Further details are available here: https://www.nuigalway.ie/business-public-policy-law/cairnes/ourstaff/noelcarroll/.

Dr. Peter Cleary is a Senior Lecturer in Accounting. He has been lecturing at University College Cork (UCC) in Ireland in the area of Management Accounting since 2002. A graduate of UCC and a qualified Chartered Management Accountant (ACMA), Dr. Cleary has worked for organisations in both Ireland and the USA prior to becoming an academic. Dr. Cleary completed his doctoral dissertation at the University of Limerick in 2007 which focused on the role of management accounting in knowledge-intensive firms. He regularly presents his research at both national and international conferences. Dr. Cleary is currently the Academic Programme Director for the BSc (Accounting) degree at UCC.

Brenda Clerkin has over 14 years' experience working in practice with a Big 4 professional services firm before her career in academia. Her experience spanned from small and medium enterprises, based in the UK and Ireland, to large multinational organisations across a number of different industries. Her interests are in Accounting, Auditing, Data Analytics and Ethics.

W. Alec Cram is an Assistant Professor in the School of Accounting & Finance at the University of Waterloo, Canada. His research focuses on how information systems control initiatives can contribute to improving the performance of organisational processes, including systems development and cybersecurity management. His work has been published in outlets including *Information Systems Journal*, *Information & Management*, *European Journal of Information Systems*, *MIS Quarterly*, *Information Systems Research* and *Journal of the Association for Information Systems*.

Andrea Crean is an Accounting Lecturer, specialising in Financial Reporting and Auditing, and also holds the position of Programme Director of the Master's in International Accounting and Analytics at NUI Galway. She obtained an undergraduate degree in Accounting and Finance and a first class Master's in Accounting from Dublin City University. She is a Fellow of the Institute of Chartered Accountants, Ireland, and prior to joining NUI Galway four years ago, Andrea has seven years' experience working in practice and industry roles. Andrea is currently pursuing her PhD in the area of innovation in auditing through the use of big data and data analytics.

Christoph Eisl is Professor for Controlling and Head of the Master's degree programme Accounting, Controlling and Financial Management. His teaching and research activities focus on controlling and performance management, business planning, information visualisation, digital accounting and accounting education.

Robert D. Galliers is the University Distinguished Professor Emeritus and former Provost of Bentley University and Professor Emeritus and former Dean of Warwick Business School. He was the founding Editor-in-Chief of *The Journal of Strategic Information Systems* up till the end of 2018 and was the President of the Association for Information Systems (AIS), of which he is a Fellow, in 1999. He received the AIS LEO Award in 2012. His work has been cited over 15,000 times according to Google Scholar.

Markus Granlund is the Dean and Professor of Accounting at the Turku School of Economics, University of Turku. Markus' key areas of expertise are strategic financial management, information system solutions and strategic management. His research has been published in highly respected scientific journals, and he is also an award-winning management educator. Markus has long been involved with various development projects in companies and the public sector. He also holds a number of positions of trust in the university sector, foundations and companies.

Steven A. Harrast, PhD, teaches accounting information systems and data analytics in the School of Accounting at Central Michigan University. He received his PhD in 1999 from the University of Memphis and is a frequent publisher and speaker on information technology topics.

Martin R. W. Hiebl is Professor of Management Accounting and Control at the University of Siegen and a Visiting Professor at the Johannes Kepler University Linz. His research concentrates on management accounting and control, risk management and digital transformation, with a focus on family firms and small businesses. He is also interested in contemporary business research methods and their further development. His work has been published in the *European Accounting Review*, *European Management Review*, *Journal of Management Accounting Research*, *Management Accounting Research* and *Organizational Research Methods*, among others.

Peter Hofer is Professor of Managerial Accounting and BI at the University of Applied Sciences Upper Austria in Steyr. His main research areas are information design, user-centred Big Data visualisation and managerial accounting. He is the author of several publications in these research areas and also speaker on conferences for researchers and practitioners. Peter Hofer is also a Lecturer at the Management Academy in Linz (LIMAK) in the field of Cost Accounting and Cost Management. Before his academic career, he has worked as an accounting manager in the automotive industry.

Esperanza Huerta is a Professor in the Department of Accounting and Finance in the Lucas College of Business at San José State University. She does research on data science, human–computer interaction, automated internal controls and blockchain. Her publications have appeared in major journals and conferences in the Accounting Information Systems area.

Scott Jensen is an Associate Professor in the School of Information Systems & Technology at San José State University focusing on big data and has published in international conferences and journals such as the *Journal of Information Systems*. Prior to his PhD in Computer Science, he worked for over 15 years in software development and professional services at Big 4 accounting firms.

Carina Knoll is an aspiring researcher in the field of Digital Accounting at the University of Applied Sciences Upper Austria. With a background in sociology and management, her interests are the humanist implications of the digital transformation in accounting and auditing. In this, she looks at new job roles, tasks, team compositions and educational avenues in the larger financial service sectors.

Gerhard Kristandl is an Associate Professor of Accounting and Technology-enhanced Learning at the University of Greenwich. He is the Faculty Business Learning Technologist and the Head of the Greenwich SAP Next-Gen Lab. He has recently published in the area of enabling technologies in higher education. He also runs a YouTube channel on enabling learning technologies and regularly blogs in this area.

Prof. Dr. Othmar M. Lehner works in the fields of AI-based accounting and impact investing. As Professor of Accounting and Finance in London at the Middlesex University, and in Helsinki at the Hanken School of Economics, with an additional background in information sciences, he uses his knowledge to drive forward the field through high-impact publications, keynotes at global industry events and through consulting in the banking and investment industry. He is also the Director of the Hanken Center of Accounting, Finance and Governance in Helsinki.

Dr. Susanne Leitner-Hanetseder is Professor of Accounting at the University of Applied Sciences Upper Austria in Steyr. Her research focuses on the digitalisation and automation of financial processes. As part of her research, she supports companies in their digital transformation. She has gained experience in the financial industry and accounting consulting. She is a Lecturer at the Johannes Kepler University (Linz/Austria) and Hanken School of Economics (Helsinki/Finland) in the field of International Accounting. Additionally, she is a speaker at Accounting and Finance conferences. She is the author of several papers in the field of national and international accounting and digitalisation and automation of accounting and finance.

Heimo Losbichler is Professor of Controlling, Head of Studies Controlling, Accounting and Financial Management, and elected Dean of the School of Business and Management at the University of Applied Sciences Upper Austria. He is the Chairman of the International Controller Association and the Chairman of the International Group of Controlling.

Theo Lynn is Full Professor of Digital Business at DCU Business School, Ireland. Professor Lynn specialises in the role of digital technologies in transforming business processes.

Danielle McConville is a Senior Lecturer (Education) in Accounting at Queen's University Belfast and a Chartered Accountant (CAI). Danielle holds a PhD in Accounting from QUB, and her research interests are in charity regulation, accountability, transparency and trust. Her teaching experience at UG/PGT level includes Accounting Information Systems, Management Accounting and Not-for-Profits. She also has extensive experience in delivering Executive Education for QUB's Clinton Leadership Institute and in teaching for CAI's professional accounting qualifications. She has been an examiner for the Information Systems paper for CPA Ireland's professional accounting qualification.

Dr. Tadhg Nagle is a Lecturer (Business Information Systems) at Cork University Business School (CUBS), University College Cork (UCC), and an Associate Faculty at the Irish Management Institute (IMI). He specialises in the business value of data. Tadhg has created a number of tools and techniques (such as the Data Value Map – http://datavaluemap.com) to aid organisations in getting the most out of data assets. He has also developed a brand of applied research (Practitioner Design Science Research) that arms practitioners with a simple and scientific methodology in solving wicked problems. He is currently an Associate Investigator on the SFI-funded FinTechNext project, investigating the value and impact of Open Banking. Tadhg has also published in a range of international journals (such as *Harvard Business Review*) and presented at several international academic and practitioner conferences.

Winnie O'Grady is a Senior Lecturer in Management Accounting at the University of Auckland. She has taught courses in Accounting Information Systems, Cost and Revenue Management, Strategic Management Accounting and Management Control Systems.

João Oliveira is an Assistant Professor at the University of Porto School of Economics and Business (FEP.UP), Director of the Master's in Accounting and Management Control, Visiting Professor at HEC Paris, Invited Professor at Porto Business School (PBS) and Board Member of the EAA – European Accounting Association.

Victoria Paulsson is a Lecturer in Information Systems at Linköping University, Sweden. She holds a PhD in Information Systems from Lund University, Sweden. She was a postdoctoral researcher in cloud computing at Dublin City University, Ireland. She is responsible for courses in Enterprise Systems, Project Management and Perspectives on Digitalisation.

Lisa Perkhofer has Bachelor's and Master's degrees in Finance and a Doctorate in Information Systems. She is employed since 2011 at the University of Applied Sciences Upper Austria where she was part of multiple research projects dealing with information processing, information visualisation and big data visualisation. Her research focus is mostly quantitative, and the methods used range from eye tracking to structural equation modelling.

Martin Quinn is Professor of Management Accounting and Accounting History at Queen's Management School, Queen's University Belfast, Northern Ireland.

Maria Céu Ribeiro is a Certified Accountant with more than 30 years of accounting experience in auditing. She is an audit Director in Oporto PwC office, responsible for carrying out, coordination and control of several auditing engagements, consolidation and internal control, and a member of the Technical Committee. She teaches Forensic Auditing/External Auditing at postgraduate level.

Paulo J. Ribeiro is Chief Financial Officer at OLI - Sistemas Sanitários, S.A (oli-world.com) and a PhD student in Management FEP Porto. His interests are in strategy and management control, business intelligence and analytics.

Pierangelo Rosati is an Assistant Professor in Business Analytics at Dublin City University and a Co-Deputy Director of the Irish Institute of Digital Business. He previously worked as a Postdoctoral Researcher in the Irish Centre for Cloud Computing and Commerce (IC4). Dr. Rosati specialises in measuring the business value of digital technologies such as big data analytics, cloud computing, social media and blockchain.

Daniel Schallmo is a Digit-Angelist, economist, management consultant, lecturer and author. He is Professor of Digital Transformation and Entrepreneurship at the Neu-Ulm University of Applied Science, Director at the Institute for Entrepreneurship and member at the Institute for Digital Transformation. His research focuses on digitalisation (digital maturity, digital strategy, digital transformation of business models and digital implementation) and the development and application of methods to the innovation of business models, mainly in business-to-business markets. He is the author of numerous publications (10+ books, 20+ articles) and a speaker (100+ speeches; 7,000+ participants). He is a member of various research societies and a reviewer.

Erik Strauss is Professor of Accounting and Control at Witten/Herdecke University, Witten, Germany.

Henri Teittinen holds a PhD in Accounting and works as an Assistant Professor in UEF Business School at the University of Eastern Finland. He has specialised in management accounting and management control issues.

Christopher Williams, MA, MBA, is a researcher in innovation management and entrepreneurship with a broad range of experience in human resource, business and innovation management in research and industry. Christopher has more than ten years of teaching and research experience in multidisciplinary and applied research.

David A. Wood is Glenn D. Ardis Professor of Accounting at Brigham Young University. David has published over 100 articles in a combination of respected academic and practitioner journals, monographs, books and cases. He also works with the EY ARC to develop curriculum that is provided for free to academics throughout the world.

INTRODUCTION TO HANDBOOK OF ACCOUNTING INFORMATION SYSTEMS

Erik Strauss and Martin Quinn

When the first edition of this *Handbook to Accounting Information Systems* was published – or *Companion* as it was called – we had thought that information technology (IT) had permeated all walks of life. Just around five years later, we find ourselves in a very different world. Even more areas of private and corporate life have been influenced, shaped, and restructured by IT. Five years ago, technologies such as robotic process automation (RPA) had been in their infancy, blockchain was just a new trend, and data visualisation played a minor role during the publication of the first edition. Today, these two technologies (and many more) are already reality in some parts of corporate practice. Therefore, we deemed it necessary to update the *Companion to Accounting Information Systems* to offer a comprehensive and contemporary guide to students and academics and reveal the state of current knowledge on accounting information systems (AIS). Particular attention is paid to providing students and academics a balanced view of both the technical underpinnings and organisational consequences of AIS, with emphasis on the latter. To achieve this aim, the book is structured in 22 chapters, which we outline below. The chapters are organised into four parts. Part 1 (Chapters 1–5) explores the basics of what we term the AIS discipline; Part 2 (Chapters 6–14) explores the organisational effects of AIS; Part 3 (Chapters 15–18) looks at the controlling of AIS; and finally, Part 4 (Chapters 19–22) looks to the future.

Chapter 1 provides general introduction to AIS. It begins by examining how accounting information is used both within and outside organisations, before describing the role occupied by information systems (IS). Rapid advances in IT have led to the development of a suite of accounting-based IS, collectively known as AIS. These systems are then critiqued before considering the future role for both accounting and accountants in the digital economy and beyond.

Chapter 2 provides a summary on the evolution of AIS, from when the first rudimentary versions of AIS were adopted to the information age with the adoption of mainframes and Enterprise Resource Planning (ERP) systems to the present with the increasing adoption of business intelligence and data analytics capabilities. The technological development of AIS is also discussed in relation to how the role of accountants has changed over time.

Chapter 3 explains the technologies underpinning AIS. After clarifying the general relationship between AIS and technology, the chapter reveals networks as a necessary technological feature of AIS, before the components that are aligned to build and run an AIS are

DOI: 10.4324/9781003132943-1

discussed, namely hardware and software. As such, this chapter adopts a drill-down approach to illustrate the technologies that underpin modern AIS.

Chapter 4 presents key considerations on developing IS for the contemporary accounting profession. Particularly, it outlines the growing capabilities of IS and the growing expectations this sets across the industry. The chapter also describes the use of AIS and how systems development and methods play a key role to inform their design and development as well as the impact of systems development within the accounting profession and the growing demands for accountants with skills in data analytics.

Chapter 5 deals with change management in the context of AIS. In this chapter, the emphasis is on describing the background behind AIS and its role in changing organisations. Even though advanced IS, in general, and modern AIS, in particular, bring new opportunities to an organisation and the management function, it is important to first understand the new context in which AIS is situated. It is also important to understand the challenges managers are facing when trying to benefit from more advanced systems and try to grasp where AIS trends are heading and what kind of change that brings.

Chapter 6 examines the significance of a holistic view on digitalisation by presenting the fundamental levels for strategically oriented digitalisation and relevant concepts to advance the field. Therefore, it presents the fundamental levels including digital strategy, digital transformation, and digital implementation. Additionally, the chapter provides procedure models for each fundamental level and additional insights (e.g. generic option for digital strategy).

Chapter 7 links AIS and decision making. It outlines how AIS can support managerial decision making in contemporary organisations. The authors suggest some future trends regarding this topic by describing the factors constituting different decision-making environments and what they call data environments. This lays a foundation for describing what kind of information is needed in different contexts and how AIS can support managers in making informed decisions.

Chapter 8 presents a mini case documenting the role of AIS in promoting the continuous improvement (CI) culture of a company. It discusses how the organisation-wide and vernacular AIS support CI culture and motivate CI initiatives. The presented evidence reveals that mutual interdependence between CI culture and AIS creates a reinforcing cycle of learning and improvement. It also shows that different components of the AIS can operate on different levels of aggregation and temporal cycles yet provide a consistent view of performance. Moreover, it demonstrates that carefully designed AIS can provide timely, relevant, and easy-to-understand information to drive CI.

Chapter 9 explores the inherent dynamics of Artificial Intelligence in Accounting (AIA) through a large-scale Delphi study based on 138 participants over three rounds. Based on Giddens' structuration theory, it critically analyses the structures of signification, legitimisation, and domination and more closely examines how powerful, highly knowledgeable actors of human and robotic natures influence the actual "enactment" of practices in AIA systems. As a result, the chapter identifies three maturity levels of the development of AI in accounting, elaborates on the role of time and geographical distance in future accounting teams, and furthermore finds new powerful actors, such as the chief financial and information officer (CFIO).

Chapter 10 discusses options for outsourcing AIS. It starts by defining outsourcing, clarifying the difference to offshoring, and providing examples of numerous ways outsourcing can be used for AIS. Following this definition, key decisions associated with outsourcing are described. When trying to appreciate issues associated with the outsourcing of AIS, the chapter reveals that it is important to realise that a large proportion of issues are the same as the ones associated with outsourcing of IS in general. Therefore, elements presented in this chapter are not limited to accounting and might also provide insights into outsourcing more generally.

Chapter 11 elaborates the influences of recent digital technologies and data sciences upon the Accounting and Finance (A&F) area. It discusses ERP systems, business intelligence and analytics, RPA, AI, machine learning, big data, cloud, internet of things, and blockchain. For each of three major A&F functions – financial accounting, management accounting, and control and treasury – the influences of these technologies are analysed.

Chapter 12 explores the transformative impact of predictive analytics on the accounting profession. It clarifies what predictive analytics is and how it differs from other techniques accountants use to support decision making and explains how predictive analytics can be valuable to people within the organisation and outside of it. In addition, it also discusses the increasing prevalence of predictive analytics for assurance purposes – its adoption, platforms developed, uses to which it is put, and personnel training.

Chapter 13 focuses on coding skills and highlights two important areas where coding skills are expected to become more useful and necessary for accountants in the future. Firstly, workflow automation is an area that would be beneficial to enhance efficiency. Secondly, the ability to analyse and extract meaningful information out of ever-increasing volume of big data would also be invaluable. This chapter further focuses on this second issue to provide readers a starting point to handle big data with illustrative examples and introduce them to Python.

Chapter 14 introduces big data visualisations to the accounting community and lay out the benefits of big data visualisations as well as propose appropriate areas of applications. Visualisation types introduced range from visualisations to display multiple hierarchies, over the display of multiple attributes and datasets with multiple and large time-series data to geographical visualisations.

Chapter 15 critically reflects on data security and quality, providing a broad overview of the role of data within AIS, with a primary focus on the risks to security and quality. It examines a range of security and quality risks, corresponding internal controls, and the organisational implications of a data security program. For practitioners, this chapter can help to establish a holistic, integrated understanding of the links between data security and quality risks, corresponding countermeasures, and organisational outcomes. For researchers, this chapter draws on a range of AIS, management IS, and cybersecurity research to highlight the integrative nature of accounting processes, technology, and information security as it pertains to the data used within today's organisations.

Chapter 16 explores audit tools and approaches to enable continuous auditing, in the context of today's connected and complex IS. It discusses how the increasingly real-time nature of business and accounting data affects auditing and highlights the contributions of a continuous auditing approach. It characterises the technological framework of continuous auditing and presents the current state of the art. Finally, it identifies the persistent challenges of current efforts of improving auditing procedures in the context of new AIS and proliferation of big data.

Chapter 17 discusses the status of RPA technology, the various choices of automation technologies, the process of automation, challenges with RPA, and questions for future research. It presents a recent framework for selecting tasks to automate and discuss opportunities for individuals to learn RPA development skills, including cases designed for educators to use in class. Finally, it also discusses several of the known RPA challenges.

Chapter 18 presents key ideas on how firms can use their AIS to support business strategy. The chapter outlines a two-by-two matrix representing a strategic AIS framework based upon two fundamental dimensions: the strategy type (cost leader versus differentiator) and the software acquisition mode (build versus buy). A key contribution of the chapter is the identification of the critical factors involved in the choice of AIS to support the business strategy. It also considers the implications for AIS of new forms of business competition afforded by platforms, networks, and ecosystems and new modes of transferring and recording value through cryptocurrencies and blockchain.

Chapter 19 explores four contemporary technologies – data analytics, AI, RPA, and blockchain – and their integration with AIS. In this vein, it discusses the advantages that accompany those technologies as well as require the change of accountants' skillset and organisational structures.

Chapter 20 discusses several perspectives on how technology is shaping "us", both individually and as a society. Several biases are outlined, such as whether we as human beings think technology is shaping us in a good way and if we think our technological future is going to be a good place for us as a society overall. The motivation for the chapter comes from a need to be mindful of the impact of technology and possibly get us to recognise our own biases and, as a result, help us make more rational decisions for the future. However, this mindfulness only comes about when we examine a wide spectrum of perspectives, from the contrarian to conformist, technophile to luddite, and utopian to dystopian. This chapter might build the starting point for more fruitful discussions that will provide a more rounded view on the socio-technical nature of IS.

Chapter 21 summarises traditional challenges in IS implementation and discusses some of the issues arising from the deployment of digital technologies including migration to the cloud, security, data protection and information and communication technologies governance, contractual issues in the cloud, big data, and mobility.

Chapter 22 presents new developments in IT and calls for action. This chapter particularly considers major developments taking place in new information technologies such as ERP systems and, more recently, so-called big data analytics, AI, blockchain technology, and algorithmic decision making. It also considers the implications of such developments, in terms of organisational capabilities, with reference to the A&F professions. It commences with a reflection on ERP systems as a potential strategic asset and then consider big data in a similar light. Implications for accounting practice and for A&F professionals are then considered.

We hope these 22 chapters provide a good scholarly overview of the current state of AIS and with some eye to the future. Having said that, the pace of technological change today is quite fast, and we cannot hope to keep up with all changes, nor can we hope to predict them. Despite this, we can take from these chapters and point to one major issue which will, we think, be the subject of much future research on the organisation consequences of AIS. While prior IT developments primarily unburdened accountants from more routine tasks such as data gathering and processing, newer developments also take over more advanced tasks such as data analyses and interpretation that are at the heart of accountants' current value adding work. Consequently, the question emerges how accountants can justify their existence in the future and how they can still use IT to leverage their own performance. We submit that accountants will need to improve their business know-how to contextualise data and analyses provided by ever improving AIS. Furthermore, they need to develop psychological skills to be able to support the acceptance of and trust in those AIS. Against this backdrop, we emphasise that the technological developments will not reduce the relevance of human actors in organisational decision-making process but quite the opposite, i.e. the human side of the human being in the sense of emotions and gut feelings becomes even more relevant as humans might detect or avoid wrong decisions.

PART 1

The accounting information systems discipline

1

INTRODUCTION TO ACCOUNTING INFORMATION SYSTEMS

Peter Cleary

Introduction

The use of accounting information has been traced back many thousands of years and originally emerged as a means to allow wealthy individuals keep track of their assets as they bought, sold and/or traded them. Double-entry bookkeeping was first described in 1494 by an Italian monk named Luca Pacioli, in referring to the system of debits and credits used by merchants in Venice. This system of recording still underpins modern (financial) accounting systems to the present day.

Over time, the commercial environment gradually evolved from primarily family-owned firms to increasingly large and complex entities, encompassing a wide variety of stakeholders (e.g. investors, suppliers, customers), each with their own information requirements. This led to a demand for more sophisticated accounting information. Consequently, two distinct forms of accounting (i.e. financial accounting and management accounting) were developed to satisfy these additional informational requirements. In recent times, rapid advances in technology, and the emergence of the internet and the digital economy, have spawned entirely new industries and have led to the creation of an interconnected society whereby the provision and utilisation of data, information and knowledge are considered amongst the key drivers of economic success. Indeed, the availability of these so-called disruptive technologies means that accounting currently exists within organisations in the form of a suite of interlinked, digitally enabled information technology (IT)[1] systems. Indeed, such is the reliance on information systems (IS)[2] nowadays that it is difficult to envisage modern organisations being able to function effectively without them.

As the first chapter of this handbook, the aim here is to provide a general introduction to accounting information systems (AIS). The chapter begins by defining what is meant by accounting before outlining the potential use of accounting-based information. It then proceeds to introduce the concept of IS, before specifically addressing AIS. After providing a brief but critical analysis of AIS, the chapter concludes by pondering the future for both accountants and accounting in the digital economy. Subsequent chapters will provide much more detailed insights from contemporary research on various topics mentioned in this chapter.

DOI: 10.4324/9781003132943-3

Accounting

Accounting has been defined as:

> The process of identifying, measuring and communicating economic information to permit informed judgements and decisions by users of the information.
>
> *(American Accounting Association, 1966, p. 1)*

Accounting is generally deemed to consist of two distinct disciplinary areas: financial accounting and management accounting. Financial accounting aims to provide a summary of the past financial performance of an entity for a particular period of time (e.g. quarterly, annually) and is primarily used by external parties (e.g. financial institutions, shareholders, suppliers) as a means to evaluate an organisation's recent financial performance. The information provided within the remit of financial accounting, and how it is to be reported upon, is dictated by specific accounting rules and standards. In this regard, the two primary standard-setting bodies in financial reporting are the International Accounting Standards Board, who are responsible for the International Financial Reporting Standards, and the Financial Accounting Standards Board, who are responsible for the US Generally Accepted Accounting Principles. Both bodies refer to the provision of "useful" information to potential decision-makers (e.g. investors), which must demonstrate the qualitative characteristics of relevance and faithful representation. Relevant information should enable a user to make an informed decision, while faithful representation refers to the scenario whereby an organisation's financial statements reflect their actual performance during the reporting period, i.e. they are complete, neutral and free from error.

From a legal perspective, the provision of financial accounting information is mandatory for organisations. As the information provided within the realm of financial reporting is relied upon by a diverse range of stakeholders, it is legally subjected to an annual external audit for the vast majority of firms. This is to ensure that – amongst other objectives – the accounting records are accurate, that they have been completed in accordance with the relevant accounting rules and regulations and that the financial statements presented fairly represent the firm's financial position at a given point in time. Simultaneously, management accounting attempts to forecast and plan the consequences of future organisational events (e.g. the budgeted total revenue or profit for the coming financial year or the expected payback period associated with the purchase of an item of new machinery). This information (both financial and non-financial) is generally used internally by management to facilitate subsequent evidence-based planning and control-based decisions. Unlike the standardised reporting requirement inherent in financial accounting, no such external requirements apply to management accounting, as its adoption by organisations is voluntary.

In the performance of their duties, all accountants are required to adhere to various rules and regulations including the rules of the particular professional accounting body of which they are a member and the commercial laws of the country in which they are employed. In this regard, the enactment of the Sarbanes-Oxley Act (SOX) in the United States of America (USA) in 2002 significantly increased the level of regulation and subsequent compliance tasks that many employed in financial roles globally were subject to. This act was introduced in response to a series of high-profile financial scandals, including Enron, WorldCom and Tyco, which collectively shook investor confidence in financial statement information (De Groot, 2020). A radical overhaul of the incumbent regulatory system was therefore required to restore the faith of investors by protecting them from further fraudulent accounting-based activities. As compliance with SOX is viewed by many as "best practice" in the area of corporate governance, many firms, both private and public, have implemented the terms of the Act, despite not being legally required to do so. According to the terms of the Act, senior management (i.e. the Chief Executive Officer and the Chief Financial Officer) is required to personally review all the financial information provided and to confirm that it does not contain any misrepresentations. They are also collectively responsible for developing and maintaining an "adequate" internal control structure, and all annual financial reports must include a report stating that this is the case coupled with an assessment by management of its effectiveness (Marden et al., 2003). From the external auditors' perspective, it is now their responsibility to confirm management's assertions in this regard coupled with reporting on the state of the overall financial control system. Collectively, the introduction of SOX has significantly increased attention on the accuracy of both the inputs and outputs of various accounting-based IS, especially as the terms of the Act also require firms to keep all of their business-related records and messages (including electronic ones) for a period of at least five years (De Groot, 2020).

As illustrated above, the discipline of accounting continues to evolve in response to changing organisational requirements. This has led some to speculate that financial accounting will ultimately become more forward-looking and, facilitated by advances in IT, will eventually converge with management accounting (Hemmer & Labro, 2008; Taipaleenmaki & Ikaheimo, 2013). Recent research suggests that this convergence has tentatively begun and, in some instances, has resulted in an enhanced level of consistency in financial reporting and better co-operation between those engaged in what traditionally were viewed as distinct financial accounting and management accounting roles (Weißenberger & Angelkort, 2011; Kabalski & Zarzycka, 2018). Indeed, as there can often be significant costs associated with maintaining separate financial and management accounting systems, many smaller organisations maintain a single system whereby their financial accounting information is often used internally by management to inform their decision-making.

From an IS perspective, it has been suggested that the accounting function was one of the first within organisations to regularly use computers from the 1950s onwards. Since then, those employed in this area have continued to embrace new technologies as a means of performing their duties in a more effective and efficient manner. Nowadays, the use of, e.g. cloud-based and mobile accounting software is becoming more prevalent within the accounting function. The next section therefore outlines the role occupied by IS in organisations.

Information systems

In the digital economy where organisations now compete, information is a critical resource that must be effectively managed to be of value as, without it, it would be extremely difficult to survive. As per the definition of IS outlined earlier by Valacich & Schneider (2010), there are various types of IS that can exist within organisations. Examples include, but are not limited to, management information systems (MIS), marketing IS, human resource IS and AIS.

Information differs from data as it has been put in a usable form, whereas data essentially refers to facts and statistics. E.g. sales data can be analysed according to customer, product, etc., therefore allowing management to make informed decisions how they might attempt to increase sales/profits on a customer and/or product basis. As this example illustrates, those occupying accounting-based roles both create and transform data and information. Within an organisational setting, information flows in different directions. e.g. information flows downwards from senior management to mid-level and low-level management in the form of budgetary targets, key performance indicators, non-financial targets, etc., whereas aggregated operational information is communicated upwards from lower levels for use by senior management for planning and control purposes. Additionally, as organisations do not exist in a vacuum, external parties such as suppliers, customers, shareholders, etc. continually exchange data/information with the firm primarily in digital form, which subsequently becomes part of the firm's internal IS.

Irrespective of the type of IS, according to McLaney & Atrill (2010), the output (i.e. information) generated from it must possess certain characteristics for it to be of value, including:

- Relevance – it must have the ability to influence subsequent decisions
- Timeliness – it needs to be provided promptly to inform the decision under consideration
- Accuracy – it should not contain any material errors
- Completeness – all pertinent elements should be included
- Understandability – it must be presented to the user in an easily comprehendible manner
- Comparability – it needs to facilitate the user in making comparisons if required
- Objectivity – any bias on behalf of the compiler(s) should be excluded
- Cost/benefit – the cost of collecting and storing the information should not exceed the likely benefit to be derived from its use

The type of information required by the end user will dictate the choice of IS best equipped to supply it. The use, scale and reliance on organisational IS have dramatically evolved over the course of the last 30 years due to the seismic developments that have occurred in technology. Indeed, the role occupied by IT within organisations has increased to such an extent that those employed in this function are generally regarded as indispensable to the successful operation of their IS and, by implication, the firms themselves.

In terms of the evolution of IS usage within organisations since their initial introduction during the 1970s, Bodnar & Hopwood (2004) report that data processing systems were initially designed to conduct repetitive transaction-oriented tasks and consequently provided little usable information for decision-making purposes. These were followed by MIS, which attempted to provide information to managers in support of their decision-making remit. Decision Support Systems emerged next and sought to process organisational data into a decision-making format suitable for the end user. Specifically, these systems were primarily aimed at supporting the ad hoc and non-routine nature of managerial decisions. Executive information systems (EIS) were then promoted as a necessity for senior management as they were capable of customisation to specific strategic informational requirements, many of whom were external to the organisation. Many EIS allowed management to "drill down" from aggregated data to more specific and detailed data, and in some instances, the data could be displayed in graphical form (Bodnar & Hopwood, 2004).

Since the 1990s, IS usage within organisations has included enterprise resource planning (ERP) systems. Prior to their development, each organisational function (including accounting) often had their own individual IS, which existed in isolation from each other. ERP systems were therefore developed to collect data from all parts of the organisation and to feed it into an application supporting all (or a majority) of a firm's activities. As all the information contained within an ERP system is held within one central database, each piece of information need only be stored once, thereby eliminating the possibility of different files containing different information about the same item. Essentially, an ERP system is a set of integrated software application modules that aims to control all information flows within an organisation, including accounting (Rom & Rohde, 2006). As all modules are fully integrated, users can access real-time information concerning various aspects of the business, a facility that was not previously available with the IS that preceded the development of these systems.

Cloud computing (incorporating cloud-based ERP systems) has also emerged as a means of consolidating an organisation's IT/IS resources (including accounting). According to the National Institute of Standards and Technology (2011, p. 2), it can be defined as "a model for enabling ubiquitous, convenient, on-demand network access to a shared pool of configurable computing resources (e.g., networks, servers, storage, applications, and services) that can be rapidly provisioned and released with minimal management effort or service provider interaction". The potential advantages for a firm to adopt cloud computing include lower IT costs/barriers to entry, global data/systems availability, automatic access to IT updates and ease of IT scalability (Avram, 2014). Potential limitations include issues surrounding data protection, reliability, service availability, privacy and security (Islam et al., 2013). More recently, some firms have begun to experiment with the use of artificial intelligence as a means of automating some of their more complicated and repetitive accounting tasks (Griffin, 2019). By doing so, they expect to realise benefits such as improved accuracy and efficiency, along with reduced operating costs.

A major issue with all IS projects relates to the fact that many of the subsequent benefits realised are often intangible in nature and, hence, difficult to quantify. Consequently, there has been sustained criticism over the years surrounding the amount of capital invested in IS projects compared with the actual "visible" benefits realised. Furthermore, IS projects have in the past also been criticised as being over-sold by the respective IT champion to try and ensure that the proposed project was ultimately developed (Brynjolfsson, 1993; Masli et al., 2011). However, as employees and managers have become more IT/IS savvy over the years, it seems reasonable to conclude that this latter criticism has in all likelihood been significantly reduced. As most investments in IS/IT are aimed at automating particular processes with a potential reduction in, e.g. staff numbers and costs, they are effectively attempting to increase organisational productivity. Nevertheless, as noted above, the perceived lack of tangible results has resulted in what has been referred to as the IT productivity paradox. Indeed, despite the significant increase in spending on digital technologies in recent times, research from the USA, United Kingdom (UK) and Germany suggests that this status quo will remain until such time as the digital economy becomes more established (van Ark, 2016). It is within this context that the next section discusses AIS.

Accounting information systems

An AIS is a technology-based system that enables an organisation to collect, store and process accounting data (financial and non-financial) and convert it into information that is then capable of supporting subsequent decision-making (Bodnar & Hopwood, 2004). Examples of such decisions include how best to allocate scarce resources, plan cash flows, determine human resource requirements, etc. As accounting information permeates most business decisions taken, the role and impact of an AIS can potentially be significant. The size and scale of the organisation will determine the most appropriate AIS suitable for their needs. E.g. a relatively simple manual system may be sufficient for a sole trader, whereas from the perspective of a global conglomerate, a sophisticated and integrated suite of AIS would most likely be required.

In terms of their composition, an AIS generally consists of three main components: (1) a transaction-processing system that supports the organisation's daily operations with the provision of relevant reports, etc.; (2) a general ledger/financial reporting system which produces the traditional financial reporting statements, i.e. income statement, balance sheet and cash flow statement; and (3) a management reporting system which produces reports and analytics and any other ad hoc information required by management to assist them in running the organisation (Belfo & Trigo, 2013). Although the use of IT is not a prerequisite for an AIS, it is difficult to imagine modern organisations developing an AIS without the use of any IT components.

The primary objective of an AIS is to provide the user with timely and reliable accounting-based information to support their subsequent decision-making. Therefore, to become an intrinsic element of the successful operation of an organisation, the AIS needs to be, at least, functional (i.e. every task requested of it needs to be undertaken in an appropriate time frame), reliable (i.e. it must function correctly as and when required), usable (i.e. it must have the capability of being tailored to the end user's individual requirements) and maintainable (i.e. it possesses the necessary functionality to allow it to adapt to new organisational circumstances as and when required) (Buljubasic & Ilgun, 2015).

According to Granlund (2011), prior research conducted in the IS arena has not considered the impact of AIS within organisations to any great extent. Indeed, those studies that have been undertaken have tended to pursue a technical orientation with a corresponding shortage of research in areas such as management decision-making and control (Granlund & Mouritsen, 2003). This fact seems at odds with the development of IS generally, as their very existence requires the provision of relevant information to support the decision-making remit of management. In this regard, it has been suggested that the interface between (management) accounting and IT represents a complex area and arguably the most unpredictable in the realm of AIS (Sutton, 2006).

At this point, it should be noted that there has been an ongoing debate as to where AIS research is most appropriately situated. Some have argued the case for IS, others have suggested that accounting represents a more natural setting, while another cohort has suggested that as AIS has its own "unique identity", it should contribute to both areas but not necessarily at the same time (Steinbart, 2009). More recently, Murthy (2016) suggested that those engaged in AIS research were too diverse in their outlook and should instead refocus their efforts on the intersection of accounting and IS. In contrast, Moffitt et al. (2016) support a broad-based AIS research agenda to encourage more researchers into the area and to allow them the freedom to consider new and innovative elements of accounting that an overly rigid approach would discourage. This questioning of the AIS research agenda is not new. Previously, Sutton (1992) had challenged much of the prior AIS research. This criticism included suggestions that the discipline appeared to lack an identity, many of the renowned AIS scholars were researching in areas that were considered outside of the AIS domain and a shortage of skilled researchers in the area along with a lack of appropriate levels of academic rigour in the research that was conducted. Although it was acknowledged some years later that research in the AIS area had evolved (Sutton, 2010), questions about its long-term sustainability as a viable research area continue to be raised. Nevertheless, AIS are essential infrastructural components in modern business environments with organisations continuing to invest significant sums of money to try and improve their efficiency and effectiveness. The next section offers a critical analysis of the use of AIS within organisations.

Critical analysis of AIS

Due to the development of the internet, e-commerce and, more recently, the digital economy, many organisations now compete on a global rather than a local basis. The advent of globalisation has meant that the basis of competition between firms has also changed. E.g. in the area of customer service, the information generated from an AIS can play a signifi- cant role in ensuring that customer satisfaction is maintained and/or enhanced by allowing management to act decisively in addressing any issue that could potentially negatively affect customer satisfaction such as an excessive amount of time to process refunds electronically. A further potential advantage of using an AIS is enhanced efficiency, as digitised and inter- connected systems are faster at processing data than humans. Consequently, the information generated by the AIS is immediately available for use by management to support their sub- sequent decision-making. This capability would not be possible by using a manual system. It has also been suggested that if an AIS is operated in an effective manner, it can potentially prevent/mitigate the occurrence of possible crises by allowing management to take pre- emptive action quickly (Ceran et al., 2016). Cost effectiveness represents another potential benefit of an AIS. By investing the necessary resources (financial and otherwise) needed for an AIS, an organisation can potentially reduce the number of staff required for manual accounting-based work and instead redeploy them into higher value-adding roles. Finally, a further benefit suggested is the possible improvement in the quality and a reduction in the cost of products by effectively monitoring the good/defective output generated by produc- tion machinery coupled with enhanced knowledge-sharing throughout the organisation and beyond. E.g. the organisation may allow their customers to directly access their inventory levels and sales order entry systems, which would reduce the cost of both their sales and marketing activities (Romney & Steinbart, 2006).

As outlined earlier, ERP systems (the majority of which incorporate an accounting mod- ule) have the potential to allow management to regularly report predetermined key perfor- mance metrics. The ability to drill down into accounting data using an ERP system may enhance the auditing of the firm with a subsequent improvement in their internal control and, hence, corporate governance. It has been further suggested that ERP systems can potentially support an organisation's incumbent management accounting practices as firms with them were found to be better off than those without them (Rom & Rohde, 2006). Furthermore, it has also been claimed that organisations that develop a dynamic AIS capability (e.g. via their use of cloud computing) may increase the flow of information internally, thereby making it more accessible and facilitating a more strategic orientation for their accounting/finance function. The net result of this could be enhanced decision-making with a subsequent pos- itive impact on organisational performance (Prasad & Green, 2015). Indeed, Quinn et al. (2014) refer to improved efficiency in business processes because of using cloud computing in their sample of firms, while Cleary & Quinn (2016) have shown enhanced business per- formance in a sample of Irish small and medium sized enterprises (SMEs) due to their use of cloud-based accounting/finance infrastructures. Furthermore, the impact of blockchain technology on AIS may also result in the avoidance of errors, a reduction in missing data and enhanced information reliability (Tarifa-Fernández et al., 2019).

Although large firms may have considerable resources at their disposal to invest in new AIS, for many smaller firms, a lack of time, resources and expertise may hinder their ability to follow suit. Indeed, in some cases, an attitude seems to exist that if the incumbent accounting systems have not been subject to sustained criticism, then no obvious reason to replace them with more advanced alternatives exists. If this is the attitude that prevails for rudimentary AIS, then it seems reasonable to suggest a lower level of adoption for more sophisticated and expensive AIS. This argument is supported by the fact that research has shown low adoption rates for the implementation of sophisticated (management) AIS, such as activity-based cost- ing (ABC), Target Costing, etc., despite the potential advantages that organisations could realise from their use (Kennedy & Affleck-Graves, 2001). However, in the case of ABC, it should be noted that Askarany & Yazdifar (2012) discovered that amongst their sample of firms in Australia, New Zealand and the UK, many ABC adopters were found to have incorrectly classified themselves as adopters of traditional accounting systems owing to a lack of understanding of ABC systems. Nevertheless, it has been reported that more basic systems such as standard costing and job costing appear to dominate (Cleary, 2015). Furthermore, research conducted by van der Steen (2009) has claimed that employees overly familiar with incumbent accounting systems make it difficult for management to implement new and potentially more beneficial ones. This scenario indicates that organisations may be managing their increasingly complex operations with basic AIS and therefore not considering the potential advantages that more advanced and robust AIS could possibly deliver.

In any AIS, once raw data is captured within the system, it can then be used to generate outputs. However, if the input data is inaccurate, the output data will inevitably follow suit, with potentially negative consequences for subsequent organisational decision-making. As accounting data contains much of an organisation's commercial and highly sensitive information, it is imperative that adequate internal controls are implemented to ensure that, e.g. suppliers are not provided with details of other suppliers' credit terms or that employees' pay levels are not made public. If any of these possibilities were to occur, it would create major "trust" issues for both the AIS and the organisation concerned, which may take a considerable amount of time, effort and money to resolve, if ever. Other reservations surrounding AIS include the possibility that firms that invest in this area may subsequently find that the levels of creativity and innovation that previously existed within their accounting functions have declined due to increased standardisation and automation (Gordon & Tarafdar, 2007). Furthermore, it was initially suggested that the use of cloud computing in the area of AIS may not be appropriate due to issues surrounding security and confidentiality (Quinn et al., 2014). However, with the installation of adequate protection, e.g. firewalls and anti-virus software, the risk of, e.g. a ransomware attack or other authorised access can be significantly reduced. Following on from this critical analysis of AIS, the next section considers the impact of AIS on both accounting and accountants.

Role of accountants/accounting

Due to the rapid pace of advances in IT, the nature of accounting and the role of accountants continue to evolve. However, it should be remembered that accountants have always performed numerous activities associated with developing AIS or their equivalent. These have included assessing end user's information requirements, developing report formats and content, identifying sources and the reliability of input data, etc. Indeed, as articulated by Malmi & Brown (2008), IT systems are not developed or do not exist in isolation and, in the context of AIS, are primarily developed in partnership between accountants and IT personnel. The integrated nature of modern AIS means that accounting information is now more readily available to more employees within the organisation than previously, such as those operating within the sales or logistics functions. This has created threats to not only the role of the accountant but also new opportunities, as modern AIS provide a "drill-down" facility to aggregate information to a much greater extent and detail than before. A potential positive consequence of this is the revelation of insights previously hidden that could make a significant difference to the organisation's future trading performance. In a similar vein, the proliferation of data generated by organisations (including via their AIS) owing to their increased reliance on digital technologies (commonly known as big data) has created opportunities for accountants to try and extract meaning/value from this data for the subsequent benefit of their respective organisation. Indeed, Cockcroft & Russell (2018, p. 329) reported that based on their research, the accounting profession was well positioned to utilise big data in areas such as "risk and fraud management, data visualisation, auditing and performance measurement".

As the IT skills required by accountants continue to increase, professional global accounting bodies such as the Chartered Institute of Management Accountants (CIMA) and the Association of Chartered Certified Accountants now explicitly require their students to study IT/IS modules in preparation for their future employment in accounting roles. Once qualified, it is a requirement for accountants to maintain and enhance their skills through a process known as Continuous Professional Development. This is to ensure that their IT skills (amongst others) are continually upgraded to realise potential benefits that may accrue from the introduction of new technologies such as blockchain, data analytics and artificial intelligence as quickly as possible. This view has been endorsed by professional accounting bodies such as the CIMA, who have stated that to succeed in the increasingly digital environment, those employed in the finance function need to enhance their skillsets in areas such as fundamental digital literacy, enhanced technological knowledge and the ability to alter mindsets and behaviours as and when required (Noah, 2019).

Furthermore, and taking ERP as an example, studies have shown that the implementation of such systems can facilitate a change in the role of accountants from traditional score-keepers to informed business analysts (Scapens & Jazayeri, 2003). Additionally, research conducted by Kanellou & Spathis (2013) found that the benefits to accounting from the introduction of ERP systems, such as quicker gathering of data, a reduction in the time needed to close off accounts and improved decision-making, have facilitated a reduction in staff in the accounting department. Post-ERP implementation, research conducted by Chen et al. (2012) found that the role occupied by management accountants changed to incorporate additional managerial-type functions such as training, education and financial analysis. The researchers also reported that this was facilitated by the use of ERP systems to replace repetitive accounting tasks.

Summary

This chapter has provided a general introduction to AIS. It began by defining accounting in its various forms before outlining the potential use of accounting-based information from an organisational perspective. The concept of IS was then introduced, with a focus on AIS. A critical analysis of AIS followed before the chapter concluded by considering the future role for both accounting and accountants in the rapidly evolving, digitally enabled global economy. Within accounting, there is an ongoing movement towards the harmonisation of global accounting standards to facilitate investors in making more informed capital allocation decisions. Simultaneously, there is also a suggestion that organisations may in the future further engage in what has been termed "integrated reporting". This proposal is in response to the view that as some elements of financial reporting rules and regulations are considered to be overly restrictive, it would allow firms to publish "extra" information (both financial and management accounting based) as a supplement to their annual report. By doing so, it will allow them to communicate with interested stakeholders as to how they are planning to manage their limited resources to create value in the short, medium and long term. Indeed, in recent times there has been a significant increase in organisations publishing sustainability reports in tandem with their annual reports. From an AIS perspective, all accounting information (both quantitative and qualitative) will need to be generated and provided in a timely manner so as to facilitate stakeholders in making informed decisions.

As the preceding section represents just some examples of the possible future use of AIS, it seems reasonable to conclude that the role and scale of AIS within organisations will continue to develop. Consequently, the role currently occupied by both accounting and accountants will also inevitably evolve, with multiple opportunities and threats likely to emerge. Based on the scale and speed of developments occurring within the realm of digital technologies, it seems clear that advances in this area will have a significant impact on this development.

Notes

1 IT is defined here as the use of hardware, software and telecommunications to provide data, information and knowledge (Attaran, 2003).
2 An IS is defined here as the combination of hardware, software and telecommunications networks that humans develop and use to collect, create and disseminate useful data, generally within an organisational setting (Valacich & Schneider, 2010).

References

American Accounting Association (1966). *A Statement of Basic Accounting Theory*. Illinois, USA: American Accounting Association.

Askarany, D. & Yazdifar, H. (2012). An investigation into the mixed reported adoption rates for ABC: Evidence from Australia, New Zealand and the UK. *International Journal of Production Economics*, 135(1), 430–439. https://doi.org/10.1016/j.ijpe.2011.08.017

Attaran, M. (2003). Information technology and business-process redesign. *Business Process Management Journal*, 9(4), 440–458. https://www.proquest.com/docview/220298568/fulltextPDF/831FCFD52F649B5PQ/6?accountid=14504

Avram, M.G. (2014). Advantages and challenges of adopting cloud computing from an enterprise perspective. *Procedia Technology*, 12, 529–534. https://www.sciencedirect.com/science/article/pii/S221201731300710X

Belfo, F. & Trigo, A. (2013). Accounting information systems: Tradition and future directions. *Procedia Technology*, 9, 536–546. https://www.sciencedirect.com/science/article/pii/S2212017313002144

Bodnar, G.H. & Hopwood, W.S. (2004). *Accounting Information Systems*. New Jersey, USA: Pearson Prentice Hall.

Brynjolfsson, E. (1993). The productivity paradox of information technology. *Communications of the ACM*, 36(12), 66–77. https://doi.org/10.1145/163298.163309

Buljubasic, E. & Ilgun, E. (2015). Impact of accounting information systems on decision making – the case of Bosnia and Herzegovina. *European Researcher*, 96(7), 460-469. https://doi.org/10.13187/er.2015.96.460

Ceran, M.B., Gungor, S. & Konya, S. (2016). The role of accounting information systems in preventing the financial crises experienced in businesses. *Economics, Management and Financial Markets*, 11(1), 294–302. https://www.proquest.com/docview/1782998836/fulltextPDF/9F8142721F734DDAPQ/34

Chen, H.J., Huang, S.Y., Chiu, A.A. & Pai, F.C. (2012). The ERP system impact on the role of accountants. *Industrial Management & Data Systems*, 112(1), 83–101. https://doi.org/10.1108/02635571211193653

Cleary, P. (2015). An empirical investigation of the impact of management accounting on structural capital and business performance. *Journal of Intellectual Capital*, 16(3), 566–586. https://doi.org/10.1108/JIC-10-2014-0114

Cleary, P. & Quinn, M. (2016). Intellectual capital and business performance – an exploratory study of the impact of cloud-based accounting and finance infrastructure. *Journal of Intellectual Capital*, 17(2), 255–278. https://doi.org/10.1108/JIC-06-2015-0058

Cockcroft, S. & Russell, M. (2018). Big data opportunities for accounting and finance practice and research. *Australian Accounting Review*, 28(3), 323–333. https://doi.org/10.1111/auar.12218

De Groot, J. (2020). What is SOX compliance? 2019 SOX requirements & more. *Data Insider - Digital Guardian*, 29th September. https://digitalguardian.com/blog/what-sox-compliance

Gordon, S.R. & Tarafdar, M. (2007). How do a company's information technology competences influence its ability to innovate? *Journal of Enterprise Information Management*, 20(3), 270–290. https://doi.org/10.1108/17410390710740736

Granlund, M. (2011). Extending AIS research to management accounting and control issues: A research note. *International Journal of Accounting Information Systems*, 12(1), 3–19. https://doi.org/10.1016/j.accinf.2010.11.001

Granlund, M. & Mouritsen, J. (2003). Problematizing the relationship between management control and information technology, introduction to the special section on "management control and new information technologies". *European Accounting Review*, 12(1), 77–83. https://doi.org/10.1080/0963818031000087925

Griffin, O. (2019). How artificial intelligence will impact accounting. *ICAEW*, October. https://www.icaew.com/technical/technology/artificial-intelligence/artificial-intelligence-articles/how-artificial-intelligence-will-impact-accounting

Hemmer, T. & Labro, E. (2008). On the optimal relation between the properties of managerial and financial reporting systems. *Journal of Accounting Research*, 46(5), 1209–1240. https://doi.org/10.1111/j.1475-679X.2008.00303.x

Islam, M.M., Morshed, S. & Goswami, P. (2013). Cloud computing: A survey on its limitations and potential solutions. *International Journal of Computer Science Issues*, 10(4), 159–163. https://www.proquest.com/docview/1470806295/fulltextPDF/F1E090BC93BF4907PQ/43?accountid=14504

Kabalski, P. & Zarzycka, E. (2018). The convergence of financial and management accounting in Poland. *Financial Sciences – Nauki O Finansach,* 23(2), 9–19. https://econpapers.repec.org/article/vrsfinsci/v_3a23_3ay_3a2018_3ai_3a2_3ap_3a9-19_3an_3a1.htm

Kanellou, A. & Spathis, C. (2013). Accounting benefits and satisfaction in an ERP environment. *International Journal of Accounting Information Systems*, 14(3), 209–234. https://doi.org/10.1016/j.accinf.2012.12.002

Kennedy, T. & Affleck-Graves, J. (2001). The impact of activity-based costing on firm performance. *Journal of Management Accounting Research*, 13, 19–45. https://doi.org/10.2308/jmar.2001.13.1.19

Malmi, T. & Brown, D. (2008). Management control systems as a package – challenges, opportunities and research directions. *Management Accounting Research*, 19(4), 287–301. https://doi.org/10.1016/j.mar.2008.09.003

Marden, R.E., Edwards, R.K. & Stout, W.D. (2003). The CEO/CFO certification requirement. *The CPA Journal*, July. http://archives.cpajournal.com/2003/0703/features/f073603.htm

Masli, A., Richardson, V.J., Sanchez, J.M. & Smith, R.E. (2011). The business value of IT: A synthesis and framework of archival research. *Journal of Information Systems*, 25(2), 81–116. https://doi.org/10.2308/isys-10117

McLaney, E. & Atrill, P. (2010). *Accounting, An Introduction*. Essex, England: Financial Times Prentice Hall.

Moffitt, K.C., Richardson, V.J., Snow, N.M., Weisner, M.M. & Wood, D.A. (2016). Perspectives on past and future ais research as the journal of information systems turns thirty. *Journal of Information Systems*, 30(3), 157–171. https://doi.org/10.2308/isys-51495

Murthy, U. (2016). Researching at the intersection of accounting and information technology. *Journal of Information Systems*, 30(2), 159–167. https://doi.org/10.2308/isys-51413

National Institute of Standards and Technology (2011). The NIST definition of cloud computing. Special Publication 800-145. https://nvlpubs.nist.gov/nistpubs/legacy/sp/nistspecialpublication800-145.pdf

Noah, A. (2019). The future of finance: How to thrive in the digital age. *CIMA Insights*. https://www.cimaglobal.com/Members/Insights/2019-CIMA-Insights/The-Future-of-Finance-How-to-thrive-in-the-digital-age/.

Prasad, A. & Green, P. (2015). Organizational competencies and dynamic accounting information system capability: Impact on AIS processes and firm performance. *Journal of Information Systems*, 29(3), 123–149. https://web-s-ebscohost-com.ucc.idm.oclc.org/ehost/pdfviewer/pdfviewer?vid=2&sid=9f18e803-b534-485a-b626-c61b5ebdb851%40redis

Quinn, M., Strauß, E. & Kristandl, G. (2014). The effects of cloud technology on management accounting and decision-making. *Financial Management*, 10(6), 54–55. https://www.cimaglobal.com/Research--Insight/The-effects-of-cloud-technology-on-management-accounting/

Rom, A. & Rohde, C. (2006). Enterprise resource planning systems, strategic enterprise management systems and management accounting: A Danish study. *Journal of Enterprise Information Management*, 19(1), 50–66. https://doi.org/10.1108/17410390610636878

Romney, M. & Steinbart, P. (2006). *Accounting Information Systems*. New Jersey, USA: Pearson Education International.

Scapens, R. & Jazayeri, M. (2003). ERP systems and management accounting change: Opportunities or impacts? A Research Note. *European Accounting Review*, 12(1), 201–233. https://doi.org/10.1080/0963818031000087907

Steinbart, P.J. (2009). Thoughts about the future of the Journal of Information Systems. *Journal of Information Systems*, 23(1), 1–4. https://doi.org/10.2308/jis.2009.23.1.1

Sutton, S.G. (1992). Can we research a field we cannot define? Towards an understanding of the AIS discipline. *Advances in Accounting Information Systems*, 1, 1–13.

Sutton, S.G. (2006). Enterprise systems and the re-shaping of accounting systems: A call for research. *International Journal of Accounting Information Systems*, 7(1), 1–6. https://doi.org/10.1016/j.accinf.2006.02.002

Sutton, S.G. (2010). A research discipline with no boundaries: Reflections on 20 years of defining AIS research. *International Journal of Accounting Information Systems*, 11, 289–296. https://doi.org/10.1016/j.accinf.2010.09.004

Taipaleenmaki, J. & Ikaheimo, S. (2013). On the convergence of management and financial accounting – the role of information technology in accounting change. *International Journal of Accounting Information Systems*, 14(4), 321–348. https://doi.org/10.1016/j.accinf.2013.09.003

Tarifa-Fernández, J., Casado-Belmonte, M.P. & Martínez-Romero, M.J. (2019). Perspective and challenges of Blockchain technology in the accountability of financial information. *Architectures and Frameworks for Developing and Applying Blockchain Technology,* IGI Global, 45–68. https://www.igi-global.com/gateway/chapter/230190

Valacich, J. & Schneider, C. (2010). *Information Systems Today – Managing in the Digital World*. New Jersey, USA: Prentice-Hall.

Van Ark, B. (2016). The productivity paradox of the new digital economy. *International Productivity Monitor*, 31, 3–18. http://www.csls.ca/ipm/31/vanark.pdf

Van der Steen, M. (2009). Inertia and management accounting change. The role of ambiguity and contradiction between formal rules and routines. *Accounting, Auditing & Accountability Journal*, 22(5), 736–761. https://doi.org/10.1108/09513570910966351

Weißenberger, B.E. & Angelkort, H. (2011). Integration of financial and management accounting systems: the mediating influence of a consistent financial language on controllership effectiveness. *Management Accounting Research*, 22(3), 160–180. https://doi.org/10.1016/j.mar.2011.03.003

2

THE EVOLUTION OF ACCOUNTING INFORMATION SYSTEMS

Pierangelo Rosati and Victoria Paulsson

Introduction

Accounting is typically seen as a slow-paced and conservative industry. Despite such a reputation, the accounting discipline and the role of accountants have both changed significantly over time (Baldvinsdottir et al., 2009; Kokina et al., 2021). Boyns & Edwards (1997a, p. 21) state that "accounting is a discipline which may be seen, at a particular point in time, to encompass a body of ideas, a number of conventions, a set of available tools/techniques and a variety of actual practices". All these components are embedded in a system, which takes the name of accounting information systems (AIS). The scope of AIS has expanded in tandem with the role of accountants as a consequence of technological developments that have shaped how accountants perform their work. AIS have developed from mere record-keeping systems to complex systems encompassing technical, organisational, and cognitive factors (Mauldin & Ruchala, 1999). AIS are not used only by accountants but also by other decision-makers within organisations who need to make their decisions based on accounting data, as well as in tasks that involve an application of accounting data (Reneau & Grabski, 1987).

Among the available definitions[1] of AIS in the literature, this chapter adopts the one proposed by David et al. (1999, p. 8) who define AIS as a discipline "that captures, stores, manipulates, and presents data about an organisation's value-adding activities to aid decision makers in planning, monitoring, and controlling the organisation."

This definition is preferred over others for the following reasons. First, this definition of AIS does not make any reference to information technology per se. Therefore, it fits particularly well in a discussion about the evolution of AIS, which is the aim of this chapter. Readers should not be confused between the terms *information systems* and *information technology* since they are not synonymous; furthermore, the former does not imply the latter as information systems existed well before the development of computers (Alikhani et al., 2013). Information technology, on the contrary, is simply a use of computers to manage information systems. Thus, considering AIS only as computerised systems, or simply information technology, would underestimate the extent of changes occurred over time. Second, the definition proposed by David et al. (1999) refers to the essential role of AIS, which is to provide both internal and external decision-makers with timely and valuable information about the organisation. Although the essential role of AIS has been substantially untouched, the extent

DOI: 10.4324/9781003132943-4

to which such information has been used to monitor, control, or plan an organisation's activities has changed over time leading to a change in AIS design (Anandarajan et al., 2004).

Leitch & Davis (1983) identified four main drivers behind the evolution of AIS:

- *Information requirements.* Information needs can be classified into two categories, i.e. *internal* and *external* information requirements. Internal information requirements have been growing over time due to the increase in firm size and business complexity, as well as changes in ownership structure. For example, a merchant, who runs a local business, has lower information requirements than a firm with offices in many different countries. External information is mostly related to financial reporting. Regulators in different parts of the world have substantially increased the information a firm has to disclose to enhance the informativeness of financial statements, which thereby increases a level of investor protection.
- *Technology development.* AIS do not always imply the use of computers. However, it would be hard to imagine modern information systems without any support from computers (i.e. information technology). Information technology has been gradually introduced to aid AIS in many aspects. The first computerised AIS were adopted to handle day-to-day operations in large organisations. Many technological developments have led to increasing computing power and rapidly decreasing cost, and the invention of the Internet led to quantum changes within AIS. Recently popularised technologies such as Artificial Intelligence (AI) (Sutton et al., 2016) and robotic process automation (RPA) have dramatically increased the speed of change within AIS (Kokina et al., 2021).
- *Systems approach.* The systems approach is a way of structuring and coordinating the activities and operations within an organisation. This approach is based on the idea that different parts of a system may, and should be, interrelated so that the value of the system as a whole is greater than the sum of its components. The systems approach is clearly visible in modern AIS, but it was extremely challenging to put it into practice prior to the 1990s, when the enterprise resource planning (ERP) system was invented. Back then, AIS typically did not interact with any other information systems adopted in other departments and vice versa. The systems approach was a result of the integration need that emerged inside companies that had grown substantially in terms of size and complexity. With the systems approach, AIS started to provide timely performance feedback to other functions.
- *Scientific approach to management.* The application of mathematical, statistical, and advanced analytical models for big data to organisational management has significantly increased the complexity of AIS. As a response to the growing complexity of companies and the business environment, AIS are required to handle increasingly larger volumes of data in different formats as well as to integrate, manipulate, and analyse this data. As a result, AIS have experienced a constant increase in the number of tasks they can execute and in their performance.

The innovation process in the AIS domain has been anything but linear, and this chapter aims to describe these main stages in this evolution. In a similar attempt, Anandarajan et al. (2004) divide the AIS history into five periods: Ancient Times, Pre-RenAISance, RenAISance, Industrial Age and Information Age. The characteristics of the first four periods are briefly summarised in the next paragraph (i.e. where it all began). This chapter extends the discussion on the post-1950s era divided into three main phases, i.e. the *Information Age* (1950s–1980s), the *Integration Phase* (1990s) and *AIS 2.0* (2000s–present).

Where it all began

The first example of AIS can be traced back to ancient Jericho around 8,000 BC where merchants kept track of their inventories and transactions using tokens (Anandarajan et al., 2004). For 5,000 years, there were just small improvements until the advent of the abacus (Brown, 2014). Originally invented in China, the abacus made its way to western civilisation and became a valuable tool for accounting calculations. Around the same time in Egypt and Mesopotamia, accounting transactions were being recorded on papyrus rolls and clay tablets. The role of these rudimentary AIS consisted only in *list making* with transactions being recorded in terms of items exchanged. Three major changes then occurred and changed the course of accounting practices. First, the invention of banking and coins attributed to the Greeks (575 BC) enabled commercial transactions to be recorded in money instead of weights or other measures (De Soto, 2009); second, the development of a basic income statement and balance sheet in ancient Rome (Anandarajan et al., 2004); and third, the development of an initial concept of corporation (Brown, 2015). Roman authorities introduced a regulated system of accounting and taxation, and merchants were required to *register* their business and report profits for taxation purposes.

During the Middle Ages, there was a period from 1000 to 1200 that saw small incremental advancements in the AIS field. The Normans invented the tally stick, which displayed the equivalent of accounts receivables and payables in our modern financial statements (Anandarajan et al., 2004). Italian merchants improved single-entry bookkeeping practices to effectively manage the increased number of transactions generated by the Crusades (Gleeson-White, 2011).

The period between 1250 and 1350 saw the so-called *commercial revolution* (Bryer, 1993). During those years, merchants' businesses grew so significantly that they formed partnerships to address their funding needs. Furthermore, between 1400 and 1600, large joint-stock companies[2] emerged to fund transoceanic expeditions. For the first time, there was a real separation between owners and managers. In such a context, efficient and reliable AIS were essential to ensure transparency between investors (owners) and administrators (managers) and to make appropriate decisions for the benefit of the companies. In contrast to single-entry bookkeeping, double-entry bookkeeping[3] did not only allow transactions to be measured and recorded, but it also explained how the profit and loss statement and the balance sheet were generated (Littleton, 1933). The enhanced level of transparency and accountability increased the level of trust in commercial and investment ventures. Thus, investments in commercial and other financial opportunities increased and enabled further economic developments.

It was during the Industrial Age (1700–1940) that double-entry bookkeeping gained importance on a global scale (Hoskin & Macve, 1986; Anandarajan et al., 2004). This period was also characterised by a significant change in AIS. AIS had to provide more information to both external and internal stakeholders. With the separation between ownership and control becoming more common in different industries (Johnson & Kaplan, 1987), financial reports had to provide owners with complete and reliable information about how financial results were generated. At the same time, internal stakeholders were constantly looking for mechanisms to reduce inefficiencies in the production process (Fleischman & Tyson, 1993). AIS had to support management activities by providing more granular information about the production process and relevant performance measures. This gave rise to a new accounting field known as management accounting.[4] Management accounting is closely related to the development of scientific management; the main concern is to identify and understand costs for the purposes of control. AIS had to be adapted to manage the increased volume of information to be processed. The same logic adopted for other operating processes was applied to AIS where the workflow was divided into minute operations performed by a worker or by a small group; in this way the performance of each worker and process could potentially have been controlled by mathematical checks. Despite all the changes to AIS up to and during the Industrial Age, the impact of technology in the office was mostly confined to various forms of office mechanisation (i.e. typewriters). It was the so-called Information Age that represented a turning point in AIS development.

The Information Age: 1950s–1980s

The Information Age spans a 40-year period in which there were many technological developments. For ease of reference, the Information Age is divided into two distinct phases: the *mainframe* phase (1950s–1960s) and *the personal computer (PCs)* and *Decision Support System (DSS)* phase (1970s–1980s).

The *mainframe phase* started with the development of the first computer with electronic circuits – which were developed by Eckert and Mauchly in 1943. A decade later, IBM released the IBM 702 Electronic Data Processing Machine. The machine's ability to process large amounts of data and handle alphanumeric variables of varying size made it suitable for accounting workloads. Thus began a revolutionary phase in AIS history (Anandarajan et al., 2004). At this time, the main role of computers was to improve the efficiency and accuracy of manual accounting work performed by accountants in voluminous and repetitive accounting activities such as inventory tracking, general ledger, account receivable/payable, and payroll. The traditional role of accountants was to summarise transactional details of how a business operated in a past period, but this time with an aid from computerised AIS. AIS were no longer operating through faith in accountants and their locally developed manual routines but through faith in computers (Baldvinsdottir et al., 2009). Despite the slowly growing importance of computerised AIS, their functions were limited to routine data gathering and processing. The introduction of computerised AIS had three main impacts. First, speed and volume increased rapidly with the introduction of machines in the accounting function. Managers could introduce new methods for performance monitoring and management control. For example, *management by exception*, a practice in which only a significant deviation from a budget/plan is brought to the attention of the management, was made possible by computerised AIS (Brownell, 1983). Second, there was a swift change of skillsets required for senior accountants. Before the introduction of computers in the AIS function, senior accountants had only needed to perfect the art of manual-based AIS. With the introduction of computers in their work routines, senior accountants faced a dual role of running not only the AIS but also the computer system so that the traditional manual-based AIS could work in perfect harmony with the computerised system (Anandarajan et al., 2004). Demand for senior accountants was high, and they were in a strong position to negotiate higher salaries. Conversely, it had an adverse impact on junior accountants. This leads to the third point. The introduction of computerised AIS meant that basic accounting clerks were no longer required and were made redundant since the work was more efficient and effective when performed by computers than humans. Only simple tasks like data entry were left to junior accounting staff. For example, a US-based multi-branch bank reported a 75% reduction of bookkeeping staff within the first 18 months of an electronic bookkeeping machine installation (Braverman, 1974). The typical *bean counter role* of the accounting profession, who provided only transactional and historical information of the business, was eroded for the first time. Despite the undeniable benefits that resulted from the introduction of mainframes, the adoption rate was initially extremely low. By 1955, there were only about 240 mainframes in use in the US (Campbell-Kelly & Garcia-Swartz, 2009). The main reasons for such low adoption were the complexity of such systems and high investment required.

The 1970s marked the beginning of the *PCs* and *DSS* phase. By this time, the number of companies adopting computerised AIS had begun to increase. The turning point was the development of PCs and accounting software, which first became available during that period. With PCs, the investment required to adopt computerised AIS fell dramatically. The MITS Altair 8800 was the first PC to be introduced to the market in 1975 at a retail price between USD 275 and 395, followed by the Apple I in 1976 at USD 666.66 (ComputerHistoryMuseum, 2016). In comparison, the cost of mainframe computers was around USD 4.6 million (Perry, 2007). Such a low cost represented a significant incentive for companies to adopt PCs in their daily activities. The software side grew along in harmony. The *ICP Quarterly* in 1974 listed 324 accounting software packages available in the market for core accounting functions such as general ledger, account receivable/payable, billing, budgeting, and costing within the price range of USD 5,000–8,400 (Campbell-Kelly, 2004).

The following decade saw the emergence of the *business controller role* within the accounting profession. The significance of this role grew over time (Baldvinsdottir et al., 2009). In this role, accountants are thought of as business advisors who analyse accounting data and provide guidance to middle management on how best to make a business decision at a strategic level. It should be noted that the 1980s marked only the very early onset of the business controller role. It was not until the 1990s that technological advancements, like ERP systems, which will be discussed in the next section, were developed enough to fully support accountants in this role.

To aid the early but steadily growing business controller role, a new kind of computerised AIS called the *DSS* was invented (Baldvinsdottir et al., 2009). *DSS* is a term that refers to any kind of computer system that can be used to support complex decision-making and problem solving (Shim et al., 2002). Many kinds of DSS are identified in the literature, such as (1) data-driven DSS, (2) model-driven DSS, (3) knowledge-based DSS, (4) communication-based DSS, and (5) document-driven DSS (Alter, 2004). The relative importance of a particular type of DSS compared to the others depends on how decision-makers use the systems in question to support decisions at hand. For example, to perform a sales forecast for the next quarter, an accountant might need access to all kinds of DSSs for information about past sales, current knowledge about the macroeconomy, and insights about a particular market. This data and information could be located within a number of different DSSs.

One of the software revolutions that marked the DSS era of the 1980s was VisiCalc, the first electronic spreadsheet software, which was launched in 1978 (Cunha et al., 2015). VisiCalc played a significant role in transforming the perception of PCs into that of a useful business tool. It had most of the features of electronic spreadsheets available on the market today, for example, a column/row tabulation programme with a *What You See Is What You Get* (WYSIWYG) interface, a cell reference (A1, A2, etc.), and recalculation of formulas (Mendes, 2012). An electronic spreadsheet provided an excellent platform to perform what-if analysis, which involved combining historical accounting data with up-to-date facts and knowledge, to forecast how a future business condition might play out. A simulation of several different business conditions (e.g. best-case, most-likely case, and worst-case scenarios) could be run through electronic spreadsheets and possibly through other statistical software. Despite the gradual growing significance of the business controller role, the role did not dominate the AIS landscape until the 1990s, as the technology required to support decision-making tasks was not fully developed. For example, VisiCalc was only the first attempt at a DSS; consequently, much manual work was left to accountants, particularly manual data entry into spreadsheets.

In summary, the Information Age can be divided into two main phases. The initial *main-frame* phase (1950s–1960s), in which AIS ran on complex mainframes adopted by a limited number of big companies, and the second – *PCs and DSS* phase (1970s–1980s) – in which revolutionary technologies, such as PCs and electronic spreadsheets, gradually reshaped AIS.

The Integration Phase: 1990s

The 1990s was a decade of great volatility in the global economy. Developed countries experienced rapid economic growth from international trades, but there were also many major financial crises in several parts of the world (Nankani, 2005). In terms of technological advancement, many key information technology developments were invented during this period to aid computerised AIS. The Internet, data warehousing, and ERP systems are some key technologies that define the computerised AIS landscape of the 1990s (Rashid et al., 2002). These technologies were complemented with advancements in cost and management control techniques, which were highly popularised throughout the decade (Meyer, 2003). These include Activity-Based Costing (ABC) (Cooper & Kaplan, 1991) and Balanced Score-card (BSC) (Kaplan & Norton, 1995). All of these challenges – macroeconomic conditions, technological advancement, along with advanced cost and management control techniques – required accountants to integrate all of these aspects together into their work function. Thus, we label this decade the *Integration Phase*.

The 1990s posed significant challenges to accountants. These included the increasing globalisation of business (Nankani, 2005), tighter controls imposed by ABC and BSC, and growing business uncertainty as signalled by various financial crises worldwide (Nankani, 2005). Accountants faced such challenges by adopting the new information technology tools and management accounting techniques, which became available during those years. There was also a shift in the role of accountants. The *business controller* emerged as the dominant role over the *bean counter role*. The business controller role, which was first introduced during the 1980s, was fully developed by the start of this decade. This progressive expansion of the business controller role in the 1990s was primarily due to the arrival of the ERP system. The remaining part of this section will explain the impact of ERP systems on the changing role of accountants.

An ERP system is, in essence, an integrated cross-functional business support system (Grabski et al., 2011) that is often available *off-the-shelf* and ready to be implemented in any business organisation. ERP systems comprise functions (or *modules* as they are commonly referred to in the business literature) that correspond to a function or department within an organisation. Common functions that were available in a typical ERP package in the 1990s consisted of (1) Financial Accounting, (2) Managerial Accounting, (3) Human Resources, (4) Supply Chain Management (SCM), (5) Project Management, and (6) Customer Relationship Management (CRM) (Rashid et al., 2002). To achieve these all-in-one functions through the use of a single software, the ERP itself comprises four key layers. An elaboration of these layers allows us to understand how the ERP system integrates with other key technologies of the 1990s, like a data warehouse and the Internet, to make a strategic impact on organisations (Møller, 2005; Paulsson, 2013; Kale, 2016). The four layers of the ERP system consist of the following:

- *The foundation layer* is built upon data warehousing technology. It provides an integrated database for different modules and outlines an application framework to make ERP modules work together in perfect harmony.

- *The process layer* provides core transaction-based functions of the ERP system such as financial accounting and material and production planning. These are the core components of the earliest ERP systems (Rashid et al., 2002).
- *The analytical layer* combines transaction data in the process layer with other databases, which might not be directly synchronised with the core-integrated database in the foundation layer, to provide a DSS to users. The Internet, and other network technologies in the 1990s, like local area network and wide area network, are the main technologies that make the connection between different databases possible. Modules like SCM and CRM are the hallmarks of the analytical layer.
- *The e-business layer* utilises Internet technology to provide electronic collaborations with other business parties outside an organisation, such as customers, business partners, and employees. The layer enables the ERP system to integrate with other business systems through enterprise application integration technology.

The ERP system of the 1990s had fully working foundation and process layers, but it also started to embrace the analytical layer into the overall ERP design. However, it was not until the 2000s that the analytical layer was fully commercialised, and the e-business layer started to take off (Møller, 2005). The next paragraph provides further details about these more recent developments.

The ERP system of the 1990s played a significant part in supporting the business controller role. To effectively utilise an ERP system, all business processes must run according to an accepted industry standard, regardless of location and local cultures – this is commonly known as *best practice* (Hong & Kim, 2002). In any ERP implementation, best practice is required in conjunction with the technological part of the ERP system to improve process efficiency (Hong & Kim, 2002; Wagner & Newell, 2004). Best practice applies a standardised data definition throughout business branches. For example, a definition for an invoice overdue is anything over 30 days through all business branches (as opposed to 15 days in a New York branch and 30 days in a London branch as it had been prior to best practice). Therefore, accountants spend less time reconciling data definitions and allow the process layer of the ERP system to do the drudgery of financial data processing and consolidation. With ERP system and best practice, accountants had more time to focus on the analytical layer of the ERP system. Accountants could therefore integrate transactional accounting data with qualitative and quantitative insights available from other business functions through the integrated database in their ERP system and the Internet to forecast and control business performance.

The period of the 1990s can be labelled as the Integration Phase because there were many factors in the AIS arena that had to be incorporated together to enable the business controller role of accountants and also because of the increasing tendency towards adopting fully integrated information systems. Technological advancements like ERP systems and the Internet, as well as consequences of the adoption ERP systems like best practice, were integrated with accounting innovations like ABC and BSC to make it possible.

AIS 2.0: 2000s–present

The term *AIS 2.0* is inspired by the term *Web 2.0*, where user-generated content and compatibility with other information technology systems are key to success. The decade from the 2000s onwards is labelled AIS 2.0 to highlight a significantly growing impact of accounting-generated business insights through ERP systems and *business intelligence (BI)*. It also enabled

AIS' ability to integrate with other innovations, like cloud computing, big data, and block-chain, to generate even more data-driven business insights.

ERP systems had become the key technology of choice in this era because of their ability to respond to ever-growing compliance requirements (Gupta & Misra, 2016). On top of that, the analytical layer and the e-business layer of ERP systems were now a prospering business. *BI* is now the common term referring to the analytical layer of business operations. BI is commonly connected to the ERP system, but it is not an absolute prerequisite, as some BI might be better positioned to gather data and information elsewhere (Elbashir et al., 2011). The most significant function of BI is to perform "data gathering, data storage and knowledge management with analysis to evaluate complex corporate and competitive information" (Negash & Gray, 2008, p. 176).

Similarly, the e-business layer integrated within the ERP system began to grow from the 2000s onwards as more and more businesses exchanged values over the Internet (Hsu, 2013) and via *cloud computing* (Marston et al., 2011). In a nutshell, cloud computing is a new technology enabled via the Internet for users to access an on-demand network of shared computing resources, for example, networks, servers, storage, applications, and services (Mell & Grance, 2011). The challenges that cloud computing creates from an AIS perspective are discussed in other sections of this volume. The trend now is that most business applications will be migrated to the cloud, including ERP systems (Raihana, 2012) and BI (Mircea, Ghilic-Micu, & Stoica, 2011). The e-business layer also holds the promise of enabling information produced through ERP systems and many other online databases to be shared among companies in a supply chain in a timely yet cost-effective fashion. This gives rise to a relatively new technology called *big data*. Big data exploits a vast amount of data available on the Internet, other online databases and internally gathered historical data from ERP systems, along with the scalable information processing power of cloud computing, to answer any data-driven question when traditional methods to data analysis could not provide such an answer in a timely, cost-effective, and satisfactory fashion (Kraska, 2013). Other chapters in this volume provide a deeper discussion about the impact of big data on AIS.

Blockchain is another technology that has the potential to influence the future development of AIS significantly (Rosati & Čuk, 2019). The Institute of Chartered Accountants in England and Wales (2018) believes that the adoption of blockchain technology will empower the accountancy profession to record more types of economic activities, therefore increasing the capacity of AIS to provide a clear and reliable representation of them. In comparison to other existing AIS technologies, blockchain offers at least the following advantages: (1) decentralisation, (2) authentication, and (3) tamper-resistance (Dai & Vasarhelyi, 2017). In its purest version, a blockchain is essentially a distributed ledger where all nodes have access to the entire list of transactions. It relies on a public-key cryptography to authenticate the parties involved in the transaction and protect their privacy. It is tamper-resistant because once a transaction has been verified and stored in the distributed ledger, it cannot be changed. As such, blockchain technology offers clear benefits for organisations, investors, and regulators. Organisations and investors may benefit from the availability of real-time and reliable information about the organisation's economic activities, therefore improving business and investment decision-making. Regulators may benefit from increased compliance to financial reporting standards and from higher data quality assurance (Rosati & Čuk, 2019).

The technological advancement in this period defines a new way of business operation such as how businesses are connected through the e-business layer of ERP systems. The power of the Internet, cloud computing, big data, and blockchain represents a new landscape for business operations in many ways. For example, consumer trends are changing at a much faster rate than before due to the explosion of information sharing via social web, e-commerce sites, and the Internet. Businesses must constantly refine and redefine their *competitive advantage* (Barney, 1991) to survive a constantly fluctuating market trend. In such a context, the analysis coming from AIS and accountants has risen to a strategic level. The business controller role of the 1990s has now escalated to the new role of *business partner* (Scapens & Jazayeri, 2003; Järvenpää, 2007). The role is similar to the *business controller* role, however, with a focus on data-driven analytics to shape effective and strategic decision-making, not just control decisions at the tactical level like it was before. The primary activities of accountants in organisations are to analyse information and advise management on how to navigate new and existing business ventures. They analyse information clues from multiple sources, both online and offline, to create a futuristic business vision (Järvenpää, 2007). The analysis role of the accountancy profession is even more pronounced given the rise of AIS technologies (Kokina et al., 2021). The term *business partner* reflects their main role in working alongside top management to shape strategic business decisions.

The AIS era from the 2000s onwards is referred to as AIS 2.0 because of the growing significance of analytics in shaping strategic business decisions. The AIS 2.0 era reflects a new way of how computerised AIS is used to support strategic decisions. New technological developments enabled through the Internet, like BI and e-business layers of ERP systems, cloud computing, and big data, present a valuable opportunity to expand the role of AIS.

Conclusion

The accounting discipline has played a critical role in economic history. AIS have the merit of having supported accountants in activities since ancient times. Although mostly associated with information technology, rudimentary AIS existed long before the development of computers. As time passed, AIS evolved to include more features, which led to increased complexity. The evolution of AIS has been anything but linear. Indeed, it is possible to identify at least three significant breakthroughs that led to the AIS that we know today: (1) the introduction of double-entry bookkeeping, which gained particular importance in the Industrial Age (1700–1940); (2) the development of computers, which opened the so-called Information Age in the 1950s; and (3) the adoption of the Internet, which allowed the Integration Phase (1990s) to commence and enable the development of AIS 2.0 (2000s–present). Double-entry bookkeeping represents the essence of AIS. The increased level of transparency enabled the separation of ownership and control, a characteristic of the modern enterprise. Computers and the Internet represent the instruments that brought AIS to a superior level of sophistication. They have significantly enlarged the scope of AIS, which is not only confined to the mere reporting or analysis of historical data but also extends to the provision of forward-looking information to help top management in their decision-making. AIS are now able to convey timely and valuable information to both internal and external stakeholders and are well recognised as a key component of companies' information systems. The effort to continuously adapt AIS to the constantly evolving business environment has brought AIS from a mere supportive role to that of a strategic one, and such a role is not likely to change soon.

Notes

1 See, for example, the ones suggested by Belfo & Trigo (2013) and Poston & Grabski (2000).
2 A well-known example of joint stock company is the East India Company founded in 1600 (Lawson, 2014).
3 The origin of double-entry bookkeeping is uncertain. However, it was attributed to an Italian mathematician whose name was Luca Pacioli who wrote, in 1494, the treatise *Summa de Aritmetica, Geometrica, Proportione et Proportinalite* where he explained how to effectively and efficiently record financial information.
4 Sometimes management accounting is also referred to as cost accounting. It emerged in Britain around the 1870s (Boyns & Edwards, 1997b).

References

Alikhani, H., Ahmadi, N., & Mehravar, M. (2013). Accounting information system versus management information system. *European Online Journal of Natural and Social Sciences*, 2(3), 359–366.

Alter, S. (2004). A work system view of DSS in its fourth decade. *Decision Support Systems*, 38(3), 319–327.

Anandarajan, A., Srinivasan, C. A., & Anandarajan, M., (2004). Historical overview of accounting information systems. In: M. Anandarajan, A. Anandarajan, & C. A. Srinivasan (Eds.), *Business Intelligence Techniques* (pp. 1–19). Berlin: Springer.

Baldvinsdottir, G., Burns, J., Nørreklit, H., & Scapens, R. W. (2009). The image of accountants: From bean counters to extreme accountants. *Accounting, Auditing & Accountability Journal*, 22(6), 858–882.

Barney, J. (1991). Firm resources and sustained competitive advantage. *Journal of Management*, 17(1), 99–120.

Belfo, F., & Trigo, A. (2013). Accounting information systems: Tradition and future directions. *Procedia Technology*, 9, 536–546.

Boyns, T., & Edwards, J. R. (1997a). Cost and management accounting in early Victorian Britain: A Chandleresque analysis?. *Management Accounting Research*, 8(1), 19–46.

Boyns, T., & Edwards, J. R. (1997b). The construction of cost accounting systems in Britain to 1900: The case of the coal, iron and steel industries. *Business History*, 39(3), 1–29.

Braverman, H. (1974). Labor and monopoly capital. *Nueva York, Monthly Review*.

Brown, B. (2015). *The History of the Corporation*. Oakland: BF Communications.

Brown, R. (2014). *A History of Accounting and Accountants*. New York: Routledge.

Brownell, P. (1983). The motivational impact of management-by-exception in a budgetary context. *Journal of Accounting Research*, 21(2), 456–472.

Bryer, R. A. (1993). Double-entry bookkeeping and the birth of capitalism: Accounting for the commercial revolution in medieval northern Italy. *Critical Perspectives on Accounting*, 4(2), 113–140.

Campbell-Kelly, M. (2004). *From Airline Reservations to Sonic the Hedgehog: A History of the Software Industry*. Cambridge, MA: MIT Press.

Campbell-Kelly, M., & Garcia-Swartz, D. D. (2009). Pragmatism, not ideology: Historical perspectives on IBM's adoption of open-source software. *Information Economics and Policy*, 21(3), 229–244.

ComputerHistoryMuseum. (2016). *Timeline of Computer History in the 1970s*. Retrieved from http://www.computerhistory.org/timeline/1975/

Cooper, R., & Kaplan, R. S. (1991). Profit priorities from activity-based costing. *Harvard Business Review*, 69(3), 130–135.

Cunha, J., Fernandes, J. P., Mendes, J., & Saraiva, J. (2015). Spreadsheet engineering *Central European Functional Programming School* (246–299): Berlin: Springer.

Dai, J., & Vasarhelyi, M. A. (2017). Toward blockchain-based accounting and assurance. *Journal of Information Systems*, 31(3), 5–21.

David, J. S., Dunn, C. L., McCarthy, W. E., & Poston, R. S. (1999). The research pyramid: A framework for accounting information systems research. *Journal of Information Systems*, 13(1), 7–30.

De Soto, J. H. (2009). *Money, Bank Credit, and Economic Cycles*. Auburn: Ludwig von Mises Institute.

Elbashir, M. Z., Collier, P. A., & Sutton, S. G. (2011). The role of organizational absorptive capacity in strategic use of business intelligence to support integrated management control systems. *The Accounting Review*, 86(1), 155–184.

Fleischman, R. K., & Tyson, T. N. (1993). Cost accounting during the industrial revolution. The present state of historical knowledge. *The Economic History Review*, 46(3), 503–517.

Gleeson-White, J. (2011). *Double Entry: How the Merchants of Venice Created Modern Finance*. Crows Nest: Allen & Unwin.

Grabski, S. V., Leech, S. A., & Schmidt, P. J. (2011). A review of ERP research: A future agenda for accounting information systems. *Journal of Information Systems*, 25(1), 7–78.

Gupta, S., & Misra, S. C. (2016). Compliance, network, security and the people related factors in cloud ERP implementation. *International Journal of Communication Systems*, 29, 1395–1419.

Hong, K.-K., & Kim, Y.-G. (2002). The critical success factors for ERP implementation: An organizational fit perspective. *Information & Management*, 40(1), 25–40.

Hoskin, K. W., & Macve, R. H. (1986). Accounting and the examination: A genealogy of disciplinary power. *Accounting, Organizations and Society*, 11(2), 105–136.

Hsu, P.-F. (2013). Integrating ERP and e-business: Resource complementarity in business value creation. *Decision Support Systems*, 56, 334–347.

ICAEW (2018). *Blockchain and the Future of Accountancy*. The Institute of Chartered Accountants in England and Wales (ICAEW). Retrieved from https://www.icaew.com/-/media/corporate/files/technical/technology/thought-leadership/blockchain-and-the-future-of-accountancy.ashx

Johnson, T., & Kaplan, R. (1987). *Relevance Lost: The Rise and Fall of Management Accounting*. New York: Harvard Business School Press.

Järvenpää, M. (2007). Making business partners: A case study on how management accounting culture was changed. *European Accounting Review*, 16(1), 99–142.

Kale, V. (2016). *Enhancing Enterprise Intelligence: Leveraging ERP, CRM, SCM, PLM, BPM, and BI*. Boca Raton: CRC Press.

Kaplan, R. S., & Norton, D. P. (1995). Putting the balanced scorecard to work. *Performance Measurement, Management, and Appraisal Sourcebook*, 66, 66–74.

Kokina, J., Gilleran, R., Blanchette, S., & Stoddard, D. (2021). Accountant as digital innovator: Roles and competencies in the age of automation. *Accounting Horizons*, 35(1), 153–184.

Kraska, T. (2013). Finding the needle in the big data systems haystack. *IEEE Internet Computing*, 17(1), 84–86.

Lawson, P. (2014). *East India Company*, The: A History. London: Routledge.

Leitch, R. A., & Davis, K. R., (1983). *Accounting Information Systems*. Hoboken: Prentice Hall Professional Technical Reference.

Littleton, A. C. (1933). *Accounting Evolution to 1900*. Tuscaloosa: University of Alabama Press.

Marston, S., Li, Z., Bandyopadhyay, S., Zhang, J., & Gjalsasi, A. (2011). Cloud computing—the business perspective. *Decision Support Systems*, 51(1), 176–189.

Mauldin, E. G., & Ruchala, L. V., (1999). Towards a meta-theory of accounting information systems. *Accounting, Organizations and Society*, 24(4), 317–331.

Mell, P., & Grance, T. (2011). *The NIST Definition of Cloud Computing*. Retrieved from http://csrc.nist.gov/publications/nistpubs/800-145/SP800-145.pdf

Mendes, J. C. (2012). *Evolution of Model-Driven Spreadsheets*. (PhD dissertation), Universidade do Minho. Retrieved from http://repositorium.sdum.uminho.pt/bitstream/1822/27889/1/eeum_di_dissertacao_pg16490.pdf

Meyer, M. W. (2003). *Rethinking Performance Measurement: Beyond the Balanced Scorecard*. Cambridge: Cambridge University Press.

Mircea, M., Ghilic-Micu, B., & Stoica, M. (2011). Combining business intelligence with cloud computing to delivery agility in actual economy. *Journal of Economic Computation and Economic Cybernetics Studies*, 45(1), 39–54.

Møller, C. (2005). ERP II: A conceptual framework for next-generation enterprise systems? *Journal of Enterprise Information Management*, 18(4), 483–497.

Nankani, G. (2005). *Economic Growth in the 1990s: Learning from a Decade of Reform*. Washington, DC: The International Bank for Reconstruction and Development/The World Bank.

Negash, S., & Gray, P. (2008). *Business Intelligence*: Springer.

Paulsson, W. V. (2013). *The Complementary Use of IS Technologies to Support Flexibility and Integration Needs in Budgeting* (PhD in Information Systems Monograph), Lund University, Lund. Retrieved from https://lup.lub.lu.se/search/publication/4022792 (Lund Studies in Informatics No. 12)

Perry, M. (2007). *Computer Prices and Speed: 1970 to 2007*. Retrieved from http://mjperry.blogspot.ie/2007/08/ibm-mainframe-computer-in-1970-pictured.html

Poston R. S., & Grabski, S. V. (2000). Accounting information systems research: Is it another QWERTY? *International Journal of Accounting Information Systems*, 1, 9–53.

Raihana, G. F. H. (2012). Cloud ERP–a solution model. *International Journal of Computer Science and Information Technology & Security*, 2(1), 76–79.

Rashid, M. A., Hossain, L., & Patrick, J. D. (2002). The evolution of ERP systems: A historical perspective. In: H. Liaquat, P. Jon David, & A. R. Mohammad (Eds.), *Enterprise Resource Planning: Global Opportunities and Challenges* (pp. 1–16). Hershey, PA: IGI Global.

Reneau, J. H., & Grabski, S. V. (1987). A review of research in computer-human interaction and individual differences within a model for research in accounting information systems. *Journal of Information Systems*, 2(1), 33–53.

Rosati, P., Čuk, T. (2019). Blockchain beyond cryptocurrencies. In: T. Lynn, T., J. Mooney, P. Rosati, P., Cummins, M. (Eds.), *Disrupting Finance* (pp. 149–170). Palgrave Studies in Digital Business & Enabling Technologies. London: Palgrave.

Scapens, R. W., & Jazayeri, M. (2003). ERP systems and management accounting change: opportunities or impacts? A research note. *European Accounting Review*, 12(1), 201–233.

Shim, J. P., Warkentin, M., Courtney, J. F., Power, D. J., Sharda, R., & Carlsson, C. (2002). Past, present, and future of decision support technology. *Decision Support Systems*, 33(2), 111–126.

Sutton, S. G., Holt, M., & Arnold, V. (2016). "The reports of my death are greatly exaggerated"— Artificial intelligence research in accounting. *International Journal of Accounting Information Systems*, 22, 60–73.

Wagner, E. L., & Newell, S. (2004). Best for whom?: The tension between 'best practice' ERP packages and diverse epistemic cultures in a university context. *The Journal of Strategic Information Systems,* 13(4), 305–328.

3

TECHNOLOGIES UNDERPINNING ACCOUNTING INFORMATION SYSTEMS

Gerhard Kristandl

Introduction

It is now widely accepted that information technology (IT) has been, and still is, a major driver for accounting to become a knowledge service profession (Granlund, 2011). Accounting information systems (AIS) have grown into complex decision-support systems (DSSs) whilst increasing the speed and accuracy of more traditional accounting tasks (Gelinas et al., 2018). IT impacts the quality of the AIS (measured in terms of scope, timeliness, aggregation, reliability, flexibility and usefulness), which, in turn, impacts the quality of accounting information (Wisna, 2013). To become the enabling and empowering tools AIS are expected to be, they require the technological infrastructure or 'underpinnings' that facilitate their smooth operation (Ghasemi et al., 2011; Wisna, 2013; Gelinas et al., 2018). Inadequate technologies underpinning AIS can burden a firm with extra maintenance and data recovery costs and issues with data reliability, security and privacy. Thus, inadequate technology can potentially corrupt the very outcomes of an AIS, namely reports and decision-relevant information (Ghasemi et al., 2011), leading to incorrect, unreliable decisions.

In the remainder of this chapter, the general relationship between AIS and technology is detailed. Further, networks are revealed as a necessary technological feature of AIS. Then, the components that are aligned to build and run an AIS are discussed, namely hardware and software. Networks, hardware and software must work together to provide a reliable basis for any AIS to perform and provide reports and decision-relevant information. Finally, the focus is moved to the emerging technologies of blockchain, the Internet of Things (IoT) and artificial intelligence (AI) that have started to heavily impact AIS in recent years. Later chapters home in on some of the topics covered here in greater detail.

Accounting information systems and technology

Accounting has experienced many improvements due to the computerisation of accounting processes (Ghasemi et al., 2011). Traditional paper-based ledgers and bookkeeping processes have been automated and mirrored in AIS, which eventually morphed into full decision-making systems (O'Donnell & David, 2000). An AIS in this context is a cohesive organisational structure (Boczko, 2007), a set of processes, functions, interrelated activities,

DOI: 10.4324/9781003132943-5

documents and technologies (Hurt, 2016) that captures, processes, outputs and stores data, and as such provides information for decision-making and control purposes to internal (Quinn & Kristandl, 2014) and external parties (Hurt, 2016). Historically speaking, an AIS was a specialised subsystem of a management information system, and thus integrated with other information systems (IS) in firms. With the rise of material resource planning and, subsequently, enterprise resource planning (ERP) systems, AIS have become even more integrated with other IS (Gelinas et al., 2018). This has an important implication for the view taken in this chapter – the technologies that enable AIS to run are the same for other types of IS. They share the same network technologies, hardware, software and other components that make up the technological basis for them to be efficiently and effectively operated. This view is in line with Gelinas et al. (2018, p. 14) who explain that the distinctions between separate IS have become somewhat blurred, and a clear differentiation between IS and AIS is less prominent today.

As discussed in more detail in other chapters of this handbook, an AIS fulfils not only a decision-oriented but also a controlling function. The cohesiveness of the AIS structure is achieved through prudent, integrated system design and the interactions of the human actors along a network of computerised resources that capture, process and deliver the required information (Boczko, 2007; Ghasemi et al., 2011; Gelinas et al., 2018). These resources can be determined as a collection of computer hardware and software, connected to one another within a network (Ghasemi et al., 2011; Quinn & Kristandl, 2014), and need to be implemented and maintained to support business processes (Gelinas et al., 2018). Although non-computerised AIS exist (Quinn & Kristandl, 2014), modern businesses that employ such systems can rarely do so without the use of computers. In very simple terms, to capture – ideally – *all* relevant, transaction-based information for accounting purposes in an organisation, the resources need to be linked to one another to input information and send the information to the right addressee (another computer or person) for processing and finally onwards to the party that requires the processed data for decision-making, reporting or controlling (including auditing).

Networks

As of the time of writing, almost every business is connected to and uses networks, particularly the Internet. As of 2019, 91% of enterprises in the European Union (EU) with at least ten persons employed had used a fixed broadband connection (Eurostat, 2020). Mobile technologies such as mobile payment systems and capturing document data (e.g. via a scan of invoices) and the IoT have a major impact on AIS and the opportunities to collect and report data in real time (Trigo et al., 2014; Brandas et al., 2015; Romney et al., 2021). This illustrates the importance and – to some extent – implicitness of networks in today's corporate environment. The interconnectedness between devices determines the infrastructure that forms the backbone of any AIS today (Romney et al., 2021).

The technological view on networks is that of a so-called hard network (as opposed to social soft-type, or the logical, more abstract semi-soft-type; see Boczko, 2007). A hard network is the physical representation of a group of devices (e.g. computers and servers) connected to one another via a network interface card (NIC) and wired/wireless links, managed by software allowing data exchange (Hall, 2019). Wired connections (e.g. copper wire, twisted pair, coaxial, fibre optic) connect the various computers in a permanent manner, typically via point-to-point links (Tanenbaum & Wetherall, 2021). Wired connections, once set up, are difficult to reconfigure. Physical links provide the infrastructure to enable networking; this includes computer-to-computer, computer-to-server, server-to-server or computer-to-periphery (e.g. shared network printers; Quinn & Kristandl, 2014) connections. Wireless networks connect via broadcast links, such as high-frequency radio signals; infrared, electromagnetic signals; or laser for short-distance networks; or mobile telephony, microwaves or satellite for long-distance networks (Boczko, 2007; Richardson et al., 2014; Tanenbaum & Wetherall, 2021). Wireless networks provide the advantages of mobility, rapid deployment, flexibility and scalability, low-cost setup and easy maintenance (Boczko, 2007; Richardson et al., 2014). However, they can be limited by the distance to the access point, as well as the number of wireless devices using the existing bandwidth at the same time. Wireless network access typically requires access to a wired intranet or Internet, linked via a wireless network interface card.

Regardless of their physical connections, all types of networks can be described using the following three attributes (Boczko, 2007):

- Architecture
- Topology
- Protocols

Architecture

The architecture describes the technological and geographical layout and configuration of a network and includes the definition of intra-network and inter-network relationships, the physical configuration, the functional organisation, the operational procedures employed, the data used and the scale of the network (Boczko, 2007; Magal & Word, 2012; Tanenbaum & Wetherall, 2021).

Network architecture can be described either in system or in hardware terms. A typical example of the former is a client-server (C-S) model that aims to interconnect and distribute software and hardware efficiently and effectively across a network (Boczko, 2007). Here, a 'client' is a computer or workstation that requests services (programs, applications, data processing) from a 'server', a computer that manages and allocates these services (Curtis & Cobham, 2005; Hall, 2019). The C-S model is an example of a multi-tier architecture (see Figure 3.1), where presentation, data/application processing and data storage/management are separated into different layers (see Chapter 4). IS such as SAP ERP are based on a C-S architecture, with only the graphical user interface (GUI) running at the user end. The C-S model is widely used in online commerce and forms the underlying idea behind cloud computing with the main difference that the data is stored on a server that is owned by a cloud provider instead of the company, accessed via the Internet (Lin & Chen, 2012; Zissis & Lekkas, 2012).

An evolution of the standard C-S architecture is service-oriented architecture, based on the concept of designing and developing inter-operable functions and applications (services) that are reusable without needing to change the underlying application (Magal & Word, 2012; Hall, 2019). Hardware architecture, on the other hand, supports the distribution of software, data and processes. Typical examples are local area networks (LANs), wide area networks (WANs) and virtual private networks (VPNs).

A LAN (see Figure 3.2) is a network within geographically close confines, often within the same room or building, privately owned by a single organisation (Quinn & Kristandl, 2014; Tanenbaum & Wetherall, 2021). Within this type of network, computers (*nodes*), servers and peripheral devices, such as printers, are connected either wired or wirelessly

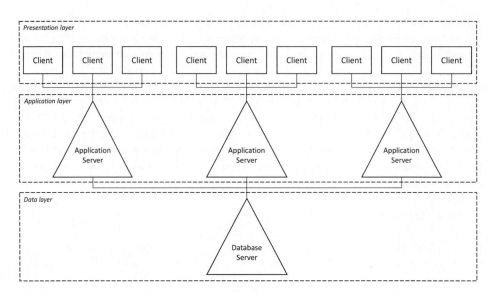

Figure 3.1 Client-server architecture.

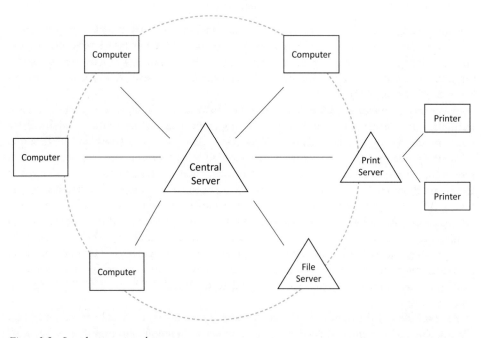

Figure 3.2 Local area network.

(WLAN) (Richardson et al., 2014). Hubs and switches (see the 'Hardware' section later) interconnect the devices and send packets (formatted, small units of data; Richardson et al., 2014) over the network. LANs allow use of a common network operating system, centralisation of shared data and programs from a central server as well as their downloading for local processing, communication of personal computers with outside networks (e.g. the Internet), sharing of scarce resources, email as well as access to and use of a centralised calendar and diary (Curtis & Cobham, 2005). Sharing resources over a network is cost-efficient since there is less need for large-storage hard disks or programs for every computer within the network. Computers may act as both clients and servers in smaller LANs – such a network is then called a peer-to-peer network (Boczko, 2007) due to the equivalent responsibilities that each workstation fulfils. In larger LANs, workstations act as clients only and are then linked to a server.

A WAN (see Figure 3.3) is a network over a larger geographical area (e.g. a country), connected via public (e.g. phone lines) or private (e.g. leased lines or satellite) communication facilities (Shinder, 2001; Hall, 2019). WANs provide remote access to employees or customers, link two or more separate LANs at sites within a company and provide the business with access to the Internet (Richardson et al., 2014).

Depending on the location of a central hub, there are two types of WAN, namely centralised and distributed. In a centralised WAN, all major functions (e.g. accounting, procurement, sales order processing) are carried out at the central hub. The computers in the network do not process transactions locally but send data processing requests remotely to the central hub (Curtis & Cobham, 2005; Boczko, 2007). All data traffic can be closely monitored, but it puts a heavy burden on the network itself. The central hub needs to queue and prioritise concurrent requests, rendering the network much more vulnerable to a complete standstill. A distributed WAN, on the other hand, is decentralised in terms of data processing (Curtis & Cobham, 2005; Boczko, 2007) and is thus better able to transmit and process individual transactions simultaneously. In a distributed environment, LANs are connected to one another, and/or to larger WANs, via bridges (linking same-type LANs) or gateways (linking different-type LANs; Hall, 2019). The largest distributed WAN to date is the Internet, and the World Wide Web is a WAN that uses a client/(web) server architecture to transmit data and process tasks (Shinder, 2001).

Variations of WANs are metropolitan area networks and campus area networks that can be quite large but are confined within a city or campus (Shinder, 2001; Tanenbaum &

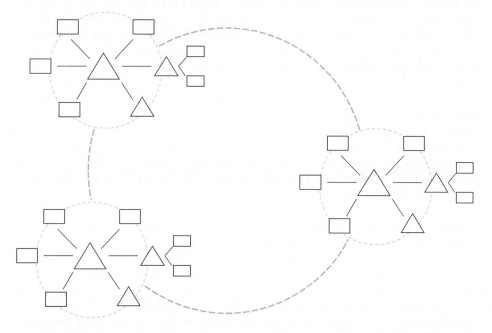

Figure 3.3 Wide area network.

Wetherall, 2021). A VPN is created using a secure tunnel between a corporate WAN and (home) offices via virtual links over the Internet rather than leased lines (Richardson et al., 2014; Tanenbaum & Wetherall, 2021). VPNs came to prominence due to the larger bandwidth availability, enabling remote access to corporate WANs from outside the business premises for salespersons, home offices and business partners that require access. Companies that use cloud technology for their networks are particularly in need of secure access points, which a VPN provides. Since they use the Internet, this network type provides a low-cost connection but suffers a lower Quality-of-Service than corporate WANs (Richardson et al., 2014).

Topology

The term 'topology' denotes the physical or logical arrangement of network devices (Boczko, 2007). Figure 3.4 shows the most common topologies utilised in networks.

A bus topology is a linear topology where clients share a central line connection (Boczko, 2007; Hall, 2019), either linear or in a daisy chain (see Figure 3.4a and b). When data is sent along the network, it contains a unique network address for the desired destination and will thus be delivered to the correct network resource. Although a bus topology is easy to set up and extend, the connected devices are competing for connection resources, as only one line is available to them (Hall, 2019). In cases where two or more clients want to use the network at the same time, this might lead to queuing and slow operation of the network – a situation that is exacerbated by every additional node added to the bus. Thus, this topology is limited in size, as it may become difficult to operate and manage (Boczko, 2007).

In a ring topology, each node is connected to two other nodes and represents a peer-to-peer arrangement (see Figure 3.4c). As opposed to a bus topology in a daisy-chain configuration, a ring topology creates a closed loop of nodes, meaning that if a signal is sent along the network, and no destination node accepts it, it returns to the sending node (Boczko, 2007; Hall, 2019). Each node has equal status, but only one node can communicate at a time. Unlike a bus topology, the nodes along a ring topology move the signal along rather than ignore it. This improves network speed; the scalability of the network is also superior to a bus topology, as additional nodes do not significantly impact network speeds. It requires more connections however than a bus network; is more costly to implement; and if one single node fails, it will impact the entire network. Both ring and bus typologies have become side-lined in favour of the more stable star typology (see Figure 3.4e; Quinn & Kristandl, 2014). A mesh topology (see Figure 3.4d) is a variation of the bus topology, where every node is connected to every other node (Boczko, 2007). Although providing a more stable and reliable network for small networks, its complexity increases considerably when the network grows. This can render network management and reconfiguration difficult and costly (Boczko, 2007). Mesh topologies are often used in WANs to connect several LANs to one another.

In a star topology (see Figure 3.4e), all devices are linked to a central computer which acts as a transmission device (Boczko, 2007; Hall, 2019). In this case, signals are transmitted via the central hub rather than along the entire network. It is relatively easy to implement, extend and monitor, and if a device fails, it rarely impacts the entire network, unless the central hub fails (Quinn & Kristandl, 2014). Other disadvantages are higher cost (maintenance, security) and higher risk of virus infection via the central hub (Boczko, 2007). This topology is often used in both centralised and distributed WANs where the central hub is a mainframe (Hall, 2019).

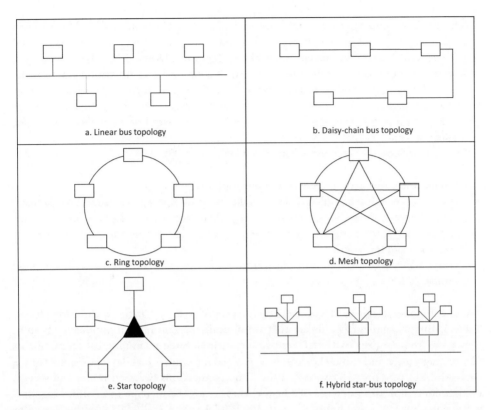

Figure 3.4 Network topologies.

The topologies above can be combined based on business needs. Examples of such hybrid topologies are star-bus or star-ring topologies (Boczko, 2007) that combine the advantages and eliminate topology-individual drawbacks. Figure 3.4f shows an example of a star-bus topology that is easier to extend and more resilient than a pure bus topology.

Protocols

Without instructions to manage the communication and flow of data between the devices, networks would merely be physical arrangements of computers and connections. A network requires protocols – formalised and uniform sets of rules and standards that govern the syntax, semantics and synchronisation of communications between nodes to enable them to communicate (Quinn & Kristandl, 2014; Hall, 2019). AIS need to comply with these standards – they define the formal rules of conduct and etiquette to avoid miscommunication and misinterpretation (Hall, 2019). Standardised reference models for network protocols such as the Open System Interconnection (OSI) standard or the more commonly used Transfer Control Protocol/Internet Protocol (TCP/IP) standard provide businesses with a framework to achieve this compliance (Tanenbaum & Wetherall, 2021).[1]

Hardware

Nodes and their periphery mentioned when discussing network architectures, topologies and protocols can be summarised as 'hardware' in IT. The term comprises all physical devices used to capture, process and store data (Curtis & Cobham, 2005). This includes not only computers and their components (e.g. keyboards, disk drives) and servers but also cloud-enabled devices such as tablets, smartphones (Quinn & Kristandl, 2014) or other smart devices (see the 'Internet of Things' section later). A computer is a workstation that provides a network-human interface, an access point to the AIS for both input and output of the required accounting data. The role of a server (see also the 'Architecture' section earlier) in a network is to process and manage the flow of information between the nodes and allocate processing resources to the task at hand.

Typically, a computer comprises (Curtis & Cobham, 2005):

- Input devices that accept, convert and transmit data
- A central processing unit (CPU) that executes program instructions, controls/coordinates data movement, carries out arithmetic and logical operations and stores programs and data
- A secondary storage that maintains a permanent record of data and programs beyond execution and for security
- Output devices that receive information from the CPU and convert it into the required format

These components can be detailed further, as illustrated by Curtis & Cobham (2005). Table 3.1 lists examples of hardware that are typically present in an individual computer. However, from an organisational perspective with elevated technological requirements (processing power and storage), it can be separated into individual devices connected via network links (Quinn & Kristandl, 2014). The connections between nodes and servers require communication devices (see below) that create and manage these links, e.g. network cards, repeaters and hubs (Boczko, 2007; Richardson et al., 2014), either wired or wireless.

Input devices accept data, convert them into a machine-readable form and transmit them within a computer system (Curtis & Cobham, 2005). Keyboards are a typical input device, where information is entered into the system and converted into binary code whilst being displayed on a screen. However, keyboards are not the only way to enter data into a system (see Table 3.1). Pointing devices – such as a mouse – are a commonplace feature in computers.

Table 3.1 Examples of computer hardware

Hardware type	Function/s	Examples
Input devices	To input/capture data	Keyboard, touchscreen, mouse, barcode reader, microphone, pointing devices, scanners, IoT sensors
Processors	To perform calculations, to execute tasks	CPU, Intel range of microprocessors, M1 chip (Apple devices)
Storage devices	To retain data when power is switched off	Hard disks, CD/DVD/Blu-ray disks, USB sticks
Output devices	To provide/display data in an understandable and useful format	Display screens, printers, (smart) speakers
Communication/network devices	To allow network devices to communicate and exchange information with each other across networks	Routers, cabling, switches, NICs (wired/wireless), hubs, firewalls, modems

Adapted from Quinn & Kristandl (2014, p. 15).

Scanners, for instance, are widely used as input devices. They employ optical character recognition (OCR) or magnetic ink character recognition (MICR) to identify relevant data from a source document. OCR is commonly used by utility companies or government departments. Documents scanned using OCR typically come with specific instructions on how to fill in the data, such as writing in capital letters, black ink and within a confined box, to correctly identify the characters written (Curtis & Cobham, 2005). MICR is mostly used in processing cheques in banks, where the cheque number, account and sort codes are printed in magnetic ink – although cheques are increasingly less common. Barcode readers are another widespread input device type, particularly in logistical processes to record the movement of goods. A good example of an industry that relies on data input that way is food retailing (e.g. supermarkets). Voice recognition via microphones is also widely used for data entry, for instance, in call centres or customer service to screen and route calls. Today, voice inputs are often processed by AI, embodied in smart assistants like Apple's Siri, Amazon's Alexa or Microsoft's Cortana. Finally, the IoT uses technologies like radio-frequency identification (RFID) tags and global positioning system (GPS) to capture data (see discussion later in this chapter). Different input devices show differences in accuracy and cost. Keyboards, for instance, are by and large inexpensive input devices but are subject to human error (Curtis & Cobham, 2005). Also, data entry can be quite slow when keyboards are being used – this is different with scanners or barcode readers where data entry is quick and less prone to error but comes with the disadvantage that they are costlier when acquired and operated.

Processors enable a computing device to decode and execute program instructions, control and coordinate data movements and perform arithmetic and logical operations (Curtis & Cobham, 2005; Quinn & Kristandl, 2014). Examples of processor manufacturers are Intel (i5, i7, i9), AMD (Ryzen series) or Apple (M1 chip). Together with the main memory unit (random-access memory, RAM), used for storage of currently used data/programs, and the operating system, processors are the heart of the computing functions of hardware (Curtis & Cobham, 2005). The history of processors has shown an exponential increase in processing power, which, in turn, allows for quicker program execution and larger RAM for program-multitasking in computers today.

Storage devices serve to maintain the input, processed data and programs on a permanent basis (Curtis & Cobham, 2005), for immediate or later use or as backup for data in case of security and integrity issues. Where the CPU only stores data whilst the computer is switched on, storage devices hold the data even if powered off. Different types of storage devices differ in speed of data retrieval, capacity, cost and robustness. Hard disks are a typical storage device in most computer systems. Types of hard disks are magnetic drives (hard drive disk), optical disks (Blu-ray, DVD/CD), flash drives (solid state drive) or cloud storage where the stored data is accessed via the Internet. The latter type has experienced a rapid increase in usage, as it allows not only large but also small and medium-sized companies to acquire and operate hitherto unaffordable AIS technology (Brandas et al., 2015). Older types of storage devices such as magnetic tapes or floppy disks still exist in some organisations (such as the US Nuclear Weapons Force; see BBC, 2016) but nowadays do not feature in modern AIS technology.

Output devices are used to display information in the required format. Typical examples are computer monitors, tablet and smartphone screens, printers and speakers (Curtis & Cobham, 2005; Quinn & Kristandl, 2014). Screens, in general, are the most common type. They are used with desktop computers, laptops, tablets, smartphones, machinery and vehicles – in fact, the IoT has had a major impact on screens added to the most unusual devices (Mazhelis et al., 2012). Printers are another output device that issue information by means of laser, ink or thermal printing technology (Curtis & Cobham, 2005). Larger type of printers are plotters, chain and drum printers, but these do not offer the quality and flexibility suitable for AIS. Finally, speakers – in conjunction with screens or as stand-alone devices – can output information to the user. Particularly when equipped with AI, smart speakers become both input and output devices that can interact with the user (Hart, 2018).

Communication/network devices are hardware that allow network resources to interconnect with one another. As discussed earlier, the actual connection between a node and network is either wired (cabling) or wireless (NIC). However, the cabling or connection alone is not enough – data that is transmitted along the network needs to find the right address. This is done by hubs, switches or routers. Hubs merely transmit incoming data packets to all other connections, whilst switches and routers intelligently determine an outgoing line for incoming data, choosing the most efficient communication path through a network to the required destination, using the IP addresses of sender and receiver (Richardson et al., 2014; Tanenbaum & Wetherall, 2021).

Networks that use hubs instead of switches are called non-switched networks, where communication links are shared by all devices (Curtis & Cobham, 2005). Typically, switched networks show a better performance than non-switched ones, as there are no data collisions, data can be transmitted simultaneously and the capacity is used more efficiently (Tanenbaum & Wetherall, 2021). From a data security point of view, switched networks are also preferable, as data traffic is only sent to the address where it is required (Tanenbaum & Wetherall, 2021). They are also more efficient to monitor, as corporate firewalls are a security system comprising hardware like switches, routers, servers and software, to allow or deny a data packet that enters or exits a company LAN to continue on their transmission path (Richardson et al., 2014).

Software

Although hardware and networks are essential in enabling a smooth-running and purpose-driven AIS, without software it would not work. 'Software' is the general term used to describe the instructions that control the operations of hardware (Curtis & Cobham, 2005; Quinn & Kristandl, 2014).[2] Software can be categorised as operating systems (OS), database systems or applications software and requires the use of programming languages to design and create them.

Operating systems software

This type of software comprises programs that enable an efficient and smooth operation of the computer system (Curtis & Cobham, 2005) and is considered the 'most important piece of software' (Richardson et al., 2014, p. 242). It is the basis for the hardware to work in the first place and provides the following four functions (Curtis & Cobham, 2005):

- Handling of data interchange between input/output devices and the CPU
- Loading of data and programs into and out of the main memory
- Allocating main memory to data and programs as needed (managing processes and memory so that all programs receive a share of the available resources)
- Handling job scheduling, multiprogramming and multiprocessing

Examples of OS available on the market are Microsoft Windows, Apple OS, Linux, Unix and Chrome OS for computers, as well as Android and iOS for mobile devices. Not all of these incur acquisition costs – Linux distributions like Ubuntu and openSUSE are free, whereas Windows may have a cost based on the licence model. All these OS provide a GUI as opposed to text-based interfaces that require the entry of command lines to work with the system – an example was MS-DOS which was eventually superseded by the more user-friendly Windows systems (which, in turn, had been inspired by Apple's OS in the 1980s).

Its crucial role in the smooth running of an AIS requires the OS to be secured against internal and external threats to its integrity. This includes intended or unintended security threats by users, computers, applications, the OS itself as well as hacking or data leaks of sensitive information to external parties (Richardson et al., 2014). The OS requires clear IT governance policies (e.g. the COBIT5 framework) that control who can manage and access the system, system and network resources and actions that are allowed by users. These security features are even more relevant in a cloud-computing environment, where several 'virtual' (rather than actual) OS share the same hardware and could potentially become permeable, allowing access to resources between two instances of an OS running on the same platform.

Database systems software

In an integrated AIS, corporate accounting data is typically stored on a central database to ensure that all relevant applications access the same kind of information when processing data. As such, databases are another crucial component in an AIS and require a database system that can record, manage and store a massive amount of day-to-day accounting data. A database system comprises two main software components, namely a data warehouse (a centralised collection of company-wide data for a long period of time) and operational databases that draw data from the data warehouse (Richardson et al., 2014). Operational databases contain the data for current/recent fiscal years, updated whenever a transaction is processed. Periodically, data is uploaded from the operational databases to the data warehouse to provide decision-useful information to identify trends and patterns – the process of analysing them as such is called data mining, using Online Analytical Processing.

Applications software

Applications software are programs that fulfil specific user functions (Quinn & Kristandl, 2014). In an accounting context, this may mean functions like sales ledger processing, budgeting, forecasting or reporting (Curtis & Cobham, 2005). Most AIS include application packages that consist of functional modules such as sales ledgers, accounts receivable/payable, payroll or credit and payment systems. These desktop accounting packages are offered and distributed by ERP software providers such as SAP or Oracle, or mid-level accounting package providers such as Sage or Xero, either as in-house or subscription-based cloud offerings.

If applications packages are unable to fulfil a specific business need, a company could develop it in-house or commission development – see Chapter 4 also. However, such specific software developments require lengthy analysis, design and testing phases (Curtis & Cobham, 2005). Commissioned software can become very costly as opposed to application packages; the cost of software development, testing and subsequent updates needs to be absorbed in full by the commissioning business (Curtis & Cobham, 2005). Further considerations stem from the frequent requirement to run the commissioned software on different types of hardware (portability) and the existence of professional documentation that enables adequate IT support. On the other hand, specially commissioned software provides a perfect fit to corporate requirements; this includes the elimination of redundant functions that may not be needed (but paid for) and the compatibility with other existing software (Curtis & Cobham, 2005). Whether a company is able to commission specially designed AIS software is mostly a question of affordability, which typically rules out smaller businesses. Interestingly, it appears that most companies prefer packaged software to self-developed or commissioned ones (Granlund, 2011).

To avoid compatibility issues, businesses often acquire entire software suites, where several programs are integrated and sold together. Suites provide inter-program compatibility in data exchange and user interface – good examples are Microsoft Office (e.g. Word, Excel, Access, Outlook) or the SAP Business Suite (containing ERP, Customer Relationship Management, Supplier Relationship Management, Supply Chain Management, and Product Lifecycle Management).

Programming languages

Software is written as a set of instructions to control computer operations. These instructions are written in a formal language to communicate them to the computer – a programming language. Table 3.2 briefly details the three main categories of programming languages and their characteristics (Curtis & Cobham, 2005):

Machine-oriented programming languages have been mostly superseded by higher level ones due to their dependence on the source program and the computer architecture it is written on/for. Task-oriented languages that require compiling can be used repeatedly, are independent of the source program and provide portability between computer systems and architectures, with a certain level of security against tampering with the compiled code (Curtis & Cobham, 2005). However, programs operate slower due to inefficiencies in the compiling process and the exclusion of the individual CPU structure. Object-oriented programming languages (OOPLs) apply a different logic to task-oriented ones, in that they do not define complex operations but rather the objects and their (changeable) attributes that take part in the operations. OOPLs offer a more natural way of reflecting the real world, objects that are reusable (saving programming time and complexity) and a simpler syntax (Curtis & Cobham, 2005). A good example for an OOPL used in AIS is ABAP Objects for SAP ERP software.

Table 3.2: Programming language categories

Category	Characteristics	Examples
Machine-oriented	Written in strings of 0s and 1s, either directly or via mnemonics (assembler), for the specific architecture the program is run on	Machine code, assembly languages
Task-oriented	Written for task rather than machine; relatively straightforward to learn using Near-English expressions; requires translation into machine code using an interpretation or compiling process	COBOL, FORTRAN, C
Object-oriented	Using objects with properties that stand in relationship to other objects and interact with them	C++, C#, Java, PHP, Python, Perl, ABAP Objects

Emerging technologies impacting AIS

In the latter half of the 2010s, a range of disruptive technologies emerged that have already shown an impact on AIS. Blockchain, the IoT and AI are chief amongst them (Sandner et al., 2020), all enabled by accelerated growth in computer technology and its processing power (Quinn & Kristandl, 2014). Within just a few years, these three emerging technologies have found purpose in a variety of business processes and functions, such as accounting and AIS. The remainder of this chapter offers a brief overview of blockchain, IoT and AI as well as their impact on AIS, as they are joining the technologies underpinning AIS.

Blockchain

After beginnings in digital time-stamping services in the 1990s, the concept of 'blockchain' was popularised in the late 2000s due to the rise of cryptocurrencies, most prominently Bitcoin (Nakamoto, 2008). Whilst cryptocurrencies have experienced large-scale falls and rises since (Dutta, 2020), blockchain as a technology has emancipated itself from this single focus and found a wide range of additional and diverse uses such as supply chain management, smart contracts, healthcare, property rights, voting or automated bank books (Wu et al., 2019; Sandner et al., 2020; Romney et al., 2021). Figure 3.5 shows the basic concept behind blockchain.

In brief, blockchain technology is a database of individual digital records (blocks), linked together in a 'chain'. Blockchain differs from 'traditional' databases in the way it stores data. Each block contains a random number (a 'nonce'), its own hash value (encrypted data on the block) and the hash value of the previous block (Wu et al., 2019; Dutta, 2020; Romney et al., 2021). Once a block is filled, it is chained to the previous block in chronological order.

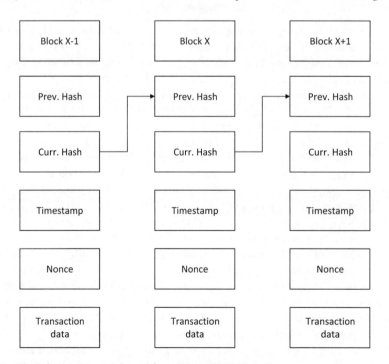

Figure 3.5   Blockchain concept (adapted from Wu et al., 2019, p. 3).

Rather than being stored in a single location, the blockchain is a decentralised database forming a distributed ledger of transactions across all nodes in a peer-to-peer network and made public to each stakeholder therein (Romney et al., 2021). It can store all kinds of transactional accounting data (e.g. bank transfers, sales records, purchases) which get exchanged between contracting parties without the need for intermediaries (such as banks; Romney et al., 2021). The entire peer-to-peer network acts as decentralised monitoring and control authority – a new block gets added only if all previous nodes agree (via a protocol) on its legitimacy and the validity of the data on it. Another key feature of blockchains is that they are immutable (Dutta, 2020), meaning that entries are irreversible and permanently recorded. Any tampering of data by a single entity would alter the hash values of the block header, highlighting the attempt to all other nodes and increasing the likelihood of not just discovery but also its origin (Wu et al., 2019).

This robustness of blockchain technology adds accuracy of transaction data and transparency of transaction details (Romney et al., 2021). The data is consistent (as there is only one database) and ensures a higher degree of privacy and security due to the underlying cryptography (Sandner et al., 2020). These advantages are beneficial to the operation and audit of AIS. Most importantly, blockchain technology increases the level of trust in the data/information, as nodes that want to join the blockchain must pass a 'proof of work' test before they can add a new block that is validated by consensus from the other nodes (Dutta, 2020; Romney et al., 2021). This 'proof of work' is basically a test of a new node's processing power. Adding a new block is designed to be difficult and costly (necessary processing power, hardware and electricity) to reduce the gains from fraudulent behaviour (Dutta, 2020). Notable examples of blockchains in use are Ethereum, Monero, Zcash and Dash.

Internet of Things

The term 'Internet of Things' was initially coined by Kevin Ashton at the Massachusetts Institute of Technology's AutoID Labs in 1999 (Kranz, 2017; Ramakrishnan & Gaur, 2019). It describes the linking of sensors embedded in previously non-networked devices, such as vehicles, household and consumer appliances, wearables, medical equipment, even entire buildings, wired or wirelessly, to the Internet (Romney et al., 2021). Physical sensors (like RFID tags, GPS, QR codes or light sensors) 'connect the unconnected' (Hanes et al., 2017, p. 21) to create smart devices that collect data and information for transmission over the Internet to a server (Wu et al., 2019). Networked devices can capture, process and communicate data that can be transmitted to and used in AIS for planning, decision-making and control. At the same time, these devices can be remotely controlled across the network to improve efficiency, accuracy, automation as well as introducing applications that these devices – the 'things' – were previously not capable of (Hanes et al., 2017). The IoT connects people, processes, data, machines and other objects on a hitherto unknown scale.

Whilst 1999 marked the emergence of the term 'IoT', its application only started to take off in the latter half of the 2000s with technological advances in high-speed broadband and computational power (Hanes et al., 2017). Although an in-depth discussion of IoT as a multifaceted ecosystem of physical devices, networks and protocols is outside the scope of this chapter, smart devices beyond the ubiquitous smartphone have entered private households and businesses on a broad scale. Smart speakers, smart lightbulbs, smart fridges or virtual assistants like Amazon's Alexa or Microsoft's Cortana have become widely used.

For AIS, the IoT means both opportunities and challenges. The increased amount of data captured can improve data analytics and DSSs in real time, allowing, e.g., auditors to test full populations instead of small samples or accountants to gain much more accurate data for cost estimates and decision support (Romney et al., 2021). Whilst the introduction of a high number of sensors might introduce additional security challenges to the AIS itself (see below), it also facilitates new types of physical controls to monitor movement of staff and visitors across premises when embedded in wearables such as key cards, name tags or wrist bands (Romney et al., 2021). When sensors are attached to raw materials and goods in various stages of completion, their movements and status can be monitored in real time between warehouses, production areas and shipping points.

As indicated above, the IoT adds considerable challenges for the information security in AIS, as every new Internet-enabled and networked device is another end point in the system (Romney et al., 2021). Traditionally, the number of input and output devices (computers, servers, printers, etc.) was limited (see the 'Hardware' section earlier), with information security and access controls focused on them. Many additional devices now add many new access points to the system (Romney et al., 2021). Internal control systems need to address this new layer of risk to the integrity of AIS, adding complexity to their design (Wu et al., 2019). Added challenges may arise from the need for adequate computational power for the AIS to process a much higher amount of data into meaningful information (Sandner et al., 2020).

Artificial intelligence

AI aims to computerise typical human processes such as learning, reasoning and self-improvement (Romney et al., 2021) to simulate the style of human decision-makers (Hall, 2019). As such, they form expert systems and DSSs that can either provide the basis for human decision-making or even automate decisions (Romney et al., 2021). In imitating human decision-making, AI can be employed in AIS to deal with complex and ambiguous situations in a fraction of the time (Gelinas et al., 2018), to automate mundane tasks (Marr, 2016) and to improve processes by detecting patterns in data and optimising outcomes (Sandner et al., 2020). Often used synonymously to 'AI' is the concept of 'machine learning' that involves coding computers to 'think like human beings' (Marr, 2016) and is a current application of AI rather than a synonym to it.

AI has gained traction with the big accounting firms, used to review tens of thousands of documents, to evaluate compliance with accounting standards or to employ machine learning for detection of anomalies and potential fraud (Zhou, 2017). Natural language processing (NLG) is used, e.g. by Deloitte to generate 50,000 tax returns annually for their clients, completing work in weeks instead of months. Chapter 9 provides some more insights on AI.

The link between blockchain, IoT and AI

These three emerging technologies should not necessarily be seen as separate or mutually exclusive. They can act as complements as they converge towards the enablement of new business models (Sandner et al., 2020). In fact, actively interconnecting or even converging them may reduce their individual risks. As discussed earlier, IoT devices attach additional risks to the AIS. The subsequent increase in data volume also increases risks of fraud and theft. Here, blockchain technology may serve as an internal control and alleviate some of the risks when data is sent and received (Wu et al., 2019; Sandner et al., 2020). At the same time, blockchain can improve data transmitted and information quality in terms of standardisation, interoperability and compatibility (Sandner et al., 2020) as well as relevance, timeliness, faithful representation and comparability (Wu et al., 2019).

Further, the IoT devices can act and even make decisions autonomously when AI is leveraged (Salah et al., 2019; Sandner et al., 2020), as algorithms enable IoT devices to learn faster due to the much higher amount of data processed (Yin et al., 2019). Blockchain also benefits from AI being able to detect patterns of illicit activities and fraud in case the blockchain is fully or partially anonymous (Sandner et al., 2020).

Summary

This chapter detailed the technological underpinnings of AIS that are predominantly the same as for general corporate IS. It detailed and discussed the technological perspective on networks, hardware and software that enable an AIS to record, process and display accounting information for reporting and decision-making. A main emphasis was placed on computer networks that not only enable AIS to record transactions in any part across a company but also furnish the business with the computing power needed to process large amounts of data. Connected within a network are hardware that provides the physical resources, as well as software that enables the smooth operation of an IS. Common standards like protocols facilitate the inclusion of various accounting software packages to create an efficient technological environment for running an AIS.

The future of AIS will continue to be inextricably linked to their technological underpinnings. With cloud computing offering processing power hitherto unavailable to many businesses (Strauss et al., 2015), emerging technological developments such as blockchain, IoT and AI have already started to rewrite the story of AIS technology in terms of higher security of and trust in data used in businesses, higher volumes of data captured and intelligent systems to automate mundane tasks and even decision-making. As such, the technological future of AIS seems a promising and bright one.

Notes

1 The details of OSI versus TCP/IP are beyond the scope of this chapter. For a detailed discussion, please see Tanenbaum & Wetherall (2021).
2 The term 'firmware' also exists, indicating an inseparable combination of hardware and software, it being a set of instructions that is permanently encoded on a microchip.

References

BBC (2016, July 6). US nuclear force still uses floppy disks. *BBC Online*. http://www.bbc.co.uk/news/world-us-canada-36385839.

Boczko, T. (2007). *Corporate Accounting Information Systems*. Harlow: FT Prentice Hall.

Brandas, C., Megan, O., & Didraga, O. (2015). Global perspectives on accounting information systems: mobile and cloud approach. *Procedia Economics and Finance*, 20, 88–93.

Curtis, G., & Cobham, D. (2005). *Business Information Systems: Analysis, Design and Practice*. 5e. Harlow: FT Prentice Hall.

Dutta, S. (2020). *The Definitive Guide to Blockchain for Accounting and Business*. Bingley: Emerald publishing.

Eurostat (2020). Digital economy and society statistics - enterprises. https://ec.europa.eu/eurostat/-statistics-explained/index.php?title=Digital_economy_and_society_statistics_-_enterprises#Access_and_use_of_the_internet.

Gelinas, U.J., Dull, R.B., Wheeler, P.R., & Hill, M.C. (2018). *Accounting Information Systems*. 11e. Boston: Cengage Learning.

Ghasemi, M., Shafeiepour, V., Aslani, M., & Barvayeh, E. (2011). The impact of Information Technology (IT) on modern accounting systems. *Procedia – Social and Behavioral Sciences*, 28, 112–116.

Granlund, M. (2011). Extending AIS research to management accounting and control issues: A research note. *International Journal of Accounting Information Systems*, 12(1), 3–19.

Hall, J.A. (2019). *Accounting Information Systems*. 10e. Boston: Cengage Learning.

Hanes, D., Salgueiro, G., Grossetete, P., Barton, R., & Henry, J. (2017). *IoT Fundamentals: Networking Technologies, Protocols, and Use Cases for the Internet of Things*. Indianapolis: Cisco Press.

Hart, L. (2018, May 21). What you should know about smart speakers at work. *CPA Insider*. https://www.journalofaccountancy.com/newsletters/2018/may/smart-speakers-work.html.

Hurt, R.L. (2016). *Accounting Information Systems – Basic Concepts and Current Issues*. 4e. New York: McGraw-Hill Education.

Kranz, M. (2017). *Building the Internet of Things*. Hoboken: Wiley.

Lin, A., & Chen, N.-C. (2012). Cloud computing as an innovation: Perception, attitude, and adoption. *International Journal of Information Management*, 32(6), 533–540.

Magal, S.R., & Word, J. (2012). *Integrated Business Processes with ERP Systems*. Hoboken: John Wiley & Sons.

Marr, B. (2016, Dec 6). What is the difference between artificial intelligence and machine learning? *Forbes*. https://www.forbes.com/sites/bernardmarr/2016/12/06/what-is-the-difference-between-artificial-intelligence-and-machine-learning/?sh=4e23c32e2742.

Mazhelis, O., Luoma, E., & Warma, H. (2012). Defining an Internet-of-Things Ecosystem, 1–14. In: S. Andreev, S. Balandin, and Y. Koucheryavy, eds. *Internet of Things, Smart Spaces, and Next Generation Networking*. Berlin: Springer.

Nakamoto, S. (2008). Bitcoin: A peer-to-peer electronic cash system. https://bitcoin.org/bitcoin.pdf.

O'Donnell, E., & David, J. S. (2000). How information systems influence user decisions: A research framework and literature review. *International Journal of Accounting Information Systems*, 1(3), 178–203.

Quinn, M., & Kristandl, G. (2014). *Business Information Systems for Accounting Students*. London: Pearson.

Ramakrishnan, R., & Gaur, L. (2019). *Internet of Things – Approach and Applicability in Manufacturing*. Boca Raton: CRC Press.

Romney, M.B, Steinbart, P.J., Summers, S.L., & Wood, D.A. (2021). *Accounting Information Systems*. 15e. Harlow: Pearson.

Richardson, V.J., Chang, C.J., & Smith, R. (2014). *Accounting Information Systems*. New York: McGraw-Hill Education.

Salah, K., Rehman, M. H., Nizamuddin, N., & Al-Fuqaha, A. (2019). Blockchain for AI: Review and open research challenges. *IEEE Access*, 7, 10127–10149.

Sandner, P., Gross, J., & Richter, R. (2020). Convergence of Blockchain, IoT, and AI. *Frontiers in Blockchain*. 3. https://www.frontiersin.org/article/10.3389/fbloc.2020.522600

Shinder, D.L. (2001). *Computer Networking Essentials*. Indianapolis: Cisco Press Core Series.

Strauss, E., Kristandl, G., & Quinn, M., (2015). The effects of cloud technology on management accounting and decision-making. *CIMA Research Executive Summary Series*, 10(6), 1-10.

Tanenbaum, A.S., & Wetherall, D.J. (2021). *Computer Networks*. 6e. Boston: Pearson.

Trigo, A., Belfo, F., & Estebanez, R.P. (2014). Accounting information systems: The challenge of the real-time reporting. *Procedia Technology*, 16, 118–127.

Wisna, N. (2013). The effect of information technology on the quality of accounting information system and its impact on the quality of accounting information. *Research Journal of Finance and Accounting*, 4(15), 69–75.

Wu, J., Xiong, F., & Li, C. (2019). Application of internet of things and blockchain technologies to improve accounting information quality. *IEEE Access*, 7, 100090–100098.

Yin, H. H., Langenheldt, K., Harlev, M., Mukkamala, R. R., & Vatrapu, R. (2019). Regulating cryptocurrencies: a supervised machine learning approach to deanonymizing the bitcoin blockchain. *Journal of Management Information Systems*, 36(1), 37–73.

Zissis, D., & Lekkas, D. (2012). Addressing cloud computing security issues. *Future Generation Computer Systems*, 28(3), 583–592.

Zhou, A. (2017, November 14). EY, Deloitte and PwC embrace Artificial Intelligence for tax and accounting. *Forbes*. https://www.forbes.com/sites/adelynzhou/2017/11/14/ey-deloitte-and-pwc-embrace-artificial-intelligence-for-tax-and-accounting/?sh=342ce9b73498.

4

DEVELOPING INFORMATION SYSTEMS FOR THE CONTEMPORARY ACCOUNTING PROFESSION

Challenges and recommendations

Andrea Crean and Noel Carroll

Accounting information systems

Accounting information systems (AIS) has been well documented in the literature (e.g. Gordon & Miller, 1992; Moscove et al., 1998; Rom & Rohde, 2007; Hall, 2012) and defined in numerous ways, all sharing many commonalities – see also Chapter 2. AIS can be defined as a specialised subset of an organisational information system that accumulates, classifies, processes, analyses, and communicates relevant financial transaction information to internal and external parties and supports management in decision-making tasks. AIS are designed to facilitate both financial and non-financial analysis and reporting by supporting various accounting tasks. Whatever the key focus is of an AIS (i.e. financial and non-financial data), this does not largely affect the systems development but rather informs the system requirements and the desired functionality of the AIS. AIS has three basic functions:

1 Efficient and effective collection and storage of financial data and activities.
2 Ensure controls are in place to accurately record and process data.
3 Supply accurate and timely information to support decisions through various reports and financial statements.

Considering the importance of accurately collecting, storing, and processing financial data, adopting AIS can automate and streamline reporting and data mining capabilities of an accounting function. AIS also ensures that managers can accurately summarise data and present it in an improved manner to support decision-making. Extracting information from a large volume of data in a database through the process of consolidation is critical to ensure analysts and key decision-makers can easily consume information. To understand how to structure an AIS, a good starting point is identifying how the various layers communicate with each other to offer various functionalities on separate servers, computers, networks, and remote locations (see also Chapter 3) – typically referred to as the three-tier architecture. Three-tier architecture is a well-established software application architecture that organises

DOI: 10.4324/9781003132943-6

applications into three logical and physical computing tiers: (i) the presentation tier, or user interface; (ii) the application tier, where data is processed; and (iii) the data tier, where the data associated with the application is stored and managed.

Systems development and methods

An information system is comprised of an integrated set of components for collecting, storing, and processing data and for providing information, knowledge, and digital products. Developing systems to integrate these key components is a challenging process which must cater for the dynamic nature of a specific context such as accountancy responding to changes in corporate governance and corporate reporting. Systems development methods provide a process for planning, creating, testing, and deploying an information system. The software development methodology plays a key role in systems development life cycle (SDLC). The SDLC provides a framework which guides a systems development team on how to meet customer or user requirements. The SDLC presents a process (Figure 4.1) for planning, creating, testing, and deploying an information system through five key stages: requirement analysis, design, implementation, testing, and evaluation.

There has been a long history of various systems development methodologies. These methodologies include the waterfall method, V-model, and others (Carroll, 2017) which have served as a foundation for the creation of sequential (i.e. a series of steps or stages) or iterative (i.e. series of versions) systems development approaches. There are a variety of traditional systems development methods for organisations, and the selection of each approach would influence the software development process. These included:

* The iterative model (Zurcher & Randell, 1968): a model that focuses on an initial, simplified implementation, which then progressively gains more complexity and a broader feature set until the final system is complete.

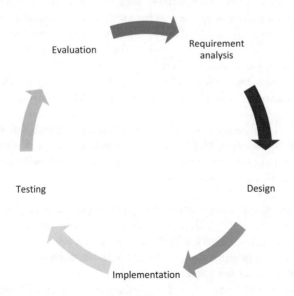

Figure 4.1 Key stages of a systems development life cycle.

- The waterfall model (Royce, 1970): comprises of six stages (requirement gathering, analysis, design, testing, implementation, and maintenance) that have specific goals at each stage of software development.
- The spiral model (Boehm, 1988): combines the features of prototyping and the waterfall model. The spiral model consists of four stages starting with planning, objectives, risk analysis, and development.
- The V-model (Forsberg & Mooz, 1991): addresses some of the problems encountered in the waterfall model. In the waterfall model, defects were found very late in the development life cycle because testing was not involved as early as the initial stage. The emphasis of the V-model is more on the testing of each stage of the development life cycle.
- The rapid application development model (Martin, 1991): aims to develop systems faster and produce high-quality results compared to linear traditional model. As a result, this enables organisations to take leadership in implementing the latest technology systems quicker.
- The agile model (Agile Alliance, 2001): an approach based on iterative development which breaks tasks into smaller iterations, or parts do not directly involve long-term planning. Plans regarding the number of iterations, the duration and the scope of each iteration are clearly defined in advance. The agile model emphasises the values of (i) individuals and interactions, (ii) focusing on working software, (iii) customer collaboration, and (iv) responding to change.

While technological advancements continue to influence the nature of the accounting profession, accountants must also play a role in shaping AIS to meet their needs through contemporary information systems development and methods.

Contemporary information systems development is generally considered to be a complex activity (Truex et al., 1999; Meso & Jain, 2006; Highsmith, 2013). For example, research carried out by Benbya & McKelvey (2006) identifies several sources of complexity in contemporary systems development, including the continuous changing of user requirements; evolving organisational needs; unpredictable nature of external competitive conditions; increased interdependencies among the involved individuals, organisations, and technologies; and the rapid advancements of information systems and information technology (IT). Within an accounting context, an AIS involves the collection, storage, and processing of financial and accounting data used by internal users to report information to investors, creditors, and tax authorities. In essence, AIS supports organisations to monitor accounting activity through IT resources. Therefore, AIS must align with key stages of an organisation's accounting cycle.

The agile method has become one of the most popular modern software development paradigms (Carroll et al., 2020). "Agile" promotes a much more fluid approach to software development and management methods. Developments across the agile community became the driving force for new initiatives such as:

1 Extreme programming: a derivative of the agile process. Extreme programming stresses customer satisfaction as the guiding force for development iteration cycles.
2 Lean development: an evolution of lean manufacturing principles and practices to support new values and principles in culture and mindset within the agile community to improve value, enhance flow, and reduce waste.
3 DevOps: provide a set of practices that combine software development (Dev) and IT operations (Ops). DevOps focus on support and automation in software development.

DevOps teams are typically tasked with building tools to automate and maintain mundane software development processes such as infrastructure maintenance.

Efforts to develop and deliver enterprise-class systems and software vary with small team involvement or with many globally distributed teams involved. For larger teams, this can imply that organisations must adopt scaled-agile methods enterprise-wide across different departments and locations. In essence, organisations are trying to mimic the success of small-scale agile methods, and large projects are increasingly adopting agile development practices. Large-scale agile development is increasingly prevalent in contemporary software development organisations. As a result, many organisations have turned to large-scale agile development frameworks (Conboy & Carroll, 2019) such as the Scaled-Agile Framework, Large-Scale Scrum, Spotify,[1] Nexus, and Scrum at Scale. Each incorporates predefined workflow patterns and routines and is supported by an ever-increasing set of tools. Although the information contained in systems varies among industries and business sizes, a typical AIS includes data relating to revenue, expenses, customer information, employee information, and tax information. Accounting professionals are often responsible for analysing data from various sources including sales orders and reports, purchase requisitions, invoices, inventory, payroll, and financial statement information.

The contemporary accounting profession and technology

Every accountant knows that accounting is the language of business. That language has gone through many changes throughout the ages. But through all the changes accounting technology played a part in making the accountant's job just a little easier.

(Pepe, 2011)

The use of machines and technology is not a new phenomenon in the accounting world. As far back as 1642 with the advent of the mathematical calculator, accountants relied on machines to help them with information accuracy. However, for centuries, most of the accountants' work centred around documentation, paper records, and physical files. The traditional accountant is portrayed as a very methodical and detail-oriented person.

Towards the end of the 20th century, the accounting profession began to take on a whole new look (Pepe, 2011). Computer and internet usage became prevalent, and the use of electronic mail for communication and Microsoft Excel and Enterprise Resource Planning systems for accounting and financial reporting purposes had a transformative impact on the profession. Fast forward 20 years, we are witnessing global trends transforming the working world and reshaping the future of the accounting profession (ACCA, 2020, p. 3):

Technology is transforming the global economy. It is changing the very fabric of businesses and organisations. This imperative provides golden opportunities for the accountancy profession to build on its strong foundations and evolve; it's a once in a lifetime opportunity to repurpose the accountancy profession for the modern working world and to transform the profession in the minds of the younger generation coming to the workplace.

In recent years, there has been widespread development in technology within the accounting profession including the use and implementation of disruptive technologies ranging from big data and data analytics, machine learning, artificial intelligence (AI), blockchain, and

Internet of Things (IoT) to perform accounting procedures. This popularity is due to 'the exponentially growing amount of information made available by developments in computing and telecommunications technology, particularly the internet and environmental sensing' (Vasarhelyi et al., 2014, p. 381).

In recent years, big data analytics (BDA) techniques are being applied to accounting processes, and in the past number of years, there has been significant investment by accounting firms to advance their technologies and leverage the use of AIS. Big data relates to the nature of data (Arnaboldi et al., 2017), whereas data analytics refers to the collection of tools developed to make sense of big data (Salijeni et al., 2019). The two concepts are interrelated – 'the real value of Big Data is the value of the analytics that can be performed with that data – the ultimate insights gleaned from the data' (Alles & Gray, 2016, p. 45). The advent of BDA presents a real opportunity to transform the accounting profession, particularly areas of audit, taxation, and consulting where particular opportunities lie such as the ability to identify business risks more rapidly through analysis of data insights. The application of BDA and the use of data mining create many opportunities for businesses to gain greater insight, predict future outcomes, and automate non-routine tasks. It also provides opportunities for the accounting profession to deliver greater value and to help businesses transform their decision-making in many different areas (ICAEW, 2019).

The field of auditing is perhaps the most widely researched area as it presents significant opportunity for technological development within the accounting world. For example, mundane audit tasks such as confirming thousands of transactions which would traditionally take an audit team member days to complete can now be completed instantaneously using BDA tools. As a result of this, the major international public accounting firms are making substantial investments in BDA software and tools capable of leveraging clients' data sets to provide reliable audit evidence. For example, KPMG has partnered with IBM's Watson AI to develop AI audit tools (Kokina & Davenport, 2017). Similarly, data analytics now form part of Deloitte's audit strategy for most audit engagements (Sheehan, 2017).

However, while the use of BDA and other disruptive technologies across some platforms such as retail and manufacturing has been hugely successful, from an accounting perspective, the transformation is more complex and presents implementation difficulties due to factors such as legal and regulatory blocks, the expertise and experience of the traditional accountant, and issues around availability of information. Therefore, integrating AIS into the accounting process is not without its challenges and presents many obstacles for the profession.

It has been reported that the accounting profession is at a crossroads (Baron & Kleinsmith, 2018), and for accountants to grow and meet the growing demands by clients, shareholders, and wider society in general, they must embrace a more forward-looking response to innovation and technological change. Accountants who seize this as an opportunity will differentiate themselves by developing new skills and new ways of thinking (ACCA, 2013). Those who do not are at risk of their roles becoming redundant. Their skills will be commoditised and may become irrelevant in time with continuous improvements in automation. However, it is a rather simplistic view of the role of the accountant to suggest that the professional will be replaced by AIS. Automation brings greater opportunities for the profession as it helps to reduce routine tasks including double-entry bookkeeping and compliance work, allowing accountants to focus on more value-added services, such as providing advice to clients and providing strategic insights on critical business transactions (Nagarajah, 2016). However, the accountant, through engaging with and embracing AIS, has the opportunity to see their responsibilities grow and develop. For example, Katz (2014, p. 20) argues that within the next five years, the availability of big data, coupled with data analytics, has the potential to make 'the finance function … a strong, formidable strategic partner to operations and sales. Finance is the natural gatekeeper of data, as information normally flows through the function'.

Systems development for the accounting profession

Developing AIS includes five basic steps – planning, analysis, design, implementation, and maintenance – and each step can be as short as a few weeks or as long as several years depending on the objectives. Yet, to successfully deliver at each step requires a collaborative effort across multiple stakeholders. While the accounting profession has evolved from what was considered to be bookkeeping, it is now experiencing growing expectations with the support of AIS. This may be achieved by exploring ways to better integrate accounting roles, systems development roles, and data science roles to:

- Enable data access and utilisation and enable value capture.
- Optimise and enable data for business and system functional value capture and value creation.
- Support business to make better accountancy-related decisions through data and improved systems.

The accounting profession will continue to face significant changes largely influenced by smart and digital technology, globalisation of standards, and new regulations. AIS functions within organisations also expect employees to be highly trained in both financial and technological matters. Accounting professionals need a balance of business skills, specialised accounting, taxation, auditing, data analytics, and information systems development. Specifically, future accountants will require education in digital technology (including cloud computing and use of data analytics), globalisation (outsourcing of accounting services), and evolving regulations (tax regulation, new forms of corporate reporting, integrated reporting regulation, etc.).

The software component of an AIS composes the computer programs used to store, retrieve, process, and analyse the organisation's financial data. Examples of AIS may include Intuit's QuickBooks, Sage 50 Cloud, SAP's Business One, Microsoft's Dynamics GP, Oracle's PeopleSoft, or SAP S/4 HANA. Such technologies will continue to shape the future of the accounting professions and further influence digital transformation across the accounting field. Digital transformation has become a global priority on leadership agendas. Leaders have growing expectations from the promise of digital transformations to make a strategic contribution to their business survival and success (Carroll, 2020), which will also impact on the accounting profession. Considering the growing demands placed on the modern accounting profession, there are growing expectations of information systems in the accounting profession.

Growing expectations of information systems in the accounting profession

Given what has been outlined thus far, a growing expectation on the role of AIS follows the increased and increasing demand on accountants. In many accounting firms, and in particular larger accounting organisations, information systems usage is becoming more and more prevalent. Disruptive technologies such as mobile, cloud, BDA, AI, blockchain, and IoT are impacting nearly every aspect of auditing, tax, management and financial accounting, and advisory services. For example, Ramlukan (cited in Tschakert et al., 2016) argues that data analytics is a skill that can be applied to many scenarios across all service lines. Accounting firms have access to ever-increasing amounts of data. The question is how these firms can use this data to derive both value and revenue (Boomer, 2018). As information system usage becomes more prevalent, Bhimani & Willcocks (2014) argue that developments in digitisation, software, and processing power and the accompanying data explosion create significant alterations, dilemmas, and possibilities for enterprises and their finance function. They note how developments in data, information, and technology are now becoming so extensive that a fundamental shift in accounting is taking place across many organisations.

In addition to BDA implementation, we are also seeing the rise of advanced technologies such as AI, blockchain, and robotic process automation (see Chapter 17 for more on this latter topic). This is a key area of focus for development within accounting firms at present. This is raising concerns among professional accountants as to what accounting and the accounting profession will resemble going forward. Bhimani & Willcocks (2014) assert that organisations need to be sensitised to different types of knowledge, the challenges in creating and applying that knowledge, and be more circumspect about what can be achieved through advances in information-based technologies and software.

For example, in management accounting, there is a growing focus on the development and implementation of AIS. Going forward, with the right training and knowledge, accountants can use their business knowledge and monitoring techniques to identify areas for key improvements and opportunities within the firm (Richins et al., 2017). For example, given accountants' ability to recognise and assess how various performance measures reflect effective operations as they relate to a firm's strategic operations, gaining data analytics skills provides accountants with additional tools to monitor operations and product quality. In addition, it enables accountants to discover opportunities to reduce costs and meaningfully contribute to decision-making (Dai & Vasarhelyi, 2016).

Ultimately, advances in technology have seen a reinvention of the accounting profession and see accountants move up the value chain in organisations. Accountants are no longer just service providers or traditional number crunchers; they are becoming strategic business partners central to decision-making across the organisation (Goretzki et al., 2013). For example, according to ACCA (2020, p. 5):

> In tomorrow's world, work will be transformed and 'jobs' will be redefined in accountancy. Parts of jobs will be reapportioned to machines or automated. But this isn't a threat to the profession, it's a world of opportunity. This 'nexus' of human capability with technology will herald a new era of brilliant careers that add value and have purpose.

With this comes a growing expectation on information systems, and this needs to be managed by the accounting profession. Many of the larger accounting firms are now hiring data scientists and data engineers to help with this transition to a new world of accounting with AIS and analytics. However, despite hiring data scientists and data engineers, the accountant needs the skills to be able to understand the processes involved in using and implementing AIS techniques. As a result of this, there is a need for postgraduate programs of study to equip accounting students with knowledge of information systems tools and techniques. For example, Figure 4.2 presents an overview of an MSc in International Accounting and Analytics, which is designed and delivered to address many of the contemporary challenges outlined in this chapter.

MSc in International Accounting and Analytics, NUI Galway, Ireland

At the National University of Ireland, Galway, the *MSc in International Accounting and Analytics* programme was launched in September 2017 in response to the above calls for accounting educators to revamp accounting and auditing curricula. The ICAS and FRC report on *Auditor Skills in a Changing Business World* (in 2016) also notes the importance of analytics skills for accountants and calls for educators to include practical courses on data interrogation and analytics. The MSc in International Accounting and Analytics is the first programme of its kind in UK and Irish Universities to offer practical hands-on modules in data interrogation and analytics and practitioner-led summer schools demonstrating practical experience using audit analytics tools for accountants.

Figure 4.2   Example of a university incorporating AIS and analytics into curriculum.

Many researchers are highlighting the need for upskilling accountants to deal with AIS implementation and development. For example, Cao et al. (2015) state that educational changes are necessary for making successful use of BDA in public accounting practice, and Yoon et al. (2015) agree, suggesting that in educating auditing and accounting students, the curriculum should reflect changing audit evidence sources and ensure more content is delivered on advanced data analytics. Griffin & Wright (2015) suggest that academics, as educators, must revamp their accounting and auditing curricula to provide the necessary skills for BDA in the accounting and auditing profession. In addition, Applebaum et al. (2017) indicate this will be a challenge as accounting faculties tend not to be prepared to teach analytics, and accounting curricula are too full to add more IT. Additionally, firms tend to have already hired specialist groups from non-accounting backgrounds who work in IT audits, external to the audit team and brought into the audit if the manager of the engagement setting out the plan sees fit.

Following on from this, current research in the area of accounting and technology implementation is highlighting the importance of the accountant in understanding how to use technological tools. In the context of auditing, Brown-Liburd et al. (2015) warn that while these new technological tools can identify patterns in data, it is the auditor who is needed to analyse and evaluate these patterns, and human interpretation and judgement are still at the core of the audit process. For example, Salijeni et al. (2019) warn that there is a danger of disappointment if BDA developments are seen as a golden ticket which will solve all audit problems and lead to a future in which audit services are universally valued. Equally, however, Salijeni et al. (2019) acknowledge the potential for AIS and technological developments to provide real tools to reconfigure, refocus, and potentially reposition contemporary audit practice and, because of such potentially significant transformative effects, should be subject to much higher level of scholarly attention and debate. Therefore, it is important for the accountant to understand how these AIS are developed and applied to enable them to complete their tasks more efficiently and effectively.

Challenges and recommendations of developing information systems for the modern accounting profession

Based on our review of the literature, it is apparent that accounting practices are shaping the development of AIS. However, AIS are also shaping the development of accountants. Therefore, for successful implementation of AIS in the accounting space, AIS must be designed and tailored efficiently and effectively to enable accountants to perform tasks, and accountants must have the skills to use these systems. Firm culture and a willingness to learn and change will determine whether to adopt and use new capabilities and capitalise on the opportunities that BDA and other technologies will bring (Boomer, 2018). The key to successful implementation has a number of facets, and each plays a part in embedding AIS into the accounting process.

Although the key principles of the accounting profession have to a large extent remained the same, the adoption of AIS has improved efficiencies of accounting practices (Ganyam & Ivungu, 2019). AIS has opened new opportunities to innovate around the use of systems and data analytics and created new roles and responsibilities across the accounting profession to facilitate more accurate predictions or support managers in their attempt to drive profitable digital agendas. However, there are many key challenges of developing AIS for the modern accounting profession.

Table 4.1 summarises seven key challenges of AIS and analytics for the modern accounting profession. To address these challenges, this section outlines recommendations to further develop AIS for the modern accounting profession.

Table 4.1 Key challenges and recommendations for the accounting profession

Challenges	*Recommendations*
The accelerating growth in AIS technology advancements and pace of change for accountants (e.g. mobile, cloud computing, BDA, and AI).	• Train accountants on the potential of emerging tools and technologies such as BDA and AIS. • Improve communication and planning between accountants and technology specialists by removing silos. • Implement a new strategy within an organisation with buy-in from all parties. The accountants must be at the centre of AIS development – asking questions and giving their opinions on these new tools and technologies.
Training and upskilling of accountants to successfully adopt AIS into their processes.	• Adopt a firm-wide approach with compulsory training in AIS adoption for all employees across the organisation. • Establish links with universities who play a key role in shaping modern accounting profession, for example, through new educational innovations and training accounting graduates on the importance of information systems and data science. • Reward a culture of learning and regular training on information systems development to enhance the role of AIS, data analytics, and other disruptive technologies in the modern accounting profession.
The growing uncertainty on how the role of accounting professions will be influenced by AIS technology innovations.	• Embrace modern technologies such as AI to automate specific accounting processes and reduce resources invested in mundane tasks. • Adoption and implementation of AIS must align with accountants' needs to support rather than hinder their skillset. • Promote need for interdisciplinary teams such as accounting, technologies, and data scientists within organisations.
The rise and potential value of big data in AIS to support the accounting profession evolve.	• Demonstrate to accountants how AIS are only as good as the information and data inputs. Data quality is essential for successful implementation of AIS within an organisation. • Examine how new data extraction techniques can optimise the capability of AIS analytics to support auditors and consultants to easily extract data, perform analytics, and inform decision-making processes. • Encourage accountants to use increasingly sophisticated and smart technologies to enhance their traditional ways of working.

Challenges	Recommendations
Globalised adoption of new standards and regulations associated with AIS.	• Increase awareness on the importance of AIS-related standards and regulations across the organisation. • Reinforce the value and impact of standards in driving transparency and creating a common terminology for high-quality financial information. • Encourage strong leadership to extend the adoption and implementation of proper legal and regulatory frameworks to exploit AIS capabilities.
The growing focus on security, data protection, and system governance compliance with AIS.	• Conduct regular AIS security audits and communicate the implications of failing to meet specific targets. • Establish multistakeholder perspectives on the governance of AIS to include accounting professionals. • Assess employee awareness of security, data protection, and system governance compliance across the organisation.
The significant initial cost outlay of implementing sophisticated AIS systems within the accounting organisation.	• Perform cost-benefit analysis to highlight how AIS will reduce costs and increase efficiencies within the profession and reduce the accountant's workload. • Increase awareness among staff that benefits of AIS implementation may not be realised immediately and it is a long-term investment that will reap rewards in future years. • Reinforce the benefits of AIS systems for the modern accounting profession including real-time reporting which provides accountants with instantaneous information about key aspects of the organisation, allowing for better decision-making among other benefits.

As outlined in Table 4.1, it is apparent that there are significant challenges associated with successful AIS implementation for this current technological revolution to be successful in the modern accounting world. The adoption of AIS not only brings with it risks but also presents several rewards. In addition to the technological challenges of implementing AIS, the accountant needs to be at the forefront of this transformation. However, buy-in is needed across the entire organisation, demonstrating how accounting firms will gain strategic and competitive advantage by effectively adopting AIS. This aligns with Trigo et al. (2014, p. 126) who note that:

> [n]owadays, some accounting activities face special concerns that represent serious challenges. Of course, the implementation success of an accounting information system depends on technological issues, but other dimensions should be considered, like the people and the organisational dimensions.

In addition to key challenges, we identified some of the key recommendations for AIS in response to the growing pressures technology innovation places on the modern accounting profession. Although AIS will continue to be shaped by advanced technologies across cloud computing, mobile, and AI in the future, developing a thorough understanding on information system development will encourage firms to discover new opportunities and benefits for new systems and their impact on the role of the accounting function.

Conclusion

This chapter provides an overview of developing information systems for the modern accounting profession. Within the development models, particular emphasis is placed on planning, design, and implementation. From this chapter, we learn that as the application of systems development becomes increasingly engrained and interwoven into the fabric of accounting in organisations, the complexities of the accounting processes and value chain define the needs of users and the requirements of AIS. Thus, while technological advancements play a key role in the planning, design, and implementation of AIS, so too do behavioural aspects of formal and informal accounting routines which interplay on a regular basis. It is this interplay that ultimately influences the AIS acceptance within an organisation.

AIS are valuable assets and are an important part of the organisational value chain. This may mean that AIS provide more efficient, reliable, and an improved service or decision-making support to enhance the accounting service provision. For accounting organisations, creating an IT strategy is important to ensure that organisational objectives will be realised through the effective deployment of service capabilities. The service capabilities must compete with the external environment to generate some form of uniqueness, differentiation, or even rarity from other competitors (Carroll & Helfert, 2015) while also optimising internal routines and capabilities though key processes. Considering the evolving nature of the modern accounting profession, it is inevitable that AIS will continue to play a key role in delivering more efficient and effective mechanisms of support. The future of AIS will therefore be influenced by new technological advancements in areas such as BDA, automation, blockchain, IoT, and AI. Therefore, there will be a growing expectation for AIS professionals to be skilled in developing and customising information systems to align with their evolving industry trends. One of the key challenges and an area for future research will include finding a balance with digital transformation for AIS innovation while adhering to legal and regulatory requirements, i.e. striking the balance between innovation and compliance within the industry. In addition, it is envisaged that this may also carve out new roles in the area of AIS where employees will play a key role in accounting, developing AIS, and exploiting BDA and other disruptive technological tools.

Note

1 The Spotify model, developed by the music streaming service company Spotify, is a people-driven, autonomous approach for scaling agile that emphasises the importance of culture and network.

References

ACCA (2013). Big data: Its power and perils. Available at: https://www.accaglobal.com/bigdata [Accessed 2 December 2020]

ACCA (2020). Future ready: Accountancy careers in the 2020s. London: ACCA. Available at: https://www.accaglobal.com/content/dam/ACCA_Global/professional-insights/FutureReady2020s/JamieLyon.FutureCareersAccoutancy2020s.fullreport.pdf [Accessed 6 November 2021]

Agile Alliance (2001). Manifesto for Agile Software Development. Retrieved 4 December 2020 from www.agilemanifesto.org.

Alles, M. G., & Gray. L, G. (2016). Incorporating big data in audits: Identifying inhibitors and a research agenda to address those inhibitors. *International Journal of Accounting Information Systems*, 22, 44–59.

Applebaum, D., Kogan, A., & Vasarhelyi, M. A. (2017). Big data and analytics in the modern audit environment: Research needs. *Auditing: A Journal of Practice & Theory*, 36(4), 1–27.

Arnaboldi, M., Busco, C., & Cuganesan, S. (2017). Accounting, accountability, social media and big data: Revolution or hype? *Accounting, Auditing and Accountability Journal*, 30(4), 762–776.

Baron, J., & Kleinsmith. J. (2018). Thriving in an age of disruption for tax and accounting. *Answers for Tax Professionals Magazine*. Available at: blogs.thomsonreuters.com/answerson/thriving-in-an-age-of-disruption-tax-accounting/ [Accessed 29 January 2021]

Benbya, H., & McKelvey, B. (2006). Toward a complexity theory of information systems development. *Information Technology & People*, 19(1), 12–34.

Bhimani, A., & Willcocks, L. (2014). Digitisation, 'Big Data' and the transformation of accounting information. *Accounting and Business Research*, 44(4), 469–490.

Boehm, B. W. (1988). A spiral model of software development and enhancement. *Computer*, 21(5), 61–72.

Boomer, J. (2018). The value of big data in an accounting firm. *CPA Practice Advisor (September)*. Available at: https://www.cpapracticeadvisor.com/firm-management/article/12424744/the-value-of-big-data-in-an-accounting-firm [Accessed 19 January 2021].

Brown-Liburd, H., Ossa, H., & Lombardi, D. (2015). Behavioral implications of Big Data's impact on audit judgment and decision making and future research directions. *Accounting Horizons*, 29(2), 451–468.

Cao, M., Chychyla, R., & Stewart, T. (2015). Big Data analytics in financial statement audits. *Accounting Horizons*, 29(2), 423–429.

Carroll, N. (2017). Systems planning, design and implementation. In Quinn, M. and Strauss, E. (Eds.), *The Routledge Companion to Accounting Information Systems*, Chapter 4, 39–54. London: Routledge.

Carroll, N. (2020). Theorizing on the normalization of digital transformations. In *28th European Conference on Information Systems (ECIS)*, Marrakech, Morocco, An Online AIS Conference, June 15–17.

Carroll, N., Bjørnson, F. O., Dingsøyr, T., Rolland, K., & Conboy, K. (2020). Operationalizing agile methods: Examining coherence in large-scale agile transformations. *8th International Research Workshop on Large-Scale Agile Development, Proceedings of the 21st International Conference on Agile Software Development (XP2020)*, Copenhagen, Denmark.

Carroll, N., & Helfert, M. (2015). Service capabilities within open innovation. *Journal of Enterprise Information Management*, 28(2), 275–303.

Conboy, K., & Carroll, N. (2019). Implementing large-scale agile frameworks: Challenges and recommendations. *IEEE Software*, 36(2), 44–50.

Dai, J., & Vasarhelyi, M, A. (2016). Imagineering Audit 4.0. Working paper, Rutgers, The State University of New Jersey.

Forsberg, K., & Mooz, H. (1991). The relationship of system engineering to the project cycle. *INCOSE International Symposium*, 1(1), 57–65.

Ganyam, A. I., & Ivungu, J. A. (2019). Effect of accounting information system on financial performance of firms: A review of literature. *Journal of Business and Management*, 21(5), 39–49.

Gordon, L. A., & Miller, D. (1992). A contingency framework for the design of accounting information systems. In C. Emmanuel, D. Otley and K. Merchant (Eds.), *Readings in Accounting for Management Control*. London: Chapman & Hall, 569–585.

Goretzki, L., Strauss, E., & Weber, J. (2013). An institutional perspective on the changes in management accountants' professional role. *Management Accounting Research*, 24(1), 41–63.

Griffin, P. A., & Wright, A. M. (2015). Commentaries on Big Data's importance for accounting and auditing. *Accounting Horizons*, 29(2), 377–379.

Hall, J. (2012). *Accounting Information Systems*. London: Cengage Learning.

Highsmith, J. (2013). *Adaptive Software Development: A Collaborative Approach to Managing Complex Systems*. Boston: Addison-Wesley.

ICAEW (2019). Big data and analytics: The impact on the accountancy profession. Available at: https://www.icaew.com/-/media/corporate/files/technical/information-technology/thought-leadership/big-data-and-analytics.ashx [Accessed 30 November 2020].

Katz, D. M. (2014) Accounting's Big Data problem. *CFO Magazine* (March 4). Available at: https://www.cfo.com/management-accounting/2014/03/accountings-big-data-problem/ [Accessed 25 January 2021].

Kokina, J., & Davenport. T. H. (2017). The emergence of artificial intelligence: How automation is changing auditing. *Journal of Emerging Technologies in Accounting*, 14(1), 115–122.

Martin, J. (1991). *Rapid Application Development* (Vol. 8). New York: Macmillan.

Meso, P., & Jain, R. (2006). Agile software development: Adaptive systems principles and best practices. *Information Systems Management*, 23(3), 19–30.

Moscove, S. A., Simkin, M. G., & Bagranoff, N. A. (1998). *Core Concepts of Accounting Information Systems*. Hoboken, NJ: John Wiley & Sons.

Nagarajah, E. (2016). 'Hi Robot What does automation mean for the accounting profession?' *Accountants Today*. Available at: https://www.pwc.com/my/en/assets/press/1608-accountants-today-automation-impact-on-accounting-profession.pdf [Accessed 30 November 2020].

Pepe, A., 2011. The evolution of technology for the accountancy profession. *CPA Practice Advisor (April)*. Available at: https://www.cpapracticeadvisor.com/home/article/10263076/the-evolution-of-technology-for-the-accounting-profession [Accessed 6 November 2021]

Richins, G., Stapleton, A., Stratopoulos, T., C., & Wong, C. (2017). Big data analytics: Opportunity or threat for the accounting profession? *Journal of Information Systems*, 31(3), 63–79.

Rom, A., & Rohde, C. (2007). Management accounting and integrated information systems: A literature review. *International Journal of Accounting Information Systems*, 8(1), 40–68.

Royce, W. W. (1970). Managing the development of large software systems. *Proceedings of IEEE WESCON*, 26(8), 1–9.

Salijeni, G., Samsonova-Taddei, A., & Turley, S. (2019). Big Data and changes in audit technology: Contemplating a research agenda. *Accounting and Business Research*, 49, 95–119.

Sheehan, K. (2017). The ongoing audit transformation. *Accountancy Ireland*, 49(6), 54–55.

Trigo, A., Belfo, F., & Estebanez, R. P. (2014). Accounting information systems: The challenge of real-time reporting. *Procedia Technology*, 16, 118–127.

Truex, D. P., Baskerville, R., & Klein, H. (1999). Growing systems in emergent organizations. *Communications of the ACM*, 42(8), 117–123.

Tschakert, N., Kokina, J., Kozlowski, S., & Vasarhelyi, M. (2016). The next frontier of data analytics. *Journal of Accountancy*. Available at: https://www.journalofaccountancy.com/issues/2016/aug/data-analytics-skills.html [Accessed 19 January 2021].

Vasarhelyi, M. A., Kogan, A., & Tuttle, B. M. (2014). Big Data in accounting: An overview. *Accounting Horizons*, 29(2), 381–396.

Yoon, K., Hoogduin, L., & Zhang, L. (2015). Big Data as complementary audit evidence. *Accounting Horizons*, 29(2), 431–438.

Zurcher, F. W., & Randell, B. (1968). Iterative multi-level modelling: A methodology for computer system design. *IFIP Congress*, 2, 867–887.

5

AIS AS A CATALYST
FOR CHANGE

Krister Bredmar

Introduction

In many businesses, managers are experiencing increased speed when it comes to how the business landscape is changing (Michels & Murphy, 2021). Manager's ability to adjust the operations and manage externally driven change, here with the help of the change power coming from within the organisation, is hard to measure. However, this capacity is becoming increasingly important, especially when it comes to the ability to stay competitive. Accounting information systems (AIS) have always been about measuring and monitoring the different aspects of the business, and in today's changing business landscape, AIS could act as a catalyst for change. In a way, there are two sides to this coin: ways of developing the function of AIS could both work as the tool that measures the organisation's power to change and facilitate change as such, for example, through implementing new AIS. Hence, the function and purpose behind an advanced system, such as modern AIS, can work as a catalyst for change.

Technology in different forms drives the renewal of how things are done in an organisation (Peppard & Ward, 2016). This can be understood by considering how technologies, as in machines, change how products or services are realised. However, technology also deals with how the work is carried out, how processes are run and who does what. When exploring how, as a function, accounting has changed over time, the most important development arose when computerised systems were introduced. Simple, well-defined and routine tasks were moved to transaction-based systems that did the simple calculations that accounting is based on (Simkin et al., 2015). By this time, the concept of AIS emerged, and new ways of structuring reports, as well as making supporting decisions, appeared along with it. The way an organisation chooses to work with its AIS informs the ability that management has to plan for and control operations (Emmanuel et al., 1990). The new ways of working with accounting issues in the form of AIS did not in and of itself bring anything new to the organisation. The accounting function was still working in the same way, but automation shortened the time and increased the possible variations when compiling financial reports. By doing so, the technology regarding computers and the way work was conducted changed.

In a more structured way, AIS can act as the catalyst for changing how operations are planned for and monitored. When changing how things are done in an organisation, a more structured process of how change itself should be carried out can be applied (Hayes, 2014).

DOI: 10.4324/9781003132943-7

This is usually referred to as change management and can be understood as the process where the different aspects of an organisation's operations, such as technical areas, personnel aspects and cultural dimensions, can be altered (Chaffey & White, 2010). From an AIS perspective, change also involves dealing with how the business is transformed, producing more efficient and improved operations and bringing about improved performance as a result. To understand how AIS deliver improved performance through change management, it is important to first understand the development of AIS as such and to understand how these new forms of AIS contribute to change in organisations. Even though advanced information systems in general, and modern AIS in particular, have brought new opportunities to an organisation and the management aspects of business, it is important to first understand how AIS have changed over time. It is also important to understand the new challenges managers are facing when trying to benefit from the new, more advanced systems and to try to grasp where AIS trends are heading and what kind of change this may bring.

When AIS is changing, its ability to support managers is changing

In organisations, accounting has always played an information system function. When Luca Pacioli wrote his *Summa* in 1494, one chapter described how merchant families in Venice used a double-entry bookkeeping methodology to keep track of goods and money (Thompson, 1994). At the time, the accounting function played the role of documenting juridical transactions but was also a means of showing ethical actions. In addition to this, the geometrical dimension was important, which helped the user document a transaction in more than one dimension. In many ways, financial reports and information have always been about understanding business and operations (Littleton, 1953). Through the gathering and structuring of accounting information, these reports add another dimension of understanding the business as such, which, in many ways, helps management in their work with planning and controlling performance.

Over the years, AIS have become more complex but also increased in ability. Earlier systems would 'just' do the work of the accountant, but in more recent systems, a widely expanded ability to do advanced analyses has become possible (Simkin et al., 2015). Here, we could say that there have been three rough phases in accounting. The first was when tasks were done by hand-in books, where the focus was on summarising columns and checking that the figures were correct. In the next phase, the computer entered the scene, and routine-based work was automated, whereby one of the immediate effects was that the need to check numbers was less important. It was, however, still important to check that the numbers entered into the system were correct. In the third and current phase, the accounting function has a more integrated role within a broader, more comprehensive system, usually called an enterprise resource planning (ERP) system. It is still an information system that deals with accounting issues, but it is integrated into an even more complex context.

Information systems

When trying to understand what drives change and how systems such as AIS contribute to it, a natural first step is to try to understand information systems. One of the first scholars who coined the phrase *information system* in a research conference in New York during the mid-1960s was Börje Langefors (Langefors, 1995). At the time, the ability to process data to process information was being discussed, eventually being termed the information system. Later, additional meanings were added, such as capturing, storing, processing and communicating information within an organisation, usually with the help of technology (Alter, 1999). It is important, however, to remember that an information system, in general, and an AIS, in particular, contribute to the management function by offering different forms of performance reports that can help managers with decision making in various ways, for example, to plan and control operations (Davis & Olson, 1984).

The more abilities the information system brings, the more the management function needs to understand how to use its features in managing the business. This idea is something that Checkland & Holwell (1998) worked on. Their approach was that instead of looking at a system as something merely technical, and in a way 'hard', they wanted to add a 'soft' dimension by also considering how real-world management problems could be addressed. One insight they elaborated on was that people in general—and managers in particular— want to act in a purposeful way. To do this, they needed some sort of information support: 'information systems exist to serve, help or support people taking action in the real world' (Checkland & Holwell, 1998, p. 10). Translated into an AIS context, this means that these systems are built to help managers act in a purposeful way by supporting them with information aimed at actions within the organisation.

Stand-alone systems

When computers were introduced on a larger scale in business sometime around the early 1980s, software was generally limited to one narrow task or function (Bradford, 2014). Accounting is a good example of this. The software was characterised as narrowly focused on a single function, and as a result, data and/or information were partitioned between the departments dealing with different functions. Another consequence of this was that the same data could be stored in two different systems, making it harder to work with in decision making. One way of describing and understanding this type of information system is that it was a stand-alone solution, or a system that did not communicate with others. In a way, it focused on a single user's tasks and needs, for example, a specific manager's request.

Another way of describing these systems is that they supported what is called end-user computing, where the user controls how the systems are used and the role they play (Chaffey & White, 2010). The end user of the information system used the system as a tool, as an optional source of information or as merely a transaction processor that kept the records in order. Advanced calculations could be done with these systems but because digital communication outside and inside the organisation was not that well developed. A simple example is that of a spreadsheet, where different forms of information systems, such as management and executive ones, calculated data from the early AIS, transforming it into information. In this way, accounting data became management information. Even though such software is an early example of information systems, the development of software over the years has taken leaps and bounds.

ERP—Enterprise resource planning

Up to and including the 1990s, there was increased development in various forms of more advanced information systems. Especially within the manufacturing industry, a new standard was set where the specific focuses were on inventory, materials planning and, later, resource planning (Bradford, 2014). In a way, this allowed managers to implement management control in the way that influential authors such as Robert Anthony (1965) stated it should be—with a focus on obtaining the resources needed to achieve organisational goals. Still, some of the early systems such as material requirements planning and manufacturing resource planning were stand-alone systems. Nevertheless, their data came from different sources, and departmental borders were somewhat erased. When the information systems used today, for example, ERP systems, were introduced, they—in different forms and ways—integrated various functions; hence expanded the possibility for management to have information systems support (Simkin et al., 2015).

A typical ERP system includes several facets of business functions (Bradford, 2014); therefore, this system can integrate data not only from accounting, but also customers, human resources, supply chain, inventory and sales and marketing, to name a few (Baltzan, 2019). Through this integration, the accounting function in general—and AIS in particular—has come to play a new role, one where it is not only the traditional financial statements that are interesting to report but rather where more detailed commentary on, for example, a specific product or customer, some parts of a process or strategic information about different scenarios, can be given. Because AIS have a new role in a more advanced information system context and a focus on management information support, these systems have begun to drive a change in the way management is using AIS information. Scholars such as Kaplan & Norton (1996) arrived at the conclusion that even though financial information in an era of advanced information systems is not enough, financial information is still crucial for the business to be able to reach its strategic goals and stay competitive. Accounting information still facilitates managers' ability to lead and make decisions about new paths and take actions that improve competitiveness.

A critical challenge—information overload

What information consumes is rather obvious: it consumes the attention of its recipients. Hence, a wealth of information creates a poverty of attention and a need to allocate that attention efficiently among the overabundance of information sources that might consume it.

(Greenberger, 1971, pp. 40–41)

When working with modern, advanced ERP systems and AIS, it has become a significant challenge to navigate the immense amount of data that are exponentially increasing around and within organisations. In some cases, the volume of data produced and stored increases at a pace which is making it almost impossible to work with these data and information in a structured way. Information is intended to support managers' decisions and actions, so its value decreases when too much unstructured information is presented. There are several ways to deal with this overload issue. One is to work with aggregated information—the bigger picture—and when there is a deviation between goals and performance, a deeper drilldown can be used. This is typically possible with modern AIS. Another way of managing information overload is through the use of different filters—for example, via key indicators or specific performance measures, which focus a manager's attention on specific results (Waal, 2013). Advanced AIS bring a multitude of opportunities, but it also comes with some important challenges, especially those relating to the amount of information produced.

What the future brings

In many ways, the ability to present a broader picture has facilitated managers with new tools and insights into what is occurring in a business. This makes it even more important for the management function to be able to interpret and incorporate new information into their everyday work. One of the challenges that managers are facing is to learn and change the way things are conducted within an operation to stay competitive. AIS and their role in ERP systems are rapidly transforming into the metaphorical backbone of companies; the ability to use the system to create increased customer value or growth is what separates the 'wheat from the chaff', per se. In the future, these new systems will play an increasingly important role, and organisations that manage to understand AIS new functionalities, for example, within an ERP system, will benefit from the opportunities they bring. Accounting will still be accounting, and information systems still be information systems, but with new functionalities, they will bring added value to management in ways and forms that were not there before (Simkin et al., 2015). As an illustration of how information systems such as AIS can contribute to change, the case of Philz Coffee is a good example.

Business case—Philz Coffee

In San Francisco, there is a chain of coffee shops called Philz Coffee. Founded by Phil Jaber, it is a family-owned and family-managed business. Over the years, they have established themselves as a quality supplier of a blend of real, authentic coffee served both in the coffee shops and sold to those who want to make it at home. When Phil's son, Jacob, became CEO, one of his challenges was to expand the business and scale up what was a known success to a larger setting. They wanted to increase the number of coffee shops and expand coffee sales. Because the core business was fundamentally about everything, from making the different flavours to selling a hot cup of coffee, there was both a demand for point-of-sale happenings and for an efficient inventory management. For the business to grow, Philz Coffee needed to change the way things were done.

Jacob decided to contact NetSuite, an ERP systems provider. They offered Philz Coffee a system solution that was cloud based, making it possible to connect over the internet, hence allowing it to be accessible from different locations. It also connected to all major functions in the operations, from production, packaging and inventory to marketing and sales. In the middle of everything was the accounting module. It keeps track of all the financial consequences of running the operation. Through the system, Jacob was able to plan for and measure the performance in different parts of the business, both financial performance and other forms of performance. NetSuite helped Philz Coffee expand its business through changes in how integrated information systems were used to manage the operations. Even though AIS are still a crucial function, they have become an even more important part of the ERP system, providing managers with financial information and, if needed, adding other integrated information into managers' work and understanding of the business.

In many ways, a new information system, particularly new and advanced AIS, brings with it new ways of working and running an operation. In this way, implementing AIS also comes with a change in the organisation, a change that needs to be managed to be successful. How management deals with change lays the foundation for the coming success of a system implementation, and the technical side of AIS implementation becomes a socio-technical challenge. In many cases, this is dealt with through different forms of change management, where the technical side of AIS implementation is accompanied by a softer organisational implementation endeavour.

Understanding AIS and management challenges

Changing how things are done and how processes are run in an organisation are typical management challenges. These not only affect how people in the organisation should behave and do their work but also are a matter of how different technological solutions are implemented, where one of the most obvious is the information system. From a work-centred perspective, operations and changes in, for example, a process are about people, information and technology. From another perspective, change in an organisation is about changing the organisation itself. This is an important distinction because changing an organisation can be both of more strategic importance and, when it is operationalised, of a lower level of importance. In many cases, change comes down to how managers alter their way of making decisions and acting on them. Different actors in an organisation—those who could be described as change agents—then drive change.

Work-centred analysis

A fruitful way of looking at an organisation and its processes is through a work-centred analysis, a model developed by Steven Alter (1999). This focuses on an information system's role in an organisation. In doing so, there is an initial need to understand what kind of product or service the organisation tries to compete with and what customers are willing to pay for. Thus, from one perspective, it is important to understand and follow what could be described as the result generated from the core business process, that is, what the organisation does. At the centre of the model are the business processes that produce the goods or services, and this is, on the other hand, built on three equally important parts: people, information and technology. To understand what is occurring within an organisation and how technology affects the core processes, one can look at the organisation from a behavioural perspective, where people and information are important for describing a process. Yet from another perspective, the technological solution that produces information is equally important to understand. These two perspectives are considered two sides of the same coin.

It is important to try to understand what kind of problem the system is supposed to solve. When Checkland (1981) (see also Checkland & Scholes, 1990) discussed the softer side of systems, he noted that there were some organisational problems that need addressing. When doing a systems analysis, it is important to describe the situation where the problem occurs in enough depth, and as a result, a specific management problem can become contextualised. Then, different solutions to the problem within the context can be presented, and the ability to implement a solution is described. Altogether, a good systems analysis, here with a focus on actual ambitions or problems within an organisational context, should form the basis for a blueprint of future possible changes. Analysing the value and contribution from systems such as AIS then forms the basis for this change to occur.

Organisational change

The processes that bring change to an organisation can be understood from different perspectives (Hayes, 2014). From one perspective, change could be about operational and incremental change, where ongoing adjustments to new circumstances or fine-tuning operations becomes the focus. On the other hand, change in an organisation can also be about more strategic decisions and radical change that have longer-term consequences. Whatever way change occurs, it is important to note whether the organisation wants to be proactive or reactive. When an incremental or minor change is decided on, it could very well be reactive, but if the change discussed in an organisation is more of strategic importance, it might be crucial to be proactive. When working with ERP systems, in general, and AIS, in particular, it is important to think through what consequences the system will have for the organisation. In many cases, it is of strategic importance, and senior management needs to be proactive in facilitating the needed change that a new system brings with it.

Inherent to organisational change is organisational learning (Senge, 1990). When an organisation changes the way it does things, usually by basing this change on experience or new insight, there is an inherent element of learning. This is effectively what happens when a new information system is implemented, such as an AIS. The organisation needs to learn how to take advantage of the new possibilities that the system brings, which are made concrete when conducting operations in a new way. Sometimes, the new system forces employees to do things differently, but learning and change frequently come from employees themselves. However, there is often a discrepancy between what people in an organisation know and what they do (Argyris, 1982). Many of the opportunities that a new system offers are not fully learned until it changes the way work is done in a permanent way. As such, organisational learning and organisational change are intertwined.

Change management and change agents

Managing change in an organisation is usually thought of as something realised over several phases (Jay & Smith, 1996). In the first phase, there is a need to understand why change is required, resulting in some sort of plan for the change process, where different milestones are identified, and a cost-benefit analysis occurs. In the next phase, different forms of preparation are realised, including an environmental analysis, critical success factors and different forms of threat to change. Then, in the third phase, the change is implemented. This also involves thinking through whether there is an additional need to change the working procedures or test the new system in one department. In the fourth and final phase, the change needs to be stabilised through support in different forms, which might also include fine-tuning and additional training. Altogether, there is usually a need to think the entire project through so that the desired change can be made.

Usually, there is also a need to have a change agent in charge of the entire process of working through the change phases (Hayes, 2014). Of course, this is done with the help and mandate of senior management. The change agent could be understood as a form of project manager who runs the change process, monitoring and ensuring that goals are met and that necessary resources are available. In addition, the change agent might be responsible for communicating why change is needed. Communication is crucial for an organisation to adapt to changes, and in many cases, an organisation needs to believe—not only understand—why change is needed. When long-term, strategic change is about to happen, this could be described as a transformational change, and here, the ability of the transformational leadership is important. If this leadership is not working as it should, it could contribute to a change project failing. To paraphrase Brown (1994), transformational leadership is key to successful management of technology change, involving the instilling of a sense of purpose in staff and encouraging them to identify emotionally with the organisation and its goals.

A critical perspective on change management challenges

In many organisations, there seems to be a never-ending search for the next change. The structures, forms and ways of doing the job seem to be continually questioned, and something new is needed. This ongoing strive to find the new 'Holy Grail' sometimes makes it difficult for an organisation to mature in the latest organisational change; therefore, they miss out on the benefits they initially hoped to achieve (Hayes, 2014). It then becomes important for senior management to evaluate if the opportunities the change brings match its needs. When it comes to changing AIS, it is even more crucial to ask that question because the accounting function is imbedded in so much of what is done, and changing such a system—especially to an ERP—brings many additional alterations (Bredmar et al., 2014). If the information processed and used today is close to what is needed from a management perspective, then the additional value of changing a system might not outweigh the cost or effort of doing so. In some cases, new AIS also mean a new internal structure or process, and the cost of changing a system must also include the change of the business process.

An even faster pace of change in the future

A problem exists that relates to the rate of change occurring in many organisations; this problem has to do with the fact that many of the earlier change theories were developed under circumstances that were more stable. Through technological innovation and new systems, such as advanced AIS and integrated ERP, old models are not applicable in the same way. As such, a form of change management also focuses on how to change an organisation's culture, getting employees to understand that change will benefit them, forming a more dynamic view of the constant state of change (Goldberg, 1992). The concept of business agility has come to encompass this new state of constant change, where the focus is on the organisation's ability to rapidly change when new expectations occur in the environment around the organisation and in a cost-efficient manner. The changes in an organisation come with a cost, and it has become even more important for senior managers to be able to estimate the benefit and value from changing the organisation compared with the cost. Implementing new AIS is not only about hardware and software costs; there is a lot more to it (Baltzan, 2019).

New technical opportunities drive the ability to use advanced information systems and data analysis to improve efficiency and increase innovation. New systems and advanced analyses drive how management understand and make decisions within a company, decisions and actions that eventually end up in AIS. Complex and advanced integrated systems, where AIS play an important part, today drive change when it comes to how operations are achieved and how businesses gain a competitive advantage.

AIS and trends that drive change

In most companies, there is a never-ending quest for increasing revenue, growth and/or increased profitability. Through modern, advanced AIS, there is an opportunity to track and monitor the various parts of an organisation that contribute to these parameters. In some industries, there is a saying that 20% of customers generate 80% of the revenue. With the help of modern AIS, this can be monitored and acted on. For example, performance that deviates from targets can be tracked through detailed AIS, hence creating new opportunities for management (Waal, 2013). Moreover, a change in how the management accounting function works can be facilitated by implementing new AIS, especially if it automates routine work and frees time for more advanced analyses. Analyses, decisions and actions are all possible through advanced digital initiatives in general, and a complex analysis of financial data may contribute to a more productive business.

Expecting the unexpected

When planning for any new system, there is an implied idea that managers know what they are planning for, that is, what they want the system to contribute. However, in many cases, it might be hard to overview all the possible contributions that a system might bring, especially if it also means changing and improving the way things are done in an organisation. One of the ideas behind ERP implementation is that it facilitates an increased ability to plan and control operations. This could be done through advanced analyses and calculations, and integrating and analysing data in a new way may also reveal findings not previously known (Chapman, 2005); these findings could be out of line with the intentions behind implementing a specific system, but when discovered, they can be valuable. From a management control perspective, these insights and discoveries might be quite valuable and, in different ways, drive the renewal and transformation of how management control is conducted.

Because the accounting function is based on norms and rules, these norms and rules are also reflected in the way an AIS is built. Nevertheless, an AIS is a technically driven solution that may not contribute to a strategic purpose. However, if the new system is integrated within an ERP so that they both can contribute to a new technical platform while implying a strategic move, there is also a possibility that the organisation will change its operations (Hyvönen, 2003). Several of the AIS software packages offered on the market are what could be called best-of-bread systems. They are developed to comply with accounting standards and have also been developed with the needs of a certain industry in mind. This makes it more difficult to use systems to facilitate major changes within an organisation because they are standardised. For an organisation to experience business value from such a system, there needs to be a clear strategic intent, which also drives and tries to maximise positive business change (Davenport, 2000).

Adopting or not adopting a new feature

Within management accounting and control research, there has been ongoing development for some years regarding new ways of managing an organisation based on financial and non-financial information. This development started with a discussion regarding the ways in which management accounting and control have developed since industrialisation. Scholars such as Johnson & Kaplan (1987) have suggested that the methods and techniques formed during industrialisation—and still used at the time—had lost their relevance. One of the new methods developed as an answer to this problem was the balanced scorecard (Kaplan & Norton, 1996) that used both financial and nonfinancial information in the work of managing an organisation in general and to transform a strategy into actions. One of the problems with that model was that it depended heavily on advanced information system support, and at that time, the systems were not that developed and difficult to use (Olve et al., 1999). Because of poor system support, it became hard to adopt new models, such as the balanced scorecard.

When more advanced ERP solutions with clear and advanced AIS functions were developed, it became easier to support new needs from management (Spathis & Constantinides, 2004). These new systems also changed accounting processes, making them automatic, at least to some extent.

> The empirical evidence confirms a number of changes in the accounting processes introduced with the adoption of ERP systems. The most frequently quoted ones involve the introduction of an internal audit function, the use of nonfinancial performance

indicators, and profitability analysis at segmental/product level. It is noteworthy though that these changes stem from the main advantages of ERP system, which have also been the driving force for managers adopting them.

(Spathis & Constantinides, 2004, p. 243)

Using advanced AIS, for example, within an ERP system, there is an opportunity to be more flexible and improve the quality of usefulness within financial reports. In many ways, this has facilitated an improved competitive position through the combined use of accounting information together with the nonfinancial, bringing a more efficient management function via the adoption of the ERP solution and changing the business processes.

Resistance to change: changing AIS but keeping operations the same

It is common for an organisation to show resistance to change, especially when it comes to changes in structure and how work is done (Hayes, 2014). This has, in a way, to do with the comfort and stability of existing processes. When implementing new AIS/ERP systems, there may be resistance to learning new techniques, as well as accepting the new responsibilities (Gupta, 2000). This may be traced back to poor training, yet there may also be additional costs associated with new systems, giving them a negative character within an organisation. This could be because of different ambitions and how the projects shift in focus and scope (Bredmar et al., 2014). Different phases in an AIS or ERP system project also focus on different areas, and new needs might be targeted that also bring new costs and decisions.

Resistance in an organisation can be described as a barrier that needs to be addressed in a conscious way. An opportunity could become a barrier if the organisation does not look at it as an opportunity but instead as a problem. There might be some initial ideas or suggestions that bring changes to operations and processes that, on implementation, suddenly become problems that the organisation does not want or think they need (Bredmar et al., 2014). One of the problems with change is that in the first phases of a change project, for example, when driven by the implementation of a new AIS, there might be some value or benefits pinpointed and communicated as a rhetorical argument as to why the change is needed. Nevertheless, in the end, the change that was implemented may look different and might not deliver the value or benefit initially thought of or argued for.

Accountants' new role and future implications

Changing the way things are done in an organisation is not something that is easily done. This makes it even more important to understand what new role the accountant might play in this process and in an organisation's quest for additional value, and by managers to find a competitive advantage. In many cases, there is an increased need among managers to get additional support from accountants just to understand the new financial information that advanced packaged systems deliver (Scapens & Jazayeri, 2003). Even though new systems usually bring about change, this is not always the case. A stand-alone AIS might not, per se, mean that functions or structures are changing because this is, to an extent, up to the accountant and the managers, especially when it comes to how the systems are used. Similarly, implementing new management accounting techniques, which could be understood as a change process, is not necessarily driven by introducing new ERP or AIS systems (Booth et al., 2000).

Generally, accountants' work has become broader today, with more of an educational and informational function because the routine work of day-to-day transactions has been narrowed (Scapens & Jazayeri, 2003). Thus, the accountant and the AIS function have come to play a new and increasingly important part in delivering value to the organisation, when change is arising in a slower, more indirect way. New software and technical solutions that bring opportunities to be evaluated, as well as increase the organisation's competitive advantage and the management function's abilities, are the ones that will find their way into the established practices of an organisation.

Concluding remarks

The technical development that organisations have faced for more than 20 years, especially when it comes to new administrative, advanced information systems, is remarkable. It has forced organisations to change the way they handle their operations, in some cases because of the demand of the customer and sometimes because of the possibilities that arise from new technical solutions. New AIS features have also created a need for more thought-out change management, driving the urgency for understanding how change in administrative processes comes about and how these new opportunities can work as a force creating a competitive advantage. More than ever, AIS constitute a system that can create the basis for an efficient business, a system that drives renewal and a system that makes a company profitable in the long run by showing what parts of an operation are the most profitable. In a way, advanced AIS have come to play a catalyst role, forcing the organisation to think through how operations are done and in what ways it could be improved to stay competitive.

References

Alter, S. (1999). *Information systems, a management perspective*. Reading, MA: Addison-Wesley.
Anthony, R. N. (1965). *Planning and control systems: A framework for analysis*. Boston, MA: Harvard University.
Argyris, C. (1982). *Reasoning, learning and action: Individual and organizational*. San Francisco, CA: Jossey- Bass.
Baltzan, P. (2019). *Business driven information systems*. New York, NY: McGraw-Hill Education.
Booth, P., Matolcsy, Z., & Wieder, B. (2000). The impacts of enterprise resource planning systems on accounting practice – The Australian experience. *Australian Accounting Review*, 10(3), 13–29.
Bradford, M. (2014). *Modern ERP - Select, implement, & use today's advanced business systems*. Raleigh, NC: North Carolina State University.
Bredmar, K., Ask, U., Frisk, E., & Magnusson, J. (2014). Accounting information systems implementation and management accounting change. *Business Systems Research*, 5(2), 125–138.
Brown, A. (1994). Transformational leadership in tackling technical change. *Journal of General Management*, 19(4), 1–12.
Chaffey, D., & White, G. (2010). *Business information management: Improving performance using information systems*. Harlow: Pearson Education.
Chapman, C. S. (2005). Not because they are new: Developing the contribution of enterprise resource planning systems to management control research. *Accounting, Organizations and Society*, 30, 685–689.
Checkland, P. (1981). *Systems thinking, systems practice*. Chichester: John Wiley and Sons.
Checkland, P., & Holwell, S. (1998). *Information, systems and information systems*. Chichester: John Wiley and Sons.
Checkland, P., & Scholes, J. (1990). *Soft systems methodology in action*. Chichester: John Wiley and Sons.
Davenport, T. H. (2000). *Mission critical. Realizing the promise of enterprise systems*. Boston, MA: Harvard Business School Press.
Davis, G. B., & Olson, M. H. (1984). *Management Information Systems*. New York, NY: McGraw-Hill.
Emmanuel, C., Otley, D., & Merchant, K. (1990). *Accounting for management control*. London: Chapman and Hall.
Goldberg, B. (1992). Managing change, not the chaos caused by change. *Management Review*, 81(11), 39.

Greenberger, M. (Eds.) (1971). *Computers, communications, and the public interest*. Baltimore, MD: Johns Hopkins University Press.

Gupta, A. (2000). Enterprise resource planning: The emerging organizational value systems. *Industrial Management & Data Systems*, 100(1), 114–118.

Hayes, J. (2014). *The theory and practice of change management*. Basingstoke, Hampshire: Palgrave Macmillan.

Hyvönen, T. (2003). Management accounting and information systems: ERP versus BoB. *European Accounting Review*, 12(1), 155–173.

Jay, K. E., & Smith, D. C. (1996). A generic change model for the effective implementation of information systems. *South African Journal of Business Management*, 27(3), 65–70.

Johnson, H. T., & Kaplan, R. S. (1987). *Relevance lost: The rise and fall of management accounting*. Boston, MA: Harvard Business School Press.

Kaplan, R. S., & Norton, D. P. (1996). *The balanced scorecard: Translating strategy into action*. Boston, MA: Harvard Business School Press.

Langefors, B. (1995). *Essays on infology*. Lund: Studentlitteratur.

Littleton, A. C. (1953). *Structure of accounting theory*. Sarasota: American Accounting Association.

Michels, D., & Murphy, K. (2021). How good is your company at change? *Harvard Business Review*, 99(4), 62–71.

Olve, N.-G., Roy, J., & Wetter, M. (1999). *Performance drivers*. Chichester: Wiley.

Peppard, J., & Ward, J. (2016). *The strategic management of information systems: Building digital strategy*. Chichester: John Wiley & Sons.

Scapens, R. W., & Jazayeri, M. (2003). ERP systems and management accounting change: Opportunities or impacts? A research note. *European Accounting Review*, 12(1), 201–233.

Senge, P. M. (1990). *The fifth discipline, the art and practice of the learning organization*. London: Century Business.

Simkin, M. G., Norman, C. S. & Rose, J. M. (2015) *Core concepts of accounting information systems*. Chichester: Wiley.

Spathis, C., & Constantinides, S. (2004). Enterprise resource planning systems' impact on accounting processes. *Business Process Management Journal*, 10(2), 234–247.

Thompson, G. (1994). Early double-entry bookkeeping and the rhetoric of accounting calculation. In A. G. Hopwood & P. Miller (Eds.), *Accounting as social and institutional practice* (24th ed., 40–66). Cambridge: Cambridge University Press.

Waal, A. D. (2013). *Strategic performance management: A managerial and behavioural approach*. Basingstoke, Hampshire: Palgrave Macmillan.

PART 2

Organisational effects of accounting information systems

6

CLARIFYING DIGITALISATION

Strategy, transformation, and implementation

Daniel Schallmo and Christopher Williams

Introduction

Understanding digitalisation has become central for all non-profit and for-profit institutions (Tidd, 2019; Schallmo & Tidd, 2021). Recent developments in digital initiatives (Niemand et al., 2020) have heightened the need to investigate holistic digitalisation. The terms 'digital transformation' and 'strategy-oriented digitalisation' contain overlapping features. However, it has been argued that certain digitalisation-level initiatives (e.g. digital process model) may also exhibit strategy-oriented perspectives (Caputo et al., 2021). In addition, with a term such as 'Industry 4.0,' companies consider the idea of digital transformation to be too abstract (Gimpel et al., 2018). A holistic view of digitalisation research provides various concrete possibilities for companies striving for best practices that can be applied in real-life business environments. Digitalisation initiatives, especially in digital maturity, strategy, transformation, and implementation, provide a path for companies' optimisation and development. Holistic digitalisation opens new networking possibilities and enables cooperation among different actors, who, for example, exchange data and subsequently initiate processes (Nikmehr et al., 2021). The key questions are what the digital drivers (Weill & Woerner, 2015) towards holistic digitalisation are and how these drivers differ among countries, industries, and company size.

The objective of this is to present a holistic view to digitalisation consisting of fundamental levels for strategically oriented digitalisation. These include digital strategy, digital transformation of business models, and digital implementation. It is posited that key drivers towards holistic digitalisation are digital strategy, digital transformation of business models, and digital implementation. The development of a digital strategy is just as integral to a company's activities as the digital transformation of business models. Although companies have recognised the need for a digital strategy (Bharadwaj et al., 2013; Peppard & Ward, 2016), developing that strategy in a structured way and integrating individual digitisation efforts into a strategic concept still present challenges (Butschan et al., 2019; Dutta & Sarma, 2020).

The digital transformation of business models concerns individual business model elements, but questions remain on how digitally transforming one element of a business model affects the other elements (Schallmo et al., 2017; Latilla et al., 2020). The key questions are how digital strategies can be developed in a more structured manner and what the effects are on a revised digital business model. Digital implementation involves enacting a digital

DOI: 10.4324/9781003132943-9

strategy and supports the digital transformation of one or more business models of a company (Schallmo et al., 2019a). Due to the complex nature of empirically investigating digital implementation, research should use a mixed method or qualitative approach to properly investigate the phenomena of implementing digital initiatives (Ivančić et al., 2019). The following are relevant to digital implementation – organisation, technical implementation, skills, and culture. The key question is how digital implementation and its essential areas can be evaluated empirically using a mixed methods approach.

Literature

As previously noted, and based on existing research, we consider the following three essential aspects in the context of digitisation: (1) digital strategy, (2) digital transformation of business models, and (3) digital implementation. These aspects are explained here based on extant literature.

Digital strategy

Based on existing research, we now outline insights on digital strategy (Schallmo et al., 2018; Schallmo et al., 2019a, 2019b). The development of a strategy involves two essential processes: (1) strategy formulation and (2) strategy implementation. The formulation of a long-term strategy requires a firm to assess its resources and capabilities to determine its competitive advantage. The resource-based view (RBV) and digital capabilities (DC) are widely cited as key concepts of strategy formulation, particularly when investigating a firm's resources and potential competitive advantage. According to Tywoniak (2007), RBV provides a fresh understanding of competitive advantage by relying on both internal and external analyses (Collis, 1991). Peteraf (1993) defined RBV as 'a model of how firms compete, which is unique to the field of strategic management.' The importance of RBV for formulating a strategy lies in its focus on optimising the use of resources and capabilities to create a competitive advantage (Wang & Ahmed, 2007). There is also evidence of effective orchestrating of resources helping those companies with limited resources still develop their innovative capabilities (Rindova & Kotha, 2001). RBV provides a framework for measuring the value of resources based on how they are valuable, rare, inimitable, and non-substitutable. While scholars praise RBV for offering both a theory for creating unique value (Peteraf & Barney, 2003) and competitive advantages (Barney, 1991), others have criticised RBV for being too static (Eisenhardt & Martin, 2000). One example of the static nature of RBV is its inability to explain how the competitive advantage changes in a dynamic environment (Teece et al., 1997). DC can be considered an answer to the static nature of RBV by connecting the capabilities to the dynamic nature of the market (Wang & Ahmed, 2007).

DC has been considered a clear extension of RBV (Barney, 2001; Helfat & Peteraf, 2003; Ahmad et al., 2018). Although differences of opinion remain, there is common consensus that Teece's (2012, p. 1395) definition of DC as 'higher-level competences that determine the firm's ability to integrate, build, and reconfigure internal and external resources/competences to address, and shape, rapidly changing business environments' embodies the essence of the concept. Based on literature, there is clear evidence that DC more effectively measures a company's competitive advantage in dynamic business environments (Lin & Wu, 2014). Although extensive research has been conducted on both RBV and DC, to date, no single study offers a generic framework for formulating a (digital) strategy. Lin & Wu (2014) suggested the complexity of combining RBV and DC (Danneels, 2011) when making strategic decisions as one explanation for this gap.

The past 20 years have seen increasingly rapid advances in the field of strategic management, particularly when researchers consider the heightened need for competitive advantages in digital environments. Koch & Windsperger (2017) offer a network perspective for understanding firms' resources and how these resources create competitive advantages in a volatile digital environment. The authors first argued that DC may provide a competitive advantage only compared to RBV in specific circumstances, but DC can also simply constitute best practices, which can be substituted as needed (Eisenhardt & Martin, 2000). Second, the authors claim that the rise of digitisation challenges the traditional approaches to strategic formulation (i.e. competitive advantage). They argue 'from a network-centric perspective, it can be concluded that firms' resources and capabilities extend beyond firm boundaries and be embedded in a set of relationships between firms' (Eisenhardt & Martin, 2000, p. 7). Too et al. (2010) posited that capabilities are the effective way a company utilises their resources and turn this into the desired output. The authors claimed that capabilities are an intermediate transformation capability between resources and their company aims.

'Digital strategy' is a term frequently used in the literature, but there is no consensus to date about a commonly accepted definition. When reflecting on the definition of digital strategy, the terms should be considered individually.[1] The terms 'digitalisation strategy,' 'digital business strategy,' 'digitisation strategy,' and 'digital transformation strategy' are used often interchangeably (see Schallmo et al., 2019a, 2019b). There are several main focuses and classification (definitions) of the digital strategy within the existing definitions and additional publications. For example, Fraunhofer IAO (2016) or Rauser (2016) considers digital strategy to be a part of the business strategy that concentrates on digitisation projects. Based on the literature, we propose the following definition of digital strategy (Schallmo et al., 2019a, 2019b):

> A digital strategy is the strategic form of digitisation intentions of companies. The short- and mid-term objectives are to maintain or create new competitive advantages. Within the digital strategy, digital technologies and methods are applied to products, services, processes, and business models. To develop a digital strategy, the company and its environment must be analysed as a basis for several future scenarios. The digital strategy consists of a vision, mission, strategic objectives, strategic success factors, values, and measures.

Within the framework of definitions and existing approaches as mentioned, there are different perspectives on the relationship between digital and corporate strategy, which are shown graphically in Figure 6.1.

Digital transformation of business models

There are many digital transformation definitions (Vial, 2021). However, in the field of information systems, we still witness the importance of providing distinct theoretical perspectives for the field. Based on our existing research, we now propose a theoretical background for digital transformation (Schallmo & Williams, 2018; Schallmo, 2019; Schallmo et al., 2017).

The digital transformation framework includes the networking of actors, such as businesses and customers, across all value-added chain segments (Bowersox et al., 2005; BMWi, 2015; Bouée & Schaible, 2015) and the application of new technologies (Westerman et al., 2011; PwC, 2013). As such, digital transformation requires skills that involve the extraction and exchange of data as well as analysis and conversion into actionable information. This

Figure 6.1 Connection between digital and corporate strategy (Schallmo et al., 2019a, 2019b).

information should be used to calculate and evaluate options to enable decisions and/or initiate activities (BMWi, 2015; Bouée & Schaible, 2015). To increase the performance and reach of a company (Westerman et al., 2011), digital transformation involves companies, business models, processes, relationships, products, etc. (Bowersox et al., 2005; Mazzone, 2014).

One of our contributions to the literature on digital transformation of business models is a definition as follows (Schallmo, 2013):

> A business model is the basic logic of a company that describes what benefits are provided to customers and partners. A business model answers the question of how the provided benefits flow back into the company in the form of revenue. The created value enables a differentiation from competitors, the consolidation of customer relationships, and the achievement of a competitive advantage.

A business model involves five dimensions: (1) customer dimension contains the customer segments, customer channels, and customer relationships; (2) benefit dimension includes products, services, and values; (3) value-added dimension includes the resources, skills, and processes; (4) partner dimension includes the partner, partner channels, and partner relations; and (5) financial dimension includes the revenues and expenses. The business model objective is to combine the business model elements such that they mutually reinforce each other. Thus, it is possible to achieve growth, and it is difficult to be imitated by competitors.

Based on the proposed definitions, we define the digital transformation of business models as follows (Schallmo, 2016; Schallmo et al., 2017; Schallmo & Williams, 2018; Schallmo, 2019):

> The digital transformation of business models relates to individual business model elements, the entire business model, value-added chains, and the networking of different actors in a value-added network. The degree of digital transformation concerns the incremental (marginal) as well as the radical (fundamental) change of a business model. The reference unit with regard to the level of novelty is primarily to the customer, but it can also affect its own business, partners, industry, and competitors. Within digital transformation of business models, enabler(s) – or, rather, technologies (e.g., big data) – are used to generate new applications or services (e.g., on-demand predictions). These enablers require skills that enable data collection and exchange as well as analysis and use them to calculate and evaluate options. The evaluated options are used to initiate new processes within the business model. Digital transformation of business models is based on an approach with a sequence of tasks and decisions related to one another in a logical and temporal context. It affects four target dimensions: time, finance, space, and quality.

Digital implementation

In one of our previous works, we proposed innovation insights on digital implementation (Schallmo & Williams, 2020). As digital implementation has had a significant relationship with organisational change, we considered Leavitt's System Model, which is also known as Leavitt's Diamond Model (Leavitt, 1965). This is seen as an integrated model for organisational change management. According to Leavitt (1965), with a change in any component of a system (= organisation), the impact on other components should be evaluated, and the proper balance should be found.

When comparing the popular digital strategy approaches, every approach includes some form of a digital implementation phase, and we now highlight some of these approaches. Kraewing's (2017) digital strategy approach targeted internationally active executives in medium-sized companies with an increased interest in digital transformation. The last step of Kraewing's (2017) approach is the implementation of the strategy with an individual implementation of the strategic objectives and continuous improvement. He also considers relevant phases of transformation within a change-management model. In the implementation phase, the following three methods are considered: (1) scrum as an agile project management method with fixed cycles (sprints), (2) digital value creation with an overview of the value-added potential of the digital as a product, and (3) a checklist of all major actions and issues for the implementation of digital strategy.

Greiner et al. (2017) developed an approach for digital strategy (here also digitisation strategy) based on theoretical findings and consulting experiences. The last step is the action plan for digital actions, which includes options for concrete measures through a prioritisation process. The approach includes two methods in this phase: (1) balanced scorecard and (2) economic efficiency calculation comparing expenses and income of the strategic measure. Rauser (2016) designed his approach to digital strategy based on experiences from consulting with companies. He considers the implementation in achievable steps as the last phase of his approach. The following methods and characteristics are mentioned: (1) agile project management, (2) iterative process, (3) UX process for obtaining user experience feedback, (4) key performance indicators (KPI) map as a representation of individual digital activities and their influence on defined corporate goals, and (5) lead nurturing funnel as an overview of the different sales initiatives of the request to purchase decision.

Petry (2016) formulated an approach aimed at executives who want to explore the implications of digitisation in the context of business and people leadership. He considers strategy implementation as the last step and includes the following methods: (1) lean start-up, (2) scrum, and (3) participatory workshops and two-speed information technology (IT) as a modular and flexible IT architecture. The foundation of Cordon et al.'s (2016a) approach is theoretical research based on existing models (classical and more modern strategic approaches) augmented by studies and practical examples. Digital strategy focuses on the use of big data, and, in the last phase, the implementation of the strategy or business model is conducted with the lean start-up method.

Holistic view of digitalisation

Based on the chapter objective of presenting a holistic view of digitalisation consisting of fundamental levels for strategically oriented digitalisation, we structure strategy-oriented digitalisation into the following three fundamental levels: (1) digital strategy, (2) digital transformation of business models, and (3) digital implementation influenced by the macro- and micro-environment (Schallmo et al., 2019a). This enables companies to gain a holistic view of digitalisation. The three fundamental levels of strategy-oriented digitalisation are shown in Figure 6.2 and are described now.

Level 1: digital strategy

Approach for the development of a digital strategy

Based on our research, including the description and comparison of eight approaches, interviews with six researchers and seven practitioners (consultants), interviews with ten practitioners (company representatives), and the description and comparison of case studies, we present an integrated approach for the development of a digital strategy (Schallmo et al., 2018; Schallmo et al., 2019a, 2019b). The integrated approach for the development of a digital strategy is based on a procedure model with six phases shown in Figure 6.3. These six phases are explained in the following sections: the strategic options (Phase 5) are explained in greater detail.

Phase 1: external strategic analysis

This phase involves analysis of influencing factors from the macro- and micro-environment (Peppard & Ward, 2016; Rauser, 2016; Greiner et al., 2017; Kraewing, 2017). The analysis of the macro-environment (PESTEL) focuses on technologies and technology trends, and the analysis of the micro-environment (Five Forces) focuses on customers and competitors.

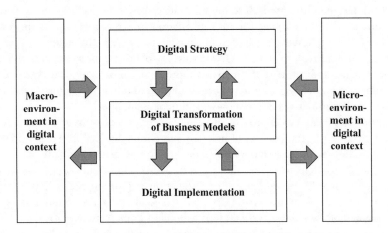

Figure 6.2   Classification in the context of digitisation (Schallmo et al., 2019a).

Figure 6.3   Procedure model for digital strategy development.

Within the framework of the analysis, a fundamental understanding of existing influencing factors is gained, which serves to develop scenarios in a digital context.

Phase 2: scenario development

The objective of this phase is to develop scenarios. The factors influencing the macro- and micro-environment will be selected regarding their future relevance in the digital context and supplemented. A typical observational horizon is ten years. After that, a forecast (e.g. ten years) is made for the development of the influencing factors, and they are subsequently prioritised. Based on these influencing factors, coherent scenarios are developed that include aspects of the macro- and micro-environment (Cordon et al., 2016b; Hille et al., 2016; Kraewing, 2017).

Phase 3: internal strategic analysis

The objective of this phase is to analyse the firm and its different divisions in the digital context (Hille et al., 2016; Rauser, 2016; Kraewing, 2017; Greiner et al., 2017). In addition, its digital maturity level is surveyed. This enables the firm to discover potential for the digital strategy.

Phase 4: digital strategy statement

The objective of this phase is to identify current and future fields of action with focus on digital initiatives based on the previous phases. The objective is also to develop a digital strategy statement for the firm (Petry, 2016; Rauser, 2016; Greiner et al., 2017; Kraewing, 2017).

Phase 5: strategic options

The objective of this phase is to derive strategic options, evaluate them, and select a strategic option (Cordon et al., 2016b; Hille et al., 2016; Kraewing, 2017). Generic digital strategies are utilised, and the results of the previous phases can be used in this phase (e.g. digital strategy statement).

Phase 6: digital strategy formulation

The aim of this phase is to formulate a digital strategy based on the strategic option selected (Cordon et al., 2016b; Peppard & Ward, 2016; Petry, 2016; Rauser, 2016; Kraewing, 2017). Projects and measures are defined and compared to the corporate strategy and the mission statement. In combination with the mission statement developed, the projects and measures represent the digital strategy.

The digital strategy is the starting point for digitally transforming existing business models or developing new digital business models. The process model above seeks to develop a digital strategy in a structured way. In addition to applying the entire process model, it is also possible to adapt the process model to company-specific requirements. For example, individual phases and activities can be combined or skipped.

Generic options for a digital strategy

Generic digital strategies are also used within the integrative approach. These generic digital strategies are based on the following two dimensions:

- Deliverables: What is the focus regarding deliverables? What services are provided? Is the focus on material services (e.g. products/components) or intangible services (e.g. services/information)?
- Roles: What is the focus regarding the role? What is the primary role? Is the focus on the creation of services or on the building/operation of a platform?

The two dimensions can be combined, resulting in a matrix with four generic digital strategies – see Figure 6.4 – namely, Product Provider, Service Provider, Product Platform Operator, and Service Platform Operator. Each is now described.

The product provider focuses on the provision of material services, such as products and components. These material services are then offered either directly or on a platform or by a platform operator. Examples of this are manufacturers of notebooks and suppliers of automotive parts. For a Service Provider, the generic digital strategy primarily provides intangibles such as services and information. These are then offered either directly or on a platform or by a platform operator, analogous to the product provider. Examples of this are insurance companies and logistics service providers. For a Product Platform Operator, in the generic digital strategy, the focus is on building and operating a product platform. In this scenario, proprietary/third-party material services are offered individually or as a bundle on a platform. Examples include online retailers of electronic goods or shoes. For a Service Platform Operator, the generic digital strategy focuses primarily on building and operating a service platform. In this scenario, proprietary/third-party intangible services are offered individually or as a bundle on a platform. Examples of this are a comparison platform for electricity and a platform for the brokerage of overnight stays. These four generic digital strategies offer different entry points and development opportunities depending on the initial situation and objectives. This means that a company might be a product provider at the moment but

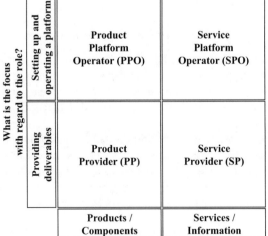

Figure 6.4 Matrix with four generic options for a digital strategy.

would like to develop into a future service platform provider. The matrix for generic digital strategies also supports a classification of competitors and their digital strategy.

Level 2: digital transformation of business models

Approach for the digital transformation of business models

Based on existing approaches to digital transformation, existing theories on business model innovation (Bucherer, 2011; Schallmo, 2013; Rusnjak, 2014; Schallmo, 2014; Thomas, 2014), and our previous research (Schallmo et al., 2017; Schallmo & Williams, 2018; Schallmo, 2019), we now present an approach for the digital transformation of business models shown in Figure 6.5. The approach consists of five phases which are explained below. Within Phase 3 (digital potential), we focus on the detailed description of digital enablers.

Phase 1: digital reality

In this phase, the firm's existing business model is sketched along with a value-added analysis related to stakeholders and a survey of customer requirements. This provides an understanding of the digital reality in different areas.

Phase 2: digital ambition

Based on the digital reality, objectives with regard to digital transformation are defined. These objectives relate to time, finances, space, and quality. Digital ambition postulates which objectives should be considered for the business model and its elements. Subsequently, objectives and business model dimensions are prioritised.

Phase 3: digital potential

Within this digital potential phase, best practices and enablers for the digital transformation are collected. This serves as a starting point in terms of digital potential and the design of a future digital business model. For this purpose, different options are derived for each business model element and logically combined.

Phase 4: digital fit

The digital fit phase looks at options for the design of the digital business model, which are evaluated to determine digital fit with the existing business model. This ensures that one fulfils customer requirements and that business objectives are achieved. The evaluated combinations are then prioritised.

Procedure Model for Digital Transformation of Business Models

Figure 6.5   Procedure model for digital transformation of business models (Schallmo, 2016, p. 23).

Phase 5: *digital implementation*

Digital implementation includes finalisation and implementation of the digital business model. The various combination options are further pursed within a digital implementation framework. The digital implementation also includes the design of a digital customer experience and the digital value-creation network that describes integration with partners. In addition, resources and capabilities are identified in this phase.

Enablers for digital transformation

Enablers allow applications or services to be used for the digital transformation of the business model. There are four categories for enablers and applications/services as now explained. First is digital data, which is the collection, processing, and analysis of digitised data to facilitate and improve predictions and decisions. Second is automation, which is the combination of classical artificial intelligence technologies that enables autonomous work and self-organising systems. This reduces error rates, increases speed, and makes it possible to reduce operating costs. Third is digital customer access, which is mobile internet enabling direct access to the clients, who, in turn, are provided with high transparency levels and new services. Fourth is networking. Mobile or wired networking of the entire value-added chain of high-broadband telecommunications allows the synchronisation of supply chains, which leads to a reduction of production times and innovation cycles. Enablers are listed with their applications/services in a digital radar, shown in Figure 6.6.

Level 3: digital implementation

Based on our research, including the review of existing approaches, we now present an integrated approach to digital implementation (Schallmo & Williams, 2020). The integrated approach for digital implementation is also based on a procedure model with five phases. These phases are iterative and are shown in Figure 6.7 and described now. The five phases of

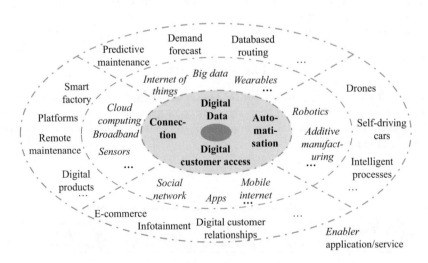

Figure 6.6 Digital radar with enablers and applications (Bouée & Schaible, 2015).

Procedure Model for Digital Implementation

Figure 6.7   Procedure model for the digital implementation.

the procedure model are now explained. We also explain the dimensions and their influence as relevant to Phase 4 (execute digital agenda).

Phase 1: derive digital initiatives

Within this phase, digital initiatives are derived, based on two main sources. First is the firm's analysis (Hille et al., 2016; Rauser, 2016; Greiner et al., 2017; Kraewing, 2017) across relevant areas (e.g. organisation, processes, IT, infrastructure, systems, technologies, capabilities, and existing initiatives) and digital maturity analysis. Ideally, these analyses are conducted in the context of digital strategy development and the defined digital strategy with projects and measures (Cordon et al., 2016a; Peppard & Ward, 2016; Petry, 2016; Rauser, 2016; Kraewing, 2017). Second is the digitally transformed business model, which is based on best practices, digital transformation enablers, the digital value network, and digital customer experiences. The derived digital initiatives are assigned to the categories of the TOSC-Model with technology, organisation, skills, and culture (Schallmo et al., 2019a).

Phase 2: prioritise digital initiatives

The derived and categorised digital initiatives are then evaluated in terms of their impact, time, cost, etc. They are also included in an influential matrix to measure their mutual influence. The result is an active and passive sum of each digital initiative revealing its influence on (active sum) and by other initiatives (passive sum) (Vester & Hesler, 1980). Then, they are included in a digital initiative matrix with four categories: (1) slow digital initiatives; (2) active digital initiatives with a prime influence; (3) passive digital initiatives, being highly influenced; (4) critical digital initiatives, making it possible to prioritise the derived digital initiatives and to focus on the most important and immediate.

Phase 3: set up digital agenda

The prioritised digital initiatives are included in a visual tool, the digital agenda. The digital initiatives are accompanied by two important propositions: change and communication management (in particular, internal communication), which includes the purpose definition applying the 'why, how, what' principle (Sinek, 2009; Cameron et al., 2014). In addition, the digital initiatives are described in detail, including responsibilities, time frames, key performance indicators, objectives, resources, actions, and a budget.

Phase 4: execute digital agenda

Within this phase, the digital agenda is executed. This means that all digital initiatives are implemented properly, applying agile methods (e.g. scrum, lean). The implementation of digital initiatives is checked and adjusted if necessary. In addition, the influence on customer experiences, operational excellence, and digital excellence is measured, and the defined digital strategy and digitally transformed business model should be considered regarding the measurement of the influence. The most relevant dimensions of the digital implementation can be represented by the TOSC-Model (Schallmo et al., 2019a):

- Technology: e.g. use of sensors, creation of databases, networking of components
- Organisation: e.g. definition of structures and responsibilities, establishment of departments, definition of processes
- Skills: e.g. IT know-how (hardware, software application/development, etc.), use of collaboration tools, development of leadership and collaboration skills, acquisition of methods
- Culture: e.g. cultural anchoring in the company, sensitisation of employees, communication within the company

These dimensions interact, are interdependent, and therefore influence each other. They support the achievement of the digital strategies' goals and contribute to the operational excellence, customer experience, and digital excellence, as shown in Figure 6.8.

Phase 5: check digital results

The last phase is to check the digital results within the three main categories of customer experience, digital excellence, and operational excellence. Thus, the previously defined objectives of Phase 3 (set up digital agenda) are relevant. The deviation is identified, and the actions, objectives, etc. are adjusted. The checked/reviewed digital results are executed permanently while still allowing for adjustments throughout the process.

Combination of approaches

Figure 6.9 combines the three approaches and procedure models for digital strategy, digital transformation of business models, and digital implementation, i.e. Level 1, Level 2, and Level 3 as described earlier. Every procedure model is iterative and can be applied separately depending on what digital maturity exists at each level. This is applicable if the effort should be reduced. The three procedure models can also be combined and interdependent. In in this case, the procedure models are not exclusive and can have redundances. For example, the 'internal strategic analysis' (digital strategy development) phase is generating output that can be applied in the 'digital reality' (digital transformation of business models) and 'derive digital initiatives' (digital implementation) phases.

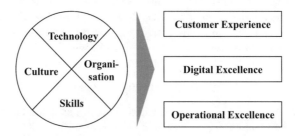

Figure 6.8   TOSC-Model and influence.

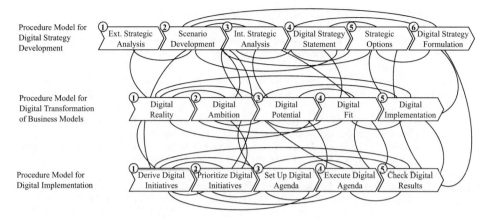

Figure 6.9   Combination of approaches.

Concluding comment

This chapter contributes a holistic view to digitalisation. This view consists of fundamental levels for strategy-oriented digitalisation. The fundamental levels include digital strategy, digital transformation, and digital implementation. We also provide procedure models for each fundamental level and additional insights (e.g. generic option for digital strategy), which closes a research gap regarding digitalisation. Further investigation and experimentation into our approaches in real-life business environment are strongly recommended to improve these complex phenomena. It is hoped that senior managers and business developers will also gain from the findings by having a holistic view of digitalisation covering three levels. The holistic view enables companies to take advantage of their digital potential. By developing each fundamental level further, companies can optimise their current situation and create a distinct competitive advantage. Specific requirements of companies should be covered by adjusting the view presented.

Note

1 For definitions of 'digital,' see Albayrak & Gadatsch, 2017; Heuermann et al., 2018; Hippmann, et al., 2018; Schawel & Billing, 2018; Wolf & Strohschen, 2018; also: digitisation. For definitions of 'strategy,' see Drucker, 1954; Ansoff, 1965; Chandler, 1962; Steiner & Miner, 1977; Mintzberg, 1979; Andrews, 1980; Henderson, 1989; Porter, 1996; Johnson et al., 2008; Hungenberg, 2014; Schallmo & Williams, 2018.

References

Ahmad, M., Papert, M. & Pflaum, A. (2018). Dynamic capabilities related implementation skills for Internet of Things solutions in the digital economy. Hawaii: *Proceedings of the 51st Hawaii international conference on system sciences*, 3996–4005.

Albayrak, C.A. & Gadatsch, A. (2017). Digitalisierung für kleinere und mittlere Unternehmen (KMU): Anforderungen an das IT-Management. In *IT-GRC-Management–Governance, risk und compliance* eds. M. Knoll, & S. Strahringer (pp. 151–166). Springer Gabler.

Andrews, K.R. (1980). *The concept of corporate strategy* (Rev. ed.). Irwin Homewood.

Ansoff, H.I. (1965). *Corporate strategy: An analytical approach to business policy for growth and expansion.* McGraw-Hill Education.

Barney, J. (1991). Firm resources and sustained competitive advantage. *Journal of Management, 17*(1), 99–120. https://doi.org/10.1177/014920639101700108

Barney, J.B. (2001). Resource-based theories of competitive advantage: A ten-year retrospective on the resource-based view. *Journal of Management, 27*(6), 643–650. https://doi.org/10.1177/014920630102700602

Bharadwaj, A., el Sawy, O.A., Pavlou, P.A. & Venkatraman, N. (2013). Digital business strategy: Toward a next generation of insights. *MIS Quarterly, 37*(2), 471–482. https://doi.org/10.25300/misq/2013/37:2.3

BMWi. (2015). *Industrie 4.0 und Digitale Wirtschaft - Impulse für Wachstum, Beschäftigung und innovation*, Bundesministerium für Wirtschaft und Energie.

Bouée, C. & Schaible, S. (2015). *Die Digitale Transformation der Industrie*. Roland Berger und BDI, Studie.

Bowersox, D.J., Closs, D.J. & Drayer, R.W. (2005). The digital transformation: Technology and beyond. *Supply Chain Management Review, 9*(1), 22–29.

Bucherer, E. (2011). *Business model innovation-guidelines for a structured approach*. Aachen: Shaker.

Butschan, J., Heidenreich, S., Weber, B. & Kraemer, T. (2019). Tackling hurdles to digital transformation — The role of competencies for successful industrial Internet of Things (IIoT) implementation. *International Journal of Innovation Management, 23*(04), 1950036. https://doi.org/10.1142/s1363919619500361

Cameron, K.S., Quinn, R.E., Degraff, J. & Thakor, A.V. (2014). *Competing values leadership*. Edward Elgar Publishing.

Caputo, A., Pizzi, S., Pellegrini, M.M. & Dabić, M. (2021). Digitalisation and business models: Where are we going? A science map of the field. *Journal of Business Research, 123*, 489–501. https://doi.org/10.1016/j.jbusres.2020.09.053

Chandler, A.D. (1962). *Strategy and structure: Chapters in the history of the industrial enterprise*. Mansfield Centre.

Collis, D.J. (1991). A resource-based analysis of global competition: The case of the bearings industry. *Strategic Management Journal, 12*(S1), 49–68. https://doi.org/10.1002/smj.4250120906

Cordon, C., Garcia-Milà, P., Vilarino, T.F. & Caballero, P. (2016b). From digital strategy to strategy is digital. In *Strategy is digital*, ed. C. Cordon, P. Garcia-Milà, T.F. Vilarino, & P. Caballero (pp. 9–45). Berlin: Springer.

Cordon, C., Garcia-Milà, P., Vilarino, T.F. & Caballero, P. (2016a). *Strategy is digital: How companies can use big data in the value chain*. Springer.

Cordon, C., Garcia-Milà, P., Vilarino, T.F. & Caballero, P. (2016b). From digital strategy to strategy is digital. In Cordon, C., Garcia-Milà, P., Vilarino, T.F. & Caballero, P. (eds.): *Strategy is digital* (pp. 9–45). Berlin: Springer.

Danneels, E. (2011). Trying to become a different type of company: Dynamic capability at Smith Corona. *Strategic Management Journal, 32*(1), 1–31.

Drucker, P.F. (1954). *The practice of management*. Harper & Brothers.

Dutta, D. & Sarma, M.K. (2020). Adoption of digital innovation — Formulating adopter categories and levels of adoption in a digital sphere in an emerging economy. *International Journal of Innovation and Technology Management, 17*(08), 2050059. https://doi.org/10.1142/s0219877020500595

Eisenhardt, K.M. & Martin, J.A. (2000). Dynamic capabilities: What are they? *Strategic Management Journal, 21*(10–11), 1105–1121.

Fraunhofer IAO. (2016). *Lightweight robots in manual assembly-Best to start simply*. Technical report.

Gimpel, H., Hosseini, S., Huber, R.X.R., Probst, L., Röglinger, M. & Faisst, U. (2018). Structuring digital transformation: A framework of action fields and its application at ZEISS. *Journal of Information Technology Theory and Applications, 19*(1), 3.

Greiner, O., Riepl, P. & Kittelberger, D. (2017). Die digitale Strategie: Der wegweiser zur systematischen digitalisierung des unternehmens. In *Digitalisierung der Unternehmenssteuerung: Prozessautomatisierung, business analytics, big data, SAP S/4HANA, Anwendungsbeispiele*, ed. Michael Kieninger (pp. 19–32). Stuttgart: Schäffer Poeschel.

Helfat, C.E. & Peteraf, M.A. (2003). The dynamic resource-based view: Capability lifecycles. *Strategic Management Journal, 24*(10), 997–1010.

Henderson, B.D. (1989). The origin of strategy. *Harvard Business Review, 67*(6), 139–143.

Heuermann, R., Tomenendal, M. & Bressem, C. (2018). *Digitalisierung in Bund, Ländern und Gemeinden*. Springer.

Hille, M., Janata, S. & Michel, J. (2016). *Digitalisierungsleitfaden: Ein kompendium für entscheider im mittelstand im auftrag der QSC AG*. Compendium.

Hippmann, S., Klinger, R. & Leis, M. (2018). Digitalisierung–Anwendungsfelder und Forschungsziele. In *Digitalisierung: Schlüsseltechnologien für wirtschaft und gesellschaft*, ed. reimund neugebauer (pp. 9–18). Springer.

Hungenberg, H. (2014). *Strategisches management in Unternehmen: Ziele - Prozesse - Verfahren* (8. Aufl.). Springer Gabler.

Ivančić, L., Vukšić, V. & Spremić, M. (2019). Mastering the digital transformation process: Business practices and lessons learned. *Technology Innovation Management Review, 9*(2), 36–50. https://doi.org/10.22215/timreview/1217

Johnson, G., Scholes, K. & Whittington, R. (2008). *Exploring corporate strategy* (8. Aufl.). Pearson Education Limited.

Koch, T. & Windsperger, J. (2017). Seeing through the network: Competitive advantage in the digital economy. *Journal of Organisation Design, 6*(1). https://doi.org/10.1186/s41469-017-0016-z

Kraewing, M. (2017). *Digital business strategie für den mittelstand: Entwicklung und konzeption mit internationaler ausrichtung* (1. Aufl.). Haufe.

Latilla, V.M.M., Urbinati, A., Cavallo, A., Franzò, S. & Ghezzi, A. (2020). Organisational re-design for business model innovation while exploiting digital technologies: A single case study of an energy company. *International Journal of Innovation and Technology Management, 18*(02), 2040002. https://doi.org/10.1142/s0219877020400027

Leavitt, H. (1965). Applied organisational change in industry: Structural, technological, and humanistic approaches. In *Handbook of organisations*, ed., J. March (pp. 1144–1170), Rand McNally & Co.

Lin, Y. & Wu, L.Y. (2014). Exploring the role of dynamic capabilities in firm performance under the resource-based view framework. *Journal of Business Research, 67*(3), 407–413. https://doi.org/10.1016/j.jbusres.2012.12.019

Mazzone, D.M. (2014). *Digital or death: Digital transformation - The only choice for business to survive, smash, and conquer.* Smashbox Consulting Inc.

Mintzberg, H. (1979). *The structuring of organisations: A synthesis of research.* Prentice Hall.

Niemand, T., Rigtering, J.C., Kallmünzer, A., Kraus, S. & Maalaoui, A. (2020). Digitalisation in the financial industry: A contingency approach of entrepreneurial orientation and strategic vision on digitalisation. *European Management Journal, 39*(3), 317–326. https://doi.org/10.1016/j.emj.2020.04.008

Nikmehr, B., Hosseini, M.R., Martek, I., Zavadskas, E.K. & Antucheviciene, J. (2021). Digitalisation as a strategic means of achieving sustainable efficiencies in construction management: A critical review. *Sustainability, 13*(9), 5040. https://doi.org/10.3390/su13095040

Peppard, J. & Ward, J. (2016). *The strategic management of information systems: Building a digital strategy.* Wiley.

Peteraf, M.A. (1993). The cornerstones of competitive advantage: A resource-based view. *Strategic Management Journal, 14*(3), 179–191. https://doi.org/10.1002/smj.4250140303

Peteraf, M.A. & Barney, J.B. (2003). Unraveling the resource-based tangle. *Managerial and Decision Economics, 24*(4), 309–323. https://doi.org/10.1002/mde.1126

Petry, T. (2016). *Digital leadership: Erfolgreiches führen in zeiten der digital economy.* Haufe.

Porter, M.E. (1996). What is strategy? *Harvard Business Review, 74*(6), 61–81.

PwC. (2013). *Digitale transformation – der größte wandel seit der industriellen revolution.* Pricewaterhouse Coopers.

Rauser, A. (2016). *Digital strategy: A guide to digital business transformation.* CreateSpace Independent Publishing Platform.

Rindova, V. P. & Kotha, S. (2001). Continuous "morphing": Competing through dynamic capabilities, form, and function. *Academy of Management Journal, 44*(6), 1263–1280.

Rusnjak, A. (2014). *Entrepreneurial business modeling: Definitionen – Vorgehensmodell – Framework – Werkzeuge – Perspektiven.* Springer Gabler.

Schallmo, D.R. (2013). *Geschäftsmodelle erfolgreich entwickeln und implementieren: Mit aufgaben und kontrollfragen.* Springer Gabler.

Schallmo, D.R. (2014). Vorgehensmodell der geschäftsmodell-innovation–bestehende ansätze, phasen, aktivitäten und ergebnise. In *Kompendium Geschäftsmodell-Innovation*, ed. D. Schallmo (pp. 51–74), Springer Fachmedien.

Schallmo, D.R. (2016). *Jetzt digital transformieren: So gelingt die erfolgreiche digitale Transformation Ihres Geschäftsmodells.* Springer.

Schallmo, D.R. (2019). *Jetzt digital transformieren. So gelingt die erfolgreiche digitale Transformation ihres Geschäftsmodells.* 2nd ed. Springer Gabler.

Schallmo, D.R & Tidd, J. (2021). *Digitalisation: Approaches, case studies, and tools for strategy, transformation, and implementation.* Series on management for professionals. Springer.

Schallmo, D.R. & Williams, C.A. (2018). *Digital transformation now!: Guiding the successful digitalisation of your business model.* Springer.

Schallmo, D.R. & Williams, C.A. (2020). An integrated approach to digital implementation: TOSC model and DPSEC-Circle. *Proceedings of the XXXI ISPIM Innovation Conference – "Innovating Our Common Future",* Berlin, Germany, June 7–10, 2020. ISBN 9789523354661

Schallmo, D.R., Williams, C.A. & Boardman, L. (2017). Digital transformation of business models – Best practices, enablers, and roadmap. *International Journal of Innovation Management, 21*(8), 119–138.

Schallmo, D.R., Williams, C.A. & Lohse, J. (2018). Clarifying digital strategy - Detailed literature review of existing approaches. *Proceedings of the XXIX ISPIM Innovation Conference "Innovation, The Name of The Game",* Stockholm, Sweden, June 17–20, 2018. ISBN 9789523352193

Schallmo, D.R., Williams, C.A. & Lohse, J. (2019a). Digital strategy: Integrated approach and generic options. *International Journal of Innovation Management, 23*(8), 1940005-1-1940005-24.

Schallmo, D.R., Williams, C.A. & Lohse, J. (2019b). Digital strategy: Integrated approach and generic options. *Proceedings of the XXX ISPIM Innovation Conference,* Florence, Italy, June 16–19, 2019. ISBN 9789523353510

Schawel, C. & Billing, F. (2018). *Top 100 Management Tools: Das wichtigste Buch eines Managers Von ABC-Analyse bis Zielvereinbarung.* (6. Aufl.). Springer Gabler.

Sinek, S. (2009). *Start with why: How great leaders inspire everyone to take action.* Penguin Random House.

Steiner, G.A. & Miner, J.B. (1977). *Text readings and cases (management policy and strategy).* MacMillan.

Teece, D.J. (2012). Dynamic capabilities: Routines versus entrepreneurial action. *Journal of Management Studies, 49*(8), 1395–1401. https://doi.org/10.1111/j.1467-6486.2012.01080.x

Teece, D.J., Pisano, G. & Shuen, A. (1997). Dynamic capabilities and strategic management. *Strategic Management Journal, 18*(7), 509–533.

Thomas, D.K.M.J. (2014). Design und entwicklung der business model-innovation. In *Kompendium geschäftsmodell-Innovation: Grundlagen, aktuelle ansätze und fallbeispiele zur erfolgreichen geschäftsmodell-innovation.* Springer.

Tidd, J. (2019). *Digital disruptive innovation (Series on technology management, 36).* WSPC (Europe).

Too, L., Harvey, M. & Too, E. (2010). Globalisation and corporate real estate strategies. *Journal of Corporate Real Estate, 12*(4), 234–248.

Tywoniak, S. (2007). Making sense of the resource-based view? *Proceedings Academy of Management,* Philadelphia, USA.

Vester, F. & Hesler, A. (1980). *Sensitivitätsmodell/sensitivity model.* Regionale Planungsgemeinschaft Untermain.

Vial, G. (2021). Understanding digital transformation: A review and a research agenda. *Managing Digital Transformation, 28*(2), 13–66.

Wang, C.L. & Ahmed, P.K. (2007). Dynamic capabilities: A review and research agenda. *International Journal of Management Reviews, 9*(1), 31–51. https://doi.org/10.1111/j.1468-2370.2007.00201.x

Weill, P. & Woerner, S. (2015). Thriving in an increasingly digital ecosystem. *MIT Sloan Management Review, 56*(4), 27–34.

Westerman, G., Calméjane, C., Bonnet, D., Ferraris, P. & McAfee, A. (2011). Digital transformation: A roadmap for billion-dollar organisations. *MIT Center for Digital Business and Capgemini Consulting, 1,* 1–68.

Wolf, T. & Strohschen, J.H. (2018). Digitalisierung: Definition und reife. *Informatik-Spektrum, 41*(1), 56–64.

7

ACCOUNTING INFORMATION SYSTEMS AND DECISION MAKING

Markus Granlund and Henri Teittinen

Introduction

Decision making plays a major, many times crucial, role in managers' work, as they aim to make their organisations prosper. Some of the decisions are operative ones and need to be made on monthly, weekly, or even daily basis. Strategic decisions, on the other hand, are made more seldom, but they may be once-in-a-lifetime type of decisions, framing the future of the organisation. Decisions also form chains, as most decisions lead to new decision-making situations in the near or more distant future (Mouritsen & Kreiner, 2016).

In order to be able to make 'wise' and justified decisions, managers need something to build their decisions on: experience, intuition, information, and their combinations, depending on the situation. During the last decade, the idea of fact-based decision making has gained more momentum. This means that decisions could and should be based more on 'cold facts' instead of intuition, beliefs, and feelings. This development is supported by recent developments in information and communications technology (ICT), such as big data and business analytics (CGMA, 2013). The need for more and better information derives from the complexity and dynamics of the global markets and its implications for 'success recipes'. In brief, the whole existence of modern ICT and accounting information systems (AIS) therein is based on information needs. But what are these needs today and in the future? And how can AIS meet such needs?

In this chapter, we outline how modern AIS can support managerial decision making in contemporary organisations. We also aim to outline some future trends regarding this topic. We start by describing the factors constituting different decision-making environments and what we call data environments. This lays a foundation for describing what kind of information is needed in different contexts and how AIS can support managers in making informed decisions (see Figure 7.1).

Decision making and its environment

Decision-making contexts vary depending on many issues. Typical contingency factors (Vaassen, 2002; Chenhall, 2003) offer a valid starting point for the analysis of such contexts and the related mechanisms. Such organisational factors include size, life-cycle stage, line of

DOI: 10.4324/9781003132943-10

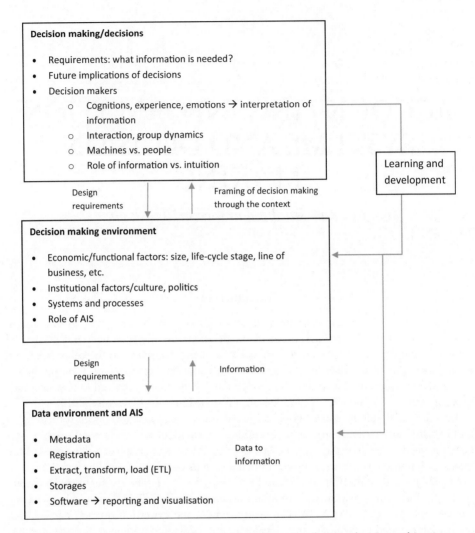

Figure 7.1 Data environment and decision-making environment framing decision making.

business, technology, strategy, culture, and so on. These factors define what kind of information is deemed relevant and valid in each context. As soon as we know about the information needs – i.e. what are the decisions to be made and in what environment – we can start designing information systems (IS) to produce relevant decision support.

Decision making is a process that can be organised in many ways. Some organisations have defined structured procedures for certain decision categories, whereas some rely more or less on ad hoc practices. Also decision-making styles vary by individuals. Some rely more on experience and intuition, while some need and want figures, calculations, and systematic analyses on which to base decision making.

It is also interesting to ponder on the human–computer relationship here. We know that automatisation and robotics are taking over many things that used to be carried out by people. Decision support is one of the fields where developments in ICT play obviously a big role in this regard. Many routine-like decisions have been handed over to IT, which can calculate the best choice under defined circumstances. Yet, even in these cases, it is people who define the parameters and algorithms and, in most cases, verify the decisions, like in case of loan decisions in banks.

In most cases, it is still people who make decisions, as decision making often requires experience-based, analytical thinking, as well as interpretation of information. Bigger decisions are typically made in groups, where different forms of expertise come together to inform decision making in a versatile and more comprehensive way. Altogether, decision making involves human action and interaction, which brings along different perceptions, interpretations, misunderstandings, disputes about estimates, and emotions. This is also the reason why there is a tendency to go for automatised, fact-based decision making; it is thought to reduce the number and magnitude of human errors in the process. In this regard it is also important to recognise that if the decision is made by a single person, there may emerge problems with cognitive and motivational biases.

Decisions are not made in a vacuum, but they are influenced by a number of factors in the decision-making environment. IS, such as AIS, can support people in these tasks by offering answers to specified questions, creating scenarios for learning purposes, as well as supporting decision influencing and legitimation (Burchell et al., 1980; Chong & Eggleton, 2003). An important issue to consider here is also the style with which decisions are made. Some people prefer fast and 'aggressive' decision-making styles, whereas others act more slowly and as followers. This has naturally implications for how they use AIS and other IS.

A relevant generic concept affecting management in organisations relates to institutionalised, taken-for-granted assumptions and beliefs, i.e. culture. Organisational culture tells 'how things are done here'. Gradually, also IS start carrying such assumptions and values, as they reflect managerial cognitions and logics (Kaplan, 2008, 2011). This way IS may also standardise behaviour towards common ways of operating.

As mentioned, all these issues alone and together define what decisions are needed and made, and especially what kind of information is needed to facilitate decision making. We will also elaborate later the fact that in addition to what information is produced, the success of decision making ultimately depends on how that information is used. Getting *information of good quality* seems to be a common challenge of contemporary organisations. This is due to many things, not least because of the large number and fast pace of changes in the networked and global operating environment. This is also the reason why ICT has been put into the core of the development agenda of most organisations: how to get more valid, timely, and relevant information to support decisions to be made regarding the short and long term. Vaassen (2002) has defined the quality of information being composed of two main characteristics: economy, i.e. the cost of producing information, and effectiveness. In this framework, effectiveness is further divided into reliability (validity and completeness) and relevance (accuracy, timeliness, understandability). This is a comprehensive basis against which to analyse contextual information needs and the design of AIS and other IS.

Data environment/ICT domain

In order to produce information that fulfils the above-mentioned quality criteria, organisations have to carry out careful IS design. The simple fact is that you cannot analyse and report something on which you do not collect data. Without going into the technical details in this chapter, we simply describe the process of producing relevant information and further knowledge as the information is applied in decision-making situations.

As Taipaleenmäki & Ikäheimo (2013) explicate, this process starts from the configuration of metadata and proceeds into data collection/registration procedures and further to data storage (databases and data warehouses) through ETL (Extract, Transform, Load) technologies. The process where these datasets are transformed into information takes place in enterprise software, stand-alone software, and spreadsheets. AIS technologies include all these elements and can be used alone or together. Some of the calculations that are run through software are automated, and some made ad hoc by user requirements.

We draw here on the definition of AIS by Vaassen (2002, p. 3). He distinguishes four related elements of AIS:

- Information Systems
  - An IS is a set of interrelated components working together to collect, retrieve, process, store, and disseminate information for the purpose of facilitating planning, control, coordination, and decision making in businesses and other organisations.
- Managerial information provision
  - The systematic gathering, recording, and processing of data aimed at the provision of information for management decisions (choosing among alternative applications) for entity functionality and entity control, including accountability.
- Accounting and administrative organisation
- Internal control

Of these four elements we focus on the two first ones, i.e. IS and managerial information provision. However, technical details in this regard are beyond the scope of this chapter. Concrete examples of this sphere are budgeting systems, performance measurement/management systems (e.g. Balanced Scorecard), costing systems, and various ad hoc analyses to support specific decisions. Regarding informed decision making, these systems alone or in various combinations support managers. The general idea of such AIS is to provide financial and non-financial (numeric) information i.e. reported in desired forms to the decision makers. Different applications from spreadsheets to enterprise systems offer nowadays a number of ways to visualise the information. The people producing such information also increasingly apply sophisticated techniques, including data mining and simulation technologies.

Framework of decision making and AIS

Figure 7.1 summarises the 'big picture' of AIS and decision making. The starting point is that managers face decision-making situations for which they need specific information; sometimes detailed, sometimes more 'rough'. This sets requirements for AIS design that are mediated by the context where the decision is being made. AIS designers then aim to design and develop systems that meet the requirements. In a similar vein, the decision-making environment mediates the information channels as relevant, and important information is filtered in the process towards the actual decisions, which themselves entail complex filtering and interaction mechanisms.

It is a reality that we are surrounded and informed by different accounting information all the time. We are using mobile devices, applications, and databases through the web and learning and getting information on businesses, like profitability of competitors and their products and services. All these, in its part, also define and constitute the accounting-information-supported decision-making environment (see Figure 7.1).

The decisions made and the experience gained in the decision-making process feed to learning and consequent development initiatives that influence, e.g. perceptions regarding the role of AIS, and, in the end, system development. The AIS needs to be constantly evaluated and developed through to keep up with and fit the operating environment and technological development, the question being, under the specific circumstances, how to produce efficiently and effectively information i.e. valid, reliable, comprehensive (yet accurate), and offered in a timely manner in an understandable visualised format (Vaassen, 2002). Increasingly, there is also pressure today to provide information i.e. forward-looking, to provide better foresight supporting decision making concerning the future.

Decision-making situations and AIS

In this section, we are discussing the roles AIS may play in different decision-making situations. At first, we will look at the Burchell et al. (1980) framework and then discuss its implications for managerial practice. Although the framework was presented already in the 1980s, it is still today highly relevant for analysing the role of AIS in organisational decision making, as the premises regarding uncertainty related to decision making have not changed.

The Burchell et al. (1980) framework

Burchell et al. (1980) argued that the uses of accounting information were extended, and accounting systems were increasingly used for enabling more detailed financial management of the firm. They explained this by the emergence of new organisational practices and forms, which include coordinating, centralised, and functional control, as well as divisional, matrix, and project organisations. Organisations were also required to fulfil more extensive needs of reporting for capital markets. They stated that accountants were more and more involved in different types of management activities, such as budgeting and standard costing, planning, and resource allocation, and thus, they became central actors in organisational management.

They also argued that these internal organisational changes and external pressures resulted in changes in accounting and institutionalisation of accounting. Accounting had become more than only a 'machine' responding to preconceived organisational needs; accountants' role was becoming more like searching for new opportunities regarding accounting practice. In addition, new professional institutes and bodies of accounting and accountants were established. The transformation also implied that accounting procedures were increasingly defined and documented in all kinds of organisations (Burchell et al., 1980).

In addition, Burchell et al. (1980) stated that the relationship between accounting and organisational decision making had been conceived as only normative; the role of accounting is simply to provide relevant information for decision making and improve the decision-making processes. However, they argued that this perspective had been taken for granted and rarely examined critically. For that reason, understanding better the role of accounting in organisations, they used the framework of Thompson & Tuden (1959) to elaborate on the roles of accounting in decision making in practice (see Figure 7.2).

The Thompson & Tuden (1959) framework is divided into categories by the uncertainty regarding cause-and-effect relations (either low or high) and uncertainty regarding objectives (either low or high). Burchell et al. (1980) presented that when objectives are clear and the consequences of actions are known/certain, decision making is possible by automation (computation). Under such circumstances, decision making may be designed and programmable, and thus accounting can serve as an 'answer machine'. When the relations between cause and effect become more uncertain, decision making will be more judgemental and subjective by the participants in decision making. In practice, this means ad hoc analyses and what-if models. Burchell et al. (1980) call this role of accounting in decision-making process as 'learning machine'. In times of big data and sophisticated analytics, including artificial intelligence, though,

Uncertainty of objectives

		Low	High
	Low	Answer machines Decision by computation	Ammunition (dialogue) machines Decision by compromise
Uncertainty of cause and effect	**High**	Answer machines/Learning machines Decision by judgement	Rationalisation machines (Idea machines) Ex post legitimation (Decision by inspiration)

Figure 7.2 Uncertainty, decision making, and the roles of accounting practice (adapted from Boland, 1979; Burchell et al., 1980).

the IS may find relevant cause-and-effect relations without users' knowledge. We may say that sometimes the IS 'knows' more than the user even in uncertain environments. However, decision making under such circumstances yet typically requires human cognition and capability to interpret whether the suggested relations are valid and reliable. When the relations between causes and effects are certain, but the objectives include political rather than computational rationales, the role of accounting in the decision-making process is seen to be an 'ammunition machine' (or 'dialogue machine'). And finally, when both uncertainty regarding objectives and uncertainty regarding cause-and-effect relations are high, the decision making tends to be of an inspirational nature, and accounting has been used for legitimising and justifying actions. This role of accounting Burchell et al. (1980) describe as a 'rationalisation machine'.

The role of AIS in different decision-making situations

We have chosen four basic decision-making situations for further analysis, including pricing, product mix, equipment replacement, and outsourcing decisions. While it is impossible to include all kinds of decision-making situations in such an analysis, we can consider these decision types to be relatively commonly relevant (capital budgeting is also excluded from the analysis as chapter 9 in this book analyses the role of AIS in investment appraisal). Overall, our approach in this analysis derives from the fact that in contemporary organisations, decision-making situations have been presented as information management questions (for more detailed descriptions and calculations, see, e.g. Burns et al., 2013).

Pricing decisions

Pricing is one of the most important decision-making situations in every organisation. Too low pricing requires higher sales volumes, whereas too high pricing means higher profit margin per unit but typically results in lower sales volume. Thus, to adjust pricing to the level where it meets the pricing strategy so that it is in line with the company's financial objectives is a demanding task.

Porter (1980) noted early on that corporate strategy has to be targeted either to cost leadership or to differentiation. If the target is to offer the lowest price, the company follows a cost leadership strategy. If the customer segment is not price-sensitive, a differentiation strategy should be applied.

In cost leadership strategy, the purpose is to win the market share having the lowest prices, or at least having the lowest price regarding value for customers.

Cost leadership strategy, in particular, requires continuous search for cost reductions in all business activities, and thus, there also exists a continuous need to make decisions, which can be supported by AIS and its automatic process controlling. Sometimes decision-making models in pricing can also be pre-programmed. This means that pricing models with different types of demands can be estimated. By giving the parameters, AIS will calculate the prices or control the processes. E.g. regarding flight tickets, decision makers have pre-programmed the pricing model for the tickets, and the prices will be changed based on the designed demand curve. Similar situations can be found in banks regarding credit lending decisions. By giving the parameters on borrowers, IS will produce a risk assessment and the interest rate (price) for the customer. If some of the parameters are changed, a new price or risk rate will be generated. In this way, decisions on price can be automatised, and the role of AIS is to support decision making and work as an 'answer machine'. In particular, the digital environment facilitates the design of the pricing process to be computational, as it enables cost-efficient collection of data for future pricing modelling. However, it is rarely possible to pre-program pricing decisions totally. Even if we would be able to pre-program the pricing model, we are not able to pre-program customer buying behaviour.

When there is no uncertainty regarding the objectives, but there is uncertainty regarding causes and effects, managers face questions such as what have the prices and volumes been previously, how did our actions affect demand and profitability, and what can be expected if we set prices now and in the near future in a particular way? Combining different datasets concerning these questions, AIS can support decision making as a 'learning machine' by producing relevant pricing scenarios for decision makers. Accountants and managers can learn about the potential consequences of decisions by experimenting with various alternatives in the pricing model and thus generate an understanding of the pricing mechanisms. The capacity of AIS to make simulations is supported by functionality combining future plans with different types of historical data from the databases. Naturally, in the end, a decision simply needs to be made based on this understanding, which may later prove to be a good one or not, depending on our ability to estimate the consequences of the actions taken.

Pricing may many times include also subjective elements. In situations where the objectives are not clear (e.g. regarding the pricing strategy in general), but we have certain ideas regarding causalities, the role of AIS may become an 'ammunition machine', as decision makers may use different scenarios offered by the AIS to influence other people involved with the decision of their view regarding the 'correct price'. This role has also been labelled as a 'dialogue machine' (Boland, 1979), meaning that AIS may in this role help managers to develop and argue different points of view which are conflicting (but consistent with the underlying facts). This view emphasises the role of AIS to encourage exploration and debate.

Regarding the 'rationalisation machine' or role, first, it may be that AIS information is used afterwards to demonstrate that the made decision was a good one. We may also state that AIS themselves may work as 'rationalisation machines'. Contemporary AIS include different types of simulation methods and embedded knowledge for pricing which may as such legitimise the role of AIS in decision making vis-à-vis other bases of decision making, such as experience and even intuition.

Product mix decisions

Product mix decisions include typically four dimensions: (1) the number of different product lines of the company, (2) the total number of items within the product lines, (3) versions of each product in one product line, and (4) consistency, which tells about the relation between the product lines. Decision making in this context may relate, e.g. to following kinds of questions: (1) should we establish new product lines or remove some of the existing ones, (2) should we add more items into certain product lines, (3) how many versions should we have regarding each product, or (4) should the product lines be more consistent with each other (e.g. Cooper & Kaplan, 1991; Drury, 2008).

As we may infer from the above questions, product mix decisions are closely related to the market situation, capacity issues, cost structure, as well as the lot sizes of production (e.g. Lea & Fredendall, 2002). The role of AIS is to connect sales, purchasing, logistics, and marketing together in order to provide data on financial and cost management issues. A sales order may start all the transactions in the supply chain: when a sales order has been entered into the system, deliveries, production, or purchasing orders may be generated. This illustrates that particularly in real time and digital environment, IS can support decision making even automatically. Uncertainty of objectives and causality are low in this context, and AIS works as an 'answer machine' in short-term planning.

In long-term planning, the role of AIS is to present historical data on demand. Managing the product mix and the supply chain is not based on sales orders but more on mixed subjective interpretations of historical data. In this type of decision-making situations, AIS can support decision making in the learning role (simulations) or, depending on the level of uncertainty regarding objectives, as an 'ammunition machine' as the different potential choices are discussed and debated. Like in pricing decisions, contemporary AIS may also be connected to different types of production planning methods, like Lean Manufacturing, Just-in-Time production, or Activity-Based-Management. Regarding the legitimising role, the same premises apply here as in case of pricing decisions illustrated above.

Equipment replacement investments

Replacement investments differ from other investments in that those involve the displacement or scrapping of an existing investment. Typically, investments are made when new assets are required for the expansion of the company. We can say that replacement investments are less complex to make, and they do not require such a massive search for alternatives as new expansion investments. One key characteristic in replacement investments is also the timing, referring here to optimising: how long to keep existing machinery before it starts to be generally more cost-beneficial to replace it (e.g. Merret, 1965; Dobbs, 2004). An interesting question also is what the replacement investments are like in contemporary organisations: in addition to parts or modifications regarding existing product lines, they may increasingly concern service type of investments, like new versions of software. This makes the evaluation of optimal replacement even more challenging, as it is very difficult to evaluate how 'worn out' the original investment is.

Today, the internet has brought the sourcing of products and services globally available. This means that comparisons can be made easily in real time worldwide. Sometimes the sourcing is based on sourcing catalogues, which may make it possible to even automatise the decisions on replacement investments. In such a case, the IS gives the decision makers clear guidelines where to source and what the item and transaction costs will be. In these situations, AIS works as an 'answer machine'.

When replacement investments involve high uncertainty regarding causalities, but there is a clear vision on objectives (at least costs of investments can be gathered and reported), AIS include all the needed data in the database which can be used in the decision-making process for simulations and to learn about the optional paths to take. Then, we can say that AIS works like a 'learning machine'.

Similarly, as in the other examples above, also here AIS can be used as an 'ammunition machine' (even in a political way) as alternative calculations are produced to back up own views and debate the options concerning the decisions to be made and actions to be taken. AIS databases typically include a lot of historical data, which can be used for such influencing purposes in situations where there is disagreement regarding the objectives of action. Typically, in post-auditing of investments, AIS can be used as a 'rationalisation machine' to evaluate and justify the decisions made. However, regarding replacement investments, this role is less apparent than in case of decisions on new expansion investments.

Outsourcing

The outsourcing decision is also known as the make-or-buy decision. This means that there may exist needs to decide whether to manufacture items or produce services in-house or purchase those from an external supplier. Two main issues have to be considered in these situations: (1) cost of outsourcing in relation to own production and (2) availability of production capacity (see, e.g., Burns et al., 2013).

Contemporary organisations are more and more part of global alliances and networks. E.g. regarding manufacturing type of organisations, they increasingly work either as subcontractors or manage their own subcontractor networks. In the leading-edge firms, the subcontractor works just like the purchaser's own product line. In this context, modern IS need to enable control of inputs, outputs, and capacity in real time. Even if the supply chain as such could be automatised, there is always an unavoidable need for supervision and control. Only people are able to manage and make decisions when something goes wrong and unexpected things happen (which are not pre-programmed into the IS). An AIS may work automatically in a 'controller' role, as an 'answer machine', when we know the consequences of actions and there is no uncertainty involved with our objectives.

In situations when the objectives are clear, but there is uncertainty around the cause-and-effect relations, AIS with its database can support decisions as a 'learning machine'. It can be used to produce different simulations on the optional paths regarding make or buy and facilitate the generation of future scenarios as the decision makers want to speculate on the outcomes of the different paths – the possible different future states of affairs.

Also, when causalities are clear (e.g. outsourcing will advance the organisation's operations), but it is not clear which products, product lines, or services should be outsourced, AIS can act as an 'ammunition machine' in debates around the specific actions to be taken.

Finally, we may suggest that the role of AIS in decision making regarding outsourcing when both the objectives and causalities are unclear (high uncertainty) is more to build the decision-making context. Contemporary AIS may thus act in a constituting role in trying to offer as many clues as possible concerning the uncertain environment; at least it may serve this role in a way to help the decision makers realise the high uncertainty surrounding the decision to be made.

Discussion – the role of AIS in decision making

To summarise, for the first, we may conclude that the task of AIS in supporting decision making, in its technical form, is to collect, retrieve, process, store, and disseminate managerially relevant information to decision makers (see Vaassen, 2002). In the digitalised environment, AIS may collect and build on massive databases in serving this task. However, as we have described, this is only one dimension in the big picture as it comes to how the decision-making environment is constituted and what factors are involved before the final decision is reached and executed. In this process, the AIS may act in different roles depending on uncertainty related to the objectives and cause-and-effect relations surrounding the particular decision situation: giving answers, facilitating learning, serving as a basis for argumentation, and legitimising the decisions (Burchell et al., 1980).

When objectives and causalities of decisions are known, in other words, when uncertainties of both objectives and causalities are low, AIS are able to present the correct options within the framework of specified parameters. Then it is possible to automatise and pre-program the decision-making models, and AIS may work as an 'answer machine'. If the objectives are clear but causalities are not well known, AIS are not able to give clear answers to the questions the decision makers may have but rather options and directions through simulations. AIS works then as a 'learning machine'. When decision makers have different opinions regarding the objectives, but the causalities are relatively clear, AIS with its capability to produce reliable figures and facts can offer a valid basis on which to build arguments as the decision makers try to influence the decision situation and convince each other about a specific option. AIS acts then as an 'ammunition machine' as it is used for purposeful prioritising. When there is uncertainty involved with both the objectives and causalities, AIS may work as a basis with which decisions are legitimised (ex post), i.e. as a 'rationalisation machine'.

We can say that all these different 'machine' roles support each other. As AIS/IS have radically increased the amount of data, we are all the time in the middle of learning about and trying to understand the environment: e.g. learning (and understanding) of general profitability of competitors and their products; learning of profitability of own products (e.g. in forms of transparency and real-time information); learning of new innovations (e.g. investment options for better profitability and efficiency); and learning (and understanding) of own profitability (working efficiency, working hours, personal scorecards, etc.). This does not mean that accounting information will be always used directly in decision making, but it is yet an essential, supporting part of the decision-making context.

Decision-making situations can be categorised either as operational or strategic. Operational decisions are of short term and repeatable nature, and they do not require huge amounts of monetary or other resources. On the other hand, strategic decision-making situations are of long-term nature, and they typically affect the whole organisation. Uncertainty in operational decisions is known to be lower than in strategic decisions. This distinction also affects the roles AIS may have. In operational decisions, the decision-making model can sometimes be pre-programmed and automated, whereas with strategic decisions, the situation typically exists only once; they do not occur repeatedly but are more or less unique. Strategic decisions also typically involve higher amounts of uncertainty and risk, which means that the 'ammunition' and 'rationalising' roles of AIS get often activated.

Nevertheless, both operative and strategic decisions involve behavioural aspects – the first typically less, the latter even quite a lot – as the long-term orientation makes the situation more difficult; whenever we look further into the future, the amount of uncertainty inevitably increases. This further relates to the amount of subjectivity and interpretation of information involved with both individual and group decision making. We may assume that decision-making models that are more or less programmable imply that interpretation of information is kind of in built into the AIS model. There is not much room or even need for interpretation, although the final decisions always require human consideration. Anyway, when decisions are made for the first time, it always requires human understanding and judgement. Later, as we have learnt from mistakes and causal effects of our actions, we can improve decision-making and information models to be increasingly programmable, especially as it comes to operational decisions.

AIS can neither make interpretations nor can they interact with their environment. The supporting role of AIS is important to note as we increasingly discuss artificial intelligence and robotics. Not even the best systems can over time accurately foresee the consequences of decisions – how customers, competitors, or employees may act in the short or, particularly, long term. Burchell et al. (1980) recognised already early on the interpretative nature of decision making and thus the complex nature of AIS therein.

In this context, we should also appreciate the role of decision-making styles. Sometimes decisions are required to be made in unexpected situations and quickly, whereas in some situations, decisions can be made slowly, following activity in the markets – the behaviour of competitors and consumers, e.g. as it comes to pricing decisions. Some decision makers have more trust in figures, whereas some may base their decisions more on intuition and feelings. AIS are part of the decision-making process, where decision makers and AIS work together. However, the role of AIS depends on the style of decision making. People's sense making and cognitive characteristics are different, which makes the design of AIS always challenging.

In addition, we should appreciate the different organisational contexts where decision makers operate. Each organisation has its own policies and processes to prepare and make decisions. Furthermore, different decision-making processes may exist also within same organisations in their different business units or divisions in different geographical locations. This is a further challenge for AIS, in the design of which it is often cost-efficient to aim for standardisation, which, on the other hand, may mean contextual trade-offs concerning the validity and relevance of the information produced. One challenge is many times the potential fragmentation of the AIS wholeness, as it is gradually built of different systems (like of different kinds of non-integrated web applications and databases). There is always need for systematic and coherent design of AIS, but at the same time, there is a need for flexibility for rapid changes when needed (see Figure 7.1 for AIS design requirements, decision-making environment, and data environment).

We also need to recognise that AIS may support decision-making processes not only in our own organisation but in our customer organisations, too. This is typical in cases where AIS collects data, analyses it, and delivers it to the customers, typically as a service. In this way, the decision-making context, data environment, and AIS can be seen even more broadly.

We have illustrated the role AIS themselves play in constituting decision-making environments. AIS design is often used to document and systematise previously undocumented or unsystematic (not transparent) processes with the aim of standardisation of practices. In this way AIS also work as security checks for decision control: the decision-making processes are expected to be followed as documented and programmed into AIS. The intention at the more general level then is to secure that the processes are in line with the organisational rules and policies. In this sense, AIS are not only technical tools but also kind of 'social actors' in organisations, as they carry common rules and procedures regarding decision-making practice. Somewhat paradoxically, the subjectivity involved with decision making may undermine or lead to bypassing of such rules, as people follow routines that may be only loosely coupled to the formal rules.

Overall, the context of decision making cannot be emphasised enough. The contingency factors framing AIS design and use are crucial to understand. e.g. in small organisations, decision-making processes are naturally different than in large ones. In small organisations, there may not exist decision-making policies. It may be that those are not even needed, if the entrepreneur-CEO is responsible for all the decisions and is responsible of their outcomes only to himself/herself. When companies grow, needs for more comprehensive systems emerge. Thus, the role of AIS in decision making is always depending on the size, line of business, life-cycle stage, etc. of the organisation.

We have been discussing the role of AIS in supporting decision making. However, in some situations, AIS may have less favourable effects; they may slow down or even create obstacles in the decision-making process. AIS are nowadays relatively complex and multidimensional, which require a lot of knowledge from their users. The process required by the rules embedded in AIS and related systems and policies may sometimes lead to unnecessarily cumbersome and complicated practices, resulting in frustration, dissatisfaction, and short-cutting. Sometimes these may be unintended consequences of the AIS design; the purpose has been something else, but for several reasons, for instance, the end users of the systems have not been engaged in the design process sufficiently to support decision makers in their real-life tasks. In this way, the AIS may have become, at least partly, an obstacle to efficient and effective decision making that not only slows down the process but may also lead to 'random behaviour' where nobody can any longer separate the facts from fiction. This is also a further indication of the role AIS may play as a part of the broader socio-technical decision-making context.

We may conclude that the role of AIS should be explored through the following perspectives: (1) data and information context, i.e. decisions are based on 'naked' facts and/or interpretation; (2) decision-making and organisational context, i.e. the decision-making process is either systematic and documented or not; and (3) decision makers' context, i.e. the decision has been made individually or in a group. These elements have been presented in Figure 7.3 summarising the role of AIS in decision making (cf. Figure 7.1).

Future trends

This chapter has explored how AIS can support decision making in organisations. We also briefly described how AIS may hinder or slow down decision making. The sophistication of AIS for decision making obviously varies a lot in practice due to different contingency factors. Our general illustration holds for most organisations, especially the larger ones. On the other hand, technology is never ready, and the most advanced companies and public-sector organisations have already moved to the era of big data and its analytics (Warren et al., 2015). When we include also non-structured data in the sphere of AIS and other IS, we enter a new world of decision support. Modern technologies including artificial intelligence and data collection through the Internet of Things facilitate already now (online) decision making regarding not only pricing and operative activities, but they transform whole business models and the processes how business is being made. Robotics and automatisation are inseparable parts of this phenomenon.

Interestingly, Burchell et al. (1980) pointed out the political and influencing roles of AIS, partly questioning the existence of a pure 'answer machine'. However, with the technological development this role gets emphasised, as the modern technology seems to enable better and better fact-based and automated decision making. This is an important observation also because this is becoming possible even if the decision-making environment (including causalities) has become more and more uncertain and turbulent, in general. Furthermore, regarding the lower right-hand corner of the framework, also an 'idea machine' role has been

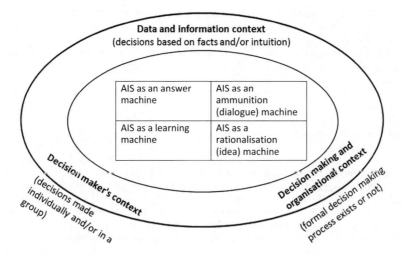

Figure 7.3 Summary of AIS and decision making.

suggested for AIS (Earl & Hopwood, 1981): a role enabling creative solutions to be found to messy problems as objectives are ambiguous and predictive models are poor. This role was earlier considered to be unrealistic to expect from a formal AIS. We suggest that the new technologies make this a realistic role to expect.

With the developing ICT comes also risks. One such risk relates to the huge amount of data being generated every second. There is a real risk of 'drowning' into data and information. Having more and versatile data, and data scientists to handle it, the role of knowledgeable managers is yet of utmost importance. This is because data/information tells little without real understanding and insight of the business. Technological complexity sets new requirements for businesses and even to existing business models. We will increasingly face radical transformations in this regard, which implies that decision making will change: what we will decide upon and how. Regarding Figure 7.1, this means that the design requirements for AIS gradually change. And who knows, if in the future, we see any longer AIS as we know them today but rather embedded technologies that together form massive decision-making systems including all kinds of data collected online. In any case, increasingly, developments in ICT enable the delivery of different software and platforms for AIS for everyone in a cost-effective way through cloud services. Previously, the bigger companies have been the pioneers in developing AIS, but this may be changing. All these also emphasise flexibility requirements and possibilities for the design of AIS (see Figure 7.1) and, further, flexibility of decision making, which may create a real competitive advantage for companies in the future.

References

Boland, R.J. (1979). Control, causality and information system requirements, *Accounting, Organisation and Society*, 4(4), 259–272.

Burchell, S., Clubb, C., Hopwood, A., Hughes, J., & Nahapiet, J. (1980). The roles of accounting in organisations and society, *Accounting, Organisation and Society*, 5(1), 5–27.

Burns, J., Quinn, M., Warren, L., & Oliveira, J. (2013) *Management accounting*. Berkshire: Mc Graw Hill Education.

CGMA, *From insight to impact. Unlocking the opportunities in big data*. London: CGMA, 2013.

Chenhall, R. (2003). Management control systems design within its organisational context: Findings from contingency-based research and directions for the future, *Accounting, Organisation and Society*, 28(2), 127–168.

Chong, V.K., & Eggleton, I.R. (2003). The decision-facilitating role of management accounting systems on managerial performance: The influence of locus of control and task uncertainty, *Advances in Accounting*, 20, 165–197.

Cooper, R., & Kaplan, R. (1991). Profit priorities from activity-based costing, *Harvard Business Review*, 69(3), 130–135.

Dobbs, I.M. (2004), Replacement investment: Optimal economic life under uncertainty, *Journal of Business Finance & Accounting*, 31(5–6), 729–757.

Drury, C. (2008). *Management and cost accounting*, 7th edition. London: Cengage Learning.

Earl, M.J., & Hopwood, A.G. (1981) From management information to information management, H.C. Lucas Jr. et al. (eds.), *The information systems environment*, Amsterdam: North Holland, pp. 315–325.

Kaplan, S. (2008). Cognition, capabilities and incentives: assessing firm response to the fiber–optic revolution, *Academy of Management Journal*, 51(4), 672–695.

Kaplan, S. (2011). Research in cognition and strategy: Reflections on two decades of progress and a look to the future, *Journal of Management Studies*, 48(3), 665–695.

Lea, B.-R., & Fredendall, L.D (2002). The impact of management accounting, product structure, product mix algorithm, and planning horizon on manufacturing performance, *International Journal of Production Economics*, 79(3), 279–299.

Merret, A.J. (1965). Investment in replacement: The optimal replacement method, *Journal of Management Studies*, 2(2), 153–166.

Mouritsen, J., & Kreiner, K. (2016) Accounting, decisions and promises, *Accounting, Organisations and Society*, 49, 21–31.

Porter, M.E. (1980). *Competitive strategy: Techniques for analyzing industries and competitors*. New York: Free Press.

Taipaleenmäki, J., & Ikäheimo, S. (2013). On the convergence of management accounting and financial accounting – the role of information technology in accounting change, *International Journal of Accounting Information Systems*, 14(4), 321–348.

Thompson, J.D, and Tuden, A. (1959). Strategies, structures and processes of organisational decision, J. D. Thompson et al. (eds.) *Comparative studies in administration*. Pittsburgh: University of Pittsburgh Press, pp. 195–216.

Vaassen, E. (2002). *Accounting information systems: A managerial approach*. Chichester: Wiley.

Warren, J.D., Moffitt, K.C., & Byrnes, P. (2015). How Big Data will change accounting, *Accounting Horizons*, 29(2), 397–407.

8

ACCOUNTING INFORMATION SYSTEMS AND CONTINUOUS IMPROVEMENT

Winnie O'Grady and Sharlene Biswas

Accounting information systems and continuous improvement

Increasingly competitive environments have prompted businesses to adopt continuous improvement (CI) strategies and cultures as ways to improve organisational performance (Mackey & Pforsich, 2019). Descriptions of CI are diverse with some focusing narrowly on CI initiatives and others more broadly on CI culture and philosophy. Much of the CI literature discusses individual improvement initiatives such as just-in-time, statistical process control, theory of constraints, six sigma, total quality management, target costing (TC) and activity-based costing and management (ABC/M) (Albright & Lam, 2006). Some CI initiatives have led to developments in accounting methods, for example, throughput accounting, lean accounting, TC and ABC. There is less discussion in the literature about how a broader CI culture or mindset is supported by accounting or how accounting information drives CI more generally. A mindset or culture of CI suggests that employees proactively seek out opportunities to improve performance by making changes, for example, enhance customer value, streamline processes or conserve resources.

A CI culture is underpinned by management's trust in and empowerment of employees at all organisational levels that enables individuals to make changes intended to improve performance. In organisations with a CI culture, time and resources are made available to promote CI activities, CI initiatives are easy to suggest and implement and unsuccessful CI efforts are viewed as opportunities for learning. The ability to improve processes and performance depends on employees' holistic understanding of operational processes, the availability of information about processes and performance, and the number of people who can access that information (Landry & Chan, 1999). Information flows are thus viewed as essential for supporting a CI culture. Information can direct employees' CI efforts and provide feedback to assess the impact of improvements on efficiency, effectiveness and profitability and to stimulate organisational learning (Turney & Anderson, 1989).

Accounting information systems (AIS) are a key source of systematic, objective and timely information that has the potential to support a CI culture (Shuhidana, Mastukib, & Nori, 2015). AIS can be broadly viewed as systems that process financially related transactional data to produce information used by decision-makers to plan, control and operate the businesses (Vaassen, Meuwissen, & Schelleman, 2009); help in the management and control of factors

DOI: 10.4324/9781003132943-11

related to firms' economic-financial areas (Grande, Estébanez, & Colomina, 2011); and collect and report important financial and non-financial information (AntónioTrigo, Belfoa, & PérezEstébanez, 2016).

Shortcomings in accounting information may limit its usefulness in driving a CI culture. Accounting information has been criticised for being too aggregated, late and obscured by allocations to be useful to managers (van der Veeken & Wouters, 2002) and ill-suited for managing CI efforts without modification (Mackey, 2005). To address these shortcomings, "[m]anagement accountants must realign systems and information delivery to meet managers' new needs in terms of continuous improvement" (Landry & Chan, 1999, p. 30). Alternately, companies might design their core AIS information to drive CI decisions and ongoing change.

The following sections present a mini case study documenting the role of AIS in promoting CI. The next three sections describe background features of the company pertinent to its CI culture and then its core AIS and supporting AIS, respectively. The subsequent sections consider how global and local AIS support CI. The final section suggests lessons offered by considering the links between AIS and CI culture in the case company.

Company background

FreightCo was founded by two partners in 1978 to provide domestic freight services. Over time, it grew into an international logistics company structured around a network comprising numerous, relatively small and independent operational branches. In 2021, the average size of FreightCo branches was 30 team members,[1] based on 9,000 team members and 297 branches recorded in its annual report. The company has always been profitable and reported $3.5 billion in revenue for the 2021 financial year.

The key activities involved in providing freight services are collecting goods from customers, sorting the goods for transport to different locations, organising transport between locations and resorting goods for local delivery (see Figure 8.3). The company owns its depots and warehouses but relies on independent operators, such as airlines, shipping companies and truck owner-drivers, to provide transport services. Branches collect and deliver goods in distinct geographical areas.

Operational branch managers (BMs) have always been expected to treat branches as their own business, to operate them profitably and to grow them each year. They are empowered to make a range of decisions including, for example, pricing, hiring and capital expenditure. BMs are enabled in their role through ready access to relevant information, which includes their own general ledgers (GL) and profit and loss (P&L) accounts.

Part of FreightCo's early corporate vision was to grow and expand the business – expressed as 'going for the moon' – while maintaining and improving service quality and team morale. The company expected 15% annual profit growth and allowed branches to set their own annual profit target – or profit pledge – to contribute to this goal. The organisational culture strongly promotes mutual support amongst team members, ongoing learning and continual improvement. FreightCo's formal statement of values and beliefs reminds team members: that education is optional but learning is compulsory, to keep reinventing the company as it ages and grows and to maintain service standards and to continually improve them. Continual improvement is achieved through a 'Ready, Fire, Aim' approach. This mantra encourages team members to make quick decisions, to learn from ongoing 'action experiments' and to avoid repeating mistakes. Information about the results of decisions made is crucial for learning. Accordingly, the company's open information policy ensures all team members, including managers and operational team members, are simultaneously provided with performance information and can scrutinise and comment on the results. The corporate culture and timely feedback together foster ongoing learning and CI. The company's core accounting systems were introduced when the company was founded and are now complemented by a range of benchmarking systems. An overview of the core accounting systems is provided next.

Core AIS systems

The heart of FreightCo's AIS is the weekly profit report, known as weeklies. This system was initiated when the company's first branch began informally tracking the profitability of consignments on scraps of paper. A senior manager described how BMs manually calculated the profitability of shipments in real time, stating:

> When we started, we knew our profits at the end of each day, for the day. In fact we used to pro-rate the consignment notes, which is the shipment document, before we loaded the truck. We would say that container's got fifteen thousand dollars revenue on it and that container's got that amount. We would know that figure as we were loading it. People used to do that, right from the start. We had that concept of knowing what our profitability was, what our margin was, on each box. We'd put down that it was going to cost us fifteen hundred dollars to deliver and there's our ... gross margin.

When FreightCo initiated computerisation of its accounting systems, it retained the practice of calculating profits on a weekly basis. According to the chief information officer (CIO):

> We took those principles of a small two-man business and continued with it. We didn't throw the principles away just because we were getting bigger. The calculations of the weekly profits and the daily profits were all offline things that people did on a piece of paper. We thought how can we keep the principles and how can we make our systems keep them? ... We don't want to change our systems for anybody. We want to keep our culture of doing the weekly profits.

Local information technology (IT) developers were tasked with developing bespoke systems that reflected how the company actually conducted business, including its weekly reporting of operational and accounting information. To ensure IT developers understood the rationale underpinning the company's systems, developers attended the company's formal induction program to learn about the corporate philosophy and business approach. The core AIS systems were then designed to reflect key operational processes, to enable managers to produce weekly profit reports and to allow accountants to produce monthly[2] accounts.

Weeklies are prepared by BMs rather than accountants. They form part of the core AIS and anticipate the results that will be produced by the monthly financial reporting system. The format for weeklies resembles a simplified P&L statement with three main sections that report financial results, operational metrics and comments about the week.

The top section of the weeklies reports financial metrics. It begins with revenues by type and direct (variable) costs and then reports allowances received from and paid to other branches for completing deliveries (i.e. transfer payments) and finally credits to customers. These figures are used to calculate gross margin (GM). Standard overheads are reported next. Average weekly figures are used to account for ongoing costs associated with running the branch office including items such as rent, salaries, insurance, interest and depreciation. Standard overheads include an allocation for head office support staff costs such as Human Resources, Legal, Corporate Accounting and senior management. Head office costs are not onerous as there are relatively few head office staff, and the head office is located in an operational branch. The costs of shared facilities such as freight processing depots are not allocated to branches. Any ad hoc expenses for the week are included as a separate line item. The net profit (NP) is the final entry in the financial section.

The remaining two sections record key operational metrics and managers' comments about the current week's performance noting items of interest, respectively. A simplified version of a weekly template is presented in Figure 8.1.

BMs typically take an hour or two to prepare the weeklies. They access a partially completed template from the core AIS system that is pre-filled with the figures for the corresponding week of the previous year. BMs use information from the operational freight system to derive the current week's figures for revenues (by mode of transport) and direct (variable) costs and then insert them into the template. A BM described the process in this way:

> Our performance measures come from our freight system. The freight system's all set up so that [managers] can ... get out their freight revenue ($) and direct costs. We give them a standard overhead. They can get ... an estimation of profit, but the freight revenue and the direct costs should be pretty accurate, and that should be driven by the operating systems. It's not the accountants running the business, it's the operating line managers.

	$ This Year	$ Last Year
Financial metrics		
1 Revenues (by Type) Allowances from sending branches		
2 Less: Direct Costs Pick Up and Delivery Allowances to receiving branches Linehaul Total Costs (all modes) Less: Credits to customers		
3 Gross Margin		
4 Standard overheads Extra overheads Additional salaries and wages		
5 Weekly profit		
Operational metrics		
6 Number of consignments Total cubic metres Total tonnage		
Commentary		
7 Branch Manager's comments e.g. Sales, margins, mix, events, weather		

Figure 8.1 Simplified template for weekly reporting.

Weeklies anticipate the figures that will be reported in the monthly accounts when the financial transactions are formally processed. The near real-time feedback the weeklies provide to managers motivates continuous efforts to improve both GM and NP. To improve margins, BMs can adjust prices, reduce direct costs for deliveries, improve utilisation of acquired capacity and control increases in standard overheads. A senior manager noted:

> It's up to the branch manager to manage his or her margins, as to how they set them and manage those margins. Now that's the key about the weeklies. The decisions managers made this week about how to move that freight and what to move it with determines what their margin looks like.

The weeklies enable managers to quickly assess the impact of their current decisions on performance. BMs can evaluate their decisions by comparing current weekly profits to those achieved for the same period last year and to the rate of growth the branch targeted in its profit pledge. The two questions BMs regularly ask each week are 'did we do better than last year?' and 'are we on track to make our profit target?' BMs closely observe weekly results to identify emerging trends in performance – defined as a change that persists over a three-week period. The weeklies provide information that regularly prompts BMs to improve branch performance. As one senior manager observed:

> It's more important that the branch manager understands what occurred in the business last week, and how the decisions he or she made in that week have impacted the profitability of the business ... you're comparing this week to the same week last year ... You can just see how well you've done or haven't done. You know if you have lost sales, lost customers, increased the costs in the business, or not managed margin well enough.

The same reporting format is used at all organisational levels. Divisional results are simply the aggregation of branch results; corporate results are the aggregation of divisional results adjusted for corporate-level expenses and tax. This reporting structure means individuals at all organisational levels interpret performance and profitability in the same way.

The preparation of monthly accounting reports, based on formal source documents, is the responsibility of the finance team. The monthly reports typically lag the weeklies by five to six weeks and are used to verify the accuracy of the weekly figures. Any discrepancies between the two are investigated and reconciled. The weeklies provide the information managers use to run the business on a day-to-day basis; the monthlies are used mainly for financial reporting. According to the CIO:

> The NCR[3] accounting systems were just used for recording after the fact, you know, this is how much the invoice is for.

Additional metrics are also supported by the AIS. The company has always relied on credit notes as an indicator of performance quality. Operational systems are designed to provide the data supporting this non-financial performance metric for service quality. As explained by the CIO:

> There was always a record kept, when I started, of how many credits were issued. How many credits were produced? There's your KPI. How many credits notes and what was

the value of the credits issued? We still run that today. That was the direct input to managers to make changes.

A league table of service quality ranks branches based on the number of customer credits issued in relation to the number of deliveries made. More specifically, there are separate ratios indicating the number of customer claims per inward and per outward consignments handled. The next section discusses how these AIS underpin the company's CI culture.

Organisational AIS and CI

The company's CI culture encourages managers to continually find ways to improve GM and NP. To improve GM, BMs can refine existing processes or identify, test and refine new offerings. Managers use data from the AIS to anticipate how changes will impact direct and indirect costs and operational volumes. BMs check the validity of their assumptions against the reality of the weeklies. Thus, the near real-time feedback provided by the weeklies allows BMs to assess the impact of decisions on margins. Two BMs explain how the weeklies help them assess improvements to their service offerings:

> For instance, we've put a line haul truck on from Newark to LA that runs on a weekly basis. It takes three or four days to get there and three or four days to get back. You immediately see what impact it has on our margin. You monitor it. You don't have to wait for the monthlies to come out, and you don't have to create a spreadsheet to theorise ... As soon as that truck leaves, we know what the cost is ... we pretty much know how much freight we've got on, the revenue and what the costs are.
>
> If we need to start a new service, we'll start a new service – we'll take a punt on it ... It might cost us a little bit to start off [with] but as long as we can see some benefit in it, we'll back ourselves. Hopefully, in three to six months that service will be very profitable ... We are more than happy to try something new, to try to be innovative, not just do the "same old, same old" ... We would do a costing – we'll look at what the cost is to set it up, and how much freight we need to make it break even ... When we look at something new we know the fixed costs and variable costs that we have within our business ... and we come up with a per-cubic-metre cost for our [new] service. We know how much freight we can get into a container ... We will assume we're not going to have a full box every time but [you work out] an average cost. Then you know what your buy rate[4] is ... then you know what your sell rate is.

Team members are also implicated in CI activities. Weekly results are posted on staff notice boards at the same time they are reported to management. Sharing this information enables team members to scrutinise performance and suggest operational improvements. Teams in every branch operate Positive Action Teams (PAT) through which they proactively review and improve operational processes. Teams are motivated to make improvements by the team-based bonus scheme, which sees team members share 10% of branch NP. Thus, the weeklies help team members recognise when improvement efforts are needed.

> In each branch, all the information is available to everyone at all times. They can see their monthly and weekly profits. It's on the branch notice boards as well as the KPIs which affect bonus. We try to create a whole lot of "capitalists" out there that want to

make that profit bigger so they can get a bigger bonus ... which helps drive that profit improvement and growth improvement.

Monthly accounts help BMs identify when control of costs needs improvement. Managers consider actual overheads in light of standard (average) overhead costs reported in the weeklies. Regular review and comparison of reported costs prompt BMs to question whether costs are proliferating and whether expenditures are delivering value for money. The questions prompted by the monthly accounts drive continuous cost improvement as noted in the following quote:

> What we're doing is basically critiquing all of our costs each month and making sure they're in line with our expectations ... that we're not only paying forwarders but paying the right rate too ... If you're going to get someone in to do the gardens, you check they are giving you a good rate, that it's competitive ... Do you need to review costs each year? You might check cleaning and find it's not being done well at the moment. Maybe you should get a couple more cleaning guys in to give some feedback on it. Is our current contract competitive?

FreightCo's CI culture is supported by benchmarking information provided by the AIS. Weekly profit reporting enables BMs to compare branches' current performance with that of the same period of the previous year. Individual BMs regularly contact peers in their informal networks[5] to compare their weekly performance. Inter-branch benchmarking through league tables informs managers how their key performance indicators (KPI) compare to that of other branches. Managers can also compare the monthly expenditures with those of similar-sized branches. Each of these comparisons helps BMs to identify where cost improvements are needed. The monthly cost review process is described by one BM in this way:

> As a manager you get to know your business, to own your financials I go through those numbers. We live these numbers, we own these numbers. We're comparing last year with this year in the same month and year-to-date, last year versus this year. We also rank the different businesses against each other [if the figures aren't comparable] then you ask what's going on? Why are we $40,000 more? Well clearly this site has got three times as many people, it's got three times as big an area. Then you start thinking about it ... We'll look at things like the light bulbs we've got, whether they're LEDs and whether we need to replace the light bulbs. Are we leaving lights on too long? We need to talk to our team and say guys the power bill's up. What the hell's going on? Turn the lights off when you leave the office. That's the sort of level of detail we'll go to. We live each line and understand those lines. Then we'll do the same for the branches that are similar. We compare every single branch across the country and then we rank them.

Benchmarking is integral to CI. Internal benchmarking of branches encourages CI by motivating lower-performing branches to improve. BMs are able to identify the 'best performers' from whom they can learn. Better-performing branches are expected to share their knowledge with other branches to help them improve performance. FreightCo's focus on internal benchmarking is characteristic of high-performance organisations who tend to avoid external benchmarks and to view competitors' best performance as the baseline for their own performance (de Waal, 2008). FreightCo's MD described the company's benchmarking focus in this way:

> We compare [amongst] ourselves … we don't do too much comparison with the competitor. We're thinking about our business, not what their level might be.

AIS support CI when they capture and report data about the key factors driving performance and make financial and non-financial information readily available to all organisational members (de Waal, 2008). FreightCo clearly understands the factors impacting its performance and has designed its AIS systems to capture relevant information. The company's AIS captures financial information and key performance metrics at the branch level, thus facilitating performance comparisons and improvements at the operational level. The use of league tables to rank branches on service quality drives branch teams to continually improve performance. Additionally, league table rankings impact bonuses; branches sitting above (below) the average ranking have bonuses increased (decreased) by up to 2%. Accordingly, branches are motivated to continually improve service quality.

The company's CI culture influences how managers and team members assess their own performance. A CI mindset encourages teams to strive for the best possible performance, i.e. to go for the moon and, no matter the results achieved, to always strive for improvement. This mindset is evident in the comments of one BM who stated:

> We understand what the numbers represent and we understand where our profitability's at. The biggest issue we have here is [our profit] is never enough. When we're asked how much did you make last week? the answer is always "not enough". Where's your gross margin at? Well, it's not high enough.

The tendency to always assess performance as 'not good enough' reflects a CI philosophy rather than a management by exception philosophy (Romney & Steinbart, 2017). Managers operating in firms with a CI culture are more likely to interpret actual results in relation to ideal performance and therefore to perceive all variances as negative, i.e. falling short of perfection. A CI culture motivates individuals to constantly strive for the best possible results and to expect the best possible effort from themselves, their colleagues and the organisation (de Waal, 2008). Striving for the 'best possible' performance drives CI efforts.

FreightCo's core AIS support a CI culture at the branch, division and corporate levels. However, information from these systems may be less informative at the work team level. In one logistics branch, the weekly financial information was found to be too aggregated to motivate improvement efforts by frontline teams. Consequently, the BM designed a local AIS to track the financial impact of decisions made by work teams and to inform their CI efforts. The following section describes how this local or vernacular AIS (Kilfoyle, Richardson, & MacDonald, 2013; Goretzki, Strauss, & Wiegmann, 2018) supported CI initiatives of work teams.

Vernacular AIS and CI

The main operational activities of the logistics branch were receiving, storing, picking and shipping products for customers. The activities were performed by six teams comprising a team leader and three to five team members who collectively managed 38 customer accounts. Customers individually negotiated their service contracts including the price of activities performed, fees for account administration, charges for consumables and the cost of other services. Customer contracts also specified agreed service levels and KPIs. The two key indicators of team performance, namely 'on time order dispatch' and 'on time order delivery', were supported by metrics for order errors, damages and stocktake accuracy. Work teams were thus keenly focused on achieving operational performance.

The financial performance of the branch, as reported in the weeklies (see Figure 8.1), indicated revenues earned for inward (unloading goods, organising goods on pallets), storage (placing goods in racking spaces) and outward activities (retrieving, checking, packing, wrapping and shipping goods), as well as fees for storage time, consumables used and house pallets' usage (pallets owned by the company). Standard branch overheads reported normal payroll and overtime hours and equipment lease costs. More variable expenses included casual or contract labour, ad hoc equipment and pallet hire or purchase costs and consumables (shrink wrap and single use pallets). The branch had not reported a profit for many months.

While work teams knew the branch weekly profit figures, they could not readily link the results with day-to-day operational activities and decisions. For example, team leaders regularly engaged additional labour and machinery in periods of high customer demand or in response to ad hoc customer service requests. While such decisions ensured teams met operational targets, it was not evident how they impacted customer and branch profitability. To make team leaders aware of the economic impact of day-to-day decisions, the BM designed a new AIS referred to as the cost centre summary (CCS). According to the BM:

> I need to break [the weekly P&L result] down because say I called in minus $10,000 [loss]. I have no idea where it was lost. Traditionally we've looked at our warehouse as an entity, but actually we've got teams [that] look after their customers. So, why wouldn't we break down the costs and get the guys involved in one of the measures that we are measured on.

The BM created an Excel template for reporting revenues, expenses and capacity usage by work team and customer. The BM manually disaggregated weekly revenues by customer to reveal income earned from inward, storage and outward activities and input the figures into the CCS template along with amounts for management fees. Team leaders subsequently completed the CCS by adding figures for weekly overtime, casual labour, machine usage (hours of use of specific types of equipment), consumables and racking and pallet utilisation. Once completed, the CCS template revealed the team's profitability and efficiency. Figure 8.2 indicates how costs were initially broken down to derive the figures for CCS reporting.

The BM initiated weekly CCS meetings with work teams. He regularly explained that the CCS was intended to help work teams identify where to focus improvement efforts, saying it would reveal "where things are going right or where there are places we can fix". As work teams became familiar with the elements of the CCS, team leaders began suggesting how they could improve the financial performance of their own teams. One early suggestion addressed casual labour costs with the team leader saying:

> A lot of my money that I am losing down there is on contract labour. I think I might be able to cut some hours down. Pretty much half a day instead of being $1,000 [per week] it would be $500.

A subsequent improvement initiative by this team leader involved reorganising the setup of the portion of the warehouse space used by his team. The CCS information had informed the team leader of the cost differences attached to the use of different types of machinery. Accordingly, he aimed to reduce his team's machine-related costs by 40% by reorganising storage spaces in

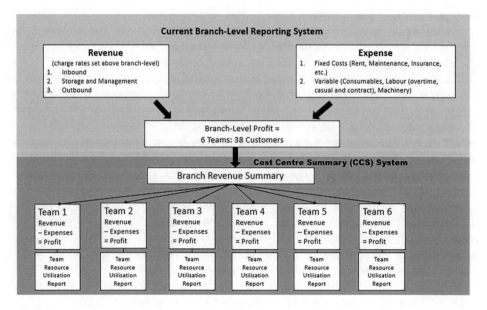

Figure 8.2 Cost breakdown for cost centre summary.

the warehouse. While the team's costs initially increased as additional machinery and overtime were used to enact the reorganisation, they quickly reduced once the changes were completed.

A second team leader reviewed her client contracts to identify which of them used single use pallets (a consumable) and billed them accordingly, thus increasing her team's weekly revenues. The remaining team leaders, surprised they had not thought of this change themselves, quickly followed suit. A third team leader noted that before the CCS, she and her team had no idea about the revenues and costs associated with their customer accounts and furthermore "didn't really care about it until it got brought to our attention". Similarly, the operations manager observed that before the CCS, the link between activity and profitability had not been that clear, noting that:

> You don't realise how much money you have been spending on all the other things because you think that you're putting out a lot of orders, but actually that's not generating as much [profit] as you think.

The CCS prompted scrutiny of activities undertaken in response to ad hoc customer requests that were not being charged for. The CCS information allowed team leaders to see that acquiescing to customer requests could lead to increased activity without generating additional revenue. Team leaders concluded that customers should be charged for these additional activities. In the words of one team leader:

> What I realised is these little side jobs that we are doing for [customers], like "can you re-price this?" … We are not charging for it. We should start recording it and charging customers.

Another improvement initiative prompted by CCS information was investigating whether key customers were in fact profitable. The CCS template was modified to track the revenues and activities of the top 12 customers with a view to renegotiating service contracts for low profitability customers.

Lessons learned

The mini case study described in this chapter reveals the central role of AIS in supporting the company's CI culture. Branches and frontline teams were expected to continuously improve profits year on year and to use their autonomy to pursue revenue enhancing and cost reduction improvement efforts. They both relied on information from the AIS to identify when and where improvements were required and to monitor the impact of CI initiatives on profitability.

The study shows how the mutual interdependence between a CI culture and the AIS establishes a reinforcing cycle of learning and improvement. The CI culture motivated team members to introduce, seek out and implement improvement initiatives. Teams relied on AIS information to assess the impact of their improvement efforts on key operational and financial metrics. AIS information helped teams focus their CI efforts by identifying where costs and revenues could be improved.

Benchmarking of financial and KPI performance prompted CI efforts by revealing shortcomings in current performance. Comparisons revealed whether, for example, branch profits exceeded those of the corresponding period of the previous year, branch profits grew at the targeted growth rate and branch financial and operational performance lagged that of peers. Shortfalls in performance motivated renewed improvement efforts. It is clear that AIS information was critical for both supporting the CI culture and motivating CI initiatives. The financial focus provided by AIS information ensured that CI efforts delivered the desired economic results (Mackey, 2005; Trigo, Belfo, & Estébanez, 2016; Mackey & Pforsich, 2019). Accordingly, the AIS information regularly reminded BMs that the ultimate objective of their CI efforts was improved profitability. Figure 8.3 depicts the dynamic relationship between AIS information and CI initiatives.

A number of design features made information from the AIS useful for CI. The AIS in the case company was designed to support a highly decentralised organisational structure. The company had many, relatively small, autonomous branches, i.e. a pooled interdependence structure (Thompson, 1967), which reduced the operational complexity individual BMs had to handle (de Waal, 2005). The AIS included a GL and supported weekly and monthly financial reporting for every branch. Disaggregating the cost and revenue information to the branch-level information was critical for enabling managers and frontline teams to understand where and when improvements were needed.

A key principle guiding the design of the AIS is that the systems should reflect business processes rather than financial reporting requirements and enable managers to monitor the key drivers of performance. The weeklies used in the case company was based on information from the operational systems, allowing BMs and frontline teams to build an integrated understanding of operational and financial performance. The evidence provided by this case study thus suggests AIS designed around work processes can overcome common criticisms of traditional accounting information (van der Veeken & Wouters, 2002) that make it useful for CI. Additionally, weeklies were shared with all team members. Thus, everyone was involved in scrutinising performance and contributing to the pool of CI ideas to improve profitability.

Another design principle was ensuring that supplemental AIS presented information that was consistent with that provided by existing systems. BMs could, for example, disaggregate AIS information – as illustrated by the CCS reporting system discussed above – as long as the

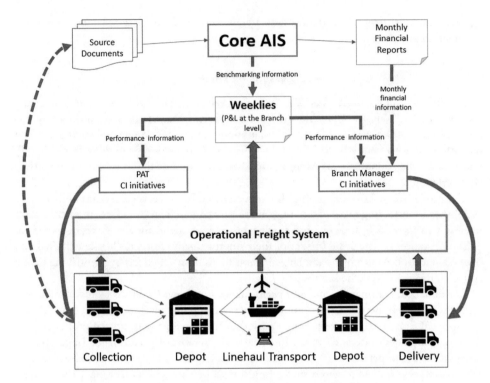

Figure 8.3   Interdependence of AIS and continuous improvement initiatives.

overall view of performance was maintained. The CCS example also shows the importance of incorporating financial metrics alongside operational performance indicators. Without financial information, operational teams couldn't assess the economic impact of their efforts to enhance customer service. This observation suggests that in highly decentralised organisations, frontline teams should have access to financial information that can be used to monitor the impact of CI efforts on economic results.

AIS can be designed with minimal allocations for overhead costs. In the case company, weeklies reported only those revenues and costs that were directly controllable at the branch level. Cost allocations were largely avoided at the branch level apart from a small share of head office salaries. This more direct costing approach, similar in nature to value stream reporting advocated by lean accounting (Maskell, 2011), ensured results were unobscured by allocations and thereby improved BMs' understanding and management of branch performance.

AIS can be designed to provide information that is timely. AIS in the case company operated on two different temporal cycles – weekly and monthly. Weeklies met the real-time information needs of branch management, while the monthly cycle supported financial reporting processes. The weeklies provided branch teams with rapid feedback that enabled CI; branches could quickly assess the impact of CI initiatives on economic performance and modify their actions as required.

AIS can be designed to present information that is simple, easy to produce and readily understood. In the case company, the weeklies could be prepared quickly – within a couple of hours – by BMs will little accounting knowledge. Team members could understand the weekly results, identify when performance was falling short and make suggestions for improvement. The simple format of the weeklies allowed more team members to engage with the financial information and to contribute to the pool of ideas for CI. Overall, the weeklies established a framework for the regular review of performance and encouraged suggestions from all organisational levels on how to improve it. According to one BM:

> We are continually reviewing our revenue that's coming in. We need to continually review the gross margin levels that we're getting from the business that's moving through the system and continually review the cost structure of our overheads to make sure that we've got it under control. It's a simple formula. As long as those three areas are where they need to be … [and] as long as our KPI's are fine … we are on the right track.

This chapter has considered how one company's bespoke AIS successfully supports its CI culture. Companies that would like to emulate this approach to developing and supporting a CI culture may need to consider how to adopt a highly decentralised structure, to simplify and openly share information with employees at all levels, to create group rewards that include frontline team members and to develop AIS that provide information that is relevant to work processes and activities, timely and easy to understand.

Notes

1 The company uses the term 'team members' instead of 'employees'.
2 The monthly accounts are based on a 4-4-5 week cycle.
3 Non-Cash Revenue.
4 Price paid to freight operators.
5 FreightCo promotes the development of informal networks by establishing cohorts for the induction program, creating buddy branches for similar operations and encouraging ongoing interactions between them, and through staff rotations between branches and divisions.

References

Albright, T., & Lam, M. (2006). Managerial Accounting and Continuous Improvement Initiatives: A Retrospective and Framework. *Journal of Managerial Issues, Summer 18*(2), 157–174.

AntónioTrigo, Belfoa, F., & PérezEstébanez, R. (2016). Accounting Information Systems: Evolving towards a Business Process Oriented Accounting. *Procedia Computer Science, 100*, 987–994.

de Waal, A. A. (2005). Is Your Organisation Ready for Beyond Budgeting? *Measuring Business Excellence, 9*(2), 56–67.

de Waal, A. A. (2008). The Secret of High Performance Organisations. *Management Online Review* (April), 1–10.

Goretzki, L., Strauss, E., & Wiegmann, L. (2018). Exploring the Roles of Vernacular Accounting Systems in the Development of "Enabling" Global Accounting and Control Systems. *Contemporary Accounting Research, Winter 35*, 1888–1916.

Grande, E. U., Estébanez, R. P., & Colomina, C. M. (2011). The impact of Accounting Information Systems (AIS) on Performance Measures: Empirical Evidence in Spanish SMEs. *The International Journal of Digital Accounting Research, 11*, 25–43.

Kilfoyle, E., Richardson, A. J., & MacDonald, L. D. (2013). Vernacular Accountings: Bridging the Cognitive and the Social in the Analysis of Employee-Generated Accounting Systems. *Accounting, Organisations and Society, July 38*(5), 382–396.

Landry, S. P., & Chan, W. Y. C. (1999). Making the Transition from Functional Cost Center "Big Brother" To Value Adding Key Team Member: A Paradigm for the Changing Role of Management Accountants in a Customer-Focused, Quality-Driven, Value-Added World. In *Role of Management Accounting in Creating Value* (pp. 24–36): International Federation of Accountants.

Mackey, J. (2005). Changing Accounting Systems to Support the Conversion and Management of a Continuous Improvement Business Culture. doi:10.2139/ssrn.773026

Mackey, J., & Pforsich, H. (2019). Using an Accounting-based Management Control System for Cultural Change. *Journal of Accounting and Finance, 19*(9), 116–141.

Maskell, B. H. (2011). *Practical Lean Accounting: A Proven System for Measuring and Managing the Lean Enterprise.* Boca Raton: CRC Press

Romney, M. B., & Steinbart, P. J. (2017). *Accounting Information Systems* (14th ed.): Pearson Prentice Hall.

Shuhidana, S. M., Mastukib, N. a., & Nori, W. M. N. W. M. (2015). Accounting Information System and Decision Useful Information Fit towards Cost Conscious Strategy in Malaysian Higher Education Institutions. *Procedia Economics and Finance, 31*, 885–895.

Thompson, J. D. (1967). *Organisations in Action: Social Science Bases of Administrative Theory.* London: Routledge.

Trigo, A., Belfo, F., & Estébanez, R. P. (2016). Accounting Information Systems: Evolving towards a Business Process Oriented Accounting. *Procedia Computer Science, 100*, 987–994.

Turney, P. B. B., & Anderson, B. (1989). Accounting for Continuous Improvement. *Sloan Management Review, Winter 30*(2), 37–47.

Vaassen, E., Meuwissen, & Schelleman, K. (2009). *AIS and Internal Control* (2nd ed.). John Wiley & Sons.

van der Veeken, H. J. M., & Wouters, M. J. F. (2002). Using accounting information systems by operations managers in a project company. *Management Accounting Research, 13*(3), 345–370.

9

THE DYNAMICS OF ARTIFICIAL INTELLIGENCE IN ACCOUNTING ORGANISATIONS

A structuration perspective

Othmar M. Lehner, Carina Knoll, Susanne Leitner-Hanetseder and Christoph Eisl

Introduction

In existing research, Artificial Intelligence in Accounting (AIA) is often used as a summarising term for a variety of research endeavours into the digitalisation and automation of accounting processes based on emerging technologies (Quattrone, 2016). Current literature – examining some core constituents of AIA – is dominated by a focus on the role of technology in accounting and auditing (Ghasemi et al., 2011; Taipaleenmäki & Ikäheimo, 2013; Güney, 2014). Examples may include the importance of the blockchain (Dai & Vasarhelyi, 2017; Kokina et al., 2017), big data (Vasarhelyi et al., 2015; Janvrin et al., 2017), AI (Sutton et al., 2016; Kokina & Davenport, 2017) or robotic process automation (Cooper et al., 2018; Kokina & Blanchette, 2019).

The phenomenon of AIA itself, however, should not be seen as a containerised development that is simply being driven by some, admittedly very important, technological advancements, but rather needs to acknowledge and, thus, find itself firmly embedded within the larger scholarly discourse surrounding the smart AI-based transformation of our society (Hinings et al., 2018; Vial, 2019; Verhoef et al., 2021). AIA thus inherits the multifaceted and varied nature of a fundamental societal change process, with necessary perspectives on, and resulting implications for, individuals, organisations and societal institutions (Tabrizi et al., 2019). Recognising the necessity of interdisciplinary approaches in this new area, scholars are already examining, e.g. integration of the "new" competences required in the accounting curricula (Janvrin et al., 2017; Sledgianowski et al., 2017) and raising ethical questions (Dignum, 2018); overall, however, research on AIA remains largely fragmented and lacks a holistic picture (Lehner et al., 2019).

Perhaps one reason for this may be the inherently complex, almost hybrid nature of AIA, as it is driven by two very different and sometimes even incompatible discourses between the technical and the normative. What is more, while much of existing Accounting Information Systems (AIS) literature (Quinn & Strauss, 2017) is concerned with the automation of processes that leads to changes in routines, information flows and organisational capabilities (Neely & Cook, 2011), we see the necessity of AIA to transcend this automation

DOI: 10.4324/9781003132943-12

perspective because of the somewhat intangible and socially loaded "promise" of an autonomous, algorithmic (Kellogg et al., 2020) cognition of complex problems and the subsequent autonomous decision making (Sutton et al., 2016; Kokina & Davenport, 2017; Jarrahi, 2018; Losbichler & Lehner, 2021) with tremendous societal implications. This ultimately leads to a "disruptive", rather than an incremental, transformation (Christensen et al., 2018), as it will change the nature of the accounting profession, with an enormous impact on the workforce and organisations (Zammuto et al., 2007; Kruskopf et al., 2019). This, however, is of course by no means limited to accounting organisations, as we are in an age of AI-driven digital transformation that impacts all aspects of society. As a result of this extended – and more radical – prospective view, we strongly agree with Vial (2019) and Hinings et al. (2018), who observe that research into such transformations needs to acknowledge the "broader individual, organisational and societal change contexts" (Vial, 2019, p. 4).

Following this line of thought, we see AIA as being the research field that allows us to critically analyse and, at the same time, drive forward the digital transformation of accounting towards holistic, cognitive-aware and largely autonomous algorithmic accounting systems. Therein, AIA research needs to acknowledge the larger context of an ongoing societal transformation through digitalisation with interdisciplinary approaches that include strong ethical perspectives. Thus, while existing research on the larger digital transformation has thus far tried to answer the question of *"What do we know?"*, thus cementing the status quo and, thereby, creating the sort of reflexive isomorphism in research that discourages critical inquiries (Gendron, 2018), our disruptive understanding of AIA rather lends itself to the question of *"What should we know?"*. That is to say, because the nature of AIA (with its various facets reaching from the technological to the normative) is in itself still poorly understood, much less so are the potential implications for (vulnerable) individuals, organisations and the larger society (Quattrone, 2016; Kokina & Blanchette, 2019; Lehner et al., 2019). Traditional functionalist (Burrell & Morgan, 2019) research may not be the optimal way forward, as Englund, Gerdin, and Burns (2011) write "that the history-less, apolitical and technical-efficiency focus of traditional functionalist research has very limited ability to help us understand how and why accounting is mobilised in and transformed" (p. 495).

In order to understand these implications, it thus seems to be necessary to shine a light upon the "whatness" of AIA (Lehner et al., 2019) and its inherent dynamics. The vast toolkit of Giddens' structuration theory (Giddens, 1984; Giddens, 1990b; Englund & Gerdin, 2014; Englund et al., 2011) seems to provide a good starting point, as it

> offers several important and largely unique contributions to the broader alternative literature as such, namely: (i) the introduction of a duality perspective, (ii) the conceptualisation of accounting as an interwoven social structure (consisting of structures of signification, legitimation, and domination), and (iii) a basis for theorising both accounting continuity and change.
>
> *(Englund et al., 2011, p. 495)*

In order to gain rich, qualitative, in-depth data as a basis, we conduct a global, triangulated Delphi study (Gallego & Bueno, 2014) on the digital future of accounting with the voices of 138 experts.

In our critical appraisal of the data, we embrace Giddens' perspectives on modernity (Giddens, 1990a, 1991; Giddens & Pierson, 1998) in order to identify the structural roots and potential power consequences of the inherent dynamics that drive the transformation in AIA by examining how the structures of signification, domination and legitimation shape the system through what Giddens calls "memory traces" of knowledgeable actors (Giddens, 1984) and how they are reproduced, in turn, through "enacted practices". Therewith, we also follow Orlikowski (2000), who compared previous models such as the technological imperative, strategic choice and technology as a trigger and considers the importance of meaning, power, norms and interpretive flexibility: "the duality of technology identifies prior views of technology as either objective force or as socially constructed product – as a false dichotomy" (p. 13).

Our specific research questions thus are:

- What are the main sources of the inherent dynamics in the current context of accounting "modernity" that drive the development of AIA, and what are the related mechanisms of this transformation?
- What are the main structures of signification, legitimation and domination that influence and control the evolvement of AIA into social systems, and how are these structures, in turn, influenced by the AIA systems that they create?
- What is the "dialectic of power" in this dynamic transformation process, i.e. who controls the expression of the structures and influences their enactment, and who are the "highly knowledgeable" actors?

Research design

For the data collection and interpretation, we used the electronic Delphi method (Okoli & Pawlowski, 2004), which is based on approaches by the RAND Corporation from the 1950s and was developed to "forecast and identify issues" (Gallego & Bueno, 2014), or as Worrell et al. (2013) put it:

> The Delphi method is especially useful in reducing ambiguity through the use of expert panels of both practitioners and experts and informing relevant and timely issues facing organisations. In essence, the Delphi method has potential to provide both rigor and relevance to AIS (note: accounting information systems) research.
>
> *(p. 193)*

We used it to structure and stepwise refine the outcome of a group communication process on the topic of the future of AIA. For this longitudinal inquiry, three refinement steps were taken over the duration of one year, each with summarising feedback for steps 2 and 3 – with the addition of a quantitative part in step 3 – and a vignette of the imagined situation "working in accounting in the year 2030" in the first step. The participants ($N = 138$ completing the final third round) comprised a global audience of expert (managerial level or above) practitioners working in the accounting profession, as well as accounting and auditing scholars attending a well-reputed annual conference on accounting. The continent-aggregated "countries of work" of respondents were Europe: 38%; North America: 22%; Asia: 20%; South America: 8%; Africa: 8%; and Australia: 4%, with an average age of 34 and a standard deviation of 6, as well as 48% males and 52% females. For this, and as a first step, we personally invited a large, theoretically identified sample ($N = 1.740$) of individuals who matched the profile of either working >2 years in accounting or auditing at the managerial level or being a scholar with at least a doctorate in accounting or finance, extracted from the database of the ACRN Oxford Research Network on Accounting, Finance and Risk.

We asked the participants to provide an open description of the field of work of AIA in the year 2030, the organisational structures, the processes and workflows, the role of technology and the new roles, corresponding duties and education of the workforce. For this, we deliberately did not provide much guidance as to not influence the answers. It was interesting to see that many of the responses dealt with functionalist angles and left out normative (amongst the ethical) perspectives. In the subsequent round, the answers were clustered and summarised, and the lead researchers subsequently identified remaining tensions and gaps within these. This then led to either the formulation of consensuses which were sent out for triangulation in the next round or to new, additional questions for potentially clarifying the identified tensions and gaps.

Finally, we ended up with in-depth narrations that were then summarised and exemplified by expert consensuses in a series of half-day (partially online) workshops consisting of the researchers, their assistants as well as selected participants (identified in the following paper by their participant numbers) from the Delphi study to enhance its qualitative validity. It has to be noted at this point that these expert voices can only be assumed as discursive consensuses; thus, we do not want to suggest that these *will* be the future (as it will most likely be *not* – see e.g. Suchman, 1995, Armstrong et al., 2014), but rather they shall help us to understand the opportunity spaces opened up by the current framing based on the field discourse. Thereafter, the insights gained were analysed and deconstructed using Giddens' structuration toolkit. In the following sections, we will critically discuss these insights in the form of a reflective narration and provide some of the exemplary expert consensuses in order to anchor our findings in the data.

Dynamism: a modernity perspective on Artificial Intelligence in Accounting

Giddens, drawing on not only the thoughts of Marx but also those of Mead and others (Giddens, 1991), sees four dimensions of modernity: capitalism, industrialism, coordinated administrative power and military power (Giddens, 1990a). In the context of AIA, one of these dimensions, which Giddens calls the "coordinated administrative power focused through surveillance" (p. 55), seems to be especially salient in its relevance, as it provides a way in which to understand the normative externalities of AIA and the increasingly technologically assisted coordination of a strong surveillance focus. Furthermore, Giddens' writings on modernity may particularly help to advance our understanding of (digital) accounting practices as being embedded in larger societal changes and the dynamic pace of change of these as discussed in the previous paragraphs. With respect to this, Giddens & Pierson (1998) argue that modernity is "vastly more dynamic than any previous type of social order. It is a society – more technically, a complex of institutions – which unlike any preceding culture lives in the future rather than in the past" (p. 94). The three main sources of such "dynamism" are identified by Giddens (1991) as:

i   Time–space separation,
ii The development of dis-embedding mechanisms, and
iii The reflexive appropriation of knowledge.

Consequently, our first research question asks: What are the main sources of the inherent dynamics in the current context of accounting "modernity" that drive the development of AIA, and what are the related mechanisms of this transformation?

The structuration of Artificial Intelligence in Accounting
across time and space

AIA can be understood to further increase time–space separation (Giddens, 1981, 1990a) of the future workforce in accounting, wherein actors can be in the same space but not in the same geographical locale. In our data we find a consensus that technological advancements such as highly flexible cloud computing and the strong inter-collaboration with robots, e.g. will even better lead to expert teams that are distributed around the globe in different time zones and work together on projects in small office hubs that may be close to their homes. Following Giddens, who observes how specific locales can still become "thoroughly penetrated by and shaped in terms of social influences quite distant from them" (1990a, p. 19), we also observe that the shaping role of the practices enacted by the dispersed workforce in the actual processes will be a strong moderating factor in opening new "opportunity spaces" (Jing & Benner, 2016). E.g. the choice of embedding robotic co-workers (and more so their inherent level of AI and the resulting agency of these) into groups will be critical in an individual organisation's path constitution (Sydow et al., 2009; Garud et al., 2010) towards what was found to be the ultimate scenario of a Fully Autonomous Accounting System (FAAS).

> Consensus Example from Expert 16 (henceforth abbreviated as CEE): "Artificial Intelligence in Accounting (AIA) systems will evolve in levels or stages with various 'optimal' expressions of each stage. The resulting systems are characterised by organisational learning. From these learnings (by individuals and groups), and also externally motivated by the ongoing evolution of technology as well as the adaptation of regulations in parallel, new opportunity spaces will open up towards potential next levels. While stages may look different for different organisations, depending on their historic choices (path dependency), they will share some common characteristics (see in the figure) due to the embeddedness in the overall digitalisation of society. Each stage, however, will need considerable time to freeze and unfreeze before it can move on to the next stage, because of limited resources and the comparatively high 'newness' that demands time to reflect upon".

It would be noteworthy at this stage to express caution with this fixed view of levels or stages, as the actual manifestation will very likely vary and express more dynamics than this static view would suggest. However, as it was clearly visible in the views of the expert participants, we chose to report it here, with the intend to propose ideal, somewhat archetypical stages that can be used as anchoring (or reference) points for practitioners. In the past, AIS changed the way in which data was collected and prepared for decision making by stakeholders (Neely & Cook, 2011). Further development of such systems (see Figure 9.1 and CEE 16) based on our data will take place, e.g. through partly autonomous robots for process automation, through advances in creating fully digital workflows with the necessary standardisations and, finally, through innovative algorithms based on data science and process mining. However, the majority of scholars would agree that the future will certainly encompass more than just collecting and processing data, as advances in AI research already predict some sort of multifunctional, cognitive capabilities and the ability to make decisions when given complex scenarios (Sutton et al., 2016; Kokina & Davenport, 2017; Jarrahi, 2018; Stancheva-Todorova, 2018). This was also identified in the data, as the majority of the experts see advanced, perhaps even yet unforeseen algorithms, which process structured and unstructured data with a strong domain awareness. Domain awareness is a form of

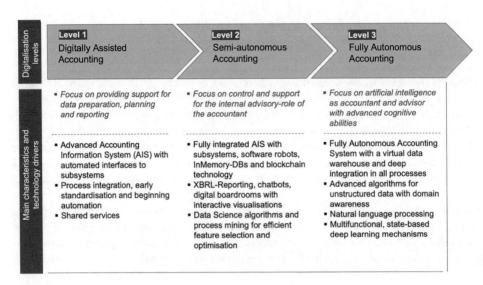

Figure 9.1   Three maturity levels of Artificial Intelligence in Accounting (AIA).

"contextual awareness", e.g. of the business model and strategy and will enable algorithms to provide much better, contextualised decision-making support with a strongly increased ability to detect fraudulent activities.

The third and "final" maturity level (in the sense of this Delphi study of AIA in 2030) thus focuses on AI in an autonomous accounting system, with self-aware cognition and (to some extent) limited decision-making power. A multifunctional, deep-learning-powered AI provides automated application and adaptation of accounting and tax regulations, implements optimisation measures, provides target-audience-specific reporting and forecasting in real time, runs simulations and scenarios and issues regular management warnings in respect of major key performance indicators with detailed analyses and recommendations. Moreover, the AI controls the deployment of specialised robots according to the necessary tasks at hand as directed by management. The participants see it use a deeply integrated virtual data warehouse that includes internal and external data and is fully managed with regard to data protection, security and availability. It should be noted that this would solve many practical problems that are currently severely inhibiting the full potential of AI (Vial et al., 2021). Managers communicate with the system via natural language processing from everywhere. The system improves its own performance through the use of deep-learning mechanisms. Internal as well as external auditing will be continuously performed as transaction data is stored in fraud-immune blockchains with encryption and full traceability.

At this stage the AIS becomes an FAAS. Based on our analysis of the future, utopian scenario, an FAAS is defined as follows:

> CEE 32: "An FAAS is a firm-wide, fully autonomous, self-aware and self-improving accounting system. The centre of an FAAS is a state-based, multifunctional, deep-learning network as Artificial Intelligence (AI) that is able to holistically simulate and potentially outpace human cognition and decision-making processes. This AI manages structured and unstructured data and regulations from various sources and delivers timely and apt information to the right audience in the right format."

Despite this consensus, the extant scholarly literature remains more cautious about this superiority claim (e.g. Grace et al., 2018).

Dis- and re-embedding and reflexivity mechanisms

Examining the above-described evolution of AIA in "time-space" more closely, we can identify Giddens' mechanisms of dis- and re-embedding as well as reflexivity (as discussed in the next two paragraphs). Giddens sees dis-embedding and re-embedding as the processes through which distant events and actions are taken from their context – thus being dis-embedded – and then become adapted and reintroduced into other contexts, thus being re-embedded. A good example in AIA of dis- and re-embedding may be the global development (as a distant event) of AI tools and algorithms (as abstract models) to be used in specific fields, e.g. in the medical profession. Thereafter, these tools and algorithms that would run, e.g. tumour-diagnostic systems are taken out of their specific contexts (dis-embedded) and will be used for fraud detection in accounting and, thus, re-embedded into the field of accounting. Giddens argues that time–space separation and dis-embedding mechanisms are mutually dependent. For this he proposes "abstract systems" as being major mechanisms (Giddens, 1990a). In our data we find ample instances of such abstract systems, e.g. a globally available cryptocurrency with blockchain-based data as "symbolic tokens" of value and also "expert systems" (meaning a system of experts, not to be confused with expert systems in the information technology (IT) terminology), e.g. social media, blogs and wikis, which are cocreated by experts and users from different areas. These abstract systems work to "bracket time and space" and engender the homogenised time–space distanciation in AIA.

> CEE 137: Tremendous efficiency enhancements have been achieved. Typical job roles and qualification profiles as well as where and when we work will have totally changed.

Reflexivity, as Giddens sees it, is at the very heart of modernity (Giddens, 1990a, 1991). Reflexivity is "introduced into the very basis of system reproduction, such that thought and action are constantly refracted back upon one another" (1990a, p. 38). Furthermore, Giddens observes "the fact that social practices are constantly examined and reformed in the light of incoming information about those very practices, thus constitutively altering their character" (ibid.). The thought of an empowered individual embedded in self-reinforcing discourses surrounding AIA, e.g. on social media, takes reflexivity to a whole new level. A permanent critical reflection of the inherent practices and conventions seems to have become the new norm rather than the exception. We are already observing the global "-post-postmodern" competition of discourses surrounding "what is true" (post-truth age) on social media; it is thus probable – given the strong embeddedness of AIA in the overall transformation of society – that such reflexivity may even have a decisive role with respect to the near future of AIA. While it was easy, e.g. to find a consensus on which technological innovations will be driving AIA forward, it was much less so in relation to interpretation of the (socially constructed) meaning of these innovations, e.g. for organisations or employees. What is more, this perception even changed over time between the rounds and sometimes strongly reversed polarity.

We may also see a new and additional dimension of reflexivity in AIA because of AI-powered "humanised" robots that use deep-state neuronal networks. To some extent, these networks are able to learn and even completely change based on their successes and failures. AI research already deals with problems of bias and the lack of transparency in the decision making of such systems (Sutton et al., 2016; Kokina & Davenport, 2017; Jarrahi, 2018), pointing out that this sort of backward-oriented learning omits evolving ethical standards based on political visions (Dignum, 2018).

In summary, reflexivity in AIA may mean both a strong acceleration for innovative accounting practices and, at the same time, utter resistance – e.g. on the dehumanisation of the workplace or based on the ethical concerns of putting too much agency into the hands of the AI – depending on individuals' norms and value systems and the change in perception based on self-reflexivity.

Two sides of a coin: systems and structures in Artificial Intelligence in Accounting

CEE 27: Artificial Intelligence in Accounting (AIA) is organised as a network of highly qualified teams empowered by (and partly consisting of) AI robots and other technologies to enhance communication, cognition and collaboration. The network is characterised by clear and accountable roles, an open physical as well as virtual environment, hands-on governance with highly agile methods, active partnerships, and a flat structure. Financial and managerial accountants, auditors, tax specialists, data scientists and software engineers work together in cross-functional teams on temporary projects. Representation in the sense of hierarchy is primarily based on company law requirements and compliance (necessity of board of directors, audit committees, supervisory board, etc.).

In his structuration theory, Giddens distinguishes between the situated practices, e.g. actual accounting practices, that form a system and can be observed and the structure(s) creating such systems, e.g. through norms and institutions. These, however, are subsequently changed and created through the enactment of practices in the system (Giddens, 1984). Due to the nature of the Delphi method enabling robust consensus-based forecasting, we were able to identify social systems of AIA over time, with more than one "optimum" system being true to the nature of path constitution, which comprises path dependence as well as path creation (Sydow et al., 2009). As Garud et al. (2010) write, "[G]iven a structurational process, our interests lie in exploring how embedded actors attempt to shape and navigate their ways through (or out of) such processes, knowing that other actors are attempting to do the same" (p. 760). Moreover, Sydow et al. (2009) earlier found: "Actors in the final phase do not simply experience the path; rather, as 'knowledgeable agents' … they have scope in interpreting the organisational patterns. This individual interpretation of the core (path) is likely to bring about some variation in actual organisational action patterns" (p. 695). In our data we find several competing potential expressions of AIA organisations, depending not only on the structures but also on the choices of individual actors, as has been discussed further in Chapter 5. Salient examples of different AIA organisations may include an almost fully automated "lean accounting organisation" that serves all external, but only limited internal, tasks with an outsourced service centre that responds to managerial change requests. Little strategic value is placed upon this system, and the focus is upon efficiency and compliance. At the opposite end of the spectrum, we find the "digitalised organisation" that strategically embraces data and any insights gained therefrom. A team of highly specialised people with vastly different skills continuously work together in order to gain a competitive advantage from the data by employing the latest innovative algorithms in AIA. The focus here is upon effectiveness and strategic value.

From these insights we further examined the structures that were dynamically creating and being created by said systems. These systems comprise the activities of human actors and were found by first identifying processes and then deriving practices in AIA in the various developmental stages. Our second question then asked: What are the main structures of signification, legitimation and domination that influence and control the evolvement of AIA into social systems, and how are these structures, in turn, influenced by the AIA systems that they create?

Examining the related structures, we can identify amongst structural archetypes a flat, hierarchical organisation in AIA teams, the importance of externalities such as regulations and technological innovations and the above-mentioned dis-embeddedness and time–space separation of the actors and activities in our data. Combining Giddens' (1984) notion of structures as "rules and resources, recursively implicated in the reproduction of social systems" (p. 377), with the specifics of AIA, we can, e.g. clearly identify the importance of "control" over the resources in the following consensus.

> CEE 135: While the development and implementation of new technologies still requires much knowhow, their usage is as simple and natural as connecting a vacuum cleaner to a power socket. All technologies and data are ultimately controlled with one fully autonomous accounting system with convenient human–computer interfaces including facial and speech recognition. The complexity lies in when to turn to the system for an answer, how to formulate the right questions, and if and when to "trust" the outcomes. Interpersonal trust may need to be replaced by institutional trust. Accountability and transparency of algorithms will thus be a core topic.

As Giddens (1984) puts it, "[S]tructure exists only as memory traces, the organic basis of human knowledgeability, as is instantiated in action" (p. 377). We were able to identify the following three dimensions of structure, or "memory traces", in AIA: signification rules, legitimation norms and the domination of resources and authority.

- Structures of signification allow people to make meaning of what they do and see by interpreting interactions in their own coding scheme. Thus, these structures of signification provide interpretative schemes or policies which enable a common understanding. AIA itself is such a term that is up for interpretation. It is often used as a structurally loaded term that signifies, e.g. innovation, dynamics and a somewhat unspecified "future". There are a number of signification structures competing with one another. We could identify a set of "positive" threads which see, e.g. *robots* standing for efficiency and the delegation of "boring" tasks to automated systems or denominating *data* as the new gold. On the other hand, and equally powerful in the discourse, there is a much more "negative" set. Therein, AIA as a whole is, e.g. seen as a major force that will drive people out of their jobs and disrupt the existing status quo of the accounting and auditing profession.
- Structures of legitimation are based on the norms and sanctions that enable but, at the same time, limit the conduct of the actors. These structures regulate practices and interactions and are often based on norms, e.g. on International Financial Reporting Standards (IFRS) or various non-financial reporting standards and on threatened sanctions in the case of deviations. Through this "corridor" of "do's and don'ts", legitimacy for those things that are classified as being "right" is created and enacted through practices – being imitated by followers – in the system. In our findings we can identify, amongst

other things, the high cognitive demand on digital accountants with respect to compliance with an even larger set of regulations in the future, driving the dynamic towards an FAAS. Additionally, our data shows that the legitimacy of AIA is largely rooted in the value assumptions of "higher efficiency and effectiveness", borrowing thus from traditional capitalist firm discourses and, at the same time, neglecting non-capitalist ideas of "better life quality" or fewer work hours with constant pay. Consequently, the delegitimisation structures are based on the negative impact on the workforce in terms of job losses, or the unwanted necessity to gain additional skills from previously untapped fields, such as IT, through intense training programs. What is more, the fear of "missing out" for organisations in terms of not embracing the promises of the new digital area of accounting was seen to be another legitimisation structure.

- Structures of domination comprise authority and resource allocation, including ideas of knowledge and power and providing facilities for the exercise of power. We find a consensus that the disposition of resources will be much more in the hands of automated robots, whereby leading to much higher efficiency. What is striking in AIA, however, is that there seems to be an "ethical void" in these structures (Baud et al., 2019). Our data shows that the human imagination falls short regarding what it might mean to give up authority (and control over resources) to an FAAS (see also Markus, 2017). Therefore, important humanist questions with regard to accountability, who has the ultimate decision-making authority and how to deal with vulnerable people may in the future be negotiated by the sheer power of "rationality" of the data and the above-mentioned legitimisation structures, instead of being guided by a normative structure based on human-centred philosophy and ethics (Dignum, 2018; Kelly & Murphy, 2021).

Finally, and based on Giddens' core structuration theory, it is vital to understand that these structures and social systems are recursively interrelated through the "duality" of structure (see Figure 9.2). The structural rules, norms and resources upon which actors draw in the production (and reproduction through enactment) of AIA as a social system are themselves the products of a preceding social system; thus, agents and structures do not constitute two independent sets of phenomena but rather can be seen as "two sides of a coin" (Giddens, 1990b; Englund et al., 2011). Figure 9.2 illustrates this continuity of production and reproduction of AIA systems. Giddens sees the structures as being relatively fixed (comprising rules and resources), forming a framework for activities in the systems. Such activities as "tacitly enacted practices" become "institutions or routines" (new structures) through their enactment by actors. Knowledgeable actors can influence this enactment through "reflexive monitoring" (as discussed above), or simply by choice (as will be elaborated upon in the next section).

In other words, while the structures create a social AIA system, the practices as well as the highly knowledgeable – and thus powerful – actors (as will be discussed further in the next section) in this system influence the structures and may even create new ones, whereby leading to new opportunity spaces. It may be noteworthy to point out that such opportunity spaces not only allow and permit changes and evolvement towards something (power to achieve) but also, at the same time, limit other and perhaps equally or more desirable opportunities for more vulnerable groups (power to control). This is especially true when resources such as technological innovations in AIA are highly dynamic and social systems are continuously confronted with, as we call it, "the dynamism of externalities".

This perspective is particularly relevant, given the context of the ever-evolving nature (changing signification rules, as mentioned above) of the "whatness" of AIA over time, as

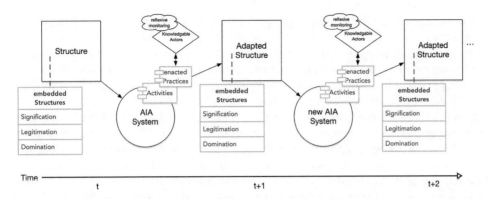

Figure 9.2   The "two sides of a coin" of the structure and system in Artificial Intelligence in Accounting and the impact of knowledgeable actors.

the structure-induced evolvement of social systems in AIA, e.g. through the implementation of specific data warehouses, software robots and the accompanying related practices, may influence the very structures through the enactment and subsequent reflection of these new practices by powerful, i.e. highly knowledgeable, actors.

Examples of this could include the integration of a data scientist as a *"highly knowledgeable actor"* within the team, who will point out, e.g. additional, innovative uses of big data in the data warehouse (Vasarhelyi et al., 2015; Janvrin et al., 2017); the introduction of blockchain access together with robotic process automation, allowing, e.g. to embrace efficient "triple-entry accounting" with encryption (Ijiri, 1986; Simoyama et al., 2017); or new Internet of Things-based "digital twins" (virtual copies of processes and products) that allow various simulations and can be accounted for as intangible assets under some circumstances.

The transformative capacity of human agents in Artificial Intelligence in Accounting

CEE 28: A digitally fluent person also understands why the use of the system is important and when it is appropriate or inappropriate and suggests necessary changes in the processes and activities of a firm in order to achieve better outcomes in terms of effectivity and efficiency. Some Information Technology (IT) knowhow will thus become part of the common domain knowhow in accounting.

It is vital to understand the importance of highly knowledgeable actors in Giddens' thoughts on the duality of structures (see Figure 9.2), which also connects to the previous notion of reflexivity with respect to practices that allow every involved actor to think about (or re-think) the system and how their own activities relate to it. We thus do not claim that any identified structure will result in an exact social system of AIA or predict human action therein, or that the specifics of an observed setting of such a system will inevitably create a certain structure. This is because, as Englund & Gerdin (2014), following Giddens (1984), write, "human agents know a great deal about the conditions for, and consequences of, what they do in day-to-day practices and, based on this, they can always choose to do otherwise" (p. 164). This goes well with Orlikowski (2000), who examines technology and constituting structures specifically and develops a practical lens in order "to examine how people, as they interact with a technology in their ongoing practices, enact structures which shape their emergent and situated use of that technology" and continues to state "viewing the use of technology as a process of enactment enables a deeper understanding of the constitutive role of social practices in the ongoing use and change of technologies in the workplace" (p. 367).

We found the concept of a "digitally fluent person" (as depicted in CEE 28) to be particularly helpful in describing the set of knowledge that would help to identify and characterise the level of power that a specific actor possesses, noting that CEE 28 does not include any mention (or necessity) of a deep understanding of humanist thoughts and ethics and is based in the very legitimisation structure of "efficiency and effectiveness" (as discussed in the previous paragraphs) – something that may be clearly alarming in light of the above-mentioned opportunity spaces. It is noteworthy at this stage that our open questions in the Delphi study about the future of AI in accounting did deliberately not put any focus on technical, functionalist or normative, ethical perspectives (or any others), and it was the free choice of the participants to select their angles to argue and describe.

Our third research question thus asks: What is the "dialectic of power" in this dynamic process towards AIA, i.e. who controls the expression of the structures and influences the enactment, and who are the "highly knowledgeable" actors? However, because of the difficulties surrounding the social "positioning" of such actors in systems with a high time–space fluidity, wherein the distanciation, dis-embedding and re-embedding mechanisms are highly prevalent, we need to pay particular attention to what Cohen (1990) calls the "reproduction of systemic activities" and the "knowledge of practices across time and space".

> CEE 97: The CFO has evolved into a CFIO (Chief Financial and Information Officer) with a strong digital fluency. The roles of IT and accounting/finance have grown together at the top. The CFIO has become one of the most important persons because he has the control over all data. His roles are Business Steward (supporting financial performance and ensuring compliance), Business Partner (supporting all business units in achieving strategic goals) and Transformation Agent (realising efficiency gains through company-wide process optimisation). The CFIO shares purpose and vision, gives actionable strategic guidance, promotes flexible resource allocation, and acts as enabler for his team.

As a particularly salient and highly knowledgeable actor, the CFIO has been identified in the findings of this study in CEE 97. The combination of controlling both data and finance in one person makes the CFIO the "ideal" transformation agent, who clearly possesses the power to change the enactment of practices and, thus, influence the opportunity space for further development of the organisation. It is a position of enormous key power that will foreseeably dominate other departments and perhaps exert an even stronger influence on the CEO because of the inherent "rationality" of data and financial information (ter Bogt & Scapens, 2019). From a critical, scholarly perspective though, it must be cautioned that this consensus might not take into account future, partly temporal and ad hoc, inter- and intra-organisational forms that may comprise various structures for different purposes. The mere existence of such an institution as a CFO or CFIO thus may be questioned (Carpenter et al., 2004, Menz, 2012).

In AIA, as in all social systems, however, people can always choose to either embrace the changes that are imposed by the structure or refuse them, or even find new and innovative ways and influence the structure, in turn. Besides the above-discussed intentionality towards change, another reason for change through knowledgeable actors may constitute the unexpected consequences of planned activities of which actors become aware through their reflexive monitoring. E.g. the introduction of new decision support systems in AIA (Jarrahi, 2018), with the intentionality of increasing the rationality of managerial decisions, may lead to the unexpected consequence of decisions that would be logically sound, compliant with existing regulations and anchored in the data but that would go completely against the corporate social responsibility culture of an organisation (Leicht-Deobald et al., 2019). In evaluating their actions, management may thus consequently (and hopefully) choose to introduce a new practice in the form of an additional check and balance level by humans.

What is more, in AIA lie the onset of and potential eye-to-eye collaboration with artificial, albeit partly humanised, actors such as robots (Cooper et al., 2018; Fernandez & Aman, 2018; Rozario & Vasarhelyi, 2018) with given names and logins such as "Roberta", with varying sets of cognitive capabilities, ranging from simple document and text interpretation skills and natural speech recognition to a full awareness of what constitutes the norm and what might potentially be fraudulent, as well as varying degrees of decision-making power.

> CEE 71: Software robots will play a vital role in Artificial Intelligence in Accounting (AIA). Besides taking over repetitive tasks that can easily be automated, the further advancement of artificial intelligence will lead to a tremendous improvement in terms of their value. Pattern and speech recognition as well as connected deep-learning, neuronal networks in the background will make them indispensable in their role as discussion and decision partners.

There was no consensus as to whether these robots would count as real AI, although the majority would pass a "Turing Test" under certain circumstances (Sutton et al., 2016; Parteke et al., 2018); however, the practice of allowing these robots to arrive at their own conclusions, with the subsequent power of (at least suggesting) resource-controlling actions and authoritative decision making, evokes the feeling that these robots might need to be accounted for in the future as empowered and highly knowledgeable individuals with the potential to change the system and reflect on the structures. As a highly problematic issue in AIA, the learning of these robots from past events and data would lead to strong biases through a sole orientation towards the past, instead of the inherently human creative potential of looking forward based on visions. What is more, the notion of "accountability" needs another dimension to be examined, as the question of *"who is responsible?"* with respect to robot-based decisions may not be easily answered (Cooper et al., 2018). Robots may be both a source of erroneous decisions (albeit fully logical ones within a set of pregiven assumptions) and the target of wrongful accusations and ex post legitimisation of erroneous decisions by human co-workers. A strong set of ethical guidelines with transparency rules and constant reviews, the inclusion of actors with a humanities background contributing additional perspectives to the business domain and an ascertained domination of human decision making may constitute ways in which to deal with these problems (Endenich & Trapp, 2018; Kelly & Murphy, 2021).

Summing up and revisiting the transformative capacity of highly knowledgeable agents (as depicted above), it is important to understand Giddens' (1984) "dialectic of control" in order to analyse power relations. It is closely related to the previous mentions of the importance of control over resources and indicates that, regardless of the power of individual actors, there are always some resources that actors who are subjected to, e.g. hierarchical power can come up with and assemble in order to influence the conduct of their "superiors"

(Englund & Gerdin, 2011; Englund et al., 2011). We see, e.g. "whistleblowing platforms" as such resources or – on an even broader societal scale – AI-powered financial technologies. Both may help to overcome dependency and empower agents, who also further form and influence these developments, e.g. through open innovation and crowdfunding. Yet, this empowerment and the resulting "situated practices" may well, in turn, create structures that exert power over others, e.g. members of the workforce who are not so tech-savvy and would prefer a personal interaction instead of a computerised AI-powered one (Goldberg et al., 2016).

Conclusion and future outlook

Within this chapter we introduce AIA as a research field that is strongly embedded in the larger societal transformation, critically deconstruct its "whatness" and provide a way in which to understand its inherent dynamics as well as structures of signification, legitimisation and domination by making use of Giddens' ample structuration toolkit and his insights into modernity. Concerning ontological considerations, we show that structuration theory (Englund et al., 2011; Conrad, 2014), with its notion of transcending the structure–agent separation towards a system of accountability (Lukka & Vinnari, 2014) with situated practices (Conrad, 2014), can be seen as being highly appropriate in understanding and, thus, guiding research into AIA.

Summarising our findings, we first identify the analogies of Giddens' modernity with AIA systems, discuss the time–space separation of technology and a globally dispersed accounting workforce and examine the related mechanisms of dis-embedding and reflexivity. Thereafter, we introduce the duality perspective as a valuable concept in understanding the constant interplay between a structure and a system in AIA through its accounting-related activities and enacted practices and find that resulting "opportunity spaces" (Jing & Benner, 2016) are consequently influenced not only by existing structures but also very much so by the individuals, the highly knowledgeable actors in their enactment and individual choices. In the persona of a CFIO, we not only found and described such a salient individual but also pointed out how "subordinates" might be empowered through technology, such as whistleblowing systems and AI, and further defined "digital fluency" as a key set of competencies. Said opportunity spaces can not only enable but also limit the future expression of AIA systems, and, therewith, we relate to the concept of path creation (Garud et al., 2010) and see AIA as a result of past choices that differ in their expressions and strategic motivations.

Finally, and as a result, in this conclusion and outlook section, we want to provide a basis for researching and theorising both change and continuity in accounting. As we were able to show from our data, any transformation of such gravity in accounting will go together with a substantial organisational transformation (Puranam et al., 2014; Oakes & Oakes, 2018; Phiri & Guven-Uslu, 2019). The interplay between the nucleus of an accounting transformation and the immediate organisational as well as the larger societal context will thus be one of the important issues for further research in the field of (critical) accounting and organisations. Our structuration approach, however, should by no means limit future research endeavours in this area, framed, e.g. in a neo-institutional theoretical setting that accepts the separation of human actors and structure and takes a certain drive for the standardisation and isomorphic adaptation of AIA for granted (Alvesson & Spicer, 2019; ter Bogt & Scapens, 2019) or looks at the legitimacy of AIA (Deegan, 2019). To understand the inherent dynamics, Latour's Actor-Network Theory (ANT), which adds non-humans as actors (Latour, 2005; Justesen et al., 2011; Lukka & Vinnari, 2017;

Robson & Bottausci, 2018) and creates fluid accounting objects that are translated into a system, would be another good choice for future research, as it overcomes the necessity for actors to be human. Finally, configuration theory (and, earlier, contingency theory), with its focus on the organisational gestalt or habitus (Bourdieu & Nice, 1977; Miller, 1987, 1996; Alvesson & Sandberg, 2014) being shaped by complex contextual interplay (Otley & Berry, 1980), may be another worthwhile perspective from which to understand and explain the organisational changes that we expect to see in the coming years (Zammuto et al., 2007). What all of these theoretical approaches have in common is that they lean towards a pragmatic worldview (Modell, Vinnari, & Lukka, 2017), which is not limited by the often artificially conjured dichotomy of a realist versus constructivist ontology in the social sciences (Ahrens, 2008) and, thus, allows researchers to embrace a variety of epistemological approaches with a range of suitable research designs.

What is more, a strong focus on the micro level – i.e. on the human factor in the transformation towards fully autonomous accounting – seems to be timely and apt (Annisette & Richardson, 2011; Gill, 2019). On the one hand, it is certainly pressing from a practical point of view, as technological advancements will inevitably have a strong impact on the existing roles, duties and corresponding skills of workers, managers and recipients of reports in the accounting profession (Neely & Cook, 2011), as well as on stakeholders in general. An interesting critical avenue for future research into this is opened by Kellogg et al. (2020), who examine "algorithmic control" in the workplace and apply labour process theory so as to identify six main mechanisms, or, as they call them, "the 6 Rs": algorithms direct workers by "restricting and recommending", evaluate workers through "recording and rating" and discipline workers by "replacing and rewarding". Corroborating our study, they observe that "the technical capabilities of algorithmic systems facilitate a form of rational control that is distinct from the technical and bureaucratic control used by employers for the past century".

On the other hand, and for the employees in the field, we need to understand the new job roles and matching qualifications that are necessary in order to not only persist in this new area (Frey & Osborne, 2017) but also help deal with the aberrations and the possible negative impact on vulnerable communities that any change process will inevitably bring (Eubanks, 2018), with the ultimate goal being to further develop the accounting profession towards accountability and societal relevance (Burchell et al., 1980; Robson, 1991). Questions in this area will be concerned not only with the career prospects, related skills and how our education systems can deal with the demand but also with the necessary tools with which to support human cognition (given the highly abstract and aggregated level of information such as visualisations and interactions) (Schick, Gordon, & Haka, 1990; Eppler & Mengis, 2004); with the psychological factors with regard to change management and the necessity to adapt (Robson, 1991; Beaubien, 2012; Langley, Smallman, Tsoukas, & Van de Ven, 2013); and, finally, with ethics, power and control (Baud et al., 2019; Domínguez-Escrig et al., 2019). Therein, Foucauldian perspectives on what constitutes power in AIA from a critical discourse perspective (Gendron, 2018) may help to identify power inequalities and allow raising the right questions in society (Hacking, 2004). The metatheories of capabilities or the Resource-Based View, finally, will provide other suitable – more functionalist and less critical – approaches with respect to understanding and guiding the interplay between organisational leadership and the role of humans in an autonomous accounting world, as these may help us to understand how a competitive advantage can be created and maintained through careful leadership and HR development in light of such rapid organisational transformations (Alexy et al., 2018; Nason & Wiklund, 2018).

References

Ahrens, T. (2008). Overcoming the subjective–objective divide in interpretive management accounting research, *Accounting, Organisations and Society*, 33(2–3), 292–297.

Alexy, O., West, J., Klapper, H. &. Reitzig, M. (2018). Surrendering control to gain advantage: Reconciling openness and the resource-based view of the firm, *Strategic Management Journal*, 39(6), 1704–1727.

Alvesson, M. & Sandberg, J. (2014). Habitat and habitus: Boxed-in versus box-breaking research, *Organisation Studies*, 35(7), 967–987.

Alvesson, M. & Spicer, A. (2019). Neo-institutional theory and organisation studies: A mid-life crisis?, *Organisation Studies*, 40(2), 199–218.

Annisette, M. & Richardson, A. J. (2011). Justification and accounting: Applying sociology of worth to accounting research, *Accounting, Auditing & Accountability Journal*, 24(2), 229–249.

Armstrong, S., Sotala, K. & Ó hÉigeartaigh, S. S. (2014). The errors, insights and lessons of famous AI predictions–and what they mean for the future. *Journal of Experimental & Theoretical Artificial Intelligence*, 26(3), 317–342.

Baud, C., Brivot, M. & Himick, D. (2019). Accounting ethics and the fragmentation of value, *Journal of Business Ethics*, 168, 373–387.

Beaubien, L. (2012). Technology, change, and management control: A temporal perspective, *Accounting, Auditing & Accountability Journal*, 26(1), 48–74.

Bogt, H. J. t. & Scapens, R. W. (2019). Institutions, situated rationality and agency in management accounting: A research note extending the Burns and Scapens framework, *Accounting, Auditing & Accountability Journal*, 32(6), 1801–1825.

Bourdieu, P. & Nice, R. (1977). *Outline of a Theory of Practice*, Cambridge University Press, Cambridge.

Burchell, S., Clubb, C., Hopwood, A., Hughes, J. & Nahapiet, J. (1980). The roles of accounting in organisations and society, *Accounting, Organizations and Society*, 5(1), 5–27.

Burrell, G. & Morgan, G. (2019). *Sociological Paradigms and Organisational Analysis: Elements of the Sociology of Corporate Life*, London: Routledge.

Carpenter, M. A., Geletkanycz, M. A. & Sanders, W. G. (2004). Upper echelons research revisited: Antecedents, elements, and consequences of top management team composition. *Journal of Management*, 30(6), 749–778.

Christensen, C. M., McDonald, R., Altman, E. J. & Palmer, J. E. (2018). Disruptive innovation: An intellectual history and directions for future research, *Journal of Management Studies*, 55(7), 1043–1078.

Cohen, S. (1990). Skepticism and Everyday Knowledge Attributions. In: Roth, M.D., Ross, G. (Eds.) *Doubting. Philosophical Studies Series*. Berlin: Springer, 48, 161–169. https://doi.org/10.1007/978-94-009-1942-6_13

Conrad, L. (2014). Reflections on the application of and potential for structuration theory in accounting research, *Critical Perspectives on Accounting*, 25(2), 128–134.

Cooper, L. A., Holderness Jr, D. K., Sorensen, T. L. & Wood, D. A. (2018). Robotic process automation in public accounting, *Accounting Horizons*, 33(4), 15–35.

Dai, J. & Vasarhelyi, M. A. (2017). Toward blockchain-based accounting and assurance, *Journal of Information Systems*, 31(3), 5–21.

Deegan, C. M. (2019). Legitimacy theory, *Accounting, Auditing & Accountability Journal*, 32(8), 2307–2329.

Dignum, V. (2018). Ethics in artificial intelligence: Introduction to the special issue, *Ethics and Information Technology*, 20(1), 1–3.

Domínguez-Escrig, E., Mallén-Broch, F. F., Lapiedra-Alcamí, R. & Chiva-Gómez, R. (2019). The influence of leaders' stewardship behavior on innovation success: The mediating effect of radical innovation, *Journal of Business Ethics*, 159(3), 849–862.

Endenich, C. & Trapp, R. (2018). Ethical implications of management accounting and control: A systematic review of the contributions from the Journal of Business Ethics, *Journal of Business Ethics*, 163, 309–328.

Englund, H. & Gerdin, J. (2011). Agency and structure in management accounting research: Reflections and extensions of Kilfoyle and Richardson, *Critical Perspectives on Accounting*, 22(6), 581–592.

Englund, H. & Gerdin, J. (2014). Structuration theory in accounting research: Applications and applicability, *Critical Perspectives on Accounting*, 25(2), 162–180.

Englund, H., Gerdin, J. & Burns, J. (2011). 25 Years of Giddens in accounting research: Achievements, limitations and the future, *Accounting, Organisations and Society*, 36(8), 494–513.

Eppler, M. J. & Mengis, J. (2004). The concept of information overload: A review of literature from organisation science, accounting, marketing, MIS, and related disciplines, *The Information Society*, 20(5), 325–344.

Eubanks, V. (2018). *Automating Inequality: How High-Tech Tools Profile, Police, and Punish the Poor*, New York: St. Martin's Press.

Fernandez, D. & Aman, A. (2018). Impacts of robotic process automation on global accounting services, *Asian Journal of Accounting and Governance*, 9, 123–132.

Frey, C. B. & Osborne, M. A. (2017). The future of employment: How susceptible are jobs to computerisation?, *Technological Forecasting and Social Change*, 114, 254–280.

Gallego, D. & Bueno, S. (2014). Exploring the application of the Delphi method as a forecasting tool in Information Systems and Technologies research, *Technology Analysis & Strategic Management*, 26(-9), 987–999.

Garud, R., Kumaraswamy, A. & Karnøe, P. (2010). Path dependence or path creation?, *Journal of Management Studies*, 47(4), 760–774.

Gendron, Y. (2018). On the elusive nature of critical (accounting) research, *Critical Perspectives on Accounting*, 50, 1–12.

Ghasemi, M., Shafeiepour, V., Aslani, M. & Barvayeh, E. (2011). The impact of Information Technology (IT) on modern accounting systems, *Procedia - Social and Behavioral Sciences*, 28, 112–116.

Giddens, A. (1981). Agency, institution, and time-space analysis, in Knorr-Cetina, K. & Cicourel, A. V. (Eds.). *Advances in Social Theory and Methodology*. Routledge & Kegan Paul, Boston, MA, 161–174.

Giddens, A. (1984). *The constitution of society: Outline of the theory of structuration*, Berkeley: University of California Press.

Giddens, A. (1990a). *The Consequences of Modernity*, Polity Press, Cambridge.

Giddens, A. (1990b). Structuration theory and sociological analysis, in Clark, J., Modgil, C. & Modgil, S. (Eds.). *Anthony Giddens: Consensus and Controversy*. Falmer Press, London, 297–315.

Giddens, A. (1991). *Modernity and Self-identity: Self and Society in the Late Modern Age*, Redwood City: Stanford University Press.

Giddens, A. & Pierson, C. (1998). *Conversations with Anthony Giddens: Making Sense of Modernity*, Polity Press, Cambridge.

Gill, M. J. (2019). The significance of suffering in organisations: Understanding variation in workers' responses to multiple modes of control, *Academy of Management Review*, 44(2), 377–404.

Goldberg, A., Srivastava, S. B., Manian, V. G., Monroe, W. & Potts, C. (2016). Fitting in or standing out? The tradeoffs of structural and cultural embeddedness, *American Sociological Review*, 81(6), 1190–1222.

Grace, K., Salvatier, J., Dafoe, A., Zhang, B. & Evans, O. (2018). When will AI exceed human performance? Evidence from AI experts. *Journal of Artificial Intelligence Research*, 62, 729–754.

Güney, A. (2014). Role of technology in accounting and E-accounting, *Procedia - Social and Behavioral Sciences*, 152, 852–855.

Hacking, I. (2004). Between Michel Foucault and Erving Goffman: Between discourse in the abstract and face-to-face interaction, *Economy and Society*, 33(3), 277–302.

Hinings, B., Gegenhuber, T. & Greenwood, R. (2018). Digital innovation and transformation: An institutional perspective, *Information and Organisation*, 28(1), 52–61.

Ijiri, Y. (1986). A framework for triple-entry bookkeeping, *Accounting Review*, 745–759.

Janvrin, D. J. & Weidenmier Watson, M. (2017). Big Data: A new twist to accounting, *Journal of Accounting Education*, 38, 3–8.

Jarrahi, M. H. (2018). Artificial intelligence and the future of work: Human-AI symbiosis in organisational decision making, *Business Horizons*, 61(4), 577–586.

Jing, R. & Benner, M. (2016). Institutional regime, opportunity space and organisational path constitution: Case studies of the conversion of military firms in China, *Journal of Management Studies*, 53(4), 552–579.

Justesen, L., Baker, C. R. & Mouritsen, J. (2011). Effects of actor-network theory in accounting research, *Accounting, Auditing & Accountability Journal*, 24(2), 161–193.

Kellogg, K., Valentine, M. & Christin, A. (2020). Algorithms at work: The new contested terrain of control, *Academy of Management Annals*, 14(1), 366–410.

Kelly, K. & Murphy, P. R. (2021). Reducing accounting aggressiveness with general ethical norms and decision structure, *Journal of Business Ethics*, 170, 97–113.

Kokina, J. & Blanchette, S. (2019). Early evidence of digital labor in accounting: Innovation with Robotic process automation, *International Journal of Accounting Information Systems*, 35, 100431.

Kokina, J. & Davenport, T. H. (2017). The emergence of artificial intelligence: How automation is changing auditing, *Journal of Emerging Technologies in Accounting*, 14(1), 115–122.

Kokina, J., Mancha, R. & Pachamanova, D. (2017). Blockchain: Emergent industry adoption and implications for accounting, *Journal of Emerging Technologies in Accounting*, 14(2), 91–100.

Kruskopf, S., Lobbas, C., Meinander, H., Söderling, K., Martikainen, M. & Lehner, O. (2019). Digital accounting: Opportunities, threats and the human factor, *ACRN Oxford Journal of Finance and Risk Perspectives*, 8, 1–15.

Langley, A., Smallman, C., Tsoukas, H. & Van de Ven, A. H. (2013). Process studies of change in organisation and management: Unveiling temporality, activity, and flow, *Academy of Management Journal*, 56(1), 1–13.

Latour, B. (2005). *Reassembling the Social: An Introduction to Actor-Network-Theory*, Oxford: Oxford University Press.

Lehner, O. M., Leitner-Hanetseder, S. & Eisl, C. (2019). The Whatness of Digital Accounting: Status Quo and Ways to Move Forward, *ACRN Journal of Finance and Risk Perspectives*, 8, 2.

Leicht-Deobald, U., Busch, T., Schank, C., Weibel, A., Schafheitle, S., Wildhaber, I. & Kasper, G. (2019). The challenges of algorithm-based HR decision-making for personal integrity, *Journal of Business Ethics*, 160, 377–392.

Losbichler, H. & Lehner, O.M. (2021), Limits of artificial intelligence in controlling and the ways forward: a call for future accounting research, *Journal of Applied Accounting Research*, 22 (2), 365–382. https://doi.org/10.1108/JAAR-10-2020-0207

Lukka, K. & Vinnari, E. (2014). Domain theory and method theory in management accounting research, *Accounting, Auditing & Accountability Journal*, 27(8), 1308–1338.

Lukka, K. & Vinnari, E. (2017). Combining actor-network theory with interventionist research: Present state and future potential, *Accounting, Auditing & Accountability Journal*, 30(3), 720–753.

Markus, M. L. (2017). Datification, organisational strategy, and is research: What's the score?. *The Journal of Strategic Information Systems*, 26(3), 233–241.

Menz, M. (2012). Functional top management team members: A review, synthesis, and research agenda. *Journal of Management*, 38(1), 45–80.

Miller, D. (1987). The genesis of configuration, *Academy of Management Review*, 12(4), 686–701.

Miller, D. (1996). Configurations revisited, *Strategic Management Journal*, 17(7), 505–512.

Modell, S., Vinnari, E. & Lukka, K. (2017). On the virtues and vices of combining theories: The case of institutional and actor-network theories in accounting research, *Accounting, Organisations and Society*, 60, 62–78.

Nason, R. S. & Wiklund, J. (2018). An assessment of resource-based theorizing on firm growth and suggestions for the future, *Journal of Management*, 44(1), 32–60.

Neely, M. P. & Cook, J. S. (2011). Fifteen years of data and information quality literature: Developing a research agenda for accounting, *Journal of Information Systems*, 25(1), 79–108.

Oakes, H. & Oakes, S. (2018). An overture for organisational transformation with accounting and music, *Critical Perspectives on Accounting*, 64, 102067.

Okoli, C. & Pawlowski, S. D. (2004). The Delphi method as a research tool: An example, design considerations and applications, *Information & Management*, 42(1), 15–29.

Orlikowski, W. J. (2000). Using technology and constituting structures: A practice lens for studying technology in organisations, *Organisation Science*, 11(4), 404–428.

Otley, D. T. & Berry, A. J. (1980). Control, organisation and accounting, *Accounting, Organisations and Society*, 5(2), 231–244.

Parteke, U. R., Yewele, N. R. & Kanoje, S. F. (2018). Artificial intelligence in various sectors, *International Journal of Research*, 5(13), 268–277.

Phiri, J. & Guven-Uslu, P. (2019). Social networks, corruption and institutions of accounting, auditing and accountability, *Accounting, Auditing & Accountability Journal*, 32(2), 508–530.

Puranam, P., Alexy, O. & Reitzig, M. (2014). What's new about new forms of organising?, *Academy of Management Review*, 39(2), 162–180.

Quattrone, P. (2016). Management accounting goes digital: Will the move make it wiser?, *Management Accounting Research*, 31, 118–122.

Quinn, M. & Strauss, E. (2017). *The Routledge Companion to Accounting Information Systems*, London: Routledge.

Robson, K. (1991). On the arenas of accounting change: The process of translation, *Accounting, Organisations and Society*, 16(5), 547–570.

Robson, K. & Bottausci, C. (2018). The sociology of translation and accounting inscriptions: Reflections on Latour and Accounting Research, *Critical Perspectives on Accounting*, 54, 60–75.

Rozario, A. M. & Vasarhelyi, M. A. (2018). How robotic process automation is transforming accounting and auditing, *The CPA Journal*, 88(6), 46–49.

Schick, A. G., Gordon, L. A. & Haka, S. (1990). Information overload: A temporal approach, *Accounting, Organisations and Society*, 15(3), 199–220.

Simoyama, F. D. O., Grigg, I., Bueno, R. L. P. & Oliveira, L. C. D. (2017). Triple entry ledgers with blockchain for auditing, *International Journal of Auditing Technology*, 3(3), 163–183.

Sledgianowski, D., Gomaa, M. & Tan, C. (2017). Toward integration of Big Data, technology and information systems competencies into the accounting curriculum, *Journal of Accounting Education*, 38, 81–93.

Stancheva-Todorova, E. P. (2018). How artificial intelligence is challenging accounting profession, *Economy & Business Journal*, 12(1), 126–141.

Suchman, L. (1995). Supporting articulation work. In Kling, R. (Ed.). *Computerization and Controversy (2nd ed.) Value Conflicts and Social Choices*. Academic Press, New York, 407–423.

Sutton, S. G., Holt, M. & Arnold, V. (2016). The reports of my death are greatly exaggerated— Artificial intelligence research in accounting, *International Journal of Accounting Information Systems*, 22, 60–73.

Sydow, J., Schreyögg, G. & Koch, J. (2009). Organisational path dependence: Opening the black box, *Academy of Management Review*, 34(4), 689–709.

Tabrizi, B., Lam, E., Girard, K. & Irvin, V. (2019). Digital transformation is not about technology, *Harvard Business Review*, 13, 1–6.

Taipaleenmäki, J. & Ikäheimo, S. (2013). On the convergence of management accounting and financial accounting – the role of information technology in accounting change, *International Journal of Accounting Information Systems*, 14(4), 321–348.

Vasarhelyi, M. A., Kogan, A. & Tuttle, B. M. (2015). Big Data in accounting: An overview, *Accounting Horizons,* 29(2), 381–396.

Verhoef, P. C., Broekhuizen, T., Bart, Y., Bhattacharya, A., Dong, J. Q., Fabian, N. & Haenlein, M. (2021). Digital transformation: A multidisciplinary reflection and research agenda, *Journal of Business Research*, 122, 889–901.

Vial, G. (2019). Understanding digital transformation: A review and a research agenda, *The Journal of Strategic Information Systems*, 28(2), 118–144.

Vial, G., Jiang, J., Giannelia, T. & Cameron, A. F. (2021). The data problem stalling AI. *MIT Sloan Management Review*, 62(2), 47–53.

Worrell, J. L., Di Gangi, P. M. & Bush, A. A. (2013). Exploring the use of the Delphi method in accounting information systems research, *International Journal of Accounting Information Systems*, 14(3), 193–208.

Zammuto, R. F., Griffith, T. L., Majchrzak, A., Dougherty, D. J. & Faraj, S. (2007). Information technology and the changing fabric of organisation, *Organisation Science*, 18(5), 749–762.

10

OUTSOURCING OF ACCOUNTING INFORMATION SYSTEMS

Benoit A. Aubert and Jean-Grégoire Bernard

Introduction

Outsourcing of information systems activities continues to grow. Companies regularly use a combination of employees, local vendors and offshore providers for their accounting information systems services. In this way they can create the optimal combination to take advantage of best prices and talents worldwide. The demand for outsourcing services was notably driven by advances in cloud computing and the provision of business processes as a service (Deloitte, 2014). Recent events have given a boost to information technology (IT) outsourcing. With the Covid-19 pandemic, many companies have relied on IT suppliers to upgrade their IT portfolio, for instance, by enabling employees to work remotely and by introducing artificial intelligence components to offer services without human intervention (UpsilonIT, 2021). IT outsourcing companies have partnered with clients to help them upgrade capabilities and adapt to a new reality (Jogani et al., 2020). In light of these facts, it is important to understand what outsourcing is. It is also essential to recognise the four key decisions a manager has to make when considering the outsourcing of accounting information systems activities, that is, the activities and technologies that enable an organisation to collect, store and process financial and non-financial accounting data and convert it into information that is then capable of supporting organisational decision-making (Cleary, 2017, p. 7).

This chapter starts by defining outsourcing, clarifying the difference with offshoring and providing examples of the numerous ways outsourcing can be used for accounting information systems. Following this definition, the key decisions associated with outsourcing are described as follows:

1 What activity to outsource, and why?
2 How to design the outsourcing contract in a way that extracts the best possible outcome from the vendor while protecting the client?
3 How to manage the relationship between vendors and client? What communication and collaboration mechanisms should be implemented?
4 How to assess and mitigate the risk of outsourcing decisions?

Finally, new managerial dilemmas posed by recent technological advances are outlined. The move of accounting information systems to a cloud-based ecosystem of service providers is

DOI: 10.4324/9781003132943-13

forcing managers to rethink how the accounting function is organised in the 21st century. When trying to appreciate issues associated with the outsourcing of accounting information systems, it is important to realise that a large proportion of issues are the same as the ones associated with outsourcing of information systems in general. Therefore, elements presented in this chapter that are pertaining to the outsourcing decision are not specific to accounting. These elements are as relevant for accounting information systems as they would be for other types of systems. However, outsourcing of accounting information systems, because of the importance of accounting data in the organisation, brings some specific challenges. These aspects are discussed in the following section detailing the managerial dilemmas. Finally, the chapter points out the necessity of future research and concludes the discussion.

Defining outsourcing

Outsourcing is fundamentally a make-or-buy decision (McLaughlin & Peppard, 2006). Companies can opt to use their own employees to perform a task or rely on a vendor to get the work done. When considering IT activities, companies can use their own infrastructure and staff to perform the activities or rely on suppliers to provide these as a service. This last option is called outsourcing. Formally, outsourcing is the decision to rely on an external party for a product or service instead of conducting the corresponding activities inside the organisation (Alaghehband et al., 2011). Outsourcing takes many forms. In some cases, activities are performed by a supplier's employees inside the client's premises. In such cases, the supplier emulates the behaviour of internal employees, ensuring daily interactions with internal staff. In other circumstances, services are provided from a different location. In those cases, companies are usually seeking economies of scale, letting their supplier pool activities with similar ones for other clients. In these situations, the activities can be conducted in the same region, or at great distance.

When companies select suppliers abroad to take advantage of other countries' lower cost structures, outsourcing becomes offshore outsourcing, often shortened to "offshoring" (Rottman & Lacity, 2006). In these situations, services are offered from foreign locations. It is important to remember that while outsourcing always refers to the use of suppliers, offshoring may involve using the company's own employees offshore. As shown in Figure 10.1, the decision to use a supplier and the decision to go offshore are two different decisions, even if they are made at the same time (Dedrick et al., 2011).

A brief history of outsourcing

While the popularity of IT outsourcing has grown significantly since the late 1980s, it is not a new phenomenon. As early as the 1960s, time-sharing services were in place to allow different companies that did not have their own computers to use computer resources in shared mode (Abbate, 2001). By the early 1980s, there was a large group of suppliers offering IT outsourcing services, though these services were not very visible in the business world. In 1989, Kodak, which was seen as a sophisticated user of IT at the time, announced that its IT services would be outsourced (Wilder, 1989). The contract was large for those times and entailed the transfer of over 500 employees to the three chosen suppliers (Brown, 1990). This contract became highly publicised and led to several more contracts, often influenced by the legitimacy given to outsourcing by the Kodak-IBM arrangement (Loh & Venkatraman, 1992). It also signalled the entry of IBM into the IT service industry (IBM, 2002). In the following years, the outsourcing industry saw the signing of several multi-billion-dollar contracts.

Geographical distance – localisation decision

		Activities performed at or near the client's main premises	Activities performed offshore
Organisational distance – make or buy decision	Activities performed by a supplier	Outsourcing	Offshore outsourcing
	Activities performed by employees of the client organisation	Internal organisation	Offshoring (offshore branch or centre)

Figure 10.1 Outsourcing and offshoring decisions.

The trend that followed outsourcing in the 1990s was offshoring. As shown in Figure 10.1, offshoring means that activities are transferred offshore. During that period, companies were not necessarily seeking to transfer activities to suppliers. They were mostly assessing where to locate their activities. Taking advantage of rapidly falling telecommunication costs and an increasingly qualified workforce in low-wage economies, companies moved some IT activities and business processes overseas. While encountering some resistance in developed countries, this contributed to the overall productivity of organisations (Blinder, 2006). In several ways, the offshoring of IT services parallels the relocation of manufacturing activities observed in the second half of the 20th century. As the skills of workers in developing countries increased, offshore companies were able to offer very competitive services to companies worldwide. Because IT services are purely digital, moving them offshore was especially easy, facilitated by the development of Internet.

Currently, outsourcing and offshoring have become part of the daily lives of managers. Client firms routinely use suppliers for IT services. This has been reinforced by the growth of cloud computing and cloud services. In general, most firms now eschew all-encompassing and very large contracts. These contracts, observed in the late 1990s, are not seen as ideal anymore. Companies use outsourcing more selectively, targeting the most appropriate services for this type of governance. They also call on multiple suppliers, taking advantage of the specific expertise of each one to gain access to expertise while avoiding lock-in problems.

Outsourcing of accounting information systems

Outsourcing takes many forms and is used for many different types of activities, including accounting information systems. Outsourcing can be used to develop and implement new accounting information systems or to operate them once they are implemented. Arrangements for outsourcing accounting system operations range from the mere provision of computer hosting services to contracting the whole accounting business process to an external provider. These various options are discussed in the following paragraphs.

Outsourcing the development of accounting information systems

Outsourcing is often used to develop and implement new information systems. It comes in two main varieties: using a provider for the software and/or consultants to configure the software. It is important to note that companies rarely rely on custom-made software in the field of accounting nowadays. There is little need to develop software from scratch unless very specific needs must be addressed inside the organisation. This is rarely the case with most business activities. Companies mostly select off-the-shelf software packages from established vendors and configure them as required. There are many applications available, often embedded in larger toolkits like Enterprise Resource Planning packages or cloud solutions. It is relatively easy for suppliers to develop a system that will serve the accounting needs of a myriad of firms (Zentz, n.d.). The fact that every company has accounting needs, combined with the standardisation provided by accounting regulations, makes production of accounting software packages financially viable. For normal use, packaged or cloud solutions provide a faster and cheaper alternative to the development of new accounting systems (Cohn, 2014). Companies can purchase a package or subscribe to a cloud solution and configure it to their needs. In so doing, they also gain access to systems having been extensively tested for reliability and accuracy.

The configuration of the software is the second way outsourcing is used. When companies select a solution, they have to ensure that it is configured to fit their specific needs. This means that specific codes have to be created to reflect the activities of the company. Areas of business have to be established to enable the company to produce the required profit and loss statements, controlling documents (used by auditors) and all other required reports. Configuring software requires a good understanding of the software itself, of accounting principles and of company operations. Adequate configuration of the accounting software will ensure that performance tracking and the information provided to managers will be correct and that regulatory requirements will be met.

Outsourcing the operation of accounting information systems

Once the systems are configured and ready to use, outsourcing can be used to support operation of the systems. The first form of outsourcing for accounting systems simply consists of using a supplier to operate, on behalf of the client, the accounting information systems. This form of outsourcing is probably the simplest. When the system is hosted by an external provider, it can still be used by employees of the firm who may not even know that the system is hosted externally.

Cloud-based solutions are used more and more for accounting information systems. Cloud companies offer standardised solutions at very competitive prices through a remote infrastructure accessible through the Internet, in comparison to an on-premise infrastructure maintained by the client (Armbrust et al., 2010). This type of solution has typically been seen as less flexible than a traditionally configured one. A cloud solution is configurable but to a lesser extent than traditional solutions (Weinhardt et al., 2009). Cloud systems were developed to cover the basic needs of most companies. In recent years, solutions have become increasingly sophisticated. Gaps in functionality can be filled through an ecosystem of modules that can be interconnected through the cloud (Rickmann et al., 2014). Cloud solutions themselves are offering increasing levels of flexibility (Allahverdi, 2017), and even traditional providers like SAP have moved their offering on the cloud (Hiter, 2021).

This suggests that the differences between hosted (cloud) solutions and traditional ones are slowly blurring. Leading companies like Sage Intacct, Xero, FreeAgent and others have become market leaders in that space (Eira, 2021) and have transformed cloud-based solutions into full-fledged ecosystems. These solutions are often called "platforms" because they enable clients (using the accounting cloud software) to connect to a wide variety of other services.

The complementary services are offered by other suppliers who connect to the cloud through the platform. This enables clients to access numerous high-end services in the ecosystem.

Finally, operation of the system can also be outsourced through accounting intermediaries. These firms primarily offer accounting services but use software (often from a cloud provider) to supply the accounting service to the company. This is usually referred to as business process outsourcing, in which a whole business process is performed by a third party (Lacity, Solomon et al., 2011). In these situations, the client does not select the software, leaving this choice to the accounting service provider. Comparison between business process outsourcing and information systems outsourcing shows that both strategies share common motivations and patterns (Lacity et al., 2011). This has been identified as one of the fastest-growing segments of the accounting industry (Eira, 2021).

Growth of outsourcing for accounting information systems

Because they are well documented and well structured, accounting activities are easier to outsource than other, less-structured management activities. The trend of outsourcing accounting and financial activities and processes continues to grow. Analysts indicate a growth rate of 8% (Byrt, 2013). This growth is, in part, fuelled by the expanding needs of clients. Outsourcing these activities enables clients to use the expertise of their suppliers to access analytics capabilities and make better use of financial information, which facilitates the standardisation of processes across multiple sites and countries (Mullich, 2013).

In light of the variety of outsourcing choices, and the growth of outsourcing, it is important to understand how outsourcing decisions are made. Thus, a key question is what should be considered before deciding to outsource an activity. This is explored next.

The outsourcing decision

There have been numerous studies looking at the decision to outsource IT activities. Very thorough reviews of the outsourcing literature, outlining what variables can influence the outsourcing decisions, can be found in Dibbern et al. (2004) and Lacity et al. (2010). The following paragraphs present the key elements explaining the choice of outsourcing as a governance mode for an information systems activity.

Economic considerations

As mentioned earlier, outsourcing is the use of a supplier to perform an activity instead of relying on employees. One approach that has been extensively used to analyse this type of decision is from economics, more precisely Transaction Costs Economics. This approach looks at the costs associated with outsourcing. When a company contracts out an activity, it has to search for the best supplier, negotiate a contract, monitor the contract to ensure compliance etc. All these activities are time-consuming and generate transaction costs. Even if a supplier is specialised and has a production cost advantage over the client, there will be situations in which the transaction costs will be too high for the transaction to be profitable to outsource. In those situations, the client reverts to internal governance.

Traditionally, transaction costs have been linked to two sources: asset specificity and uncertainty (Williamson, 1985). A specific asset is one that is unique to a specific transaction and that has no residual value for another transaction. If a firm controls a specific asset, it can ask a higher price of a party that needs the asset. The client firm will try to protect itself against such opportunistic behaviour, thus generating transaction costs (Williamson, 1985). The second element generating transaction costs is uncertainty, which takes many forms. First, there can be uncertainty about the nature of activities to perform. This means that the contract will need to establish contingencies, which are costly to develop (Williamson, 1985). The second form is uncertainty about the measurement of the activities. Activities that are difficult to measure entail additional transaction costs since much effort is needed to monitor the supplier to ensure it delivers the services promised (Alchian & Demsetz, 1972).

There is one exception to this logic of avoiding transaction costs. Companies will willingly pay higher transaction costs for activities that are infrequent in nature. Transactions organised within a firm have to be recurrent to ensure that staff and assets are used on a continuous basis. This means that companies are likely to outsource activities that are occasional to avoid hiring employees just for that purpose. In this case, they will be willing to accept higher than usual transaction costs (Williamson, 1985).

Asset specificity has not been found to be a significant factor in IT outsourcing decisions (Lacity et al., 2010; Aubert et al., 2012). It seems that most assets linked with IT activities are generic (hardware, software) and can be repurposed easily. The few assets that could be specific are likely to be associated with knowledge. In this case, they are difficult to include in contracts since they are not owned by the companies but instead are kept by employees. It is difficult to include the control of knowledge in a contract, just as it is difficult to control knowledge inside the minds of employees (Aubert & Rivard, 2016). This suggests that asset specificity does not seem to play a significant role when deciding to outsource an IT activity.

The variables that have been found to be the best predictors of outsourcing of information systems activities are all related to uncertainty in its various forms. Uncertainty around the type of activities to be delivered is a deterrent to outsourcing. If activities cannot be specified in advance in a contract, it becomes very difficult to outsource them. When activities are well standardised, they are much easier to detail in a contract and thus easier to outsource (Aubert et al., 2012). This means that companies considering outsourcing have to be able to predict the nature of their activities over a period of time at least as long as the contract. In the case of accounting activities, there is a core group of activities that are easy to predict. These activities are required for the organisation on an ongoing basis. Other activities may be more difficult to predict, notably when they are associated with changes in the organisation (mergers, acquisitions, spin-offs) that are not expected. Typically, organisations will sign contracts covering the core needs and will use separate arrangements to cover unexpected events as those events unfold.

Measurability is also very important. When a contract is signed, the client has to be able to assess the work of the supplier, and the supplier has to be able to demonstrate that the services delivered meet specifications. When client and supplier cannot agree on the services delivered, both in quality and quantity, they cannot enforce a contract. This is easier said than done. In outsourcing contracts, the client cannot easily monitor services performed by the supplier and is usually unable to tell whether a problem is due to an unforeseeable event or to some negligence on the part of its supplier. Suppliers, knowing that their behaviour cannot be observed easily, can avoid responsibility for poor performance or exaggerate their level of effort (and thus their costs) when informing their client (Aubert et al., 2003). Therefore, clients will try to outsource activities for which measurement is as easy as possible.

Political considerations

Transaction Costs Economics offers guidelines for identifying activities that should be outsourced (Lacity et al., 2011; Aubert et al., 2016). It is a rational method for determining the governance of IT activities in the organisation. However, there are cases in which organisational logic and best interest do not always align with individual logic and best interest. When assessing why different managers choose (or not) to outsource a set of activities, it is important to realise that they make those decisions in a way that often reflects their own personal benefit. In some instances, the use of outsourcing was introduced by managers to create impetus for a change they were promoting, to justify a budget increase for their department, to increase the visibility of their role etc. (Lacity & Hirschheim, 1993).

In some instances, outsourcing is also used to benchmark activities. By asking suppliers to offer a service, companies obtain a cost comparison and can see how their own internal services are performing (Lacity & Hirschheim, 1993). Outsourcing can also be used to transform services. For instance, when trying to integrate different systems, some managers use outsourcing to increase the push for integration. It can serve as a means to raise awareness of the proposed change in other departments (finance, marketing, production) and draw attention on the possibilities offered by information systems. By bundling services in a large contract, IT costs suddenly become visible and receive more attention from the company's board and leadership team.

Designing the contract

When outsourcing is used, it is important to remember that services will be managed through a contract between the client and its supplier. Agency theory provides key insights into the incentives, pitfalls and strategies that can be associated with such contract (Sappington, 1991). When designing a contract, the client hopes that suppliers will work in a way that is in the client's best interests. However, clients are aware that suppliers tend to work in their own best interests. Clients have to be aware of three challenges when trying to develop outsourcing contracts: adverse selection, imperfect commitment and moral hazard (Sappington, 1991).

Adverse selection

Adverse selection is the first challenge to overcome when considering awarding an outsourcing contract. If asked about ability, a supplier is likely to overstate its capabilities to ensure it gets the contract. No supplier will admit being incompetent. This suggests that contracts should be designed in a way that discourages the less capable suppliers and encourages the competent ones. In IT, contracts have traditionally been labelled "time and material," in which the client and the supplier agree on hourly rates for work, but for which the number of hours remains flexible. These contracts are attractive for less competent suppliers, since they are likely to need more hours (and make more money) than efficient suppliers. There are also fixed-price contracts, for which the total price is agreed in advance and for which the supplier becomes responsible to exert the efforts required to deliver the service promised. These contracts are more likely to attract efficient suppliers, since efficient suppliers are more likely to make a profit (by requiring less hours) than inefficient ones. The caveat is that the deliverables have to be clearly specified for such contracts to be feasible. In some cases, this is relatively easy to do. In other circumstances, the definitive specifications may not be available when the contract is signed.

Imperfect commitment

Imperfect commitment represents the difficulty any party faces in promising something and honouring its promise. Very often, in contracts, unexpected events arise, and parties will use these surprises to renege on their promises. For example, suppliers can claim that requirements were not clear enough and seek to increase the price initially agreed upon for a piece of software. Contractual measures preventing imperfect commitment are difficult to implement. They often rely on a long-term horizon. If a supplier hopes to secure additional contracts in the future, it may be more "honest" in its early engagements with the client. Bonds are sometimes used for information systems projects but not very frequently. In IT outsourcing, the promise of future contracts and the protection of reputation are probably the strongest incentives for a vendor to remain committed to its promises (Aubert et al., 2003).

Moral hazard

Finally, IT outsourcing is vulnerable to moral hazard. Moral hazard is created by the client's inability to observe what the supplier is doing. The supplier can therefore claim that it is exerting great efforts and that poor performance is due to external circumstances. It is very difficult for the client to challenge these claims successfully. Examples of behaviour falling under the moral hazard label include cheating, shirking, free-riding, cost padding, exploiting a partner or simple negligence. In order to curb moral hazard, clients have to rely on competition. Multi-sourcing is often used in those cases. If more than one supplier knows the client firm and systems, then any underperforming supplier can be replaced easily. It becomes easier to press suppliers for better prices and higher quality (Wiener & Saunders, 2014). Designing the contract is only a first step in ensuring a good outsourcing arrangement. Outsourcing relationships have to be managed throughout the duration of the contract.

Managing the contract

When managing outsourcing contracts for accounting information systems, it is important to consider two aspects of contract management: formal and informal (Barthélemy, 2003). Both aspects are important to ensure a good working relationship with the supplier and a satisfactory outcome for the client.

The formal part involves managing the activities associated with service-level agreements and other elements directly associated with the contract. Every contract is expected to explicitly define the responsibilities of each party, how activities are measured, who owns each process etc. (Goo et al., 2009). Agreements are expected to be as clear and complete as possible, dictating expected performance levels and associated penalties when these are not met (Kim et al., 2013). These elements have to be actively tracked to ensure that the outsourcing relationship is successful and, notably, that it generates the cost advantages expected by the client (Barthélemy, 2003).

Good contract management serves as a foundation for a good relationship between the client and the supplier. Such a contractual foundation enables client and supplier to establish common norms and ultimately trust in the relationship (Goo et al., 2009). However, the formal elements associated with management of the contract are not the only elements of the outsourcing relationship that have to be managed. Relationship management is essential and includes all the mechanisms used to work with the supplier after the contract is signed (Qi & Chau, 2012). These relationship mechanisms traditionally enable client and supplier to exchange information about the needs of the client and the activities performed. For example, coordination will involve a series of committees bringing together personnel and executives from the client and the vendor. Escalation of any issue will follow a well-established path

(Balaji & Brown, 2014). Relationship management can also include social events between the parties, informal meetings and other integration activities between the client and the vendor (ibid.).

All these activities increase knowledge sharing between the parties. The client will take advantage of these communication forums to share future growth plans with the vendor, who, in turn, can plan ahead, offer information about technological opportunities and support the client beyond the simple execution of the activities. The quality of the communication between the parties is very important for a successful outsourcing relationship (Qi & Chau, 2012). When performed consistently, relationship management enables the creation of shared values. These greatly facilitate interactions between the client and the vendor (Goo et al., 2009). A combination of formal contractual management and informal relationship management has been found to be the preferable solution for outsourcing management. It enables the client to get the best combination of short-term gains from the vendor and long-term performance from the outsourcing strategy (Barthélemy, 2003).

Risk assessment

Like any other business activity, the outsourcing of accounting information systems entails some risk. These operational risks have to be adequately assessed and reported. IT outsourcing risk has traditionally been measured in terms of risk exposure, which is defined as a combination of the probability that an undesirable outcome associated with the contract will occur and the magnitude of the loss associated with this outcome (Aubert et al., 2005).

There are many potentially undesirable outcomes associated with outsourcing contracts. Unexpected costs are the most common and can come from high transition costs, lock-in situations, costly contractual amendments, escalation or hidden costs. The client can also experience reduced quality of service, lose organisational competencies and face litigation (Earl, 1996; Aubert et al., 2005). Finally, the client can face compliance issues if the outsourcing contract is not set up properly (Gandhi et al., 2012). The potential damage associated with each of these possible undesirable outcomes has to be weighed. The likelihood of each undesirable outcome can be determined by looking at a series of associated risk factors, which act as proxies for the probability of an undesirable outcome. This approach is common to many fields. For example, when assessing the risk of a heart attack, physicians will look at the associated risk factors: smoking, drinking, lack of physical exercise, poor dietary habits, genetic antecedents etc. These, in turn, can lead directly to risk management strategies. For IT outsourcing, the most common risk factors are presented in Table 10.1 (Aubert et al., 2005). These factors are characteristics of the client, the vendor, the activities themselves or the environment in which the company operates.

It is important to note that these characteristics will vary with each situation and the type of outsourcing chosen. For instance, evidence suggests that cloud vendors carry more debt (relative to assets) than non-cloud ones, compromising their financial stability (Alali & Yeh, 2012). Managing the risk of an outsourcing arrangement thus involves the following steps: (1) evaluating the impact of possible negative outcomes, (2) evaluating the various associated risk factors to determine the likelihood of each possible negative outcome and (3) devising corresponding risk mitigation mechanisms. While a full description of these mitigation mechanisms is beyond the scope of this chapter, one can easily see that risk factors offer a first source of mitigation mechanisms. Once the client knows what the "sources" of risk are, it can adjust its strategy to reduce the risk. For example, if the highest risk factors are associated with the vendor, the client may decide to select a better-suited vendor. If the highest

Table 10.1 Risk factors

Associated with the client:	• Client's lack of experience or expertise with the outsourced activity
	• Client's lack of experience and expertise with contract management
	• Client's lack of experience with outsourcing
Associated with the vendor:	• Supplier's lack of experience and expertise with the activity outsourced
	• Supplier's size
	• Supplier's financial instability
Associated with the interaction or with the activities in the contract:	• Poor cultural fit between client and supplier
	• Size of the contract
	• Interdependence between the activities in the contract and the activities kept inside the firm
	• Measurement problems
	• Task complexity
Environmental characteristics	• Technological discontinuity
	• Uncertainty about the legal environment

risk factors are associated with the client, it can decide to get additional expertise before entering an outsourcing relationship, or gain experience by first awarding a small and easily monitored contract. Similarly, activity-specific risk factors can be managed by modifying the portfolio of activities considered for outsourcing. Each category of risk factors listed in Table 10.1 has to be evaluated carefully before finalising the outsourcing decision. In most organisations risk has to be assessed and reported on a regular basis. Outsourcing is a significant endeavour for an organisation. It can provide significant benefits. However, it is not a risk-free solution. Adequate risk reporting and management is essential when considering outsourcing as a solution for information systems activity.

Future managerial dilemmas in accounting information systems outsourcing

Accounting information systems are constantly evolving. In terms of technological platforms, a decade ago the main change was the integration of accounting systems into larger software packages (Sutton, 2006). More recently, the changes mostly consist of advances in cloud computing and service providers (Asatiani & Penttinen, 2015). These advances are changing not only how accounting information is produced and recorded in organisations but also how the accounting function is organised. These changes pose new dilemmas for managers considering exploiting these technological advances.

Data accessibility and confidentiality

When introducing a vendor, the company gives a third-party access to its accounting systems. What are the consequences of this access? On the one hand, it might reduce the security of the data since the systems can be accessed on public networks, shared technological infrastructure and by more people, some of whom are not even employees of the firm. On the other hand, it might increase security since the third party, not being part of the organisation, has no incentive to tamper with the data since it is not concerned with its operations.

Insights can be gained from studies of auditing outsourcing. It has been observed that internal auditors are less objective than auditors from an external provider (use of outsourcing). The internal auditor, being an employee, is more vulnerable to internal pressures, which could affect its recommendations (Ahlawat & Lowe, 2004). This provides support for the idea that outsourcing accounting information systems is more secure. The vendor's employees have nothing to gain (and probably a lot to lose) by tampering with the data and are more isolated from pressures emanating from the client than internal employees would be. This means that the risk of data being altered is probably lower when the systems are outsourced. In addition, the use of an external provider for accounting activities can also lead to knowledge sharing, which can benefit the company (Prawitt et al., 2012).

Data ownership and portability

The proliferation of cloud computing in recent years has exposed a new challenge with accounting information system outsourcing. In some cases, client companies sign a contract directly with their cloud provider. In other cases, the contract is signed with an accounting firm offering the accounting service. This accounting firm, in turn, has a contract with a cloud provider to host the system (Asatiani & Penttinen, 2015). In those situations, who owns the client's data? Is it the client, or is it the accounting firm? It turns out that this can be a muddy situation, and in some cases, the client firm might actually not control its own data (Macpherson, 2014). Depending on the type of contract signed, the client company could be locked in with the accounting firm. Even cloud providers take the time to explain these differences and advise clients to have a clear discussion with their accounting firm before agreeing on an outsourcing contract (Ridd, 2014). Ownership of data is becoming a more salient consideration with the development of big data approaches in organisations. Companies are trying to leverage their data to gain insights into their activities and their customers. The ability to control data and knowledge (property rights) is therefore a growing concern in outsourcing decisions (Kotlarsky et al., 2020).

Data integrity and regulatory compliance

Unlike other types of organisational information, the production of accounting information and financial statements is subject to regulation. Regardless of the form of the outsourcing arrangement considered, the ultimate responsibility for integrity of the information produced by accounting systems lies with the organisation, not with the cloud or service provider. If a cloud or service provider fails to meet reporting standards and requirements due to a technological or process breakdown, the organisation can incur a risk of penalties for non-compliance. However, if the organisation does not have the resources or competence to keep up to date with regulation, the cloud or service provider might be in a best position to do so on its behalf.

While some cloud and service providers hire independent auditors to provide assurances that their practices follow regulatory standards, managers should also develop internal controls to assess their supplier's compliance. The challenge in developing such controls lies in the fact that the accuracy and integrity of accounting information can be difficult to verify without independently reprocessing the transactions that produced the accounting information in the first instance. Also, the production of accounting information will tend to become fragmented across an ecosystem of cloud providers, which will complicate tracing the source of integrity and non-compliance problems.

Ecosystems' complexity and associated risks

Cloud-based ecosystems have emerged in the past decade, thus providing greater choices for adopting and configuring accounting systems that align with company needs. Such ecosystems can be more or less open, depending on the rules and interfaces set by the vendor for governing outside participation in the ecosystem via application programming interfaces, developer toolkits and the sharing of data (Sebastian et al., 2020).

For companies, ecosystems complicate the decision to adopt a cloud-based accounting solution in at least three ways. First, they magnify the aforementioned challenges posed by data accessibility, data ownership and data integrity because accounting data becomes distributed among the multiple technological platforms used by the vendor and the complementary module producers. Companies have to assess the risks posed by an ecosystem's governance, in terms of the allocation of obligations and decision rights among the ecosystem's vendor and the module producers, as well as in terms of the mechanisms that ensure compliance by the module producers with the ecosystems' policies and standards.

Second, adopting a cloud-based accounting solution from an ecosystem may generate unexpected costs in comparison to a stand-alone cloud solution. Companies need to evaluate and compare the functionalities provided by the modules of an ecosystem, thus possibly making compromises when organisational needs can't be met perfectly across the modules. Dependence on a particular module of the ecosystem that cannot be used in a stand-alone fashion because of data or functionality interdependence can generate significant lock-in and transition costs, thus preventing a switch to another ecosystem for the full accounting solution.

Third, ecosystems are prone to cross-side network effects, that is, the value gained by users of the ecosystems is dependent on the size and growth of the module producers' side and vice versa (Song et al., 2018). Cross-side network effects can benefit companies looking to adopt accounting solutions when they involve a great diversity of complementary modules, thus broadening choice. Yet, they may pose new kinds of risks. Cross-side network effects can increase the market power of an ecosystem vendor over time, especially if they engender the dynamics of winner-take-all or oligopolistic markets, where only one or a few ecosystems survive over time. In those circumstances, ecosystem vendors can unexpectedly raise the costs of solution usage or developer participation in the ecosystem (Rietveld et al., 2020). They can also engage in platform envelopment, a tactic where an ecosystem vendor develops or takes control of a module, possibly undermining competitive alternatives in the ecosystem (Eisenmann et al., 2011). If a company is dependent on a competitor of the enveloped module for its accounting systems, it could face the risks of discontinuance and transition costs.

Research avenues

A significant body of knowledge on outsourcing has developed as outsourcing became commonly used. However, the forms outsourcing can take are increasingly complex. This creates several opportunities for additional research on accounting information systems outsourcing. For example, we now observe several layers of contracting. Contracts are nested, and vendors sub-contract some services to other providers, who, in turn, use the capabilities of external sources (Jansen, 2011). These layers of sub-contracts dilute the knowledge related to the activities performed and the data used and can limit the accountability of vendors. At the same time, they enable more complete services at very competitive prices. How should contract design and reporting mechanisms evolve to take into account the layering of contracts? Most of the literature has been looking at the relationship between a client and a vendor or between a client and multiple vendors. What happens when the vendor is also a client in another relationship? The mesh of relationships may lower the accountability of contracting parties and dilutes the control over data and activities (Aubert & Rivard, 2020).

Because accounting information systems hold critical information for the firm, the ability to use this information may become a strategic consideration in future outsourcing decisions. The flexibility allowed by some outsourcing solutions to interconnect data with other services can provide an advantage to the firm. Asatiani et al. (2019) noted that accounting information systems relying on cloud solutions were facilitating the dissemination of data inside the organisation and with the organisation's partners and the optimisation of work processes when compared to more traditional arrangements. This could accelerate the trend towards outsourcing arrangements relying on cloud solutions. This suggests that better understanding future options associated with data, beyond the delivery of accounting services themselves, is required.

Another area in which research is needed is the international dimension of outsourcing and offshoring. When activities are managed by vendors, they can be moved from one country to another to take advantage of different cost structures. The data can be stored in one country, while the employees working with it are in other countries. This creates risks (Nassimbeni et al., 2012). Regulations differ from one country to another, and understanding each country's privacy laws, government surveillance strategies and intellectual property regulation is a challenge. In addition, these can change depending on political pressures. New risk management strategies will need to be developed to assess and manage those risks.

The compliance challenge associated with the practices of suppliers and their sub-contractors also requires additional research efforts. Companies are relying on multi-sourcing arrangements, involving numerous vendors (Könning et al., 2019). How managers organise accounting functions in response to such dilemmas is an interesting line of inquiry. Data must be traced through an increasingly complex maze of systems. Auditing cannot be an afterthought. Auditing strategies have to be developed in parallel with contract development to ensure their soundness. Even when auditing strategies are being developed (Wang et al., 2015), how to implement them into auditing standards and practices and how to embed them into contracts remain a challenge.

Conclusion

The use of outsourcing is growing steadily. Companies use it to increase their flexibility and adapt to changes in regulations or in technological landscapes (Jogani et al., 2020). For accounting information systems, the outsourcing option must be considered. Managers must assess the extent to which their activities are predictable and measurable. The more they are, the better candidates they are for outsourcing. Managers must remain aware that political games may influence the decisions. They also must remember that internal factors are not the only ones to consider. The ecosystem in which the firm operates is increasingly influential when making technological choices. Once the decision to outsource is taken, it is important to devise a contract that will motivate the vendor to exert maximal effort and protect the client from any lock-in situation or unwanted sub-contracting. Competition should be maintained while active management of the relationship takes place. Outsourcing is a major governance decision for organisations and can have long-term implications. Cognisant managers will recognise that good outsourcing management is a balancing act.

References

Abbate, J. (2001). Government, business, and the making of the Internet. *Business History Review*, 75(1), 147–176.

Ahlawat, S. S., & Lowe, D. J. (2004). An examination of internal auditor objectivity: In-house versus outsourcing. *Auditing: A Journal of Practice and Theory, 23*(2), 147–158.

Alaghehband, F. K., Rivard, S., Wu, S., & Goyette, S. (2011). An assessment of the use of transaction cost theory in information technology outsourcing. *The Journal of Strategic Information Systems, 20*(2), 125–138.

Alali, F. A., & Yeh, C. L. (2012). Cloud computing: Overview and risk analysis. *Journal of Information Systems, 26*(2), 13–33.

Alchian, A. A., & Demsetz, H. (1972). Production, information costs, and economic organization. *The American Economic Review, 62*(5), 777–795.

Allahverdi, M. (2017). Cloud accounting systems and a SWOT analysis. *Proceedings of the International Symposium on Accounting and finance (ISAF)*, Macedonia, July 3–5, 92–105.

Armbrust, M., Fox, A., Griffith, R., Joseph, A. D., Katz, R., Konwinski, A., Lee, G., Patterson, D., Rabkin, A., Stoica, I., & Zaharia, M. (2010). A view of cloud computing. *Communications of the ACM, 53*(4), 50–58.

Asatiani, A., Apte, U., Penttinen, E., Rönkkö, M., & Saarinen, T. (2019). Impact of accounting process characteristics on accounting outsourcing-comparison of users and non-users of cloud-based accounting information systems. *International Journal of Accounting Information Systems, 34*, 100419.

Asatiani, A., & Penttinen, E. (2015). Managing the move to the cloud–analyzing the risks and opportunities of cloud-based accounting information systems. *Journal of Information Technology Teaching Cases, 5*(1), 27–34.

Aubert, B. A., Houde, J. F., Patry, M., & Rivard, S. (2012). A multilevel analysis of information technology outsourcing. *Journal of Strategic Information System, 21*(3), 233–244.

Aubert, B.A Patry, M., & Rivard, S. (2003). A tale of two contracts, an agency-theoretical perspective. *Wirtschaftsinformatik, 45*(2), 181–190.

Aubert, B. A., Patry, M., & Rivard, S. (2005). A framework for information technology outsourcing risk management. *Database, 36*(4), 9–28.

Aubert, B. A., & Rivard, S. (2016). A commentary on "The role of transaction cost economics in information technology outsourcing research: A meta-analysis of the choice of contract type". *The Journal of Strategic Information Systems, 25*(1), 64–67.

Aubert, B. A., & Rivard, S. (2020). The outsourcing of IT governance. In Hirschheim, R., Heinzl, A. & Dibbern, J. (eds). *Information Systems Outsourcing* (pp. 43–59). Springer, Cham.

Aubert, B. A., Saunders, C., Wiener, M., Denk, R., & Wolfermann, T. (2016). How adidas realized benefits from a contrary it multisourcing strategy. *MIS Quarterly Executive*, 15(3), 179-194

Balaji, S., & Brown, C. V. (2014) Lateral coordination mechanisms and the moderating role of arrangement characteristics in information systems development outsourcing. *Information Systems Research, 25*(4), 747–760.

Barthélemy, J. (2003). The hard and soft sides of IT outsourcing management. *European Management Journal, 21*(5), 539–548.

Blinder, A. S. (2006). Offshoring: The next industrial revolution? *Foreign Affairs-New York, 85*(2), 113.

Brown, B. (1990). Kodak turns nets over to IBM and DEC. *Network World, 7*(3), 1, 61.

Cleary, P. (2017). Introduction to accounting information systems. In Quinn, M., & Strauss, E. (eds). *The Routledge Companion to Accounting Information Systems* (pp. 3–12). Milton Park: Routledge.

Cohn, C. (2014). Build vs. Buy: How to know when you should build custom software over canned solutions, *Forbes*, www.forbes.com/sites/chuckcohn/2014/09/15/build-vs-buy-how-to-know-when-you-should-build-custom-software-over-canned-solutions/ (accessed 28-4-2016).

Dedrick, J., Carmel, E., & Kraemer, K. L. (2011). A dynamic model of offshore software development. *Journal of Information Technology, 26*(1), 1–15.

Deloitte (2014). Deloitte's 2014 global outsourcing and insourcing survey 2014 and beyond, 24 pages. https://www2.deloitte.com/content/dam/Deloitte/global/Documents/Process-and-Operations/gx-2014-global-outsourcing-survey-report.pdf

Dibbern, J., Goles, T., Hirschheim, R., & Jayatilaka, B. (2004). Information systems outsourcing: A survey and analysis of the literature. *ACM SIGMIS Database, 35*(4), 6–102.

Earl, M. J. (1996). The risks of outsourcing IT. *Sloan Management Review*, 37, 26-32.

Eira, A. (2021). 11 Accounting trends for 2021/2022: New forecasts & what lies beyond?, https://financesonline.com/accounting-trends/ (accessed 12-7-2021).

Eisenmann, T., Parker, G., & Van Alstyne, M. (2011). Platform envelopment. *Strategic Management Journal, 32*(12), 1270–1285.

Gandhi, S. J., Gorod, A., & Sauser, B. (2012). Prioritization of outsourcing risks from a systemic perspective. *Strategic Outsourcing: An International Journal, 5*(1), 39–71.

Goo, J., Kishore, R., Rao, H. R., & Nam, K. (2009). The role of service level agreements in relational management of information technology outsourcing: an empirical study. *MIS Quarterly, 33*(1), 119–145.

Hiter, S. (2021). SAP ERP software: S/4HANA cloud review for 2021, *CIO Insight*, June 21, https://www.cioinsight.com/enterprise-apps/sap-erp-software/ (accessed 12-7-2021).

IBM Corporate Archives (2002). IBM global services: A brief history (May), 19 pages. www-03.ibm.com/ibm/history/documents/pdf/gservices.pdf (accessed 23-2-2016).

Jansen, W. A. (2011). Cloud hooks: Security and privacy issues in cloud computing. In *System Sciences (HICSS), 2011 44th Hawaii International Conference on* (pp. 1–10). IEEE.

Jogani, R., Khan, N., Lala, W., Ramaa, R., Van Kuiken, S. (2020). How CIOs can work with outsourcing providers to navigate the coronavirus crisis. *McKinsey Quarterly*, April 15, https://www.mckinsey.com/business-functions/mckinsey-digital/our-insights/how-cios-can-work-with-outsourcing-providers-to-navigate-the-coronavirus (accessed 12-7-2021).

Kim, Y. J., Lee, J. M., Koo, C., & Nam, K. (2013). The role of governance effectiveness in explaining IT outsourcing performance. *International Journal of Information Management, 33*(5), 850–860.

Könning, M., Westner, M., & Strahringer, S. (2019). A systematic review of recent developments in IT outsourcing research. *Information Systems Management, 36*(1), 78–96.

Kotlarsky, J., Oshri, I., Dibbern, J., Mani, D. (2020). IS sourcing research curation (hosted by MIS quarterly), https://www.misqresearchcurations.org/blog/2018/6/26/is-sourcing (accessed 12-7-2021).

Lacity, M. C., & Hirschheim, R. (1993). The information systems outsourcing bandwagon. *Sloan Management Review, 35*(1), 73.

Lacity, M. C., Khan, S., Yan, A., & Willcocks, L. P. (2010). A review of the IT outsourcing empirical literature and future research directions. *Journal of Information Technology, 25*(4), 395–433.

Lacity, M. C., Solomon, S., Yan, A., & Willcocks, L. P. (2011). Business process outsourcing studies: A critical review and research directions. *Journal of Information Technology, 26*(4), 221–258.

Lacity, M. C., Willcocks, L. P., & Khan, S. (2011). Beyond transaction cost economics: Towards an endogenous theory of information technology outsourcing. *The Journal of Strategic Information Systems, 20*(2), 139–157.

Loh, L., & Venkatraman, N. (1992). Diffusion of information technology outsourcing: Influence sources and the Kodak effect. *Information Systems Research, 3*(4), 334–358.

Macpherson, S. (2014). Why you should always hold your own cloud software subscription, April 30, www.digitalfirst.com/you-hold-software-subscription/ (accessed 6-9-2016).

McLaughlin, D., & Peppard, J. (2006). IT backsourcing: From 'make or buy' to 'bringing IT back in-house'. *Proceedings of the European Conference on Information Systems (ECIS 2006)*, Göteborg, 117.

Mullich, J. (2013). The benefits of outsourcing finance and accounting, *Forbes*, www.forbes.com/sites/xerox/2013/07/12/the-benefits-of-outsourcing-finance-and-accounting/ (accessed 25-4-2016).

Nassimbeni, G., Sartor, M., & Dus, D. (2012). Security risks in service offshoring and outsourcing. *Industrial Management & Data Systems, 112*(3), 405–440.

Prawitt, D. F., Sharp, N. Y., & Wood, D. A. (2012). Internal audit outsourcing and the risk of misleading or fraudulent financial reporting: Did Sarbanes-Oxley get it wrong?. *Contemporary Accounting Research, 29*(4), 1109–1136.

Qi, C., & Chau, P. Y. (2012). Relationship, contract and IT outsourcing success: Evidence from two descriptive case studies. *Decision Support Systems, 53*(4), 859–869.

Rickmann, T., Wenzel, S., & Fischbach, K. (2014). Software Ecosystem Orchestration: The Perspective of Complementors (2014). AMCIS 2014 Proceedings. 7. https://aisel.aisnet.org/amcis2014/e-Business/GeneralPresentations/7.

Ridd, C. (2014). Managing your Xero subscription, www.xero.com/blog/2014/04/managing-xero-subscription/ (accessed 9-6-2016).

Rietveld, J., Ploog, J. N., & Nieborg, D. B. (2020). Coevolution of platform dominance and governance strategies: Effects on complementor performance outcomes. *Academy of Management Discoveries, 6*(3), 488–513.

Rottman, J. W., & Lacity, M. C. (2004). Twenty practices for offshore sourcing. *MIS Quarterly Executive, 3*(3), 117–130.

Sappington, D. E. (1991). Incentives in principal-agent relationships. *The Journal of Economic Perspectives, 5*(2), 45–66.

Sebastian, I. M., Weill, P., & Woerner, S. L. (2020). Driving growth in digital ecosystems. *MIT Sloan Management Review, 62*(1), 58–62.

Song, P., Xue, L., Rai, A., & Zhang, C. (2018). The ecosystem of software platform: A study of asymmetric cross-side network effects and platform governance. *MIS Quarterly, 42*(1), 121–142.

Sutton, S. G. (2006). Enterprise systems and the re-shaping of accounting systems: A call for research. *International Journal of Accounting Information Systems, 7*(1), 1–6.

UpsilonIT (2021). Top 10 IT outsourcing trends that will matter in 2021, https://upsilon-it.medium.com/top-10-it-outsourcing-trends-that-will-matter-in-2021-4c2fbf5aa6e6 (accessed 12-7-2021).

Wang, J., Chen, X., Huang, X., You, I., & Xiang, Y. (2015). Verifiable auditing for outsourced database in cloud computing. *IEEE Transactions on Computers, 64*(11), 3293–3303.

Weinhardt, C., Anandasivam, A., Blau, B., Borissov, N., Meinl, T., Michalk, W., & Stößer, J. (2009). Cloud computing–a classification, business models, and research directions. *Business & Information Systems Engineering, 1*(5), 391–399.

Wiener, M., & Saunders, C. (2014). Forced coopetition in IT multi-sourcing. *The Journal of Strategic Information Systems, 23*(3), 210–225.

Wilder, C. (1989). Kodak hands processing over to IBM, *Computerworld, 23*(31), 1.

Williamson, O.E., (1987). Transaction cost economics: The comparative contracting perspective. *Journal of Economic Behavior & Organization*, 8(4), 617-625.

Zentz, M. (n.d.). Custom vs. off-the-shelf software, *Marketpath*, www.marketpath.com/digital-marketing-insights/custom-applications-vs-off-the-shelf-software (accessed 28-4-2016).

11

TECHNOLOGICAL DEVELOPMENTS AND NEW HYBRID ROLES IN ACCOUNTING AND FINANCE

João Oliveira and Paulo J. Ribeiro

Introduction

This chapter discusses how recent developments in digital technologies and data sciences have influenced, and will influence, major functions within Accounting and Finance (A&F) and its professionals. The relevance of these technological developments can hardly be overstated for the A&F function, but the literature provides disparate, even antagonistic accounts and predictions about their influence upon its professionals. Accounts in the professional and academic literature range from fantastic opportunities and dire prospects for A&F professionals (Schmidt et al., 2020). These prospects, whether bright or grim, are related with the potential roles played by the A&F professionals. Accountants' roles have been extensively researched (e.g. Herbert & Seal, 2012; Goretzki et al., 2013; Burns et al., 2014; Quinn, 2014; Goretzki & Messner, 2019) but mostly focusing on the interplay between accountants and managers, leading to the well-documented potential transition from a 'bean-counter' to a 'business partner' and to the notion of hybridity in the function and professionals (Caglio, 2003). This chapter studies how recent technological developments have the potential to introduce new dimensions, tensions and outcomes to these topics of A&F roles and hybridity.

Among the many 'digitalisation topics' in the A&F area (Möller et al., 2020, p. 2), this chapter covers both well-established information systems and recent emerging developments – including the most relevant ones highlighted by Schmidt et al. (2020). In the first category, we include Enterprise Resource Planning (ERP) systems and Business Intelligence and Analytics (BI&A) – even though both, and particularly BI&A, continue to expand and evolve. The second category is more diversified and related with automation (Robotic Process Automation (RPA), Artificial Intelligence (AI) and Machine Learning (ML)), data expansion (Big Data, Cloud and Internet of Things (IoT)) and the decentralised database blockchain. These technologies are often interdependent: e.g. the more established BI&A technology has become even more relevant by the recent data expansion related with Big Data. Some impacts are somewhat transversal to all A&F functions, while others are particularly important for specific areas, and the impacts from different technologies may be interdependent as well.

While other chapters in this handbook cover some of the technology developments mentioned, this chapter focuses on A&F roles. While any categorisation of the A&F area is controversial (Gerdin et al., 2014), we focus on three major functions: financial accounting,

DOI: 10.4324/9781003132943-14

management accounting and control (MAC) and treasury. Research tends to emphasise the MAC function and the role of its professionals; we aim to rebalance the debate, by also focusing on the two other areas (Mouritsen, 1996). Furthermore, research has identified hybridisation between accounting and management professionals (Burns et al., 2014) and their skills. We reposition this focus, revealing how technological developments create new tensions and dimensions around roles, skills and hybridity. The present day is decisive for the A&F profession's future – for how it may evolve, expand or lose relevance to other competing professionals, due to these developments. Therefore, this chapter contributes to support A&F practitioners and academics, highlighting emerging insights and trends, and calls for in-depth empirical research about these ongoing phenomena.

This chapter is structured as follows. The next section adopts a mostly technological perspective to overview the main technological developments relevant to A&F. Building on this overview, the following section focuses on the three mentioned A&F functions and the most relevant technologies and respective impacts for each one. The ensuing section reflects about opportunities and challenges for A&F professionals, particularly considering the required and existing levels of IT and data science skills. It then goes on to discuss new dimensions of the 'hybridisation' and 'business partner' topics, created by the ongoing technological evolution. A final section concludes this chapter.

An overview of Accounting and Finance-related technologies

This section starts by exploring relatively established technologies relevant to the A&F areas (ERPs and BI&A systems) and then analyses more recent ones (RPA, AI, ML, Big Data, Cloud, IoT and blockchain). The development of accounting systems over recent decades has moved from a quest for integration to a current explosive expansion. Initially, decoupled systems, based on generic purpose solutions like spreadsheets or best-of-breed solutions of specific areas, had scarce or no integration with operational systems and required time-consuming and error-prone manual data entry. Integration was pursued first by coupling those systems through interfaces and then, more fundamentally, by implementing ERP systems.

ERPs have spread from large to small organisations and are now commonplace. Within one single, organisation-wide database, data flows seamlessly across multiple ERP modules, promoting single data entry and generating greater data quality, and these integration effects expand when business partners' ERPs are connected and transfer transaction data. Since accounting activities typically occur at the end of business processes (Kanellou & Spathis, 2013), manual data entry in accounting is drastically reduced. Integration was further enhanced when ERPs became established as the major backbone of the information systems architecture to which other systems can connect, such as Shop Floor Control, Customer Relationship Management and Supplier Relationship Management. However, ERPs remained mostly transactional systems, with limited analytical capabilities (Scapens & Jazayeri, 2003; Rom & Rohde, 2006). This limitation was first addressed by data warehouses/data marts, enabling data exploration by drilling-down data, and then, in a more robust and sophisticated way, through their connection to BI&A systems.

BI&A includes multiple technologies and methodologies to collect, prepare and analyse internal and external data and then provide results to users through reports, scorecards, dashboards and dynamic visualisations (Rikhardsson & Yigitbasioglu, 2018) – see also Chapter 14. BI&A improves the timeliness and quality of inputs for decision-makers by translating semi-structured and structured data to suitable information, which is then analysed to become knowledge. Its analytical focus makes it particularly relevant to an organisational function like A&F and, in particular, to those A&F areas – and professionals – more focused on analysis and support of data-driven decisions. While BI&A has existed for decades, its development and diffusion have drastically increased during the last decade, leveraged by, and leveraging, other technologies, both mature (like ERPs) and more recent ones, to which we now turn.

The recent developments of Cloud computing, Big Data and IoT have been instrumental for A&F. Cloud computing has become an established alternative to having hardware and applications, such as ERPs or BI&A systems, on premises, accessing them online wherever or whenever required. Cloud computing reduces upfront costs, changes fixed costs into variable costs and is highly scalable. It promotes agility and cooperation in deploying or updating a single system or in accessing and sharing data, from and to anywhere, including mobile devices. In A&F, Cloud-based solutions and collaborative work based on consistent information and reliable systems promote a more adaptive finance function (CIMA, 2010; Quinn & Strauss, 2017), including for small and medium enterprises (Kristandl et al., 2015). Big Data technology seeks valuable patterns in huge amounts of data from multiple origins, structured or unstructured in form. Big Data is characterised by the 4 Vs of high volume, velocity, variety and uncertain veracity (more variety leads to more uncertainty), requiring new analytical approaches with high-value potential, generating insights for rapid reactions and boost data-driven decisions (Bhimani & Willcocks, 2014; Gepp et al., 2018). Finally, IoT increasingly links networks of computers, machines, objects and even animals and people, with unique identifiers and transferring data without human intervention. By sensorising and connecting billions of objects, it continuously increases available data, dwarfing the until recently considered large amounts of structured data stored in ERPs (Schmidt et al., 2020) and enabling new high-value areas to deploy real-time analytics.

Automation is a major recent trend in A&F, through RPA and AI. In less than a decade, RPA has become established in many large organisations and is now expanding to smaller ones (Kokina & Blanchette, 2019; Deloitte, 2020a; IT Central Station, 2020). RPA is based on software (robots) programmable to execute human tasks – i.e. they become 'digital workers', replacing or complementing human workers. Ideal tasks for automation with RPA are relatively low value-added, labour-intensive, repetitive, high volume and rules-based, with few exceptions and changes, already digitalised, involving multiple systems and structured data, and requiring low human interaction and judgement (Kokina & Blanchette, 2019). An important area is data transfer across non-integrated business applications, using existing user interfaces – i.e. RPA 'plugging-in' not-yet integrated processes. RPA therefore works alongside ERPs towards the objective of integration and increases processes traceability (Kokina & Blanchette, 2019). And, like ERPs did, applying RPA to finance enables radical cost efficiencies and increased control and allows skilled resources to focus on value creation (SAP, 2016; Deloitte, 2020a). Finally, cognitive or intelligent RPA has recently emerged, handling unstructured data and carrying out non-routine tasks involving judgement and performing basic analyses for more advanced assessment by experts (E&Y, 2016; Kokina & Blanchette, 2019).

AI and ML are also transforming the A&F function, generating new ways to improve decision-making support and strengthen businesses' competitive advantage. Originating in the 1950s, AI has recently gained a major importance in data sciences given the explosion of computer processing power and storage, combined with the advent of social media and technological companies. AI concerns the possibility of machines being able to interpret data, in a given predetermined context, and act accordingly (Kokina & Davenport, 2017). Therefore, AI mimics human cognitive functions, while RPA mimics human actions (Deloitte, 2020b). The development of ML algorithms and the vast amounts of available data enabled computers to learn, solve problems and make decisions. From analysing numbers using ML and neural networks, to interpreting words and images via text mining, natural language processing and deep learning algorithms, AI is transforming the way A&F tasks are performed. For example, AI can provide cost-effective and time-saving benefits, streamlining routine A&F processes and freeing teams from low-value administrative tasks (Deloitte, 2020a). Not only does this provide the time to focus on higher-value activities but AI can also assist in carrying out such activities, like scenario planning and predictive analysis. Within AI, the sub-area of data mining, and more specifically process mining, assists in making processes more efficient and can usefully complement RPA. Process mining constructs a visualisation of how business processes are actually structured and how activities are carried out, enabling the identification of areas for automation through RPA, eliminating bottlenecks and enhancing efficiency (Deloitte, 2020a).

Finally, blockchain is a recent data technology, consisting of a new type of decentralised database where data flows and is stored in a secure way (Maffei et al., 2021). Unlike traditional databases, no one owns the decentralised database, which is scattered across different and dispersed servers. The data is cryptographically recorded and stored, and since all records are connected to one another and are part of the cryptographic key used, no record can be deleted or modified. Decentralisation, transparency to authorised users and the immutability of records are therefore the key characteristics of blockchain, allowing for a secure and transparent way of registering data and performing transactions. Blockchain enables the exchange of value between entities across the world, without any intermediaries or trustful third parties to validate transactions (Tiron-Tudor et al., 2021). By applying blockchain to accounting, transactions can be posted in a decentralised public ledger without a central authority, or in a private distributed ledger accessible to predetermined and authorised entities. Due to its characteristics, this technology can both reduce costs and improve reliability and assurance, reducing fraud risk (Cai, 2021), with particular impacts in financial accounting (Tiron-Tudor et al., 2021).

This section provided an overview of the technological developments most relevant for the A&F area, ranging from relatively mature and established technologies to more emergent ones. These technologies can be complements or substitutes to one another (e.g. BI&A complements ERPs, and AI/ML complements BI&A; and an ERP-based structural integration can substitute a temporary RPA-based integration); others tend to be relatively independent (e.g. blockchain). The next section builds on this overview to discuss specific impacts of these developments upon three major A&F functions.

Technological developments and Accounting and Finance functions

In this section, we distinguish three major functions within the wide area of the A&F in organisations: financial accounting, MAC and treasury. They mirror the three categories (accounting, controlling and cash management) mentioned in Mouritsen (1996), and while overlaps and gaps are inevitable, they suitably cover the main functions in A&F and enable a characterising of how each one was and/or will be affected by technological developments. While some technologies are particularly relevant for only some functions, other technologies (ERPs, RPA and BI&A) potentially impact all functions (e.g. Deloitte, 2020a; Spraakman et al., 2021).

The financial accounting function

Financial accounting traditional activities range from record-keeping to reporting, including administrative and auditory[1] controls, and are typically beyond and detached from core organisational activities (Mouritsen, 1996), focused on the resulting financial transactions. However, this function has evolved to become more analytical, future-oriented and concerned with value, including seeking efficiency improvements, in the entire organisation and in its own functioning – a shift greatly enhanced by technological developments.

ERP-enabled integration has had dramatic effects upon financial accounting. Information flows seamlessly from the operational modules (e.g. sales and distribution, production and human resources) to the financial accounting module, avoiding much low-value-added work of bookkeeping manual data entry. Overall, ERPs' efficiency in transaction processing, relevant for many high-volume, repetitive tasks of financial accounting, has been amply demonstrated. For example, in Kanellou & Spathis's (2013) survey, the two major benefits of ERPs are key to financial accounting: efficiency in gathering data and generating results and less time to period-end accounts close and issue financial statements. Financial consolidation also benefits from an ERP, and consolidation solutions interfaces draw data from most financial accounting solutions; however, while this integration eliminates much manual effort, the complexity of consolidation still leaves many areas requiring intervention and judgement by skilled accountants.

Seamless, automated and real-time information flows with an ERP are not without issues. As Quattrone & Hopper (2005) point out, errors in records by non-accounting staff (such as a shop floor employee producing a shipping document or issuing a receipt) have immediate repercussions in financial accounting. Therefore, spreading awareness and knowledge among non-accounting staff about their actions' repercussions within the accounting area is required. Indeed, this challenge increases in scale and complexity when it becomes inter-organisational, as information about transactions is exchanged across organisations' interconnected ERPs. Inter-organisational cooperation between the respective accounting (and other) departments becomes essential, e.g. a supplier including a particular code in its documents to assist the customer when recording the transaction. In addition, as not only accounting records but also controls become more real-time, ranging from management controls to internal and external auditing controls (see Chapter 16 on continuous auditing), the challenges posed by this tight integration must be considered.

RPA has found an ideal implementation setting in financial accounting, given the significant component of high-volume, repetitive, rule-based tasks – see also Chapter 17. Examples from the record-to-report process include performing manual or reclassification journal entries, reconciliations, fixed asset accounting, financial close activities and data aggregation for, and preparation of, all sorts of reports (e.g. trial balances, balance sheet, profit and loss and management, statutory and regulatory reports) (Kokina & Blanchette, 2019; IT Central Station, 2020). AI/ML algorithms, individually or combined with other technologies, are also transforming financial accounting practices. AI can process documents using natural language processing and computer vision, making bookkeeping tasks, such as invoicing or producing expense reports, more efficient and reliable, and even easier to approve, including through mobile devices. Moreover, these systems, coupled with embedded business rules and regulations, can identify compliance issues.

Turning to blockchain, its distributed ledger technology can be programmed, and controls can be implemented to ensure that the stored information is reliable and complies with business rules or with standards and legal regulations (Dai & Vasarhelyi, 2017). Data integrity, instant sharing, security and traceability have a direct impact upon financial accounting activities, automating transactional tasks and improving reporting, contributing to the development of new accounting systems, public or privately held (Pimentel & Boulianne, 2020). Big Data and IoT have potential to be relevant to financial accounting (Vasarhelyi et al., 2015) but have had relatively limited impacts so far, when compared to other mentioned technologies, particularly due to the nature of most tasks and data involved. Gepp et al. (2018)'s systematic literature review identified relevant impacts in three areas of the finance field (financial distress modelling, financial fraud modelling and stock market prediction and quantitative modelling) but somewhat tangential regarding financial accounting. Specific applications may be, for example, exploring Big Data to identify trends with a negative impact upon a company's brands, using those insights when estimating potential impairment and drawing upon Big Data gathered by IoT included in machinery to provide data on usage and physical condition, to determine depreciation and potential impairment.

The treasury function

Treasury activities involve tracking and managing information on account balances, transaction details and cash and currency positions; executing fund transfers and short-term investments; controlling customers' credit, managing liquidity and working capital needs; and making cash-flow forecasts. Like the financial accounting function, the treasury function is traditionally beyond and detached from core business activities, which are merely 'a context for its work' (Mouritsen, 1996, p. 297), although changes are emerging in this function as well.

ERPs have specific modules to deal with treasury, and cash management, in particular – an increasingly popular alternative *versus* interfacing best-of-breed solutions with the ERP. ERPs' efficiency in gathering data and generating results (Kanellou & Spathis, 2013) is also felt in this area, for example, reconciling operational and banking transactions. Linking the organisation's treasury management system with the banks' information system is now common, even in smaller organisations, and it has virtually eliminated manual entry of financial transactions data.[2] However, SAP's (2015) survey revealed that when multiple systems are involved, gathering data across multiple bank accounts, entities and geographies still requires significant manual efforts, making group-wide cash assessment and management difficult and time-consuming.

AI is transforming treasury activities by improving transactional efficiency, implementing reliable controls, and assisting data-driven decision-making. ML and advanced process automation tools can assist treasurers in bookkeeping and integration, shifting manual and repetitive tasks to machines. Business rules and event triggers can automate controls and increase transaction security and reliability. Outliers and fraudulent transactions can be easily spotted by ML algorithms (Roszkowska, 2021). Rating and credit score activities can be automated and benefit from ML algorithms able to classify customers and transactions and alert for possible non-compliance. Predictive analytics tools enable to accurately forecast cash flows and anticipate cash needs or surpluses, improving decisions on liquidity allocation and management.

BI&A tools enable the analysis of treasury data quickly and accurately and aggregate and visualise it at a corporate level, allowing better cash-flow management and a more efficient allocation of resources (Polak et al., 2020). Most respondents in the survey by SAP (2015) indicated that treasury had to become not only faster in preparing and delivering cash reports and forecasts but also better in delivering more in-depth, forward-looking cash analyses – even using advanced forecasting to leverage Big Data (e.g. to manage exposure to markets' financial risks). And, as already mentioned, treasury has been highlighted as an area where RPA can be most effectively deployed (E&Y, 2016).

The management accounting and control function

The MAC function is often very broadly conceived, and its two components are often examined together (Goretzki & Messner, 2019; Oesterreich et al., 2019; Möller et al., 2020). This chapter conceives the MAC function as aggregating a controlling role, associated with budgeting and budgetary control, recording performance data and ensuring managers' compliance with budgeted figures, and a consulting role, supporting organisational activities through specialised, often *ad hoc* analyses, as an internal consultancy, involved in business matters (Mouritsen, 1996).

Cost accounting, budgeting and variance analysis have traditionally been carried out through spreadsheets, whose stand-alone nature requires significant manual work in gathering and entering data from multiple sources. Interfaces with accounting and non-accounting systems were valuable whenever available, but sometimes data had to be manually gathered from physical devices. Data manipulation, calculations and reporting in spreadsheets tended to be complex and error prone (Goretzki et al., 2013; Schmidt et al., 2020). Moreover, when these activities are carried out at a local level, visibility and comparability at a higher, corporate level are limited (Oliveira & Clegg, 2015). Managerial usefulness was also limited by delays in data gathering, manipulation and reporting, of both financial and non-financial information (see Ribeiro & Oliveira, 2017). Furthermore, technological constraints imposed a focus on periodical information production rather than on its continuous analysis.

Systems integration and greater data availability significantly changed cost accounting and budgeting procedures. An ERP costing module directly retrieves the required diversified types of information from the ERP database, and an even higher degree of integration in more recent ERP versions contributes to more reliable and granular cost accounting (Weber, 2022). IoT applied to production processes provides real-time information, replacing data gathering manually. Control and analysis become less periodic and historic, and more continuous (daily, for each batch or even real time), incorporating still 'fresh' operational explanations, and become more future-oriented and predictive. ERPs facilitated measuring and controlling more than the cost and profitability of products (the traditional cost object). Detailed, integrated information about sales and distribution promotes more accurate and faster customer profitability analysis. For example, information about the products and locations involved in each sales transaction enables estimating distribution costs. Integrated systems eased gathering data about actual performance for budgeting control, and tools including what-if models and scenario planning facilitated planning activities and hence budgets' construction (Politano, 2003).

Although ERPs provided management accountants with greater data storage and computational power (Appelbaum et al., 2017) and improved transactions processing efficiency and data quality, early on, they were considered as limited in supporting higher-value, flexible analyses (Hyvönen, 2003; Rom & Rohde, 2006). As already noted, this limitation was addressed, first, by using data warehouses/data marts to extract and consolidate data to enable deeper exploration and then by using BI&A systems to analyse data in multiple perspectives. Indeed, ERPs have affected MAC and the roles of professionals, particularly when supplemented by analytical systems (Herbert & Seal, 2012; Goretzki et al., 2013; Appelbaum et al., 2017). For example, for the MAC function to provide valuable insights to managers,

ERPs' 'organisational accounting' benefits (flexibility in information generation, applications integration, timely and reliable information for decision-making and improved quality of reports – Kanellou & Spathis, 2013) are particularly salient, especially when leveraged by BI&A; this combination enables to support flexible analyses of internal and external information, with greater depth and breath.

BI&A, deploying suitable analytical tools, enables the drawing of data from the entire population, gathered from different sources, developing real-time analyses and value-added insights and promoting data-based efficient decisions, and even generating competitive advantages from data, in particular from Big Data. Even cost accounting, typically working with 'small financial data', is affected by the wide variety of information of Big Data (Weber, 2022).

Beyond cost accounting, Bhimani & Willcocks (2014) highlighted that consumers' online tracking prior to purchases is extremely valuable. Capturing and combining this non-financial information with the actual economic transactions offers 'the potential of developing financial intelligence and shaping cost management as well as pricing and operational control decisions' (pp. 475–476). MAC professionals that can use tools to extract, transform and use data in the form of data collecting, cleaning, reporting and visualisation, through spreadsheets, SQL queries and data visualisation and reporting, will be prepared to answer questions related to descriptive analytics. However, this is only the starting point of BI&A. If they can use statistical analysis, and more advanced tools such as algorithms for data mining, knowledge discovery or ML, they will be prepared to answer crucial questions related to predictive analytics.

Technologies, roles and skills in Accounting and Finance: contributions, opportunities and challenges and new dimensions of hybridity

While the previous section explored impacts of technological developments upon three major functions in A&F, this section takes a more global view. After aggregating the technologies according to particular types of contribution to generate value, it discusses opportunities, challenges and consequences to the A&F profession(s), their roles and their skills.

Major types of contributions from technologies

A significant type of contribution from technologies is cost reduction, in particular through headcount reductions. ERPs, RPA and AI/ML have greatly automated data entry and basic manipulation, drastically reducing manual tasks and enabling the release of personnel, to other functions or not. However, automation generates value beyond cost reduction; it also creates value (Deloitte, 2020a). Data quality was also greatly improved by ERPs, based on single data entry points in a single database, and by RPA and its more reliable execution of mechanical tasks – despite the inherent dangers of integration (Dechow & Mouritsen, 2005) and the limitations of automation when dealing with errors and exceptions (Kokina & Blanchette, 2019). Increased speed has been achieved through ERP and RPA, not only in transactional matters but also, alongside BI&A and AI/ML, in analytics. Indeed, faster retrieval and preparation of data are essential for timely analyses and managerial decisions. This goes hand in hand with increased data availability, first when ERPs facilitated immediate access to vast amounts of detailed, non-financial data and, more recently, when Big Data (including IoT data) started providing unprecedented amounts of unstructured, potentially real-time data. Indeed, Big Data greatly promoted the further development of BI&A, which cannot be analysed by traditional tools like spreadsheets.

While it is tempting to suggest that the most recent innovations have a more substantial impact, in particular Big Data, BI&A and AI/ML, these actually build upon the contributions enabled by ERPs and RPAs (and indeed, by the Cloud supporting these technologies). Paraphrasing John Merino, FedEx's Chief Accounting Officer, cited in AICPA & CIMA & ORACLE (2019, p. 5), these are multiple legs of a large, solid stool. Focusing on RPA, advanced analytics and AI/ML, he considered that

> the combination of those technologies and the ability to deliver them in an agile manner without long lead times and extensive interface complexities creates a tremendous opportunity to capitalise on some really big efficiency gains in virtually every staff function. The big win for us is to liberate that time and move finance up the value chain in what it delivers to the organisation.

While a focus on technologies highlights great opportunities for the A&F function, the consideration of the human component – the professionals in and around this function – paints a more complex and paradoxical picture. As Schmidt et al. (2020, p. 165) aptly summarise, articles on technological developments 'alternate between warnings of dire consequences and proclamations of fantastic opportunities that lie ahead for the accounting profession', related with an emerging type of professional hybridity.

Opportunities and challenges for the profession

The developments of ERPs and other connected systems, automation technologies like RPA and AI/ML and Big Data and Analytics, and even blockchain, promote the evolution of the A&F area, across the three functions analysed above, in two opposing ways.

First, there is a reduction of low-value activities, in a process often depicted as the 'death of the bean-counter' dealing with low-value-added tasks, driven mostly by integration and automation technologies like ERPs, RPA and ML. In this perspective, A&F staff become the victims of the first type of contribution from technologies, identified above: cost reduction. Second, there is a continuing need of A&F staff – albeit in smaller numbers – to deliver the second type of contribution from technologies: value creation. They configure and maintain software, solve exceptions in human-machine shared processes and engage in richer data analysis requiring subjective insights and assessment to enable business insights. A&F staff become more engaged with the rest of the organisation, introducing a consulting role even in areas traditionally with a more detached back-office role (Mouritsen, 1996), such as financial accounting and treasury. Indeed, even in new activities still closely related with transactional ones, such as dealing with exceptions in RPA-driven processes, shifting from task performance to task review (of activities carried out by robots) may be considered an important success for employees (Kokina & Blanchette, 2019).

These are the 'fantastic opportunities' for the profession (Schmidt et al., 2020), in line with the ascension of A&F professionals up the value chain, and even becoming part of the decision-making team. As Safra Catz, Oracle's Chief Executive Officer, argued in AICPA/CIMA, & ORACLE (2019, p. 3), recent technological developments enable the finance function to 'be a true co-pilot to the business, working in tandem with the CEO'.

The academic literature has long explored this more attractive role, mostly in MAC but also across a wide spectrum of functions in A&F. At stake is the proverbial shift from 'a bean-counter' to a 'business partner' role (Goretzki & Strauss, 2018; Goretzki & Messner, 2019). The derogatory 'bean-counter' caricature, associated with an organisational role with minor relevance, can certainly be linked to limitations of past technologies. Developments related with integration and automation have contributed to improve data access, accuracy and timeliness. However, technological developments, by themselves, were limited in changing the *cliché* of the (cost) accountant as 'knowing the costs of everything and the value of nothing'. Goretzki et al. (2013) reported that an ERP implementation provided a crucial information base but only after subsequent developments, including business intelligence portals to develop reporting and planning processes, did a more substantial role shift emerge, towards controllers as business partners.

This shift in roles, promoted by technological developments, entails changes in operations, identities and skills. Operational changes concern the tasks performed, redefinitions of the actors involved (including across professional and specialisation boundaries), and, importantly, the contributions made by each one. Occupational identity changes require complex identity work by accountants, through interactions with other organisational actors to position themselves as business partners contributing to 'value creation' (Goretzki & Messner, 2019). Finally, changes in required skills deserve a closer look, given the increasing pervasiveness of new technologies, some of which drastically different from established ones.

Skills in a technology-intensive Accounting and Finance function

While technology mastery (along with business knowledge and interpersonal skills) has long been recognised as essential for an accountant to become a successful business partner, the IT skills traditionally required involved mostly spreadsheet and database knowledge to deal with ERPs' highly structured approach – a type of knowledge in line with the traditional, structured work of accountants. However, Big Data, BI&A and AI/ML require both IT and statistical knowledge at a level often above the accountants' traditional toolkit. Deploying, even dealing with BI&A or AI/ML without suitable skills, leads to a black-box effect, undermining the understanding of how the algorithms work and the usage and communication of the generated knowledge.

However, A&F professionals seem far from fully embracing BI&A (Appelbaum et al., 2017; Oesterreich et al., 2019; Schmidt et al., 2020). There appears to be resistance to adopting more advanced techniques and solutions and a preference to remain with traditional solutions such as spreadsheets (Schmidt et al., 2020). Spraakman et al. (2021) found that data analytics practices remained largely restricted to descriptive and financial data analyses through the analytics provided by spreadsheets, without exploring and modelling external and operational data through more complex techniques and solutions.

Even RPA, a more structured technology which 'merely' mirrors users' existing practices, presents similar challenges (and opportunities) for accountants. Kokina et al. (2021) highlighted that accountants are well positioned to take various roles related with RPA implementation. These roles are identifier (spotting RPA opportunities), explainer (communicating with RPA developers), sustainer (managing the robot post-implementation) and analyser (providing better insights by leveraging on RPA-enhanced processes). However, the trainer role (training, i.e. programming the robot) was typically taken by IT professionals, with coding skills hard to develop for most accountants. And while software vendors emphasise that prior coding expertise is not essential, and while Kokina et al. (2021) have direct anecdotal evidence of that, Kokina & Blanchette (2019) caution against underestimating the IT skills required for an RPA implementation. This apparent difficulty, in some cases even resistance, to develop new skills and engage with new technologies poses obvious risks for

A&F professionals. The A&F profession has long evolved within a context with hybridity of functions, in particular between A&F and managers; however, the new technological context opens up a new dimension of hybridity.

A new dimension of hybridity in the accounting profession

The literature has long documented that becoming closely related and aligned with the business has led to hybridisation of the A&F function in a dual direction – labelled here as the traditional dimension of occupational hybridity (for the multiple areas of hybridity, see Besharov & Mitzinneck, 2020). On the one hand, managers became increasingly able to monitor and analyse budgets, variances and other performance data, leveraging on BI&A systems and underlying data sources, designed by controllers, but dispensing their intervention on a daily basis (Goretzki et al., 2013). The control role becomes diffused, a 'collective affair' (Dechow & Mouritsen, 2005) across accountants and managers becoming 'hybrid accountants'. On the other hand, a second type of 'hybrid accountants' are technology-empowered accountants, combining accounting knowledge and business knowledge, who provide insights to explain past performance and to improve performance. They are often integrated as business team members (Goretzki et al., 2013; Burns et al., 2014), expanding the traditional controlling, 'bean-counter' role into a consulting, 'business partner' role.

With the recent wave of technological developments, a new type of hybridisation is emerging. The difficulty and resistance of the A&F profession to develop new skills in IT and BI&A make many professionals unable to meet the expectations, even requirements, from organisations pursuing these developments. Consequently, companies are hiring IT and data science professionals to deliver these new tasks and contributions, aspirationally attributed to accountants, but that these are not fully taking over. While this recruiting trend was still low in the recent past (Oesterreich et al., 2019, based on job postings to 2017), the quick uptake of these technologies suggests that this is an actual, increasing and inexorable trend. In Schmidt et al.'s (2020) survey of A&F professionals, even though there were favourable perceptions of switching benefits and value from embracing new technologies, respondents perceived switching costs as more significant, leading to an overall resistance. Appelbaum et al. (2017) and Oesterreich et al. (2019) report similar insights.

Therefore, the next wave of hybridisation in A&F may well consist of IT and data scientists taking over the high-value tasks of advanced analytics of large volumes of data and managerial advice – the basis of a future 'business partner'. Those are the 'dire consequences' that Schmidt et al. (2020) identified, should the accounting profession continue to 'wait and see', leaving new technologies entirely to IT and data science professionals, and become increasingly obsolete or reduced to a small niche of technical accounting specialists.

Future avenues for a technologically hybrid profession

The solution to the above challenges is not that all A&F staff become IT professionals or data scientists. This will be more the exception than the norm. However, all A&F professionals should advance their IT and data science skills, including statistics, beyond the typical current level. This upskilling to at least a basic level will be increasingly required to carry out many core activities of A&F and to interact with other organisational actors in a technology-advanced work environment. As Deloitte (2020b, p. 3) humorously put it, an alternative to A&F staff to become a data scientist/AI expert is to 'at least learn how to sound like one', arguing that 'cross-functional partnering' will contribute to 'gain fluency' (p. 5).

In an RPA context, accountants need to be able to communicate, to software designers and RPA developers, the steps and internal controls of processes to be dealt with by RPA and to assist RPA developers to improve the robot resilience and error-handling (Kokina et al., 2021). They also need to communicate with managers and internal and external auditors about the robots' actions. Finally, they also need to develop metrics for the robot as a digital worker, just as they would for human workers. To make all these tasks possible, accountants should have the capacity to at least read (though not necessarily to program) the RPA code.

In addition, the emergence in A&F of multidisciplinary teams including IT and data scientists seems inevitable. Whereas this solves the current (and likely future) difficulty of a massive upskilling of A&F professionals, this implies at least some upskilling to enable successful communication and cooperation within those teams, including members with IT/data science education but lacking business and accounting knowledge. This challenges the adage of defining accounting (and finance) based on 'what accountants do'. On the contrary, we should perhaps wonder what an accountant, or indeed an A&F professional, is. The answer may be that A&F professionals are those who deliver what managers increasingly expect to obtain from this field, ranging from traditional reporting and compliance to forward-looking business advice to create value. They will increasingly be members of heterogeneous, multidisciplinary teams, with diversified educational backgrounds, ranging from traditional A&F degrees to IT and data science degrees.

Under this scenario, two new types of 'hybrid accountants' emerge, different from the ones discussed in the literature: the professionals with a traditional A&F education and experience who strongly embrace the new technologies and the IT and data science specialists dedicated to the new A&F tasks. Indeed, the location in the organisational structure and the associated reporting lines in these new configurations of hybridity are issues still requiring research.

Conclusion

This chapter aimed to reflect, and envision, how recent technological developments have influenced, and will continue to influence, the A&F area, its tasks, its contributions and its professionals, in particular reflecting on the skills required and the various profiles of professionals involved, traditionally and in the future.

The initial overview of the main technological developments related with the A&F area and their applicability and relevance to three A&F functions set the stage to identify the technological developments leading to different types of contributions and highlighted interrelationships between them. Identifying those technological developments more directed towards cost reduction, and those more directed towards value generation, assists in identifying what they may entail for A&F professionals. Opportunities and challenges of traditional A&F professionals to master those developments, particularly considering the level of IT and data science/statistical skills required and typically existing among these professionals, were also examined. The still scarce evidence of a strong need, search for and offer of advanced IT and data science skills in A&F (Oesterreich et al., 2019) may not be representative of a near-future scenario.

Upskilling in IT and data sciences is likely to occur in a continuum. On one extreme, a few professionals may indeed become IT experts in specific tools and data scientists; this is unlikely to be highly representative. On the other extreme (and ignoring the no-go option of not upskilling at all), upskilling may involve developing skills at a still relatively basic level yet sufficient to enable to successfully carry out traditional A&F tasks in a technologically advanced environment and cooperate with IT specialists and data scientists as members of multidisciplinary teams. As technologies evolve at an increasing pace, requiring increasingly sophisticated and extended learning, most A&F professionals are likely to tend towards this pole of the upskilling continuum.

The above analysis revealed the emergence of a variation of two extensively discussed topics: hybridisation and the 'business partner' role. The literature has typically considered hybridisation across the accounting and the managerial areas and located the 'business partner' concept within the relation between these two areas. This chapter suggested that a new phenomenon of hybridisation is unfolding between the A&F and the IT/data science areas and between professionals originating from each area. Furthermore, it was suggested that the 'business partner' role may be taken by professionals coming from the latter areas, not from the traditional A&F area.

The previous broad-brush conclusions are, of course, not deterministic. The evolution of A&F and of the (various types of) professionals involved is subject to both macro-level factors (e.g. the technological developments at an industry level, or overall competitive and economics forces, not analysed here) and micro-level factors, which are highly context-specific (Mouritsen, 1996). Changes do not occur naturally and free from resistance; on the contrary, they are dependent on explicit or hidden strategies by organisational actors pursuing particular objectives, including through securing ambitioned key roles (Goretzki et al., 2013). This chapter privileged reported empirical relationships between technology and A&F, rather than assuming these relationships, although some normative/aspirational literature was also used. However, as Dechow et al. (2007, p. 633) concluded, this relationship 'is one to be untangled rather than to be assumed'. Hopefully, this chapter we hope encourages future in-depth empirical research, with practical and academic relevance, aiming to untangle the new, emerging relationships between ongoing technological developments, the quickly shifting A&F area and the new, emerging hybrid roles of its professionals.

Notes

1 While financial accounting and auditing are linked, auditing technologies are explored in Chapter 16.
2 This has also been promoted by the European Union's open banking regulation; see www.open-bankingeurope.eu.

References

AICPA/CIMA, & ORACLE (2019). Agile finance unleashed – The key traits of Digital finance leaders. https://www.uipath.com/resources/automation-whitepapers/agile-automation

Appelbaum, D., Kogan, A., Vasarhelyi, M., & Yan, Z. (2017). Impact of business analytics and enterprise systems on managerial accounting. *International Journal of Accounting Information Systems, 25*, 29–44. https://doi.org/10.1016/j.accinf.2017.03.003

Besharov, M.L., & Mitzinneck, B.C. (Eds.). (2020). Organizational hybridity: Perspectives, processes, promises. *Research in the Sociology of Organizations, 69*, 313–320.

Bhimani, A., & Willcocks, L. (2014). Digitisation, Big Data and the transformation of accounting information. *Accounting and Business Research, 44*(4), 469–490. https://doi.org/10.1080/00014788.2014.910051

Burns, J., Warren, L., & Oliveira, J. (2014). Business partnering: Is it all that good?, *Controlling & Management Review, 58*(2), 36–41. https://doi.org/10.1365/s12176-014-0907-6

Caglio, A. (2003). Enterprise resource planning systems and accountants: Towards hybridization? *European Accounting Review, 12*(1), 123–153. https://doi.org/10.1080/0963818031000087853

Cai, C.W. (2021). Triple-entry accounting with blockchain: How far have we come? *Accounting & Finance, 61*(1), 71–93. https://doi.org/10.1111/acfi.12556

CIMA (2010). Cloud computing could lead to a more adaptive finance function. *CIMA Insight E-Zine.* http://www.cimaglobal.com/Thought-leadership/Newsletters/Insight-e-magazine/Insight-2010/ Insight-December-2010/Cloud-computing-could-lead-to-more-adaptive-finance-function/

Dai, J., & Vasarhelyi, M.A. (2017). Toward blockchain-based accounting and assurance. *Journal of Information Systems, 31*(3), 5–21. https://doi.org/10.2308/isys-51804

Dechow, N., Granlund, M., & Mouritsen, J. (2007). Management control of the complex organization: Relationships between management accounting and information technology. In C. Chapman, A. Hopwood, & M. Shields (Eds.), *Handbook in Management Accounting Research*, Vol. 2, 625–640. Pergamon Press.

Dechow, N., & Mouritsen, J. (2005). Enterprise resource planning systems, management control and the quest for integration. *Accounting, Organizations and Society, 30*(7–8), 691–733. https://doi.org/ 10.1016/j.aos.2004.11.004

Deloitte (2020a). Automation with Intelligence – Pursuing organisation-wide reimagination. https:// documents.deloitte.com/insights/AutomationwithIntelligence2020.

Deloitte (2020b). Why CFOs should have artificial intelligence on their minds. https://www2.deloitte. com/us/en/pages/finance/articles/cfo-insights-why-cfos-should-have-artificial-intelligence-on-their-minds.html.

E&Y (2016). Robotic process automation in the Finance function of the future. https://webforms. ey.com/Publication/vwLUAssets/EY-robotic-process-automation-in-the-finance-function-of-the-future/$FILE/EY-robotic-process-automation-in-the-finance-function-of-the-future.pdf

Gepp, A., Linnenluecke, M.K., O'Neill, T.J., & Smith, T. (2018). Big data techniques in auditing research and practice: Current trends and future opportunities. *Journal of Accounting Literature, 40*, 102–115. https://doi.org/10.1016/j.acclit.2017.05.003

Gerdin, J., Messner, M., & Mouritsen, J. (2014). On the significance of accounting for managerial work. *Scandinavian Journal of Management, 30*(4), 389–394. https://doi.org/10.1016/j.scaman.2014.09.004

Goretzki, L., & Messner, M. (2019). Backstage and frontstage interactions in management accountants' identity work. *Accounting, Organizations and Society, 74*, 1–20. https://doi.org/10.1016/j.aos.2018.09.001

Goretzki, L., & Strauss, E. (2018). *The Role of the Management Accountant: Local Variations and Global Influences.* Routledge.

Goretzki, L., Strauss, E., & Weber, J. (2013). An institutional perspective on the changes in management accountants' professional role. *Management Accounting Research, 24*, 41–63. https://doi.org/ 10.1016/j.mar.2012.11.002

Herbert, I., & Seal, W. (2012). Shared services as a new organisational form: Some implications for management accounting. *The British Accounting Review, 44*, 83–97. https://doi.org/10.1016/j. bar.2012.03.006

Hyvönen, T. (2003). Management accounting and information systems: ERP versus BoB. *European Accounting Review, 12*(1), 155–73. https://doi.org/10.1080/0963818031000087862

IT Central Station (2020). Realizing the benefits of RPA in accounting and finance. https://www. uipath.com/resources/automation-whitepapers/it-central-station-peer-paper-finance-accounting

Kanellou, A., & Spathis, C. (2013). Accounting benefits and satisfaction in an ERP environment. *International Journal of Accounting Information Systems, 14*, 209–234. https://doi.org/10.1016/j.accinf.2012.12.002

Kokina, J., & Blanchette, S. (2019). Early evidence of digital labor in accounting: Innovation with Robotic process automation. *International Journal of Accounting Information Systems, 35*, 100431. https://doi.org/10.1016/j.accinf.2019.100431

Kokina, J., & Davenport, T.H. (2017). The emergence of artificial intelligence: How automation is changing auditing. *Journal of Emerging Technologies in Accounting, 14*(1), 115–122. https://doi. org/10.2308/jeta-51730

Kokina, J., Gilleran, R., Blanchette, S., & Stoddard, D. (2021). Accountant as digital innovator: Roles and competencies in the age of automation. *Accounting Horizons, 35*(1), 153–184. https://doi. org/10.2308/HORIZONS-19-145

Kristandl, G., Quinn, M., & Strauss, E. (2015). Controlling und cloud computing – Wie die Cloud den Informationsfluss in KMU ändert. *ZfKE – Zeitschrift für KMU und Entrepreneurship*: 63, Controlling in und für KMU, *63*(3–4), 281–304. https://doi.org/10.3790/zfke.63.3-4.281

Maffei, M., Casciello, R., & Meucci, F. (2021). Blockchain technology: Un-investigated issues emerging from an integrated view within accounting and auditing practices, *Journal of Organizational Change Management, 34*(2), 462–476. https://doi.org/10.1108/JOCM-09-2020-0264

Möller, K., Schäffer, U., & Verbeeten, F. (2020). Digitalization in management accounting and control: An editorial. *Journal of Management Control, 31*, 1–8. https://doi.org/10.1007/s00187-020-00300-5

Mouritsen, J. (1996). Five aspects of accounting departments work. *Management Accounting Research, 7*, 283–303. https://doi.org/10.1006/mare.1996.0017

Oesterreich, T.D., Teuteberg, F., Bensberg, F., & Buscher, G. (2019). The controlling profession in the digital age: understanding the impact of digitisation on the controller's job roles, skills and competences. *International Journal of Accounting Information Systems, 35*, 100432. https://doi.org/10.1016/j.accinf.2019.100432

Oliveira, J., & Clegg, S. (2015). Paradoxical puzzles of control and circuits of power. *Qualitative Research in Accounting & Management, 12*(4), 425–451. https://doi.org/10.1108/QRAM-02-2015-0023

Pimentel, E., & Boulianne, E. (2020). Blockchain in accounting research and practice: Current trends and future opportunities. *Accounting Perspectives, 19*(4), 325–361. https://doi.org/10.1111/1911-3838.12239

Polak, P., Nelischer, C., Guo, H., & Robertson, D.C. (2020). 'Intelligent' finance and treasury management: What we can expect. *AI & Society, 35*, 715–726. https://doi.org/10.1007/s00146-019-00919-6

Politano, A. (2003). Taking performance management to the next level: How to measure the state of your business and achieve optimal what-if scenarios. *Strategic Finance, 8*. https://sfmagazine.com/wp-content/uploads/sfarchive/2003/08/Taking-Performance-Management-To-The-Next-Level.pdf

Quattrone, P., & Hopper, T. (2005). A 'time–space odyssey': Management control systems in two multinational organisations. *Accounting, Organizations and Society, 30*(7/8), 735–64. https://doi.org/10.1016/j.aos.2003.10.006

Quinn, M. (2014). The elusive business partner controller. *Controlling & Management Review, 58*(2), 22–27. https://doi.org/10.1365/s12176-014-0905-8

Quinn, M., & Strauss, E. (2017). The cloud and management accounting and control. In E. Harris (Ed.), *The Routledge Companion to Performance Management and Control*, 124–138. Routledge.

Ribeiro, C., & Oliveira, J. (2017). The uses (and non-usage) of the balanced scorecard: A case study. *Revista Contabilidade & Gestão, 20*, 9–64.

Rikhardsson, P., & Yigitbasioglu O. (2018). Business intelligence and analytics in management accounting research: Status and future focus. *International Journal of Accounting Information Systems, 29*, 37–58. https://doi.org/10.1016/j.accinf.2018.03.001

Rom, A., & Rohde, C. (2006). Enterprise resource planning systems, strategic enterprise management systems and management accounting – a Danish study. *Journal of Enterprise Information Management, 19*(1), 50–66. https://doi.org/10.1108/17410390610636878

Roszkowska, P. (2021). Fintech in financial reporting and audit for fraud prevention and safeguarding equity investments. *Journal of Accounting and Organizational Change, 17*(2), 164–196. https://doi.org/10.1108/JAOC-09-2019-0098

SAP (2015). Next generation needs for cash management. http://go.sap.com/documents/2015/07/966ef4a4-357c-0010-82c7-eda71af511fa.html

SAP (2016). Digital finance – Transforming finance for the digital economy. http://go.sap.com/documents/2016/03/a4d16bd0-627c-0010-82c7-eda71af511fa.html

Scapens, R.W., & Jazayeri, M. (2003). ERP systems and management accounting change: Opportunities or impacts? A research note. *European Accounting Review, 12*(1), 201–233. https://doi.org/10.1080/0963818031000087907

Schmidt, P., Riley, J., & Church, K. (2020). Investigating accountants' resistance to move beyond excel and adopt new data analytics technology. *Accounting Horizons, 34*(4), 165–180. https://doi.org/10.2308/HORIZONS-19-154

Spraakman, G., Sanchez-Rodriguez, C., & Tuck-Riggs, C.A. (2021). Data analytics by management accountants. *Qualitative Research in Accounting & Management, 18*(1), 127–147.

Tiron-Tudor, A., Deliu, D., Farcane, N., & Dontu, A. (2021). Managing change with and through blockchain in accountancy organizations: A systematic literature review. *Journal of Organizational Change Management, 34*(2), 477–506. https://doi.org/10.1108/JOCM-10-2020-0302

Vasarhelyi, M.A, Kogan, A., & Tuttle, B.M. (2015). Big Data in accounting: An overview. *Accounting Horizons, 29*(2), 381–396. https://doi.org/10.2308/acch-51071

Weber, J. (2022), Zukunftsfähige Kostenrechnung, *Controlling & Management Review, 66*, 8–15. https://doi.org/10.1007/s12176-021-0439-9

12

PREDICTIVE ANALYTICS IN ACCOUNTING INFORMATION SYSTEMS

Esperanza Huerta and Scott Jensen

Introduction

Predictive analytics can be used in many areas of accounting, including financial, managerial, taxes, forensics, and auditing. In 2014, for instance, KPMG uncovered fraud totalling hundreds of thousands of dollars at a United States (US) call centre where a dozen operators had issued multiple small refunds to themselves and others (McGinty, 2014). Given the large number of transactions for small amounts, it is unlikely that the fraud would have been uncovered but for the use of predictive analytics.

The predictive analytics sector was valued at $5.7 billion in 2018 and expected to continue growing at a compound annual growth rate of 23.2% from 2019 to 2025 (Grand View Research, 2020). As in many industries, predictive analytics can transform the way accountants make decisions. Considering the substantial impact that predictive analytics could have on the accounting profession, it is important to understand how predictive analytics can use data from an accounting information system (AIS) and other sources to support the typical accounting areas within an organisation. In addition to its use within an organisation, data from an AIS may also be used by people outside the organisation (who are granted access), including regulatory agencies.

To explore the transformative impact that predictive analytics might have on the accounting profession, this chapter is organised as follows. We first define predictive analytics and discuss each of the elements in the definition. Although the definition applies to many domains, in this chapter we focus on how predictive analytics differs from other techniques accountants have traditionally used to predict outcomes. We then discuss the use of predictive analytics in different areas of accounting. Given the relevance of external audit in the accounting profession, we dedicate a section to the use of predictive analytics in assurance practices and present an example of its use at a Big 4 firm. The chapter concludes with suggestions for future research.

Definition

Predictive analytics is an area of data analytics that builds mathematical 'models that make predictions based on patterns extracted from historical data' (Kelleher et al., 2015, p. 1). As

DOI: 10.4324/9781003132943-15

simple as that definition is, several nuances need to be addressed to understand the advantages and disadvantages of predictive analytics in AIS.

The first element of the definition identifies predictive analytics as an area of data analytics. Considering that there is no standard definition of data analytics, it is not surprising that different authors propose alternative ways to categorise data analytics. Richins et al. (2017), for instance, propose the categorisation of data analytics along two dimensions: analysis approach and data. They classify the analysis approach as being either problem-driven or exploratory. In problem-driven analysis, data analytics focuses on identifying problems, the causes of those problems, and potential solutions (Richins et al., 2017). In exploratory analysis, data analytics focuses on summarising data and identifying its main characteristics (Richins et al., 2017).

A broadly accepted classification of data analytics distinguishes between descriptive and predictive analytics (Prabhu et al., 2019). Descriptive analytics is what Richins et al. (2017) refer to as exploratory analysis, and it summarises the data in terms of its tendency, variability, and other descriptors. Descriptive analytics is not by itself the goal in predictive analytics but rather a necessary preliminary step in conducting predictive analytics. Predictive analytics is equivalent to what Richins et al. (2017) call problem-driven analysis. Classifying data analytics into descriptive and predictive might portray the incorrect idea that these two areas are mutually exclusive. Descriptive and predictive analytics are intertwined. Predictive analytics relies on the results reported by descriptive analytics to determine which models would be suitable considering the characteristics of the data. Attempting to use predictive analytics without first engaging in descriptive analytics can lead to meaningless models (Kelleher et al., 2015).

Data analytics can also be classified based on its use, resulting in three or four data analytics areas. Tschakert et al. (2016), for instance, classify data analytics in four areas: descriptive, diagnostic, predictive, and prescriptive. Based on their definition, diagnostic, predictive, and prescriptive analytics involve building models, but they are used to answer different business questions. Diagnostic analytics uses models to identify the causes of business problems, predictive analytics uses models to forecast future events, and prescriptive analytics uses models to select among alternatives. This classification can be useful in identifying how predictive analytics can be used by businesses. However, at its core, predictive analytics builds mathematical models, and it is the user who decides how the models are used.

A common misunderstanding is to believe that predictive analytics focuses exclusively on foretelling the outcome of future events. This misunderstanding arises from the everyday use of the word 'prediction', which is associated with temporality - some event in the future (Kelleher et al., 2015). Predictive analytics can, of course, be used to build models to predict future outcomes. For instance, predictive analytics could be used to estimate whether an organisation has the resources to remain in operation in the future or whether there are going concern issues. That is, based on data, predictive analytics estimates the expected future outcome. However, from a data analytics perspective, prediction only means 'the assignment of a value to any unknown variable' (Kelleher et al., 2015, p. 2). There is no temporality constrain inherent in the modelling. The example discussed at the start of this chapter illustrates the use of predictive analytics to predict which past transactions were fraudulent. The distribution pattern of past data (digit occurrence in the refund amounts given at a call centre) was compared to the expected pattern (pattern of digit occurrence according to the Newcomb-Benford Law) to identify significant differences. As in all predictive analytics, in that example, historical known trends were used to build a model to predict the status (fraudulent or not) of transactions the model had not evaluated before. Regardless of how data analytics are classified, or how they are used, accountants should understand that using predictive analytics requires descriptive analytics as the first step. It is also the responsibility of accountants to understand that predictive analytics can be used to assign unknown values not only to future events but also to past events that the model had not previously evaluated.

The second element in the definition of predictive analytics by Kelleher et al. (2015) is the building of mathematical models. The models produced in predictive analytics are mathematical functions that take data inputs and produce an output to solve ill-posed problems – 'a problem for which a unique solution cannot be determined using only the information that is available' (Kelleher et al., 2015, p. 7). Models are built iteratively using different statistical methods depending on the type of data input and desired output. The building of the models is the domain of data analysts with strong mathematical and statistical backgrounds. However, accountants, as users of the models produced, should have a basic understanding of the limitations of these models.

The third and last element in the definition of predictive analytics as defined by Kelleher et al. (2015) is the extracting of patterns from data. The characteristics of the data determine the type of mathematical models that can be built, but as noted by Kelleher et al. (2015 p. 2), one aspect the models have in common is that they are supervised machine learning models trained using historical data. The use of historical data is necessary since the training data uses labelled instances (e.g. whether a transaction is fraudulent or not). While the labelled events are historical, they could include real-time data – as soon as a data point is captured, it can be used in refining the model. Predictive analytics for customer behaviour is an example where the data can change very fast, and the data used to build a predictive model is constantly updated with data from current website activity and online searches (Loten, 2021). The historical nature of the data used in predictive analytics not only differentiates it from predictive forecasting, which may incorporate the results of predictive analytics, but also includes projected future data, which can be particularly relevant in fast-changing and dynamic environments (Wiegmann et al., 2021). In using predictive analytics, accountants need to be aware of the limitations of these models, and one of these limitations is whether the historical data is similar enough to the events being predicted (Boone et al., 2019).

Not explicitly stated in the definition is this assumption that models can reasonably predict unknown instances (e.g. if a transaction is fraudulent) because they behave similarly to known transactions (e.g. which have been identified as fraudulent or not). For instance, a model predicting the likelihood of a tax return being fraudulent would be useful if the determinants in the data used to build the model are the same determinants in the return being predicted. The COVID-19 pandemic in 2020, for instance, created many data irregularities, making models unreliable for estimating customer demand or the movement of goods (Loten, 2021). The volatility that resulted from the pandemic caused some organisations to revert to models built using data gathered before the pandemic (Loten, 2021).

One of the many differences that distinguish predictive analytics from other models used for prediction purposes is the large volume of data required (O'Leary, 2018). For instance, auditors evaluating whether an organisation is likely to continue in operations may calculate financial ratios to make predictions, but this is not predictive analytics. Similarly, models to predict inventory reorder points and safety stock rely on past data but are not predictive analytics. The use of a large amount of data is a non-explicit requirement of predictive analytics, so much so that it is sometimes called big data predictive analytics. The iterative process and the statistics behind these models require large amounts of data to build useful models (O'Leary, 2018). The general rule of thumb is that the more data, the better. However, data is perishable; its value can decrease over time (Committee on National Security Systems,

2022). Historical data that is not similar to the instances an accountant wants to predict might not only be useless but also misleading (Kelleher et al., 2015). Including additional historical data just for the sake of increasing the size of the data available might harm a model's predictive capabilities. The estimated useful life of data is subjective and would require accountants to determine when the data have lost their predictive value. Although these evaluations should be part of a larger data management plan (Gajbe et al., 2021), accountants need to be involved because the estimated life of data depends on the context in which it is used. As the custodians and auditors of accounting data, accountants have the competence and expertise to identify when accounting data has lost its value.

Predictive analytics in different accounting areas

Predictive analytics models can rely on the data stored in the AIS as well as other data sources. In the following discussion, we classify users based on the access they have to the data stored in the AIS. Typical users can be classified as internal users (with potentially unlimited access) or external users (with limited access). We further classify external users into those with access provided at the discretion of the organisation (voluntary disclosure) and those with access provided to comply with regulations (compliance disclosure). However, this classification is not exhaustive. Additional stakeholders, such as investors, stock market analysts, and competitors, could use public data generated by the AIS in their own predictive models. Figure 12.1 shows the AIS within the boundaries of the organisation and the three types of users.

Internal users

Internal users are employees of the organisation and, as such, have unlimited access (depending on their organisational hierarchy) to the data stored in the AIS. Internal users include accountants (internal audit, managerial accounting, financial accounting, and taxes) as well as employees in other areas of the organisation who use data from the AIS to support operations (maintenance, sales). Accountants in different roles, such as banking and controlling, might benefit from the insights that predictive analytics can provide (Oliveira, 2018).

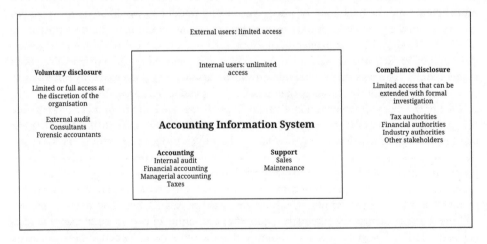

Figure 12.1 Typical users of accounting information systems for predictive analytics.

Internal auditors not only have full access to the data in the AIS but also are responsible for designing and implementing the controls necessary to provide reasonable assurance of its reliability. In contrast to external auditors who would use predictive analytics based on data from the AIS during the duration of an engagement, internal auditors may build predictive analytics models that access data on an ongoing basis. Internal auditors might use predictive analytics for fraud detection, information technology risk, audit, and enterprise risk management (Rakipi et al., 2021).

As the role of managerial accountants has evolved, the data sources and methodologies used have also evolved. Appelbaum et al. (2017a) propose a managerial accounting data analytics framework to supplement data from the AIS with external data for performance measurement and decision making. The framework proposes data analytics to improve the performance of traditional managerial accounting tasks, such as measuring the efficiency of processing, and more recently adopted tasks, such as continuous monitoring. There is evidence that managerial accounting is adopting and benefiting from predictive analytics. Huikku et al. (2017), for instance, documented how accounting departments at companies located in Finland are initiating projects to utilise predictive analytics for forecasting financial and operational data. Similarly, Wiegmann et al. (2021) documented how two multinational corporations benefited from the use of predictive analytics, combined with traditional budgeting techniques, to prepare more accurate budgets.

Financial accounting, with its responsibility for preparing financial statements and compliance, may utilise predictive analytics to detect bribes and other illegal activities. Regulators in the US have shown leniency towards organisations that provide their compliance office with access to financial and operational data to screen for risks (Tokar, 2020). Microsoft, for instance, was assessed for a reduced fine in a foreign bribery case due to its use of analytics and transaction monitoring (Tokar, 2020).

Relative to other internal functions in an organisation, the tax function has been a late adopter of predictive analytics since its work is focused mainly on tax compliance (Deloitte, 2016). However, the tax function can benefit from the use of predictive analytics to identify anomalies and risk areas, analyse unstructured documentation, and even interpret tax laws (Deloitte, 2016). For instance, a predictive analytics tool developed by Wolters Kluwer uses natural language processing (NLP) to interpret legal texts and estimate external factors, both positive and negative, that affect the tax bill (PR Newswire, 2017). Also, using NLP, KPMG patented a tool to analyse text and predict which elements would be relevant for tax returns (PR Newswire, 2021). In addition to the functional areas that are the competency of accountants, an AIS also provides data to other functional areas, such as sales, marketing, purchasing, and operations. Diageo, for instance, uses predictive analytics to predict the return on marketing campaigns and to target advertisement more precisely (Trentmann, 2019).

Voluntary disclosure users

Voluntary disclosure users are external to the organisation and have been granted access to the AIS to provide services at the discretion of the organisation. The scope of the data access provided to this type of user depends on their engagement. Examples of voluntary disclosure users are external auditors, forensic accountants, and consultants. Considering the relevance of external auditing in the accounting profession, we discuss predictive analytics for external auditing in a separate section.

Although forensic investigations can be prompted by regulators, organisations may also hire external forensic accountants to investigate anomalies. Forensic investigations often supplement the data from the AIS with other sources such as emails, texts, or voicemails (Todd & Gill, 2018). Analytics performed on financial transactions can reveal suspicious transactions that deserve further investigation. Predictive analytics can also be used on other data sources to identify evidence then used in an investigation (Todd & Gill, 2018).

Compliance disclosure users

Compliance disclosure users are external to the organisation and are typically government agencies that receive summary data produced by the AIS and reported for various regulatory compliance purposes. Examples include tax returns and financial statements. Compliance users are increasingly supplementing the data they receive through these compliance processes with other data sources. In 2011, the Internal Revenue Service (the government tax agency in the US) established the Office of Compliance Analytics, which uses predictive models that combine compliance data with publicly available data such as social media and commercial data to identify potential fraud and identity theft (Houser & Sanders, 2018).

Although their access to the AIS is initially limited, compliance disclosure users may gain full access when a formal investigation is launched. When Airbus admitted to paying bribes and entered into a deferred prosecution agreement, it allowed forensic investigators access not only to its AIS containing millions of transactions but also to many other data sources (Dempsey, 2021). In that case, investigators used predictive analytics to identify payments made using fake names and coded emails (Katz, 2020).

External users who only have access to publicly available financial information may also use predictive analytics to supplement their analysis. For instance, financial investors used cell phone data to determine whether Tesla ramped up production as it had promised (Dezember, 2018). Similarly, stock market analysts, competitors, and others could use public financial information to build their own predictive analytics models.

Predictive analytics in external auditing

When compared to other business functions, accounting has been late in realising the value of analytics. Thomas Davenport, a professor of Information Technology at Babson College and Senior Advisor to Deloitte US, noted:

> The accounting function is probably one of the least analytical functions in large organisations, clearly, it has a very strong transactional orientation, at best doing descriptive analytics focused only on structured small data. … Accounting not only has to catch up with analytics, but also needs to keep up with this rapidly changing field on an ongoing basis.
> *(Tschakert et al., 2016, p. 61)*

Although accountants and accounting practices, in general, may have been slow to adopt analytics, in a 2014 study, Earley (2015) found that the tax and advisory practices of public accounting firms were the first to embrace analytics, with the auditing practice lagging. At that time, he questioned whether the investments being made in data analytics by auditing firms would pay off, or if longer-term analytics was more in the domain of the consulting practices. While Davenport and Early saw accounting, and audit in particular, as being slow to adopt analytics, Salijeni et al. (2019) argue that the increasing use of data analytics within auditing firms could be seen as motivated by a desire to maintain or restore legitimacy to audits, like the motivation for statistical sampling and the development of the Audit Command

Language (ACL) and Interactive Data Extraction and Analysis (IDEA) back in the 1980s. The use of analytics by auditors has also started to concern regulators. To grow their analytics business, the accounting firms need to attract analysts with data skills, which are 'not in the natural skill set of the auditor', so it was expected that they would need to boost the services side of their businesses, possibly running the risk of auditing their own work (Katz, 2014). Earley (2015) also noted that if analytics became a growth area for advisory services, such services would likely be prohibited transactions under the Sarbanes-Oxley Act. Salijeni et al. (2019) also raised the question of whether requiring accountants to also master analytics skills might result in the de-skilling of accountants instead of better audit outcomes.

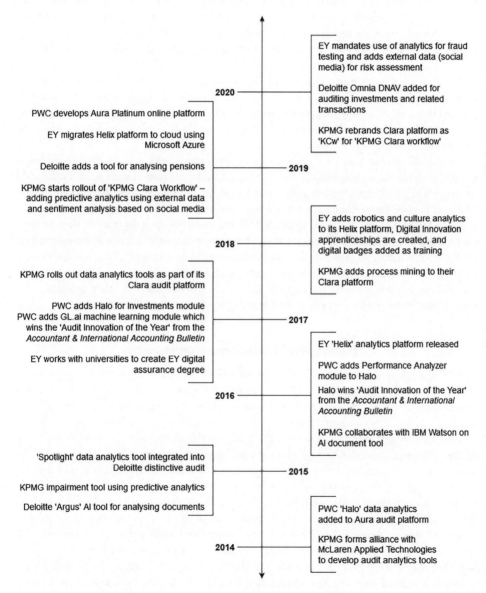

Figure 12.2   Timeline of audit analytic milestones in the UK transparency reports for each of the Big 4 firms (2012–2020).

A timeline of analytics in public accounting

In examining the factors motivating or hindering the adoption of data analytics and other decision support technologies by external auditors, Meredith et al. (2020) identified firm size as an important factor, in part due to more limited resources at smaller firms and budget pressures being a dominant factor in auditor reluctance to adopt these technologies. Similarly, a survey by CPA Canada (2017) found that firm size was an impediment to smaller firms adapting audit analytics. For these reasons, we have focused on the adoption of analytics by audit practices at the Big 4 accounting firms, which have been working on embedding analytics into their audit workflow systems and training their personnel on the use of these tools since 2015. A timeline of the audit analytics milestones mentioned in the United Kingdom (UK) transparency reports for each of the Big 4 firms from 2012 to 2020 is shown in Figure 12.2. Before 2014, there was limited discussion of analytics related to assurance services by any of the firms, and what minimal discussion was included had a forward-looking context.[1] In its 2013 transparency report, Deloitte was the first firm to mention using analytics in its assurance practice. Although it had not branded its analytics tools at that time, it claimed that analytics would transform audit. In a section on the 'audit of the future', PWC made a similar claim in 2013 that sophisticated analytics would allow auditors to assess huge data sets in seconds.

During the period 2014–2016, all the Big 4 firms announced the development and branding of their proprietary analytics platforms that would be integrated with their digital auditing workflow platforms. PWC was the first to announce a branded data analytics tool named 'Halo' as part of their Aura auditing software platform in 2014 as a replacement for ACL and IDEA (Salijeni et al., 2019). In 2015, Deloitte revealed their 'Spotlight' data analytics tool and EY announced 'Helix', as an integrated component of its Canvas auditing platform. KPMG took a different approach by first forming a ten-year strategic alliance with McLaren Applied Technologies in 2014 to develop analytics tools and a collaboration with IBM Watson to develop new artificial intelligence (AI) tools. These tools were then integrated into their 'Clara' audit platform but were not branded separately from Clara.

Training and educational requirements

For auditing firms to get widespread adoption of analytics tools on audit engagements and realise any of the potential cost and audit quality benefits, they needed to train their personnel both in the use of these tools and how to use and interpret the results. Initially, one of the bottlenecks to incorporating analytics more broadly in the audit process was the lack of expertise among auditors (Salijeni et al., 2019). Analytics training was needed at all levels of the audit engagement. Although the software tools would mainly be used by junior-level personnel, senior personnel would be responsible for interpreting the results and deciding the impact on the audit outcome (Tschakert et al., 2016). Salijeni et al. (2019) found that if the senior personnel were not comfortable with the analytics performed, they would ask for the analysis to be repeated using traditional audit approaches. They also found cases where there was disagreement between engagement and analytics partners regarding the additional work to be performed on outlier transactions, since the additional work required would strain the audit budget. In addition to training their staff, auditing practices needed to convince clients of the value in adopting an approach where all the transactions in a journal would be analysed instead of using statistical sampling. Deloitte found that it would usually take three years to realise cost savings on an audit using advanced analytics. In the first year of adoption, audit costs would increase due to the additional work of setting up the data wrangling process needed to format and reconcile the data. It could be expected to break even in year two and then start to see savings in year three (Tysiac, 2020). A recent survey of public accounting partners on audits using analytics found disagreement as to how the use of analytics would impact audit fees. Some partners thought fees would eventually need to decrease due to client expectations that analytics should result in a more efficient audit, whereas other partners anticipated no decrease due to the cost of the investment their firm made in developing the analytic tools (Austin et al., 2021).

To train their personnel, auditing firms not only created their own internal training programs but also looked to academia to train the next generation of auditors. In 2013, the Association to Advance Collegiate Schools of Business (AACSB) added standard A7 on the additional information technology skills accounting graduates should possess. A 2014 white paper interpreting that standard clarified that although the additional analytics courses did not need to be taught by the accounting department, 'data analytics or business analytics along with appropriate IT skills and knowledge development should be a key component of accounting curricula' (AACSB, 2014). In 2015, PWC (2015) published a white paper on what students need to learn for this changing environment, and it advocated for curriculum enhancements similar to the AACSB's revised standard. PWC also expected increased demand for students with dual majors in accounting and information systems – a combination similar to AIS programs. They foresaw a need for accounting students who were not software developers but could understand and be able to work with the tools that were starting to emerge. In 2015, KPMG identified the same need for accountants with data analytics skills and initiated partnerships with nine schools to create accounting programs focused on analytics (Moore & Felo, 2021). In December of that same year, the American Institute of Certified Public Accountants (AICPA) and CPA Canada announced the *Rutgers AICPA Data Analytics Research* initiative with the College of Business at Rutgers University, to explore how analytics could be incorporated at a foundational level in the audit process to improve audit quality (AICPA, undated).

A 2021 study of university accounting programs found that standard A7 has had the desired impact of providing accounting students with analytics skills since 91.6% of the accredited accounting programs reviewed offered dedicated data analytics courses in accounting, but only 30.3% of accounting programs without any AACSB accreditation had such courses (Moore & Felo, 2021). However, Moore & Felo (2021) also validated the concern voiced by Salijeni et al. (2019) that a focus on data analytics could result in the de-skilling of accountants since 31% of new accounting hires in 2018 were from degree programs outside of accounting.

Regulatory barriers to the adoption of analytics

Although all the Big 4 have emphasised their increasing investments in analytics, the slow adoption of analytics in auditing compared to other fields is not solely due to the lack of analytics skills among their staff. The director of professional standards at the Public Company Accounting Oversight Board (PCAOB) stated he did not want auditing standards to inhibit the adoption of audit analytics (Davenport, 2016), but the lack of guidance from regulators and the lack of professional standards addressing the role of analytics in assurance have made auditors hesitant to rely on analytics instead of traditional audit procedures in establishing substantive evidence for an audit opinion (EY Reporting, 2015; Eilifsen et al., 2020; Austin et al., 2021). In 2018, the AICPA issued the *Guide to Audit Data Analytics* (AICPA, 2018), which, although not authoritative, provided an overview to financial statement auditors on Audit Data Analytics (ADAs). ADA is defined as:

> [t]he science and art of discovering and analyzing patterns, identifying anomalies, and extracting other useful information in data underlying or related to the subject matter of an audit through analysis, modeling, and visualisation for the purpose of planning or performing the audit.
>
> *(Byrnes et al., 2014, p. 5)*

Despite the AICPA providing this guidance, Alles & Gray (2016) argue that advanced analytics is a disruptive technology and will require a significant change in auditing standards. The International Audit and Assurance Standards Board working group on data analytics has been looking at the use of data analytics, but Sue Almond, a member of the working group, noted that there are many challenges, including that the standards need to apply to all audits, and there needs to be enough flexibility to foster innovation, and any standards created today would apply in the future when analytic capabilities have evolved (ACCA, 2019).

In the initial period from 2014 to 2016, each of the Big 4 firms developed their own proprietary analytics tools. The initial goals for each of these analytics platforms were (1) improving audit quality through better risk analysis, (2) utilising 100% of the transactions in a ledger instead of auditing a sample of the data, and (3) being able to summarise the results and communicating them visually to clients. During this time frame, many firms claimed that analytics would transform the audit process (Davenport, 2016; Sidhu, 2017). However, researchers found that analytics tools did not result in new audit procedures but instead were used largely to perform recomputations, reconciliations, and recalculations that previously had been done manually (Salijeni et al., 2019). Even those firms investing in analytics acknowledged that they were early in the process of adopting advanced analytics and that using analytics involved a massive change from the traditional audit approach (EY Reporting, 2015). At a PCAOB standing advisory group meeting in 2015, some audit committee members commented that they found a gap between the sophistication of the audit technology capabilities discussed at the firm level and what the engagement teams were delivering. This gap in actual use continues to be an issue. A survey of audit partners and managers at five Norwegian international accounting firms in 2019 (Eilifsen et al., 2020) found that although the global firms were making a push to use advanced ADA, and these were more often used on new audits where the clients had asked about the firm's ADA capabilities, there was little use of advanced ADA and almost no use of big data or NLP techniques.

Rollout of analytics in audit practices

In their transparency reports for the years 2017–2020, each of the Big 4 discusses their continued investment and development of integrated advanced data analytics, machine learning, AI, NLP, and process mining in its cloud-based audit platform (Raphael, 2017; Werner et al., 2021). Over the longer term, it will be interesting to see if audit engagement teams catch up and implement the capabilities being developed at the firm level, or if the pattern of limited use that Eilifsen et al. (2020) found persists. Alles & Gray (2016) point out that accounting firms have a mixed history regarding the implementation of new audit technologies. They point out that an article in 1991 found the Big 6 were developing or had deployed 43 different expert system tools, but despite having spent millions of dollars developing these systems, none were regularly used in financial audits. They also point out that continuous auditing and continuous monitoring have long been promoted by researchers, but there has not been a significant uptake.

However, not all components of the 'digital audit' have seen such slow adoption. Krieger et al. (2021) see the digitisation of audits as consisting of two components, the first being the management aspect, which includes the workflow and communication with clients, and the second being the fieldwork of assessing risk and obtaining audit evidence. The use of ADA, which would be part of the fieldwork, has seen slow adoption, but the digitisation of the management aspect has already been widely implemented. By 2020, all the Big 4 were touting their audit analytics platforms as market-leading or world-class. Deloitte claims its Omnia global audit platform is the first audit platform that is 100% cloud based and includes cognitive technologies, customised workflows, and advanced data analytics (Deloitte, 2020). In their 2020 transparency report, EY describes its EY Canvas audit platform and EY Helix analytics platform as world-class technological tools it has deployed to enhance audit quality (EY UK, 2020, p. 87). KPMG's 2020 transparency report notes that 'KPMG Clara work-flow', which incorporates advanced analytics, is their largest technology investment to date. According to KPMG, Clara is 'the most modern audit platform and methodology in the Big 4' (p. 6). PWC describes its Halo analytics platform as market-leading in their 2020 transparency report (PwC UK, 2020, p. 75).

One aspect of advanced analytics that is likely to hinder its adoption in risk assessment is the lack of explainability for the complex calculations used in predictive analytics. Anthony (2021) points out that in investment banking, software has now replaced many of the quantitative calculations previously performed by junior staff, and that at both the junior and senior levels, some investment bankers relied on the algorithms in the software without understanding how they worked – effectively treating them as a 'black box'. Since both investment banking and risk assessment rely on quantitative analysis, to the extent that software is automating existing calculations, increased training can provide an understanding of the underlying algorithms, increasing transparency and making the calculations a 'glass box' (Anthony, 2021). However, for novel approaches based on machine learning techniques such as support vector machines or AI methods such as deep neural networks, additional training would not suffice since the engineers building these systems cannot fully explain how they make decisions, and deep learning, in particular, has been described as a deep black box (Knight, 2017; Asatiani et al., 2021). Beyond whether the inner workings of such systems are transparent to software developers, different types of system transparency and explanation may be required for different stakeholders as well as for different purposes. In discussing explainable AI systems in general, Weller (2019) identifies eight different types of transparency with different goals, including developers who need an understanding of how a system works (type 1), society in general for developing trust in the system (type 3), users understanding a particular decision (type 4), regulators being able to evaluate the system (type 5), and even the firms deploying a system that would want users to be comfortable with the decisions so they continue using it (type 7). When applied to risk analysis in auditing, there could be different explanations required for different stakeholders with different goals, such as system developers, auditors using the software, accounting firms rolling out the software, regulators, audit clients, and users of a company's financial reports who are relying on an auditor's opinion.

To explore one platform in more detail as an example, in the following section, we discuss the evolution of EY's Helix suite of analytics tools, which were first introduced in 2016 and have been integrated into its Canvas audit management platform.

Helix

EY Helix is the analytics component of EY's cloud-based audit platform, but it was not originally cloud based. In 2018, EY began its cloud migration as the available cloud platforms became more mature. Back in 2016, when Helix was originally rolled out to the audit practice, it was hosted on EY's servers, and EY emphasised the data security achieved by having staff access Helix through the EY corporate network to data hosted on servers managed by EY personnel, with none of the data infrastructure outsourced, and the operation of the datacentres being performed only by EY personnel. Although the use of cloud offerings from Amazon, Microsoft, IBM, and others was becoming more common, many large companies initially viewed the cloud as a data security risk, particularly for confidential data. More recently, the Big 4 have all migrated their audit platforms to cloud-based infrastructures. In 2018, EY started work with Microsoft on migrating its analytics platform to Microsoft's Azure Synapse Analytics hosted on the Azure cloud (Microsoft, 2021a). Azure Synapse leverages Microsoft's Power BI as a way for end users to be able to visualise data and underneath leverages Azure machine learning, SQL, and Apache Spark to analyse and query both structured and unstructured data stored in Microsoft's cloud-based Azure Data Lake (Microsoft, 2021b).

The migration to a cloud-based platform mirrors trends in the software industry in general, and some of the reasons for EY's migration are the same advantages cited by other software companies, such as the elasticity of paying only for computing resources as needed, which is particularly relevant for processing that experiences seasonal peaks. According to Rahul Misra, EY Helix Product Director, 'that kind of flexibility and elasticity is a game changer' (Microsoft, 2021a). Other reasons cited for the move to a cloud environment include being able to store the data in datacentres located in specific countries (to comply with the European Union's General Data Protection Regulation) and the improved data security as cloud platforms have matured. The migration to a cloud platform is not unique to EY in that all the Big 4 now emphasise that their analytics platforms are cloud based, and Deloitte's Omnia audit platform also uses Microsoft's Azure cloud (Agile Thought, undated).

Since Microsoft's Azure Synaptic Analytics leverages Microsoft's Power BI, an end-user data visualisation tool, Helix allows audit staff to analyse large volumes of data stored in an Azure data lake and then generate visualisations of the results without the need for data scientists on the audit engagement (Microsoft, 2021b). EY's stated goal is to use analytics tools to augment the auditor instead of replacing the auditor. Although much attention has been given in the popular press to predictions that accountants would be automated out of a job – both for routine tasks and those requiring judgement (Roose, 2021) – in promoting its concept of the 'digital audit', EY sees the use of analytics and automation as enabling auditors to spend more time on risk identification and tasks requiring professional judgement.

The Helix platform is composed of an array of 'analysers', and audit staff at member firms worldwide have been trained in their use, allowing the tools to be applied consistently on global audits (EY, 2021). At the start of each audit engagement (for data security reasons), a separate instance of Synapse Analytics is started in Helix for that specific engagement; EY states that there are 70,000 such instances being used worldwide (EY, undated). Since 'analyser' is not a common term in the accounting field nor data analytics, machine learning, or AI, it is not immediately clear what an analyser is.

Analysers can be thought of as modules in EY's Helix platform, and the term predates its migration to a cloud platform. Each analyser is focused on a specific purpose, but some are more general, such as the 'group scope analyser', which is based on aggregated financial

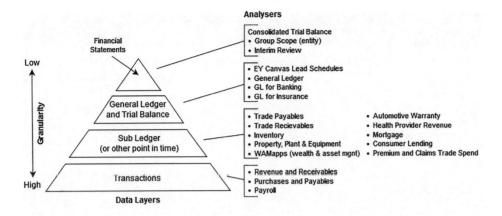

Figure 12.3 Data layers and analysers in EY Helix.

statement data and used to inform overall audit strategy (EY, undated). Others, such as the payroll analyser, are more specialised and use granular transaction-level data. In discussing the array of analysers available to audit teams, EY groups analysers into four data layers based on the granularity of the data they utilise. Figure 12.3 shows the four data layers, with the most granular transaction-level data at the bottom. The analysers are then listed by data layer. Integrated into Helix is the ability to ingest data from multiple sources, which is then stored in the Azure Data Lake. Deloitte noted that due to the data wrangling required to ingest highly granular data for analytics, their audit fees were higher in the first year of an engagement (Tysiac, 2020). EY is using robotic process automation for data wrangling and workpaper generation, and it is unclear if this process is automated in subsequent years after the initial setup in the first year of an engagement.

Shown in Figure 12.4 is a view of the user interface for EY's Trade Receivables Analyzer.[2] The aim when using this analyser is not to automate audit decisions but instead to identify patterns or trends that could suggest where the auditor should focus their effort, or predicting where problems may exist and greater effort should be focused. From the analyser dashboard shown in Figure 12.4, the audit staff can drill down to the transaction level of data granularity. If the analysis shows a result that could impact the audit opinion, the staff can then export the results shown to EY Canvas to be included in the audit workpapers. There is also a separate export button for creating a report to share information with the audit client. As can be surmised from Figure 12.4, auditors are the end user of these analytics tools and need to be trained on what the visualisation is communicating, and understand the risks, but using the Power BI interface in EY Helix does not require the auditor to be a programmer. Instead, EY is separately recruiting programmers and data scientists and creating hubs of excellence in data science.

In addition to clients finding value in audit analytics capabilities, and regulators accepting revised procedures that may not align with generally accepted practices, for the analysers and other components of Helix to provide value over the long term, programmers and data scientists need to work closely with the auditors in building these tools. When engaged to develop Deloitte's Omnia cloud-based audit platform, Agile Thought (undated) emphasised the importance of having Deloitte's audit practitioners fill the role of product owner on each of the 30 agile teams delivering software every two weeks. Although other public accounting firms, including EY, do not directly discuss their development methodology, it is

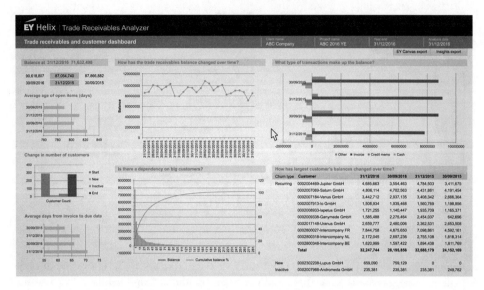

Figure 12.4   Screen capture of EY Helix Trade Receivables Analyzer (with permission).

most likely similar to Deloitte's agile approach since domain expertise would be required to determine which features would be useful on an engagement.

In addition to the Helix Analysers, which are primarily focused on audit risk, EY is investing in further research using machine learning and predictive analytics and bringing in external data such as from social media into an audit. Examples include text analytics for analysing documents such as leases and contracts, experimenting using deep learning to evaluate restatement risk or detect fraud, and creating a fraud prediction model to calculate the probability of financial misstatements. EY Japan is also piloting an AI-driven tool for detecting data anomalies that may indicate fraud, and the EY practice in Australia is using AI on audits to automate bank confirmations. AI is also being used to automate data capture, such as a proof-of-concept project using drones and computer vision to perform an inventory count of cars at an automobile factory and then pushing that data into EY's Canvas audit workflow platform.

Future research areas

The application of advanced analytics to audit has lagged other areas of accounting, and although the Big 4 have made substantial investments in their audit analytics platforms, these same firms previously made substantial investments in expert systems that never were widely implemented. This raises a question as to whether their current investment in analytics and machine learning will lead to widespread adoption of analytics on audit engagements.

Additionally, interviews of Big 4 personnel and their clients (Eilifsen et al., 2020), as well as a review by the Financial Reporting Council (FRC), have highlighted gaps between the analytics capabilities touted at the firm level and their implementation on actual audit engagements. Similarly, there is a gap in expectations between the accounting firms and their clients as to the impact of audit analytics on fees – clients see analytics as potentially reducing fees and auditors see it as increasing audit fees since they need to recoup their investment in analytics (Austin et al., 2021). For audit analytics to be widely adopted, audit engagement partners must see a value in adding analytics to the audit, the audit staff must be skilled in using the tools that the firms create, clients must perceive analytics as adding value to the audit, auditing standards need to be updated to allow alternate procedures based on analytics, and regulators must see analytics as generating better audit results. Prior researchers have identified several issues related to the use of analytics in assurance and proposed a research agenda (Alles & Gray, 2016; Sutton et al., 2016; Salijeni et al., 2019). Some of these issues are discussed below, as well as open issues we see as being in the path to widespread adoption of auditing analytics.

One focus of audit analytics in large auditing practices has been on analysing 100% of the transactions instead of using statistical sampling. It has previously been argued (Appelbaum et al., 2017b) that looking at all transactions could enable continuous auditing and auditing by exception, but a question arises as to whether continuous auditing is necessary for there to be value in looking at all the transactions. Despite continuous auditing being widely discussed as a research topic, it has seen minimal adoption in practice since audit clients have not perceived its value to exceed its cost (ACCA, 2019). An open question is whether audit clients will see a value in auditors analysing 100% of their transactions instead of using sampling, particularly if that approach initially results in higher audit fees.

Prior research has identified the need for regulatory guidance on the use of analytics since it is a disruptive technology (Alles & Gray, 2016), but an open question is whether the use of analytics results in better audits. As noted by Violino (2019), some significant audit failures have been due to budget pressures or a lack of staff expertise in a client's industry, so it is unclear whether analytics could help prevent such failures. Similarly, Salijeni et al. (2019) questioned whether auditors possessing technology skills will make better audit judgements. In a thematic review of the use of audit analytics and their impact on audit quality, the FRC found that when firms rolled out a limited set of analytics tools, they were more likely to see an improvement in audit quality since staff were able to gain confidence in their use of the tools (Financial Reporting Council, 2017). However, in the FRC's 2020 review of the top seven auditing firms, they found overall audit quality to be unacceptable in that 33% of the audits required more than limited improvements. Of the Big 4, only Deloitte was able to reach the target of having 90% of reviewed audits requiring no more than minimal improvement (Sweet, 2020). In the FRC's firm reports for 2020, there was limited discussion of analytics, but one of the good practices observed at Deloitte was the use of bespoke data analytic procedures in auditing unbilled revenue, and one of the good practices observed at PWC was the comprehensive use of data analytics in the auditing of revenue. Given the FRC's earlier thematic review involved the 2016 audit cycle, an open question is whether ADA contributed in a meaningful way to improvements in audit quality by 2020 and beyond.

One last issue that deserves further research is the impact of analytics training on the long-term career prospects of accounting graduates. There has been an effort by accounting educators and the AACSB to increase the level of education in analytics and data science. Additionally, all the Big 4 firms are looking for analytics skills in the accounting graduates they hire. However, analytics are performed by junior audit personnel, and other researchers have raised concerns as to whether a greater emphasis on data and analytic skills could reduce the learning of traditional accounting skills. An open question is whether analytic skills are being rewarded over the longer term. Are students who pursue analytics in accounting increasing their initial employment prospects at a risk to their long-term career advancement?

Conclusions

Predictive analytics uses historical data to build models to estimate unknown values. The usefulness of these models has the potential to transform the accounting field in all areas, including financial, managerial, taxes, and forensics. Predictive analytics models in accounting draw from the vast amounts of data stored in AIS and may supplement the models with other sources of data.

Commonly performed tasks, such as estimating whether there is a going concern issue, could be transformed using predictive analytics models by including many variables of interest from multiple data sources. Although predictive analytics could impact all accounting areas, its potential has been discussed predominately in external auditing, with the Big 4 making significant investments. Implementing predictive analytics poses technical challenges, but overcoming other challenges, such as enriching the skill set of accountants and enacting regulations that permit its use, may be equally or more critical to its widespread use.

To reap the benefits of predictive analytics, more research is needed to understand the nature of the challenges to its adoption in the accounting field, from the perishability of data to the transformation of the workflow. Researchers can also address open research issues, such as investigating the impact of predictive analytics on audit quality and career advancement.

Notes

1 The transparency reports used to create the timeline can be downloaded from https://bit.ly/Big4Transparency.
2 Screen capture from video available at: https://player.vimeo.com/video/244350616. Used with permission.

References

AACSB. (2014). *AACSB international accounting accreditation standard A7: Information technology skills and knowledge for accounting graduates: An interpretation.* Association to Advance Collegiate Schools of Business. Retrieved December 20 from https://www.aacsb.edu/-/media/aacsb/publications/white-papers/accounting-accreditation-standard-7.ashx?la=en
ACCA. (2019). *The impact of digital and artificial intelligence on audit and finance professionals: Harnessing the opportunities of disruptive technologies.* Retrieved May 1 from https://www.accaglobal.com/gb/en/technical-activities/technical-resources-search/2018/december/impact-of-digital-and-ai-on-audit-.html
Agile Thought. (undated). *Transforming Deloitte's audit experience with next-gen, azure-based platform.* Retrieved May 1 from https://agilethought.com/client-stories/transforming-deloittes-audit-experience-with-next-gen-azure-based-platform/
AICPA. (2018). *Guide to audit data analytics.* John Wiley & Sons, Incorporated.
AICPA. (undated). *Rutgers AICPA Data Analytics Research Initiative (RADAR).* AICPA. Retrieved May 1 from https://www.aicpa.org/interestareas/frc/assuranceadvisoryservices/radar.html
Alles, M., & Gray, G. L. (2016). Incorporating big data in audits: Identifying inhibitors and a research agenda to address those inhibitors. *International Journal of Accounting Information Systems, 22,* 44–59. https://doi.org/10.1016/j.accinf.2016.07.004
Anthony, C. (2021). When knowledge work and analytical technologies collide: The practices and consequences of black boxing algorithmic technologies. *Administrative Science Quarterly, 66*(4), 1173–1212. https://doi.org/10.1177/00018392211016755
Appelbaum, D., Kogan, A., & Vasarhelyi, M. A. (2017a). Big Data and analytics in the modern audit engagement: Research needs [Article]. *Auditing: A Journal of Practice & Theory, 36*(4), 1–27. https://doi.org/10.2308/ajpt-51684
Appelbaum, D., Kogan, A., Vasarhelyi, M., & Yan, Z. (2017b). Impact of business analytics and enterprise systems on managerial accounting. *International Journal of Accounting Information Systems, 25,* 29–44. https://doi.org/10.1016/j.accinf.2017.03.003
Asatiani, A., Malo, P., Rådberg Nagbøl, P., Penttinen, E., Rinta-Kahila, T., & Salovaara, A. (2021). Sociotechnical envelopment of artificial intelligence: An approach to organisational deployment

of inscrutable artificial intelligence systems. *Journal of the Association for Information Systems*, *22*(2), 325–352. https://doi.org/10.17705/1jais.00664

Austin, A. A., Carpenter, T. D., Christ, M. H., & Nielson, C. S. (2021). The data analytics journey: Interactions among auditors, managers, regulation, and technology. *Contemporary Accounting Research*, *38*(3). https://doi.org/10.1111/1911-3846.12680

Boone, T., Ganeshan, R., Jain, A., & Sanders, N. R. (2019). Forecasting sales in the supply chain: Consumer analytics in the big data era. *International Journal of Forecasting*, *35*(1), 170–180. https://doi.org/10.1016/j.ijforecast.2018.09.003

Byrnes, P. E., Criste, T., Stewart, T. R., & Vasarhelyi, M. A. (2014). *Reimagining auditing in a wired world*. AICPA. Retrieved May 1 from https://us.aicpa.org/content/dam/aicpa/interestareas/frc/assuranceadvisoryservices/downloadabledocuments/whitepaper-blue-sky-scenario-pinkbook.pdf

Chartered Professional Accountants of Canada. (2017). *Audit data analytics alert. Survey on use of audit data analytics in Canada Results and possible implications*. CPA Canada https://www.cpacanada.ca/en/business-and-accounting-resources/audit-and-assurance/canadian-auditing-standards-cas/publications/audit-data-analytics-alert-ada-survey-results

Committee on National Security Systems. (2022). *Glossary*. Retrieved from https://www.cnss.gov/CNSS/openDoc.cfm?JDuV5sVEdc5egZ4Fk6NkAw==

Davenport, T. H. (2016). *The power of advanced audit analytics*. Deloitte. Retrieved May 1 from https://www2.deloitte.com/us/en/pages/deloitte-analytics/articles/us-the-power-of-advanced-audit-analytics.html

Deloitte. (2016). *Tax data analytics*. Deloitte. Retrieved May 1 from https://www2.deloitte.com/content/dam/Deloitte/us/Documents/Tax/us-tax-data-analytics-a-new-era-for-tax-planning-and-compliance.pdf

Deloitte. (2020). *Deloitte Wins 2020 'Audit Innovation of the Year' at the digital accountancy forum & awards*. Deloitte. Retrieved May 1 from https://www2.deloitte.com/us/en/pages/about-deloitte/articles/press-releases/deloitte-wins-2020-audit-innovation-of-the-year-at-digital-accountancy-forum-awards.html

Dempsey, M. (2021). *How to investigate a firm with 60 million documents*. BBC. Retrieved March 1st, 2021 from https://www.bbc.com/news/business-55306139

Dezember, R. (2018, Nov 02). Your smartphone's location data is worth big money to wall street; the phone in your pocket is dishing info on where you spend your time and, likely, money. *Wall Street Journal (Online)*. https://www.wsj.com/articles/your-smartphones-location-data-is-worth-big-money-to-wall-street-1541131260

Earley, C. E. (2015). Data analytics in auditing: Opportunities and challenges. *Business Horizons*, *58*(5), 493–500. https://doi.org/10.1016/j.bushor.2015.05.002

Eilifsen, A., Kinserdal, F., Messier, W. F., & McKee, T. E. (2020). An exploratory study into the use of audit data analytics on audit engagements. *Accounting Horizons*, *34*(4), 75–103. https://doi.org/10.2308/HORIZONS-19-121

EY. (2021). *Three lessons in resiliency from the data-driven audit*. FEI. Retrieved July 1 from https://www.financialexecutives.org/FEI-Daily/May-2021/Three-Lessons-in-Resiliency-from-the-Data-Driven.aspx

EY. (undated). *EY Helix*. Retrieved May 1 from https://www.ey.com/en_gl/audit/technology/helix

EY Reporting. (2015). *How big data and analytics are transforming the audit*. EY. Retrieved May 1 from https://www.ey.com/en_gl/assurance/how-big-data-and-analytics-are-transforming-the-audit

EY UK. (2020). *Transparency report*. https://www.ey.com/en_uk/about-us/transparency-report-2020

Financial Reporting Council. (2017). *The use of data analytics in the audit of financial statements*. Financial Reporting Council. Retrieved May 1 from https://www.frc.org.uk/getattachment/4fd19a18-1beb-4959-8737-ae2dca80af67/AQTR_Audit-Data-Analytics-Jan-2017.pdf

Gajbe, S. B., Tiwari, A., Gopalji, & Singh, R. K. (2021). Evaluation and analysis of Data Management Plan tools: A parametric approach. *Information Processing & Management*, *58*(3), 102480. https://doi.org/10.1016/j.ipm.2020.102480

Grand View Research. (2020). *Predictive analytics market analysis report*. Grand View Research. Retrieved May 1 from https://www.millioninsights.com/industry-reports/predictive-analytics-market

Houser, K. A., & Sanders, D. (2018). The use of big data analytics by the IRS: What tax practitioners need to know. *Journal of Taxation*, *128*(2), 6–11.

Huikku, J., Hyvönen, T., & Järvinen, J. (2017). The role of a predictive analytics project initiator in the integration of financial and operational forecasts. *Baltic Journal of Management*, *12*(4), 427–446. http://dx.doi.org/10.1108/BJM-05-2017-0164

Katz, B. (2020, Feb 01). Airbus settles bribery probe for $4 billion. *Wall Street Journal*. https://www.wsj. com/articles/airbus-reaches-international-deal-over-corruption-probe-11580195579

Katz, D. (2014). *Regulators fear big data threatens audit quality*. CFO. Retrieved May 1 from https://www. cfo.com/auditing/2014/04/regulators-fear-big-data-threatens-audit-quality/

Kelleher, J. D., Mac Namee, B., & D'Arcy, A. (2015). *Fundamentals of machine learning for predictive data analytics: Algorithms, worked examples, and case studies*. The MIT Press.

Knight, W. (2017). The dark secret at the heart of AI. (Cover story). *MIT Technology Review, 120*(3), 54–65.

Krieger, F., Drews, P., & Velte, P. (2021). Explaining the (non-) adoption of advanced data analytics in auditing: A process theory. *International Journal of Accounting Information Systems, 41*, 100511. https:// doi.org/10.1016/j.accinf.2021.100511

Loten, A. (2021, Jul 01). Companies adjust predictive models in wake of covid; FedEx and other firms are leaning more heavily on real-time live data to gauge demand. *Wall Street Journal (Online)*. https:// www.wsj.com/articles/companies-adjust-predictive-models-in-wake-of-covid-11625160587

McGinty, J. C. (2014, Dec 05). Accountants increasingly use data analysis to catch Fraud; auditors wield mathematical weapons to detect cheating. *Wall Street Journal (Online)*. https://www.wsj. com/articles/accountants-increasingly-use-data-analysis-to-catch-fraud-1417804886

Meredith, K., Blake, J., Baxter, P., & Kerr, D. (2020). Drivers of and barriers to decision support technology use by financial report auditors. *Decision Support Systems, 139*, 113402. https://doi.org/ 10.1016/j.dss.2020.113402

Microsoft. (2021a). *EY Helix transforms audit by using analytics powered by Azure Synapse Analytics*. Microsoft. Retrieved May 1 from https://customers.microsoft.com/en-us/story/ 1376231533824549115-ey-professional-services-azure-en-united-states

Microsoft. (2021b). *Three ways analytics can help: Respond, adapt, save*. Microsoft. Retrieved July 1 from https:// azure.microsoft.com/en-us/resources/three-ways-analytics-can-help-you-respond-adapt-and-save/

Moore, W. B., & Felo, A. (2021). The evolution of accounting technology education: Analytics to STEM. *Journal of Education for Business*, 1–7. https://doi.org/10.1080/08832323.2021.1895045

O'Leary, D. E. (2018). Big Data and knowledge management with applications in accounting and auditing. In M. Quinn & E. Strauss (Eds.), *The routledge companion to accounting information systems* (pp. 145–160). Routledge.

Oliveira, J. (2018). Accountants' roles and accounting-related technologies. In M. Quinn & E. Strauss (Eds.), *The routledge companion to accounting information systems* (pp. 133–144). Routledge.

PR Newswire. (2017, Sep 14). Wolters Kluwer introduces ai-powered predictive analytics to federal developments knowledge center: Collaboration with Skopos Labs, Inc. will enable practitioners to predict the likelihood of bills becoming law. *PR Newswire*.

PR Newswire. (2021, Apr 01). KPMG's new tax data reader tool automates analysis of financial data, simplifying tax filing season: Firm receives patent on natural language processing and character recognition technology. *PR Newswire*.

Prabhu, C. S. R., Chivukula, A. S., Mogadala, A., Ghosh, R., & Livingston, L. M. J. (2019). *Big data analytics: Systems, algorithms, applications* (1st 2019. ed.). Springer Singapore. https://doi. org/10.1007/978-981-15-0094-7

PwC. (2015). *Data driven, what students need to succeed in a rapidly changing business world*. PwC. Retrieved May 1 from https://www.pwc.com/us/en/faculty-resource/assets/pwc-data-driven-paper-feb2015.pdf

PwC UK. (2020). *Transparency report for the year ended June 2020*. https://www.pwc.co.uk/annualreport/ assets/2020/uk-transparency-report-2020.pdf

Rakipi, R., De Santis, F., & D'Onza, G. (2021). Correlates of the internal audit function's use of data analytics in the big data era: Global evidence. *Journal of International Accounting, Auditing and Taxa-tion, 42*, 100357. https://doi.org/10.1016/j.intaccaudtax.2020.100357

Raphael, J. (2017). *Rethinking the audit*. AICPA. Retrieved May 1 from https://competency.aicpa. org/media_resources/211236-rethinking-the-audit/detail

Richins, G., Stapleton, A., Stratopoulos, T. C., & Wong, C. (2017). Big data analytics: Opportunity or threat for the accounting profession? *Journal of Information Systems, 31*(3), 63–79. https://doi. org/10.2308/isys-51805

Roose, K. (2021, March 17). The robots are coming for Phil in accounting. *International New York Times*, NA.

Salijeni, G., Samsonova-Taddei, A., & Turley, S. (2019). Big Data and changes in audit technology: Contemplating a research agenda. *Accounting and Business Research, 49*(1), 95–119. https://doi. org/10.1080/00014788.2018.1459458

Sidhu, H. (2017). *How audit can benefit from a dive into deep data*. EY. Retrieved May 1 from https://www.ey.com/en_gl/assurance/how-audit-can-benefit-from-a-dive-into-deep-data

Sutton, S. G., Holt, M., & Arnold, V. (2016). "The reports of my death are greatly exaggerated"—Artificial intelligence research in accounting. *International Journal of Accounting Information Systems, 22*, 60–73. https://doi.org/10.1016/j.accinf.2016.07.005

Sweet, P. (2020). *AQI 2020: FRC finds a third of audits need improvement*. Accountancy Daily. Retrieved May 1 from https://www.accountancydaily.co/aqi-2020-frc-finds-third-audits-need-improvement

Todd, K. J., & Gill, L. H. (2018). *Using data analytics in forensic investigations*. Accounting Today. Retrieved May 1 from https://www.accountingtoday.com/opinion/using-data-analytics-in-forensic-investigations

Tokar, D. (2020, Sep 22). Corporate compliance programs hit refresh with data-analytics tools; authorities show leniency to companies with data-driven anticorruption systems. *Wall Street Journal (Online)*. https://www.wsj.com/articles/corporate-compliance-programs-hit-refresh-with-data-analytics-tools-11600767001

Trentmann, N. (2019, Apr 25). Predictive analytics give a boost to Diageo's cost-savings efforts; technology helps spirits maker improve forecasts of customer demand, creditor payments and commodity prices. *Wall Street Journal*. https://www.wsj.com/articles/predictive-analytics-give-a-boost-to-diageos-cost-savings-efforts-11556208946

Tschakert, N., Kokina, J., Kozlowski, S., & Vasarhelyi, M. A. (2016). The next frontier in data analytics. *Journal of Accountancy, 222*(2), 58–63.

Tysiac, K. (2020). *How firms are delivering value with audit analytics*. Journal of Accountancy. Retrieved May 1 from https://www.journalofaccountancy.com/news/2020/jan/cpa-firm-value-audit-data-analytics-22751.html

Violino, B. (2019). *Upgrading the engagement*. CFO. Retrieved May 1 from https://www.cfo.com/auditing/2019/12/upgrading-the-engagement/

Weller, A. (2019). Transparency: Motivations and challenges. In W. Samek, G. Montavon, V. Andrea, L. K. Hansen, & K.-R. Müller (Eds.), *Explainable AI: Interpreting, explaining and visualizing deep learning*. Springer. https://doi.org/10.1007/978-3-030-28954-6_2

Werner, M., Wiese, M., & Maas, A. (2021). Embedding process mining into financial statement audits. *International Journal of Accounting Information Systems, 41*, 100514. https://doi.org/10.1016/j.accinf.2021.100514

Wiegmann, L., Schäffer, U., & Löhlein, L. (2021). The impact of predictive forecasting on corporate control: A comparison of two multinational corporations. *17*(1). https://www.cimaglobal.com/Documents/8976%20Impact%20of%20Predictive%20Forecasting%20Report.pdf

13

CODING SKILLS FOR ACCOUNTANTS

Bibek Bhatta and Martin R. W. Hiebl

Introduction

Recent advancements in computer technology have transformed the working landscape. Computerisation and information technology (IT) have helped workers performing abstract,[1] task-intensive jobs by increasing the scope of information and analysis while lowering the cost, thus enabling the workers to specialise further in their area of comparative advantage (Autor, 2015). At the same time, warnings have been issued at various times in history about the dangers of job losses due to work automation; for example, the economic depression that engulfed countries like France, Germany, Great Britain and the USA in the late 19th century was most severe where employment of machinery was high, among other things (Rosenbloom, 1964). Likewise, there is evidence from the early 20th century that the introduction of new typewriters, which allowed for some automation in accounting, resulted in staff reductions among accountants (Martínez Franco & Hiebl, 2019). However, job automation not only leads to job losses, but it can also complement job creation (Miller, 1964).

From the perspective of the accounting profession, an open question is how current technological changes will impact the labour market and what it means for practicing accountants (e.g. Rikhardsson & Yigitbasioglu, 2018). Another pertinent issue relates to the opportunities and challenges the accounting profession could face (or is already facing) owing to these recent advancements in computer technology (e.g. Spraakman et al., 2020). Among these challenges, the accounting profession may be subject to the phenomenon of job polarisation, which has been well documented in the economics literature (see Goldin & Katz, 2007; Goos et al., 2014). Job polarisation, in this context, refers to rise in employment shares for high-paid and low-paid jobs at the expense of middle-paid jobs. In the past few decades, jobs at the top and bottom of skill and income distribution have witnessed disproportionately high wage gains (Autor, 2015). Existing studies show that job polarisation is pervasive across industries and across developed countries, mainly due to technological change.

If the accounting profession is considered to lie at the middle of the income/skill distribution, then this points towards the necessity to acquire new skills to counter the threats of technological advancement to the profession. But accounting does not necessarily only involve rather repetitive tasks such as bank reconciliation and financial report preparation but may also involve support for strategic decision-making (e.g. Burns et al., 2013; Oliveira, 2018). Hence, if accounting is

DOI: 10.4324/9781003132943-16

considered to be towards the top of the skill/income distribution table, then there are benefits to be had by adapting to the changing technological landscape. Either way, the key point is that technological change is likely to necessitate additional skills accountants need to acquire to deal with emerging challenges (Kokina & Blanchette, 2019; Oesterreich & Teuteberg, 2019; Wolf et al., 2020; Kokina et al., 2021). The 'additional skills' we focus on in this chapter are coding skills. Coding skills may have been perceived as the sole preserve of computer programmers and software engineers but, as we discuss below, are becoming increasingly useful in the accounting domain (e.g. Cooper et al., 2019; Bertomeu, 2020; Ding et al., 2020; Kokina et al., 2021).

Therefore, this chapter aims to assess and illustrate the relevance of coding skills, and associated challenges, for individuals working in the accounting profession. Due to a dearth of research looking specifically into the relevance of coding skills for contemporary accountants (Tsiligiris & Bowyer, 2021), we aim to address our aims for this chapter with the help of examples from and insights into accounting practice. Thus, the more detailed purpose of this chapter is twofold. First, we highlight two important areas – Robotic Process Automation (RPA) and Big Data – where coding skills are expected to become more useful and necessary for accountants in the future. RPA and Big Data are certainly not the only areas where coding skills could be beneficial for accountants but are arguably two important such areas (e.g. Warren et al., 2015; Gärtner & Hiebl, 2018; Moffitt et al., 2018; Cooper et al., 2019; Kokina & Blanchette, 2019). With the help of these two examples, we aim to make accountants aware of the opportunities and threats to their profession arising out of rapid technological change. Second, we aim to illustrate how accountants can make use of coding skills. To this end, we draw on four small but hopefully attractive examples of how accountants can use coding in data analysis, data visualisation, problem-solving and market research. These illustrations cannot cover the myriad of available coding options and languages. We draw on practical examples that are programmed in Python – the coding language that is often perceived as best suited for beginners in coding (Kaggle, 2020), including those in the accounting profession (e.g. Oesterreich & Teuteberg, 2019; Tsiligiris & Bowyer, 2021).

Before proceeding further, it is pertinent to note that learning the programming logic is of more importance than merely learning any programming language. This idea is associated to the notion of 'computational thinking', which can be described as the thought processes used in formulating a problem and expressing its solution so that a computer can effectively carry out the task (Wing, 2006, 2008). Wing (2008), who has been very influential in her ideas about computational thinking, argues that it should be taught in early years of childhood and its application is relevant for the wider society and not just accounting. Further discussion on computational thinking is beyond the scope of this chapter.

In the remainder of this chapter, we will first define the scope of 'coding' and 'accounting' we will use on in the rest of this chapter. By drawing on the examples of RPA and Big Data, we then discuss the enhanced usefulness of coding in the accounting domain. Afterwards, we provide four illustrations of coding skills for accountants and discuss some practical steps towards learning coding skills to benefit from the rising challenge of Big Data. Finally, we provide concluding remarks along with limitations of this chapter.

Terminology

What is 'coding'?

The Oxford dictionary defines coding[2] as the 'process or activity of writing computer programs'. Traditionally, one of the first exercises in introductory computer science textbooks consists of printing out *Hello World!* in the console or display box of the program (e.g. Sande & Sande, 2019). Likewise, a common task of inserting a formula within a spreadsheet, producing a pivot table or recording steps for repetition (using macros) could also be considered components of coding. One could argue that recording an auto-reply message in email or arranging for different emails to be delivered to different folders depending on the subject matter or sender is also a coding exercise. Similarly, a myriad of activities in technological environment could be considered to be within the premise of coding. In this chapter, however, we take coding in a rather limited, but nevertheless important, sense. The coding we discuss in this chapter is more aligned with the task of using programming language to analyse data for decision-making from a management accounting perspective (cf. Oesterreich & Teuteberg, 2019). Some related research publications refer to the same phenomenon as 'programming skills' for accountants (e.g. Oesterreich &Teuteberg, 2019; Kokina et al., 2021). For our purposes, coding and programming can be considered synonyms. In the rest of this chapter, we will therefore stick to the term 'coding'.

Accounting within the context of this chapter

Now we focus on the scope of accounting. Accounting practice is broadly divided into two categories: financial accounting and management accounting (Burns et al., 2013; Drury, 2018).[3] While some common ground exists between these two categories, they mainly differ in purpose, focus, reporting standards and reporting interval and are aimed at different primary users (see Bhimani et al., 2019, p.5). In simpler terms, financial accounting mainly consists of following established accounting standards to prepare financial statements based on past financial data so that shareholders and other stakeholders can get a true picture of a firm. Management accounting is aligned with analysing and reporting financial as well as non-financial information primarily for the purpose of decision-making, including controlling and strategic decisions. Bhimani et al. (2019, p. 7) further notes:

> The shift towards managerial and strategic engagement rather than just acting as providers of largely information about enterprises allows management accountants to alight their work to the changing business and organisational landscape.

Hence, it should be clear that management accounting has a close link with high volumes of structured and unstructured data being generated by businesses in a fast-paced manner so that useful information can be gleaned out of such Big Data for decision-making (e.g. Gärtner & Hiebl, 2018). Due to this very characteristic, practical coding skills that we discuss in this chapter are more relevant from a management accounting perspective (Oesterreich & Teuteberg, 2019). However, the issues we highlight especially related to RPA and thus automation – which we discuss below – make this chapter relevant for financial accountants as well (Cooper et al., 2019).

Areas of enhanced usefulness of coding skills for accountants

Robotic process automation

RPA refers to the growing tendency in firms to rely on computing power to executive, day-to-day, repetitive tasks in an automated environment. Considering the rule-based repetitive tasks that need to be executed in accounting, RPA is no doubt an issue of interest for accountants (e.g. Moffitt et al., 2018; Cooper et al., 2019; Kokina & Blanchette, 2019). A survey conducted by the consulting firm Deloitte (2018) indicates substantial efforts by firms towards RPA that could lead to 'near universal' (p. 4) adoption of RPA by 2022. The same report finds that more than half of the deployment of RPA among Deloitte's clients are taking place within accounting and finance. These processes within accounting and finance include processing transactions in accounts receivables and payables, inventory accounting, fixed asset accounting, tax accounting, cash management, management reporting, external reporting, etc. Deloitte (2015) provides a lucid example of RPA in action whereby a specific account-ing task used to be performed by ten employees in 10–15 minutes being executed by bots in about four minutes. This points towards the need for people within the accounting profession to adapt to this changing environment by bringing their personal skills in better alignment with the expected changes in the near future. This is particularly important in the context of Keynes's observation in the 1930s that our advances in technological efficiency outpace the search for new uses for labour, leading to 'technological unemployment' (Keynes, 2010[4]).

While some human skills remain to be valuable despite the accelerated computerisation, other human skills have lost their shine, and people possessing the latter skills have little to offer to employees (Brynjolfsson & McAfee, 2011). Existing studies indeed show that increased computerisation has led to declines in employment, especially in occupations that mainly consist of routine-intensive and well-defined steps that can be replicated by computer algorithms (Frey & Osborne, 2017). This is important considering that accounting is consid-ered to be one of the most routine-intensive occupations (Autor & Dorn, 2013). However, recent accounting studies reveal that accountants can play important roles within the RPA process, and it is imperative for accountants to acquire new technical skills to play these im-portant roles (Kokina et al., 2021).

Brynjolfsson & McAfee (2011, p. 14) liken the advancements in computing technology to the 'second half of the chessboard', referring to the exponential nature of growth. In a similar fashion, though the encroachment of technology into the domain of human labour has accelerated in the past decades, it has been manageable so far and thus can be considered as the first half of the chessboard, but this encroachment is set to make exponential inroads in the coming years into tasks hitherto undertaken by humans. As such, recent advancements in computer technology are expected to impact not just the accounting profession but most if not all occupations in general. Brynjolfsson & McAfee (2011) suggest that the way forward is not to compete against computers but to compete with computers; a prerequisite for this is to invest in human capital so that the labour force can keep pace with the accelerating technological dominance. In a similar vein, Davenport & Kirby (2015) argue that automation should be seen as an opportunity rather than a threat, and our mindset needs to be developed to treat smart machines as partners and collaborators for creative problem-solving.

More recent studies have brought to light the potential threat of this increased computeri-sation in the field of accounting. Frey & Osborne (2017) examine the susceptibility of various occupations to this increasing dominance of computer technology. Out of 702 occupations examined in the USA, they find that 47% are at 'high risk' of being replaced by comput-erisation. From an accounting perspective, particularly important are the findings that four specific occupations, namely, 'accountants and auditors', 'bookkeeping, accounting and au-diting clerks', 'new accounts clerks' and 'tax preparers' were all under high risk, with at least 94% probability of being automated within the foreseeable future. Out of the 702 detailed occupations, these four occupations related to accounting were ranked 114th, 32nd, 10th and 8th, respectively, in terms of their probability of being replaced by increased automation.

Building on these estimates, Cooper et al. (2019) have examined the extent of increasing computerisation of tasks in public accounting firms and provide evidence that firms are making substantial efficiency and effectiveness gains with up to 80% reduction in processing times due to adoption of RPA. Interviews with 14 accounting professionals within the Big 4 accounting firms reveal that though computerisation has been pervasive across all areas of accounting,[5] most of the computerisation has taken place in the accounting firms' tax, advisory and assurance services. Though this computerisation has not (yet) led to reductions in headcount of employees within these firms, it had led to reductions in outsourcing. So, in a way, this is consistent with the predictions of Brynjolfsson & McAfee (2011) that increased computerisation could have a negative impact on employment.

Given these developments, it seems even more pertinent that accountants develop a thorough understanding of automation potentials of their own and others' work. Not least, such understanding could be used to identify the most attractive use cases of RPA and bots more generally to provide better services to clients (Cooper et al., 2019). Consequently, there is a need to be conversant with various tools (like Microsoft Power Automate, IBM Robotic Process Automation, UiPath and Automation Anywhere, to name a few) that are readily available to many accountants. Processes that could be automated could be as simple as sending out specific company emails at specific times to more complex tasks like bank statement reconciliation, invoice processing, inventory control, etc. In a business setting, a classic example of RPA involves the three-way matching of invoice, purchase order and inventory receipt to process payments automatically so that the more tedious tasks of accountants are transferred to the computer leaving the accountants available to handle any exceptions that may arise (see Figure 13.1). Although these tools usually require very little coding skills, those limited coding skills are expected to be important for accountants to be capable of improving efficiency by streamlining workflows. Given that the most widely used RPA tools as noted above do not require commanding a specific programming language and are quite intuitive in use, we encourage the reader to explore these tools independently to identify potentials for increasing work efficiency in their organisations. Behind the user interface, of course, there is some coding or programming going on, which warrants the inclusion of

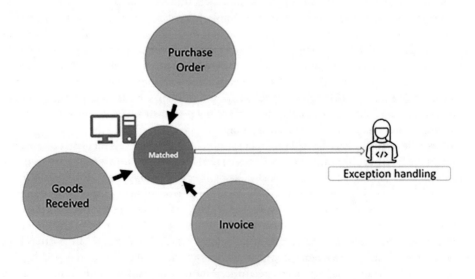

Figure 13.1   An illustration of three-way matching to automating payment processing.

RPA in this chapter. But for our illustrative coding examples below, we will focus on showcasing how accountants may use coding for handling Big Data.

Big Data

Big Data has become a commonly used term and is generally associated with exponential growth and availability of data in various forms. Industry analyst Doug Laney in 2001 characterised Big Data in terms of three Vs, namely, Volume, Velocity and Variety. Volume, in this case, is associated with the unprecedented amount of data that is being generated nowadays in our society; Velocity refers to the sheer pace in which data is being created; and Variety is the various forms of structured and unstructured manner (e.g. audio, video, emails, social media posts, photos) in which data is being generated from various sources. Other Vs such as Veracity and Value were added later to characterise Big Data. Incorporating such extensions, more comprehensive definitions of Big Data have been offered, for example, by Gärtner & Hiebl (2018, p. 163), which we take as a starting point – 'Big Data refers to the generation, storage, processing, verification and analysis of large, highly versatile and quickly growing volumes of data with the objective of creating valuable information'.

A growing number of firms are utilising Big Data in conjunction with established data sources for the purpose of managerial decisions (Davenport, 2014). Big Data is adding value to many firms by the sheer accumulation of information and from the consequences that can arise by evaluation of such data (Brynjolfsson & McAfee, 2014). Big Data poses both challenges and opportunities to accountants (Gärtner & Hiebl, 2018). The challenge is that Big Data arises from various information pools and could be structured or unstructured, formal or informal and social or economic in nature, and is also dynamic in its content and representation (Bhimani, 2015). While the IT departments established in many firms may have the capability to store and preserve such Big Data, the IT team itself may not have the capabilities to turn the data into valuable insights to drive key business decisions (Beath et al., 2012). As such, individuals within firms who are able to evaluate the data and draw insights from such Big Data for strategic decision-making are likely to be influential within the firms (Bhimani, 2015). This portends well for management accountants but only if they can develop the skills for evaluation of Big Data (Gärtner & Hiebl, 2018).

Big Data has implications not just for management accountants but also for financial accountants. The information contained in Big Data can be used to enhance the quality and relevance of accounting information, which, in turn, can lead to better transparency, and Big Data can also be of assistance in accelerating the convergence of accounting standards like US General Accepted Accounting Principles (GAAP) and International Financial Reporting Standards (IFRS) (Warren Jr et al., 2015). If accountants are keen to 'race with the computers rather than race against the computers' (Brynjolfsson & McAfee, 2011), it is imperative that they learn the necessary skills to handle Big Data for decision-making.

One contemporary field where accountants may use or may need to draw on Big Data is accounting for environmental issues. For instance, environmental, social, and governance (ESG) criteria are interconnected, and they should be viewed in an integrated way (Richardson, 2009; Galbreath, 2013). Management accountants have been criticised for not providing sufficient details regarding ESG issues within management accounting information systems (Drury, 2018, p. 629), and many firms do not track their environmental costs extensively. However, other research has found that there is a positive association between the tracking of such environmental costs and taking initiatives to address environmental concerns (Henri et al., 2016). Drury (2018) further notes that most accounting systems rely on traditional and arbitrary cost-assignment bases when it comes to assigning environmental costs, and this results in such environmental costs being concealed under other general overheads. Consequently, Bhimani et al. (2019) argue that techniques and strategies in management accounting must be updated to recognise and present the environmental cost from an organisational perspective in what they term Environmental Management Accounting. However, calculating environmental costs of firms is a tricky business. Anecdotal evidence suggests that firms are under increased pressure to reveal the extent of their environmental costs or externalities to outside stakeholders, which may lead to change in accounting models (Balch, 2021). For the collection and analysis of data to compute monetary costs of such externalities, Balch (2021) further reports a new technological approach that uses a combination of data on social, natural, human and financial capital along with more than 17,000 equations. It is important that as the stakeholders' appetite for ESG disclosure increases, and considering the costs of such disclosures (Aggarwal & Dow, 2012), management accountants should equip themselves to meet this demand in a cost-effective and time-efficient manner. Not least, cost-effective and time-efficient approaches to creating such information may rest on making smart use of new technology, which are likely to include coding skills for accountants. In this spirit, we now turn to some practical questions accountants may face when wanting to increase their coding skills.

Starting point – which programming language?

Given the challenges as discussed in the above sections, a natural question that can arise to individuals within the accounting profession with very limited coding skills is, where is the starting point for learning coding skills? And what kind of coding skills should to be learned to deal with the existing and upcoming challenges? And which programming language should one start to learn? With the plethora of programming languages being used widely in academia and industry, it can be easy for beginners to be overwhelmed with choices. For example, should one start learning C, C++, Java, Julia, Matlab, Octave, Perl, Python, R or various other programming languages? These questions are obviously without one best answer, but we will try to propose a recommendation based on the assumption that the reader is relatively new to coding and is interested in learning programming language that is least difficult to learn.

We suggest Python programming language as the starting point for learners, for two important reasons. First, Python has a relatively wide user base. In a 2020 survey published at the popular data science website Kaggle.com, when asked what programming language participants used on a regular basis, it was observed that 78% respondents used Python on a regular basis (see Figure 13.2), whereas another popular open-source programming language (i.e. R) was used by 21% of the respondents. Python was the predominant package in the survey conducted in the previous years as well.

Python invariably gets compared with R within the data science community (e.g. Ozgur et al., 2017), and the debate on whether Python is better than R or whether R is better than Python is an ongoing debate not likely to be settled soon.[6] Indeed, as noted by the IBM Cloud Team (2021), 'most organisations use a combination of both languages, and the R vs Python debate is all for naught'. It would be akin to debating whether Real Madrid or FC Barcelona is better at football, or a similar debate between Chicago Bears and Green Bay Packers in the USA. Instead of wading into this debate, we note that there is anecdotal evidence that Python is more intuitive and has a smoother learning curve

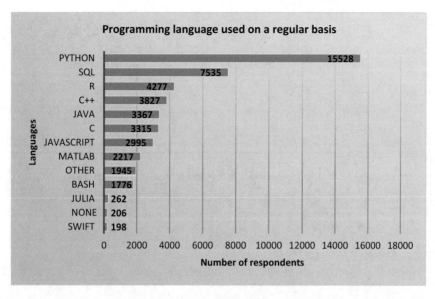

Figure 13.2 Programming languages used by respondents on a regular basis.

Notes: Respondents were allowed to choose multiple options. Total number of respondents: 20,036. This visualisation is based on the authors' calculations based on data from Kaggle (2020).

compared to R (e.g. Coursera, 2021). In addition, it may be argued that people who have more of a programming background prefer Python, while people with a statistical background prefer R (Ozgur et al., 2017).

Python is also mentioned in the small number of existing research papers that touch upon coding skills for accountants as one of the programming languages that are most likely to be useful to the above-noted purposes of coding skills for accountants (e.g. Oesterreich & Teuteberg, 2019; Tsiligiris & Bowyer, 2021). Learners can expect to be engaged with other professionals, at some stage, on the pros and cons of Python versus R, and it can easily confuse novices on whether to give up one in favour of the other, or whether to learn both at the same time. We suggest viewing both of these popular languages as healthy competitors but rather choose Python in the initial stage merely due to its relative ease of learning and intuitive syntaxes (cf. IBM Cloud Team, 2021).

Second and relatedly, Python is considered to be relatively easy to learn. In fact, in the above-mentioned survey conducted by Kaggle (2020), Python was the most recommended package to learn whereby 80% of the respondents recommended Python to someone new to programming language, followed by R recommended by 7% (see Figure 13.3). The relative ease with which Python can be learned is also reflected in a large and growing number of Python courses designed to complement regular university studies. For example, the Software Carpentry organisation (software-carpentry.org) was founded ten years ago to enable researchers to use Python for data analysis – tasks shared by many of the potential use cases for accountants outlined below. Additionally, Python has wide applicability and is free to use and distribute, even for commercial purpose (Python Software Foundation, 2021).

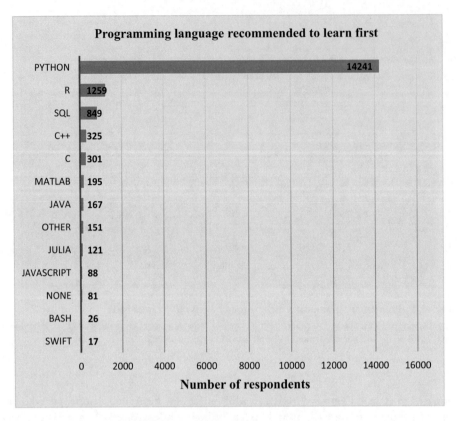

Figure 13.3 Programming language recommended to learn first.

Notes: Respondents were allowed to choose only one option. Total number of respondents: 17,821. This visualisation is based on the authors' calculations based on data from Kaggle (2020).

Online use of Python without installation

Assuming that the reader has decided to proceed with Python as programming language of choice, the next logical step is to start using Python to get the feel of it. It is encouraging that users can go to various online platforms that have made it possible for users to use Python in the cloud without installing it in their local machine. One of the first sites we recommend, at least initially, is the Try Jupyter website (https://try.jupyter.org/) that allows users to use Python without even registering. This site has been around since 2014 and is a non–profit project. More information on how to start using it is provided later in this chapter. Many other sites are also available for free, but these may require initial registration requiring individual email address. Some of the more reputable sites requiring registration before use include Kaggle.com, Google Colab and Replit.com, all of which provide free platforms to try Python (and other programming languages). All these three sites allow users to upload their codes and data for sharing with others. It is worth noting that Kaggle.com is supported by Google and is hugely popular with data enthusiasts who like to share their codes and learn from each other. As such, readers with very little or no knowledge on Python can still explore these datasets and run code – uploaded by others – online at the click of a button and see the results interactively. In short, learners not yet ready for installing Python on their local machines can simply try it first online before deciding on installing Python.

Python installation

Assuming that the reader has decided to proceed with installing Python to their local computer, we next discuss the installation process and try to avoid some common pitfalls in installation of Python. At the official Python webpage (www.python.org), various versions of Python are available for download. Readers should be aware at this stage that Python comes pre-packed with basic tools called 'modules' (or packages) to handle basic and common tasks, but users may need to install additional packages to handle specific tasks like image processing, extracting text from PDF files, web-scraping, visualisation, etc. For illustration purposes, this can be thought of as buying a house (for free) with rooms containing basic furniture, while occupants may need to add/install additional items like a printer, a toaster, a dryer, a shower or a dishwasher, depending on what they plan to do in the various compartments. Of course, the occupants can decide not to add a printer if they do not plan to print anything. Similarly, depending on what the user needs to do (e.g. interactive visualisation), additional packages may need to be installed in Python. An important thing to note here is that the various packages in Python could be dependent on a specific version of another package, and this can lead to compatibility issues (and much frustration) as new libraries are added to Python later. Though there is nothing wrong in installing a given version of Python from the official webpage (e.g. version 3.9), novice users especially could face compatibility issues later when they install other modules. To avoid this issue, we suggest learners to exercise caution and not to install Python independently unless they are confident of what they are doing. Instead, novice users may first install a package called Anaconda from the official Anaconda Inc. website (www.anaconda.com/). Anaconda comes with a Python distribution along with various popular packages for data analysis pre-added so that learners can use Python out of the box (i.e. without having to install additional libraries) for basic data-analysis-related tasks. Anaconda provides an intuitive interface (Graphical User Interface) for users to manage, install and upgrade packages in a simplified way with few mouse clicks only and without having to use command prompts.

The Anaconda Individual Edition is open source and available for different operating systems, including Windows, Linux and MacOS. The official Anaconda, Inc. (2021) website reports that the 'Anaconda Individual Edition is the world's most popular Python distribution platform with over 25 million users worldwide'. Learners are suggested to install the latest available version of Anaconda Individual Edition – as of December 2021, this would be version 2021.11 – which comes with more than 100 packages for data extraction, visualisation and analysis. Anaconda also installs other useful tools like Jupyter and Spyder, which can be invaluable for beginners, as we shall discuss later. When installed on a Windows PC, Anaconda will appear in the Windows menu as a separate folder containing additional items such as Jupyter Notebook and Spyder.

Once installed, users can turn to the Anaconda Navigator and the official Anaconda documentation for upgrading and managing their Python environment and packages. As mentioned previously, Anaconda helps in these endeavours to avoid compatibility issues. If the users are going to engage in tasks of very different nature like data analysis, web-scraping and image processing, it is suggested to create separate 'environments' for these within Anaconda for these different tasks. Using separate environments for separate kinds of tasks helps avoid compatibility issues later. To draw an analogy with our earlier example, imagine installing a toaster, a shower and a dryer in the same room or 'environment'. This may produce issues later, whereas keeping these in different environments or different rooms but within the same Anaconda house could be more helpful to avoid compatibility issues.

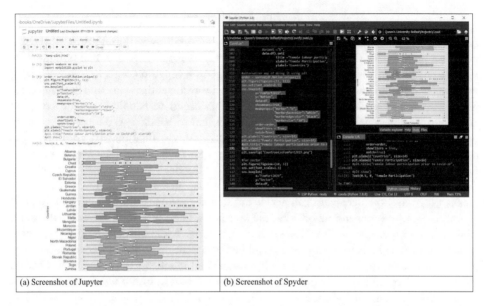

| (a) Screenshot of Jupyter | (b) Screenshot of Spyder |

Figure 13.4   Screenshots of Jupyter (a) and Spyder (b) to demonstrate frequently used user interfaces while running commands in Python.

As indicated above, Anaconda comes with Jupyter Notebook, which can be used to run Python commands. Jupyter allows users to run Python commands in a user-friendly way, one or few lines at a time with instant results and errors flagged. It also allows for easy checking and eyeing of data on a piecemeal basis, thus providing a useful learning experience. This is especially useful for beginners as complex commands and frequently occurring errors, while learning a new programming language can quickly bring frustration to a new learner. Jupyter notebooks also allow accountants to easily document their process using markdown, which is automatically compiled into a well-formatted document. Jupyter is designed to make the learning experience much more positive for beginners, and as illustrated below with some practical examples, new learners are encouraged to use Jupyter Notebook to try out Python commands. While Spyder, which is also installed with Anaconda and comes with its own Python console and variable explorer, we encourage new users to get familiar with Jupyter first before deciding to use Spyder. This is because Jupyter allows the codes to be written in a more organised manner and also allows for subset and summary of data to be displayed in a more organised way. To give new learners a visual example of Jupyter and Spyder, we provide screenshots of both in Figure 13.4.

Illustrative practical examples

In this section, we provide four basic examples to illustrate practical uses of Python in data analysis, data visualisation, problem-solving and market research. Readers can execute these examples interactively online without the need for registration and without installing any package in their local computer by going to the Binder website (https://mybinder.org/) and using the GitHub link (https://github.com/bibekbhatta/CodingForAccountants) in the URL field, as illustrated in Figure 13.5a. Clicking the 'Launch' button,[7] as shown in the figure, will lead to a page displaying the four examples on the left-hand pane in the webpage

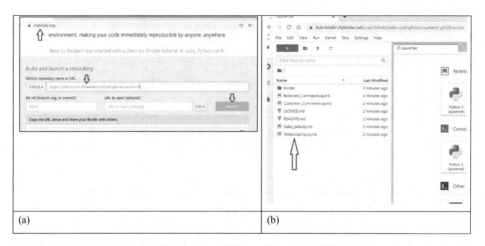

(a)   (b)

Figure 13.5   Using Binder.org website to open Jupyter Notebooks from GitHub repository.

as shown in Figure 13.5b. Readers can double-click on any of the four examples and work with the provided codes interactively. Readers also have the option to download the files from the GitHub repository directly using the given link.

Data analysis and visualisation

The first illustration is related to a situation where a management accountant in a company wants to get an overview of the sales data from three stores located in three different cities, based on the most recent 5,000,000 transactions in each store. More specifically, the focus is on the amount of money being spent by customers in each store per transaction. In a real-life setting, the accountant would have access to such data, but for our purpose, we will artificially create the data in Python with the codes as shown in uploaded file 'Sales_data.ipynb'. The first few lines of code[8] are used to artificially create the data using the 'NumPy' package. Then we import a package called 'pandas' for any manipulation and visualisation of data.[9] We execute the last three lines of command separately in the online notebook to show the results separately and present the results in Appendix 1. After the data has been loaded, a single line of code provides us with summary statistics on the sales figures for each of the stores and helpful statistics like average transaction value (mean), number of observations (count), minimum transaction value (min), spending figures at different percentiles, etc. (see Appendix 1). To provide a basic visualisation of such data, the next line of code provides box plots for the transaction figures for the three stores (see Figure 13.6). Another line of command provides a frequency distribution of amount spent in one of the stores (see Figure 13.6); in the given example, it can be observed that most of the customers spent an amount of £/$/Eur of 435 (16,550 times) within the most recent 5,000,000 transactions. A simple exercise like this allows the accountant to get useful information about the current state of the business with the help of some coding, whereas more complex techniques will have to be used to gain deeper insights.

Problem-solving

The second illustration is related to cost optimisation where an imaginary catering firm is planning to provide lunch packs for a large number of customers on a regular basis. More

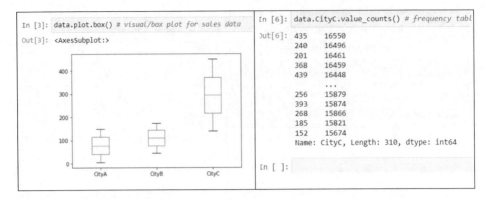

Figure 13.6   Basic data visualisation and frequency table.

information regarding the ingredients to be included in the lunch pack, along with pricing and other constraints, are provided in Appendix 2. As can be observed in the given information, there are constraints related to the minimum and maximum levels of calories, proteins, vitamins, etc. to be included in the pack for each customer from the given list of ingredients. If the management of the firm is keen on minimising the cost of the lunch pack while meeting all the given dietary constraints, one of the options is to use linear programming in Python to figure out the amount of ingredients to be used in the pack for cost minimisation. For illustration, we use a package called 'PuLP' in Python and solve the optimisation function. The actual lines of codes are provided in online file 'Balanced_Lunchpack.ipynb'. As shown in Figure 13.7, the results show that only four of the ingredients should be used for cost minimisation in the given proportion (e.g. 0.84 units of carrots should be included along with 0.27 units of meat). In this rather simple example, we had only a few variables (ingredients) and constraints; more realistically, optimisation problems could have dozens of variables and constraints, which can be listed in tabular form in spreadsheets. Such spreadsheets can be directly loaded into Python for such problem-solving situations.

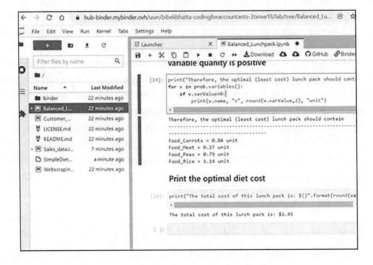

Figure 13.7   Solving problems with multiple constraints using Python.

Market research

Our third illustration is related to market research where a book-selling firm is interested in checking the kinds of books being sold by competitors. One option is trying to find the relevant information online from the competitors' websites or other such sites selling books. For this purpose, we use a website Books to Scrape, which is specifically designed to allow learners of web-scraping techniques to scrape data from the site. To keep things simple, we focus on the kinds of travel books being sold by this 'competitor'. Using a Python package called 'BeautifulSoup', we are able to gather information about the book titles, prices and stock availability by using the codes as shown in online file 'Webscraping.ipynb'. The fairly simple and basic result from this operation, as shown in Figure 13.8, reveals the list of books sold online by the competitor along with the prices and stock availability for each of the books.

While this illustration may provide a flavour of possible utilisation of coding skills to gather information from the internet, it has to be taken into account that website structures do change from time to time. Such changes require the codes to be changed accordingly to capture the required information of interest. In other words, codes working today on a given website may not be successful in getting the required information when the website changes its structure. But the bigger challenge lies with speed and volume of information. Market research will likely require gathering information from hundreds if not thousands of online sources, and such information may come in various forms including texts, images, videos and live feed. To add to this complexity, websites are increasingly providing dynamic information, and some information may be displayed only after an interaction with the user (e.g. a click on a button to get further information on something). While the approach we used in our simple example may be appropriate for getting information from a small number of websites, various other packages like Scrapy would have to be deployed when dealing with larger numbers of websites (see also Anand et al., 2020). To gather information from dynamic webpages which requires user interaction, packages like Selenium provide functionality to automatically interact with the website (e.g. clicking a given button or inputting usernames and passwords) and then extract the required information. While we have not analysed any text in our example, firms may want to extract information from their own

A	B	C
Book	Price	Availability
It's Only the Himalayas	£45.17	In stock
Full Moon over Noah's ...	£49.43	In stock
See America: A Celebration ...	£48.87	In stock
Vagabonding: An Uncommon Guide ...	£36.94	In stock
Under the Tuscan Sun	£37.33	In stock
A Summer In Europe	£44.34	In stock
The Great Railway Bazaar	£30.54	In stock
A Year in Provence ...	£56.88	In stock
The Road to Little ...	£23.21	In stock
Neither Here nor There: ...	£38.95	In stock
1000 Places to See ...	£26.08	In stock

Figure 13.8   Market research of a competitor examining the availability and price of books.

website and other online sources (e.g. social media) on what customers are commenting about their products and services. For the purpose of text analysis, packages like NLTK and Spacy can be useful. Last but not the least, gathering information from external websites using automated processes can lead to unwanted consequences if correct protocols are not followed; hence, users should familiarise themselves with basic etiquette of web-scraping and act in a fair manner to avoid negative consequences (cf. Scassa, 2020; Bosse et al., 2022).

In a similar way, Python can be used to extract visual reflections of what users think about a firm's products. To illustrate this use case, we extend our example on market research by analysing artificial data related to a new product that has been released on the market. Let us imagine we have already extracted comments and feedback provided by social media users regarding our new product. The sample text provided in Appendix 3 shows that users have made generous use of emojis (like 🙏, 😎, etc.) in their comments (text1), and this could be useful for getting general feedback on how customers feel about this product. Using available packages, we can quickly filter out the various emojis along with their relative frequencies to get some idea on what the customers think about the product. Results shown in Figure 13.9 reveal that most of the customers seem to be enjoying the product, while one sad emoji can also be seen. This simple exercise, which can be scaled up to incorporate more voluminous customer feedback, can be considered just another example of how data in structured and unstructured form could be used to gather new sources of relevant information and to guide management decisions.

Handling Big Data

As discussed earlier in this chapter, the challenges that come with Big Data include the difficulty of extracting useful insights from such data (Bhimani, 2015; Gärtner & Hiebl, 2018). However, the examples we have looked into so far are fairly basic in terms of volume and structure of data. And the Python packages like pandas, NumPy, etc. that we have used in the earlier examples were not designed to be used across clusters. Big Data itself is often viewed as not fitting into one machine (e.g. Singh & Kaur, 2014). Thus, the next logical step is to discuss how Python can be useful in processing Big Data so as to gain useful insights

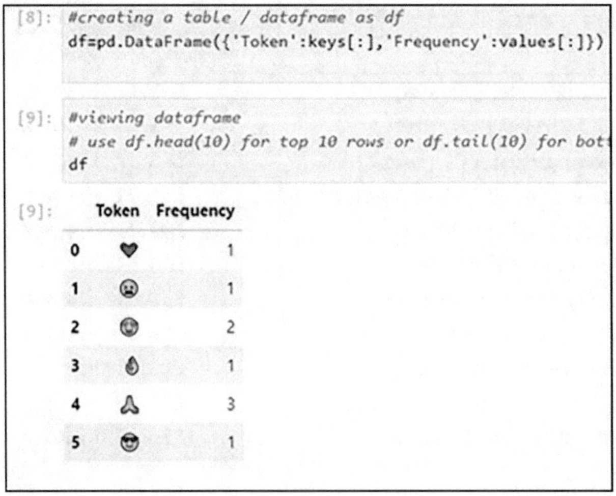

Figure 13.9 Examining the use of emojis by customers.

and information from such data. By its very definition, due to its sheer volume, speed and complexity, traditional data processing software cannot manage Big Data, and additional challenges include integrating and managing such data before they can be analysed (Oracle, n.d.). The integration and management/storage of such data require new technologies and strategies and resources. Parallel or distributed computing and cloud computing form a part of these new technologies and strategies.

Starting from the mid-2000s, Big Data storage and analysis frameworks like Hadoop (currently Apache Hadoop) started gaining popularity, but more recently, Apache Spark (Spark) has emerged as a dominant force for handling Big Data. Though Spark is written in a different language (Scala), it can be used interactively from within Python through the use of a specific library called PySpark. Another application that is gaining popularity in handling Big Data is Dask, which is written in Python. As such, Python can be used to analyse Big Data through Dask as well, with relatively little change in code as Dask is co-developed and integrates well with the Python ecosystem. It has to be emphasised though that additional resources might be needed to transform or maintain the required data architecture. Dask can then be used to execute computational tasks either in a single machine or across a distributed cluster. Put differently, Dask[10] can be used to scale up the utility of Python packages beyond a single machine to handle Big Data. In short, Python can be a valuable tool for analyses of Big Data regardless of whether users choose to use applications like PySpark or Dask.

Concluding remarks and limitations

In this chapter, we have highlighted recent technological advancements in the labour market and the resulting need for coding skills in the accounting profession. Though job polarisation is thought to introduce wage gains mainly at the top and the bottom (in terms of wage and skills) of the labour market, we have tried to highlight the importance of coding skills in the accounting profession regardless of where (top, middle or bottom) a given accounting task sits. We argue that coding skills can enhance value at the highest level by allowing the accountants to garner meaningful information from Big Data for the purpose of decision-making and also at the lower level by enhancing efficiency through automation. Based on the existing literature (e.g. Frey & Osborne, 2017; Bertomeu, 2020; Ding et al., 2020; Tsiligiris & Bowyer, 2021), it is reasonable to assume that accountants need to upgrade their existing skills, and coding skills can be an additional tool in their armoury to thwart any threat of inefficiency or redundancy.

Assuming that the reader is new to the domain of coding, this chapter proposes Python as the programming package to learn due to its perceived intuitive syntaxes and ease of learning. This chapter provides readers with some options of using Python with or without installing it on their local computers. However, if the reader decides to install it, a user-friendly approach to installing Python was discussed. It is worth reiterating that the suggested approach using Anaconda can help avoid common pitfalls and technical issues in Python, thus providing a more conducive learning environment.

In addition, we have provided various illustrations related to data analysis, visualisation, problem-solving and market research with actual codes and results. These examples are not meant to be exhaustive but highlight some use cases for accountants and fellow researchers and educators. We envisage that readers may try out these basic codes either on their computers or through the online Python platforms – which allows use of Python without installation on a local machine – to get familiar with coding skills. We also provide a brief discussion on how existing knowledge on Python can be scaled up to handle Big Data through specific packages like Dask and PySpark. Beyond the initial motivation that this chapter is expected to provide, readers will have to explore further to build on the knowledge they acquire from this chapter. We have attempted to provide useful links as and where applicable, which we hope to be useful to the readers for this further exploration.

This focus of our chapter on use cases and illustrative examples of coding skills is due to our above assessment that the current research literature has not provided much insight into the specific relevance and the outcomes of coding skills for accountants. We thus call for more research on how use cases of such coding skills – including the ones sketched out above – play out in practice and in how far accountants' increased coding skills shape their future roles in providing information to managers and supporting their decision-making (cf. Wolf et al., 2020).

This chapter, like any other book chapter, has its limitations. First, this chapter does not offer specific prescriptions for dealing with RPA. Our attempt in this chapter has been to make readers aware of opportunities and threats related to RPA from the perspective of an accounting professional. As we have mentioned earlier, various proprietary packages are available to automate workflows and work processes. We encourage readers to explore these tools independently. The purpose of this chapter hence is just to make readers aware of need for efficiency and possible tools for automating routine tasks without prescribing any specific tool for RPA. Second, our dive into various packages within Python, let alone Python itself, is cursory in nature. For example, the documentation of the pandas package alone is extensive. However, the aim of this chapter is to motivate the readers in trying out the various tools available within Python to get a sense of what is possible. Third and finally, there are various tasks that are hard to codify; these tasks include those requiring judgement, flexibility, problem-solving capabilities, creativity, common sense, etc. and are difficult to computerise (Autor, 2015). Coding skills will only be able to complement these skills, not replace them completely. Therefore, we would like to add the warning that future accountants cannot expect to rely on coding skills only, but that coding skills are likely to augment the skill set of typical accountants, either in managerial or in financial accounting roles (e.g. Wolf et al., 2020; Tsiligiris & Bowyer, 2021).

Notes

1 Abstract tasks in this context refer to professional, technical and managerial occupations requiring high level of education and analytical capability.
2 https://www.lexico.com/definition/coding.
3 We recognise that there are finer classifications of accounting practice than the simple distinction between financial accounting and management accounting. For instance, depending on the regulatory environment of the respective country, some authors consider tax accounting as a separate area of accounting (e.g. Weißenberger & Angelkort, 2011), while others consider it part of and related to financial accounting (e.g. Tzovas, 2006). For the purposes of this chapter, we consider the distinction between financial accounting and management accounting sufficient to clarify our arguments.
4 The first edition of this book was published in 1931, but we refer to the latest edition of Keynes's book, which is available electronically and thus easier to find for today's readers.
5 See also Chapter 12.
6 See https://www.datacamp.com/community/blog/when-to-use-python-or-r.
7 It might take a few minutes for the required environment to be loaded in the cloud.
8 Place the cursor in the top cell in the Notebook; then press Shift+Enter to run the code in that cell.

9 For more information and documentation on the packages NumPy and pandas, see the official websites, https://numpy.org/ and https://pandas.pydata.org, respectively.

10 For readers interested to get a feel of Dask, their website (https://dask.org/) provides working environment with pre-written codes. Use the 'Try Now' button to enter the Python environment, and choose any of the workbooks.

References

Aggarwal, R., & Dow, S. (2012). Corporate governance and business strategies for climate change and environmental mitigation. *The European Journal of Finance, 18*(3–4), 311–331. https://doi.org/10.1080/1351847X.2011.579745

Anaconda Inc. (2021). *Anaconda Individual Edition.* https://www.anaconda.com/products/individual

Anand, V., Bochkay, K., Chychyla, R., & Leone, A. J. (2020). Using Python for text analysis in accounting research. *Foundations and Trends in Accounting, 14*(3–4), 128–359. http://dx.doi.org/10.1561/1400000062

Autor, D. H. (2015). Why are there still so many jobs? The history and future of workplace automation. *Journal of Economic Perspectives, 29*(3), 3–30. https://doi.org/10.1257/jep.29.3.3

Autor, D. H., & Dorn, D. (2013). The growth of low-skill service jobs and the polarisation of the US labor market. *American Economic Review, 103*(5), 1553–1597. https://doi.org/10.1257/aer.103.5.1553

Balch, O. (2021). *Big Data Helps Put Numbers on Sustainability.* Financial Times. https://www.ft.com/content/2a405cf6-9592-4de2-960b-4c3e5d0df030

Beath, C., Becerra-Fernandez, I., Ross, J., & Short, J. (2012). Finding value in the information explosion. *MIT Sloan Management Review, 53*(4), 18–20.

Bertomeu, J. (2020). Machine learning improves accounting: Discussion, implementation and research opportunities. *Review of Accounting Studies, 25*(3), 1135–1155. https://doi.org/10.1007/s11142-020-09554-9

Bhimani, A. (2015). Exploring big data's strategic consequences. *Journal of Information Technology, 30*(1), 66–69. https://doi.org/10.1057/jit.2014.29

Bhimani, A., Datar, S. M., Horngren, C. T., & Rajan, M. V. (2019). *Management and Cost Accounting* (7th ed.). Pearson.

Bosse, S., Dahlhaus, L., & Engel, U. (2022). Web data mining: Collecting textual data from web pages using R. In U. Engel, A. Quan-Haase, S. Xun Liu, & L. Lyberg (Eds.), *Handbook of Computational Social Science, Volume 2: Data Science, Statistical Modelling, and Machine Learning Methods* (46–70). London: Routledge.

Brynjolfsson, E., & McAfee, A. (2011). *Race against the Machine: How the Digital Revolution Is Accelerating Innovation, Driving Productivity, and Irreversibly Transforming Employment and the Economy.* Digital Frontier Press.

Brynjolfsson, E., & McAfee, A. (2014). *The Second Machine Age: Work, Progress, and Prosperity in a Time of Brilliant Technologies.* WW Norton & Company.

Burns, J., Quinn, M., Warren, L., & Oliveira, J. (2013). *Management Accounting.* McGraw-Hill Higher Education.

Cooper, L. A., Holderness Jr., D. K., Sorensen, T. L., & Wood, D. A. (2019). Robotic process automation in public accounting. *Accounting Horizons, 33*(4), 15–35. https://doi.org/10.2308/acch-52466

Coursera (2021). *Python or R for Data Analysis: Which Should I Learn?* https://www.coursera.org/articles/python-or-r-for-data-analysis

Davenport, T. H. (2014). *Big Data at Work: Dispelling the Myths, Uncovering the Opportunities.* HBS Press.

Davenport, T. H., & Kirby, J. (2015). Beyond automation. *Harvard Business Review, 93*(6), 58–65.

Deloitte (2015). *The Robots Are Coming.* https://www2.deloitte.com/uk/en/pages/finance/articles/-robots-coming-global-business-services.html

Deloitte (2018). *Internal Controls Over Financial Reporting Considerations for Developing and Implementing Bots.* https://www2.deloitte.com/content/dam/Deloitte/us/Documents/audit/us-audit-internal-controls-over-financial-reporting-considerations-for-developing-and-implementing-bots.pdf

Ding, K., Lev, B., Peng, X., Sun, T., & Vasarhelyi, M. A. (2020). Machine learning improves accounting estimates: Evidence from insurance payments. *Review of Accounting Studies, 25*(3), 1098–1134. https://doi.org/10.1007/s11142-020-09546-9

Drury, C. (2018). *Management and Cost Accounting* (10th ed.). Cengage Learning EMEA.

Frey, C. B., & Osborne, M. A. (2017). The future of employment: How susceptible are jobs to computerisation? *Technological Forecasting and Social Change*, *114*, 254–280. https://doi.org/10.1016/j.techfore.2016.08.019

Galbreath, J. (2013). ESG in focus: The Australian evidence. *Journal of Business Ethics*, *118*(3), 529–541. https://doi.org/10.1007/s10551-012-1607-9

Gärtner, B., & Hiebl, M. R. W. (2018). Issues with Big Data. In M. Quinn & E. Strauss (Eds.), *The Routledge Companion to Accounting Information Systems* (pp. 161–172). Routledge. https://doi.org/10.4324/9781315647210-13

Goldin, C., & Katz, L. F. (2007). The race between education and technology: The evolution of U.S. educational wage differentials, 1890 to 2005. *National Bureau of Economic Research Working Paper Series, No. 12984*. https://doi.org/10.3386/w12984

Goos, M., Manning, A., & Salomons, A. (2014). Explaining job polarisation: Routine-biased technological change and offshoring. *The American Economic Review*, *104*(8), 2509–2526. https://doi.org/10.1257/aer.104.8.2509

Henri, J.-F., Boiral, O., & Roy, M.-J. (2016). Strategic cost management and performance: The case of environmental costs. *The British Accounting Review*, *48*(2), 269–282. https://doi.org/https://doi.org/10.1016/j.bar.2015.01.001

IBM Cloud Team (2021). *Python vs. R: What's the Difference?* https://www.ibm.com/cloud/blog/python-vs-r

Kaggle (2020). *2020 Kaggle Machine Learning & Data Science Survey*. https://www.kaggle.com/c/kaggle-survey-2020/overview

Keynes, J. M. (2010). Economic possibilities for our grandchildren. In J. M. Keynes (Ed.), *Essays in Persuasion*. (3rd ed.), Palgrave Macmillan. https://doi.org/https://doi.org/10.1007/978-1-349-59072-8_25

Kokina, J., & Blanchette, S. (2019). Early evidence of digital labor in accounting: Innovation with Robotic Process Automation. *International Journal of Accounting Information Systems*, *35*, 100431. https://doi.org/10.1016/j.accinf.2019.100431

Kokina, J., Gilleran, R., Blanchette, S., & Stoddard, D. (2021). Accountant as digital innovator: Roles and competencies in the age of automation. *Accounting Horizons*, *35*(1), 153–184. https://doi.org/10.2308/HORIZONS-19-145

Martínez Franco, C. M., & Hiebl, M. R. W. (2019). The introduction of accounting machines at Guinness. In M. Quinn & J. Oliveira (Eds.), *Accounting for Alcohol: An Accounting History of Brewing, Distilling and Viniculture* (pp. 11–27). Routledge. https://doi.org/10.4324/9781315185477-2

Miller, J. J. (1964). Automation, job creation, and unemployment. *Academy of Management Journal*, *7*(4), 300–307. https://doi.org/10.5465/254939

Moffitt, K. C., Rozario, A. M., & Vasarhelyi, M. A. (2018). Robotic process automation for auditing. *Journal of Emerging Technologies in Accounting*, *15*(1), 1–10.

Oesterreich, T. D., & Teuteberg, F. (2019). The role of business analytics in the controllers and management accountants' competence profiles: An exploratory study on individual-level data. *Journal of Accounting & Organisational Change*, *15*(2), 330–356. https://doi.org/10.1108/JAOC-10-2018-0097

Oliveira, J. (2018). Accountants' roles and accounting-related technologies. In M. Quinn & E. Strauss (Eds.), *The Routledge Companion to Accounting Information Systems* (pp. 133–144). Routledge. https://doi.org/10.4324/9781315647210-11

Ozgur, C., Colliau, T., Rogers, G., & Hughes, Z. (2017). MatLab vs. Python vs. R. *Journal of Data Science*, *15*(3), 355–371. https://doi.org/10.6339/JDS.201707_15(3).0001

Python Software Foundation (2021). About Python. https://www.python.org/about/

Richardson, B. J. (2009). Keeping ethical investment ethical: Regulatory issues for investing for sustainability. *Journal of Business Ethics*, *87*(4), 555–572. https://doi.org/10.1007/s10551-008-9958-y

Rikhardsson, P., & Yigitbasioglu, O. (2018). Business intelligence & analytics in management accounting research: Status and future focus. *International Journal of Accounting Information Systems*, *29*, 37–58. https://doi.org/10.1016/j.accinf.2018.03.001

Rosenbloom, R. S. (1964). Men and machines: Some 19th-century analyses of mechanisation. *Technology and Culture*, *5*(4), 489–511. https://doi.org/10.2307/3101215

Sande, W., & Sande, C. (2019). *Hello World! Computer Programming for Kids and Other Beginners* (3rd ed.), Manning.

Scassa, T. (2020). Ownership and control over publicly accessible platform data. *Online Information Review*, *43*(6), 986–1002. https://doi.org/10.1108/OIR-02-2018-0053

Singh, K., & Kaur, R. (2014). Hadoop: Addressing challenges of big data. *2014 IEEE International Advance Computing Conference (IACC),* 686–689. https://doi.org/10.1109/IAdCC.2014.6779407

Spraakman, G., Sanchez-Rodriguez, C., & Tuck-Riggs, C. A. (2020). Data analytics by management accountants. *Qualitative Research in Accounting & Management, 18*(1), 127–147.

Tsiligiris, V., & Bowyer, D. (2021). Exploring the impact of 4IR on skills and personal qualities for future accountants: A proposed conceptual framework for university accounting education. *Accounting Education, 30*(6), 621–649. https://doi.org/10.1080/09639284.2021.1938616

Tzovas, C. (2006). Factors influencing a firm's accounting policy decisions when tax accounting and financial accounting coincide. *Managerial Auditing Journal, 21*(4), 372–386. https://doi.org/10.1108/02686900610661397

Warren Jr, J. D., Moffitt, K. C., & Byrnes, P. (2015). How big data will change accounting. *Accounting Horizons, 29*(2), 397–407. https://doi.org/10.2308/acch-51069

Weißenberger, B. E., & Angelkort, H. (2011). Integration of financial and management accounting systems: The mediating influence of a consistent financial language on controllership effectiveness. *Management Accounting Research, 22*(3), 160–180. https://doi.org/10.1016/j.mar.2011.03.003

Wing, J. M. (2006). Computational thinking. *Communications of the ACM, 49*(3), 33–35. https://doi.org/10.1145/1118178.1118215

Wing, J. M. (2008). Computational thinking and thinking about computing. *Philosophical Transactions. Series A, Mathematical, Physical, and Engineering Sciences, 366*(1881), 3717–3725. https://doi.org/10.1098/rsta.2008.0118

Wolf, T., Kuttner, M., Feldbauer-Durstmüller, B., & Mitter, C. (2020). What we know about management accountants' changing identities and roles–a systematic literature review. *Journal of Accounting & Organisational Change, 16*(3), 311–347. https://doi.org/10.1108/JAOC-02-2019-0025

14

NOVEL VISUALISATION TECHNIQUES TO UNDERSTAND AIS DATA

Lisa Perkhofer, Peter Hofer, and Heimo Losbichler

Introduction

One of the key activities in management accounting is to provide decision-makers with relevant information to aid in an easy, accurate, fast, and rational decision-making process (Dilla et al., 2010; Ohlert & Weißenberger, 2015; Appelbaum et al., 2017). To keep up with today's dynamic markets and challenges, management accountants need to drastically change their long-standing reporting practices. First and foremost, their scope needs to be shifted from historical data reporting to real-time data processing and predictions, their data pool needs to be expanded from using only in-house data to the inclusion of external data sources, and the form of reporting needs to change from being paper based to interactive and web-based dashboarding to enable self-service (Goes, 2014; Appelbaum et al., 2017). To achieve this shift, new tools and technical instruments such as algorithms, appropriate accounting information systems, and business intelligence (BI) tools are necessary (Janvrin et al., 2014; Ohlert & Weißenberger, 2015; Bačić & Fadlalla, 2016; Pasch, 2019; Perkhofer, Hofer, Walchshofer et al., 2019).

As soon as traditional (retrospective and static) reporting is adapted to the above-stated changes and the quality of management information is enriched by data generated from business analytics (predictive (why did something happen) and/or prescriptive (how can this event be recreated or prevented)), datasets, as well as correlations among the variables of interest, become highly complex. This is particularly true for situations when datasets and tasks increase in volume and traditional and static business charts are no longer able to convey all necessary information (Perkhofer et al., 2019). Therefore, dashboarding and the inclusion of newer forms of visualisations (also known as big data visualisations) need to be taken into account (Dilla et al., 2010; Bačić & Fadlalla, 2016; Appelbaum et al., 2017).

Big data visualisations are intended to present more intuitive ways to visualise large amounts of data (for examples, visit https://D3js.org) (Elmqvist et al., 2011; Chen & Zhang, 2014; Perkhofer et al., 2020), and their inherent goal is to present the whole dataset (based on a predefined feature, such as analysis by dimension or analysis by attribute) within one frame. This approach allows us to uncover otherwise hidden information (Perkhofer et al., 2019); however, it also introduces a lot of challenges, such as visual clutter (Huang et al., 2017), a general lack of experience on how to work with and read the visualisations (Grammel et al.,

DOI: 10.4324/9781003132943-17

2010), the necessity for coding skills or BI support, and a high risk of information overload (Perkhofer et al., 2019). Nonetheless, there seems to be a common belief that visual analytics, 'the science of analytical reasoning facilitated by interactive visual interface' (Bačić & Fadlalla, 2016, p. 78), can help decision-makers to draw new and helpful insights from large datasets in the field of management accounting (Appelbaum et al., 2017).

In this chapter, we want to increase knowledge within the community of new visualisation types, convey methods of how to successfully integrate them into the decision-making process, and thus reduce the barriers and existing preconceptions associated with them.

How to visualise information

Visualising data means organising information by spatial location and supporting perceptual inferences (Perkhofer et al., 2019). Visualisation enhances the ability of both, searching and recognising, and thus significantly enhances sense-making capabilities (Munzner, 2014; Bačić & Fadlalla, 2016). It thereby enriches the discoveries and fosters profound and unexpected information to stand out (McCornick et al., 1987). However, the right visualisation and an appropriate format need to be chosen, allowing insights to appear. Consequently, for specific information-seeking tasks, particular visualisation types seem to best support its performance (Brehmer & Munzner, 2013). Nonetheless, for an accurate matching of the task and the visualisation cognitive (user-dependent) and data-dependent differences also need to be acknowledged, making the pick often less obvious than the general recommendations make them out to be (Hichert & Faisst, 2017; Eisl et al., 2018; Perkhofer, 2019).

In this context, one of the most important factors that needs to be considered is experience, which helps the decision-maker to decode the visual information presented to them in an efficient and effective way (Falschlunger et al., 2016). Consequently, new forms of visualisations, which cannot rely on experience but are of high complexity at the same time, need (1) explanation (e.g. through storytelling), (2) active engagement from the decision-maker, (3) multiple views (multiple visualisations showing the same dataset but each time in a slightly different format), and (4) possibilities to reduce the load through interaction. In particular, the last two points are institutionalised by the concept of dashboarding and need more explanation.

Multiple views/dashboarding

Dashboards are a response to the challenges faced by the information age, and they help in organising and streamlining information, in performing information processing and collaboration, in resource allocation as well as decision-making, and they empower employees to utilise self-service (McKeen et al., 2005; Pauwels et al., 2009). 'Using several graphics allows you to present a selection of views, with each one making an additional contribution to the overall picture' (Gelman & Unwin, 2013, p. 9) – in other words, through the help of information systems, information can be pulled together and presented in one display as a simple answer to the increasing problem of information overload (McKeen et al., 2005). A dashboard is thus a 'visual and interactive performance management tool that displays on a single screen the most important information to achieve one or several individual and/or organisational objects, allowing the decision-maker to identify, explore and communicate problem areas that need corrective action' (Yigitbasioglu & Velcu, 2012, p. 44).

Dashboards not only improve decision-making by concentration on abstract information, but they also attract the interest of the decision-maker by allowing deviations and anomalies to stand out due to their consistent content and design over time (McKeen et al., 2005; Yigitbasioglu & Velcu, 2012). Once a source of concern is identified (e.g. an unexpected development or a negative deviation), the decision-maker can uncover causes of poor or unexpected performance through interaction (Pauwels et al., 2009), another highly important feature of dashboarding.

Interaction

Interaction in this context means using filter or selection techniques, drilling down to the next layer of a data dimension, or also interchanging data dimensions or value attributes for further analysis (Heer & Shneiderman, 2012; Perkhofer et al., 2019). In addition, these changes are visible not only in one particular chart within the dashboard but also through the use of coordinated views in all linked visualisations – meaning, a change in one chart (e.g. the selection of a data dimension such as the country of origin) is highlighted in other charts as well (Dörk et al., 2008).

When working interactively, the analysis of the data does not end by finding a proper answer to the initial task but rather allows the generation and verification of additional and different hypotheses (Pike et al., 2009). These are generated only because the decision-maker interactively works with the dataset, and the process of doing so increases engagement, opportunity, and creativity (Dilla et al., 2010; Brehmer & Munzner, 2013; Perkhofer et al., 2020). Thus, interaction demonstrates the 'discourse the user has with his or her information' (Pike et al., 2009, p. 273).

Further, the sequence of actions is not predefined but rather individual and dependent on the decision-maker. It thereby particularly supports the user's knowledge base and perceptual abilities (Dörk et al., 2008; Dilla et al., 2010; Elmqvist et al., 2011; Liu et al., 2017). Consequently, interaction requires active physical and mental engagement, and throughout this process, understanding is increased and decision-making capabilities are enhanced (Buja et al., 1996; Shneiderman, 1996; Dix & Ellis, 1998; Pretorius & van Wijk, 2005; van Wijk, 2005; Wilkinson, 2005; Pike et al., 2009).

How to optimally use big data visualisations

In managerial accounting, areas of application and challenges associated with big data increase. While the first use cases dealt with internal audit, risk management, and fraud detection (Christensen, 2020), current discussions deal with key tasks in managerial accounting such as allocating budgetary resources, forecasting (predictive analytics), or cost reduction while maintaining product quality (Appelbaum et al., 2017). As already explained, a countermeasure to deal with the negative effects of large and complex datasets, as well as the challenges associated with analytics, is the use of interactive dashboarding and appropriate visualisations. Choosing appropriate visualisation, however, is a non-trivial task given the large options available (including big data visualisations).

For an optimal choice, the features of the visualisation need to target the core task, and their respective user groups need to be classified by previous experience and introduced to various options accordingly. With respect to business communication, and in particular managerial accounting, one needs to distinguish between *two major activities*: data exploration and communication.

1 *Data exploration:* In the first steps of data analysis, visual analytics and/or big data visualisations help to discover, identify, and verify new patterns, trends, and correlations (Brehmer & Munzner, 2013; Gelman & Unwin, 2013; Huang et al., 2017). In this initial phase, specific big data visualisations given each purpose do exist; however, they are hard to read and need experienced analysts/accountants to be able to extract information (Perkhofer et al., 2019). Visualisations belonging to this category, such as the parallel coordinates plot or the scatterplot matrix, are recommended for use by a small and specialised group to evaluate hypotheses and uncover new insights (Aigner et al., 2011). Nonetheless, an integration of these visuals into standardised reporting practices is *not* advised.

This is not only due to the fact that the user needs enhanced analytical skills but also because the obtained insight on patterns and correlations does not change to the same frequency (weekly or monthly) as decision-makers use dashboards in managerial accounting to check for a change in performance and a possible need for interference. Thus, using big data visualisations from this category not only confuse and irritate most potential users, but they also do not add any value if reported continuously (e.g. daily, weekly, or monthly). Rather, once a new logic is uncovered, the standardised dashboard used in managerial decision-making is enriched by the insight obtained through the visualisation (e.g. a newfound correlation tells us that variable X (e.g. order intake) can be used as a predictor of Y (e.g. sales) – then X is reported and actions can be taken at an earlier time).

2 *Communication of insights/results*: The communication of insights can follow two ways: either for the purpose of (a) *storytelling* during a presentation or for *(b) self-service*, included in a standardised dashboard (Perkhofer et al., 2019). Big data visualisations that are not too complex should be used in a presentation to convince the audience because they support telling a data-driven story, which supports trust through providing evidence. Further, the decision-maker or user is not completely left alone during the process of information acquisition but rather is guided by the presenter. However, highly complex visualisations (see Dataset 2 – Analysis of multiple attributes) should only be used if the audience shows interest and if they are skilled/experienced in deriving information from these kinds of visualisations and have a basic knowledge of statistics (Eckerson, 2010; Grammel et al., 2010; Perkhofer et al., 2020).

With respect to self-service, a small group of big data visualisations, those which present multiple hierarchies (see Dataset 1 – Analysis of multiple hierarchies) and also those representing geographical information (see Dataset 4), can be included in a dashboard as their complexity is manageable and their design is similar to traditional visualisation use (e.g. the sunburst visualisation is an extension of the pie chart and extracting information works in a very similar way) (Keim et al., 2006; Eckerson, 2010). Additionally, the information they represent – analysing a particular indicator using multiple dimensions – is of continuous interest to the management. Nonetheless, the willingness and the ability of the decision-maker to deal with new visualisations should always be taken into account.

The next section gives an overview on appropriate big data visualisations with a focus on their use in managerial accounting. This overview does not claim to be exhaustive; rather it shows visualisations the authors believe to have high potential based on previous research and practical experience. For better readability, the icons in Table 14.1 are used for classification of the different areas of application of big data visualisation, namely the above-described differentiation between exploratory data analysis versus communication (storytelling and self-service). Further, visualisations are categorised based on the authors' experience and knowledge.

Table 14.1 Classification of visualisation activities

Purpose 1:	Purpose 2:	Purpose 3:
Explorative data analysis	*Storytelling*	*Self-service*

Note: As discussed, the category 'explorative data analysis' means that the visualisation's sole purpose is to identify trends or correlations, while those visualisations categorised as 'self-service' can be used in all three stages without any restrictions.

Big data visualisations in accounting information system (AIS) – an overview

Big data visualisations can be clustered in multiple ways; however, a common method is to distinguish them based on the dataset they represent (Shneiderman, 1996; Keim, 2001; Brehmer & Munzner, 2013), which is also used to classify big data visualisations in this chapter. In the following, the different visualisation types will be briefly introduced by describing

- The intended purpose
- Necessary and helpful interaction techniques
- Design specifications for better readability and
- The advantages as well as disadvantages of each visualisation type

Due to restrictions in applicability, we limit our example to the four datasets: analysis of multiple hierarchies, analysis of multiple attributes, analysis of time series, and analysis of geographic information. The datasets are named Dataset 1 through 4 here. We specifically excluded visualisation of textual information and networks, as their main area of application lies in social media analysis and process optimisation – both interesting and important but not the core focus in managerial accounting.

For a better understanding of the visualisations discussed, QR codes are included which are linked to interactive visualisations created with Microsoft Power BI. For many years, Microsoft Power BI and Tableau were the front runners when it comes to BI support; however, in recent years, the distance between the two products is increasing with Power BI winning the race (Richardson et al., 2021). Further, information visualisation researchers often publish their research in open access platforms (e.g. GitHub or D3.js). These visualisations often show an increased usability due to higher interactivity. Thus, for most visualisations, an optimised D3 version is also included in the following tables (again included via QR codes).

Dataset 1: analysis of multiple dimensions (hierarchies)

Contemporary enterprise resource planning systems allow the use of varying and deep-levelled hierarchies (Parush et al., 2007). Thus, you can save and consequently analyse information in a fine-grained and targeted way. Unfortunately, the currently dominating form of interaction with the use of traditional visualisations in this context – the use of filters – often struggles in presenting an appropriate overview on dimensions and possible combinations of different dimensions. Further, next to the problem of identifying possible filter options, multiple filters and/or multi-select options can lead to misinformation and confusion of the decision-maker (e.g. too many filters are active and hidden in the filter area). Thus, a combination of two or three dimensions is mostly the limit. In contrast, big data visualisations designed to visualise hierarchies allow us to analyse multiple dimensions at the same time, reducing the risk of confusion and presenting an overview of the dataset at the same time. Still, problems arise as soon as five to eight dimensions are exceeded (Bertini et al., 2011).

More precisely, big data visualisations for multiple hierarchies allow us to analyse one specific attribute (in an accounting-related context, this is very often the analysis of revenues, units sold, or costs) and evaluating it based on specific but multiple hierarchies/dimensions (product group, sales regions, sales representative, etc.) at the same time. An interchangeable order of dimensions and the possibility of filtering data based on your information need are of high importance (Perkhofer et al., 2020).

With respect to the classification introduced in Table 14.1, these visualisation types also add value to dashboards for self-assessment as they are easy to understand and interact with, they represent very space-efficient options for analysis by dimensions, and they are similar to already-known visualisations used in business communications (pie chart, bar chart, etc.) (Perkhofer et al., 2020). Example visualisations are presented in Figures 14.1–14.3, with notes in Tables 14.2–14.4. The visualisations can be downloaded from the library available on d3js (https://d3js.org/).

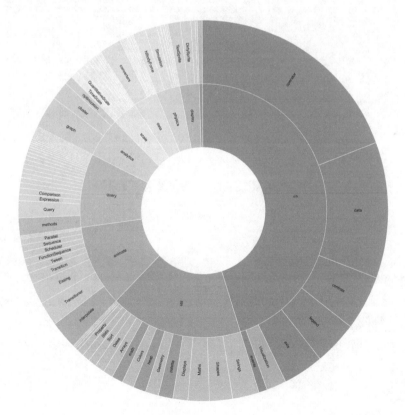

Figure 14.1   Sunburst visualisation (Link to original Visualisation: https://observablehq.com/@d3/zoomable-sunburst).

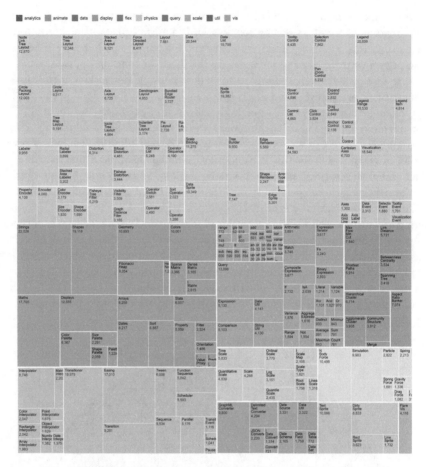

Figure 14.2 Treemap visualisation (Link to original Visualisation: https://observablehq.com/@d3/treemap).

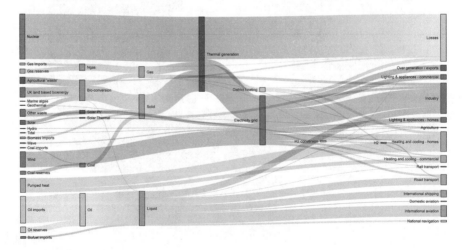

Figure 14.3 Sankey visualisation (Link to original Visualisation: https://observablehq.com/@d3/sankey-diagram).

Table 14.2 Sunburst visualisation, Dataset 1

Adjusted D3   *Power BI visual*

Visual mapping of the data: The sunburst is created by introducing additional category levels in hierarchical dependency to a one-dimensional pie chart and is a further development of the pie/ring diagram. It is a space-filling, polar-coordinates-based, comprehensive representation that maps the different dimensions of the dataset into rings. This visualisation uses radius and arc length to display the value of the attribute. Analysis is done by following a straight line from the inner circle to the outer rings (Keim et al., 2006; Rodden, 2014) whereby the innermost circle represents the highest level of the hierarchy. Also helpful during analysis are filters to reduce the visual display to focusing on particular dimensions.

Interaction techniques: The hierarchies need to be interchangeable to order dimensions depending on your information interest; a drill-through or filter based on a pre-selection of dimensions increases readability for smaller sub-dimensions; mouse-over effects including numerical information and active filters increase the readability of the display and add important information to each visual node (Rodden, 2014; Perkhofer et al., 2020).

Design specifications: Varying colours should be applied to distinguish between the different categories of the first hierarchy level, while different shades of the same colour should be used for a differentiation in the next hierarchy levels. Too many rings/hierarchies might overwhelm the decision-maker.

Advantages: The visualisation is very similar to the popular pie chart and, therefore, rather self-explanatory (Rodden, 2014). By rearranging the dimensions, the visualisation becomes very space-efficient and offers a lot of information at a glance. Up to six dimensions can be presented at once in a sunburst, and therefore, an overview is given concerning the available dimensions. Thus, the visualisation can be used as a visual filter for the rest of the dashboard.

Disadvantages: Very small sub-dimensions might be overlooked due to the proportional scaling of the data. Radial representations can be misleading – angle and area cannot be interpreted (Rodden, 2014; Perkhofer et al., 2020). Conclusions are often less effective (Kim & Draper, 2014), and side-by-side comparison and analysis might be difficult with two sunbursts (similar to comparisons of pie charts). Further, it is harder to assess the size of a sub-component.

Table 14.3 Treemap visualisation, Dataset 1

Dimensions   *Adjusted D3*   *Power BI visual*

Visual mapping of the data: This visualisation type is again a space-filling hierarchical display (Gorodov & Gubarev, 2013). This time, each dimension is represented by a rectangle, and the total of all sub-dimensions visually represents the amount of the higher dimension (Keim et al., 2006). This results in a nesting of smaller rectangles within the rectangle of the first dimension (Severino, 2015). Thus, only a limited number of dimensions are presented at once, and the remaining dimensions become visible through interaction.

Interaction techniques: In order to work with the treemap visualisation, interaction techniques such as filtering and arranging are of great importance (to change the order of dimensions). Also, navigating (zooming) is a crucial part in exploring this visualisation. A thorough analysis of deep hierarchies is possible but only if the decision-maker can jump to the next hierarchical layer of the diagram (and back) and drill through the data.

Design specifications: The size of each rectangular space (or sub-segment) displays the corresponding value of the dimension, while colours are often used to delineate different structures from each other at the same hierarchical level. Areas for headings and figures (both in terms of ordering by size and concrete values) should be defined, and, with respect to colours, there should be a concept that allows for the labels to be readable in all instances (e.g. dark colouring + bright font colours, and vice versa).

Advantages: All levels of the first dimensions are visually mapped (size is proportionate to the value of the rectangle) and visible. Thus, it is easy to assess large as well as small categories, and all sub-dimensions become clearly visible. By drilling through the data, the lower levels of the hierarchy also become clearly visible (one needs to be careful to visualise the process of drilling through, in order for the decision-maker to not lose focus).

Disadvantages: Prior studies have revealed that the integration of too many dimensions can negatively affect the perceptiveness of decision-makers (Liu et al., 2017). Deeper hierarchical structures only become visible through interaction – only two dimensions are visible without interaction. Having an overview of the data's structure is missing, which is a huge disadvantage of this visualisation.

Table 14.4 Sankey visualisation, Dataset 1

Adjusted D3   Power BI visual

Visual mapping of the data: The Sankey visualisation has a Cartesian-based layout and visualises the quantitative information of flow between multiple entities or hierarchies (Chou et al., 2016). The different dimensions are presented next to each other as nodes, and the sub-dimensions are integrated vertically in each node, while the size is representative for its value. By selecting and unselecting different sub-dimensions, the flow between the multiple dimensions becomes visible.

Interaction techniques: In terms of storytelling and sense-making, interactions such as rearranging and filtering are vital. In addition, it is crucial to highlight information across nodes with the use of selectable options in order to ensure an in-depth data analysis. It is essential that multiple options are allowed to be active at the same time in order to select different sub-dimensions across nodes, as only then can the full potential of these visualisations be unlocked. Furthermore, a reordering or a reduction of nodes might be necessary to reduce visual clutter and facilitate information processing (Chou et al., 2016). For a detailed analysis, mouse-over effects, including further information, should also be enabled (e.g. exact numerical values presented in the display and additional information such as previous year comparison).

Design specifications: Highlighted information should be presented in a more intense colour than unselected information. Colour coding for different data dimensions helps in immediate differentiation.

Advantages: All sub-dimensions are clearly visible, and their interplay also becomes visible by selecting various nodes. The visualisation is easy to understand and intuitive to work with. Selecting different nodes allows us to combine information on multiple dimensions, such as distribution channels, geographical areas, managing partners, or product groups, in a very space-efficient way.

Disadvantages: From the selected nodes, which are needed for data analysis, all data records stay visible, and thus high information load can be a consequence. The concept of flow might not be useful in every analysis and, thus, distract the decision-maker from their original processing intent.

Dataset 2: analysis of multiple attributes

An attribute is a measure which can be allocated to a scale (Lehmann et al., 2010). A multi-attribute dataset is one consisting of multiple (more than two) attributes, such as cost, revenue, and units sold, as well as temperature, stock price development, and customer satisfaction index. It can also be called multivariate (Kehrer & Hauser, 2013). Time (and or date) can be used just like any other attribute (Kehrer & Hauser, 2013), but time-related developments can also be ordered using a hierarchy and need special attention – as are discussed in the next section (Dataset 3 – Analysis of temporal data).

If a dataset is unknown, one of the first steps is to analyse descriptive statistics as well as simple inferences, such as correlations. Typically, this means analysing each variable's sum, median, mode, mean, variance, quantiles, and possible correlations between two or more variables within the dataset. The measures are well known and allow for a very quick assessment of the data's distribution while also acting as an indicator for finding possible patterns and relationships.

A table is the simplest form for presenting multi-attribute data; however, extracting information out of tables on trends, outliers, or correlations is extremely difficult. When visualising the data, very often new patterns and correlations become apparent that would otherwise stay hidden (Lehmann et al., 2010). Thus, these kinds of visualisations are particularly helpful and important tools in visual analytics. Unfortunately, despite their unique ability to uncover correlations, trends, and distributions, they are often difficult to read, cluttered, and require an experienced analyst to extract information (Huang et al., 2017). Also, especially for multimodal data (different sources using different units or scales), normalising the data before visualising it is often required for reasonable data mapping and analysis (Kehrer & Hauser, 2013). Examples are presented in Figures 14.4–14.7, with notes in Tables 14.5–14.8. They can be downloaded from the library available on d3js (https://d3js.org/).

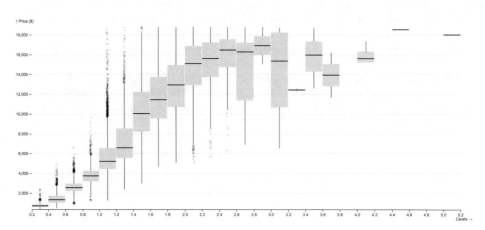

Figure 14.4 Box plot visualisation (Link to original Visualisation: https://observablehq.com/@d3/box-plot).

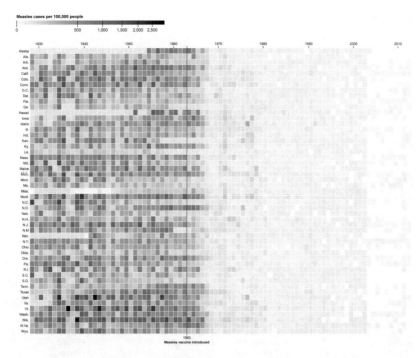

Figure 14.5 Heatmap visualisation (Link to original Visualisation: https://observablehq.com/@ mbostock/the-impact-of-vaccines).

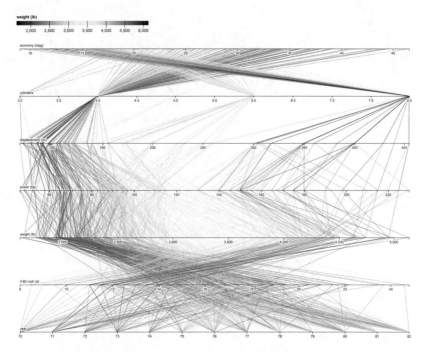

Figure 14.6 Parallel coordinates plot (Link to original Visualisation: https://observablehq.com/@d3/ parallel-coordinates).

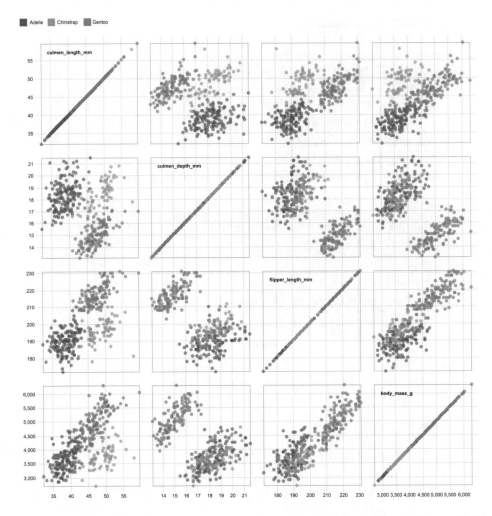

Figure 14.7 Scatterplot matrix (Link to original Visualisation: https://observablehq.com/@d3/brushable-scatterplot-matrix).

Table 14.5 Box plot visualisation, Dataset 2

Dimensions

Attributes

Power BI visual

Visual mapping of the data: A box plot is designed to indicate important descriptive statistics of the primary data within one glyph. The upper and lower ends of the box plot show outliers or extrema (indicated by a line, also called whiskers), while the core of the box plot, the bar including the median, indicates where 50% of the data is positioned (Spitzer et al., 2014). Next to the obvious statistics – minimum, maximum, median, upper quintile, lower quintile – information on the size of the variable's standard deviation is also revealed. Using a box plot allows for comparison of multiple variables at the same time while comparing them with respect to these well-known statistical parameters (Potter, 2006). For big data, the focus on outliers is highly relevant.

Interaction techniques: Mouse-over effects are helpful in showing more detailed information. Applying filters to focus on different clusters within the dataset helps in understanding more fine-grained nuances in the large datasets. Reordering the variables to cluster similar data is also essential.

Design specifications: Consequent labelling and putting labels and values in juxtaposition are crucial to avoid misunderstandings. Different colours should only be applied if useful in the context of the information. A lot of modifications exist to add additional information concerning the variable's distribution, and the width of the box plot is often adjusted to represent size (Spitzer et al., 2014).

Advantages: The box plot is a widely known visualisation that helps present descriptive information of a variable in a simple and understandable format, and it is particularly helpful in identifying outliers. Further, using such a standardised schema for visualisation allows for an easy comparison of different variables (Spitzer et al., 2014).

Disadvantages: Summary statistics describing the distribution are displayed; however, the distribution itself is hidden, and thus, differences among two variables might be missed – especially when dealing with skewed data. Thus, a completely different distribution can result in the same measures (Potter, 2006). Further, only a limited amount of information can be included in the box plot.

Table 14.6 Heatmap visualisation, Dataset 2

Dimensions / Attributes / *Adjusted D3*

Visual mapping of the data: A heatmap represents data through a colour-coded system, and the format resembles a table as it consists of rows and columns. Although no numerical values are presented, they can be inferred by colour: very dark and very light colours are an indication for extremities (Perrot et al., 2017). Also, a heatmap can always show the sum, maximum, or minimum values, or it shows the computed average per attribute (Severino, 2015). Which information is used is usually selectable by a drop-down menu. Insights obtained by a heatmap are outliers, patterns, and possible correlations of two or more attributes.

Interaction techniques: An option list or drop-down menu (as already mentioned above) is mostly added to change the computation of the attributes (e.g. from sum to average). Further, to identify patterns or correlations across attributes, reordering and putting similar variables in juxtaposition are highly important. Also, mouse-over to specify a field (e.g. include figures) and the possibility of highlighting a column or a row are necessary to focus analysis.

Design specifications: When displaying values, a distinction is made between categorical data, which relies on a defined colour code (e.g. Low, Medium, High), and numerical data, which requires the use of a colour scale. The colour scale represents flowing colour gradients from minimum to maximum and can be monochrome or multi-coloured. In both cases, however, a legend is indispensable for understanding the colour meaning (Severino, 2015). Care should be taken not to create visualisations that are too colourful, as these very quickly overload the decision-maker (Liu et al., 2017). With respect to the colour code used, a business logic similar to traffic lights should be applied (McKeen et al., 2005).

Advantages: The heatmap is a very space-efficient visualisation, and it permits intense areas to stand out. Further, minimum and maximum values are clearly visible through the used scale, and the interpretation of high and low is very easy through the colour support.

Disadvantages: By switching between the different methods of computation, existing patterns might fade, while comparing different patterns that might exist between computation methods is highly difficult. Also, a heatmap always shows condensed information; thus, for checking the visually induced hypothesis, a deeper analysis is often required. Caution is advised when applying the commonly used business logic (red and green) as an 8% proportion of the population (primarily male) suffer from colour blindness and can't distinguish between green and red (this also applies to all other visualisations using this logic, of course).

Table 14.7 Parallel coordinates plot, Dataset 2

Adjusted D3   Power BI visual

Visual mapping of the data: The parallel coordinates plot is a very popular and strongly recommended visualisation in the InfoVis (Information Visualisation) community. This is due to the fact that the parallel coordinates plot is one of the few visualisations that is able to present multiple attributes – without the need for normalisation – in one chart (Hofer et al., 2018; Perkhofer et al., 2019). Two or more horizontal attribute axes are connected via polygonal lines at the height of the respective attribute value (Keim, 2002). To do so, data is geometrically transformed (Keim, 2001), and each line represents one specific data record (e.g. order number, a sales entry). With respect to interpretation, Inselberg introduced common rules for the identification of correlations and trends (Inselberg & Dimsdale, 1990). Lines which are parallel to each other suggest a positive correlation, lines crossing in an X shape suggest a negative correlation, and lines crossing randomly show no particular relationship.

Interaction techniques: A user has to be able to re-arrange the axes, as only neighbouring axis can be interpreted in a meaningful way, e.g. to analyse relationships between two attributes (Perkhofer et al., 2019). Further, filtering different sections within one or more axes is useful for uncovering correlations, which might only exist in particular parts. Also, through a concentration on particular sections, visual clutter can be reduced.

Design specifications: Colour coding for a differentiation on dimensions (e.g. different years, different vendors, different geographical areas) is very helpful. Axes should be clearly labelled, and each should start with its minimum and end with its maximum value, while the lines should be thin but clearly visible.

Advantages: The visualisation is one of few that allows multiple attributes to be displayed in one visualisation. By making use of categorical/sequential single-hue colour scales and filtering options, cluster analysis is also possible (Perkhofer et al., 2019).

Disadvantages: Unfortunately, managers in managerial accounting are widely unfamiliar with this visualisation type. The visualisation is very hard to read and interpret if unknown (Huang et al., 2017). Negative correlations tend to stand out more than positive correlations. Too much information (too many lines) can introduce visual clutter, and thus correlations, might still be missed. Therefore, large datasets can require pre-processing at the cost of data loss.

Table 14.8 Scatterplot matrix, Dataset 2

Attributes

Dimensions

Power BI visual

Visual mapping of the data: A scatterplot depicts two variables by presenting a collection of points on two continuous, orthogonal dimensions and is designed to emphasise the spatial distribution of the data presented (Sarikaya & Gleicher, 2018). The degree of the correlation is described by the correlation coefficient and ranges from 1 (100% positive correlation) to −1 (100% negative correlation). A scatterplot matrix orders multiple scatterplots horizontally and vertically in the same order, and it duplicates them relative to the diagonal (Kanjanabose et al., 2015). In doing so, one can cancel out the negative aspect of low dimensionality of a single scatterplot but, at the same time, also draw on the readers' ability to extract information from the well-known visualisation type (Elmqvist et al., 2008; Sarikaya & Gleicher, 2018).

Interaction techniques: It is important to allow highlighting selected information to easily find the right column and row. Also, if different clusters are visualised within one chart, using filters to reduce the visible data to those data points is of utmost importance. In doing so, the axes need to be rescaled to their respective minimum and maximum, and consequently, correlations within a specific sub-dimension among the variables become apparent.

Design specifications: For an easy assessment of the strength and direction of the correlation, a trend line should be included. It is best to use distinguishable colours or shapes to differentiate between data clusters. Too little information reduces the likelihood of correlations to be identified, and thus, a larger dataset is necessary. Also, for a better description of the variables, histograms should be included in the diagonal of the visualisation, and colour-coded correlation coefficients (see heatmap) should be included below the diagonal.

Advantages: The visualisation type (the single scatterplot) is very well known, and thus, almost everyone can extract useful information from a scatterplot matrix. This is true for information on both correlations and distributions (especially if a histogram is included).

Disadvantages: Compared to the parallel coordinates plot, less attributes can be displayed in one chart, and this is often deemed to be space-inefficient due to the high redundancy (Huang et al., 2017). More than eight scatterplots reduce the ability of users to extract information. Further, correlations on datasets showing a high kurtosis or skewness are significantly harder to assess (Perkhofer, Walchshofer et al., 2019).

Dataset 3: analysis of temporal data

Time is one of the most important dimensions, and it has distinct characteristics that predefine data analysis. This is the case, as time itself comes with a hierarchy (seconds, minutes, hours, days, weeks, months, years, decades, etc.) and thus has an inherent order. It also comes with the challenge of working with different forms of divisions within this predefined hierarchy (e.g. 60 minutes is an hour but one day has 24 hours) (Aigner et al., 2011; Blázquez-García et al., 2021). 'Therefore, time-oriented data, i.e., data that is inherently linked to time needs to be treated differently than other kinds of data and requires appropriate visual and analytical methods to explore and analyse it' (Aigner et al., 2011, p. 2).

An additional reason why time-series data is problematic in data analysis is that more and more data get automatically collected and saved from sensors (Walker et al., 2015). Thus, data is very often recorded continuously (Moritz & Fisher, 2018), and next to the sheer volume of data, unfortunately, time-oriented data comes with a lot of data quality issues (e.g. missing values, outliers, drifts, precision degradation, faulty data) (Blázquez-García et al., 2021). Visualisations, in this context, not only enable data analysts or managerial accountants to visually process information (spot patterns, trends, and sequences), but they also help identify problems in pre-processing (Friedl et al., 2021). Therefore, visualisations for temporal big data can be used before, instead of, or after algorithmic analysis, potentially adding value to multiple process steps in data analytics (Aigner et al., 2011).

Due to the distinct characteristics of this particular dimension, a lot of different visualisations do exist, each supporting a different task or a different kind of computation (e.g. daily tracking of records vs. a calendar view) with the aim of identifying repetitive patterns and trends (van Wijk & van Selow, 1999). Examples are presented in Figures 14.8–14.10, with notes in Tables 14.9–14.11. They can be downloaded from the library available on d3js (https://d3js.org/).

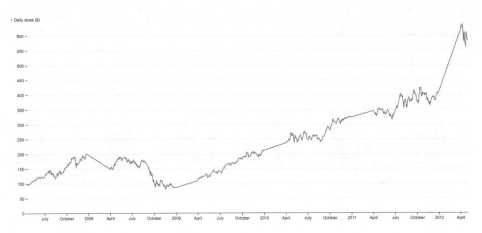

Figure 14.8   Interactive line chart (Link to original Visualisation: https://observablehq.com/@d3/line-with-missing-data).

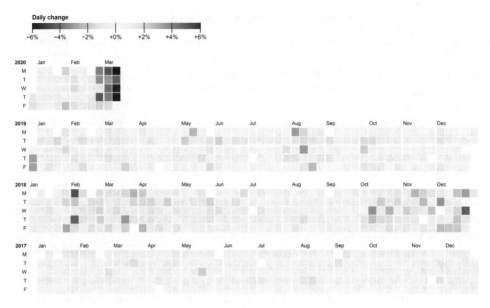

Figure 14.9 Calendar visualisation (Link to original Visualisation: https://observablehq.com/@d3/calendar-view).

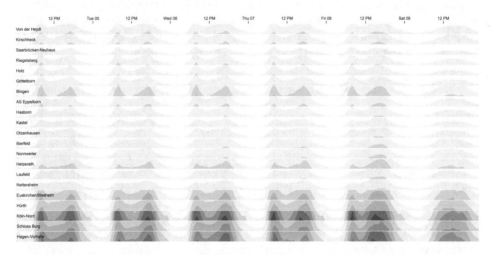

Figure 14.10 Horizon graph (Link to original Visualisation: https://observablehq.com/@d3/horizon-chart).

Table 14.9 Interactive line chart, Dataset 3

Adjusted D3   Power BI visual

Visual mapping of the data: When analysing time series, the most common way to visualise temporal data is the line chart (Potter, 2006; Aigner et al., 2011). With respect to the visual mapping, data is plotted along the x-axis representing time from left to right and a scale representing the variable of interest (Potter, 2006). The focus lies on the overall shape of the data over time (Aigner et al., 2011). For a multivariate dataset, multiple lines can be displayed within one chart, or multiple small visualisations can be used which are positioned on a single screen (= small multiples) (Moritz & Fisher, 2018). Further colour, line width, and line shape can be used for distinction. For very large datasets, an overview showing the whole dataset in addition to a detailed view focusing on a particular time frame is very helpful (see adjusted D3 visual) (Friedl et al., 2021).

Interaction techniques: Panning is a helpful technique for changing the focus of the visualisation to another time frame (Friedl et al., 2021). Interaction helps in identifying a specific data point by allowing us to connect the data point with the x-axis. Mouse-over effects help in differentiating and adding additional information (Ware, 2012; Eisl et al., 2018). Also drill-in and drill-out can be helpful to jump through different hierarchy levels (e.g. from months to years).

Design specifications: Explicit colours should be used to differ between variables. Further, it is of importance to use the same scale for direct comparison. If patterns and sequences reoccur, highlighting those using colours is helpful. The area chart is a variation of the line chart and shows the computed sum of all lines (Moritz & Fisher, 2018).

Advantages: The visualisation is very well known, and spotting trends over time from left to right is comparably easy for humans to do. Different aggregation (e.g. cycle plot) also allows us to uncover seasonal trends (Aigner et al., 2011).

Disadvantages: Line charts are easy and effective for small data space; however, for large datasets, they become ineffective due to visual clutter if too many lines/data points are presented within one chart (Potter, 2006). Another problem lies in overplotting, which can occur if multiple line charts are presented on one screen, each showing one chart (Moritz & Fisher, 2018). As a result, patterns and trends become very hard to detect (Potter, 2006). The alternative, e.g. presenting the data on a higher hierarchy, is also problematic as it can hide patterns or outliers. Also, missing values can result in false interpretation (Aigner et al., 2011).

Table 14.10 Calendar visualisation, Dataset 3

Power BI visual

Visual mapping of the data: The calendar visualisation is a specific form of a heatmap visualisation. It presents the particular hierarchy of time (days, months, hours, etc.) and highlights in distinct colours if a variable performed good or bad at this point/period in time. The two-dimensional matrix allows users to identify patterns (long term – years – as well as short term – weeks) (Aigner et al., 2011). This way of clustering information is supposed to give a quick overview on both standard and exceptional patterns. However, through computation (sums, averages), visualisations often lose information on interesting patterns and outliers. An illustrative example concerning this problem is given by van Wijk and van Selow (1999, p. 2), who state: 'Many data patterns on holidays show strong similarities to data patterns on Sundays. If the data for each weekday is averaged separately, the holidays will disturb the results'. Also, using mathematical models to eliminate the hierarchical structure considering the different divisions are available might be helpful, but interpretation of the outcome is much harder and needs skilled analysts (van Wijk & van Selow, 1999).

Interaction techniques: Related to time-series data, a priori hypotheses are rare, and thus, interacting with the data, such as jumping through hierarchy levels, changing the variable of interest, changing the computation of the variable (sum, average, min, max), etc. is of great importance (van Wijk & van Selow, 1999).

Design specifications: Colours should be used in accordance with common interpretation standards – e.g. a business logic with green for favourable and red for unfavourable developments, or the logic applied to temperatures, blue for low and red for high values, should be taken into account.

Advantages: A calendar is well known and easy to interpret. The use of different colour shades allows for an immediate understanding and for patterns to pop out.

Disadvantages: Interesting patterns and outliers might be missed due to the need for computation (e.g. sums, averages). Caution is again advised when applying the commonly used business logic (red and green) due to colour blindness.

Table 14.11 Horizon graph, Dataset 3

| Time | Power BI *visual* |

Visual mapping of the data: The horizon graph visualises layered bands to compress vertical extremes (Moritz & Fisher, 2018). Thus, it is a condensed visualisation that allows to show the performance of a lot of individual variables over time. To do so, distinct colours for positive and negative values (e.g. green for positive and red for negative developments) are used. Further, to differentiate between moderate and extreme values within each direction, bands using colour grading are utilised (Heer et al., 2009). The idea is very similar to a heatmap – the darker the colour, the higher the value, and thus, outliers are easily detected. To condense the display, the negative values are integrated into the positive design space, and the colour bands are also presented on top of each other, resulting in only one line of visualised data. Thus, the distinction between positive and negative, as well as high and low, values can no longer be deduced from the distance to the *x*-axis but rather through the colour coding used (Aigner et al., 2011). The condensed display and the use of the colours allow us to find similar patterns within the whole dataset (across time sequences and variables).

Interaction techniques: By hovering over a variable, more information should become apparent (e.g. a visualisation showing a traditional line chart). Also, the row of interest should be highlighted or even enlarged when clicking on it. To uncover similar trends, not only enlarging and limiting the time frame but also reducing visible variables or reordering them are highly recommended interaction techniques.

Design specifications: The visualisation is two-toned (Saito et al., 2005) and integrates the development below the zero axis within the positive space while signalling it through a different (mostly blue or red) colour (Reijner, 2008).

Advantages: The visualisation is very space-efficient and allows us to detect outliers, exceptional behaviour, and predominant patterns across multiple variables (Reijner, 2008). It is very useful for stock price developments and portfolio management.

Disadvantages A simple normalisation technique needs to be applied before visualising the data – not the actual values are plotted but the percentage changes from one particular timestamp until today (Reijner, 2008). Further, the visualisation is far from being self-explanatory, and if red and green should be used for colour coding, again colour blindness needs to be considered.

Dataset 4: analysis of geographical data

Geographic maps provide visual information for the spatial domain (Dörk et al., 2008). The aim is to identify not only regions of particular interest (through the detection of outliers) but also patterns with respect to regional areas (cities tend to show increased sales or differences between western and eastern regions) and patterns over time – either through interaction or by comparing different time stamps next to each other (Han et al., 2019; Leung et al., 2020).

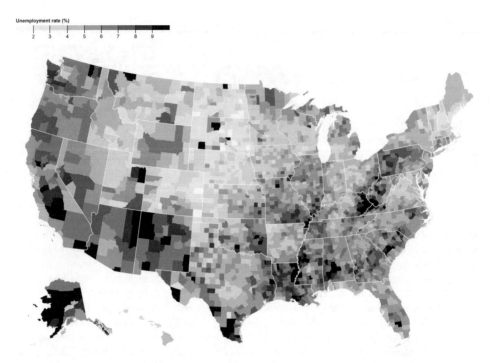

Figure 14.11 Choropleth visualisation (Link to original Visualisation: https://observablehq.com/@ d3/choropleth).

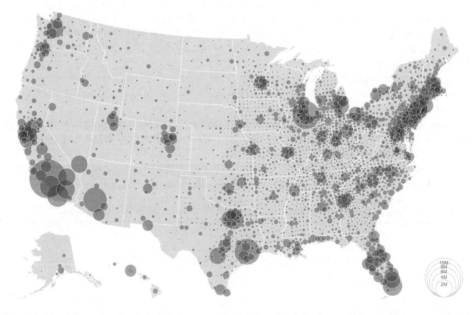

Figure 14.12 Map visualisation (Link to original Visualisation: https://observablehq.com/@d3/ bubble-map).

Widespread use of geographic visualisations has been witnessed since the beginning of the COVID-19 crisis. Graphics on newspapers, television, etc. make regular use of choropleths and other geographic visualisations to introduce areas with outbreaks, regional lockdowns, and the effect of measures (Leung et al., 2020; Shaito & Elmasri, 2021). Examples of popular geographical visualisations are presented in Figures 14.11 and 14.12, with notes in Tables 14.12 and 14.13. They can be downloaded from the library available on d3js (https://d3js.org/).

Table 14.12 Choropleth visualisation, Dataset 4

Adjusted D3

Visual mapping of the data: This visualisation is one of the most used geographic visualisation types (Besancon et al., 2020). It applies the concept of the heatmap and transforms a colour code onto a map, conveying different regions with different granularity (countries, states, or districts). Colours in different shades are used to distinguish between regions with high and low values. This structure reveals spatiotemporal patterns of one variable, but choropleths can also be used to compare the geographical patterns of multiple variables (Han et al., 2019).

Interaction techniques: The most important interaction techniques in the context of land maps are zooming and panning. If a region attracts interest, a deeper analysis should be made possible by jumping into the next hierarchy level, and if more choropleths are used to visualise different variables, interactions should be linked to view the changes induced simultaneously in other variables (Han et al., 2019). Further, additional information via mouse-over should be available to the decision-maker.

Design specifications: No more than seven colour shades should be used to differentiate between classifications; otherwise, differentiation could become very difficult. The map design should be reduced (no or limited information on lakes, rivers, etc.) but display regions in accordance with regional districts, federal states, or countries to draw on people's ability and experience with cartography. Caution should again be paid to colour blindness.

Advantages: The visualisation is very easy to read for most decision-makers, and it shows information on a particular variable in a highly condensed form, adding information on geographic regions when compared to the heatmap itself. Thus, geographical patterns can be identified by the decision-maker. It is also a very helpful way to include a filter (by region) into a dashboard display (using coordinated views).

Disadvantages: Regional differences (size of the region) impact the interpretation of the user. Larger areas tend to focus the attention, which can be misleading. This is especially problematic in highly populated areas, as they tend to be the most concentrated locations, in contrast to low populated areas where the districts or regions are larger but mostly have less impact on economic and business-related data. It can only display one attribute.

Table 14.13 Map visualisation, Dataset 4

| | | Adjusted D3 | Power BI visual |

Visual mapping of the data: In regard to map visualisations, the most common type used is the bubble map. The bubble indicates the size of a variable given a specific geographic location using its radius. However, instead of a bubble, small business charts (e.g. pie charts or bar charts) can be placed onto the map, and thus, a second dimension can also be integrated into the display. Also, the radius needs not to necessarily represent the sum, but other descriptive information (e.g. average, max, min) can also be used (Leung et al., 2020).

Interaction techniques: The most important interaction techniques in context of land maps are zooming and panning (Leung et al., 2020). One needs to be able to dive into the map and analyse the values in more detail if an interesting pattern pops up. Further, the value and the exact location (district, region, or country) should appear as a pop-up if one hovers over a bubble with the mouse.

Design specifications: Again, the map design should be reduced (no or limited information on lakes, rivers, etc.), but display regions in accordance with regional districts, federal states, or countries to draw on people's ability and experience with cartography should be maintained. Further, business charts should be designed in accordance with visualisation design principles (Ware, 2012; Eisl et al., 2018).

Advantages: Geographic regions with high values can be identified with high efficiency. Bubbles and standard business charts are easy to read and interpret.

Disadvantages: If a map is divided into small regions, bubbles (or business charts, respectively) can overlay and thus be hard to distinguish from each other (Leung et al., 2020).

Conclusion and research agenda

The above-mentioned trends in reporting, namely storytelling and self-service, are evoked by the increasing availability of big data and imply the need for significant technological changes in management reporting. As a consequence, in the recent years, the number of BI tools to support managerial decision-making has skyrocketed (Hoelscher & Mortimer, 2018). With these tools, a lot of visualisation options, from traditional business charts, such as bar, line, and pie charts, to newer forms of interactive visualisations (e.g. the parallel coordinates plot or the heatmap visualisation), have become available to their potential decision-makers (Bačić & Fadlalla, 2016).

Knowledge on when and how to use new visualisation types is a key success factor in dealing with the challenges brought about by the area of big data. These visualisation types support the analysis of datasets including large time-series data and datasets including multiple attributes for uncovering correlations and trends. The benefits of big data visualisation options are described and presented (including links to the interactive visualisations integrated via QR code). Especially with respect to multi-dimensional and geographic visualisations, we hope to see an increased use, also in self-service in AIS, to empower employees and managers as well as increase decision-making quality.

Hopefully, this chapter adds to the understanding of big data visualisations and reduces the prevalent hesitance or unawareness concerning interactive forms of novel visualisations, as they limit usage and hence the potential impact of big data in AIS (Chen & Zhang, 2014; Bačić & Fadlalla, 2016).

References

Aigner, W., Miksch, S., Schumann, H., & Tominski, C. (2011). *Visualisation of time-oriented data.* Springer.

Appelbaum, D., Kogan, A., Vasarhelyi, M., & Yan, Z. (2017). Impact of business analytics and enterprise systems on managerial accounting. *International Journal of Accounting Information Systems, 25,* 29–44.

Bačić, D., & Fadlalla, A. (2016). Business information visualisation intellectual contributions: An integrative framework of visualisation capabilities and dimensions of visual intelligence. *Decision Support Systems, 89,* 77–86.

Bertini, E., Tatu, A., & Keim, D. A. (2011). Quality metrics in high-dimensional data visualisation: An overview and systematisation. *IEEE Transactions on Visualisation and Computer Graphics, 17*(12), 2203–2212.

Besancon, L., Cooper, M., Ynnerman, A., & Vernier, F. (2020). An evaluation of visualisation methods for population statistics based on choropleth maps. *Computing Research Repository.*

Blázquez-García, A., Conde, A., Mori, U., & Lozano, J. A. (2021). A review on outlier/anomaly detection in time series data. *ACM Computing Surveys, 54*(3), 1–33. https://doi.org/10.1145/3444690

Brehmer, M., & Munzner, T. (2013). A multi-level typology of abstract visualisation tasks. *IEEE Transactions on Visualisation and Computer Graphics, 19*(12), 2376–2385.

Buja, A., Cook, D., & Swayne, D. F. (1996). Interactive high-dimensional data visualisation. *Journal of Computational and Graphical Statistics, 5*(1), 78. https://doi.org/10.2307/1390754

Chen, C. P., & Zhang, C.-Y. (2014). Data-intensive applications, challenges, techniques and technologies: a survey on big data. *Information Sciences, 275,* 314–347.

Chou, J.-K., Wang, Y., & Ma, K.-L. (2016). Privacy preserving event sequence data visualisation using a Sankey diagram-like representation. In W. Chen & D. Weiskopf (Eds.), *9th ACM siggraph conference and exhibition on computer graphics and interactive techniques* (1–8). ACM.

Christensen, B. (2020). Adapting to the dynamic risk environment: Internal audit needs to move beyond analog processes to assess risks in a digital world. *Internal Auditor, 77*(5), 22–23. http://search.ebscohost.com/login.aspx?direct=true&db=bsh&AN=146221114&site=ehost-live

Dilla, W. N., Janvrin, D. J., & Raschke, R. L. (2010). Interactive data visualisation: New directions for accounting information systems research. *Journal of Information Systems, 24*(2), 1–37.

Dix, A., & Ellis, G. (Eds.) (1998). *Starting simple: Adding value to static visualisation through simple interaction. AVI '98.* ACM New York, NY, USA.

Dörk, M., Carpendale, S., Collins, C., & Williamson, C. (2008). Visgets: Coordinated visualisation for web-based information exploration and discovery. *IEEE Transactions on Visualisation and Computer Graphics, 14*(6), 1205–1212.

Eckerson, W. W. (2010). *Performance dashboards: Measuring, monitoring, and managing your business* (2nd ed.). John Wiley & Sons, Inc.

Eisl, C., Perkhofer, L., Hofer, P., & Losbichler, H. (2018). *Exzellenz im Reporting Design: Leitfaden für messbar bessere Berichte.* Haufe.

Elmqvist, N., Dragicevic, P., & Fekete, J.-D. (2008). Rolling the dice: Multidimensional visual exploration using scatterplot matrix navigation. *IEEE Transactions on Visualisation and Computer Graphics, 14*(6), 1141–1148.

Elmqvist, N., Moere, V. A., Jetter, H.-C., Cernea, D., Reiterer, H., & Jankun-Kelly, T. J. (2011). Fluid interaction for information visualisation. *Information Visualisation, 10*(4), 327–340.

Falschlunger, L., Lehner, O., Treiblmaier, H., & Eisl, C. (2016). Visual representation of information as an antecedent of perceptive efficiency: The effect of experience. In *Proceedings of the 49th Hawaii international conference on system sciences (HICSS)* (668–676). IEEE.

Friedl, J., Zimmer, B., Perkhofer, L., Zenisek, J., Hofer, P., & Jetter, H.-C. (2021). An empirical study of task-specific limitations of the overview+detail technique for interactive time series analysis. *Procedia Computer Science, 180,* 628–638.

Gelman, A., & Unwin, A. (2013). Infovis and statistical graphics: Different goals, different looks. *Journal of Computational & Graphical Statistics, 22*(1), 2–28.

Goes, P. B. (2014). Big data and is research. *MIS Quarterly, 38*(3), 3–8.

Gorodov, E. Y.'e., & Gubarev, V. V.'e. (2013). Analytical review of data visualisation methods in application to big data. *Journal of Electrical and Computer Engineering, 2013.* https://doi.org/10.1155/2013/969458

Grammel, L., Tory, M., & Storey, M. (2010). How information visualisation novices construct visualisations. *IEEE Transactions on Visualisation and Computer Graphics, 16*(6), 943–952.

Han, Rey, Knaap, Kang, & Wolf (2019). Adaptive choropleth mapper: An open-source web-based tool for synchronous exploration of multiple variables at multiple spatial extents. *ISPRS International Journal of Geo-Information, 8*(11), 509. https://doi.org/10.3390/ijgi8110509

Heer, J., Kong, N., & Agrawala, M. (2009). Sizing the horizon: The effects of chart size and layering on the graphical perception of time series visualisations. In *Proceedings of the SIGCHI conference on human factors in computing systems* (1303–1312). ACM.

Heer, J., & Shneiderman, B. (2012). Interactive dynamics for visual analysis. *Communications of the ACM, 55*(4), 45–54. https://doi.org/10.1145/2133806.2133821

Hichert, R., & Faisst, J. (2017). *International business communication standards: Conceptual, perceptual, and semantic design of comprehensible business reports, presentations, and dashboards.* IBCS Association.

Hoelscher, J., & Mortimer, A. (2018). Using tableau to visualize data and drive decision-making. *Journal of Accounting Education, 44*, 49–59.

Hofer, P., Walchshofer, C., Eisl, C., Mayr, A., & Perkhofer, L. (2018). Sankey, sunburst & co: Interactive big data visualizierungen im usability test. In L. Nadig & U. Egle (Eds.), *Proceedings of CARF 2018: controlling, accounting, risk, and finance* (92–112). Verlag IFZ.

Huang, T.-H., Huang, M. L., Nguyen, Q. V., Zhao, L., Huang, W., & Chen, J. (2017). A space-filling multidimensional visualisation (SFMDVis) for exploratory data analysis. *Information Sciences, 390*, 32–53. https://doi.org/10.1016/j.ins.2015.06.031

Inselberg, A., & Dimsdale, B. (1990). Parallel coordinates: A tool for visualizing multi-dimensional geometry. In *Proceedings of the first IEEE conference on visualisation: Visualisation `90* (361–378). IEEE Computer Society Press. https://doi.org/10.1109/VISUAL.1990.146402

Janvrin, D. J., Raschke, R. L., & Dilla, W. N. (2014). Making sense of complex data using interactive data visualisation. *Journal of Accounting Education, 32*(4), 31–48.

Kanjanabose, R., Abdul-Rahman, A., & Chen, M. (2015). A multi-task comparative study on scatter plots and parallel coordinates plots. *Computer Graphics Forum, 34*(3), 261–270.

Kehrer, J., & Hauser, H. (2013). Visualisation and visual analysis of multifaceted scientific data: A survey. *IEEE Transactions on Visualisation and Computer Graphics, 19*(3), 495–513.

Keim, D. A. (2001). Visual exploration of large data sets. *Communications of the ACM, 44*(8), 38–44.

Keim, D. A. (2002). Information visualisation and visual data mining. *IEEE Transactions on Visualisation and Computer Graphics, 8*(1), 1–8. https://doi.org/10.1109/2945.981847

Keim, D. A., Mansmann, F., Schneidewind, J., & Schreck, T. (2006). Monitoring network traffic with radial traffic analyzer. In Wong, Pak, Chung & D. A. Keim (Chairs), *IEEE Symposium On Visual Analytics Science And Technology (VAST).* Symposium conducted at the meeting of IEEE Computer Society, Baltimore, MD, USA.

Kim, M., & Draper, G. M. (2014). Radial vs. Cartesian revisited: A comparison of space-filling visualisations. In *7th International Symposium on Visual Information Communication and Interaction VINCI'14*, Sydney, Australia.

Lehmann, D. J., Albuquerque, G., Eisemann, M., Tatu, A., Keim, D. A., Schumann, H., Magnor, M., & Theisel, H. (2010). Visualisierung und analyse multidimensionaler datensätze. *Informatik-Spektrum, 6*(33), 589–600.

Leung, C. K., Chen, Y., Hoi, C. S. H., Shang, S., Wen, Y., & Cuzzocrea, A. (2020, September 7–11). Big data visualisation and visual analytics of covid-19 data. In *2020 24th international conference information visualisation (iv)* (415–420). IEEE. https://doi.org/10.1109/IV51561.2020.00073

Liu, S., Maljovec, D., Wang, B., Bremer, P.-T., & Pascucci, V. (2017). Visualizing high-dimensional data: Advances in the past decade. *IEEE Transactions on Visualisation and Computer Graphics, 23*(3), 1249–1268.

McCornick, B. H., DeFanti, T. A., & Brown, M. D. (1987). Visualisation in scientific computing. *Computer Graphics Forum, 21*(6), 61–70.

McKeen, J. D., Smith, H. A., & Singh, S. (2005). Developments in practice xx - digital dashboards: Keep your eyes on the road. *Communications of the Association for Information Systems, 16*. https://doi.org/10.17705/1CAIS.01652

Moritz, D., & Fisher, D. (2018, August 18). *Visualizing a million time series with the density line chart.* http://arxiv.org/pdf/1808.06019v2

Munzner, T. (2014). *Visualisation analysis and design* (1st ed.). *AK Peters Visualisation Series.* CRC Press.

Ohlert, C. R., & Weißenberger, B. E. (2015). Beating the base-rate fallacy: An experimental approach on the effectiveness of different information presentation formats. *Journal of Management Control, 26*(1), 51–80.

Parush, A., Hod, A., & Shtub, A. (2007). Impact of visualisation type and contextual factors on performance with enterprise resource planning systems. *Computers & Industrial Engineering, 52*(1), 133–142.

Pasch, T. (2019). Strategy and innovation: The mediating role of management accountants and management accounting systems' use. *Journal of Management Control, 30*(2), 213–246.

Pauwels, K., Ambler, T., Clark, B. H., LaPointe, P., Reibstein, D., Skiera, B., Wierenga, B., & Wiesel, T. (2009). Dashboards as a service: why, what, how, and what research is needed? *Journal of Service Research, 12*(2), 175–189. https://doi.org/10.1177/1094670509344213

Perkhofer, L. (2019). A cognitive load-theoretic framework for information visualisation. In O. Lehner (Ed.), *Proceedings of the 17th conference on finance, risk and accounting perspectives* (in Print, 9–25). ACRN Oxford.

Perkhofer, L., Hofer, P., & Walchshofer, C. (2019). Big data visualisierungen 2.0: optimale gestaltung und einsatz neuartiger visualisierungsmöglichkeiten. In L. Nadig (Ed.), *Proceedings of CARF 2019: controlling, accounting, risk and finance* (76–104). Verlag IFZ.

Perkhofer, L., Hofer, P., Walchshofer, C., Plank, T., & Jetter, H.-C. (2019). Interactive visualisation of big data in the field of accounting. *Journal of Applied Accounting Research, 5*(1), 497–525.

Perkhofer, L., Walchshofer, C., & Hofer, P. (2019). Designing visualisations to identify and assess correlations and trends: an experimental study based on price developments. In O. Lehner (Ed.), *Proceedings of the 17th conference on finance, risk and accounting perspectives* (294–340). ACRN Oxford.

Perkhofer, L., Walchshofer, C., & Hofer, P. (2020). Does design matter when visualizing big data? An empirical study to investigate the effect of visualisation type and interaction use. *Journal of Management Control, 31*(1), 55–95. https://doi.org/10.1007/s00187-020-00294-0

Perrot, A., Bourqui, R., Hanusse, N., & Auber, D. (2017). Heatpipe: High throughput, low latency big data heatmap with spark streaming. In *Information Visualisation 2017.* Symposium conducted at the meeting of IVS, London, UK. https://hal.archives-ouvertes.fr/hal-01516888/document

Pike, W. A., Stasko, J., Chang, R., & O'Connell, T. A. (2009). The science of interaction. *Information Visualisation, 8*(4), 263–274. https://doi.org/10.1057/ivs.2009.22

Potter, K. (2006). Methods for presenting statistical information: the box plot. In H. Hagen, A. Kerren, & P. Dannemann (Eds.), *Visualisation of large and unstructured data sets: GI-edition lecture notes in informatics* (97–106).

Pretorius, J., & van Wijk, J. (2005). Multidimensional visualisation of transition systems. In E. Banissi, M. Sarfraz, J. C. Roberts, B. Loften, A. Ursyn, R. A. Burkhard, . . . G. Andrienko (Chairs), *International Conference on Information Visualisation (IV'05).* Symposium conducted at the meeting of IEEE Computer Society, London, UK.

Reijner, H. (2008). The development of the horizon graph. In *Proceedings of the visweek workshop from theory to practice: Design, vision and visualisation* (p. 1). Columbus.

Richardson, J., Schlegel, K., Sallam, R., Kronz, A., & Sun, J. (2021). *Magic quadrant of analytics and business intelligence platforms.* Gartner. https://www.gartner.com/doc/reprints?id=1-1YOXON7Q&ct=200330&st=sb

Rodden, K. (2014). Applying a sunburst visualisation to summarize user navigation sequences. *IEEE Computer Graphics and Applications, 34*(5), 36–40.

Saito, T., Miyamura, H. N., Yamamoto, M., Saito, H., Hoshiya, Y., & Kaseda, T. (2005, October 23). Two-tone pseudo coloring: Compact visualisation for one-dimensional data. In *IEEE symposium on information visualisation, 2005. Infovis 2005* (173–180). IEEE. https://doi.org/10.1109/INFVIS.2005.1532144

Sarikaya, A., & Gleicher, M. (2018). Scatterplots: tasks, data, and designs. *IEEE Transactions on Visualisation and Computer Graphics, 24*(1), 402–412.

Severino, R. (2015). *The data visualisation catalogue - an online blog: heatmap*. Tableau. https://datavizcatalogue.com/methods/heatmap.html

Shaito, M., & Elmasri, R. (2021). Map visualisation using spatial and spatio-temporal data: Application to covid-19 data. In *The 14th pervasive technologies related to assistive environments conference* (284–291). ACM. https://doi.org/10.1145/3453892.3461336

Shneiderman, B. (1996). The eyes have it: A task by data type taxonomy for information visualisations. In *Proceedings of the international workshop on multi-media database management systems*. IEEE Computer Society Press.

Spitzer, M., Wildenhain, J., Rappsilber, J., & Tyers, M. (2014). Boxplotr: A web tool for generation of box plots. *Nature Methods, 11*(2), 121–122. https://doi.org/10.1038/nmeth.2811

Van Wijk, J. J. (2005, October). The value of visualization. In VIS 05. *IEEE Visualization*, 2005 (pp. 79–86). IEEE, Minneapolis, MN, USA. van Wijk, J. J., & van Selow, E. R. (1999, October 24). Cluster and calendar based visualisation of time series data. In *Proceedings 1999 IEEE symposium on information visualisation (infovis'99)* (4–9). IEEE Computer Society https://doi.org/10.1109/INFVIS.1999.801851

Walker, J., Borgo, R., & Jones, M. W. (2015). Timenotes: a study on effective chart visualization and interaction techniques for time-series data. *IEEE transactions on visualization and computer graphics, 22*(1), 549–558.

Ware, C. (2012). *Information Visualisation: Perception for design* (3rd ed.). Elsevier Ltd.

Wilkinson, L. (2005). *The grammar of graphics*. Springer-Verlag. https://doi.org/10.1007/0-387-28695-0

Yigitbasioglu, O. M., & Velcu, O. (2012). A review of dashboards in performance management: Implications for design and research. *International Journal of Accounting Information Systems, 13*(1), 41–59.

PART 3

Controlling accounting information systems

15

DATA SECURITY AND QUALITY

W. Alec Cram

Introduction

Business operations, including managerial decision-making and executive-level strategising, include a fundamental reliance on secure and high-quality data. To maximise the value of such data, companies aim to achieve objectives corresponding to confidentiality, integrity, availability, accuracy, and completeness (Boritz, 2005; Neely & Cook, 2011; Cohen et al., 2014; Otero, 2015). Within the context of accounting information systems (AIS), the growing quantity and complexity of data have led to increasing scrutiny on the risks and controls associated with both emerging technologies and governance approaches (Cram et al., 2022). Recent incidents at LinkedIn, Facebook, and Marriott highlight the financial, reputational, and strategic implications of companies that encounter ineffective data security (Holmes, 2021; Morris, 2021; Whittaker, 2020).

Much of the difficulty in avoiding such incidents lies in the variety of security threats and the speed that such threats transform over time. For example, external parties including hackers, nation states, and competitors can infiltrate systems to steal data, as well as disrupt availability through ransomware and denial-of-service attacks. Internally, both malicious and non-malicious employees pose a significant threat to data security and quality through theft, accidental change/deletion, fraud, and sabotage (Probst et al., 2010; IBM, 2021).

Fortunately, there are a wide variety of internal controls that can be employed as countermeasures to prevent and detect data-related concerns associated with AIS (as explained below). On the one hand, controls that attempt to influence the behaviour of employees can be employed in the form of policies, managerial monitoring, and independent audits. On the other hand, technical controls that are embedded within systems can be used to provide and restrict access to sensitive data and business transactions (Karimi et al., 2014). Past research suggests that a balanced portfolio of preventive and detective controls is a necessary condition to achieving an acceptable standard of data security and quality (Fenz et al., 2011). The resulting positive outcomes can be a reduction of downtime due to security incidents, a reduction of time to contain attacks, and improved employee compliance with security policies.

The objective of this chapter is to first provide a broad overview of the role of data within AIS, with a primary focus on the risks to security and quality.[1] It then examines a range of security and quality risks, corresponding internal controls, and the organisational implications of a data security program. For practitioners, this chapter can help to establish a holistic, integrated understanding of the links between data security and quality risks, corresponding countermeasures, and organisational outcomes. For researchers, this chapter draws on a range of AIS, management information systems, and cybersecurity research in order to highlight the integrative nature of accounting processes, technology, and information security as it pertains to the data used within today's organisations.

The role of data in accounting information systems

The discussion of data security and quality within this chapter is framed within the context of AIS, which is defined as "a specialised information system that collects, processes, and reports information related to the financial aspects of business events" (Gelinas et al., 2014, p. 685).[2] In short, AIS data is unique in its role of aiding stakeholders in making decisions based on financial transactions and reporting activities (e.g. sales, payments, receipts, assets), while data related to non-financial aspects of an organisation (e.g. customer relationship data within a marketing application) are considered as a separate topic (Neely & Cook, 2011).

A variety of useful frameworks can be applied to the objectives of data security and quality to examine the relevant risks and countermeasures. The first is the CIA triad, which refers to the fundamental objectives of confidentiality, integrity, and availability. This framework is a mainstay within the information security field, as it helps to distinguish between the risks that an information asset is faced with (related deviations of the framework include the McCumber Cube (McCumber, 2004) and Parkerian Hexad (Parker, 1998)). For example, where an external hacker gains unauthorised access to a company network, managers investigating the implications of the breach can consider whether their data was read (i.e. confidentiality was violated), the data was changed (i.e. integrity was violated), or the data was rendered inaccessible (i.e. availability was violated).

An alternative set of factors to consider when evaluating the role of financial data is to draw on the assertions commonly associated with audit practices, such as accuracy, completeness, occurrence, and cut-off (Boritz, 2005). Although these assertions apply to data within a security context to varying degrees and can overlap depending on the security incident being considered, they remain useful in evaluating the broader risks to an organisation. For example, a denial-of-service attack (i.e. the flooding of an information technology (IT) resource with data to render it unavailable to others) may cause an online retailer's website to crash, resulting in issues related to availability (the sales processing system is offline), completeness (some transactions may be interrupted by the attack), and cut-off (if the attack crosses multiple accounting periods, the transaction may be recorded incorrectly). Refer to Table 15.1 for an overview of the factors considered most relevant from a data security and quality perspective.

Because of the range of factors at play, it is unsurprising that the relationship between data quality and data security has been interpreted in different ways within past research. Some commentators, such as Tayi & Ballou (1998), argue that the two concepts are largely analogous; however, others such as Wang & Strong (1996) consider data quality to encompass intrinsic, contextual, representational, and accessibility characteristics, of which access security links to the accessibility element. In another perspective, Boritz (2005) suggests that system security contributes to both availability and processing integrity, which together provide a foundation for complete, current, accurate, and valid data. In this chapter, the view that data security is one of a series of contributors to data quality is adopted. That is, security alone cannot ensure that an organisation's data is complete, relevant, and reliable but is a key factor in driving towards this goal.

In the following section, the risks to data security (and their subsequent impacts on quality) are discussed. This is followed by a discussion of the relevant detective and preventive controls that can act as countermeasures to those risks. Finally, a discussion of the organisational outcomes and implications of an effective data security and quality program will be outlined. Refer to Figure 15.1 for an illustration of the integrated nature of these concepts.

Data security and quality risks

By understanding the consequences that result from data security and quality issues, organisations may be able to more effectively motivate both business and IT stakeholders to

Table 15.1 Data security and quality objectives

Objectives	Definition
Confidentiality	Data is protected from unauthorised access and/or disclosure.
Integrity	Data is protected from unauthorised modification and/or destruction.
Availability	Data can be reliably accessed in a timely fashion.
Accuracy	Transactions are recorded for the correct amount.
Completeness	All transactions are recorded.
Occurrence	The transactions that are recorded actually took place.
Cut-off	Transactions are recorded in the correct reporting period.
Relevance	The data is predictable and dependable.
Reliability	The data is free from bias.
Usability	The data is perceived to be useful and easy to use.

Adapted from Boritz (2005), ISACA (2012) and Andress (2014).

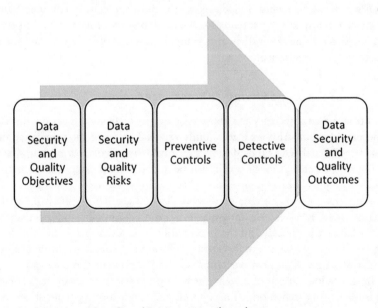

Figure 15.1 Data security and quality objectives, controls, and outcomes.

243

undertake appropriate actions. However, the approach that an organisation employs in response to security threats should consider both the source of the threat and the nature of the threat.

From a source perspective, data security threats originate both internally and externally. Internal threats refer to an organisation's current or former employees, contractors, and business partners, whose malicious or non-malicious actions result in a security incident (Software Engineering Institute, 2015). Malicious insider actions include the theft of data for profit or a disgruntled employee who intentionally deletes data. In comparison, non-malicious employees may be poorly trained or reckless in their actions (e.g. victimised by a phishing attack and mistakenly disclosing a password), causing accidental leaks of data or unintentional changes to data (Probst et al., 2010). External, outsider threats from hackers are commonly what is thought of when considering security risks, but past research shows that the cost and impact of insider threats can be even greater (Posey et al., 2011; Wall, 2013).

The nature of data security and quality threats is a serious concern for organisations. Reports suggest that 82% of Boards of Directors are concerned or very concerned about information security but that only 40% of security professionals believe their staff can handle complex attacks (ISACA, 2016). The impact of data breaches to organisations is significant, with an average cost of $148 per record, but stretching to $429 per record in the healthcare industry (Ponemon Institute, 2020).

All companies are faced with a wide range of security-specific circumstances that, if they came to fruition, could cause damage. The extent that these risks have the potential to evolve into actual security incidents depends on a variety of vulnerability factors, including an organisation's industry, location, the value of its data (e.g. credit cards, personal information, proprietary information), and the countermeasures it currently has in place. In discussing these risks, those typically initiated by external parties (e.g. hackers, hacktivists, nation states, competitors) from those initiated from within the organisation (e.g. employees, contractors) are distinguished. Although the confidentiality, integrity, and availability consequences of such security incidents may be comparable regardless of the source of the attack, this categorisation can be helpful in identifying the most appropriate countermeasures. The threats discussed below are not intended to be an exhaustive inventory of all the possible issues that could occur; however, they aim to highlight some of the most common incidents that occur in today's AIS environment.

External data security threats

External threats to data security are those that originate from the actions of individuals outside the organisation. Although commonly referred to using the somewhat ambiguous term 'hackers', external actors include activists, competing firms, nation states, and terrorists. The impact of natural disasters can also be added to this category, as environmental events present unique risks to the operation of technology resources. The impact of external threats is primarily focused on data confidentiality and availability of financial data, with less emphasis generally placed on integrity. From a confidentiality perspective, the target of an external attack is typically on the organisational data that has utility for them, either by selling the data (e.g. stolen credit cards) or through the resulting competitive benefits (e.g. access to strategic plans or other propriety data). Access to this data can be gained by outsiders from a wide variety of attacks, including malicious software (e.g. virus, worm, Trojan), insufficiently patched operating systems and application systems, stolen or guessed user credentials, or via social engineering attacks (i.e. manipulating individuals to provide confidential information, such as by requesting that a password be provided to a fabricated IT Help Desk email address).

When considering availability threats from external actors, the aim of the attackers is to prevent legitimate users from accessing organisational data. This can be achieved through malicious software (e.g. ransomware), as well as distributed denial-of-service attacks, which refers to the inoperability of a device (e.g. web server) due to the receipt of excessive data from a variety of sources. Recent reports suggest that both attack vectors are on the rise in terms of frequency and intensity (Verizon, 2020).

Natural disasters introduce a unique form of external threats to financial data. These are primarily oriented around concerns related to availability due to power outage or physical damage to equipment (e.g. flood, hurricane) (Junglas & Ives, 2007). As a result, data integrity issues can occur in situations where the processing of data is abruptly halted due to a sudden power outage or other disruption.

Insider security threats

In contrast to threats originating outside the company, insider threats are the acts of employees, contractors, and partners (Software Engineering Institute, 2015). These threats are typically categorised as either malicious or non-malicious. With malicious attacks, the insider intends to cause harm through actions such as theft of data (i.e. confidentiality), alteration of mission-critical data (i.e. integrity), or sabotage of IT resources (i.e. availability). In comparison, non-malicious users introduce risk to the enterprise but do so without intending to cause harm. These issues could arise through accidents (e.g. inadvertently deleting a transaction) or using unauthorised IT resources, sometimes referred to as shadow IT (e.g. posting confidential company files on non-sanctioned websites, such as Dropbox).

Implications for accounting information systems

The broader organisational implications of external and insider security events have been well documented in practitioner publications, including fines, reputational risk, legal expenses, and loss of business (Federal Trade Commission, 2008; Muncaster, 2015; ISACA, 2016). From an AIS perspective, the impacts are largely focused around the objectives noted in Table 15.1. On the one hand, a security incident has the capability to temporarily disrupt the conduct of business, which leads to questions of completeness (did all the transactions get recorded prior to the denial-of-service attack?) and availability (did the system's downtime impact sales for the period?). On the other hand, attacks can also lead to a degree of uncertainty for organisations. These could be questions of integrity (did the attackers change the data or just steal it?) as well as confidentiality (exactly what data was stolen?). Particularly where audit logs are not enabled within the financial systems, managers may be unable to conclusively determine what activities have actually occurred. Although the theft of data (i.e. copying but not modifying) may have little impact on the financial statements themselves, there can be future implications such as financial penalties (e.g. fines, lawsuits) that remain of interest to company stakeholders.

Controlling for data security and quality: insights from research and practice

Although absolute protection of a company's data is not possible, a portfolio of internal controls can be designed and implemented to adequately address the risk appetite of the organisation (i.e. the extent that risks are willing to be taken to achieve goals). One of the fundamental aspects of protecting organisational data from security threats is clearly understanding what data exists, how important it is, where it resides, and what its value is (Andress, 2019). Although this can be a relatively simple exercise in a small company with a straightforward technology configuration, the challenge should not be underestimated in large companies, particularly those with a complex technology infrastructure. By conducting a thorough risk assessment focusing on the organisation's financial data, managers can more easily assess the nature of the data that needs to be protected (e.g. credit card numbers), the confidentiality/integrity/availability considerations related to the data, the location of the data (e.g. locally stored, cloud storage), and the value of the data to the organisation (e.g. considers reputational impact of a breach and inability to operate for a period of time). Evaluating these contextual factors can allow managers to make more informed decisions regarding the design of security controls.

Identifying data security and quality controls

To identify a collection of internal controls to address the relevant security risks, organisations commonly draw on the available frameworks and standards, including COBIT, ISO 27001/27002, and PCI DSS. These frameworks provide a variety of control objectives, control activities, and control practices that can be implemented to address a wide range of security concerns (von Solms, 2005; Ataya, 2010; Wallace et al., 2011; ISACA, 2012). However, managers and employees are often wary of implementing too many controls, due to the high costs and corresponding bureaucracy that can often result. Instead, recent research suggests that companies may be better off by considering the alignment of controls with the organisation's environment, the socio-emotional behaviour of staff, and the employment of controls within technology processes in order to configure an efficient approach (Cram et al., 2016).

Preventive controls

Security policies play an important role within organisations by establishing a guideline for appropriate employee behaviour, setting technical configurations, and outlining the sanctions for non-compliance. Such policies tend to be established at either an organisational level, covering a wide range of technology resources and behaviours, or at a very detailed level, typically for specific technologies (e.g. email use, anti-virus software). A wide range of research has examined employee compliance with security policies, which is viewed as a key antecedent to achieving objectives related to security of the data stored within organisational systems (Siponen & Oinas-Kukkonen, 2007; D'Arcy & Herath, 2011; Moody et al., 2018; Cram et al., 2019). These studies have employed a variety of theory bases, including deterrence theory (e.g. Bulgurcu et al., 2010)), protection motivation theory (e.g. Herath & Rao, 2009), and control theory (e.g. Boss et al., 2009). Among the many antecedents to policy compliance that have been identified in the literature, the certainty of non-compliance detection (D'Arcy & Greene, 2014), employee attitude (Siponen et al., 2014), and normative beliefs (Ifinedo, 2014) have been noted as having a particularly strong effect.

The topic of access control is a key preventive measure to ensure that only authorised staff have access to data and that their access is appropriate for their role in the organisation. In order to achieve this objective, the first step is to verify the identity of employees. Although this activity has typically relied on passwords (i.e. something an employee *knows*), supplementary mechanisms are increasingly being added to defend against easy-to-guess passwords and stolen credentials. These additional measures commonly include a physical token that displays a temporary code (i.e. something an employee *has*) or relies on the physical attributes of the employee, such as fingerprints or iris (i.e. something an employee *is*). Although authentication is traditionally employed only at the beginning of a user's session as they log in, research suggests that a continuous model of authentication that challenges users on an ongoing basis may be a valuable alternative (Calderon et al., 2006).

Biometrics are increasingly becoming an important supplementary authentication mechanism, particularly for high-risk areas such as data centre access. Since physiological and behavioural traits tend to be less ambiguous than a factor that relies on user knowledge (e.g. password) or user possession (e.g. token), biometrics add strength to authentication controls (Chandra & Calderon, 2003). In considering the type of biometric authentication to employ, managers can consider a range of factors including accuracy (i.e. what proportion of legitimate users are denied access?), cost (i.e. what is the expense of implementation?), intrusiveness (i.e. how invasive is the biometric assessment on employees?), permanence (i.e. to what extent does the characteristic being evaluated, such as voice or signature, change over time?), and circumvention (i.e. how easily can a biometric characteristic be falsified?) (Chandra & Calderon, 2003; Andress, 2014).

The second key component of access control is that of authorisation: the provisioning of appropriate access to files and application transactions to employees. Particularly in the context of AIS, the risk of fraud due to inappropriate segregation of duties is a notable concern (Elsas, 2008). Authorisation controls rely on the principle of least privilege, which aims to grant employees the level of access to the systems resources that they need to do their job, but no more. This can be an extremely challenging activity within large organisations, particularly those with multiple application systems or complex enterprise resource planning systems (Kobelsky, 2014; Ferroni, 2016). Ideally, organisations will establish set lists of authorised application permissions by job role (e.g. Accounts Payable Manager, Controller, Chief Financial Officer), which have been checked for segregation of duties violations. When employees are hired to these pre-defined rolls, they are granted those permissions, and any permissions from previous positions in the organisations are removed from their access (Ferraiolo et al., 1992).

One approach that is increasingly being adopted to address the concerns related to authorisation and access control, particularly when multiple software applications are involved, is the use of identity and access management technology. These centralised systems are able to manage collections of user credentials, authenticate users, and provide authorised permissions (Sharma et al., 2015). Using a federated model, users can sign on in one location and establish trust within the system that streamlines authentication with other, linked systems (Baldwin et al., 2010). Because of its centralised nature, identity and access management systems can enable user management efficiencies for the IT department, increased security, and a more streamlined audit process (Bradford et al., 2014).

Although organisations routinely purchase off-the-shelf financial applications, other companies develop such software themselves or outsource the development to a third party. A customised system provides highly tailored software, but a series of important preventive controls are necessary to mitigate confidentiality, integrity, and availability risks during development. These controls also apply to companies with purchased software that are responsible for installing periodic upgrades or have made customisations to the software themselves. The first of these controls is oriented around the concept of change control, whereby developers should not have sufficient access to allow them to make technical changes to a financial application without independent review and approval. A key control in this area is to restrict developer access to only the test and development environments (where evaluation of updated systems takes place) but to prevent their access to the live, production system. In addition, all changes to the financial software should undergo detailed testing and receive formal approval by management prior to installation. In the case of outsourced development, past research has highlighted the importance of control related to communication tools (Gantman & Fedorowicz, 2016), knowledge sharing (Tiwana & Keil, 2007; Gopal & Gosain, 2010), and trust (Mao et al., 2008; Rustagi et al., 2008).

The encryption of data represents a key control for both data at rest (e.g. stored in a database) and data 'in transit' (e.g. credit card information being sent over the internet by a customer) (ISACA, 2012). Encrypting confidential accounting data primarily guards against confidentiality attacks, as the data is rendered unreadable unless a key is entered to unscramble the data. Because the specific algorithms used to encrypt data are periodically rendered obsolete, managers must be diligent in ensuring that proper precautions are taken to secure decryption keys and update the tools as required.

The eXtensible Business Reporting Language (XBRL) refers to a programming language that can tag financial data, allowing rapid reporting, accessibility, and the identification of errors (Pinsker & Li, 2008). Beyond cost reductions and administrative efficiencies, the use of XBRL can also aid in the enhancement of corporate governance (Alles & Piechocki, 2012; Cong et al., 2014). Specifically, by employing formal business rules using XBRL formulas, the quality of data existing in the financial reports can improve by avoiding incorrect calculations or inadvertent user errors (Du et al., 2013; Li & Nwaeze, 2015). Although XBRL elements can be viewed as application controls or reporting controls, they can also be viewed through the lens of security (specifically integrity). Indeed, past research highlights the importance of maintaining security over XBRL-formatted reports, particularly in regard to attaining assurance around the integrity and availability of the reported data (Boritz & No, 2005; Cohen et al., 2014). Solutions in the form of document hosting (e.g. auditor versus client), digital signatures, and the broad adoption of security standards are considered in past research.

Detective controls

In comparison to preventive controls, detective controls aim to identify when security incidents occur and respond to remedy the situation. These controls are particularly important in the face of quickly changing threats that are difficult to design preventive controls for. One of the key elements of detective security controls is the knowledge of existing issues. Sometimes referred to as threat intelligence, vendors and members of the security community share resources and information that highlight current attacks, malicious activity, and blacklists (Greene, 2015). This information can aid the effectiveness of traditional information systems controls, such as intrusion detection, anti-virus, and network monitoring.

Continuous auditing is one approach that can aid in the rapid detection of data issues, including those related to a security incident. Continuous auditing refers to the real-time evaluation of internal control systems to verify that they are operating in line with expected norms in regard to the reliability and accuracy of financial information (Flowerday et al., 2006). Such an approach relies on the collection of data, followed by the evaluation of the data against expected trends. Where deviations exist from the anticipated results (e.g. data has unexpectedly changed), exception reports and notifications can be created automatically. Monitoring of these exceptions may be the responsibility of management, internal audit, or the information security department (Hardy, 2014). Beyond the assurance that continuous auditing can provide for financial reporting (Flowerday & Von Solms, 2005), it can contribute assurance around the absence of unauthorised data manipulation, which may indicate that a security incident has occurred.

Traditional internal and external audit approaches also provide detective control benefits to AIS data. Standardised approaches such as periodic control assessments (Otero, 2015) and security program evaluations (Steinbart et al., 2016) can aid in uncovering security controls that are absent or not operating as designed. Such audits can be conducted by external financial auditors, IT departments, or internal auditors while engaging stakeholders such as business management and users. In fact, past research indicates that benefits can result when the parties work together on security assessments (Spears & Barki, 2010; Steinbart et al., 2012, 2013).

Although the preventive versus detective nature of data governance could be disputed, the approach itself is an important factor in addressing data security and quality risks. Weber et al. (2009) define data governance as the "decision rights and accountabilities to encourage desirable behaviour in the use of data" (p. 6). Although this activity can include some of the controls outlined above, including policies and standards, it can also include an enhanced infrastructure of data-centric roles and tasks within the organisation. These include the broad domains of data principles (the role of data), data quality (intended use of data), metadata (ensuring interpretability by users), data access (specifying access requirements), and the data lifecycle (the definition, production, and retention of data) (Khatri & Brown, 2010). Although data governance is an important topic on its own, its relevance in the context of this chapter centres mainly on those domains of 'quality' and 'access'. In particular, data governance supplements the aspects of more general IT governance that may already be in place within an organisation to more specifically focus on the data-centric elements (Otto, 2011). By clearly specifying data owners, data quality managers, data security officers, and technical security analysts (as data governance principles advise), organisations can be better placed to not only effectively prevent AIS data issues from occurring (e.g. establish accepted standards to store and maintain financial data) but also detect data issues when they arise (e.g. assign roles responsible for monitoring and evaluating the quality of data).

Data security and quality outcomes

Information security threats are in a constant state of flux, and the countermeasures employed by organisations need to evolve to keep up. Where a comprehensive information security program is implemented, including the controls noted above, managers are provided with the tools to enable an agile and robust defence. However, the broader benefits of security investments can be difficult to quantify (Ryan & Ryan, 2006), placing an increased responsibility on managers to demonstrate the value of security initiatives.

The investment in preventive and detective measures can be viewed by some stakeholders as a 'negative deliverable', as it has the potential to minimise the impact of undesirable events but is not directly connected to bottom line performance. Indeed, establishing a clear picture of the return on a security investment can be difficult to arrive at (Mercuri, 2003; Cavusoglu et al., 2004; Bodin et al., 2005). Despite this, the nature of the preventive and detective controls contributes to developing a strong security culture that appreciates the risks and implications of security incidents and aims to achieve desirable outcomes.

A variety of benefits specific to AIS can result from effective data security and quality, which go beyond the high-level objectives highlighted in Table 15.1. For example, past research shows that top management support is a key predictor of an organisation's information security culture (Knapp et al., 2006). That is, the organisational benefits that may accrue as a result of attempting to secure financial data may also serve to benefit other aspects of data security in the organisation. Driving effective data security and quality can also contribute to the avoidance of unnecessary costs. For example, effectively encrypting customer credit card data to achieve confidentiality can aid the organisation in avoiding the regulatory fines and penalties that would result from a breach, as well as the (often mandatory) expense of credit report monitoring services.

Although it is unclear if effectiveness in achieving secure and quality data can prove to be a competitive advantage, some research suggests that ignoring security can lead to a competitive disadvantage (Kankanhalli et al., 2003). To the extent that executives and managers rely on complete and accurate financial data to make decisions, the investment made in the corresponding internal controls is likely to make a fundamental contribution to the organisation.

Conclusion

This chapter has outlined the objectives of data security and quality and the associated threats that jeopardise the achievement of these objectives. A discussion of the internal controls highlighted the preventive and detective measures that managers can employ in response to data security and quality risks. Finally, the organisational consequences of an effective program of data security and quality are noted. In response to the continued concerns from executives, managers, and other stakeholders, this chapter provides an overview of the current state of AIS data security and quality research findings, as well as a range of practical organisational considerations.

Notes

1 Although a wide range of data quality research has been conducted (e.g. see Neely & Cook 2011), the scope of this chapter is restricted to the data quality issues that directly relate to information security incidents. I primarily frame such incidents within the context of AIS data, but broader information security/cybersecurity concepts are also considered.
2 See also Chapters 1 and 4 for other definitions.

References

Alles, M., & Piechocki, M. (2012). Will XBRL improve corporate governance? A framework for enhancing governance decision making using interactive data. *International Journal of Accounting Information Systems, 13*(2), 91–108.

Andress, J. (2014). The basics of information security: Understanding the fundamentals of InfoSec in theory and practice. In Andress, J. (ed.). *The Basics of Information Security*, 2nd Edition, Oxford: Syngress.

Andress, J. (2019). *Foundations of Information Security: A Straightforward Introduction*. San Francisco, CA: no starch press.

Ataya, G. (2010). PCI DSS audit and compliance. *Information Security Technical Report, 15*(4), 138–144.

Baldwin, A., Mont, M. C., Beres, Y., & Shiu, S. (2010). Assurance for federated identity management. *Journal of Computer Security, 18*(4), 541–572.

Bodin, L. D., Gordon, L. A., & Loeb, M. P. (2005). Evaluating Information Security Investments Using the Analytical Hierarchy Process *Communications of the ACM, 48*(2), 79–83.

Boritz, J. E. (2005). IS practitioners' views on core concepts of information integrity. *International Journal of Accounting Information Systems, 6*(4), 260–279.

Boritz, J. E., & No, W. G. (2005). Security in XML-based financial reporting services on the Internet. *Journal of Accounting and Public Policy, 24*(1), 11–35.

Boss, S. R., Kirsch, L. J., Angermeier, I., Shingler, R. A., & Boss, R. W. (2009). If someone is watching, I'll do what I'm asked: Mandatoriness, control, and information security. *European Journal of Information Systems, 18*(2), 151–164.

Bradford, M., Earp, J. B., & Grabski, S. (2014). Centralized end-to-end identity and access management and ERP systems: A multi-case analysis using the Technology Organization Environment framework. *International Journal of Accounting Information Systems, 15*(2), 149–165.

Bulgurcu, B., Cavusoglu, H., & Benbasat, I. (2010). Information security policy compliance: An empirical study of rationality-based beliefs and information security awareness. *MIS Quarterly, 34*(3), 523–548.

Calderon, T. G., Chandra, A., & Cheh, J. J. (2006). Modeling an intelligent continuous authentication system to project financial information resources. *International Journal of Accounting Information Systems, 7*(2), 91–109.

Cavusoglu, H., Mishra, B., & Raghunathan, S. (2004). A model for evaluating IT security investments. *Communications of the ACM, 47*(7), 87–92.

Chandra, A., & Calderon, T. G. (2003). Toward a biometric security layer in accounting systems. *Journal of Information Systems, 17*(2), 51–70.

Cohen, E. E., Debreceny, R., Farewell, S., & Roohani, S. (2014). Issues with the communication and integrity of audit reports when financial reporting shifts to an information-centric paradigm. *International Journal of Accounting Information Systems, 15*(4), 400–422.

Cong, Y., Hao, J., & Zou, L. (2014). The impact of XBRL reporting on market efficiency. *Journal of Information Systems, 28*(2), 181–207.

Cram, W. A., Brohman, M. K., Chan, Y. E., & Gallupe, R. B. (2016). Information systems control alignment: Complementary and conflicting systems development controls. *Information & Management, 53*(2), 183–196.

Cram, W. A., D'Arcy, J., & Proudfoot, J. G. (2019). Seeing the forest and the trees: A meta-analysis of the antecedents to information security policy compliance. *MIS Quarterly, 43*(2), 525–554.

Cram, W. A., Wang, T., and Yuan, J. (2022). Cybersecurity research in accounting information systems: A review and framework. *Journal of Emerging Technologies in Accounting*. Forthcoming.

D'Arcy, J., & Greene, G. (2014). Security culture and the employment relationship as drivers of employees' security compliance. *Information Management & Computer Security, 22*(5), 474–489.

D'Arcy, J., & Herath, T. (2011). A review and analysis of deterrence theory in the IS security literature: making sense of the disparate findings. *European Journal of Information Systems, 29*(6), 643–658.

Du, H., Vasarhelyi, M. A., & Zheng, X. (2013). XBRL mandate: Thousands of filing errors and so what? *Journal of Information Systems, 27*(1), 61–78.

Elsas, P. I. (2008). X-raying segregation of duties: Support to illuminate an enterprise's immunity to solo-fraud. *International Journal of Accounting Information Systems, 9*(2), 82–93.

Federal Trade Commission. (2008). *Agency Announces Settlement of Separate Actions Against Retailer TJX, and Data Brokers Reed Elsevier and Seisint for Failing to Provide Adequate Security for Consumers' Data.* Retrieved from http://www.ftc.gov/opa/2008/03/datasec.shtm

Fenz, S., Ekelhart, A., & Neubauer, T. (2011). Information security risk management: In which security solutions is it worth investing? *Communications of the AIS, 28*, 329–356.

Ferraiolo, D. F., Cugini, J. A., & Kuhn, D. R. (1992). *Role-based Access Control (RBAC): Features and Motivations.* Paper presented at the Proceedings of the 15th National Computer Security Conference.

Ferroni, S. (2016). Implementing segregation of duties: A practical experience based on best practices. *ISACA Journal, 3*, 1–9.

Flowerday, S., Blundell, A. W., & Von Solms, R. (2006). Continuous auditing technologies and models: A discussion. *Computers & Security, 25*, 325–331.

Flowerday, S., & Von Solms, R. (2005). Continuous auditing: Verifying information integrity and providing assurances for financial reports. *Computer Fraud & Security, 7*, 12–16.

Gantman, S., & Fedorowicz, J. (2016). Communication and control in outsourced IS development projects: Mapping to COBIT domains. *International Journal of Accounting Information Systems, 21*, 63–83.

Gelinas, U. J., Dull, R. B., & Wheeler, P. (2014). *Accounting Information Systems* (10th ed.). Stamford, CT: Centage Learning.

Gopal, A., & Gosain, S. (2010). The role of organizational controls and boundary spanning in software development outsourcing: Implications for project performance. *Information Systems Research, 21*(4), 1–23.

Greene, F. (2015). Cybersecurity detective controls—Monitoring to identify and respond to threats. *ISACA Journal, 5*, 1–3.

Hardy, C. A. (2014). The messy matters of continuous assurance: Findings from exploratory research in Australia. *Journal of Information Systems, 28*(2), 357–377.

Herath, T., & Rao, H. R. (2009). Protection motivation and deterrence: A framework for security policy compliance in organisations. *European Journal of Information Systems, 18*(2), 106–125.

Holmes, A. (2021, April 3, 2021). 533 million Facebook users' phone numbers and personal data have been leaked online. *Business Insider*. Retrieved from https://www.business insider.com/stolen-data-of-533-million-facebook-users-leaked-online-2021-4?op=1&scrolla=5eb6d68b7fedc32c19ef33b4&r=US&IR=T

IBM. (2021). *IBM X-Force Threat Intelligence Report 2021*. Retrieved from Somers, NY: https://www.ibm.com/security/data-breach/threat-intelligence

Ifinedo, P. (2014). Information systems security policy compliance: An empirical study of the effects of socialisation, influence, and cognition. *Information & Management, 51*(1), 69–79.

ISACA. (2012). *COBIT 5*. https://www.isaca.de/sites/default/files/attachements/cobit_5_streubel_0.pdf

ISACA. (2016). *State of Cybersecurity: Implications for 2016*. Retrieved from Rolling Meadows: http://www.isaca.org/cyber/Documents/state-of-cybersecurity_res_eng_0316.pdf

Junglas, I., & Ives, B. (2007). Recovering IT in a disaster: Lessons from Hurricane Katrina. *MIS Quarterly Executive, 6*(1), 39–51.

Kankanhalli, A., Teo, H.-H., Tan, B. C. Y., & Wei, K.-K. (2003). An integrative study of information systems security effectiveness. *International Journal of Information Management, 23*(2), 139–154.

Karimi, V. R., Cowan, D. D., & Alencar, P. S. (2014). An approach to correctness of security and operational business policies. *International Journal of Accounting Information Systems, 15*(4), 323–334.

Khatri, V., & Brown, C. V. (2010). Designing data governance. *Communications of the ACM, 53*(1), 148–152.

Knapp, K. J., Marshall, T. E., Rainer, R. K., & Ford, F. N. (2006). Information security: Management's effect on culture and policy. *Information Management & Computer Security, 14*(1), 24–36.

Kobelsky, K. W. (2014). A conceptual model for segregation of duties: Integrating theory and practice for manual and IT-supported processes. *International Journal of Accounting Information Systems, 15*(4), 304–322.

Li, S., & Nwaeze, E. T. (2015). The association between extensions in XBRL disclosures and financial information environment. *Journal of Information Systems, 29*(3), 73–99.

Mao, J.-Y., Lee, J.-N., & Deng, C.-P. (2008). Vendors' perspectives on trust and control in offshore information systems outsourcing. *Information & Management, 45*(7), 482–492.

McCumber, J. (2004). *Assessing and Managing Security Risk in IT Systems: A Structured Methodology*. Boca Raton: Taylor & Francis.

Mercuri, R. T. (2003). Analyzing security costs. *Communications of the ACM, 46*(6), 15–18.

Moody, G. D., Siponen, M., & Pahnila, S. (2018). Toward a unified model of information security policy compliance. *MIS Quarterly, 42*(1), 285–331.

Morris, C. (2021, June 30, 2021). Massive data leak exposes 700 million LinkedIn users' information. *Fortune*. Retrieved from https://fortune.com/2021/06/30/linkedin-data-theft-700-million-users-personal-information-cybersecurity/

Muncaster, P. (2015, July 10). OPM comes clean: Dual breaches exposed 22.1 million individuals. *Infosecurity Magazine*. Retrieved from http://www.infosecurity-magazine.com/news/opm-dual-breaches-exposed-221/

Neely, M. P., & Cook, J. S. (2011). Fifteen years of data and information quality literature: Developing a research agenda for accounting. *Journal of Information Systems, 25*(1), 79–108.

Otero, A. R. (2015). An information security control assessment methodology for organizations' financial information. *International Journal of Accounting Information Systems, 18*, 26–45.

Otto, B. (2011). Organizing data governance: Findings from the telecommunications industry and consequences for large service providers. *Communications of the Association for Information Systems, 29*, 45–66.

Parker, D. B. (1998). *Fighting Computer Crime: A New Framework for Protecting Information*. New York: Wiley.

Pinsker, R., & Li, S. (2008). Costs and benefits of XBRL adoption: Early evidence. *Communications of the ACM, 51*(3), 47–50.

Ponemon Institute. (2020). *Cost of a Data Breach Report.* Retrieved from https://www.ibm.com/security/data-breach

Posey, C., Bennett, R. J., & Roberts, T. L. (2011). Understanding the mindset of the abusive insider: An examination of insiders' causal reasoning following internal security changes. *Computers & Security, 30*(6–7), 486–497.

Probst, C. W., Hunker, J., Gollmann, D., & Bishop, M. (2010). *Aspects of Insider Threats.* New York: Springer.

Rustagi, S., King, W. R., & Kirsch, L. J. (2008). Predictors of formal control usage in IT outsourcing partnerships. *Information Systems Research, 19*(2), 126–143.

Ryan, J. J. C. H., & Ryan, D. J. (2006). Expected benefits of information security investments. *Computers & Security, 25*(8), 579–588.

Sharma, A., Sharma, S., & Dave, M. (2015). *Identity and Access Management: A Comprehensive Study.* Paper presented at the 2015 International Conference on Green Computing and Internet of Things.

Siponen, M., Mahmood, M. A., & Pahnila, S. (2014). Employees' adherence to information security policies: An exploratory field study. *Information & Management, 51*(2), 217–224.

Siponen, M., & Oinas-Kukkonen, H. (2007). A review of information security issues and respective research contributions. *The DATA BASE for Advances in Information Systems, 38*(1), 60–80.

Software Engineering Institute. (2015). *Analytic Approaches to Detect Insider Threats.* Retrieved from http://resources.sei.cmu.edu/asset_files/WhitePaper/2015_019_001_451069.pdf

Spears, J. L., & Barki, H. (2010). User participation in information systems security risk management. *MIS Quarterly, 34*(3), 503–522.

Steinbart, P. J., Raschke, R. L., Gal, G., & Dilla, W. N. (2012). The relationship between internal audit and information security: An exploratory investigation. *International Journal of Accounting Information Systems, 13*(3), 228–243.

Steinbart, P. J., Raschke, R. L., Gal, G., & Dilla, W. N. (2013). Information security professionals' perceptions about the relationship between the information security and internal audit functions. *Journal of Information Systems, 27*(2), 65–86.

Steinbart, P. J., Raschke, R. L., Gal, G., & Dilla, W. N. (2016). SECURQUAL: An instrument for evaluating the effectiveness of enterprise information security programs. *Journal of Information Systems, 30*(1), 71–92.

Tayi, G. K., & Ballou, D. P. (1998). Examining data quality. *Communications of the ACM, 41*(2), 54–57.

Tiwana, A., & Keil, M. (2007). Does peripheral knowledge complement control? An empirical test in technology outsourcing alliances. *Strategic Management Journal, 28*(6), 623–634.

Verizon. (2020). *2020 Data Breach Investigations Report.* Retrieved from https://enterprise.verizon.com/resources/reports/dbir/

von Solms, B. (2005). Information security governance: COBIT or ISO 17799 or both? *Computers & Security, 24*(2), 99–104.

Wall, D. S. (2013). Enemies within: Redefining the insider threat in organizational security policy. *Security Journal, 26*(2), 107–124.

Wallace, L., Lin, H., & Cefaratti, M. A. (2011). Information security and Sarbanes-Oxley compliance: An exploratory study. *Journal of Information Systems, 25*(1), 185–211.

Wang, R. Y., & Strong, D. M. (1996). Beyond accuracy: What data quality means to data consumers. *Journal of Management Information Systems, 12*(4), 5–33.

Weber, K., Otto, B., & Osterle, H. (2009). One size does not fit all: A contingency approach to data governance. *ACM Journal of Data and Information Quality, 1*(1), 1–27.

Whittaker, Z. (2020, March 31, 2020). Marriott says 5.2 million guest records were stolen in another data breach. *Tech Crunch.* Retrieved from https://techcrunch.com/2020/03/31/marriott-hotels-breached-again/

16

CONTINUOUS AUDITING

Developments and challenges

Maria Céu Ribeiro and João Oliveira

Introduction

This chapter addresses the emergence of continuous auditing (CA), a phenomenon profoundly affecting auditing[1] practice and research, directly related with technological developments, in accounting information systems (AIS) and beyond. CA is a new approach to monitoring and auditing information, addressing and leveraging the transformative impact of technological advances in business practices. The spread of automated routines and interfaces led to new business models for enterprise architectures and, consequently, new AIS. Today's process of recording and storing business transactions (data and processes workflows) into those integrated information systems handles millions of transactions, in a real–time approach to conducting business. Within the accounting domain, the computerisation of financial business processes has affected everything, from accounting recording and ledger posting to system reports. This evolution in business and accounting systems has created new opportunities and challenges for auditing to shift towards the paradigm of CA (Vasarhelyi et al., 2010).

There is a striking contrast between contemporary business and AIS, on one hand, and traditional auditing tools, on the other. Business and AIS are increasingly leveraged for cross–application integration and intertwining sequential business processes (e.g. internet-based electronic data interchange, manufacturing, inventory flows, sales) allowing continuous information collection. By contrast, traditional auditing tools are based on data extraction, cumbersome spreadsheets, manual manipulation and limited automation (Chan & Vasarhelyi, 2011), although the appearance of new technologies in recent years with capacity to analyse massive data is transforming it. Given the resulting effects on auditing, both researchers and practitioners are progressively paying more attention to the demands and opportunities for audit tasks to be performed automatically, continuously and even in real time (Chiu et al., 2014). This entails the concept of CA and new auditing practices. The traditional auditor extracts sample data from information systems, using spreadsheets and basic sampling and analytical techniques, and more recently, using data analytic (DA) tools (CPAB Exchange, 2019). By contrast, the future auditor will remotely have a periodical (daily, monthly) look at a dashboard into an automated audit system, even using interactive visualisations, to check if any audit status indicators have been flagged for further investigation or if statistical reports indicate any unusual trends (Byrnes et al., 2014; Salijeni et al., 2021).

DOI: 10.4324/9781003132943-20

This chapter is organised as follows. The next provides a review of traditional auditing issues, recent – though non-disrupting – improvements and increasing limitations in the context of the new real-time business systems. Then the framework of CA and CA's state of the art are described. This is followed by an analysis of the impact of the recent phenomenon of Big Data on CA. Then focus is given to the development of continuous monitoring (CM) activities, one of CA components, and the final section provides concluding remarks and highlights still unsolved issues and challenges.

Traditional auditing in today's technological environment

The traditional auditor focuses on time intensive manual procedures (Rezaee et al., 2002, Chan & Vasarhelyi, 2011). All work is performed several months after the occurrence of relevant events, and any anomalies detected are investigated only after the end of the audit period. Auditors deal with the introduction of technology and current complex AIS by tailoring some computer programs to do traditional audit procedures and by developing generalised audit software to provide information on data files. Furthermore, a digital journey through DA, developed internally or by third parties, has begun. However, overall, and as experienced by the first author during her career of more than 30 years at a Big 4 firm, auditors still depend on traditional tools to support the audit process. We now analyse those minor, incremental changes and improvements in audit tools, still within the traditional auditing approach.

Information technology (IT) and traditional auditing

With changes to business systems architecture, related with internet/cloud-based applications and Enterprise Resource Planning (ERP) systems, enabling more automated controls, the IT audit function gained a more critical role. During internal control evaluations and transactional testing, auditors connect to client systems over networks, on-site or remotely, to periodically check audit logs, run analytical tests and test for anomalies pulling sample transactions through macros (Teeter et al., 2010). As complex AIS became ubiquitous, there was a need to adapt auditing to this computerised environment. Therefore, Computer-Assisted Audit Tools (CAATs) were designed to aid in automating the audit process and obtaining data from the ERP systems.

Computer-assisted auditing techniques and current data analytics tools

Nowadays, auditors use CAATs for retrieving data, analysing transactional data to detect anomalies or verifying system controls, such as checking who performed a control, since documentary evidence may not exist. These tools are useful to choose statistical samples and use the computer's speed to process large volumes of data; however, they are mainly extraction tools to perform data analysis through queries activated only periodically – i.e. well *after* transactions have occurred and data has been processed in the system (Byrnes et al., 2014). In substance, this is still the once-a-year, traditional, backward-looking audit practice, relying on a sample basis. There is no continuous process, and the analytical tools, even if remote or by applying CAATs, are still limited to basic statistical techniques, such as ratio or trend analyses (Alles et al., 2008).

As traditional paper trail audits became impossible because documents were electronically stored, new technologies emerged through DA tools. DA allows the auditor to interrogate and test a larger volume of transactions through matching accounts and/or transactions (CPAB Exchange, 2019). Current DA enables to produce visualisations and assist auditors in understanding the data more clearly and efficiently, through graphic trends and identification of outliers in the figures (FRC, 2017; Salijeni et al., 2021). DA procedures can result in many exceptions/outliers, and anomalies are still tested by pulling sample transactions. However, auditors may sometimes view the reliability of DA sceptically, as mere "add-ons", rather than an alternative, to traditional audit techniques, leading to over-auditing (Salijeni et al., 2021).

In recent years, to address real-time transaction processing and stakeholders' demand for continuous reporting, a fundamentally different auditing stream has emerged. The next two sections examine the CA methodology and its recent framework developments – a fundamental redesign of audit processes using today's technology.

Continuous auditing for a real-time approach

In the current business environment, information is processed, collected and reported so that it can provide near immediate feedback to stakeholders. In addition to its strong infrastructure of automation, what distinguishes CA from traditional auditing performed today is CA's *real-time* approach. There is no standard definition for CA yet (Brannen, 2016), but the initial definition by Canadian Institute of Chartered Accountants/American Institute of Certified Public Accountants (CICA/AICPA) (1999) was restated and expanded in Bumgarner & Vasarhelyi (2015, p. 48) as:

> a methodology that enables auditors to provide assurance on a subject matter for which an entity's management is responsible, using a continuous opinion schema issued virtually simultaneously with, or a short period of time after, the occurrence of events underlying the subject matter. The continuous audit may entail predictive modules and may supplement organisational controls. The continuous audit environment will be progressively automated with auditors taking progressively higher judgment functions. The audit will be analytic, by exception, adaptive, and cover financial and non-financial functions.

Therefore, CA is a new conceptualisation of the whole auditing process. In a nutshell, CA's ultimate goal is to bring audit results closer to the occurrence of relevant events, hence enabling a significant improvement in reacting to problems as they occur and prompting an immediate resolution.

Overview of the continuous auditing components

In a CA environment, data flowing through the system are analysed continuously (e.g. daily). Software continuously running as an analytical review technique compares expected results with the characteristics of the whole population of transactions being monitored (Chan et al., 2011). In this "future-oriented" audit, historical data helps to model expectations for future data. When the software detects an anomaly, it notifies the auditor through emails, notification systems and/or system reports, prompting timely further investigation (Kuhn & Sutton, 2010).

CA was initially targeted to external auditors, as a pilot data analysis to deal with the issue of auditing large paperless database systems (Vasarhelyi & Halper, 1991). However, CA became a phenomenon increasingly affecting internal auditors as well (Vasarhelyi et al., 2010).

Its concept was first expanded by Alles et al. (2006) in an implementation for controls testing at Siemens as a reaction to Sarbanes Oxley (SOX).[2] The CA framework evolved to a composite model with two key primary components: procedures for monitoring business process controls – Continuous *Controls* Monitoring (CCM); and procedures for detailed transactions testing – Continuous *Data* Audit (CDA) (Alles et al., 2006). Vasarhelyi et al. (2010) proposed a third element in the CA methodology, the Continuous *Risk* Monitoring and Assessment (CRMA), and Bumgarner & Vasarhelyi (2015) added a fourth element, Continuous *Compliance* Monitoring (COMO). We now analyse these four primary components of the CA framework, focusing first on CCM and CDA and then on CRMA and COMO.

Continuous controls monitoring and continuous data audit

Typically, the expected result of monitoring is to obtain information about the performance of a process, a system or data. CCM consists of a set of procedures used for monitoring internal controls and helps to ensure that procedures and business processes are operating effectively (Alles et al., 2006). The validation of the implemented controls is rooted in the shift from manual controls assessment to automated platforms. CCM procedures include, for instance, continuously monitoring user access controls, user account authorisations and workflows related with business processes (Vasarhelyi et al., 2010). Alongside CCM, CDA verifies the integrity of data flowing within and between systems to ensure that errors in the data are minimised (Chan et al., 2011). CDA includes procedures for verifying underlying master data (e.g. comparing prices in the master file with prices in invoices), transactional data flows and key process metrics using analytics (Vasarhelyi et al., 2010), through which transactional data are continuously tested for anomalies.

CCM is a part of the wider CM activities. Although CM and CA as terms are often used interchangeably, and both consist of data analysis on a real-time basis against benchmarks, they are separate concepts and activities. The key difference between these two terms is related to a process ownership. CM is owned by management, as a management function to ensure processes are working as defined and approved. By contrast, CCM is owned by auditors, as an auditing process that continually tests controls implemented by the management based upon criteria defined by auditors (Alles et al., 2006). As such, in the context of technology, auditors have seen CM as applying to *testing controls* (Brannen, 2016). However, with the need to issue opinions on the adequacy of internal controls (e.g. a SOX requirement), it became clear that CCM insights and analytics would also be of interest to management in assessing the effectiveness of such controls.

Hence, CA is a technological innovation of the traditional audit process being used by a variety of actors. It continually gathers data to support not only auditing, for the issuance of the mandated annual audit opinion, but also management objectives and activities for business process reviews (Alles et al., 2006; Chan & Vasarhelyi, 2011). After the above analysis of CCM and CDA, we now analyse the two remaining components of CA: CRMA and COMO.

Continuous risk monitoring and assessment and continuous compliance monitoring

The 2008 sub-prime crisis made it obvious that existing enterprise risk management was not adequate to assess business risks (Bumgarner & Vasarhelyi, 2015). Auditors have systematised approaches that are heavily reliant on periodic and relatively unstructured assessment of risk and judgement (Vasarhelyi et al., 2010). Having real-time information of changes in business and audit environments is critical in CA. Technological advances allow for closer and more realistic measurements of risk and CRMA. CRMA uses algorithms and probability models to assess judgements and risk evaluations, as well as to monitor operational and environmental risks (Vasarhelyi et al., 2010; Moon & Krahel, 2020). Hence, the aim of CRMA is to make CA dynamic by reflecting risk management practices in the audit itself. With CRMA, new CCM and CDA resources may be updated as entity risks change. For example, Moon & Krahel (2020) proposed a methodology for CRMA implementation, to build leading and lagging indicators to monitor and assess business risks. The methodology potential was illustrated by drawing upon real-time postings in social media websites, as a basis to develop a leading indicator of reputational damage. It was then applied to Twitter messages involving two large US corporations, to assess their potential reputational damage.

Although much of the traditional world of compliance is qualitative, monitoring organisational compliance with regulation is progressively being implemented using IT (COMO) (Ly et al., 2015; Rikhardsson & Dull, 2016), in particular by financial institutions (Becker & Buchkremer, 2019). Regulators of financial institutions have deployed machine learning and natural language processing to improve automated supervisory processes and CM (KPMG, 2021), and similar approaches can be deployed by auditing firms as well.

Implementing CRMA and COMO is still a slow-moving work in progress, as it will first require the formalisation of the practice and solution on how it can be automated (Bumgarner & Vasarhelyi, 2015) – a prerequisite not fully attained yet. However, recent advances, such as Becker & Buchkremer (2019) and Moon & Krahel (2020), presented above, reveal their gradual practical application.

Continuous auditing: beyond audit automation

CA must be based upon computer-assisted tools and techniques. It is only feasible if implemented as an automated process with full access to relevant events (Kogan et al., 1999). This explains why the terms "audit automation" and "continuous auditing" may be confused or interchangeably used (e.g. Chiu et al., 2014). In fact, identification of exceptions, analysing numeric patterns, reviewing trends and testing controls are all automated, so IT plays a key role in CA activities.

Nevertheless, CA is not a simple automation of the traditional audit procedures. All auditors have tools and audit automation to support their work, such as electronic working papers in customised audit databases and data analysis tools. However, this is not the concept of the CA methodology. CA requires *formalised* audit procedures programmed into an automated audit system that can run continuously. CA uses automated tools to evaluate if organisational data is maintained accurately and if internal controls function properly (Vasarhelyi et al., 2010). However, if organisational processes and data are still largely manual, traditional auditing should be maintained. Hence, before attempting to implement a CA approach, it is critical to evaluate the extent to which data, controls and key processes are, or should be, formalised and automated.

In CA, as CM of internal controls and testing of transactions are automated, the main role of the auditor will be to investigate exceptions reported by the audit system and to focus on the high-level judgemental audit areas. Therefore, while automation is an essential ingredient to CA, manual involvement remains important, particularly in situations where extensive judgement is required and where exceptions and outliers are identified (Vasarhelyi et al., 2004; Tysiac, 2022). Human factors will, thus, continue to be integrated in the audit process, although not so prominently as in traditional audit.

Continuous auditing: a proactive audit

Extensive research (e.g. Kogan et al., 1999; Brown et al., 2007; Chiu et al., 2014) has been conducted regarding the functionality, benefits and challenges of CA. In theory, the technological feasibility of CA appears simple as accounting information is now electronically recorded and computer networks allow remote access to that information. However, in practice, the great variety of software systems used in organisations makes it difficult for auditors to develop auditing tools and, furthermore, to make the implementation of these audit tools economically feasible (Kogan et al., 1999). CA is a capital-intensive technology, which requires sizable investments not only in hardware but also in software and networks, whose development in practice is analysed in the following section.

CA can be seen both as a technology (our focus so far) and as a process (our focus now) (Bumgarner & Vasarhelyi, 2015). As a process, CA is a rethink of auditing. It fundamentally changes every part of auditing, from the way that data is made available to the auditor, to the kind of tests the auditor conducts, how alarms are dealt with, what kinds of reports are issued, how often and to whom they are issued for follow-up (Vasarhelyi et al., 2010). It allows the auditor to actively detect and investigate exceptions as they occur. Depending on system capabilities, transactions involving internal control violations and transaction anomalies can even be aborted or suspended in real time until duly investigated and eventually approved.

Hence, CA can be considered a *proactive* rather than a *reactive* audit, as it has been since its inception (Chan & Vasarhelyi, 2011). With CA, a predictive audit will rely on models to predict results in an account or transaction, which are compared with actuals in near-real time to detect substantive variances (Kogan et al., 2014). While conceptually this may seem simple, the actual uptake of CA in practice has been low, as discussed in the next section.

Continuous auditing in practice – the state of the art

The real-time environment generated by advances in AIS gave birth to the CA process, and some implementation experiences of technologies have progressively been prototyped (Vasarhelyi & Halper, 1991; Vasarhelyi et al., 2004, Alles et al., 2006; Kogan et al., 2014; Singh & Best, 2015). Since the pilot implementation of CCM as a proof of concept in a large transnational company, internal auditors have increased their use of technology with the goal of automating the internal audit process (Alles et al., 2006; Codesso et al., 2020; Freitas et al., 2020). However, although the concept of CA has been researched for many years and some applications have been made, auditors, and external auditors in particular, have struggled to turn this concept into practice. To understand this, we now analyse the alternative architectures to support CA and the development of predictive models to define the benchmarks to be deployed in CA.

Technical architecture of continuous auditing

The CA cycle starts with the auditor connecting to the processing system and ends when the auditor disconnects (Chan & Vasarhelyi, 2011). There are two major issues regarding this connection. We start by analysing the first issue, related to the access to the processing system and data – direct access (either to the transactional database or to the application layer), or intermediated access through a data warehouse. After that, we analyse the second issue, related with the connection access security.

To understand the first access issue, we need to consider that CA and auditing system architectures to capture the data are based on two main designs: Embedded Audit Modules

(EAM) (Vasarhelyi & Halper, 1991) and Monitoring and Control Layer (MCL), introduced by Vasarhelyi et al. (2004). Through EAM, audit programs are integrated *directly* within the application to provide CM of the processing of transactions through examination of each transaction as it enters the system, using the language of the application itself (Rezaee et al., 2002). However, having those modules running in the background of the system may reduce its transactional processing capability and efficiency. Moreover, as the audit application is permanently resident within the processing system, possible manipulation by the auditee's personnel and dependency of its IT department to make changes create concerns about the integrity of the EAM approach.

The alternative design is based on MCL, an external software module operating independently from the information system being monitored or audited; it is merely *linked* to the system (Vasarhelyi et al., 2004). Unlike EAM, with MCL the CA system receives data periodically, as determined by the auditor. This data is then processed against pre-defined rule-sets of audit programs, outside the processing system, and stored in a different computer. Alles et al. (2006) have documented a system prototype based on MCL for controls testing at Siemens. As pointed out by those authors, in contrast with EAM, the MCL approach has fewer issues related to software maintenance, client independence and reliance on IT personnel.

To make CA possible and cost-effective, many controls were once expected to become integrated controls (CICA/AICPA, 1999). However, organisations have not yet implemented the end-to-end centralised and automated controls required by CCM. There are issues in both EAM and MCL: EAM requires implementing several modules, one in each application, and MCL implies the existence of a variety of systems, making the required connections more challenging. Rezaee et al. (2002) proposed a conceptual technical architecture for building CA systems that combine the use of audit data warehouses (integrating data from all application systems throughout the organisation) and audit data marts (smaller warehouses that focus on only one functional area, such as accounting). Each data mart loads appropriate data from the data warehouse; then, audit tests are periodically run on the data mart, generating exception reports. Kogan et al. (2014) also designed a data-oriented system for organisations in which data derived from multiple legacy systems are deployed in a single data warehouse. In terms of the platform for the audit software, an audit data warehouse, linking with the disparate systems and integrating the relevant data, has been considered a viable technical solution (Rezaee et al., 2002).

We now turn to securing CA, the second issue identified above concerning the auditor access and crucial for CA architecture. Moving data over the network for remote processing and opening new channels between auditors and auditees using the networking infrastructure of the internet creates security risks. This access has to be supported by security technologies and policies to ensure that the audit applications are protected against unauthorised alteration. Furthermore, reliable and efficient electronic communication methods need to be in place.

The next subsection discusses how to build standardised audit tests, resident in the EAM or in audit data warehouses, running continuously and generating exception reports based on business process modelling and DA.

Business processes modelling and data analytics

Preceding the stage of modelling data, developing benchmarks and deploying DA, audit procedures should be automated at a relatively low level, down to the level of individual processes (Vasarhelyi et al., 2004; Alles et al., 2006). Audit systems only detect anomalies that the auditor anticipates and, even more specifically, those anomalies that those applications are programmed to seek. Therefore, irregularities to be monitored must be previously defined.

In developing a CA system for verifying key process metrics, the assumption is that access to transaction-level data will enable auditors to design expectation models for analytical procedures at the business process level. This contrasts with the traditional practice of relying on ratio or trend analysis at a higher level of aggregation (Vasarhelyi et al., 2010). Performing analytical procedures requires determining what can be expected and a level of precision – i.e. how accurate the auditor wants the model to be, according to the auditor's perception.

Data modelling and DA techniques, developed from statistics and data mining, are used for analytical procedures for monitoring and testing transaction details (controls exceptions and transactions verifications) and account balances (Chan & Vasarhelyi, 2011). For CCM, internal control policies serve as the benchmark against which employees' actions are compared and any violation is flagged for verification. For CDA at the account level, DA helps to understand the evolution of the activity. Data modelling involves the use of *historical audited* transaction data and account balances to generate a prediction of data through empirical models of expected behaviour, such as linear regressions. Based on the assumption that future transaction data and its behaviour characteristics should be similar to the past, DA is used to compare *present unaudited* transactions and account balances (metrics) against the benchmarks created by data modelling considering an acceptable range (Chan & Vasarhelyi, 2011).

Estimates of the coefficients of the variables in the models should be statistically significant, to ensure higher precision on the metrics generated (Kogan et al., 2014). Variances from these metrics are treated as an alert. Hence, imperfect models will generate false positive errors (false alarms, i.e. exceptions detected that are not actually anomalies) and false negative errors (actual anomalies not detected by the system).

Aggregation and benchmarks for continuous auditing analytics

Much recent research on CA has focused on developing improved models for actual and more reasonable comparisons (Chiu et al., 2014; Kogan et al., 2014). Creating a metric that will prove effective in detecting exceptions is not a trivial task, since it must be based on what is "usual" for an observation (Kogan et al., 2014). In an environment where disaggregated data is available (in contrast to the traditional audit), financial and/or non-financial metrics can be used, such as document counts or number of transactions. Auditing on different metrics would enable auditors to have a more diverse set of patterns and benchmarks (Kogan et al., 2014).

There is, however, a trade-off regarding aggregation of data. The more disaggregated the metrics are, the more variability is observed among individual transactions; this is more likely to lead to unstable analytical models and generate more errors. Depending on the accuracy of those analytical criteria, problems may emerge from the flow of false positives, generating alarm floods and information overload, and, on the contrary, from the failure in detecting exceptions (Kuhn & Sutton, 2010). However, on the positive side, using disaggregated metrics will narrow down the scope of the auditor's follow-up. In addition, to address the problem of many false positives due to disaggregated data in CA, Yoon et al. (2021) developed a CA system with a three-layer structure, showing that it enhances audit effectiveness and efficiency.

A major issue in CA research is the feasibility of using statistics in practice. The willingness of auditors to model CA applications in practice has been questioned (Kuhn & Sutton,

2010), although there are increasing examples (e.g. Codesso et al., 2020; Freitas et al., 2020). Academics have a clear competitive advantage to innovate the stages of data modelling and DA to fit reality into a benchmark. However, that research will be fruitless without its implementation and validation in practice (Chan & Vasarhelyi, 2011; Kogan et al., 2014).

While not yet an established methodology, interest in exploring CA processes has advanced, particularly in internal audit (Vasarhelyi et al., 2012; Codesso et al., 2020; Freitas et al., 2020). The drivers and constraints of CA have proven to be economic and regulatory, given that auditing is a business practice, not a piece of software (Alles et al., 2008). Key concerns underpin auditors' reluctance, or at least caution, towards CA. Is the absence of exceptions, or actual data being close to the estimates of the predictive models, enough to conclude that controls are effective and that transactions and balances are accurate (Titera, 2013)? How to integrate in the audit working papers CA alerts, weaknesses of automatic controls, exceptions and bases of predictive models or evidence from technological innovations, such as camera devices monitoring a warehouse and being used to confirm deliveries of materials (Chiu et al., 2014)? Furthermore, additional challenges have arisen with the emergence of Big Data, which has changed the landscape of CA by becoming an important source for analytics. This is the focus of the next section.

Big Data in a continuous auditing environment

Big Data originates from traditional transaction systems and many exogenous new sources, such as emails, telephone calls, social media and security videos. Much of this Big Data informs and affects corporate decisions that are important to both internal and external stakeholders. Therefore, auditors need to go beyond the analysis of traditional financial, structured data (e.g. general ledger or transaction data in accounting and transactional systems). Auditors need to expand to non-financial and non-structured data, such as company emails, social networks logs, newspaper articles and even environmental data, to identify potential transactional anomalies and trends (Brown-Liburd et al., 2015; Cao et al., 2015; Holt & Loraas, 2021).

Big Data in the audit environment

The advent of Big Data means that there is extensive relevant audit evidence outside the organisation in the form of non-financial, non-structured data. However, traditional analytical tools, such as Excel and Access, require structured data to perform effectively. Moreover, existing CAATs, due to limited use of advanced statistical techniques, do not have the capability to import such information (Brown-Liburd et al., 2015).

Incorporating Big Data into the audit process is overall value-adding for auditors, but it creates serious challenges. Big Data analyses are limited to *correlations*, by looking for patterns that might help in determining expectations in analytical procedures (Cao et al., 2015) and then identify anomalies that direct the auditor's attention to investigate their causes. This focus on correlations is problematic because correlations do not point out causations – a critical aspect in auditing – and such anomalies alone do not provide sufficient and appropriate audit evidence (Brown-Liburd et al., 2015).

Big Data is a powerful predictor for auditors' expectations of financial data. However, the so-called four "Vs" of Big Data – high volume, velocity, variety and uncertain veracity – present challenges for the capabilities of CA methods (Zhang et al., 2015). Therefore, an effective development of the CA methodology to accommodate Big Data analytics requires updating the infrastructure for accessing and retrieving data with diverse formats. This is particularly challenging, in a context where CA is neither fully implemented nor an established technology yet, as previously discussed.

How Big Data is transforming the continuous audit

While collecting Big Data is relatively easy, the same cannot be said about processing and extracting useful information from large amounts of data (Brown-Liburd et al., 2015). A major concern is data quality, as noise in Big Data leads to an overload of false positive alarms (Cao et al., 2015). Data consistency, identification, integrity and aggregation are concerns for the current CA architecture, for the layer dealing with data provisioning, filtering and diagnostics (Zhang et al., 2015).

The new CA approach needs to verify relationships among data sources and to manage data inconsistencies, such as data formats and, most importantly, any contradictions between data from different sources. The unstructured nature of the data and its many formats, such as text, image or video, complicates the data management and processing software, as well as the data identification (Brown-Liburd et al., 2015). For example, the revenue amount for a given sale can be easily identified by the CA system, but it may be challenging to automatically connect this information with the associated sales terms and conditions, which are in an unstructured textual format (Zhang et al., 2015). In even more unstructured settings, revenue transactions may be compared with weather patterns, in order to select specific sales transactions to undergo substantive testing (Cunningham & Stein, 2018).

Furthermore, the volume and variety of Big Data create difficulties to identify data that has been modified or deleted, in order not to lose reliable data for audit analysis purposes. Current methods of verifying data integrity, such as reasonability, edit checks and comparison with other sources, may not be practical for Big Data audit applications. There is a need to find how to integrate techniques of data inconsistency checks in the audit data warehouse or MCL without losing efficiency and how to evaluate the suitability of current methods to address the data identification issue for the CA with Big Data (Zhang et al., 2015). In addition, modified and incomplete data detecting and repairing techniques are also imperative in CA systems (Zhang et al., 2015).

As Big Data originates from different sources, CA needs to aggregate it in order to meaningfully summarise and simplify it. However, as already discussed, there is a trade-off in data aggregation. Furthermore, auditors' processing limitation is particularly relevant with Big Data, related to information overload, information relevance and ambiguity (Brown-Liburd et al., 2015). For example, an experiment revealed that more varied data leads to more conservative risk assessments and write down recommendations, when compared with a traditional memo format, particularly under time pressure (Holt & Loraas, 2021). To counteract this higher risk aversion caused by cognitive overload, Holt & Loraas (2021) suggested using interactive visualisation tools (rather than merely static presentations) to enable auditors to flexibly choose the representation most suited to their various thought processes (for another example of Big Data visualisation in auditing, see Cunningham & Stein, 2018; see also, Chapter 14). In the same line, Salijeni et al. (2021) highlight visualisation capabilities as essential to identify client inefficiencies and areas of audit concern and improve auditors' capacity to communicate with their clients and justify their claims and judgements. Therefore, CA may be enhanced by Big Data, but, given the persistent challenges and disparate experiences, auditors both laud and lament the efficacy of Big Data and analytics and overall remain reticent about using it (Gepp et al., 2018; Salijeni et al., 2021).

Technological advancements have also increased the importance of internal controls and CCM. The next section describes recent developments of CM techniques.

Development of continuous monitoring and control activities

Today, thousands of data flows are captured in different business processes, and hundreds of controls to generate transactions and reports are used through ERPs. As already stated, CA can be defined as a process that continually tests controls based upon criteria defined by the auditor, and DA models may also be a direct test of control. We now turn to CCM, introduced earlier, to further explore how controls can be monitored on a continuous basis.

Monitoring of control settings in the CA conceptual model

In a traditional audit, controls testing is performed on a sample basis through inquiries, observation, inspection or re-performance, and it is generally phased to be performed at an interim date and the remaining portion at period-end. However, traditional manual audit activities, such as observation and inspection, are becoming less applicable or even impossible within the current environment (Chiu et al., 2014), as the following examples illustrate. The documentation of business events is increasingly conducted through computer-based processes that automatically collect data, and businesses are progressively implementing electronic documents and signatures. Drones have started being used for inventories controls testing (PwC, 2019); however, DA for internal control testing (e.g. for testing the nature of journal entries or log-ins in the system) is not widely deployed (FRC, 2017), even with the emergence of new technologies.

Process analytics involves the analysis of data drawn from different points in a transaction flow and, consequently, involves more complex datasets (FRC, 2017). To detect control violations, the CCM audit software looks, for instance, for master data tables to check approved business partners (e.g. customers, suppliers). However, obtaining data to use process analytics efficiently is still a difficult barrier for auditors.

Practical implementation of CCM, whether by using MCL or EAM, is still lower than envisaged some years ago (Vasarhelyi et al., 2012). One possible reason is that the validation of the effectiveness of any manual control through a CCM methodology should be formalised by the conversion of the manual control to automated platforms (Vasarhelyi et al., 2010). However, instead of using formalised audit programs in a computer executable format integrated into the CCM software, process mining (PM), analysed next, has been seen as an alternative.

Process mining as an audit tool

PM is a DA method to evaluate ERP log files, gathering insight into what steps people actually take when performing their tasks to identify transactions that do not follow an approved workflow (Jan et al., 2013; Chiu & Jans, 2019; Werner et al., 2021). Information is extracted from an event log, which is a chronological record of computerised activities. PM is distinctive as an audit tool because it focuses on the path of transactions and not directly on the validation of the values in the related process and uses the full population of data instead of a sample. It is, thus, a powerful tool for tests of controls, contrasting with the traditional approach. The data recorded by an ERP system includes not only entries made by users of that system, the *input-data*, but also *meta-data*, which is information automatically recorded by the system about that input and, as such, of particular interest to the auditor (Jan et al.,

2014). To create an event log, both types of data are extracted from various tables throughout the ERP system database and assembled into a structured database to allow for an adequate analysis of the input (activity) and other information about the actual operation of the process. However, the major challenge is the ERP system capturing the meta-data located across numerous tables into a structured and usable event log (Jan et al., 2014).

Besides obtaining meta-information about individual data entries, PM provides the ability to detect patterns across transactions and the users entering that data, such as whether certain transactions are regularly associated with a third party, at a certain time, or in a certain order (Jan et al., 2013). Chiu & Jans (2019) explored how PM may be used to evaluate internal control effectiveness, and Jan et al. (2013) identified the sources of value added of PM when applied to auditing. Overall, it is clear that PM can be useful when deployed as a complementary analytical procedure tool for CA, particularly in the CCM context.

Contribution of process mining in continuous auditing

As already discussed, one major issue with analytics is the potentially high number of false positives. As a follow-up procedure, PM may be of great value to explore in depth the circumstances that gave rise to the anomalies resulting from the analytical testing, to either identify a control failure or, alternatively, to improve the models to reduce future false positives (Jan et al., 2013; Werner et al., 2021). Singh & Best (2015) developed a prototype continuous monitoring system that relies exclusively on recorded transaction activity of profile users to recreate transaction histories and relationships among individuals as soon as events occur. The authors demonstrated that it is feasible to implement CM in practice using the full population of input-data and meta-data from an ERP system to enrich the audit process. Becker & Buchkremer (2019) deployed a PM application in a financial institution and used it to monitor in real time the compliance of real-life execution of business processes and to analyse in detail potentially non-compliant activities and durations.

PM can be used in conjunction with other analytical procedures to narrow down the auditors' investigation; however, PM may also be used as a primary analytical procedure instead of only as business process modelling (Jan et al., 2014). Whether PM may complement rather than replacing CCM analytics needs further research. Given the difficulties and high cost of applying PM to all the data of an organisation on a timely basis, there may be advantages in confining PM to the event logs of the anomalous transactions to be checked and investigated (Jan et al., 2014).

Conclusion

The traditional auditing paradigm based on sampling is still dominant presently, although a significant increase of DA usage is transforming the audit process (CPAB Exchange, 2019). Technology develops at an astonishing pace, and businesses have been fast in adopting it. However, auditing has not been so fast. The development of ERP systems provides the necessary infrastructure for the effective shift of auditing from a periodic review to a real-time (or near-real-time) process through CA and PM applications. Despite substantial challenges, there has been some applicability of the concepts, particularly by internal auditors; external auditors have been substantially slower to adopt them.

The lesson from CA implementations is simple: organisations and auditors should start small, with regard to the technologies involved (Chan & Vasarhelyi, 2011) and the organisations in which these are deployed (Tysiac, 2022). Since automation related with data, processes and controls is essential for CA development, organisations already possessing strong automated processes and controls are better suited to a CA approach.

Some questions, however, remain. Information systems, both within the accounting and the business realm, are continuously evolving technologies, and CA systems need to adapt to the Big Data phenomenon and ensure data quality processing. Will the existing CA architecture, not yet broadly implemented, be effective for those future ERPs and adaptable to Big Data challenges? Will hybridisation of continuous and traditional auditing procedures be the way for a most effective dynamic of the CA approach in the current and forthcoming environment? Expectation models must be developed for each business process and may vary between processes and times of the year (Kogan et al., 2014); will PM be a better CCM methodology? As business risks are constantly changing, CDA and CCM procedures may have to be constantly adapted, but how to use technology to continuously monitor and assess those risks and organisational compliance, in order to redirect audit procedures? These are relevant questions, but only partly answered, in theory and in practice. In the meantime, auditors will continue to develop and refine tools to extract information supporting greater use of DA, before actually shifting to a new paradigm of *continuous* DA and moving to CA.

Finally, while system architecture and software components are important cornerstones to successfully deploy CA, the auditors' skill sets are also fundamental. These skills range from hard skills (e.g. Cunningham & Stein, 2018) to soft skills (e.g. Codesso et al. (2020) identified the innovative tone of the audit team as a success factor to implement CA). The DA environment will result in auditor judgement playing a much more significant role, due to potentially large numbers of exceptions to evaluate and metrics to be continuously reviewed (Vasarhelyi et al., 2010; Tysiac, 2022). Do students joining auditing firms, now and in the future, have the skills required by CA (e.g. Cunningham & Stein, 2018), and are they capable of developing their auditor judgement, without the experience gained through the traditional audit tasks and knowledge? Recruiting and retaining the right people, with the right skills to interpret the resulting DA, may not be easy (PwC, 2019).

The evolution towards CA may take time, and implementing it may be complex, but it will not be an insurmountable challenge. Indeed, in a changing business and IT context, CA is not only an imperative but also an enormous opportunity for the improvement of the auditing profession.

Notes

1 In this chapter, the term "auditing" encompasses internal and external auditing, unless otherwise stated.
2 SOX 404 mandates that all publicly traded companies must establish, document, test and maintain internal control procedures to ensure their effectiveness.

References

Alles, M., Brennan, G., Kogan, A., & Vasarhelyi, M.A. (2006). Continuous monitoring of business process controls: a pilot implementation of a continuous auditing system at Siemens. *International Journal of Accounting Information Systems*, 7(2), 137–161. https://doi.org/10.1016/j.accinf.2005.10.004

Alles M., Kogan, A., & Vasarhelyi, M.A. (2008). Putting continuous auditing theory into practice: Lessons from two pilot implementations. *Journal of Information Systems*, 22(2), 195–214. https://doi.org/10.2308/jis.2008.22.2.195

Becker, M., & Buchkremer, R. (2019). A practical process mining approach for compliance management. *Journal of Financial Regulation and Compliance, 27*(4), 464–478. https://doi.org/10.1108/JFRC-12-2018-0163

Brannen, L. (2016). Demystifying continuous audit. *Business Finance, 29*(3), 4–4.

Brown, C., Wong J., & Baldwin, A. (2007). A review and analysis of the existing research streams in continuous auditing. *Journal of Emerging Technologies in Accounting, 4*, 1–28. https://doi.org/10.2308/jeta.2007.4.1.1

Brown-Liburd, H., Hussein I., & Lombardi, D. (2015). Behavioral implications of Big Data's impact on audit judgment and decision making and future research directions. *Accounting Horizons, 29*(2), 451–468. https://doi.org/10.2308/acch-51023

Bumgarner, N., & Vasarhelyi, M.A. (2015). Continuous auditing - A new view. Audit Analytics and Continuous Audit: Looking toward the Future, AICPA, New York, 3–51.

Byrnes P., Criste, T., Stewart, T., & Vasarhelyi, M.A. (2014). Reimagining auditing in a Wired World, *AICPA,* New York.

Canadian Institute of Chartered Accountants/American Institute of Certified Public Accountants (CICA/AICPA). (1999). *Continuous auditing,* Research Report, Toronto, Canada.

Cao, M., Chychyla R., & Stewart, T. (2015). Big data analytics in financial statement audits. *Accounting Horizons, 29*(2), 423–429. https://doi.org/10.2308/acch-51068

Chan, D.Y., & Vasarhelyi, M.A. (2011). Innovation and practice of continuous auditing. *International Journal of Accounting Information Systems, 12*, 152–160. https://doi.org/10.1016/j.accinf.2011.01.001

Chan, K., & Wu, D. (2011). Aggregate quasi rents and auditor independence: Evidence from audit firm mergers in China. *Contemporary Accounting Research*, 28(1), 175-213.

Chiu, T., & Jans, M. (2019). Process mining of event logs: A case study evaluating internal control effectiveness. *Accounting Horizons, 33*(3), 141–156. https://doi.org/10.2308/acch-52458

Chiu, V., Liu Q., & Vasarhelyi, M.A. (2014). The development and intellectual structure of continuous auditing research. *Journal of Accounting Literature, 33*(1), 37–57. https://doi.org/10.1016/j.acclit.2014.08.001

Codesso, M., Freitas, M.M., Wang, X., Carvalho, A., & Filho, A. (2020). Continuous audit implementation at Cia. Hering in Brazil. *Journal of Emerging Technologies in Accounting, 17*(2), 103–118. https://doi.org/10.2308/JETA-2020-006

CPAB Exchange. (2019). *Enhancing Audit Quality through Data Analytics.* http://www.cpab-ccrc.ca/Documents/ News% 20and % 20Publications/Data% 20Analytics% 20EN.pdf.

Cunningham, L.M., & Stein S.E. (2018). Using visualization software in the audit of revenue transactions to identify anomalies. *Issues in Accounting Education, 33*(4), 33–46. https://doi.org/10.2308/IACE-52146

FRC (2017). *Audit Quality Thematic Review. The Use of Data Analytics in the Audit of Financial Statements.* https://www.frc.org.uk/getattachment/4fd19a18-1beb-4959-8737-ae2dca80af67/AQTR_Audit-Data-Analytics-Jan-2017.pdf.

Freitas, M.M., Codesso, M., & Augusto, A.L.R. (2020). Implementation of continuous audit on the Brazilian Navy Payroll. *Journal of Emerging Technologies in Accounting, 17*(2), 157–171. https://doi.org/10.2308/JETA-2020-047

Gepp, A., Linnenluecke, M., O'Neill, T., & Smith, T. (2018). Big Data techniques in auditing research and practice: Current trends and future opportunities. *Journal of Accounting Literature, 40*, 102–115. https://doi.org/10.2139/ssrn.2930767

Holt, T.P., & Loraas, T.M. (2021). A potential unintended consequence of big data: Does information structure lead to suboptimal auditor judgment and decision-making?. *Accounting Horizons, 35*(3), 161–186. https://doi.org/10.2308/HORIZONS-19-123

Jan, M., Alles, M., & Vasarhelyi, M.A. (2013). The case for process mining in auditing: Sources of value added and areas of application. *International Journal of Accounting Information Systems, 14*, 1–20. https://doi.org/10.1016/j.accinf.2012.06.015

Jan, M., Alles, M., & Vasarhelyi, M.A. (2014). A field study on the use of process mining of event logs as an analytical procedure in auditing. *The Accounting Review, 89*(5), 1751–1773. https://doi.org/10.2308/accr-50807

Kogan, A., Alles, M., Vasarhelyi, M.A., & Wu, J. (2014). Design and evaluation of a continuous data level auditing system. *Auditing: A Journal of Theory and Practice, 33*(4), 221–245. https://doi.org/10.2308/ajpt-50844

Kogan, A., Sudit E.F., & Vasarhelyi, M.A. (1999). Continuous online auditing: A program of research. *Journal of Information Systems, 13*(2), 87–103. https://doi.org/10.2308/jis.1999.13.2.87

KPMG (2021). *Ten Key Regulatory Challenges of 2021.* https://assets.kpmg/content/dam/kpmg/cn/pdf/en/2021/02/ten-key-regulatory-challenges-of-2021.pdf

Kuhn, J.R. Jr., & Sutton, S.G. (2010). Continuous auditing in ERP system environments: The current state and future directions. *Journal of Information Systems, 24*(1), 91–112. https://doi.org/10.2308/jis.2010.24.1.91

Ly, L.T., Maggi, F.M., Montali, M., Rinderle-Ma, S., & Van Der Aalst, W.M.P. (2015). Compliance monitoring in business processes: Functionalities, application, and tool-support. *Information Systems, 54*, 209–234. https://doi.org/10.1016/j.is.2015.02.007

Moon, D., & Krahel, J.P. (2020). Continuous risk monitoring and assessment - New component of continuous assurance. *Journal of Emerging Technologies in Accounting, 17*(2), 173–200. https://doi.org/10.2308/JETA-18-01-09-1

PwC. (2019). *PwC Completes Its First Stock Count Audit Using Drone Technology.* https://www.pwc.co.uk/press-room/press-releases/pwc-first-stock-count-audit-drones.html.

Rezaee, Z., Sharbatoghlie, A., Elam, R., & McMickle, P.L. (2002). Continuous auditing: Building automated auditing capability. *Auditing: A Journal of Practice & Theory, 21*(1), 147–163. https://doi.org/10.2308/aud.2002.21.1.147

Rikhardsson, P., & Dull, R. (2016). An exploratory study of the adoption, application and impacts of CA technologies in small businesses. *International Journal of Accounting Information Systems, 20*, 26–37. http://dx.doi.org/10.1016/j.accinf.2016.01.003

Salijeni, G., Samsonova-Taddei, A., & Turley, S. (2021). Understanding how big data technologies reconfigure the nature and organization of financial statement audits: A sociomaterial analysis. *European Accounting Review, 30*(3), 531–555. https://doi.org/10.1080/09638180.2021.1882320

Singh, K., & Best, P.J. (2015). Design and implementation of continuous monitoring and auditing in SAP enterprise resource planning. *International Journal of Auditing, 19*, 307–317. https://doi.org/10.1111/ijau.12051

Teeter, R.A., Alles, M.G., & Vasarhelyi, M.A. (2010). The remote audit. *Journal of Emerging Technologies in Accounting, 7*, 73–88. https://doi.org/10.2308/jeta.2010.7.1.73

Titera, W.R. (2013). Updating audit standard – Enabling audit data analysis. *Journal of Information Systems, 27*(1), 325–331. https://doi.org/10.2308/isys-50427

Tysiac, K. (2022). Embracing technology in the audit. *Journal of Accountancy, 2*, 8–11.

Vasarhelyi, M.A., Alles, M., & Kogan, A. (2004). Principles of analytic monitoring for continuous assurance. *Journal of Emerging Technologies in Accounting, 1*, 1–21. https://doi.org/10.2308/jeta.2004.1.1.1

Vasarhelyi, M.A., Alles, M., Kuenkaikaew, S., & Littley, J. (2012). The acceptance and adoption of continuous auditing by internal auditors. *International Journal of Accounting Information Systems, 13*, 267–281. https://doi.org/10.1016/j.accinf.2012.06.011

Vasarhelyi, M.A., Alles, M. & Williams, K.T. (2010). Continuous Assurance for the Now Economy. http://www.charteredaccountants.com.au/Industry-Topics/Audit-and-assurance/Publications-and-tools/Other-audit-resources/Resources.

Vasarhelyi, M.A., & Halper, F.B. (1991). The continuous audit of online systems. *Auditing a Journal of Practice and Theory, 10*(1), 110–125.

Werner, M., Wiese, M., & Maas, A. (2021). Embedding process mining into financial statement audits. *International Journal of Accounting Information Systems, 41*, 100514. https://doi.org/10.1016/j.accinf.2021.100514

Yoon, K., Liu, Y., Chiu., T., & Vasarhelyi, M.A. (2021). Design and evaluation of an advanced continuous data level auditing system: A three-layer structure. *International Journal of Accounting Information Systems, 42*, 100524. https://doi.org/10.1016/j.accinf.2021.100524

Zhang, J., Yang, X., & Appelbaum, D. (2015). Toward effective big data analysis in continuous auditing. *Accounting Horizons, 29*(2), 469–476. https://doi.org/10.2308/acch-51070

17

THE STATUS OF ROBOTIC PROCESS AUTOMATION

Steven A. Harrast and David A. Wood

Introduction

Modern information technology (IT) has greatly expanded the capability of companies to coordinate activities and process large numbers of transactions. Unfortunately, large companies often support thousands of individual applications, and the data necessary for financial reporting is scattered across these applications. As applications and data proliferate, companies must link together the applications and systems, often using spreadsheets and expending significant amounts of time in manual data entry and manipulation. This manual work is slow, expensive, and error prone and lacks useful business insights. Also, the employees who must perform these tasks are often overwhelmed and unsatisfied with the mundane work.

Until recently, there have been no great alternatives outside of expensive new systems or patched-together spreadsheets to deal with the issue of connecting data across the organisation. However, in the early 2000s, several technologies were combined including character recognition (artificial intelligence), screen scraping, and workflow automation, and by 2003, commercial products were being released to automate human–computer interactions (Mullakara, 2019). Robotic process automation (RPA) technology, as it was called by software pioneers (Mullakara, 2019), permits the automation of many human interactions with a computer, including aggregating and entering data. RPA has nothing to do with a physical robot, in spite of its name. Rather, the name connotes eliminating the 'robotic' parts of a process that a human does and replacing them with easily implemented, computerised procedures.

The benefits of RPA have been quite compelling to the market. According to a recent global industry survey of companies across various geographic regions, industries, and sizes, every company in a sample of 450 plans to expand its use of RPA (Protiviti, 2019). The Institute for Robotic Process Automation & Artificial Intelligence estimates cost reductions of 25% to 50% through RPA technology (ISD, 2018). There is a trend of rapid realisation of Return on Investment (ROI) on RPA projects (AIIA Network Research, 2019). While still a relatively modest technology industry, RPA revenue exceeded $1.3 billion in 2018 and is the fastest-growing segment of the global enterprise software market (Gartner Group, 2019). Figure 17.1 shows 2018 vendor revenue for the six highest-grossing RPA products.

DOI: 10.4324/9781003132943-21

RPA Software Revenue 2018 (in $ Millions)

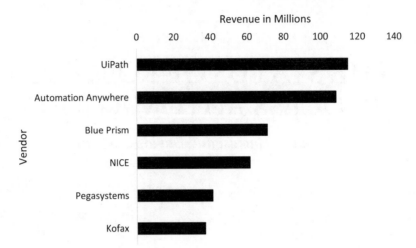

Figure 17.1 RPA software revenue.

Prepared from data contained in 'Gartner Says Worldwide Robotic Process Automation Software Market Grew 63% in 2018' (Gartner Group, 2019).

RPA is being used across all areas of business, but some functions show greater benefits. EY suggests that the accounting, finance, and related industries have the most to gain by using RPA (EY, 2015). The type of activities performed in accounting and finance are often repetitive and involve processes where data is collected from various operational sources, combined and/or consolidated and sometimes rekeyed. Frequently, data is collected from one system and transferred to another, a task for which RPA is well suited. Simple bots can log on, open email, read contents, scrape relevant data, and enter the data into an application. While these tasks are by no means unique to accounting, accounting processes repeat themselves frequently, and large organisations process a high volume of similar transactions. Implementing RPA in accounting and finance thus picks the low-hanging fruit from the efficiency tree.

While it is difficult to predict the future, the trend in commerce certainly seems to be increasing use of IT with the goal of reducing costs or reassigning them to more value-added pursuits. Entities can gain efficiency from bots by automating work that is structured and repetitive. Rather than using a small army of financial reporting staff to aggregate, transform, and re-enter data, bots can be developed to do the data-handling work, so long as it is computerised. We may not see the day when a complex financial document, such as a 10K in the USA, is filed with the touch of a button, but many of the repetitive processes could be automated. This will likely mean that a smaller headcount could do the same job; yet, we are not currently seeing reduced headcount because of RPA; rather employees are able to reallocate the hours saved to more value-adding tasks because of RPA (Cooper et al., 2019).

All things considered, the current status of RPA as a fundamental tool to automate human interaction with a computer is highly regarded, particularly in developed countries with high labour costs. Many companies are dedicated to large-scale automation, and there appears to be little to slow the advance of RPA technology, other than perhaps governance issue as the technology becomes a significant part of business operations and financial reporting. Like the internet in the early 1990s, the potential opportunities of RPA are only beginning to be realised.

In the remainder of this chapter, we take a deep dive into the issues surrounding RPA, when and why it may be the best choice to automate a human data process; how to automate processes, including methods of selecting projects and obtaining training; challenges with bots that have manifested themselves as the technology spreads; and finally, we offer a few thoughts on RPA research topics.

Automation choices

As we discuss various automation technologies in this chapter, we point out that our discussion focuses mainly on RPA technology used to automate data aggregation and transfer previously performed by humans. There are, however, other automating technologies employed for other purposes. For example, financial robots, or FINBOTS, are used heavily in the banking industry to automate answering customer queries using speech recognition and artificial intelligence. Unlike RPA, FINBOTS are generally designed to be customer facing and are used as a substitute for call centre staff. In this chapter, we will focus on RPA rather than FINBOTS or other similar technologies.

RPA is one of several possible choices among automation technologies. In this section, we discuss why one should consider using RPA instead of other automation techniques, including macros or data analysis languages like Python or R (see also Chapter 13). We also discuss RPA relative to the traditional system development lifecycle approach of analysis, design, coding/configuration, testing, and deployment (Romney et al., 2020).

Visual Basic

To begin, we discuss a basic accounting automation technique that has existed for decades, the use of Microsoft's Visual Basic (VBA) coding language as part of Microsoft Excel. VBA is an appropriate tool to automate a process when the data is entirely contained within Excel. Once written, VBA macros can be stored in a macro library and made available to multiple spreadsheets, making them reusable as needed. The shortcoming of macro languages is that they have little ability to interact with other applications. Hence, a macro language is useful for automations within a program, say Excel, but is unable to help with the many accounting tasks that require multiple applications. Also, macro languages require learning a programming language and thus take more time to learn than bots. In summary, macros, while useful for automating single-application tasks, are limited to working within applications and often require programming skills beyond those possessed by the typical business user.

Python/R

As for other options for automating human–computer interactions, computer languages like Python and R are very powerful and adaptable with their many libraries of functions, including the ability to read Excel spreadsheets and many other file formats, to manipulate data to a desired format, and to output data to a file. Nevertheless, Python and R are not designed to interact with other computerised systems at the presentation level (what the user sees), so using these to interact with an application such as SAP requires significant knowledge of the underlying system and is far above the knowledge level of most users.

Systems development

Developing a solution through systems analysis, design, coding/configuration, testing, and deployment is an option for those who are patient and well-funded. Many of the systems' ills arise because of rapidly changing business environments. These rapid changes must be addressed expeditiously, and waiting for an entire systems development cycle to run its course may not be feasible. Take, for example, the acquisition of an entity that now needs to have its accounting reporting combined with other entities. Assuming the company has to file public financial statements every quarter, it may not be possible to even do the analysis before the first quarterly reporting cycle is due. To develop a solution, programmers would need a knowledge of the existing system and program the various applications to integrate together. The various programs involved may not provide application program interfaces (APIs) that allow the programmer to access multiple programs and obtain the objects needed to complete the task, and the entire process is time consuming and expensive.

RPA

Many repetitive accounting/finance projects lend themselves to RPA. RPA technology works with the presentation layer of a system—what a human sees on the screen. Thus, a bot does not interfere with the program's normal functioning, nor must it be programmed to integrate deeply with the software it manipulates. Instead, a bot has a relatively low technical barrier, allowing for much more efficient implementation than a programmed solution (Asquith & Horsman, 2019). The use case for a bot is a situation where multiple programs are accessed, data is collected, transactions are entered, and final reports are generated. This tends to be the type of work performed by accounting and finance professionals.

In summary, while there are a number of automation tools available for accounting and finance tasks, each tool has its limitations, including RPA. Macro languages, like VBA, are largely confined to working within the specific application and require learning a programming language. Data analysis languages, like Python and R, are powerful tools, but they require programming skills that most users simply do not possess. A full systems development process, assuming it includes custom programming, is resource-intensive and may not be warranted for the myriad of small automation tasks required by accountants. The strength of RPA is that it is relatively easy to learn, and it can work across many applications. This makes RPA more available to teams that do not necessarily have a strong programming background.

The automation process

The automation process requires both a macro-level (enterprise) process methodology and a micro-level (individual) training strategy. The macro-level process methodology has been developing in theory and practice, and there are many useful ideas in the academic literature, which we discuss below. We do not wish to assert a one-size-fits-all methodology or that current methods should be adopted entirely—each organisation may have different needs, and we recommend browsing the buffet for the most attractive morsels. At the micro level, individuals will have to be trained in RPA development. Educators may have an interest in RPA from the perspective of training students. In any case, we discuss micro-level training options that could apply in education or industry while highlighting resources that are exclusive to education.

We will begin with a modest example of what an RPA bot can do, as discussed in recent research by Eulerich, Pawlowski et al. (2021). In this instance, an internal audit function for a large company in Europe developed a bot that automatically validates employee mileage reimbursements. Previously, an internal auditor would take a sample of submitted mileage and manually enter the data into an internet mapping service and compare the distance with the employee's self-reported distance. This task was performed annually, and the auditor could only examine a relatively small number of the 4,000+ transactions. However, after learning about RPA, the internal auditors programmed a bot in a few hours to automatically input the addresses into the online mapping service, plot the routes, and compare the results to the employees' self-reported mileage. The auditor then reviewed the output for every single reimbursement. This bot is estimated to save the company 19 hours of work per year while also increasing audit coverage for employee reimbursements to 100%. While 19 hours is a modest number of hours saved, this was one of many bots implemented by the internal audit function.

On its surface, this example is no different from other computer automations where a program is designed to do a manual task. However, beneath the surface is an important difference that highlights the value of RPA. Most computer automations require the involvement of a computer programmer. In contrast, RPA bots can be programmed by internal auditors. That is because of the low-code/no-code approach of RPA; the user of the bot can program it themselves rather than relying on a programming expert who does not have the domain knowledge (e.g. accounting knowledge) of the user. Because of the low-code/no-code approach, accountants can learn to create and deploy simple bots in a timely manner, sometimes in less than day. Thus, RPA allows any user to develop their own automations and does not require waiting (and hoping) for the IT department to develop a solution. Furthermore, RPA can work with existing systems and does not require a time-intensive system development project.

Recent research suggests a four-step process for RPA development (Huang & Vasarhelyi, 2019):

1   Procedure selection
2   Procedure modification
3   Implementation
4   Evaluation and operation.

We use this framework to discuss other prior research that helps users decide what to automate—a key decision in the use of RPA.

Procedure selection

The first step, or stage, in the RPA project completion process involves a review of procedures using a number of criteria to identify those most amenable to RPA. Eulerich, Pawlowski et al. (2021) developed a bot-evaluation framework to help users identify which tasks are most appropriate for automation and prioritise the order of tasks for automation. The framework has three steps: (1) identify if bots are allowable, (2) score tasks, and (3) evaluate scores. We will highlight each of the procedure selection steps below.

Identify if bots are allowable

The framework asks the users to identify whether bots are allowable. Such things as legal requirements, government regulations, ethical considerations, etc. may prohibit the use of bots. Also, users must determine if there is correct and sufficient data available to complete the task.

Score tasks

The framework requires the user to score the task on two dimensions: (1) the technical feasibility of using a bot and (2) the benefits of automation. In assessing technical feasibility, the framework specifies evaluating the following (quoted from Eulerich, Pawlowski et al., 2021):

- **Activity type** refers to the extent to which the audit activity requires human judgement or learning. Despite progress in artificial intelligence and machine learning, bots still tend to struggle with activities that require judgement and learning but do well with rule-based activities.
- **Data structure** refers to the extent to which bot technology is capable of processing the underlying format of the audit data. Bots do better with structured data (e.g. organised number and text data) and not unstructured data (e.g. images). Bots also do better when they can utilise APIs.
- **Process stability** refers to the frequency with which the underlying process changes. Some processes remain the same over time, whereas other processes are constantly fluctuating. Frequent changes to the underlying process will require constant updates to the bot or advanced programming.
- **Development requirements** refer to the amount of time, money, and expertise needed to create the bot. Development requirements tend to increase as the complexity of the process increases or if data requires extra fees (e.g. accessing an API). Development requirements also increase when the task is especially sensitive or must be 'right' every time. Examples of items that increase complexity include the number of exceptions or alternative paths and the number of data sources.
- **RPA as preferred solution** refers to the fact that there are different ways to automate tasks; RPA is just one tool useful for automation. Consider whether other tools would perform the other task more effectively and/or efficiently. RPA is often the best tool when there are multiple systems to work with. For example, if something is to be automated just within Microsoft Excel, a macro would likely be superior, but if the task requires interacting with Excel, the company ERP, and an internet website, RPA is likely superior.

In assessing potential benefits of the bot, the framework specifies evaluating the following (quoted from Eulerich, Pawlowski et al., 2021):

- **Effort needed for activity** refers to the amount of time and/or mental energy needed to perform the audit activity (and not the creation of the bot). Audit activities that require a large amount of time across all team members or that are boring and result in mental exhaustion provide greater benefit once automated.
- **Frequency of activity** refers to the number of times the activity occurs within a given time period. Activities that occur more often are more beneficial to automate.
- **Need for quality improvement** refers to the extent to which the current audit activity needs to improve in terms of quality. This can include benefits of increased scope, meaning auditors can now audit 100% or near 100% of populations. Also, it is more

beneficial to automate activities that have higher risk and therefore require higher degrees of quality and fewer errors. Current audit processes with high error rates are also good targets.

- **Useful life** refers to the amount of time the bot will be useful. If the audit activity changes or is discontinued, then this can shorten the useful life of a bot.
- **Organisational value** refers to the extent to which the bot is useful to other groups within the organisation outside of audit. Bots developed by auditors may be leveraged by other groups (e.g. advisory or support functions), resulting in additional benefits to the organisation.

These attributes are similar to those specified in other studies (e.g. see Fung, 2014; Lacity et al., 2015; Willcocks & Lacity, 2016; Vishnu et al., 2017; Leshob et al., 2018; Moffitt et al., 2018; Schuler & Gehring, 2018; Kokina & Blanchette, 2019; Santos et al., 2019; Harrast, 2020). These studies also often include some other considerations. Eulerich, Pawlowski et al. (2021) took the list of attributes from these studies, and a few others identified by professionals, and validated the list with working professionals and academics. Thus, the above items provide a strong set of validated characteristics necessary to consider for automating a task with RPA.

Evaluate scores

The framework has the user plot scores for the technical feasibility and benefits of the bot scores, and that helps the user visualise the various bots and select those that are both possible to automate and will bring the highest rewards. This step prioritises bot development for the bots that will yield the greatest return.

This framework was validated with a case study of a Big 4 accounting firm, external auditors, and internal auditors. It was also used by the internal audit function of a large corporation to help in the process of automating (and decision not to automate) several processes and tasks. Overall, it was deemed helpful by all these groups.

Procedure modification

Even after selecting a process for automation, it may be necessary or advantageous to amend the process before undertaking automation. There is a debate often held at professional conferences about whether it is better to automate a poorly functioning process or to fix the process first and then automate the fixed process. While it seems obvious to first fix a poorly functioning process, practitioners at several RPA conferences argued against this for a few reasons. It can often be a time-consuming task to redesign a poorly functioning process. Taking the time to do this can remove focus from the potential for RPA and thus lose supporters for RPA within the organisation. Also, the professionals argue that poorly functioning manual processes can often result in significant time loss, but poorly functioning automated tasks lose very little time (i.e. the time loss may be seconds or minutes on a computer rather than hours and days for a manual process). Thus, automating a poorly functioning process may result in 80% of the benefit, and the redesign may result in only 20% improvement, but the redesign may take 80% of the time to perform, whereas the RPA automation would only take 20% of the time. This is an area where professionals would benefit from academic research and guidance that can shed light on this important issue.

Implementation

If RPA software has not been licensed, this will have to be worked out with the chosen RPA vendor. Major vendors include Automation Anywhere, UiPath, and Blue Prism, as well as other smaller players. Once the software licences are acquired, development can begin according to the governance philosophy of individual companies. Some companies prefer to commission a group to lead development of RPA projects (often creating a 'centre of excellence'), while others are more laissez-faire, leaving bot development up to the time and talents of individuals. With relatively little training, individuals without a programming background can create bots, and we agree with the philosophy of allowing some 'grassroots' bot development. Nevertheless, a philosophy of pure 'grassroots' development may not be optimal, particularly in accounting and finance functions where internal controls, business continuity, and other risks need to be managed.

Our thoughts are that developing a group of individuals to support and provide oversight into RPA development has a better chance of developing a useful portfolio of bots than a pure laissez-faire approach, and a hybrid approach may be most effective—especially in larger organisations. Under a hybrid approach, a centralised group could oversee and develop bots at the enterprise level, while individuals could undertake smaller-scale, individual projects. The centralised group could also maintain a catalogue of bot information such as purpose, usage, and credential information. This would help identify popular bots, their purpose, and how to run them so that bots continue to function despite staff turnover. This group could also review and improve highly used bots to make sure they function appropriately. Bots involved in the financial reporting process might require additional documentation and monitoring to remain compliant with auditing regulations.

Evaluation and operation

Huang & Vasarhelyi (2019) suggest that parallel testing be used to validate the operation of the bot, at least in the case of an audit task where detection risk is an issue (for an example of parallel testing, see Christ, Emett et al., 2021). To do a parallel test, manual operations and the bot would each receive the same data inputs. The bot would operate independent of the manual process, and when completed, the outputs of the two processes would be compared and/or reconciled. This will ensure the completeness and accuracy of outputs from RPA. Once validated, the RPA process could be used in the future. In addition, in any process that impacts the reliability of financial reporting, documentation of the procedure will need to be maintained for review by either internal or external auditors to provide a basis for relying upon the information outputs. Also, almost all RPA software has programmed diagnostics that help in the evaluation of bot performance. These diagnostics can help identify where exceptions are occurring in the bot processing. All of these should be reviewed to determine and document whether the bot is reliable enough to be moved into production.

Learning to develop bots

In the sections above, we have discussed RPA development from a macro or general methodology perspective. Below we discuss RPA development from the micro or individual perspective. This involves describing the various trainings available for both academic and industry users.

Training and software

Training in a specific RPA technology is an important aspect of a successful bot development strategy. Most major vendors have invested significantly in free online training, as well as live training, for those living in major metropolitan areas or willing to travel. Most bot vendors also offer certifications as an incentive to progress through training, and most offer trial and student licences for those wanting to train without the fixed cost of a software licence. Simple bots can be constructed within a day of instruction, but deeper expertise takes time. Continual training is also necessary, as RPA products are rapidly changing and growing in their abilities and complexity. To facilitate getting started with training, we include the names of three large vendors, their websites, and resources, in Table 17.1.

Resources for academics

For academic institutions, there are several additional teaching resources available. The largest set of teaching resources is provided for free by the EY Academic Resource Center (EY ARC). The EY ARC has produced six case studies and overview materials as part of their 'Innovation Mindset' materials. The materials can be accessed by university professors by going to https://www.ey.com/us/arc and requesting access permission. Each case comes with case material, solutions (in this case working bots), full data sets, videos showing exactly how to build the bots, and notes on how to use the cases in class. For ease of use, we provide the summary description of each case below:

- Billing case: students help automate an existing manual process to bill customers for wood products sold by Wood's Amazing Woods Inc. This case has three parts, which increase with complexity.
- Tax form preparation case: students help automate the preparation of tax Form 8805 for each foreign partner from RiverBend Technologies whose earnings derive from the US and abroad. Students are required to create a separate tax form (a pdf file) for each foreign partner using the tax data provided.
- Sales reporting case: students help automate the creation of sales reports for Pure Guitar Inc. Students are required to generate a report in Microsoft Word with the information segregated by employee and by quarter and displayed using an Excel bar chart. Students will use the data from two.csv files and an Access database.

Table 17.1 Major RPA vendors, URLs, and resources

Vendor	URL	Resources
Blue Prism	https://blueprism.com/	Evaluation licence, training, educator licence
UIPath	https://www.uipath.com/rpa/academic–alliance/join	Evaluation licence, training, educator licence
AutomationAnywhere	https://university.automationanywhere.com	Evaluation licence, training, educator licence

- Audit sample selection case: students are expected to automate the selection of a sample of expenses for testing for audit purposes based on (1) a systematic selection of key transactions above or below a specified threshold and (2) a random selection of non-key transactions that do not meet the specified threshold. The case also requires students to automate the documentation of the selection procedures performed within audit working papers. This case is complex.
- Travel expense audit case: students gather data to perform an internal audit of travel expenses. Employees have submitted trips for reimbursement that include the address from which the employee left, the address to where they travelled, and the employee's self-reported mileage for the trip. Students will manually perform the task of mapping distances using a commercial mapping service (Google Maps). Students will next write a bot that automates this process and then calculates the difference between the distances the bot collected and the employees' self-reported distances. This bot is patterned after the use case previously discussed and contained in the article by Eulerich, Pawlowski et al. (2021).
- Bot-a-thon case: students will identify a process in business or in their personal life that can be automated using RPA and develop the bot to automate this process. Students can develop a bot that has different levels of sophistication in terms of how many programs it interacts with and that uses various principles (variables, looping, if/then logic, try/catch activity). Students are also encouraged to learn on their own and teach themselves an additional principle, technique, activity, or anything else unique that they can demonstrate with the bot.

There are many low-cost options available for learning RPA. Both academics and private-sector employees can access many of the resources, although there are resources available only to academics. Individuals tend to learn RPA skills at a fast pace and can become productive bot developers within a short time.

Challenges with bots

RPA technology has reached the level of maturity where bot problems are surfacing (Eulerich, Wagener et al., 2021). While some issues could have been expected, there are always unknowns that surface over time and need to be addressed. In this section of the chapter, we discuss some of the bot issues that have surfaced including maintenance needs of bots, bot quality compared to conventional systems development, substituting bots for needed system development, internal controls considerations, and issues with employee acceptance.

Maintaining bots

While bots are reliable in terms of following a defined process, they do depend partly on artificial intelligence, such as optical character recognition to read text and values from screens. Over time, as websites and other applications change, bots may require maintenance to correct degraded performance. Unfortunately, maintenance is a reality that needs to be planned as part of the overhead of using bots. Clues about the need for maintenance can be found in diagnostic files, which should be monitored to detect issues with performance. Where the skills exist, internal audit might examine and test bot functions periodically (Christ, Eulerich et al., 2021). Whatever the case, bots cannot be set free and forgotten. As systems change, some maintenance is likely.

Bot quality

In spite of, and perhaps because of their popularity, bots tend to be more fragile than applications developed through programmed solutions. There simply is not the same depth of analysis and design normally required in a full systems development project using a programmed/coded solution. While bots have development speed on their side, quality is sometimes sacrificed. Bots also depend on the ability to interface with other systems, which may be an issue if the bot's underlying technology is incompatible with a particular system. Many of the major RPA vendors report limitations on bot compatibility (Asquith & Horsman, 2019).

Bot quality can be partly a governance issue. While formal systems development procedures for coded solutions are well established, governance is still an evolving issue with bots. Because simple bots can be created by individuals and non-technical users, there can be grassroots, user development. There are several risks to quality with user development, including the risks inherent in what has become known as shadow IT. Shadow IT involves user-developed applications that may not be supported within the IT structure of the enterprise. Because these applications are unsupported, risks may exist that are not properly documented and controlled. Likening bots to producing Excel workbooks, most business users can prepare an Excel workbook; however, when the workbook becomes more complex (e.g. using advanced formulas, multiple worksheets), the probability of errors increases dramatically without a commensurate increase in scepticism and auditing of these worksheets (e.g. see Myers et al., 2017). If something similar happens to bots, we could see substantial issues with quality for companies that allow user developers.

Development substitute

Another possible issue is that bots may be substituted for needed systems development (Eulerich et al., 2021). In the short run, bots may be a cost-saving 'band aid,' at the cost of long-term benefits from maintaining an adequate investment in IT. Bots also add a layer of complexity to the IT infrastructure that complicates future development projects. While researchers have only tangentially studied this issue, overusing bots to gloss over system defects could be a sign of insufficient IT investment and eventually lead to performance as well as governance issues. There is a need for researchers to address these potential limitations and concerns with RPA moving forward.

Internal control

Creating a bot in the accounting and finance area is likely to require some type of auditable control to ensure that control goals are met. For example, a bot might extract invoice information and send electronic payments to vendors. As assets need to be secured, there would need to be controls around this to prevent the loss of assets and ensure the reliability of the reporting process. Even if the risk of asset loss is absent, there may be critical processes where risks to completeness, accuracy, and validity must be controlled.

Internal controls also involve separation of duties to ensure that incompatible functions are not performed by the same individual. In the domain of RPA, proper authorisation takes on greater importance, as the bot will execute once activated—a bot will do exactly what it is programmed to do. Access to bots should be controlled, as anyone with the bot credentials may activate the bot and execute transactions. Similarly, bots that record transactions should be separated from custody and safeguarding to ensure that asset discrepancies cannot be covered up by changing accounting records. As an example, warehouse employees should not have access to a bot (or other means) that would allow them to update inventory records.

Employee acceptance

Employee attitudes about technology can vary dramatically, often by employee experience level (Cooper et al., 2021). Experienced employees may feel that new technologies threaten their human capital, tilting the advantage towards younger employees who may have greater technological agility. At any level of experience, technology can be disruptive as old systems give way to new and employees are asked to adapt. Some will see technology as a threat to job security, while others may tolerate the new technology and hope it goes away. One way to view RPA technology is that it gives individuals an opportunity to take control of their work. In other words, if aggregating data and entering transactions consume much of the workday, RPA offers an opportunity to automate these tasks so that employees can undertake more value-added activities. RPA skills are sought after and may pave the way to better opportunities. Nevertheless, employees are all different, and some will accept and leverage RPA, while others may see the new technology as a threat. There is a large and interesting body of knowledge on organisational change and change resistance in the management literature; nevertheless, the topic is beyond the scope of this chapter.

Headcount reduction

Automation of manual tasks often raises understandable concerns about job loss. An early example of the concern over automation dates to the early 1800s. The Luddites were a secret organisation of English textile workers who agreed to destroy any textile machinery because of concerns that the machines would take human workers' jobs. Since those times, automation of all sorts has garnered strong fears that jobs will be destroyed. Indeed, significant research has studied employees' resistance to change for technology and other reasons (e.g. see the following meta-analyses on the topic: Thundiyil et al., 2015; Peng, Li, Wang, & Lin, 2020).

There are predictions that recent forms of automation, including RPA, will significantly reduce headcount. For example, the Everest group estimates that automation (including RPA) will decrease full-time equivalent employees by 25% to 40% (Everest Group, 2014). Anecdotal evidence does not support the idea that RPA, as currently being implemented, will reduce headcount. The accounting firms are investing enormous resources into technology. For example, PwC has reported they will spend $12 billion on technology and related issues and hire 100,000 new employees by 2026—the current headcount at PwC is 284,000 employees (DiNapoli, 2021). If technology, including RPA, reduces headcount, then it is difficult to understand the positive correlation of hiring and technology investment reported by PwC.

Related to headcount, RPA is not a technology designed to displace employees' entire jobs. Rather, RPA typically automates portions of an employee's work—10% of one task and 15% of a different task. If each employee has 10% to 30% more time, it seems likely the company will redeploy those resources into value-adding activities rather than reducing headcount. As additional anecdotal evidence, we spoke with one executive at a Fortune 50 company, and he said currently their analysts spend 80% to 90% of their time just preparing data to analyse and not adding value by doing the analyses they were hired to do. This executive hoped to increase automation so the analysts could 'do their job' of providing recommendations and suggestions and adding value. The executive stated that if the analysts could shift to doing more value-adding work, the company would likely increase hiring to implement all of the new recommendations that the analysts would be providing. Thus, it was this executive's opinion that RPA would not decrease hiring but could actually increase it. Overall, the decision to retain employees is a multifactor decision, and technology is only one factor.

Future research

Within the chapter, we have mentioned several ideas for future research in RPA. In this section we consolidate those ideas and augment with a few additional thoughts. The ideas are presented in three sections: (1) Education Research, (2) Practice-Relevant Research, and (3) Theory Contribution Research.

Education research

We believe that teaching RPA in a university setting is supported for several reasons, including the need for increasing digital acumen and technology skills among new professionals (AICPA/NASBA, 2021). Recent research by Harrast et al. (2021) shows that accounting professionals support the introduction of critical technologies in education and would likely welcome the idea that students have some exposure to RPA coming into practice. If RPA does have a place in the curriculum, there are several issues to consider including:

- How do we teach RPA technology skills most effectively?
- What content is best taught at university versus in practice?
- What is more effective, teaching technology to accountants or teaching accounting to technical people?
- Is RPA more important to students than computer programming using Python or R?
- If RPA is taught, what should be removed from the curriculum to make room for this new content?
- How can RPA, or related technologies, be used in academic settings to make professors' work more efficient?

Practice-relevant research

In general, education lags behind practice in technology usage, and often conducted research is not relevant to practice (Burton et al., 2021a, 2021b). In the RPA realm, there are many important, practice-relevant questions where academics can add value. One important area is RPA governance, but there are others. An issue that all service firms are facing is how to price services in a digital world. As processes become more efficient, how will this affect pricing? Below are a few practice issues to consider:

- How to encourage bot development without losing control of it?
- Centralised versus decentralised bot development and bot quality. What is the measure of quality, and what structure is most likely to achieve quality?
- How do we audit these approaches?
- How to implement RPA? For example, fix the process first and then automate second, or automate first and fix the process second.
- How do we price services in this new digital world?

Many of these issues are already being addressed in practice, so it might be useful to use field or survey research to learn which approaches are being taken. Once the modal techniques are known, more diagnostic questions can be pursued.

Theory contribution research

Theoretical research could answer useful questions about the differences between human and machine—what are humans best at, and what can be turned over to a machine? Some cultures severely limit technology and seem to be doing well enough without it (Kraybill et al., 2018), while people employed by large organisations spend the majority of their workdays on a computer. Computers certainly make us more efficient, but this often leads to more tasks. So how can, or should, humans and computers coexist? And, although the idea of automating tasks is appealing, is there a downside? We list several possible research topics below:

- What can and cannot be automated in accounting? What must the human do and why?
- Is RPA slowing down or speeding up system development? Is the 'band-aid' healing or hurting the overall system development life cycle? How can we tell if RPA is being substituted for needed systems development? What is the effect of delaying systems development?
- Does RPA help or hurt the IT department?

While we see RPA as a very useful technology, it is still part of a proliferation of applications that help us manage our work lives, as well as making our lives more difficult when the applications fail to function as designed. Technology is great—when it works.

Conclusions

In this chapter, we have discussed the current status of RPA, including when and why it may be the best choice to automate a data-handling process involving a human and a computer, its effects on employment in industry, the automation process, training opportunities and ideas for future research.

RPA technology was developed to permit the automation of many human interactions with a computer, including the aggregation of data from multiple systems, data transformation and data entry into production systems, and/or reports. Companies are attracted to RPA because of the potential to make processes more efficient and accurate. RPA technology works with the presentation layer of a computerised system—what a human sees on the screen. Thus, a bot does not interfere with the program's normal functioning, nor does it integrate with the software it operates. The strength of RPA is that it is relatively easy to learn. This makes RPA more available to teams that do not necessarily have a strong programming background.

RPA is most successful in processes that are well defined, highly repetitive, and mature (Lacity et al., 2015; Eulerich et al., 2021). Other things being equal, a process that consumes more time resources is likely to yield a greater ROI (Harrast, 2020). Conversely, high-level processes, such as strategic management tasks, requiring unstructured data and unique analyses are less likely to benefit from RPA. Manual processes not employing a computer, such as manual check writing or completing other business forms, cannot currently leverage RPA technology without computerising the process. Creating a bot in the accounting and finance area is likely to require some type of auditable control to ensure that control goals are met.

Educational faculty can obtain training materials online for classroom use from EY ARC at https://www.ey.com/us/arc. In addition to resources available to educators, most RPA software vendors have a significant portfolio of training options available. Many also offer certifications as an incentive to progress through training, as well as offering trial and student licences for those wanting to train but not yet ready to purchase the software. Simple bots are not difficult to write and can be constructed within a day of instruction.

There is little evidence that RPA technology is reducing employee headcount, at least currently for domestic workers. RPA reduces the amount of time spent on repetitive tasks, allowing more time for value-added analyses. This allows employees to engage in more value-added activities. Companies that are investing significant resources in RPA have announced increases in hiring.

Since bots are a relatively new technology, there are many interesting questions for researchers to investigate. Perhaps the most immediate question is whether and how RPA should be taught to students. There are many other possible research topics for those interested. This is a ripe area for researchers, and we hope this chapter has helped to steer future researchers towards areas for further investigation.

References

AICPA/NASBA. (2021). *Accounting Program Curriculum Gap Analysis*. https://www.evolutionofcpa. org/Documents/Accounting%20Program%20Curriculum%20Gap%20Analysis%20Report%20 3.15.2021.pdf

AIIA Network Research. (2019, February 11). *Rapid ROI from RPA: Synergy Case Study*. https://www. intelligentautomation.network/intelligent-automation/case-studies/rapid-roi-from-rpa

Asquith, A., & Horsman, G. (2019). Let the robots do it! – Taking a look at robotic process automation and its potential application in digital forensics. *Forensic Science International: Reports, 1*.

Burton, F.G., Summers, S.L., Wilks, T.J., & Wood, D.A. (2021a). Do we matter? The attention policy makers, academics, and the general public give to accounting research. *Issues in Accounting Education*, 36(1), 1–22.

Burton, F.G., Summers, S.L., Wilks, T.J., & Wood. D.A. (2021b). Relevance of accounting research (ROAR) scores: Ratings of abstracts by accounting professionals. *Accounting Horizons*, 36(2), 7–18.

Christ, M.H., Emett, S.A., Summers, S.L. & Wood. D.A. (2021). Prepare for takeoff: Improving asset measurement and audit quality with drone-enabled inventory audit procedures. *Review of Accounting Studies*, 26, 1323–1343.

Christ, M.H., Eulerich, M., Krane, R., & Wood, D.A. (2021). New frontiers for internal audit research. *Accounting Perspectives*, 20(4), 449–475.

Cooper, L., Holderness, D.K., Sorensen, T., & Wood, D.A. (2019). Robotic process automation in public accounting. *Accounting Horizons*, 33(4), 15–35.

Cooper, L., Holderness, D.K., Sorensen, T., & Wood, D.A. (2021). Perceptions of robotic process automation in Big 4 public accounting firms: Do firm leaders and lower-level employees agree? *Journal of Emerging Technologies in Accounting*. Forthcoming.

DiNapoli, J. (2021, June 15). PwC planning to hire 100,000 over five years in major ESG push. *Reuters*. https://www.reuters.com/business/sustainable-business/pwc-planning-hire-100000-over-five-years-major-esg-push-2021-06-15/

Eulerich, M., Pawlowski, J., Waddoups, N.J., & Wood, D.A. (2021). A framework for using robotic process automation for audit tasks. *Contemporary Accounting Research*. 39(1), 691–720.

Eulerich, M., Wagener, M., Waddoups, N.J., & Wood, D.A. (2021). The dark side of robotic process automation. [Working Paper]. University of Duisburg-Essen, University of Denver, and Brigham Young University.

Everest Group. (2014, October 28). Automation could replace 25–40% of FTEs. https://www.everest-grp.com/tag/robotics/page/4/

EY. (2015). *Robotic Process Automation* [White Paper]. https://www.ey.com/Publication/vwLUAssets/-ey-robotic-process-automation-white-paper/$FILE/ey-robotic-process-automation.pdf

Fung, H.P. (2014, July). Criteria, use cases and effects of Information Technology Process Automation (ITPA). *Advances in Robotics and Automation, 3*(3), 1–10. https://www.researchgate.net/publication/274378872_Criteria_Use_Cases_and_Effects_of_Information_Technology_Process_Automation_ITPA

Gartner Group. (2019, June 24). Gartner says worldwide Robotic Process Automation software market grew 63% in 2018 [Press release]. https://www.gartner.com/en/newsroom/press-releases/2019-06-24-gartner-says-worldwide-robotic-process-automation-sof

Harrast, S. (2020). Robotic process automation in accounting systems. *The Journal of Corporate Accounting & Finance, 31*(4), 209–213.

Harrast, S., Olsen, L., & Sun, Y. (2021). Critical technologies and their importance to career success [Working Paper]. Central Michigan University.

Huang, F., & Vasarhelyi, M. (2019). Applying Robotic Process Automation (RPA) in auditing: A framework. *International Journal of Accounting Information Systems, 35*, 100433.

ISD. (2018). The automation of knowledge work will be this decade [sic] engine of growth. https://www.isd-community.com/actualites/the-automation-of-knowledge-work-will-be-this-decade-engine-of-growth.html

Kokina, J., & Blanchette, S. (2019, November). Early evidence of digital labor in accounting: Innovation with Robotic Process Automation. *International Journal of Accounting Information Systems, 35.* https://www.researchgate.net/publication/337358544_Early_evidence_of_digital_labor_in_accounting_Innovation_with_Robotic_Process_Automation

Kraybill, D., Johnson-Weiner, K. & Nolt, S. (2018). *The Amish.* Johns Hopkins University Press.

Lacity, M., Willcocks, L.P., & Craig, A. (2015). Robotic process automation at Telefonica O2 [Working paper]. https://www.umsl.edu/~lacitym/TelefonicaOUWP022015FINAL.pdf

Leshob, A., Bourgouin, A., & Renard, L. (2018). Towards a process analysis approach to adopt Robotic Process Automation. 2018 IEEE 15th International Conference on e-Business Engineering. https://www.researchgate.net/publication/330030061_Towards_a_Process_Analysis_Approach_to_Adopt_Robotic_Process_Automation

Moffitt, K., Rozario, A., & Vasarhelyi, M. (2018). Robotic process automation for auditing. *Journal of Emerging Technologies in Accounting, 15*(1), 1–10.

Mullakara, Nandan (2019, April 10). The remarkable history of Robotic Process Automation (RPA). *Nandan Mullakara.* https://nandan.info/history-of-robotic-process-automation-rpa/

Myers, N., Starliper, M., Summers, S., & Wood, D. (2017). The impact of shadow IT systems on perceived information credibility and managerial decision making. *Accounting Horizons, 31*(3), 105–123.

Peng, J. Li, M., Wang, Z., & Lin, Y. (2020). Transformational leadership and employees' reactions to organizational change: Evidence from a meta-analysis. *The Journal of Applied Behavioral Science, 57* (3), 369–397.

Protiviti. (2019). 2019 Robotic Process Automation Survey. https://www.protiviti.com/US-en/insights/rpa-survey

Romney, M., Steinbart, P., Summers, S., & Wood, D. (2020). *Accounting Information Systems* (15th ed.). Pearson.

Santos, F., Pereira, R., & Vasconcelos, J. (2019, September). Toward Robotic Process Automation implementation: An end-to-end perspective. *Business Process Management Journal.* https://www.researchgate.net/publication/336151940_Toward_robotic_process_automation_implementation_an_end-to-end_perspective

Schuler, J., & Gehring, F. (2018). Implementing robust and low-maintenance Robotic Process Automation (RPA) solutions in large organisations [SSRN Working Paper]. https://papers.ssrn.com/sol3/papers.cfm?abstract_id=3298036

Thundiyil, T. G., Chiaburu, D. S., Oh, I., Banks, G. C., & Peng, A. C. (2015). Cynical about change? A preliminary meta-analysis and future research agenda. *The Journal of Applied Behavioral Science,* 51 (4): 429–450.

Vishnu, S., Agochiya, V., & Plakar, R. (2017, April 1). Data-centered dependencies and opportunities for Robotic Process Automation in banking. *Capco.* https://www.capco.com/Capco-Institute/Journal-45-Transformation/Data-centered-dependencies-and-opportunities-for-robotics-process-automation-in-banking

Willcocks, L., & Lacity, M. (2016). *Service Automation Robots and the Future of Work.* SB Publishing.

18

ACCOUNTING INFORMATION SYSTEMS

Supporting business strategy

Victoria Paulsson and Malcolm Brady

Introduction

Businesses in the 21st century are supported by accounting information systems (AIS). Among the most widely known AIS in business organisations are enterprise resource planning (ERP) systems and business intelligence (BI). Newcomers such as cloud computing technology for software, platform and infrastructure services over the Internet, cryptocurrencies and blockchains have recently become prevalent. These AIS have become more and more significant in the past two decades across departments and business organisations around the globe (Berry et al., 2009; Brukhanskyi & Spilnyk, 2019). Arguments to invest in AIS are multiple, but two key themes suggested in the literature are the potential for cost saving from improved operations and the capacity to support business strategies (Svejvig and Jensen, 2012).

This chapter examines the latter of these two themes: the use of AIS to support business strategy. The chapter takes as its starting point Porter's (1980) two generic business strategies: cost leadership and differentiation. The chapter also considers two approaches to AIS acquisition: bespoke development and off-the-shelf purchase. These two dimensions – generic business strategy and software acquisition mode – provide a framework for analysis of AIS support for firms with the four quadrants of the framework providing the basis for this chapter. The chapter ends with a discussion of new developments in strategy and the ability of AIS to continue supporting business strategies, given the recent advent of platform businesses, artificial intelligence, cryptocurrencies and blockchain technologies. This leads to an enhanced framework for AIS taking into account three key dimensions: the generic strategy adopted, the make or buy decision for software and the extent of sharing of the ledger using blockchain technology. A key contribution of the chapter is the identification of the critical factors involved in the choice of AIS to support the business strategy.

According to Porter (1980), business strategies fall under two main headings: cost leadership and differentiation. Cost leadership emphasises the cost element of the business profit formula; firms that follow such a strategy place continual emphasis on keeping their costs down. A differentiation strategy emphasises the revenue element of the profit; firms that follow such a strategy emphasise adding value by meeting customer needs more precisely, and charging a premium price for doing so. Given that each of these strategies can be followed

DOI: 10.4324/9781003132943-22

across a broad or narrow range of the market, Porter (1980) suggests that cost leadership and differentiation strategies can be either broadly based or focused. Strategies, in turn, are implemented by carrying out activities in the firm's value chain (Porter, 1985). The activities to concentrate on must be carefully chosen: first, they must be effective; second, they must be carried out efficiently. Among the activities carried out by firms are providing firm infrastructure: this includes the provision of the information systems that underpin the firm.

Two decisions to take into consideration when thinking about investing in any AIS application are: what AIS will best support the firm's generic strategy? and what software acquisition mode should the firm employ? With respect to generic strategy, a decision to be a differentiator may require companies to create their own AIS, one that best fits their unique business requirements. On the other hand, a decision to be a cost leader will more likely take companies down the packaged software route, better known as an *off-the-shelf* solution, to save on software development costs (Daneshgar et al., 2013). However, this may not always be the case: Walmart, an archetypal cost leader, gains significant competitive advantage from its proprietary and specific use of information technology (IT). With respect to the second question – software acquisition mode – the available options tend to cluster around building the AIS in-house or buying a solution. Two critical elements of this build or buy decision are the level of access to IT expertise and security of data and software.

Elements of AIS strategy

Costs

All costs associated with AIS, such as software development, licence fee, implementation and other ongoing costs, should be taken into consideration in a strategic decision. Traditionally, buying software incurs lower costs than developing software. However, hidden costs from off-the-shelf software, like implementation costs, ongoing support and maintenance fees, may be significant in the long run. Larger organisations may find it easier to gain access to financial resources required to develop their own AIS applications, but smaller organisations may find such commitment daunting (Daneshgar et al., 2013).

For a buy decision, the typical AIS acquisition process can be lengthy and expensive. Using an example of an ERP system, it is reported that a standard ERP implementation project lasts on average 15.7 months, with a mean project cost around $4.5 million and with more than 55% of projects exceeding their budgets (Kimberling, 2015). A recent report from Panorama Consulting, an ERP consulting firm, suggests that reasons behind an ERP project cost overrun include an unplanned expansion of project scope and an underestimation of project staff required, in addition to many other technical, organisational and data issues (Panorama, 2021). Regardless of a decision to build or buy AIS, cost overrun is a risk that should always be taken into consideration. Although every organisation is different and each has substantially different requirements in responding to their business strategies, an in-house-developed AIS solution will likely cost more than a purchased AIS solution (Daneshgar et al., 2013).

Business strategies

Companies with a unique set of requirements corresponding to their business strategies are likely to end up developing their own software. Bespoke AIS can support either cost leadership or differentiation strategies but in different ways. A large retailer such as Walmart may invest heavily in technology to allow it to gain efficiencies in distribution and logistics. Technology is a key factor in Walmart's implementation of its low-cost strategic approach and also in Dell's low-cost, direct-sales business model. On the other hand, differentiators may use IT to provide extra value to customers, as car manufacturer Lexus does with its service centres.

Firms, both cost leaders and differentiators, may buy their AIS from a vendor rather than build it from scratch. The important factor is that the AIS, whatever its origin, fits with and supports the business strategy. e.g. an off-the-shelf ERP system may support a low-cost strategy by providing detailed cost and value information for products, resources, equipment and facilities. The same off-the-shelf ERP system may support a differentiation strategy by providing detailed, precise information that allows the firm tailor its offering to meet particular customer needs. Such suitable off-the-shelf ERP systems can support business strategy at potentially much lower cost than can bespoke systems which are typically more expensive.

Customisation provides a middle ground between a pure build or buy decision. It allows companies to combine advantages from using more cost-efficient, off-the-shelf solution and abilities to answer their strategic needs. However, issues can arise. Customisation is highly complicated, costly and likely to cause problems in the long run for software updates and maintenance. The customised software may not be compatible with the vendor's standard updates and maintenance releases in a future period (Quattrone & Hopper, 2006). Therefore, customisation should be kept at a minimum level, tending towards what is known as *plain vanilla* implementation (Finney & Corbett, 2007).

One factor that is likely to affect a decision to build, buy or customise is firm size. This is particularly so for multi-business firms or conglomerates: the more diverse the range of business units within the firm, the more strategies it may need to employ. Child (1972) suggests that as a firm increases in size, it obtains more opportunities for specialisation; however, this can render strategic coordination among diverse organisational units more challenging. Thus, larger firms often find standard, off-the-shelf software solutions unsuitable for supporting the business strategies for each and every business unit that they have. For larger organisations, which tend to have demanding business requirements, many types of AIS must be purposefully implemented together to support them. At an operational level, the ERP system is key as it provides a single database to consolidate operational data across organisations (Mabert et al., 2003). At a strategic level, decision support systems, e.g. BI, retrieve ERP transactional data to forecast and support strategic business decisions (Chen et al., 2012). The *big data* technology could harvest data outside the ERP system, e.g. census, labour and macro-economic data, which strengthen business decision making (Warren et al., 2015).

Generally speaking, smaller firms find it easier than larger firms to implement off-the-shelf AIS solutions as they have simpler business requirements (Markus & Tanis, 2000). An empirical study reports a significant difference between large and small firms with regard to ERP customisations (Mabert et al., 2003). Over 50% of large companies went through either significant or major customisations, but small firms only made minor customisations. The research suggests that large firms may find it impossible not to customise. After all, their complex operations and organisational structure create a pressure for more tailor-made processes and reports.

Access to IT expertise

To build and maintain software and data in-house requires a high level of IT expertise within firms. The overall key competency in the IT industry has shifted from *delivering a technology-based solution* to *managing a solution delivery process* (Bullen et al., 2009). In other words, the focus of the IT industry is no longer on software development but on implementing and customising existing software to fit business requirements. Therefore, firms might find it challenging to find competent IT professionals to deliver technology-based solutions in-house. Additionally, a complication of using in-house expertise is that firms must continually find new projects for these people to work on. Smaller organisations might not have sufficient project work in the long run.

An alternative to building in-house expertise is to outsource the development work to a third-party organisation. Outsourcing is a practice that has been greatly utilised in the IT industry since the 1990s (Lacity & Hirschheim, 2012). It promises European and US Chief Information Officers (CIOs) a saving of 10%–50% on their IT expenditures, along with a superior level of performance. Outsourcing can help companies eliminate the problems of recruiting, managing and maintaining an in-house IT competency. However, recent research suggests that outsourcing is not a silver bullet (Kobelsky & Robinson, 2010, Lacity & Hirschheim, 2012). Many organisations find themselves worse off from outsourcing agreements in comparison to their prior in-house IT departments. e.g. Lacity & Hirschheim (2012) remark that it is tricky to think of outsourcing companies as a strategic partner. Outsourcing companies exist to earn profits in their own right, not to share their profits[1] with any other party. This is contradictory to the business partner concept, in which firms engage in mutual activity to gain reciprocal benefit.

Another solution to compensate for a lack of in-house IT expertise is to hire IT consultants (Chang et al., 2013). Hiring consultants is a common practice for many AIS implementation projects, especially ERP system projects. Consultants are perceived as carriers of knowledge, as they are involved in a similar job function with multiple organisations. Their main duties are to provide technical and business expertise to reduce the client's learning burden, give suggestions on AIS configurations and deliver user training (Chang et al., 2013). However, engaging with IT consultants represents another form of risk. The more firms rely on external expertise, the higher agency[2] risk they incur. Therefore, firms must be careful to select consultants that best fit their problem area; they must be aware of potential problems in a typical IT consultant engagement and put in place mechanisms to control IT consultants in order to minimise any agency risk (Wang et al., 2008).

Security

Security is one of the biggest concerns in AIS since they deal with confidential financial information and other key business information (CIMA, 2015). A decision to either build or buy has its own merits and issues when it comes to security. Purchasing an off-the-shelf system has the advantage that security for the system is developed and simultaneously tested by IT professionals. Earlier versions of off-the-shelf solution have also been tested in real life in many firms, locally or internationally. System bugs or security holes have very likely already been discovered and fixed. On the other hand, any security vulnerability in an off-the-shelf solution, if known to the wrong people, will introduce a serious risk to an organisation that has purchased that software. Most AIS today are connected with other systems through both internal and external networks, especially the Internet (Ellison & Woody, 2010). This interconnectedness has made it more difficult for firms to protect themselves against hackers.

The security merits and demerits for a self-developed system are the opposite from the off-the-shelf solution. Self-developed software is not likely to be subjected to the same level of stringent source code reviews, inspections and walkthroughs, as in off-the-shelf development. This is because a firm has more limited financial resources, expertise and time. This is in contrast to off-the-shelf solutions in which there are many firms pouring resources into source code reviews and software testing. However, although source code is largely proprietary to the organisation, there is still no guarantee that self-developed software will not be a target for hackers as most of these systems are connecting over the Internet.

Regardless of a build or buy decision, other dimensions of security are always of a significant priority to firms. Some of the key security issues are access control, access authentication, data encryption, firewalls, logs and audit trails and human factors (DPC, 2022). An access control protocol ensures that data is accessible only on a need-to-know basis. Those who have access to data must be able to authenticate their accesses through means such as a secure password and an access card with pin code to a computerised data centre. Data encryption is a technology to encode data and information stored on a device in such a way that only intended recipients can decode them. It is a key technology to ensure data is securely transmitted over networks. Firewalls are an essential tool that protects computers, or computer networks, against unauthorised access attempts from outside networks, especially from the Internet. In addition to that, they also prevent internal confidential information from leaving the internal network. Logs and audit trails are put in place to identify system use and to detect abuse. A system should be able to identify who the user is, time of access and any alterations to data files. The logs should be regularly reviewed for abnormal activity.

Human factors also play a key part in ensuring system security. The practice of exploiting humans to get sensitive information is known as *social engineering*. It is one of the biggest threats in cybersecurity (Salahdine & Kaabouch, 2019). No amount of state-of-the-art software security systems can prevent simple human ignorance of security issues. Staff should be informed about their responsibilities for security, e.g. passwords should not be written down and suspicious email attachments should not be opened without a prior virus scan. Security policies and procedures must be put in place and requirement for compliance made clear to staff. Monitoring and control procedures must also be put in place. Cutting-edge technological advancements must be combined with proper staff training and communication.

An AIS strategy framework

The two key questions discussed in the previous section provide the fundamental dimensions for a matrix of AIS strategies that a company may employ (see Figure 18.1). The two-by-two matrix contains four quadrants, each one a key AIS strategy: Differentiator and Build, Differentiator and Buy, Cost leader and Build, and Cost leader and Buy. Each of these AIS strategies is now discussed in more detail.

Differentiator and build

When firms decide to adopt this route, they should ensure that building their own AIS would allow them to build necessary competitive advantages they wish to attain. Paulsson (2013) reports a business case in which a global soft drinks company is employing a self-developed BI, on top of a packaged ERP system, to support the budgeting process within their global chain of organisations. The decision to invest in an in-house BI solution is directly linked with the company's strategy to be present in every corner of the world. As they produce soft drinks, of which water is the major component, it does not make sense from a cost point of view to distribute the product from a few production facilities around the world. To implement the strategy, the company must engage with a large number of

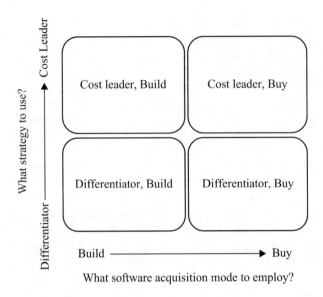

Figure 18.1   Matrix for AIS strategy.

local production facilities to produce and distribute the product, minimising distribution costs. To attract and retain local business partners, revenues are shared between the company and its local partners, depending on business strategies and circumstances in each country. As there is no standard formula to determine the revenue sharing structure between them, employing a standard off-the-shelf software solution was not possible. To accommodate this complicated system of revenue sharing, the company decided to build its own customised BI. In this case, the custom-built BI serves the company's strategy to make their product available around the world.

For strategy-sensitive business decisions, many business controllers and executives around the world rely on spreadsheets to make one-off business decisions (Panko & Port, 2012). This is because there is no predefined formula on how to make a decision on these one-of-a-kind business decisions. Business managers must rely on their understanding of the complex business problem at hand, gather relevant data and formulate a model to support their decisions. Spreadsheets, commonly used in such end-user computing solutions, are not an ideal type of AIS. They can contain errors in calculation formulae since they are rarely tested for bugs or reviewed by third parties. They might not cost money in real terms, as a company has already employed the very person who develops the spreadsheets, and the company does not have to hire anyone to do this work. However, there may be a significant opportunity cost because every minute that business managers spend on developing spreadsheets is lost time, time in which that they could have carried out their primary responsibilities in managing and running the business. Also, business managers typically are not trained in spreadsheet development, and therefore, they are likely to spend significantly more time than would an IT professional. Despite their advantages in supporting one-off business decisions, the literature suggests that end-user-developed spreadsheets should be kept at a minimum (Panko & Port, 2012).

In brief, in-house AIS[3], such as BI and spreadsheets, have significant potential to support a differentiator business strategy, as firms are able to tailor these systems to support their business strategy. However, costs are noted as a key concern. Costs associated with a build decision are not just the firm's out-of-pocket expenses but also opportunity costs: the time and effort that business managers could have spent on performing their primary responsibilities rather than designing and developing AIS to support a unique business strategy.

Differentiator and buy

With this approach, firms enjoy the benefit of being able to pick and choose a packaged software system available on the market. Consultants may then customise and implement the software based on their competitive business advantages and business strategies (Rashid et al., 2002). However, a flaw with this approach is that most packaged AIS are developed following the software house's broad assumptions about business processes and industry's best practices. These are not always compatible with how a particular firm conducts its businesses. This results in a *misfit* between the functionalities that AIS can provide and the performance expected by firms (Soh et al., 2000). While misfits can occur at all levels of business organisations – operational, tactical and strategic – there is a particular concern when misfits occur at strategic level. This can lead to a situation where firms find that their AIS poorly supports their strategic business direction. e.g. a firm wanting to pursue an online business strategy must have their AIS connected to the Internet; otherwise, it simply would not be able to support the online strategy. Given this logic, it is difficult to imagine an offline AIS that would effectively support a business like Amazon.com. Some examples of misfit at the strategic level addressed in the literature are a misfit with organisational philosophy and organisational structure, a misfit with business model and a misfit with business strategies.

Current research suggests that customisation is the most accepted method to tackle the problem of misfit at strategic level (van Beijsterveld & van Groenendaal, 2015). This is a process that allows firms to tailor *vanilla* AIS to fit their unique business strategies. It should be noted that customisation is not the only option to tackle misfit. Other available options such as workaround, acceptance of misfit, process adaptation and purchase of other software are suggested in the literature. Regardless of the option explored, there are trade-offs to make, e.g. customised software may not be compatible with future vendor update releases. A key debate when it comes to addressing a misfit is: should we change strategies to accommodate AIS? or should we change AIS to accommodate strategies? Generally speaking, firms should stick with their strategy and not alter it to suit AIS misfit. Strategy guides the firm, whereas AIS supports the strategy. Customisation may be a necessary evil for firms that choose the differentiator and buy route.

Sarker et al. (2012) point out that *technology adaptability*, i.e. the level of malleability of AIS to changing requirements and business strategies today and in the future, is a key factor that firms should look for when they compare packaged systems. This adaptability fits with current strategic thinking, which views strategy making as a craft – a blend of planned action and adaptive reaction to changes in the environment (Mintzberg & Waters, 1985). Technology adaptability through customisation at source code level was a main reason behind the success of Navision, a Danish ERP vendor acquired by Microsoft in 2002 (Antero & Bjørn-Andersen, 2013). European firms prefer customisation at the source code level – *deep customisation* – to customisation on top of the source code because this does not create unnecessary add-on modules. Such add-on modules risk altering business procedures and creating inconsistency across business functions.

An example may illustrate this more clearly. Assume that a national tax authority requires companies submitting a value-added tax return to include supplier names and their tax identification numbers. Each of a particular supplier's branches is assigned a different tax identification number under local law. In a general ERP system, supplier master data is not maintained at such a granular level, i.e. branch information is typically not included in the master data, only the headquarter data is maintained. In this case, a company is required to create an add-on module that will allow the company to manage supplier data at both headquarter and branch levels. This results in an inconsistency in the purchase cycle's core business procedure. That is, when the company issues a purchase order to a supplier, it is acceptable to refer to a supplier's headquarter master data since the company does not always know in advance which branch of the supplier will deliver the goods or service. However, when the company receives the goods or service from the supplier along with an invoice, which may come from a branch other than the supplier's headquarter, the company has to be careful to refer to the branch information and branch tax identification number from this point onwards. Otherwise, information shown on the value-added tax return would be incorrect.

This is an example of an inconsistency in business practice caused by add-on modules where it is not possible to do a deep customisation. There are many similar examples for European businesses, which are subject to European Union law alongside local laws and regulations. The case is more pronounced for multinational companies, which may use a single ERP system, but with local entities subject to local laws and regulations. Therefore, European firms might find it difficult to change their streamlined business practice to reflect new add-on modules. These are a consequence of restricted ERP system adaptability (van Beijsterveld & van Groenendaal, 2015). The case is even more pronounced given the new type of ERP system based on the cloud computing technology – *the cloud ERP system*. There are limited opportunities for cloud ERP customisation, especially in the public cloud space. Companies that are considering the cloud ERP solution, but look for a more flexible customisation condition, should investigate the private cloud solution (Gupta et al., 2017).

Cost leader and build

Traditional wisdom suggests that, all else being equal, a build decision costs more than a purchase decision (Daneshgar et al., 2013). Nevertheless, in some cases, firms pursuing a cost-leader strategy might find themselves better off by building their own AIS at a competitive price point to serve their cost-leader strategy. Recent innovations – especially from the cloud computing paradigm – make it possible for smaller companies to design, build and deploy their own AIS solutions based on their business requirements to support the cost-leader strategy.

The National Institute of Standards and Technology in the USA defines cloud computing as "a model for enabling ubiquitous, convenient, on-demand network access to a shared pool of configurable computing resources (e.g. networks, servers, storage, applications, and services) that can be rapidly provisioned and released with minimal management effort or service provider interaction" (Mell & Grance, 2011). Integration-platform-as-a-service (iPaaS) and Cloud Service Brokerage (CSB) are two examples of innovative cloud-based solutions suitable for firms adopting a cost-leader strategy.

iPaaS is defined by Gartner Group as "a cloud service that provides a platform to support application, data and process integration projects, usually involving a combination of cloud-based applications and data sources, APIs and on-premises systems" (Guttridge et al., 2016). e.g. RunMyProcess DigitalSuite is an iPaaS that allows firms to build, integrate and run workflow-based applications. The process design is simple and intuitive as it uses a drag-and-drop scheme to create a workflow. Firms have choices to integrate their application with other cloud-based applications, on-premises software, web services or even social network sites. Deployment is made easy with a built-in advanced testing mode. On top of that, a cloud-based platform like RunMyProcess allows business flexibility, i.e. firms have freedom to alter their AIS solutions to embrace a new business model and changing business environments. Costs for using such services can be competitive compared to traditional AIS solutions.

CNIEL (Maison du Lait: The French Dairy Interbranch Organisation) is an example of an organisation that has adopted an iPaaS solution to manage its financial system. CNIEL is a non-profit association that promotes a smooth relationship between milk producers and processors, reinforcing a positive image of the French milk and dairy industry. It receives membership fees from dairy producers and processors and imposes a strict financial control on the association's expenditure budgets to ensure it gains maximum utility from these fees. Prior to the cloud computing revolution an Excel sheet was sent back and forth between departments, as each and every department had to input their invoiced amounts and reserve the budget for any quote received from vendors. This was inefficient, and controls were inadequate (see discussion above on use of spreadsheets as AIS). A new budgeting application was launched on the iPaaS to streamline the entire expense-related budgeting process (RunMyProcess, 2014).

For firms looking for additional professional services on top of the IT platform, CSB may be a better alternative for an AIS initiative using the cloud. According to the US National Institute of Standards and Technology, CSB is "an entity that manages the use, performance, and delivery of cloud services, and negotiates relationships between Cloud Providers and Cloud Consumer" (Sill et al., 2013). The scope of services and IT solutions that CSB provides is much wider than any iPaaS, i.e. CSB focuses on offering end-to-end solutions to a certain specific problem by aggregating IT solutions from multiple cloud vendors with optional consulting services to business clients. An iPaaS, in contrast, offers an IT integration platform to connect multiple cloud and/or non-cloud solutions together.

Dell Boomi is an example of a CSB that extends its iPaaS offerings with professional services to help firms design, tailor, implement, run and manage their AIS solutions from start to finish. The professional service includes architectural design and validation, process development and best practice review, providing insight that firms cannot get from an iPaaS provider alone.

In short, innovative cloud-based solutions offer a vast array of opportunities for firms to tailor their AIS application based on their cost leadership strategy. Cloud-based solutions like iPaaS and CSB are nothing short of a revolution. Firms having a high concern for capital investment and operating cost now have a cost-effective opportunity to tailor their AIS to support their cost leadership strategy (Bellamy, 2013).

Cost leader and buy

There are many options for cost-leader firms of all sizes to have access to a *plain vanilla* AIS. While traditional solutions like ERP systems and BI are the norm, it is up to firms and their IT staff/consultants to select a package that is most suitable for the firm's requirements and budget. However, one thing that firms must keep in mind is that such solutions typically require a large investment upfront, e.g. licence fee, consultants fee, annual maintenance and support fee, and hosting fee. These costs can prove to be high and may not suit a cost-leader strategy.

Cloud computing services may provide solutions for cost leaders looking to buy AIS, and cloud-based developments in this regard are occurring at a fast pace. Most traditional AIS vendors already provided offerings in the cloud. e.g. SAP – the leading ERP vendor for most industries – launched SAP HANA, a cloud platform in May 2015. Tableau, a leading BI solution, is also available in the cloud.

Practitioner publications suggest that cloud-based AIS are suitable for firms in the following situations: (1) emerging businesses in a highly competitive sector, as a cloud-based solution allows them move faster and gives them an advantage in responding to changing business conditions; (2) smaller firms, especially small and medium-sized enterprises (SMEs), that have limited resources in terms of money and time, because cloud-based AIS solutions are more cost effective; and (3) firms which follow a cost-leader strategy, because pay-for-usage cloud-based solutions allow firms to keep up front investments to a minimum (Essex, 2015; Wallström, 2015).

Key advantages that the cloud solution offers over other traditional AIS – which reside and need to be maintained on the firm's own infrastructure – are cheaper implementation costs, faster implementation times, faster speed of system[4] and scalability (Armbrust et al., 2010). In the cloud model, cloud subscribers pay annual subscription fees to cloud service providers for hardware, software and IT infrastructure services. Cloud subscribers do not have to worry about ongoing system maintenance, which would generate a significant additional cost under the traditional approach.

One downside often reported about cloud solutions is weaker security, as cloud data is stored on servers that need to be Internet-accessible. However, cloud-based AIS need not necessarily have weaker security than on-premises AIS. Each solution has its own security merits and demerits. To store data on premise, physical access control to a data centre that houses the database server is needed, e.g. a surveillance system is required along with a data centre room specially designed to prevent unauthorised access to the data. The physical access control must be complemented with logical access control (e.g. passwords) and a regular audit procedure to ensure its effectiveness (Sandhu & Samarati, 1994). However, the professional fees corresponding to these activities can be hefty for smaller organisations, especially SMEs (Leimbach et al., 2013).

A decision to store data online through a cloud network eliminates the need for these security controls. However, it does bring a new set of problems – issues around data ownership, usage, integrity and confidentiality become more prominent compared to the on-premises model. Once physical control to the data is handed over to cloud-based data centre, data owners have little control on how these data might be accessed, transferred or used. Current technological advancements, like data encryption, are in place to ensure a certain level of data security, but they are not without limitation. e.g. static data used by cloud-based applications, especially software-as-a-service and platform-as-a-service applications, is not encrypted due to technical difficulties in indexing and query writing. The presence of un-encrypted data in multi-tenancy situation, e.g. a cloud database in which data from multiple organisations are stored together, poses a serious threat to data security if there is no standard security policy and practice in place (Chen & Zhao, 2012).

Towards the future AIS – strategy and technology developments to observe

AIS as a field is developing at a rapid speed due to influences both from new business strategy, enabled through technologies, and from advances in technology. This section presents upcoming business strategy and technology developments to observe as these may play a significant role in shaping the future AIS.

Strategy: pipeline versus platform businesses

The AIS strategy framework discussed above was devised with traditional pipeline firms in mind, i.e. firms that follow the systems-based input-process-output mode. These firms take in components from suppliers, carry out manufacturing or service processes to transform these components into a finished product and then sell the finished product to their customers. The recent advent of the platform-based business is a new strategic form of carrying out business and is fundamentally different in nature to the traditional pipeline-based business (van Alstyne et al., 2016; Cennamo, 2021). Whereas pipelines are linear in nature with clear progression of elements down the value or supply chain from firm to firm, platforms are networks in nature and have several different kinds of customers linked together through a central platform (Eisenmann et al., 2006). Recent developments in digital and Internet technologies have allowed a range of platform-type businesses to evolve (Zhu & Iansiti, 2019). Platform businesses may charge one or more customer groups for their platform service: customer groups may be provided with the full platform service for free, others may obtain a restricted service for free and others a complete service for a fee. Many different charging mechanisms can be applied – e.g. transaction charges, service fees or time-based subscription fees. Digital and Internet developments afford new strategic advantages gained from development of ecosystems and cooperation between competitor business firms (Jacobides, 2019; Brandenburger & Nalebuff, 2021), from network and data effects (Hagiu & Wright, 2020), from the ability to connect continuously with customers through wearable and non-wearable devices and through the Internet of Things (Siggelkow & Terwiesch, 2019). A separate but related technological development that also has implications for business strategy is the incorporation of robotics, algorithms and artificial intelligence into firm strategies (Kiron & Schrage, 2019; Iansiti & Lakhani, 2020; Lindebaum et al., 2020). Some authors imply that generic strategies such as differentiation do not apply, at least in the early stages, in these new types of market (McDonald & Eisenhardt, 2020). However, others advise that success in a platform business is not guaranteed and that strategic thinking and common sense still have relevance (Cusumano et al., 2020).

It is clear that AIS will need to evolve in conjunction with these Internet, digital and platform-based technology changes and with the new emphasis on ecosystems and cooperation among firms. AIS may need to manage the information flows between systems located in different parts of the world and between the different firms that comprise a network or ecosystem. AIS will have to manage information flow between the firm and a much greater variety of *things*, including people. This may require an AIS to manage information across the boundaries of firms, industries and states including all the intellectual property, security, privacy and data protection issues that will arise therefrom.

Technology: cryptocurrencies and blockchains

Two major technology developments over recent years may have implications for how AIS are built and maintained and for the manner in which AIS support business strategy. These are new technologies for storing and moving value (cryptocurrencies) and for recording and accounting for value (blockchains).

Cryptocurrencies were invented with an intention of becoming a means of self-regulated yet global medium of exchange, in lieu of traditional currencies which are regulated by a central government agency (Brukhanskyi & Spilnyk, 2019). Bitcoin is one of the most recognised examples of a cryptocurrency. Some major properties of cryptocurrencies are security, irreversibility, controlled supply and pseudonymity (Brukhanskyi & Spilnyk, 2019). Cryptocurrencies hold a power to become the financial instrument of choice for the future, especially crowdfunding. However, before we could get there, there is still much debate taking place on their legal status and use, especially in the accounting context. Firms should closely monitor developments in this area and adjust their business strategies accordingly.

Shared ledger technology based on blockchain principles has extended beyond its initial use in underpinning cryptocurrencies to supporting firms' business models and supply chains more broadly (Hughes et al., 2019; Morkunas et al., 2019). Blockchain holds much promise for AIS including *smart contract*, a key feature that is of special interest for AIS as it allows contractual terms of agreements to be executed automatically and without a trusted third party's involvement (Zheng et al., 2020). This feature may enable future AIS, built on the basis of blockchain, to rapidly verify transactions based on pre-specified business rules and accounting standards. Blockchain also has the potential to create an automatic system that keeps track of tokenised items, e.g. inventory and accounting documents (Dai & Vasarhelyi, 2017).

Although the application of blockchain to AIS is currently in its infancy, given the fundamental way in which it reorganises the recording of transactions and accounting for assets, it may become a key technology in AIS in the not-too-distant future. For this reason, we have extended the original matrix, shown in Figure 18.1, to include a third dimension based on an additional key strategic decision: to what extent will the firm move from its own proprietary ledger to a shared immutable ledger based on blockchain principles. Our decision to extend the original matrix is inspired by the platform business strategy and the blockchain technology. Such strategy-and-technology combination drives firms to simultaneously operate businesses in a tightly knitted manner, i.e. a drive towards a shared ledger based on blockchain principles. We posit that such change corresponds to the nature of AIS to manage information across boundaries.

Figure 18.2 shows this enhanced matrix together with four additional resulting approaches to AIS-supporting business strategy. We will not elaborate on each of these four approaches separately but will provide some general points to consider in moving towards a shared ledger. The business strategy will likely still drive the approach to a shared ledger. Where the business strategy is cost leadership, the firm will likely seek out the cost reduction and efficiency advantages of a shared ledger. Where the business strategy is based on differentiation, the firm may seek out advantages from a shared ledger that support differentiation, e.g. improved security, reduced risk, improved trust, increased transaction speed and improved partnerships with other organisations. Regarding the second decision – build or buy – it is likely the choice of a shared ledger will also have an impact here. While the advantages and disadvantages of both build and buy discussed earlier in this chapter still apply,

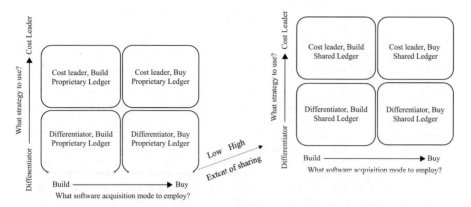

Figure 18.2   Enhanced matrix for AIS strategy (includes additional dimension referring to extent of use of shared ledger technology).

it is possible that a middle-ground approach will become available under blockchain. This middle-ground approach could be in the form of a shared or consensus-based development of AIS and ledger technology between the firm and its partners. We see the three decisions occurring in this order: first, the business strategy is chosen – low cost or differentiation; second, the level of ledger sharing is determined – proprietary or blockchain; third, the approach to software provision is decided – build or buy.

Conclusion

This chapter presents key ideas on how firms can use and, in particular, develop their AIS to support their business strategy. It is critical for organisational success that the AIS fit and support the generic business strategy, be it low cost or differentiation. The chapter outlined a two-by-two matrix representing a strategic AIS framework based upon two fundamental dimensions: the strategy type (cost leader versus differentiator) and the software acquisition mode (build versus buy). Four distinct AIS strategies are identified and discussed: Differentiator and Build, Differentiator and Buy, Cost leader and Build, and Cost leader and Buy (see Figure 18.1).

The chapter also points out that business strategy and technology developments are mutually affecting each other. Internet developments are converting business from being based along traditional pipeline value chains to being centred around platform-based ecosystems. Technology developments have created new ways to store and move value through a myriad of cryptocurrencies and new ways to account for value using blockchains. These changes will have implications for the ways and means by which AIS are developed and used in the future. The chapter therefore suggests that a third decision dimension may become relevant: the extent to which firms remain with their proprietary ledger or move to a shared ledger based on blockchain principles. The third dimension in incorporated into our enhanced framework (Figure 18.2).

Just as effective strategy making is a combination of good formulation and good implementation, so too effective AIS strategy is a combination of good selection and good execution. This chapter has examined the elements of selection in terms of acquisition cost and matching to firm strategy and the elements of execution in terms of buying an off-the-shelf software solution or building one's own bespoke system. As with all strategic decisions, consistency with the internal organisational situation and consonance with an ever-changing external environment are critical.

Notes

1 We acknowledge that this is a limited view towards the concept of business partner in outsourcing. However, our intention is to highlight a worst-case scenario when an outsourcing contract goes wrong. We believe that firms should be cautious, rather than overly optimistic, when they enter into any outsourcing agreement.

2 This refers to the risk incurred when a principal employs an agent to carry out work on their behalf: there is a risk that the agent will not act in the best interests of the principal.

3 The term *in-house AIS* excludes ERP systems because it is uncommon to find ERP systems developed in-house. In fact, a standard definition of ERP system already assumes that the system is available off-the-shelf only (Grabski et al., 2011).

4 Faster speed of the system has a direct relationship with scalability. In the cloud computing model, firms are able to increase and/or decrease information processing capability on the cloud based on the volume of business transactions. The concept is known as *scalability*. An ability to process voluminous transactions with more processing capability results in a *faster speed of the system*.

References

Antero, M. C. & Bjørn-Andersen, N. (2013) Why a partner ecosystem results in superior value: A comparative analysis of the business models of two ERP vendors. *Information Resources Management Journal, 26*(1), 12–24.

Armbrust, M., Fox, A., Griffith, R., Joseph, A. D., Katz, R., Konwinski, A., Lee, G., Patterson, D., Rabkin, A. & Stoica, I. (2010) A view of cloud computing. *Communications of the ACM, 53*(4), 50–58.

Bellamy, M. (2013) Adoption of cloud computing services by public sector organisations. in *Services (SERVICES), 2013 IEEE Ninth World Congress on*: IEEE. 201–208.

Berry, A. J., Coad, A. F., Harris, E. P., Otley, D. T. & Stringer, C. (2009) Emerging themes in management control: A review of recent literature. *The British Accounting Review, 41*(1), 2–20.

Brandenburger, A. & Nalebuff, B. (2021) The rules of co-opetition. *Harvard Business Review, 99*(1), 48–57.

Brukhanskyi, R. & Spilnyk, I. (2019) Cryptographic Objects in the Accounting System. In proceedings of *The 9th International Conference on Advanced Computer Information Technologies* (ACIT).

Bullen, C. V., Abraham, T., Gallagher, K., Simon, J. C. & Zwieg, P. (2009) IT workforce trends: Implications for curriculum and hiring. *Communications of the Association for information Systems, 24*(1), 9.

Cennamo, C. (2021) Competing in Digital Markets: A Platform-Based Perspective. *Academy of Management Perspectives, 35*(2), 265–291.

Chang, J. Y. T., Wang, E. T. G., Jiang, J. J. & Klein, G. (2013) Controlling ERP consultants: Client and provider practices. *Journal of Systems and Software, 86*(5), 1453–1461.

Chen, D. and Zhao, H. (2012) Data security and privacy protection issues in cloud computing. in *Computer Science and Electronics Engineering (ICCSEE), 2012 International Conference on*: IEEE. 647–651.

Chen, H., Chiang, R. H. & Storey, V. C. (2012) Business intelligence and analytics: From Big Data to Big Impact. *MIS Quarterly, 36*(4), 1165–1188.

Child, J. (1972) Organizational structure, environment and performance: The role of strategic choice. *Sociology, 6*(1), 1–22.

CIMA (2015) *Accountants Missing Out on Cloud Technology Revolution Due to Unfounded Security Fears.* Available: https://www.cimaglobal.com/Press/Press-releases/2015/Accountants-missing-out-on-cloud-technology-revolution-due-to-unfounded-security-fears/ [Accessed 10 Juaunary 2022].

Cusumano, M., Yoffie, D. & Gawer, A. (2020) The future of platforms. *MIT Sloan Management Review*, February 11th 2020.

Dai, J. & Vasarhelyi, M.A. (2017) Toward Blockchain-Based Accounting and Assurance. *Journal of Information Systems, 31*(3), 5–21.

Daneshgar, F., Low, G. C. & Worasinchai, L. (2013) An investigation of 'build vs. buy' decision for software acquisition by small to medium enterprises. *Information and Software Technology, 55*(10), 1741–1750.

DPC (2022) *Data Security Guidance.* Available: https://www.dataprotection.ie/en/organisations/know-your-obligations/data-security-guidance [Accessed 10 January 2022].

Eisenmann, T., Parker, G. & von Alstyne, M. (2006) Strategies for two-sided markets. *Harvard Business Review, 84*(10), 92–101.

Ellison, R. J. & Woody, C. (2010) Supply-chain risk management: Incorporating security into software development. in *System Sciences (HICSS), 2010 43rd Hawaii International Conference on*: IEEE. 1–10.

Essex, D. (2015) *Is Your Company Suited to ERP in the Cloud?* Available: https://searcherp.techtarget.com/tip/Is-your-company-suited-to-ERP-in-the-cloud [Accessed 10 October 2021].

Finney, S. & Corbett, M. (2007) ERP implementation: A compilation and analysis of critical success factors. *Business Process Management Journal, 13*(3), 329–347.

Grabski, S. V., Leech, S. A. and Schmidt, P. J. (2011) A review of ERP research: A future agenda for accounting information systems. *Journal of Information Systems, 25*(1), 37–78.

Gupta, S., Misra, S.C., Singh, A., Kumar, V., & Kumar, U. (2017) Identification of challenges and their ranking in the implementation of cloud ERP A comparative study for SMEs and large organizations. *International Journal of Quality & Reliability Management, 34*(7), 1056–1072.

Guttridge, K., Pezzini, M., Malinverno, P., Iijima, K., Thompson, J., Thoo, E. & Golluscio, E. (2016) *Magic Quadrant for Enterprise Integration Platform as a Service, Worldwide*. Available: https://www.gartner.com/doc/reprints?id=1-2C7HEYF&ct=150324&st=sb&mkt_tok=eyJpIjoiTnpBeE0yRTFZalk1TW1WbSIsInQiOiI5dUhzakdRRERvYjdvS2tTUVpuY1FyRzQwbWxvSWVtQjdzaVk4c3NNKSEwwOUVzRUhxeDFReVwvWkFLSGlBbk53OTM1SCtTRUpGGdHFlamxEUkRcLzdydDh2XC9CejZQQ2EyRUxIM3lFdDDAzSVIrTT0ifQ%3D%3D [Accessed 11 April 2016].

Hagiu, A. & Wright, J. (2020) When data creates competitive advantage, *Harvard Business Review, 98*(1), 94–101.

Hughes, A., Park, A., Kietzmann, J. & Archer-Brown, C. (2019) Beyond Bitcoin: What blockchain and distributed ledger technologies mean for firms. *Business Horizons, 62*(3), 273–281.

Iansiti, M. & Lakhani, K. (2020) Competing in the age of AI, *Harvard Business Review, 98*(1), 60–67.

Jacobides, M. (2019) In the ecosystem economy, what's your strategy? *Harvard Business Review, 97*(5), 128–137.

Kimberling, E. (2015) *2015 ERP Report*. Available: https://www.panorama-consulting.com/wp-content/uploads/2016/07/2015-ERP-Report-3.pdf [Accessed 10 January 2022].

Kiron, D. & Schrage, D. (2019) Strategy for and with AI. *MIT Sloan Management Review, 60*(4), 30–35.

Kobelsky, K. W. & Robinson, M. A. (2010) The impact of outsourcing on information technology spending. *International Journal of Accounting Information Systems, 11*(2), 105–119.

Lacity, M. C. & Hirschheim, R. (2012) The information systems outsourcing bandwagon. *Sloan Management Review, 34*, 73.

Leimbach, T., Hallinan, D., Weber, A., Jaglo, M., Hennen, L., Nentwich, M., Straub, S., Nielsen, R., Lynn, T. & Hunt, G. (2013) *Impacts of Cloud Computing*. Deliverable No.3 of the STOA Project: European Technology Assessment Group (ETAG).

Lindebaum, D., Vesa, M. & den Hond, F. (2020) Insights from "The Machine Stops" to better understand rational assumptions in algorithmic decision making and its implications for organizations. *Academy of Management Review, 45*(1), 247–263.

Mabert, V. A., Soni, A. & Venkataramanan, M. A. (2003) The impact of organization size on enterprise resource planning (ERP) implementations in the US manufacturing sector. *Omega, 31*(3), 235–246.

Markus, M. L. & Tanis, C. (2000) The enterprise systems experience-from adoption to success. *Framing the domains of IT research: Glimpsing the future through the past, 173*, 173-207.

McDonald, R. & Eisenhardt, K. (2020) The New-Market Conundrum. *Harvard Business Review, 98*(3), 74–83.

Mell, P. & Grance, T. (2011) *The NIST Definition of Cloud Computing*. National Institute of Standards and Technology, US Department of Commerce.

Mintzberg, H. & Waters, J. A. (1985) Of strategies, deliberate, and emergent. *Strategic Management Journal, 6*, 257–272.

Morkunas, V. Paschen, J. & Boon, E. (2019) How blockchain technologies impact your business model, *Business Horizons, 62*(3), 295–306.

Panko, R. R. & Port, D. N. (2012) End user computing: The dark matter (and dark energy) of corporate IT. in *System Science (HICSS), 2012 45th Hawaii International Conference on*: IEEE. 4603–4612.

Panorama (2021) *2021 ERP Report*. Available at: https://f.hubspotusercontent40.net/hubfs/4439340/Reports/ERP%20Report/2021-ERP-Report-Panorama-Consulting-Group.pdf [Accessed 17 June 2021].

Paulsson, W. V. (2013) *The Complementary Use of IS Technologies to Support Flexibility and Integration Needs in Budgeting*. PhD dissertation in Information Systems Monograph, Lund University, Lund.

Porter, M. (1980) *Competitive Strategy.* New York: The Free Press.

Porter, M. E. (1985) *Competitive Advantage: Creating and Sustaining Superior Performance.* New York: The Free Press.

Quattrone, P. & Hopper, T. (2006) What is IT?: SAP, accounting, and visibility in a multinational organisation. *Information and Organization, 16*(3), 212–250.

Rashid, M. A., Hossain, L. & Patrick, J. D. (2002) The evolution of ERP systems: A historical perspective. in Liaquat, H., Jon David, P. and Mohammad, A. R., (eds.) *Enterprise Resource Planning: Global Opportunities and Challenges,* Hershey, PA, USA: IGI Global. 1–16.

RunMyProcess (2014) *CNIEL Case Study.* Available: https://www.runmyprocess.com/case-studies/cniel/ [Accessed 10 January 2022].

Salahdine, F. & Kaabouch, N. (2019) Social Engineering Attacks: A Survey. *Future Internet,* 11, 89.

Sandhu, R. S. & Samarati, P. (1994) Access control: Principle and practice. *Communications Magazine, IEEE, 32*(9), 40–48.

Sarker, S., Sarker, S., Sahaym, A. & Bjørn-Andersen, N. (2012) Exploring value cocreation in relationships between an ERP vendor and its partners: a revelatory case study. *MIS quarterly, 36*(1), 317–338.

Siggelkow, N. & Terwiesch, C. (2019) The age of continuous connection, *Harvard Business Review,* 97(3), 64–73.

Sill, A., Sokol, A., Lee, C., Harper, D., Luster, E., de Vaulx, F., Massaferro, G. & Pilz, G. (2013) *NIST Cloud Computing Standards Roadmap.* Available: http://www.nist.gov/itl/cloud/upload/NIST_SP-500-291_Version-2_2013_June18_FINAL.pdf [Accessed 10 January 2022].

Soh, C., Kien, S. S. & Tay-Yap, J. (2000) Enterprise resource planning: cultural fits and misfits: is ERP a universal solution? *Communications of the ACM, 43*(4), 47–51.

Svejvig, P. & Jensen, T. (2012) Making sense of enterprise systems in institutions: a case study of the re-implementation of an accounting system. *Scandanavian Journal of Information Systems, 25*(1), 3–36.

van Alstyne, M., Parker, G. & Choudary, S P. (2016) Pipelines, Platforms, and the New Rules of Strategy. *Harvard Business Review, 94* (4), 54–62.

van Beijsterveld, J. A. A. & van Groenendaal, W. J. H. (2015) Solving misfits in ERP implementations by SMEs. *Information Systems Journal,* n/a–n/a.

Wallström, M. (2015) *Få affärssystem i molnet håller måttet.* Available: http://computersweden.idg.se/2.2683/1.615030/fa-affarssystem-i-molnet-haller-mattet?queryText=aff%E4rsystem [Accessed 15 September 2021].

Wang, E. T., Shih, S.-P., Jiang, J. J. & Klein, G. (2008) The consistency among facilitating factors and ERP implementation success: A holistic view of fit. *Journal of Systems and Software, 81*(9), 1609–1621.

Warren, J. D., Moffitt, K. C., & Byrnes, B. (2015) How big data will change accounting? *Accounting Horizons,* 29(2), 397–407.

Zheng, Z., Xie, S., Dai, H., Chen, W., Chen, X., Weng, J., & Imran, M. (2020) An Overview on Smart Contracts: Challenges, Advances and Platforms. *Future Generation Computer Systems,* 105, 475–491.

Zhu, F & Iansiti, M. (2019) Why some platforms thrive and others don't. *Harvard Business Review,* 97(1), 119–125.

PART 4

Future directions of accounting information systems

19

INTEGRATING AIS AND CONTEMPORARY TECHNOLOGIES

Brenda Clerkin and Danielle McConville

Introduction

In this chapter, we explore four contemporary technologies – data analytics, artificial intelligence (AI), robotic process automation (RPA) and blockchain – and their integration with accounting information systems (AIS) – see also some earlier chapters. We consider AIS as including the data, human actors, software, hardware, processes and controls that work together to record accounting transactions, prepare financial statements and support decision making. Each technology will be discussed, in turn, including a definition from current literature, how the technology has been/may be integrated into AIS and the implications of this technology for AIS, including benefits and challenges. In our conclusion, we highlight common themes from our discussion of the four technologies, with a focus on the implications of these for the future AIS and the future accountant. We also suggest areas of further research, reflecting the relatively early stage of research into the implications of these technologies in AIS.

Data analytics

Industry 4.0, or the Fourth Industrial Revolution, has created an explosion of data, driven by technological developments and automation, and commonly known as 'big data'. Gartner (2013, p. 5) defined big data as 'high-volume, high-velocity and high-variety information assets that demand cost-effective, innovative forms of information processing for enhanced insight and decision making'. In other words, data is generated in large quantities, at speed and in a variety of forms including image, text, video and audio. This unstructured data, extracted from a wide range of sources, often on a near-real-time basis, contrasts to the structured data from limited sources that traditionally impact on AIS. This drives the need for innovative forms of data processing, going beyond familiar accountants' tools (such as Microsoft Excel) towards techniques to understand and interpret the data, such as data analytics. Data analytics is defined as 'the process of using structured and unstructured data through the applications of various analytic techniques such as statistical and quantitative analysis and explanatory and predictive models to provide useful information to decision makers' (Schneider et al., 2015, p. 720). Typically, there are four categories of analytics – descriptive,

DOI: 10.4324/9781003132943-24

diagnostic, predictive and prescriptive. Descriptive and diagnostic are backward looking and outline what has happened and why, while predictive and prescriptive analytics are forward focused, highlighting what will happen and what actions need to be taken to achieve the desired outcome. Davenport & Fitts (2021) outline how data analytics will develop and become more automated and supported by AI, with analytics software automatically finding patterns in data. This will allow data to be queried or predictions to be made based on trends and anomalies found. Overall the data analytical process should become more effective and require less specialised skills in data science.

Considering the role of accountants, in particular management accountants, whose work is less prescriptive than that of financial accountants, in preparing financial statements, measuring performance and providing decision-related information (Cokins, 2016), there are many possible applications of analytics in AIS. Appelbaum et al. (2017) suggest that descriptive analytics have a role in financial reporting, summarising past events and transactions into a set of financial statements. Descriptive and diagnostic analytics help analyse past performance of a company, while predictive analytics can provide predictions on future performance and support decision making, alongside prescriptive analytics (Appelbaum et al., 2017). Table 19.1 sketches an example of this relating to sales.

Going beyond this analysis, accountants need to ensure they communicate effectively the insight they have gained, especially in cases where management may not have been involved in the data analysis process or have a financial background. As noted in Huerta & Jensen (2017, p. 105), 'a visualization is worth a million numbers' – see also Chapter 14. We outline below tools that can assist with this element of the data analytics process.

A range of options are available to organisations integrating data analytical technology into AIS. Microsoft Excel is still cited as the most common tool for data analytics due to its prevalence and ease of use, but it has limitations when it comes to handling big data and presenting visualisations (ACCA, 2020a). Increasingly, analytical tools are built into, or can be bolted onto, accounting software: from cloud-based software such as QuickBooks or Sage for smaller companies to large-scale enterprise resource planning (ERP) systems such as SAP or Oracle. These user-friendly tools allow users to perform analytics in-house and without the intervention of an IT department. These tools also have a data visualisation function within them, aiding effective communication of insights.

Alternatively, stand-alone data analytics systems are offered by vendors such as Microsoft Power BI, Tableau and Alteryx. These tools generally sit outside the AIS but utilise information from within it for analysis, often combining this with other data, including from legacy systems. Alteryx, in particular, is considered a data blending tool enabling users to blend, cleanse and transform data from multiple sources and combine this into a dataset for analysis

Table 19.1 Example integration of types of analytics

Type of analytic	Example
Descriptive	Calculation of the top five performing stores based on sales in the last quarter
Diagnostic	Understanding the behaviour of these high performing stores – look for common traits or patterns in their operations
Predictive	Calculate expected future sales in the stores based on past history
Prescriptive	Based on the outcome of the future sales analysis above, determine inventory and staffing levels to meet customer demand

(ACCA, 2020a). All such systems incorporate advanced statistical or machine learning (ML) techniques to gain insights from data and have varying levels of visualisation capabilities (ACCA, 2020a). Another option to gain benefit from data analysis within AIS would be to design and develop purpose-built tools for the organisation to exist alongside the AIS if full integration wasn't possible. This may be more applicable for specialised entities who would benefit from a more bespoke approach to data analytics.

Some of the key benefits of big data/analytics in AIS have been reported as follows:

- Better decision making – Nielsen (2015) reported that by improving the ability of accountants to make predictions using analytics, it would allow them to better consider risk and uncertainty in their decision making. Marr (2020) provides an example of predictive analytics in action within Otto, a German retail company. They analysed 3 billion past transactions and were able to build a model that would predict what consumers were going to buy in the next 30 days with 90% accuracy.
- Real-time analysis – With the increase in the breadth of data that can be utilised for data analytics and the tools available, analytics tools can provide much faster, real-time (or near-real-time) insights versus human analysis (Schneider et al., 2015).
- Improved operations – Data analytics can detect operational inefficiencies within organisations (Dai et al., 2019), such as the identification of bottlenecks with the production process.
- Better performance evaluation – Data analytics allows better prediction of financial accounting discrepancies and evaluation of current financial performance (Eaglesham, 2013).

There are also challenges with big data/analytics. Some key challenges are:

- Data quality – For data analytics to work well, the data needs to be complete, accurate, reliable and timely (Redman, 2008). Therefore, accountants need to be cognisant of the source of their data and validate its authenticity before performing analytical work.
- Management culture – Huerta & Jensen (2017) document the importance of management support for the successful implementation of data analytics in an organisation. They argue that there is a need for a change in mindset, away from traditional, hierarchy-driven management and towards data-driven management. This level of change in an organisation could lead to resistance.
- Storage challenges – Very often, big data utilised in data analytics is stored in the cloud, with risks of data loss due to lack of control of data processing systems. Systems availability and business continuity concerns arise around interruptions of the cloud infrastructure and recovery for business continuity (Brandas et al., 2015).
- Privacy and security concerns – Many studies highlight the need to be mindful of the data being collected and how it is analysed and kept secure (Huerta & Jensen, 2017; ICAEW, 2019; ACCA, 2020a). Knowledge of regulations is also important to ensure legal obligations are fulfilled, e.g. general data protection regulations. Huerta & Jensen (2017, p. 106) note that 'security of big data includes protecting new and evolving data platforms and tools, such as data repositories and analytical and visualization tools, that were not initially designed with a focus on security'.
- System compatibility – Appelbaum et al. (2017, p. 34) refer to the difficulties of integrating external big data streams and the increasing volume of internal data becoming 'unmanageable', unless systems are 're-engineered to accommodate the new complexities presented by different data streams and advanced business analytics'.

We are seeing the emergence of big data and more sophisticated data analytical tools. There is a shift from the use of historical data, to incorporating more predictive and prescriptive analysis. Successful implementation of analytics may involve organisations integrating data analytics further into their AIS and becoming data-driven organisations.

Artificial intelligence

AI has been defined as 'the theory and development of computer systems able to perform tasks normally requiring human intelligence, such as visual perception, speech recognition, decision making, and translation between languages' (Petkov, 2020, p. 100). Within this definition of AI, there are also various subtypes: Gotthardt et al. (2020) suggest that AI includes a range of linked technologies, including data mining, ML, speech and image recognition and semantic analysis. Some authors include RPA in their discussions of AI, while others suggest these are 'at opposite ends of an intelligent automation continuum' (Gotthardt et al., 2020, p. 91), and in this chapter, we present RPA separately but note increasing links with AI.

ML is often discussed synonymously with AI. Cho et al. (2020) describe ML as a computer *automatically* learning patterns and trends from a data set (i.e. instead of being explicitly programmed by humans) and iteratively improving its learning performance. Big data has a role here, as extremely large and varied data sets enable the recognition of patterns, creation of rules and then testing and improvement of these rules, leading to increased ML effectiveness (Cho et al., 2020).

AI and ML are already a consistent presence in everyday living through the likes of facial recognition, digital assistants such as Apple's Siri or Amazon's Alexa, search and recommendation tools, chatbots and more. Some examples of uses of AI in AIS reflect these everyday uses. Cho et al. (2020) give the example of using a chatbot to take customer calls, which can simultaneously speak with customers, place an order, generate a sales invoice and transmit the data to the AIS. Many authors cite the potential for AI to assist or even replace the accountant in common accounting tasks such as forecasting – Institute of Chartered Accountants in England and Wales (ICAEW) (2018a) suggests using ML-based predictive models to forecast revenues, while Bakarich & O'Brien (2021) argue drones can be used to count cars in a car park as a proxy for retail sales. Cho et al. (2020) see uses in control processes such as stock taking, combining a visual recognition system linked to ML to identify objects, count them and assess their condition for stock valuation purposes. ICAEW (2018a) notes the potential for analysis of unstructured data, such as contracts and emails, needed in a number of accounting processes including estimation of liabilities, revenue recognition and more.

Petkov (2020) presents a model to be used by organisations seeking to form and structure their systems to accommodate AI. This includes a substantial list of standard, day-to-day accounting tasks and how these could feasibly be delegated to AI – see Petkov (2020). Example tasks include preparing estimates of accrued expenses by training AI to analyse historical data and to make relevant journal entries on demand, or identifying transactions related to non-current asset purchases or disposals by scanning bank statements. Noting that not all of their suggestions will be applicable to all companies, and that it is not an all-inclusive list, they comment that 'these suggested activities should provide users with the thought processes involved in identifying and rethinking the accounting function and defining opportunities for the use of AI' (Petkov, 2020, p. 100). They also clarify the particular importance of allowing AI to identify and record economic events from primary documents such as bank statements – arguing that once this is done, the potential for AI increases, as do the advantages that can be derived.

In terms of technical implementation of AI in AIS, systems can be developed in-house using a range of technologies including coding languages such as Python and R. ICAEW (2018a) notes that this requires significant investment, and that given the data volumes involved, substantial hardware and processing power may be needed, even if it is accessed on a cloud basis. They comment that 'as a result, AI investments will likely focus on areas that will have the biggest financial impact, especially cost reduction opportunities, or those that are crucial for competitive positioning or customer service' (p. 12). Alternatively, increasingly tailored solutions are available from a range of suppliers – ACCA (2020b) gives examples of market leaders including Google Cloud, Microsoft Azure, IBM Watson and AWS SageMaker. These providers cite advantages such as users can engage quickly and easily with their products (even with varying levels of technical skills), pick and choose the underlying technologies that are most suitable (e.g. Jupyter) and have all of this integrated with secure data storage and user-friendly, comprehensive interfaces (as an example, see Microsoft, 2021a). As a further alternative, some providers offer AI tools integrated within ERP solutions (an example of this is SAP S/4 HANA; see SAP, 2021). Going forward, ICAEW (2018a) expects ML to be increasingly integrated into business and accounting software – so that many accountants, and especially smaller businesses, will be benefitting from ML without realising it.

Depending on the use and subtype of AI, various means of recording accounting transactions from these systems into the AIS need to be carefully developed in-house and/or with the service provider. Where these systems are intended to have the capability to post transactions to the AIS, there will be a need for careful creation of these interfaces, mindful of the need for control and impact on audit work (ICAEW, 2018a).

Benefits of AI in AIS include the following:

- Efficiency – In many instances, AI can complete tasks much more efficiently than humans, due to faster processing of information and decision making – Petkov (2020) cites the time delays associated with manual creations of estimates versus almost instantaneous ML estimation based on historical data analysis. Requirements for detailed manual internal control processes to check manual estimates are also reduced.
- Accuracy – Petkov (2020) notes that if AI is 'trained well' (p. 102), then information will be more accurately and consistently prepared. There are suggestions (Cho et al., 2020) and some limited empirical evidence (Ding et al., 2020) that ML can improve the accuracy of accounting estimates. Removing humans from the process has the potential to reduce some forms of bias in decision making, including confirmation and availability bias (ICAEW, 2018a).
- Increased scope – AI enables the detection of patterns and trends in very large data sets that might not otherwise be possible (ICAEW, 2018a). ML can adapt itself to new data over time as the rules written by the system constantly evolve and refine, meaning that outcomes will improve with experience (Cho et al., 2020).
- Fraud reduction – Petkov (2020) highlights the potential to reduce some opportunities for fraud, where organisations apply AI with predefined principles and auditors test the AI for compliance with rules and/or for anomalous interventions by control owners. Cho et al. (2020) go further to discuss the potential use of AI in predicting accounting fraud (see also ICAEW, 2018a) and countering biases.

There are also challenges of AI in AIS, as follows:

- Cost – Petkov (2020) highlights the initial costs associated with creating, planning and implementing new AI systems but also cautions of the need for continued investment in monitoring and improving the system over time.
- Data availability – ICAEW (2018a, p. 9) notes that 'success depends on having sufficient data of the right quality', with many ML applications requiring very large data sets as training data to be effective. ICAEW (2018a) flags particular issues in small businesses, which may have less available data, in pulling together data from multiple, complex and legacy systems, and in the sometimes prohibitive cost of acquiring external data.
- Data security – AI based on incomplete or corrupted data is very likely to be misleading or inaccurate (ACCA, 2020b). Petkov (2020) highlights the critical cost of total reliance on a system: 'if such a system is attacked, and there is no back up based on human engagement, it might become more of a liability rather than an asset' (p. 102).
- Complexity – AI often becomes extremely complex, which can cause issues in applying professional scepticism, control and auditing (ACCA, 2020b). Explainable AI (XAI), which provides the user with supporting information on how the system reached a particular conclusion, is one response to this (Cho et al., 2020), but this is also something of increasing concern to auditors (ICAEW, 2018a).
- Bias/harm – AI can learn biases that are present in the underlying data sets reflecting existing bias and prejudice (ICAEW, 2018a) and replicate these biases in their rules. Examples include decision making relating to customers with specific characteristics or excessive prudence/confidence in accounting estimations.

Estimates of the scale at which AI is being introduced and impacting on AIS vary. An Oracle survey of 700 global finance executives in 2019 established that only 11% have implemented AI in their finance function (Oracle, 2019). Bakarich & O'Brien (2021) indicate limited implementation or training on AI by accountants in practice but a very wide-scale expectation that this will change substantially over the next five years.

Robotic process automation

RPA is 'an umbrella term for tools that operate on the user interface of other computer systems in the way a human would do' (van der Aalst et al., 2018, p. 269). Sometimes referred to interchangeably as bots (Cooper et al., 2019), RPA are software programs that follow structured commands to perform if, then, else statements on structured data – in other words: if you see this, then do this, or else that. Processes that suit this type of automation are therefore generally highly structured, repetitive, simple and routine (van der Aalst et al., 2018; Cooper et al., 2019).

Cooper et al. (2019) explain that RPA mimics the actions of a human in completing its tasks. This includes performing process tasks such as communicating with other digital systems and humans, sending email notifications, capturing data, manipulating data, retrieving information, structured decision making, processing transactions and more. In particular, RPA is often used to automate processes that are low value-added, monotonous and time-consuming: examples in everyday life include credit card applications, scheduling systems and automated help desks (Marr, 2021a).

Many opportunities to use RPA exist within AIS – see also Chapter 17. Marr (2021a) gives examples relating to the sales process, including setting up new customers on the system, updating customer relationship management (CRM) systems and inputting data into sales metrics and monitoring systems. Cooper et al. (2019) give examples including bank reconciliations (also McCann, 2018), expense processing, inventory tracking, timesheet administration and supplier and purchase order validations. McCann (2018) identifies increasing automation of core finance functions including financial closing and consolidation, cashflow statement preparation and tax reporting. McCann (2018), van der Aalst et al. (2018) and Cooper et al. (2019) highlight the use of RPA in pulling together data from legacy or stand-alone applications for further processing. Cooper et al. (2019) cite significant uptake of RPA in tax compliance work – including calculating accounting-tax differences, applying these to the trial balance, reconciling intercompany transactions and completing tax return workbooks.

Implications for AIS can differ dramatically. Where the RPA is simply acting as an agent in place of a human, the existing information system remains unchanged (van der Aalst et al., 2018). However, in practice, it is also common to see improvements to the process and changes in controls because of the greater reliance that can be placed on the RPA (McCann, 2018).

RPA can be set up in-house using coding languages – ultimately, this is simply writing a software programme to follow specific commands. Some authors suggest this can be done at relatively low cost (McCann, 2018) albeit that they do not state their assumptions of existing IT skills and support in the organisation. When implementing RPA in organisations, Cooper et al. (2019) found a combination of accountants and software programmers involved. Alternatively, hosted solutions are increasingly being offered by dedicated RPA vendors, such as AutomationEdge, Automation Anywhere, Blue Prism and UiPath (van der Aalst et al., 2018; Cooper et al., 2019; Gotthardt et al., 2020). Solutions are also being offered by general vendors – e.g. Microsoft offers Power Automate, a platform that allows organisations to 'create automated workflows with step-by-step guidance and an intuitive, no-code interface anyone can use, regardless of their technical expertise' (Microsoft, 2021b, p. 1). Increasingly, RPA is being embedded into other business tools – van der Aalst et al. (2018) give examples including Pegasystems and Cognizant who also offer CRM and business intelligence tools. McCann (2018) suggests that automation processes can also be hard coded into ERP software, noting benefits including increased robustness, rigour and integration to the systems. However, they also caution that this is a much more expensive approach than stand-alone RPAs for most businesses.

There are several benefits of RPA in AIS:

- Accuracy – If set up correctly, then RPA can more accurately and efficiently complete process tasks, as the potential for human error in completion is removed (Cooper et al., 2019).
- Efficiency – Many examples of RPA operate without direct human supervision, so these can operate 24 × 7 without breaks, increasing efficiency (Cooper et al., 2019). Marr (2021a, p. 1) gives the example of a large bank using 85 software bots to run 13 processes that handled 1.5 million requests in a year: 'this allowed the bank to add capacity that equalled 230 full-time employees at just about 30 per cent the cost of recruiting more staff'.
- Process improvement – McCann (2018) suggests that the process of implementing RPA allows organisations to carefully consider and, as necessary, redesign their processes: e.g. to improve the logic, to skip steps that humans might take or to bring in more data to improve decision making.

- Employee impacts – Joshi (2019) indicates that some lower-level employees would find their jobs more fulfilling with RPA handling their mundane tasks. McCann (2018) and Cooper et al. (2019) express similar sentiments and note that some organisations have used RPA as a means of staff development, empowering lower-level staff to suggest processes suitable for RPA.

It also presents some challenges in AIS, as follows:

- Process suitability – Care should be taken in choosing which processes to automate. RPA is best suited to processes that are highly structured, rule-based and repetitive (Cooper et al., 2019; McCann, 2018), so trying to apply RPA where judgement is needed will be problematic.
- Robustness – McCann (2018) notes starkly that 'bots break' (p. 43), referring to the fact that many bots will cease working until recoded when there is an update to software or a change to a web page with which it interacts. This has significant implications for change management and IT resources. Gotthardt et al. (2020) note that the data contained and used in an RPA is subject to a range of security threats, but also that these are not different from other IT systems and that countermeasures are readily available.
- Controllability – Gotthardt et al. (2020) highlight the importance of understanding the risks introduced by RPA and the need to ensure controls are well designed and effective to mitigate these. How, e.g. will performance of the RPA be supervised (PWC, 2017)? If these challenges are not properly addressed, then RPA may not operate effectively and inaccurate data may flow unchecked into the AIS. Cooper et al. (2019) note that while RPA has been seen as relatively uncontroversial by regulators to date (as bots are part of an existing process, complete defined tasks and largely prevent mistakes); this may change as RPA becomes further integrated with AI.
- Employee impacts – Alongside traditional change management concerns, Joshi (2019, p. 1) flags that some employees, 'especially the ones who aren't tech-savvy, may be increasingly concerned about training and upgrading their skills for adapting to RPA'. This indicates the need for careful management, training and potentially difficult decisions around staff who are unable to adapt. Concerns are commonly expressed about reducing headcount due to RPA, but this has not been observed in practice (Cooper et al., 2019), with RPA instead being used to increase capacity and scale in organisations (McCann, 2018).

Cooper et al.'s (2019) survey of accounting professionals engaged with RPA strongly indicated that they saw RPA 'as a stepping stone to more sophisticated automation' (p. 16), with RPA vendors adding AI in the form of ML and cognitive computing (see also McCann, 2018) to traditional rules-based bots. In other words, the future of RPA may be less rules-based and have more space for judgement, allowing more sophisticated tasks to be performed.

Blockchain

Blockchain can be defined as 'a database – a storage infrastructure for data – that's secured by both encryption and by being decentralised. With many copies spread across many locations, all kept up-to-date simultaneously, changes can only be made to the data when there is consensus that it is correct to do so' (Marr, 2021b, p. 1) – see also Chapter 3. In other words, blockchain is a technology based on the premise of a decentralised ledger for storing data that operates through the internet. It enables transactions between parties in a network (peer to peer) without the need for an authoritative body or intermediary. Participants in the network work together to create and approve transactions in an open and transparent manner.

In a blockchain system, when a transaction has taken place, say between a buyer and a seller, details are recorded by both parties, including the value, date and details of the transaction. These details are then available to all participants in the network. All participants hold the same information, and it takes the agreement of all participants in the chain to update their records for the transaction to be accepted. Approval of transactions can occur online where predefined rules are built into the system, which ensures only valid transactions are accepted. Once approved, the transaction gets added to a block within the blockchain and a time stamp added. Each block within the blockchain contains three elements – data from its transactions, a cryptographic hash made up of letters and numbers (fingerprint) for that block and also a cryptographic hash of the previous block. This structure provides security: it prevents transactions already recorded within the blocks from being altered, as to do so would require adjustment to all previous blocks and therefore approval of all participants. This is often cited as a key characteristic of blockchain: Fullana & Ruiz (2021) note a blockchain as being immutable and transparent, while *The CPA Journal* (2017) describes blockchain technology as decentralised, strongly authenticated and tamper resistant.

Blockchain ledgers can be either public (permissionless) or private (permission) blockchains. The most infamous public blockchain is Bitcoin, where no approval is required to take part and anyone with the required software and knowledge can participate, usually in return for monetary rewards such as Bitcoin itself. Private blockchains are set up to serve a particular purpose between a particular group of people; participants are approved before being allowed to engage in the blockchain (ICAEW, 2018b).

Swan (2015), cited in Inghirami (2019), noted the following categories of blockchain:

- Blockchain 1.0 – Cryptocurrency-based blockchain such as Bitcoin, which facilitates payments and remittance services.
- Blockchain 2.0 – Smart contract-based ledgers, a more sophisticated blockchain which involves a computer program automatically completing elements of a contract, e.g. automatically making payments when conditions have been met or fulfilled. Smart contracts are making the formation and performance of contractual agreements more efficient, cost-effective and transparent (Crosby et al., 2016).
- Blockchain 3.0 – A blockchain system that extends beyond decentralised money and markets to governments, art and culture. It allows for greater scalability and interoperability with other blockchains.

Blockchain is suggested as having the potential to revolutionise the accounting profession – it brings to the world of accounting a new way of storing, recording and authenticating transactions. There are even discussions on how cryptocurrencies (which operate on blockchain technology) could replace/supplement fiat currencies. However, potential AIS incorporating blockchain would likely be within Blockchain 2.0 including the use of smart contracts. Carlin (2019, p. 310) defines smart contracts as

> executable programs that operate within a blockchain ecosystem that automatically carry out defined actions when defined triggering conditions arise. These autonomous rules-based programs continuously verify, enforce and execute the terms of contracts, resulting in the potential for material reductions in cost, dispute frequency and substantially improved predictability and transparency.

These contracts will automate tasks, and many smart contracts exist already, e.g. purchasing a chocolate bar at a vending machine or implementing standing orders/direct debits. ICAEW (2018b) notes that, within a blockchain, smart contract code can be written directly onto a blockchain and is examinable by the contracting parties ahead of time, just like a traditional legal contract. If it is agreed to, then the smart contract – armed with appropriate rights – will automatically execute its own terms, e.g. releasing a payment following a certain trigger.

Dai & Vasarhelyi (2017) explain the potential shift to blockchain as akin to moving from a double-entry to a triple-entry system. They characterise a double-entry system as centralised, with a high risk of manipulation, and as labour-intensive due to the volume of data and the relationships between them. A double-entry system precludes the use of smart contracts. With blockchain, transactions are entered on a blockchain ledger between parties (the third entry), as well as being recorded in the traditional double-entry system. However, as this third entry is on an open platform, i.e. the blockchain, where all parties must agree to the entries and are protected with cryptography to prevent manipulation, it instantly provides assurance over the transactions and therefore verifies the entries in the double-entry system.

One of the key functions of AIS is the production of the financial statements. Inghirami (2019) offers an interesting proposition, that if an entity posted all its transactions on a blockchain ledger, then by virtue of the characteristics of the technology, the transactions would be available instantaneously with a date stamp. Anyone with access to the blockchain could aggregate the transactions to prepare a set of financial statements in real time. However, they also point out that there are no studies of the application of this in AIS to date. Exploring why this is the case, they highlight some structural elements of the technology. Blockchain would require significant modification to a number of elements of organisations' ERP systems; therefore, it is believed that ERPs will not be upgraded to integrate blockchain technology (Inghirami, 2019). This idea is also supported by Fullana & Ruiz (2021), who outline that it is more likely that organisations will slowly start to implement blockchain for certain elements of their business (see also Tysiac, 2017) and that blockchain will have to exist alongside legacy and ERP systems. Tan & Low (2019) highlight that the technology, as it stands, is not sophisticated enough to enable key accounting tasks in the preparation of financial statements, such as estimates and judgements. They quote an example within Bitcoin to support this, where the logic written into the Bitcoin blockchain provides no scope for choice or judgement, e.g. the reward for Bitcoin mining is predetermined. Taken together, these suggestions indicate that blockchain is unlikely to be able to stand on its own in preparing financial statements.

As an alternative, Blockchain as a Service enables engagement with blockchain without such ERP modification and avoiding the capital cost of investment. There are several service providers emerging offering and managing various elements of the blockchain infrastructure. Inghirami (2019) cite a list of blockchain providers and their offerings, which include Microsoft (Azure), SAP cloud platform blockchain (Leonardo) and Deloitte (Rubix Core).

Companies' efforts to integrate blockchain technology into their AIS are in their infancy, but some examples are available. Tysiac (2017) noted companies are implementing blockchain into their ERP systems for tasks such as procurement and supplier management. Marr (2020) provides some examples of procurement and supply chain applications in practice, including Walmart, which utilises blockchain to verify the safety of its leafy greens. Farmers are required to input detailed records of their produce into a blockchain, and should a contamination arise in the future (e.g. *E. coli*), Walmart will be able to pinpoint affected batches more easily. They also cite the example of IBM, which utilises blockchain to understand the status and condition of every product in the supply chain from raw materials to distribution.

The blockchain facilitates a shared record of ownership and location of parts and products in real time. They suggest that these uses lead to unprecedented transparency and increased operational efficiency.

The benefits of blockchain for AIS can be summarised as follows:

- Security – Due to the requirement for consensus among the participants in the blockchain, it minimises the risk of fraud and corruption (*The CPA Journal*, 2017). However, Fullana & Ruiz (2021) note that blockchain can only provide confidence that a transaction occurred, not whether it is legal or has been authorised nor can it verify whether a transaction happened in the real world.
- Real-time reporting – Data on transactions are available to all parties in the blockchain on a real-time basis as opposed to having to wait until the end of the reporting period, as under traditional systems, it also aids the identification of fraud in real time (Wang & Kogan, 2018).
- Transparency and trust – Information available to all members of the blockchain will directly improve governance and transparency for company stakeholders as they have immediate and accurate access to data about the company (ICAEW, 2018b; Fullana & Ruiz, 2021).
- Improves the audit process – Inghirami (2019) suggests that auditors will be able to verify large portions of data within financial statements automatically, reducing the work associated with sampling and validating transactions associated with traditional AIS.

There are some challenges of blockchain in AIS, as follows:

- Lack of privacy – All participants in the blockchain have access to all transaction data. While this may be seen as an advantage in some instances, it may pose issues if the data is of a sensitive or competitive nature (Hughes et al., 2019); this may be overcome by having limited participants on a private blockchain.
- High costs – The costs of having the data spread across all participants in the blockchain are computationally expensive. It is costly to store information across all participants and to add new blocks to the blockchain (Hughes et al., 2019).
- Security model – Blockchain transactions are secured by way of public and private keys, which are used to authenticate transactions. If an individual loses their private key or accidently publishes it, there is no safety mechanism to provide additional security (Hughes et al., 2019).
- Flexibility limitations – Once transactions are approved, they are immutable unless participants agree to a change in the data (Fullana & Ruiz, 2021); this restricts flexibility and acts as a barrier to transactions that require amendments (Hughes et al., 2019).
- Non-technical limitations – Issues may include lack of user acceptance and lack of acceptance from legal and regulatory bodies (ICAEW, 2018b; Hughes et al., 2019).
- Performance – As all transactions require approval, this can slow processing within the database (ICAEW, 2018b).

In summary, it is suggested that there are benefits of blockchain technology but the why, how and, indeed, when to integrate in the AIS will require careful thought and consideration. Some organisations will be early adopters of the technology, and others will take a 'wait and see' approach; however, either way, there will be many challenges of integrating this with AIS.

Discussion and conclusions

In the preceding sections, we have outlined four contemporary technologies and their implications for AIS. Each has different implications for AIS, or indeed suggested implications, as some, particularly blockchain, are at earlier stages of implementation and research than others. Nonetheless, some common themes arise from the discussions above.

Efficiency is a commonly cited benefit of implementing these technologies – whether in replacing human agents by bots or software tools (Cooper et al., 2019), speeding analysis of data (Petkov, 2020), improving processes and controls (Dai & Vasarhelyi, 2017) or enhancing robustness/transparency with implications for audit (Inghirami, 2019). This efficiency has, in turn, been suggested as improving decision making (Cho et al., 2020; Marr, 2020) and risk assessment (Nielsen, 2015) and enabling new business activities (McCann, 2018).

Opportunities to improve the effectiveness of processes and controls are also commonly cited, including efficiency as above but also building in better analysis (Marr, 2020), accuracy of task completion (Cooper et al., 2019; Petkov, 2020) and facilitating more effective control and audit procedures (McCann, 2018; Inghirami, 2019). The corollary of this is that other authors warn of the potential risks of increasingly complex systems, making it difficult to apply professional scepticism, control and audit techniques (PWC, 2017; ICAEW, 2018a).

In many studies, the need for a changing skillset among accountants is emphasised. In the ACCA (2020b, p. 22) report, 'access to the right skills for analysing data' was one of the top three challenges identified for using analytics, with similar comments made in respect of AI and RPA. Blockchain is such a fundamental potential change that the impact on accountants has not yet been fully explored. Taken together, there is widespread acknowledgement that the skillset of an accountant is changing, and whether it is new graduates (Cooper et al., 2018) or current employees, both groups need to be adequately trained and prepared (Huerta & Jensen, 2017). This may lead to substantial positive and negative employee impact (Joshi, 2019) and potential resistance to change.

Relatedly, successful implementation of these technologies is suggested as both driving and requiring change in organisational culture, including top-level support and increasingly data-driven management (Huerta & Jensen, 2017; Cooper et al., 2019). Authors also cite a range of interrelated logistical issues with implementing these technologies, including technical compatibility with existing systems (Appelbaum et al., 2017; Inghirami, 2019; Joshi, 2019), internal IT resource availability (McCann, 2018; Bakarich & O'Brien, 2021) and cost (ICAEW, 2018a; Hughes et al., 2019; Petkov, 2020).

Threats including risk to data and security concerns are also regularly cited in respect of these technologies, including the negative impact on AIS. While these are not different from the threats to other IT systems, and countermeasures are readily available (Gotthardt et al., 2020), there is a need for care in relying on analysis based on potentially incomplete data (Petkov, 2020) and ensuring regulatory obligations are met (ACCA, 2020a).

Following on from the point above, a number of authors note increasing concern from regulators about implementation of these technologies (ICAEW, 2018a; ACCA, 2020b; Cho et al., 2020). There is potential for change to regulations including to accounting standards, auditing standards, legal requirements on company reporting and reporting to tax authorities (van der Aalst et al., 2018). Of the technologies discussed in this chapter, implementation of blockchain and AI may be particularly affected by regulatory change (ICAEW, 2018b; Hughes et al., 2019).

Our understanding of the implications of these technologies for AIS will be enhanced by further peer-reviewed empirical work. Key research questions for the future may include:

- What is the scale of uptake of these technologies in organisations, and to what extent are these integrated into the AIS?
- When taken up, what is driving the decision to implement? Is there influence from external actors, e.g. consultants, profession, regulators?
- Are suggested benefits and challenges observed, and/or are other benefits and challenges seen?
- To what extent are ethical concerns addressed, and/or what is done to build in processes for ethical behaviour?

In summary, each of the four contemporary technologies discussed in this chapter has the potential to significantly impact on AIS and accountants going forward, with some already having marked effects. For all, greater levels of implementation and research will be needed to more fully understand the implications, including the benefits and challenges. Given the rapid pace of change over the last decade, and predictions of even faster change in the next, it is likely that these technologies will develop and combine and that new technologies will emerge quickly. Considering this, regulators, professional bodies, organisations and individual accountants would be well advised to engage critically with these developments for future success.

References

ACCA. (2020a). *Professional Insight Report: Analytics in Finance and Accountancy.* https://www.accaglobal.com/in/en/professional-insights/technology/analytics_finance_accountancy.html

ACCA. (2020b, February 12). *Explainable AI: Putting the User at the Core.* https://www.accaglobal.com/in/en/professional-insights/technology/Explainable_AI.html

Appelbaum, D., Kogan, A., Vasarhelyi, M., & Yan, Z. (2017). Impact of business analytics and enterprise systems on managerial accounting. *International Journal of Accounting Information Systems, 25,* 29–44. https://doi.org/10.1016/j.accinf.2017.03.003

Bakarich, K. M., & O'Brien, P. E. (2021). The robots are coming... But aren't here yet: The use of artificial intelligence technologies in the public accounting profession. *Journal of Emerging Technologies in Accounting, 18*(1), 27–43. https://doi.org/10.2308/JETA-19-11-20-47

Brandas, C., Megan, O., & Didraga, O. (2015). Global perspectives on accounting information systems: Mobile and cloud approach. *Procedia Economics and Finance, 20,* 88–93.

Carlin, T. (2019). Blockchain and the journey beyond double entry. *Australian Accounting Review, 29*(2), 305–311. https://doi.org/10.1111/auar.12273

Cho, S., Vasarhelyi, M. A., Sun, T., & Zhang, C. (2020). Editorial: Learning from machine learning in accounting and assurance. *Journal of Emerging Technologies in Accounting, 17*(1), 1–10. https://doi.org/ 0.2308/jeta-10718

Cokins, G. (2016). The top seven trends in management accounting. *Edpacs, 53*(4), 1–7. https://doi.org/10.1080/07366981.2016.1148957

Cooper, L. A., Holderness, D. K., Sun, T., & Wood, D. A. (2019). Robotic process automation in public accounting. *Accounting Horizons, 33*(4), 15–35. https://doi.org/0.2308/acch-52466

Crosby, M., Pattanayak, P., Verma, S., & Kalyanaraman, V. (2016). Blockchain technology: Beyond bitcoin. *Applied Innovation, 2*(6–10), 71. https://j2-capital.com/wp-content/uploads/2017/11/AIR-2016-Blockchain.pdf

Dai, J., Byrnes, P., Liu, Q., & Vasarhelyi, M. (2019). Audit analytics: A field study of credit card aftersale service problem detection at a major bank. In Dai, J., Vasarhelyi, M. A., & Medinets, A. F. (Eds.), *Rutgers Studies in Accounting Analytics: Audit Analytics in the Financial Industry* (pp. 17–33). Emerald Publishing Limited.

Dai, J., & Vasarhelyi, M. A. (2017). Toward blockchain-based accounting and assurance. *Journal of Information Systems, 31*(3), 5–21. https://doi.org/10.2308/isys-51804

Davenport, T., & Fitts, J., (2021). AI can help companies tap new sources of data for analytics. https://www.tomdavenport.com/published-articles/

Ding, K., Lev, B., Peng, X., Sun, T., & Vasarhelyi, M. A. (2020). Machine learning improves accounting estimates. *Review of Accounting Studies, 25,* 1098–1134. https://doi.org/10.1007/s11142-020-09546-9

Eaglesham, J. (2013). Accounting fraud targeted. *Wall Street Journal C, 1,* C7. http://online.wsj.com/news/articles/SB10001424127887324125504578509241215284044

Fullana, O., & Ruiz, J. (2021). Accounting information systems in the blockchain era. *International Journal of Intellectual Property Management, 11*(1), 63–80. https://doi.org/10.1504/IJIPM.2021.113357

Gartner. (2013). Big Data means Big Business. http://media.ft.com/cms/4b9c7960-2ba1-11e3-bfe2-00144feab7de.pdf

Gotthardt, M., Koivulaakso, D., Paksoy, O., Saramo, C., Martikainen, M., & Lehner, O. (2020) Current state and challenges in the implementation of smart robotic process automation in accounting and auditing. *ACRN Journal of Financial and Risk Perspectives, 9,* 90–102. https://doi.org/10.35944/jofrp.2020.9.1.007

Huerta, E., & Jensen, S. (2017). An accounting information systems perspective on data analytics and Big Data. *Journal of Information Systems, 31*(3), 101–114. https://doi.org/10.2308/isys-51799

Hughes, L., Dwivedi, Y. K., Misra, S. K., Rana, N. P., Raghavan, V., & Akella, V. (2019). Blockchain research, practice and policy: Applications, benefits, limitations, emerging research themes and research agenda. *International Journal of Information Management, 49,* 114–129. https://doi.org/10.1016/j.ijinfomgt.2019.02.005

ICAEW. (2018a). *Artificial Intelligence and the Future of the Accountancy Profession.* https://www.icaew.com/-/media/corporate/files/technical/technology/thought-leadership/artificial-intelligence-report.ashx?la=en

ICAEW. (2018b). *Blockchain and the Future of Accountancy.* https://www.icaew.com/technical/technology/blockchain/blockchain-articles/blockchain-and-the-accounting-perspective

ICAEW. (2019). *Big Data and Analytics: The Impact on the Accountancy Profession.* https://www.icaew.com/-/media/corporate/files/technical/technology/thought-leadership/big-data-and-analytics.ashx

Inghirami, I. E. (2019). Accounting Information Systems in the Time of Blockchain. *[Conference paper] İtaıs 2018 Conference, 1–16. Pavia: Researchgate. Net.*

Joshi, N. (2019, 28 June). *Leverage RPA but Plan for Its Inherent Risks Too.* https://www.forbes.com/sites/cognitiveworld/2019/06/28/leverage-rpa-but-plan-for-its-inherent-risks-too/?sh=489f409611d1

Marr, B. (2020). *Tech Trends in Practice: The 25 Technologies that Are Driving the 4th Industrial Revolution.* United Kingdom: Wiley.

Marr, B. (2021a). *10 Amazing Examples of Robotic Process Automation in Practice* https://bernardmarr.com/default.asp?contentID=1909#:~:text=Robotic%20process%20automation%20reduces%20labour,million%20requests%20in%20a%20year.&text=Imagine%20RPA%20being%20the%20arms,artificial%20intelligence%20is%20the%20brains

Marr, B. (2021b). *The Six Biggest Blockchain Trends Everyone Should Know about in 2021.* https://www.forbes.com/sites/bernardmarr/2021/03/12/the-six-biggest-blockchain-trends-everyone-should-know-about-in-2021/?sh=fd9b43066315.

McCann, D. (2018, September 28). Special report: Robotic process automation. The new digital workforce. *CFO.* https://www.cfo.com/applications/2018/09/special-report-the-new-digital-workforce/

Microsoft. (2021a). *Azure AI: Make Artificial Intelligence (AI) Real for Your Business Today.* https://azure.microsoft.com/en-au/overview/ai-platform/

Microsoft. (2021b). *Power Automate: Go from Tedious to Automated with a Single RPA Solution.* https://flow.microsoft.com/en-us/robotic-process-automation

Nielsen, S. (2015). The impact of business analytics on management accounting. http://dx.doi.org/10.2139/ssrn.2616363

Oracle. (2019). *Agile Finance Unleashed: The Key Traits of Digital Finance Leaders.* https://go.oracle.com/LP=79114?elqCampaignId=169045

Petkov, R. (2020). Artificial Intelligence (AI) and the accounting function—a revisit and a new perspective for developing framework. *Journal of Emerging Technologies in Accounting, 17*(1), 99–105. https://doi.org/0.2308/jeta-52648

Pwc. (2017). *Who Minds the Robots?* https://www.pwc.com/it/it/services/robotic-process-automation/assets/docs/who-minds-robots.pdf

Redman, T. C. (2008). *Data Driven: Profiting from Your Most Important Business Asset.* Harvard Business Press.

SAP. (2021). *SAP S/4HANA Cloud.* https://www.sap.com/uk/products/s4hana-erp.html

Schneider, G. P., Dai, J., Janvrin, D. J., Ajayi, K., & Raschke, R. L. (2015). Infer, predict, and assure: Accounting opportunities in data analytics. *Accounting Horizons, 29*(3), 719–742. https://doi.org/10.2308/acch-51140

Swan, M. (2015). *Blockchain: Blueprint for a New Economy.* 'O'Reilly Media, Inc.'

Tan, B. S., & Low, K. Y. (2019). Blockchain as the database engine in the accounting system. *Australian Accounting Review, 29*(2), 312–318. https://doi.org/10.1111/auar.12278

The CPA Journal. (2017). *Why Blockchain Has the Potential to Serve as a Secure Accounting Information System.* https://www.cpajournal.com/2017/09/20/blockchain-potential-serve-secure-accounting-information-system-cpe-season/

Tysiac, K. (2017). Blockchain: An opportunity for accountants? Or a threat. *Journal of Accountancy.* https://www.journalofaccountancy.com/news/2017/nov/blockchain-opportunity-for-accountants-201717900.html

van der Aalst, W. M. P., Bichler, M., & Heinzl, A. (2018). Editorial: Robotic process automation. *Business Information Systems Engineering, 60*(4), 269–272. https://doi.org/10.1007/s12599-018-0542-4

Wang, Y., & Kogan, A. (2018). Designing confidentiality-preserving Blockchain-based transaction processing systems. *International Journal of Accounting Information Systems, 30*, 1–18. https://doi.org/10.1016/j.accinf.2018.06.001

20

TECHNOLOGY, THE FUTURE, AND US

Tadhg Nagle

Introduction

The conceptualisation of Information Systems (IS) as being an integration of people, process, and technology has been around for over 50 years,[1] yet from personal experience with organisational engagements, the embedded assumption of IS equals technology is still ingrained in their fundamental conceptualisation of the domain. In fact, academics can have similar issues as I have seen the simple request to define IS create quite a stir in an IS viva voce. However, the narrow technological view of IS serves only to make the use and exploitation of systems more difficult as it overemphasises the importance of technology over the human factor. This oversight precipitates a failure to recognise that technology will always do what it is told (follow its program), whereas people rarely do. In fact, the irrationality of human beings is becoming more understood in the context of areas such as economics (Kahneman, 2011), marketing (Ariely, 2008), and even sports (Peters, 2013). Most notably, the work of Daniel Kahneman (which won him the Nobel Memorial Prize in Economic Sciences) detailed several cognitive biases that lead to irrational decision-making. While his work was originally applied in economics, it can also be applied in IS. For instance, biases such as risk and loss aversion, the endowment effect, status quo bias, and the paradox of choice all impact our decision-making capability when it comes to IS. As a result, it can be argued that the notion of overlooking people in IS discussions will result in limited output. Furthermore, taking direction from socio-technical theories, such as Adaptive Structuration Theory (Desanctis & Poole, 1994), this discussion aligns with the notion that technology shapes us as much as we shape technology. Adaptive Structuration Theory also criticises the technocentric view of technology use and emphasises the social aspects. For instance, it denotes that people/groups using technology dynamically create perceptions about the role and utility of the technology and how it can be applied to their activities. While these perceptions can vary widely, they strongly influence the way technology is used.

Taking this line of discussion, this chapter explores several perspectives on how technology is shaping us, both individually and as a society. Several biases will be outlined especially on whether we think technology is shaping us in a good way and if we think our technological future is going to be a good place for us as a society overall. The motivation for the chapter comes from a need to be mindful of the impact of technology and possibly get us to

DOI: 10.4324/9781003132943-25

recognise our own biases and, as a result, help us make more rational decisions for the future. However, this mindfulness only comes about when we examine a wide spectrum of perspectives, from contrarian to conformist, technophile to luddite, and utopian to dystopian. The output will be food for more fruitful discussions that will provide a more rounded view on the socio-technical nature of IS. Moreover, these discussions will help provide a universal backdrop to the challenges facing Accounting Information Systems (AIS) professionals in understanding future problems, designing/implementing future solutions, and evaluating the success of these solutions.

Finally, the relevance of this discussion to AIS is also underlined by the worryingly high rate of IS failure across all types. Standing as high as 70%, the failure rate has changed very little over the last 30 years (Cecez-Kecmanovic et al., 2014), and while many factors attribute to the success and failure of IS, the focus of this chapter is on the socio-technical aspects of IS development, implementation, and usage. In particular, the chapter explores potential change driven by young people (our future business leaders) and their different attitudes to technology, the rise of new information technologies that are changing society, the bidirectional relationship between them, and the risk of not understanding either.

How technology is shaping us individually

To gauge how technology is shaping us individually, the use of generations is an effective method as it enables the tracing of adaptations made as a result of the influence of environmental changes. With each generation comes a set of new/different beliefs, abilities, and outlooks on life and living that are shared among that generation. More importantly, with new generations arises not only a sense of opportunity and evolution but also several challenges to the status quo resulting in jarring outlooks on life. Such clashes can be best viewed in large organisations, which can have up to four different generations working together at any one time (from Baby Boomers to Generation Z). For instance, in such environments, you will have people who have yet to fully adopt email as a communication tool, whereas the newer generations tend to bypass email in favour of more mobile, social, and open communication tools such as instant messaging. Given the importance of the medium of the message (McLuhan & Fiore, 1964), one can see the challenge that emerges when you try to connect to all generations.

Given the rise of technology and particularly the internet, a new generation labelled as 'Digital Natives' has come about, which details the common characteristics embodied by the individuals who have grown up in the digital era. 'Digital Native', a widely used term popularised by Prensky (2001), can be defined as an individual who has grown up in the digital era immersed in digital technology and is technologically adept (Bennett, 2012). Moreover, Digital Natives are described as digitally literate, highly connected, experiential, social, and in need of immediate gratification (McMahon & Pospisil, 2005). A key characteristic of Digital Natives is that they do not resist technology and, in particular, the internet. So much so that the internet is an indispensable part of the fabric of their life, and their norm is to be active participants and they are constantly connected (Ahern et al., 2016). In addition, Digital Natives have intertwined the digital world and its numerous technologies as part of their daily lives. For instance, ubiquitous digital connectivity can be seen in the indispensability of the internet for Digital Natives (Vodanovich et al., 2010). More importantly, Digital Natives represent the first generation to grow up surrounded by information and communications technology.

Table 20.1 Conflict of visions on Digital Natives

Constrained	Unconstrained
They're dumb	Smarter
Socially inept	Civically active
No shame	Customisers
They steal	Natural collaborators
They don't care	Innovation expected

Adapted from Tapscott (2009) and Sowell (1987).

While Digital Natives embody the adaptations to our digitally empowered world, not everybody perceives these adaptations in a positive light. In line with Sowell's (1987) *A Conflict of Visions*, which notes our disposition to have one of two totally opposing views on the nature of people, Tapscott (2009) outlined two very distinct views on Digital Natives (see Table 20.1). Mapping to Sowell's dichotomy, on the one hand, you have the unconstrained vision that Digital Natives exemplify all that is good about how technology can make us better people by providing us with new skills and abilities to do things for the good of society. On the other hand, the constrained view provides a more self-gratifying vision that leads to laziness and indifference rather than productivity and engagement. Describing this dichotomy, the work of Tapscott (2009) conducted a comprehensive investigation that included a $4 million research project and interviewed nearly 6,000 Digital Natives from around the world, disseminating the results in over 40 reports. The two contrasting views on Digital Natives are now detailed, and some interesting insights were made within both the constrained and unconstrained views.

Constrained

Digital Natives Are Dumb – it may be surprising to read there has been work done on the impact of the internet on the way we read, learn, and think. In Nicholas Carr's book *The Shallows* (2010), the argument put forward is that the internet is changing the way we think and is supported by analysing brain scans of Digital Natives. The underlying view is that the internet has enabled people to know about a lot of things as a substitute for knowing a lot about one thing.

Socially Inept – the mass substitution of face-to-face communication with social networking tools such as Facebook, SnapChat, and TikTok has created a perspective that Digital Natives are unable to socially interact with other human beings. A case in point is the sound of notification alerts replacing the sound of conversations around the dinner table. Moreover, the trend of recording and posting moments or events has become more of a priority than enjoying or living in the moment.

No Shame – Digital Natives' attitudes to sharing their lives through posts/pictures on social media have become a social norm. Moreover, this sharing often depicts the same Digital Natives in a less than favourable light – so much so that recruiters are actively using social networks to find out more about their potential candidates.

They Steal – the rise of peer-to-peer networks and the use of BitTorrent services have seen a proliferation of copyright infringement across all types of digital media. There is almost the expectation that newly created digital products will be available for free regardless of the legal implications of sourcing the digital products from unofficial channels.

They Do Not Care – one of the key aspects of the constrained view is the lack of empathy for others. The actions of Digital Natives can be viewed as totally self-serving, with no appreciation of the impact of their actions on others. For instance, the notoriety of creating a viral post has often come at an unfair cost to unsuspecting people at the focus of the post. Such cases have a requirement for search engines to implement the 'right to be forgotten' rule (in Europe) and delete any search results to such cases.

Unconstrained

Digital Natives Are Smarter – with ubiquitous access to information through smart devices and future AIS, Digital Natives can make better decisions. When deciding to buy a product or go to a movie, they can consult the opinions of hundreds of reviews or even a meta-review on those reviews. Using wearable devices, they now have the ability to create a dashboard from which they are more informed about how they live their lives. Through the utilisation of online educational resources, Digital Natives have been able to self-direct their learning outside of formal methods. One such resource, the Khan Academy, has over 10 million unique users per month, which highlights the demand for online education by Digital Natives (Murphy et al., 2014).

Natural Collaborators – the frictionless nature of the internet and ease in which people can connect make it a perfect environment for collaboration. As a result, collaboration platforms that allow people to connect and collaborate to solve real problems are now commonplace in organisations. For instance, CrowdANALYTIX is one of the most recent platforms that focus on data problems like predicting airline delays in the US. In addition, collaboration features are becoming standard in AIS and Enterprise Systems.

Innovation Is Expected – one of the most striking characteristics of Digital Natives is their ability to adapt to new technologies. Living in a world where technology lifecycles are continually reducing while the number of new technologies is increasing, the new generation has come to expect disruption as the new norm. The rise of businesses such as Airbnb and Uber points to an appetite to disrupt current systems and value chains in favour of a more innovative solution.

They Are Keen Customisers – just observe the multitude of creative pieces on Musical.ly to see how keen Digital Natives are on customisation. But while Musical.ly is an indication of their desire to customise, the real impact will come from the proliferation of 3D printers and the resulting universe of designs and products. In addition, the open community is providing opportunities for Digital Natives to customise existing open-source products to a flavour that suits their needs.

They Are Civically Active – the activity of Digital Natives in civic matters can be seen in the importance that political campaigns include a strong focus on social media channels. An in-depth study on the use of social media and participation in civic matters (Boulianne, 2015) highlighted that while the data is inconclusive and hard to quantify the impact of social media, it did show that in general, it 'plays a positive role in participation'. Again, one need only look at the use of social media in the Obama campaigns of 2008 (Aaker & Chang, 2009) and the Arab Spring in 2011 (Khondker, 2011) for evidence of this.

Bridging the gap

In contrast to Digital Natives, Digital Immigrants are those who were not born into a digitally connected world. Within accounting departments, we need to be mindful of the conflicts that arise between Digital Natives and Digital Immigrants. Such conflicts will manifest in situations where Digital Natives will expect social media tools to aid communication and collaboration and ultimately support better productivity in their role. As it stands, college students are spending an average of four hours or more on social media each day (Kettle et al., 2016; Ahmed, 2019). This may go against the views of their traditional counterparts as social media may be perceived as primarily a social tool used only for gossip and sharing photos. As a result, AIS will have to bridge the needs of those two groupings while taking the advantages of both outlooks and minimising any downsides. This sounds like a big task; however, organisations are starting to tackle such challenges but implementing tools such as slack.com. A tool for managing projects, at first glance, it looks to be more suited to Digital Natives with an interface that is very similar to Twitter or Facebook. However, the more you delve into the system, the more traditional communication features are included. Also, with compliance, security, and data retention features, many of the risks associated (e.g. data loss, hacking, and unauthorised access) with using a social media type system within an organisation are mitigated. Moreover, there is no reason why future AIS will not be able to harness the potential of this generation to the benefit of users and customers alike.

Another and possibly more robust solution is the implementation of Design Thinking when developing or embedding new AIS. Design Thinking is a human-centred approach to solving problems, which embraces integrative thinking, optimism, experimentation, collaboration, and stakeholder empathy (Brown, 2008). By taking into account multiple perspectives and being able to empathise with those perspectives is a key aspect that enables the development of solutions that better fit the people component of an IS. There is no doubt that differences will emerge from the way people see their world, but even the attempt of building a shared understanding between these perspectives will create a much more valuable output than if it was never attempted. Moreover, the tools and techniques needed to apply Design Thinking and build a shared understanding are very simple and straightforward. For instance, 'Draw How to Make Toast' (http://www.drawtoast.com/) is an excellent example of how the human-centred approach can be incorporated into systems design and problem-solving. Using similar techniques, inclusive bottom-up solutions are developed that in my experience have a much stronger success rate.

How technology is shaping our society

Having looked at how technology is shaping us at a micro (individual) level, this section explores how technology is shaping us at a macro (societal) level. There are again many differing views presented, but to preface those views, it is worth noting that we have for the most part become a society that accepts each technological juggernaut with a sense of optimistic adoption that each innovation is making our lives easier and better. Exploring these themes, two key social and economic affordances of technology are discussed (connectedness and productivity) with respect to the impact on us and our future.

Connectedness

One of the greatest benefits of technology has been our increased ability to communicate and connect with each other. The ability and hunger for conversation and communication is something that defines the human race. Thus, it is no surprise that we are constantly demanding more ways to connect and communicate with others through technology. However, the impact of the level of connectedness we have achieved has gone well beyond the increased facilitation of conversations to new economic realities in which the trade-off of richness and reach no longer applies. As a result, societies/organisations/groups can more easily be structured in the form of networks in contrast to hierarchies (Evans & Wurster, 1997).

This need to be connected is fully evident in the popularity of social media sites and a significant amount of 'friends' or 'connections' that users amass through their profiles. Does the question arise if such a volume of friends is natural or even valuable? On the face of it, we seem to have more 'friends', but studies have shown that loneliness is at epidemic levels and rising for both young and old. In addition, we have been described as living in an 'age of loneliness' where loneliness is twice as deadly as obesity and as potent as smoking 15 cigarettes a day (Monbiot, 2014). In his research, Dunbar (1992) suggests that humans can only support a limited number of relationships. That 150 number (the Dunbar Number) incorporates the number of people one knows and keeps social contact with and is linked to our cognitive ability or size of our neocortex. This number was further substantiated by the size of historic communities/settlements, which tended to fall in line with the number. But if our cognitive limit is 150 and the average amount of connections or friends is well in excess of that number, it is a case of 'our eyes being bigger than our bellies' as our hunger for connections outstrips our ability to make those relationships meaningful in any way. However, seminal research on these types of relationships – which labelled them as weak ties – did find that people benefited from the relationships (Granovetter, 1973, 1983). In his research, Granovetter found that people with more weak ties were able to secure employment much faster than those with fewer weak ties. This theory suggests that weak ties provide people with access to information and resources beyond those available in their own social circle. So in the case of searching for employment, the weaker ties you have, the better chance you have of hearing about potential opportunities in the labour market. However, this does not diminish the value of strong ties as they have greater motivation to be of assistance and are typically more easily available. So, while you may find it easier to get a new job through your weak ties, make sure you do not overlook your strong ties as they are more important for your overall well-being.

Since the rise of telecommunications, the notion of the global village has become a reality. Online communities are a core part of the internet and have enabled like-minded people to collaborate at a level that is arguably richer and more efficient than face-to-face. There are three types of online communities (Hunter & Stockdale, 2009): (i) socially constructed communities, (ii) business-sponsored communities, and (iii) volunteer-orientated communities. Socially constructed communities are built to support specific interests by providing information and support through community activities. Business-sponsored communities are developed for the sole purpose of supporting a commercial entity. For instance, many tech companies now have a sponsored community for their customers to engage with other customers and solve common problems. Finally, there are volunteer-orientated communities that can be created by local groups for the likes of sports teams or global groups for wider issues like the environment. However, given this increased ability to connect and engage with communities has made them a channel for false information that private citizens can consume directly. Indeed, during the Covid-19 pandemic, the spread of false information was so prevalent that it was labelled as an 'infodemic' by the World Health Organization.[2] Moreover, infodemics are fuelled by three types of information.

Disinformation: this is essentially false information that is spread with the sole purpose of causing confusion and harm.

Misinformation: information that is not complete or taken out of context. The motive is not malicious but can still be harmful. Decisions based on misinformation are rarely sound ones.

Amateur analysis: this describes analysis often based on trusted datasets but conducted or presented poorly, leading to misinterpretation. We are constantly being exposed to data visualisations presenting data in very innovative ways. Yet many lack details or indeed an explanation of what the data does and does not tell us.

While organisations or adopters of AIS may feel insulated from such risks, they should take note that social features are being integrated into many applications, increasing the opportunity to spread all three types of information. However, even more relevant is the amount of bad data that is already in organisations. For instance, a recent study showed that only 3% of organisations met basic data quality standards (Nagle et al., 2018). One need only read the 'Horror Story' section[3] of the European Spreadsheet Risks Interest Group to see the impact of amateur analysis.

Productivity

In the early 1930s, John Maynard Keynes, an economist whose work is still held in high regard, wrote the paper 'Economic Possibilities for Our Grandchildren' (Keynes, 1930), which contained some interesting observations about the future they were facing at the time. Of particular interest are the observations on technology and its potential impact on the economy. Overall, Keynes painted a positive picture of the future role of technology as it would bring about greater productivity and enable people to have a 15-hour workweek as this would be enough to fulfil our economic needs. In addition, our needs would be met with the abundant creation of almost free goods and services by automated machines, liberating our focus from economic necessities to more hedonic pursuits. With the benefit of hindsight, it is possible to reflect on these observations on technology and make some inferences as to the economic possibilities of our grandchildren.

It is evident that the 15-hour workweek is not a reality. Ferris (2007) did attempt to convey a path to the 4-hour workweek, yet this has been viewed by some people as more of a fantasy or psychological tenet (the person that likes their work, never works a day in their lives) (Clark, 2012). However, reflecting on the other aspects of his observation, there are indications of an abundant supply of free goods and services, particularly information-based goods and services. Since the 1990s, the marginal cost of producing, storing, and delivering information has dropped to almost zero (Rifkin, 2014). A case in point is the book publishing industry, where Rifkin (2014, p. 4) noted:

> [A] growing number of authors are writing books and making them available at a very small price, or even for free, on the Internet – bypassing publishers, editors, printers, wholesalers, distributors, and retailers. The cost of marketing and distributing each copy is nearly free. The only cost is the amount of time consumed by creating the product and the cost of computing and connecting online. An e-book can be produced and distributed at near zero marginal cost.

Indeed, the World Wide Web itself is a free service that democratises access to information and further allows people access a huge range of other free services. However, Intellectual Property Rights (IPR) still play a big part in the commercialisation of most information services. The key argument for IPR is that it stimulates innovation as it provides an incentive to invest in innovative ventures with the guarantee that any revenue from successful outputs will be protected, thus ensuring a return on investment. This is extremely important where research and development costs are substantial, and the risks associated in bringing the innovation to market are high. On the other hand, there is the view that IPR stifles innovation as it locks down the knowledge embedded in the innovative advancement and stops the proliferation of further innovation. To work around this obstacle, several open movements have been developed: Open-Source Software, Open Innovation, and Open Data. Indeed, an indication of the maturity of these movements is their adoption into mainstream industries such as it is the case of open-banking for the banking industry.

These movements have been about opening boundaries and making information/ knowledge more accessible as they feel this is a fundamental right of people. In the case of open banking, consumers are empowered to control and securely share their data with organisations beyond their incumbent bank. It does this using Application Programming Interfaces and aims to increase competition in retail banking by developing innovative products and services, which will bring increased value to those same customers (O'Leary et al., 2021). What is interesting about open banking is that it gives us an insight into how the data-driven economy is progressing as well as how we are beginning to appreciate the value of data. For instance, the conceptually simple task of allowing customers to share their data is set to provide a range of benefits that include access to new products, improved recommendations, stronger customer relationships, increased competition, lower barriers to entry for new firms, better products, and new banking business models. In addition, the intrinsic value of data, which is very difficult to measure and account for (Short & Todd, 2017), is becoming more transparent as businesses are proposing to offset access to customer data against the price of products/services provided. However, as the value of openness and data are becoming more apparent, so too are the risks and challenges. The first challenge is around the data, digital, and financial literacy of customers. There is no benefit in affording customers the features of open banking if they don't have a basic understanding of data, technology, or finance. On the other hand, organisations may utilise open banking to implement 'sharp digitisation', which focuses on extracting maximum value from data without fully comprehending the consequences it may have on customers. In line with many other industries, the ethics of businesses will be a key factor in ensuring that the implementation of open initiatives provides benefits to all and not just the data processors.

Keynes (1930) in his paper also included the term 'technological unemployment' where automation would displace much employment in the short term but ultimately to our benefit in the long term. True to his prediction, 'technological unemployment' has taken place and is now beginning to eat away at the margins of knowledge workers. Presently, the roles of teachers, doctors, lawyers, authors, accountants, and financial advisors are being eroded by automation (Davenport & Kirby, 2016). AIS are being developed to complete specific automated audits, while robo-advisors have certainly grabbed the attention of banks by encroaching on one of their key markets. Where this erosion is going to end is of course uncertain, but there are several ongoing discussions that give some indications as to the directions it may take us.

Davenport & Kirby (2016) provide an optimistic view, with these new technologies falling into the role of human augmentation. In their book *Only Humans Need Apply*, they set out five strategies that provide an indication of how jobs will change in response to the increasing of automation. The five strategies include (i) step in – humans master the details of the system, know its strengths and weaknesses, and when it needs to be modified;

(ii) step up – humans examine the results of computer-driven decisions and decide whether to automate new decision domains; (iii) step aside – humans focus on areas that they do better than computers, at least for now; (iv) step narrowly – humans focus on knowledge domains that are too narrow to be worth automating; and (v) step forward – humans build the automated systems. Overall, the advice is to understand how computers make decisions and take action in positioning your expertise. A gloomier and stark outlook is given by Ford (2015) in his book *Rise of Robots*. Ford traces the optimistic view back to post–World War II (not too long after Keynes's paper), when a virtuous cycle of technological unemployment was replaced with more productive jobs that demanded increased wages, which drove increased demand for new products and thus more high-value jobs. However, this is not the case today as Ford (2015) observes (in the US economy) that over the last 40 years since 1973, the wages of a production worker have dropped by 13%, while productivity has increased by over 100%. Also, more worrying is the fact that in the first decade of the 21st century, there were zero new jobs created, highlighting a displacement of 10 million jobs that were supposedly needed to keep the economy ticking over.

Such a pattern also fits the impact of the internet, as seen by Keen (2015) in which he posits our tendency to be blinded by the promise of democratisation, openness, and a collaborative networked society but ultimately sleepwalking into a world that is only fuelling huge inequalities. Such inequalities are best seen in the mass transfer of wealth that has taken place from the development of networked entities like Facebook and Google as they are heading towards trillion-dollar valuations (LaMonica, 2016). These companies are very young in comparison to more traditional companies in that league and need a fraction of the amount of human capital to run them. Moreover, the nature of these entities means that they need a fraction of the human capital, which enables them to be highly scalable and efficient. It is staggering to think that Google is now generating over $1.2 million per employee, along with Facebook's $1.4 million per employee, which is still well short of Apple's $2.1 million per employee (Rosoff, 2016), which has risen to $2.3 million as per the 2021 Form 10K. If this trend is to continue, it seems that there are some very big but very few winners in the economy and society. Inequality will continue to widen, and technological unemployment will become more of a long-term phenomenon, as opposed to the short-term inconvenience as described by Keynes. What is also worth noting is that these companies do offer a host of free goods and services as Keynes described, but they are only free at a superficial level. In the case of companies like Google and Facebook, you are not really getting the goods for free as opposed to selling your data for free.

Final words

Rather than focusing on technologies, this chapter has purposefully focused on a wider socio-technical discussion. This should provide a balance to the deep discussions of specific AIS technologies and provide a reminder of the wider trends that are happening in all IS domains. AIS as a domain is inextricably linked to the technologies that are continually transforming the way we work within organisations and society. To fully appreciate this, the discussion pushes beyond AIS to a certain extent. For instance, one discussion views technology as one of our defining characteristics or an extension of who we are. Whether this is a positive development, only the future will tell. To help us navigate these wider trends within AIS, this chapter serves to promote certain types of discussions and to constantly challenge ourselves on the merits of technology for us, now and in the future.

Notes

1 First mention of people, process, and technology can be traced back to Leavitt (1965) but was brought into the IS/IT by Keen (1981) and later refined in Keen (1993).
2 https://www.who.int/health-topics/infodemic.
3 http://www.eusprig.org/horror-stories.htm.

References

Aaker, J., & Chang, V., 2009. Obama and the power of social media and technology. https://www.gsb.stanford.edu/faculty-research/case-studies/obama-power-social-media-technology, 131.

Ahern, L., Feller, J., & Nagle, T. (2016). Social media as a support for learning in universities: An empirical study of Facebook Groups. *Journal of Decision Systems*, 25(1), 35–49.

Ahmed, N., 2019. Generation Z's smartphone and social media usage: A survey. *Journalism and mass communication*, 9(3), 101–122.

Ariely, D. (2008). *Predictably Irrational*. New York: HarperCollins.

Bennett, S. (2012). Digital natives. In Zheng, Y. (ed.), *Encyclopedia of Cyber Behavior* (pp. 212–219). Albany: IGI Global.

Boulianne, S. (2015). Social media use and participation: A meta-analysis of current research. *Information, Communication & Society*, 18(5), 524–538.

Brown, T. (2008). Design thinking. *Harvard Business Review*, 86(6), 1–9.

Carr, N. (2010). *The Shallows: What the Internet Is Doing to Our Brains*. London: WW Norton & Company.

Cecez-Kecmanovic, D., Kautz, K., & Abrahall, R., 2014. Reframing success and failure of information systems. *MIS Quarterly*, 38(2), 561–588.

Clark, D. (2012). The truth behind the 4-hour workweek fantasy. *Harvard Business Review, 2016*. Retrieved from https://hbr.org/2012/10/the-truth-behind-the-4-hour-fa/

Davenport, T. H., & Kirby, J. (2016). *Only Humans Need Apply: Winners and Losers in the Age of Smart Machines*. New York: HarperCollins.

Desanctis, G., & Poole, M. S. (1994). Capturing the complexity in advanced technology use - adaptive structuration theory. *Organization Science*, 5(2), 121–147.

Dunbar, R. (1992). Neocortex size as a constraint on group size in primates. *Journal of Human Evolution*, 22(6), 469–493.

Evans, P. B., & Wurster, T. S. (1997). Strategy and the new economics of information. *Harvard Business Review*, 75(5), 70–83.

Ferris, T. (2007). *The 4-Hour Workweek: Escape the 9-5, Live Anywhere and Join the New Rich*. New York: Crown Publishing Group.

Ford, M. (2015). *Rise of the Robots: Technology and the Threat of a Jobless Future*. London: Oneworld Publications.

Granovetter, M. (1973). The strength of weak ties. *American Journal of Sociology*, 78(6), 1360–1380.

Granovetter, M. (1983). The strength of weak ties: A network theory revisited. *Sociological Theory*, 1(1), 201–233.

Hunter, M. G., & Stockdale, R. (2009). *Taxonomy of Online Communities: Ownership and Value Propositions*. Paper presented at the System Sciences, 2009. HICSS'09. 42nd Hawaii International Conference on System Sciences, Hawaii

Kahneman, D. (2011). *Thinking, Fast and Slow*. New York: Macmillan.

Keen, A. (2015). *The Internet Is Not the Answer*. London: Atlantic Books Ltd.

Keen, P. G. W. (1981). Information systems and organizational change. *Communications of the ACM*, 24(1), 24–33.

Keen, P. G. W. (1993). Information technology and the management difference - a fusion map. *IBM Systems Journal*, 32(1), 17–39.

Kettle, P., Gilmartin, N., Corcoran, M. P., Byrne, D., & Sun, T. (2016). Time Well Spent? A survey of student online media usage. *Maynooth University*.

Keynes, J. M. (1930). Economic possibilities for our grandchildren. In Keynes, J. M. (ed.), *Essays in persuasion* (pp. 358–373). London: Palgrave Macmillan.

Khondker, H. H. (2011). Role of the new media in the Arab Spring. *Globalizations*, 8(5), pp. 675–679.

LaMonica, P. (2016). Why Facebook could one day be worth $1 trillion. *CNN Money, 2016*. Retrieved from http://money.cnn.com/2016/04/28/investing/facebook-trillion-dollar-market-value/

Leavitt, H. J. (1965). *Applying Organizational Change in Industry: Structural, Technological and Humanistic Approaches* (1st ed.). Chicago, IL: Rand McNaily.

McLuhan, M., & Fiore, Q. (1964). The medium is the message. In Durham, M. G. & Kellner, D. M. (eds.), *Understanding Media: The Extensions of Man, 23–35.* New York: Signet.

McMahon, M., & Pospisil, R. (2005). Laptops for a digital lifestyle: Millennial students and wireless mobile technologies. *Proceedings of the Australasian Society for Computers in Learning in Tertiary Education, 2,* 421–431.

Monbiot, G. (2014). The age of loneliness is killing us. *The Guardian, 2016.* Retrieved from https://www.theguardian.com/commentisfree/2014/oct/14/age-of-loneliness-killing-us

Murphy, R., Gallagher, L., Krumm, A. E., Mislevy, J., & Hafter, A. (2014). *Research on the Use of Khan Academy in Schools.* Retrieved from https://www.sri.com/sites/default/files/publications/2014-03-07_implementation_briefing.pdf:

Nagle, T., Redman, T. C., & Sammon, D. (2018). Waking up to Data Quality. *European Business Review.* Retrieved from http://www.europeanbusinessreview.com/waking-up-to-data-quality/

O'Leary, K., O'Reilly, P., Nagle, T., Filelis-Papadopoulos, C., & Dehghani, M. (2021). *The Sustainable Value of Open Banking: Insights from an Open Data Lens.* Paper presented at the Proceedings of the 54th Hawaii International Conference on System Sciences.

Peters, S. (2013). *The Chimp Paradox: The Mind Management Program to Help You Achieve Success, Confidence, and Happiness.* New York: Tarcher.

Prensky, M. (2001). Digital natives, digital immigrants. *On the Horizon, 9*(6), 1–6.

Rifkin, J. (2014). *The Zero Marginal Cost Society: The Internet of Things, the Collaborative Commons, and the Eclipse of Capitalism.* New York: Macmillan.

Rosoff, M. (2016). Here's how much each employee at a big tech company like Apple or Facebook is worth. *Business Insider, 2016(June).* Retrieved from http://uk.businessinsider.com/revenue-per-employee-at-apple-facebook-google-others-2016-2?r=US&IR=T

Short, J., & Todd, S. (2017). What's Your Data Worth? *Mit Sloan Management Review, 58*(3), 17.

Sowell, T. (1987). *A Conflict of Visions.* New York: Morrow.

Tapscott, D. (2009). *Grown Up Digital.* New York: McGraw-Hill.

Vodanovich, S., Sundaram, D., & Myers, M. (2010). Research commentary—digital natives and ubiquitous information systems. *Information Systems Research, 21*(4), 711–723.

21

CHALLENGES TO TECHNOLOGY IMPLEMENTATION

Pierangelo Rosati and Theo Lynn

Introduction

Technologies to support the processing and distribution of data evolved over the past five decades from systems for mere data processing to systems designed to support decision making from a wide range of perspectives, whether at the organisation, group or individual level or the operational, tactical or strategic level. More recently, the emergence of digital technologies is challenging our assumptions around technology adoption. More powerful and intelligent infrastructure combined with unparalleled access to data is creating new business models that introduce new complexities; complexities that accounting information systems (AIS) are not insulated from. Similarly, research on the adoption of information systems is not new, and these are, for the most part, applicable to AIS. Like other disciplines, accountants and financial professionals face emerging adoption challenges resulting from new technologies, not least external and internal compliance reporting (Belfo & Trigo, 2013).

This chapter starts with a discussion of the traditional challenges in information systems adoption. We examine the empirical literature from five perspectives, i.e. project management, technology, user resistance, organisational/environmental and outsourcing challenges. One could argue that cloud computing, and in particular public cloud computing, is a natural extension of outsourcing, in that firms outsource not only their information systems but also their entire infrastructure on a shared distributed basis. The traditional AIS market has been disrupted by cloud computing with legacy software vendors migrating to the cloud often merely to compete with native cloud accounting service providers, such as Xero. However, cloud computing both exacerbates traditional information systems challenges and creates new ones. The final section of this chapter discusses some of the emerging challenges for AIS adoption related to cloud computing, big data analytics and mobile technologies. This includes a discussion on challenges related to migration to the cloud, security, data protection and information and communication technologies (ICT) governance and contractual issues.

Traditional challenges to information systems implementation

There is a well-established literature base on the traditional challenges of information systems implementation providing evidence of the negative consequences for organisations

DOI: 10.4324/9781003132943-26

both in terms of financial losses (Nelson, 2007; Laumer & Eckhardt, 2012; Maier et al., 2013) and litigation (Wailgum, 2009). In addition, commentators report information technology (IT) project failure rates remain high. The Standish Group (2020) reports that roughly two out of three IT projects typically fail, a relatively constant rate since 2011. Causal analysis of such implementation failures suggests that failure can be attributed to well-known issues in IT management studies, which we label as *Traditional Challenges*, namely Project Management Challenges, Technology Challenges, User Resistance Challenges, Organisational/Environment Challenges and Outsourcing Challenges. These challenges should not be viewed as independent from each other. On the contrary, they are deeply interconnected and interdependent. All these potential issues should be evaluated but also the relationships between them.

Project management challenges

Information systems projects are particularly challenging from a management perspective mainly because of their hidden complexity and uncertainty (Peffers et al., 2003). Furthermore, information systems projects require the intense collaboration of several different groups of stakeholders, e.g. IT staff, users and management (Dechow & Mouritsen, 2005; Quattrone & Hopper, 2005). Therefore, the ability to communicate and coordinate the activities of the group is extremely important (Ewusi-Mensah, 1997; Sumner, 1999).

Nelson (2007) shows that mistakes concerning processes or people account the majority of failures, i.e. 45% and 43%, respectively. The remaining 12% is due to product (8%) or technology mistakes (4%). This highlights the importance of process and people management in information systems projects. Nelson (2007) analyses 99 projects conducted by 74 organisations over a seven-year period and comes to the conclusion that project failure is rooted in a series of missteps by project managers. Such mistakes (i.e. *Classic Mistakes*) can be grouped into four categories[1] – people, process, outputs and technology. From a people perspective, two key challenges emerge. First, careful implementation of the team configuration is critical to ensure the team has all the individual capabilities required in the project, and members can create productive working relationships (Lakhanpal, 1993; Fui-Hoon Nah et al., 2001). Second, it is important to keep the team members motivated throughout the project since motivation is a well-known driver of productivity and quality (Borcherding et al., 1980; Boehm, 1981). Problems amongst team members typically arise, and in such cases, the project manager should deal with a problematic team member as soon as possible and, ideally, achieve a win-win solution. Conflicts may compromise group motivation or intra-group relationships resulting in project failures (Larson & LaFasto, 1989).

The second category of challenges in information systems projects is around process issues. Smith & Reinertsen (1998) term the earliest stage of a project as the "fuzzy front end". The fuzzy end denotes all time and activity spent on an idea prior to the first official group meeting. Understanding the "fuzzy front end" has been a challenge for different types of organisations (Reid & De Brentani, 2004). Detailed and better understanding of the project requirements and the activities envisaged within a project may lead towards a successful implementation. Commentators suggest project management tends to waste time in this phase due to ineffective governance processes (Khurana & Rosenthal, 1997; Umble & Umble, 2001), thus resulting in an aggressive implementation schedule. Such overly optimistic schedules put excessive pressure on team members (McConnell, 2006). An acceptable trade-off in terms of time dedicated to project planning and implementation would increase the likelihood of project success. Finally, it is important to assess and control project risk (Aloini et al., 2007). Project managers may feel somewhat helpless managing risk particularly when risks are outside of their immediate control. However, risk management is critical (Cervone, 2006). Risk can be reduced (or eliminated) through problem remediation activities in the project plan, transferred to other activities or third parties (e.g. software vendor), absorbed by simply planning the required actions or avoided by implementing quality controls. A honest risk assessment during the project planning phase will lead to more effective and efficient decision making throughout the project lifetime and has a clear impact on the project outcomes (Chapman & Ward, 2003).

The third category concerns the output of the project (i.e. product). Often developers and project managers tend to add additional features, capabilities or changes, which are expected to increase user satisfaction or systems effectiveness (Addison & Vallabh, 2002; Elliott, 2007; Malhotra et al., 2012). This so-called feature-creep can lead to unnecessary costs, higher project complexity and delay (Landis et al., 1992; Murray, 2001). Therefore, it is important that project managers define clearly what the outputs and the boundaries of the project are.

The final category relates to technology. New technologies can be viewed as a panacea for problems. Nelson (2007) labels this tendency as the "silver-bullet syndrome". However, new technologies change constantly and are, therefore, unstable (Fraser et al., 2007). What seems the best solution today might not be so tomorrow, and the search for silver bullets prevents deeper analyses in organisational needs and priorities (Lyytinen & Robey, 1999). As technology evolves, management may be tempted to switch tools in the middle of a project, which can be detrimental from a technological and motivational perspective.

Technology challenges

Traditionally, information systems tend to present as large integrated, process-oriented packaged software designed to meet most needs of organisations (Pulakanam & Suraweera, 2010; Strong & Volkoff, 2010; Grabski et al., 2011). However, Markus (2000) points out that such systems address only 70% of the needs of the average organisation. Both providers and organisations have improved their ability to configure and implement enterprise systems over time, but a certain misfit between organisational needs and system characteristics still persists (Strong & Volkoff, 2010). Existing misfits create significant challenges in adopting such systems and in evaluating the success of the implementation. Strong & Volkoff (2010) classify possible misfits into six categories and identify, for each category, two types of misfits, namely deficiencies and impositions. A deficiency is a system feature that the organisation needs but is missing in the system, while an imposition is a problem that the organisation has to face because of the system's inherent characteristics.

Functionality. In some instances, the usage of an information system may reduce process efficiency or effectiveness. Functionality deficiencies are due to the impossibility of performing simple tasks because of system restrictions (e.g. minimum amount required for a purchase order); these issues are usually fixed with little customisation or future releases. Functionality impositions arise when the system prevents users from performing tasks in a non-standard order. Information systems may not allow such actions because of the level of integration and standardisation of the business processes required by the system (Gattiker & Goodhue, 2005; Volkoff et al., 2005).

Data. Data misfits arise when data or data characteristics provided or needed by the system lead to data quality issues, e.g. inaccuracy or inaccessibility. A data deficiency issue, for example, may emerge when the number of product attributes is not sufficient. In contrast, a data imposition issue may arise where a common data definition has not been implemented across the system.

Usability. A usability misfit occurs when the system requires more non-value-added steps to complete a task. A common usability deficiency is inappropriate report designs. The difficulty in using data because of different identifiers (e.g. product code versus purchase order) is, instead, an example of usability imposition.

Role. Role misfits can be one of the most problematic. These occur when the end user roles in the information system are inconsistent with the roles that end users hold in the organisation. These may create workload imbalances and bottlenecks causing a significant loss in efficiency. A role deficiency occurs when a role in the organisation is diffused across many roles in the systems. A role imposition misfit, instead, arises when a role in the system has more responsibility than in the organisation; this creates additional role misfits for some employees that cannot be easily alleviated by other end users because of the restrictions on the authority of each role.

Control. Control misfits occur when the controls embedded in the system are so strict that they constrain productivity or, on the contrary, are so weak that they do not allow adequate monitoring of the performance of a function. A control deficiency may occur when the system rules would require too much unproductive work for little control benefit (e.g. moving inventories back and forth from the warehouse). In contrast, a control imposition misfit may occur when stringent system controls cause production delays.

Organisation and Culture. The final category relates to organisational and culture misfits. Tan et al. (1998) show significant differences between individualistic (US) and collectivistic (Singapore) cultures, and their results are further confirmed regarding other Asian countries (Soh et al., 2000; Davison, 2002; Martinsons, 2004). Nevertheless, the adoption of information systems may conflict also with organisational culture (Markus, 2004). In the context of organisational misfits, there are only impositions. This type of misfits is particularly challenging because it can require modification of the company culture as well as the relationship between organisational functions. Indeed, information systems typically place more focus on finance and financial controls, and this might create significant internal frictions that need to be addressed.

User resistance challenges

One of the main reasons for information systems project failures is user resistance (Keen, 1981; Markus, 1983; Krasner, 2000). User resistance should not be ignored since minor resistance can reduce the speed of change, and major resistance can lead management to abandon the project. There are different levels of resistance behaviours and, therefore, potential consequences. Users can decide to not adopt the new system (Joseph, 2005), to not cooperate, to sabotage the project (Carnall, 1986) or even to engage in physically destructive actions (Marakas & Hornik, 1996). Klaus & Blanton (2010) identify 12 determinants of user resistance that managers should consider in adopting information systems and classify these factors into four categories as summarised in Table 21.1

To lower user resistance, managers should first identify the main user(s) of the system. Research shows that regarding the implementation of AIS, the system adoption (i.e. acceptance) by accountants within the organisation is a key factor for a successful implementation (Pulakanam & Suraweera, 2010; Vatanasakdakul et al., 2010). As a second step, managers should carefully assess what users need and what they expect from the new system, make them aware of the key objectives of the project and provide them with adequate support during the early stage of the adoption.

Table 21.1 Categories and determinants of user resistance in information systems projects

Category	Determinants	Description
Individual Issues	Uncertainty	Users are unclear of the future and view a new system as a potential threat to their job.
	Input	A new system is usually forced upon users without being able to contribute to the change process.
	Power	A new system can cause a loss of control or recognition as an "expert" inside the organisation.
	Self-efficacy	A new system may cause a lack of confidence in the skill set needed.
System Issues	Technical	Users are suddenly required to use a system with bugs and features that do not work, and they do not have figured "work-arounds" to these problems.
	Complexity	Users experience confusion when using a new system, which typically consists of many modules.
Organisational Issues	Facilitating Environment	Users working in a static organisation (i.e. bureaucratic) are more likely to resist to the adoption of new information systems since they expect (are used) to face only small incremental changes.
	Communication	Users who have not been informed about the benefits of the system, and the reasons behind the change are more likely to create resistance.
	Training	Users tend to perceive training as a waste of time while it is a key element of a successful implementation.
Process Issues	Job or Skill Change	Users may be required to perform different tasks following the adoption of a new system, and it might cause a learning process which requires a certain effort.
	Workload	The adoption of a new system usually requires additional effort during the implementation and in the daily usage. This aspect is particularly detrimental if users do not feel compensated for the workload change.
	Lack of Fit	A new system may force the organisation to change the organisational structure with consequences on users' daily activities.

Organisational/environment perspective

The definition of successful implementation of an information system rests mostly on subjective evaluation and depends on the context of application (Heeks, 2002). In deciding whether to adopt an information system, and which system to implement, management should assess the alignment between the organisation's information and business strategy (Parker & Benson, 1989; Henderson & Venkatraman, 1993; Davenport, 1998; Belfo & Trigo, 2013). According to Smits et al. (2003), managers should examine (at least) six factors which define the organisation's competitive environment. These include the organisation's position in the industry, distribution channels, special events (e.g. mergers and acquisitions), organisation size, the degree of organisation innovativeness and the presence of an existing legacy information system. These factors all impact the decision-making process and risk profile for information systems implementation.

The sector (public versus private) in which the organisation operates has also been found to have a significant effect on its culture. According to Bannister (2001), there are many important organisational differences between the public sector and the private sector in terms of culture, structure, technology and resources. Public-sector projects tend to have the following characteristics – large scale, unproven technology, hierarchical and bureaucratic decision making – and are often implemented as a result of statutory, parliamentary or supranational regulations (Jones, 2008). Furthermore, such projects are usually shaped by strong political factors (Introna, 1997; Gauld, 2007). Consequently, the differences in terms of management's incentives, objectives and leverages in the public and private sector should lead towards different information strategies.

Heeks (2002) suggests that the country or region(s) in which an information system will be implemented may also impact its potential success. Historically, information systems were designed in developed countries (Barrett et al., 2001), but the contexts of the designers and end users may be very distant in physical, cultural and economic ways (Heeks, 2002). Heeks (2002) argues that the gap between design and reality (i.e. design–actuality gap) is the main reason behind the high failure rate in information system implementation projects in developing countries and suggests that management should pay attention to three main factors in adopting a new information system in these contexts. First, the flexibility of the system. The system should not embed too many assumptions about users' roles and activities' organisation. Second, the potential for customisation. System customisations may lead to a better fit between the organisation and the system itself. Third, the availability of local resources since the involvement of people who know both the system and the local reality is essential for project success.

Outsourcing challenges

Outsourcing is generally defined as the commissioning of third-party management of IT assets/activities to required result (Willcocks & Lester, 2000). As of the early 1990s, management and accounting scholars have endorsed outsourcing as a promising business strategy (Bardi & Tracey, 1991; Sonnenberg, 1992; Apte & Mason, 1995; Lei & Hitt, 1995; Anderson & Sedatole, 2003; Christ et al., 2014). There is a general argument that organisations should focus on their core competencies and outsource all other activities to optimise the resource allocation (Lambert & Peppard, 2013). Famous companies (e.g. AstraZeneca, Procter & Gamble and Texas Instruments)[2] have successfully outsourced part of or their entire manufacturing processes generating significant operational efficiencies.

Outsourcing AIS, or information systems more generally, is a more recent trend. Technological advancements have significantly improved the extent, speed and reliability of global communications and have made easier to outsource critical activities (Levy, 2005; Blinder, 2006; Stratman, 2008; Contractor et al., 2010). As a result, outsourcing information systems has become a common business practice (Jay, 2009; Fitoussi & Gurbaxani, 2012; Han & Mithas, 2013), and its trend is still upward.

Despite the growing importance of outsourcing in the IT domain, and despite the lower technology barriers, outsourcing AIS still represents a significant challenge for both users and providers. Indeed, the decision to outsource AIS generates significant and specific risks that can be classified into three broad categories:

Relational risk. This is the risk that the partnership fails due to poor cooperation and opportunistic behaviour (Das & Teng, 1996). Relational risk arises mainly because of the intangible nature of information (Christ et al., 2014). Indeed, deliverables are hard to define and difficult to measure, thus creating an adequate contractual regime, and monitoring it over the implementation period represents a real challenge (Banker et al., 2006). Furthermore, opportunistic behaviours may arise when a user becomes too dependent from its provider (i.e. lock-in), and the latter takes advantage of the situation by increasing service price or lowering service quality (Aron & Liu, 2005).

Performance risk. This is the risk that operational or performance factors undermine the success of the partnership despite full cooperation amongst partners (Das & Teng, 1996). Difficulties in defining what the expected deliverables are and how to measure their quality can lead to an increase in performance risk. The risk of misunderstanding between users and providers and, therefore, the risk of failure are significantly higher in this situation (Michell & Fitzgerald, 1997; Willcocks & Lacity, 1999). Furthermore, AIS management requires extensive implicit knowledge (Leonardi & Bailey, 2008). Such knowledge is typically difficult to transfer, and the sharing process may require long time, significant effort and strong commitment to both users and providers as well as the alignment of their objectives. Finally, performance risk also rises when the function is off-shored, when a user engages multiple service providers (Bierstaker et al., 2013) or when the service provider does not have the expertise, sophistication, experience or knowledge of the user's business (Christ et al., 2014).

Compliance and regulatory risk. This is the risk that the user fails to adhere to regulatory standards because of the provider's errors (Anderson et al., 2014). Outsourcing AIS involves sharing data, lowering control over the outsourced system and relying upon information generated by a third party (Christ et al., 2014). Compliance and regulatory risks are particularly high in this context since the user remains responsible for the work performed by the provider, and inaccurate or non-compliant data may result in fines and penalties (Christ et al., 2014). In addition to regulatory penalties, reporting irregularities may cause a loss in terms of company reputation and value (Dechow et al., 1996), making the potential consequences of non-compliance even worse.

Mitigating these risks is a main concern of companies willing to outsource their AIS, and three key factors may provide a significant contribution towards such achievement (Blaskovich & Mintchik, 2011; Christ et al., 2014). First, managers should adopt a strategic approach to outsourcing. Investing time in clarifying expectations, choosing appropriate monitoring tools and defying long-term objectives may prevent future pains (Saunders et al., 1997; Osei-Bryson & Ngwenyama, 2006). Second, the selection of the right provider is key, and managers should evaluate both its business-specific knowledge and past experiences (Lee & Kim, 1999; Lee, 2001). Third, effective communication and knowledge sharing between partners may make it easier to align their objectives and to implement effective monitoring mechanisms (Lee, 2001, Bandyopadhyay & Pathak, 2007, Han et al., 2008).

Emerging challenges

The last decade has seen the emergence and increasing adoption of digital technologies that have resulted in ubiquitous access to the Internet for billions of users and generate unprecedented volumes of data. For enterprises, there are much cited benefits in the adoption of some of these technologies such as cloud computing, big data analytics and mobile computing; however, there are new challenges and risks to overcome in order to garner the value promised by them. This section discusses some of the challenges presented by cloud computing, big data and mobile working.

Cloud computing

Cloud computing represents a horizontal technology that enables several other digital applications and has emerged as one of the major paradigms in information systems research and practice. Cloud computing represents a convergence of two major trends in IT (Kim, 2009):

- IT efficiency, whereby modern computers are utilised more efficiently via highly scalable distributed hardware and software resources.
- Business agility, whereby IT can be used as a competitive tool through rapid deployment, parallel batch processing, use of computer-intensive business analytics and mobile interactive applications that respond in real time to consumer requirements.

The US National Institute of Standards and Technology (NIST) defines cloud computing as:

> a model for enabling ubiquitous, convenient, on-demand network access to a shared pool of configurable computing resources (e.g. networks, servers, storage, applications and services) that can be rapidly provisioned and released with minimal management effort or service provider interaction.
>
> *(Mell & Grance, 2011)*

The NIST definition of cloud computing refers to three service models (Software as a Service (SaaS), Cloud Platform as a Service (PaaS) and Cloud Infrastructure as a Service (IaaS)) and four deployment models (Private cloud, Community cloud, Public cloud and Hybrid cloud) (Mell & Grance, 2011). Organisations of all sizes and sectors are adopting cloud computing to exploit the advantages of the agility and scalability (up and down) inherent in cloud computing (Sclater, 2009; Sultan, 2010; Lian et al., 2013; Oliveira et al., 2014). Commonly cited benefits include work efficiencies, reduced IT costs (including IT capital expenditure, maintenance and support costs and related environmental costs), business continuity and scalability (Buyya et al., 2009; Hogan et al., 2011; Low et al., 2011). Unsurprisingly, a wide variety of software vendors have adopted cloud computing across the range of software functions including sales and marketing (Salesforce.com, Hubspot, Marketo), HR (Oracle Taleo, SAP SuccessFactors, Workday) and, of course, accounting (Xero, Big Red Book, Sage Live).

Despite the many perceived and actual benefits, cloud computing provides unique implementation challenges and perceived barriers to adoption. These include general technological challenges (migration, interoperability and portability), security, data protection and ICT governance and contractual issues (Leimbach et al., 2014). We discuss these now in some detail.

Technological challenges

There are a number of technological challenges for those seeking to exploit cloud computing, which largely revolve around migration to a cloud service, between cloud services and off a cloud service (Church et al., 2020). Many organisations make use of legacy systems either developed entirely within an organisation or extended and customised from a generic software base over time. The extent of customisation and/or embeddedness of these systems with other software systems or organisation processes can make it challenging, both technologically and culturally, to migrate to the cloud. Andrikopoulos et al. (2013) present four primary strategies for migration to the cloud, which present their own challenges:

- Replace components with cloud offerings;
- Partially migrate some of the application functionality to the Cloud;
- Migrate the whole software stack of the application to the Cloud;
- Cloudify the application: a complete migration of the application takes place.

At a more granular level, enterprises will face technological challenges at different layers within their information systems stack whether it is the data, business or presentation layer. Migrating the database layer of an application may result in incompatibilities with the legacy database layer (including schema, consistency models and support for atomicity, consistency, isolation und durability [ACID] of transactions), synchronicity and the accidental disclosure of confidential data (Andrikopoulos et al., 2013). These may have a significant impact on the business layer and ultimately the presentation layer. While there is an established literature base on adapting business processes, managing dependencies between cloud computing architectures and other architectures can introduce challenges. Due to the enterprise scope and complexity of most information systems, and in particular AIS, it is difficult to generate an integrated migration model so that dependencies on components being moved to the cloud can be identified. Discovering, creating and maintaining such a model can be significant challenges in themselves. Once a model has been created, the services and supporting infrastructure to migrate must be (i) identified, (ii) extracted, (iii) adapted and optimised, (iv) deployed to the Cloud and (iv) removed from the source environment. This must be done with the least impact possible on operations and ideally with improvement to performance post-migration.

The logical and physical distribution of a migrated application also provides significant challenges (Andrikopoulos et al., 2013). These include regional variances in data protection compliance, performance and cost (Reese, 2009; Schad et al., 2010). Scalability, a much cited advantage of cloud computing, is not without challenges. Horizontal scaling, adding more instances as required, depends on the application components and the application as a whole to support it as an option, the complexity of which is exacerbated where there is high transactionality such as in an AIS (Andrikopoulos et al., 2013). What, how, when and how much to scale are application-specific challenges for IS decision makers to consider.

Migrating from one cloud provider to another is challenging due to a lack of standards in interoperability and portability. Interoperability issues may arise between and within layers (Pahl et al., 2013). Both the lack of standards and the lack of adoption of existing standards by cloud service providers exacerbate the issue (Nguyen et al., 2012). Indeed, it may not be in the best interest of cloud service providers to adopt standards and common application models. Designing an application for optimal performance on a specific cloud infrastructure may result in lock-in to that cloud service provider, thereby negating the flexibility cloud computing purports to offer. As a result, a future portability issue is created when the customer wishes to migrate from one cloud service provider to another or indeed repatriate from the cloud. Whereas this is a disadvantage to the customer, it has strategic value to the service provider.

Security issues in cloud computing

Each of the three cloud computing service models has their own security issues (Kandukuri & Rakshit, 2009). The SaaS deployment model is the most widely used by enterprise IT services involving the software vendors deploying their software applications remotely in the cloud and accessible via the Internet. For the most part, the cloud service provider is responsible for security. Subashini & Kavitha (2011) identify 13 security elements that need to be considered in SaaS. These are summarised in Table 21.2.

Enterprises have more control over security as they move from SaaS to PaaS and IaaS deployment models. In PaaS, any security below the application level is still the responsibility of the service provider, and many of the issues listed in Table 21.2 still apply. At the IaaS level, the cloud service provider is often only responsible for a minimal level of security, e.g. physical security, environmental security and virtualisation security. As virtualisation security is the only element within a developer's immediate control, care needs to be taken on assuring that there are no vulnerabilities in the virtualisation manager.

Table 21.2 Software-as-a-Service security issues and challenges

Security issue	Challenge
Data Security	Data residing outside the enterprise boundary is no longer subject to its physical, logical and personnel security and access control policies, thus increasing risk from application vulnerabilities and malicious insiders.
Network Security	All data flow between the enterprise and cloud service provider over the network needs to be secured to prevent leakage of sensitive information.
Data Locality	The location of data in transit, storage and while being processed must be reliably known and secure.
Data Integrity	Data integrity issues are exacerbated by the distributed and multi-tenant nature of the cloud. Issues could be introduced by lack of support for different service and availability levels for different types of transactions.
Data Segregation	As data from multiple tenants is stored at the same location, data intrusion by hacking or application vulnerabilities is a risk.
Data Access	In addition to security and access policies and controls for their own employees, enterprises need to consider the policies and controls of their cloud service provider.
Authentication and Authorisation	Enterprises must synchronise their user management not only for internal systems but also for all cloud services. Identity management should be flexible and compliant with enterprise policies. Credentials should be secure in-transit and storage. Trust relationships and validations should be established where federation is used.
Data Confidentiality	Use of cloud computing may result in perceived or actual disclosure of personal or confidential data to the cloud service provider potentially resulting in legal ramifications.
Web Application Security	Cloud services are typically accessed using web applications. Vulnerabilities in these web applications introduce security risks.
Data Breaches	Malicious insiders are a key cause of data breaches. Cloud service provision extends the risk of malicious insiders beyond the enterprise to include cloud service employees.
Virtualisation Vulnerability	Control of administrator on host and guest operating systems, imperfect isolation and bugs in virtual machine monitors introduce vulnerabilities.
Availability	Cloud service providers need to ensure plans that offer resilience to hardware/software failures as well as denial of service attacks. Enterprises need to have plans for business continuity and disaster recovery independent of the cloud service provider.
Backup	All data must be backed up for quick recovery and protected to prevent accidental leakage. This may not be a default.

Adapted from Subashini & Kavitha (2011).

Data protection and ICT governance

Cloud computing exacerbates AIS challenges with regard to data protection and ICT governance (Coss & Dhillon, 2020). Due to the distributed nature of cloud computing, the location of data in transit (during processing and storage) may not be known by the user. This raises two key challenges. First, enterprises may find themselves subject to laws and regulations in unintended jurisdictions raising issues of compliance. Second, lack of clarity on the identity of actors raises issues of the role of various actors and associated responsibilities (and potential liabilities) under data protection legislation.

The global and distributed nature of cloud computing combined with dominance by US firms introduces significant challenges from an ICT governance perspective. In particular, there is currently widespread uncertainty between data protection regimes in the US and the European Union. This relates to the debate on actions of intelligence agencies, and specifically the US intelligence community, and their ability and actions to require telecommunications service providers to store and provide access to data under a valid court order. Such disclosure may or may not be revealed to the ultimate owners of the data. This jurisdictional ambiguity may result in compliance issues, increasing both financial and legal risks to the firm.

From an accounting perspective, existing regulations relating to the management and auditing of internal control frameworks for information technologies and systems are pertinent in the context of the use of AIS in the cloud – e.g. Statement of Auditing Standards No. 70 and Statement on Standards for Attestation Engagements No. 16. Commentators have highlighted the need under international standards for auditors to understand a firm's business processes and internal controls to complete a thorough risk assessment of these processes, controls and indeed the financial statements (Singleton, 2010; Alali & Yeh, 2012; Smith et al., 2019).

Contractual issues in the cloud

Cloud computing introduces a range of high-level contractual issues (see Table 21.3), which in themselves provide challenges for enterprises seeking to implement systems in the cloud. Cloud computing contracts typically are made up of one or more of the following documents (Bradshaw et al., 2011; Leimbach et al., 2014; Lynn, 2021):

- Terms of Service (provisions regarding the overall relationship between parties)
- Service Level Agreement (details regarding the level of service to be provided and related penalties for not meeting agreed levels)
- Acceptable Use Policy (a policy to protect cloud service providers from the actions of clients or customers of clients)
- Privacy Policy (the cloud service provider's policy for handling and protecting data)

The negotiation of cloud service contracts is a relatively rare event, often limited to the largest organisations (Bradshaw et al., 2011; Leimbach et al., 2014; Opara-Martins et al., 2014). Yet, contracts can be a source of risk and friction for firms adopting the cloud resulting in a loss of control and/or contractual lock-in.

Big data

Big data is a sobriquet for datasets that are characterised by scale differences in volume (size), velocity (rate) and variety (range of formats and representations) than conventional

Pierangelo Rosati and Theo Lynn

Table 21.3 High-level contractual Issues and challenges in cloud computing agreements

Contractual issue	Challenge
Choice of Law and Legal Jurisdiction	Choice of law may provide advantages to cloud service providers including recognition of disclaimers and limitation of liabilities.
Data Location and Transfer	Transfer of data in-transit or for processing or storage may result in compliance issues or exposure to unanticipated liabilities.
Data Integrity and Availability	Although availability is typically dealt with in the Service Level Agreement, cloud service providers may seek to disclaim liabilities associated with a wide range of causes of unavailability and limit remedies to service credits (based on continued use).
Security of Data	Accommodating discrete security requirements for each client is challenging. As such, agreements are typically standardised and benefit the cloud service provider. Many cloud computing service agreements may not address security for data in-transit, while being processed or in storage.
IP Issues	IP ownership is often not addressed or addressed clearly in cloud service agreements. The ownership in IP in software applications developed by clients should be clearly addressed, particularly where cloud service provider tools are used. Cloud computing service providers are typically exempt of copyright infringement by clients or customers of clients, and the Acceptable Use Requirements may allow termination of contract in such cases. Cloud service providers may inadvertently or by intention make use of metadata that contains client data and therefore infringe copyright. Agreements should therefore state clearly what data is being collected by the cloud service provider and for what purpose and require cloud service providers to warrant against third-party patent infringement and indemnify their clients against liabilities associated with such infringements.
Liability and Indemnities	Cloud service providers may attempt to limit direct, indirect and consequential liabilities that may arise from service provision. The extent to which such liabilities and disclaimers are permitted varies across jurisdictions.
Acceptable Use Requirements	There are deterrence mechanisms to protect cloud service providers from the actions of clients or customers of clients. These can be used as the basis for service termination and may contain language unsuitable to the client's customer base, thus requiring either disclosure or permission from affected customers.
Service Levels and Performance	Service levels are often standardised, simplistic and designed to protect the cloud service provider, not the client. Monitoring of service levels and performance is typically dependent on tools provided by the cloud providers, which may have limited transparency on overall performance.
Variation of Contract Terms	Many cloud computing agreements include a reservation of rights to vary the terms of an agreement unilaterally and by reference to changes on a cloud service provider website.
Backup	Cloud service providers may not warrant to back up client data and in fact may stipulate that the responsibility for backup is with the client.
Termination	Termination may occur as expected or due to breach of contract. Agreements should address in detail how and when the term of service and (non-) renewal of service will be addressed, termination event definition and data (including metadata) preservation, deletion and transfer following termination. Common issues in termination events include available support and time.

Adapted from Leimbach et al. (2014).

datasets, and as such conventional, data processing infrastructure, applications and tools are often found inadequate (Laney, 2001). Today, big data is driven by increased connectivity and usage of Internet-based systems and devices, accelerated by cloud computing and social media amongst other technologies. From an accounting perspective, big data is generated not only by the volume of transactions and related operations within a firm but also by the increasing volume of machine-generated data (including the so-called Internet of Things), metadata and supplemental and complementary data available from internal and third-party sources (Vasarhelyi et al., 2015). Commentators suggest that this additional big data and the ability to analyse it to make decisions have the potential to dramatically improve corporate performance across all functions (LaValle et al., 2011; Manyika et al., 2011). From an accounting perspective, big data provides additional data and evidence to assist management in making decisions. As such, it has the potential of impacting a wide range of accounting-related functions including the audit function, business measurement and business intelligence (Moffitt & Vasarhelyi, 2013; Vasarhelyi et al., 2015).

With the widespread use of cloud computing infrastructure for big data analytics, it is unsurprising that many of the challenges of cloud computing are shared with big data implementations. However, big data, by its nature, provides new challenges driven by the size and complexity of the datasets and the technologies needed to process such datasets (Ward & Barker, 2013). These include new embedded architectures and systems that can both manage and scale with data as it grows including internal ICT governance and data management infrastructure and processes (LaValle et al., 2011). Designing and migrating to such an architecture is a major challenge. Big data involves a specialist set of analytical technologies, tools and techniques that can handle both structured and unstructured data and generate insights from such data (Lynn et al., 2015). Such infrastructure can be extremely costly from a computational perspective, and such toolsets are still at an early stage of development with significant issues even in terms of analytical validity. The high dimensionality and sample size of big data can result in noise accumulation, spurious correlations and incidental homogeneity and, at the same time, heterogeneity issues caused from multiple sources, time points and biases (Fan et al., 2014). As such, firms seeking to exploit big data require not only analysts who can understand their business but also data scientists and ideally a combination of both. Unsurprisingly, there is a significant shortage in the labour market of such personnel (Manyika et al., 2011). As this shortfall is unlikely to be filled in the near future, some have argued that the accountants' mindset lends itself to such bimodal thinking and data-driven analysis; however, a significant upskilling would be required (Bhimani & Wilcocks, 2014).

While big data promises enterprises greater insights and ultimately value, it also represents a significant challenge for internal controls and specifically data protection and compliance. The value of such data increases the likelihood for large-scale theft and/or breaches related to sensitive data in the form of unauthorised access for financial gain, intelligence or merely to compromise the interpretation/analysis process (Fhom, 2015). In addition to security, there is widespread concern from policymakers in relation to individual control over personal data and related issues regarding the provenance of data and consent management (Leimbach et al., 2014; Fhom, 2015). While these might be considered ethical and social challenges, they have very real implications for those responsible for internal controls particularly where such data is integrated into AIS. Accounting and financial professionals, including auditors, may face increasing pressure and scrutiny from policymakers and regulators to ensure adequate controls are in place to protect such big data (Huerta & Jensen, 2017).

Mobile working and bring your own technology

Increasingly employees and customers have ubiquitous access to the Internet. Technological advances in mobile broadband, combined with widespread adoption of cloud computing and social media, have driven extremely high penetration and usage of mobile devices and specifically smartphones and tablets. Major software vendors, including those in enterprise resource planning and accounting software, typically have mobile access offerings. Mobile computing provides a wide range of benefits covered extensively in the teleworking literature (Baruch, 2000; Morgan, 2004). However, like outsourcing and cloud computing, it redefines the organisational boundaries and thus creates challenges particularly in relation to security and control. Lost devices, theft, security vulnerabilities in mobile access networks, devices, apps and devices are just some of the challenges to enterprises supporting enterprise mobile computing (Harris & Patten, 2014; Romer, 2014).

A particular phenomenon worth noting is "BYOD" or "Bring Your Own Device", which refers to employees using their own hardware to access company's information. However, to limit it to devices is a misnomer. People are not only bringing their own hardware but increasingly software too; "Bring Your Own Technology" or "BYOT" is more appropriate (Miller et al., 2012). The trade press has popularised the benefits of the BYOT phenomenon including teleworking, technology familiarity, improved morale, increased access and availability of employees, increased working hours and reduced cost (Boomer, 2012; Chaudhry, 2012; Singh, 2012). However, BYOT also introduces security and internal control risks. Here security is an afterthought; the employee has not bought the device for enterprise security but for a range of personal motivations (Morrow, 2012; Romer, 2014). "Personal" is a very important attribute of BYOT. As a result of personal decisions, the enterprise risks change and intensify. Lost devices, data contamination, new forms of malware, phishing attack success and risky file sharing become more likely (Miller et al., 2012; Morrow, 2012; Romer, 2014). The personal nature of the technology in BYOT scenarios undermines enterprise control and transparency over data to an unprecedented scale introducing new management, control and compliance complexities (Crossler et al., 2014).

During the COVID-19 pandemic, remote working from home became the norm for many worldwide. While this undoubtedly contributed significantly to business and economic continuity, it highlighted the unpreparedness of organisations and individuals for home working and the associated cybersecurity threats (Furnell & Shah, 2020). As well as a rise in home working, there was a significant increase in cybercrime attempts including scams and phishing, malware and distributed denial of service attacks (Pranggono & Arabo, 2021). The COVID-19 pandemic has highlighted the need for robust cybersecurity risk management processes, and cyber-literacy in general, but specifically for AIS given the sensitive nature of the information stored on these systems and for their critical role within the day-to-day business operations.

Conclusion

Challenges to the adoption and successful implementation of AIS are not dissimilar to those in other enterprise contexts. Enterprises face many of the same challenges that feature in the general information systems academic literature, namely project management, technology, user resistance, organisation/environment and outsourcing challenges. Due to the sensitive nature of accounting information, trends towards outsourcing and the extended enterprise accelerated by the emergence of cloud computing provide specific challenges for enterprises as they redefine their organisational boundaries and grapple with control and compliance issues associated with such strategies. Increased mobility and the BYOT phenomenon only further complicate enterprise management of mission-critical and sensitive systems. The emergence of big data provides not only similar but also different challenges for accounting and financial professionals. It is not difficult to foresee a time in the very near future where big data, whether sourced from internal or external sources, will become a major component of the business intelligence, business measurement and audit evidence activities of enterprises. Together and individually, cloud computing, big data and mobile computing are transforming business processes and creating new competitive advantages. While the changes to accounting and auditing processes, systems and standards have not integrated these technologies at the same pace as other enterprise functions, greater focus by practitioners and researchers is required if only to reduce risk.

Notes

1 See McConnell (1996) for further details.
2 See Heric & Singh (2010) and George (2012) for further details.

References

Addison, T. & Vallabh, S. (2002). Controlling software project risks: An empirical study of methods used by experienced project managers, *Proceedings of the 2002 Annual Research Conference of the South African Institute of Computer Scientists and Information Technologists on Enablement through Technology*, 2002. South African Institute for Computer Scientists and Information Technologists, 128–140.

Alali, F. A. & Yeh, C. L. (2012). Cloud computing: Overview and risk analysis, *Journal of Information Systems*, 26(2), 13–33.

Aloini, D., Dulmin, R. & Mininno, V. (2007). Risk management in ERP project introduction: Review of the literature, *Information & Management*, 44(6), 547–567.

Anderson, S. W., Christ, M. H., Dekker, H. C. & Sedatole, K. L. (2014). The use of management controls to mitigate risk in strategic alliances: Field and survey evidence, *Journal of Management Accounting Research*, 26(1), 1–32.

Anderson, S. W. & Sedatole, K. L. (2003). Management accounting for the extended enterprise: Performance management for strategic alliances and networked partners, in Bhimani, A., ed., *Management Accounting in the Digital Economy*, 36–73. Oxford:Oxford University Press.

Andrikopoulos, V., Binz, T., Leymann, F. & Strauch, S. (2013). How to adapt applications for the Cloud environment, *Computing*, 95(6), 493–535.

Apte, U. M. & Mason, R. O. (1995). Global disaggregation of information-intensive services, *Management Science*, 41(7), 1250–1262.

Aron, R. & Liu, Y. (2005). Determinants of operational risk in global sourcing of financial services: Evidence from field research, *Brookings Trade Forum*, 1, 373–398.

Bandyopadhyay, S. & Pathak, P. (2007). Knowledge sharing and cooperation in outsourcing projects—A game theoretic analysis, *Decision Support Systems*, 43(2), 349–358.

Banker, R. D., Kalvenes, J. & Patterson, R. A. (2006). Research note-information technology, contract completeness, and buyer-supplier relationships, *Information Systems Research*, 17(2), 180–193.

Bannister, F. (2001). Dismantling the silos: Extracting new value from IT investments in public administration, *Information Systems Journal*, 11(1), 65–84.

Bardi, E. J. & Tracey, M. (1991). Transportation outsourcing: A survey of US practices, *International Journal of Physical Distribution & Logistics Management*, 21(3), 15–21.

Barrett, M., Sahay, S. & Walsham, G. (2001). Information technology and social transformation: GIS for forestry management in India, *The Information Society,* 17(1), 5–20.

Baruch, Y. (2000). Teleworking: Benefits and pitfalls as perceived by professionals and managers. New technology, *Work and Employment*, 15(1), 34–49.

Belfo, F. & Trigo, A. (2013). Accounting information systems: Tradition and future directions, *Procedia Technology*, 9, 536–546.

Bhimani, A. & Willcocks, L. (2014). Digitisation, Big Dataand the transformation of accounting information. *Accounting and Business Research*, 44(4), 469–490.

Bierstaker, J., Chen, L., Christ, M. H., Ege, M. & Mintchik, N. (2013). Obtaining assurance for financial statement audits and control audits when aspects of the financial reporting process are outsourced, *Auditing: A Journal of Practice & Theory*, 32(1), 209–250.

Blaskovich, J. & Mintchik, N. (2011). Information technology outsourcing: A taxonomy of prior studies and directions for future research, *Journal of Information Systems*, 25(1), 1–36.

Blinder, A. S. (2006). Offshoring: The next industrial revolution?, *Foreign Affairs*, 85(1), 113–128.

Boehm, B. W. (1981). An experiment in small-scale application software engineering, *IEEE Transactions on Software Engineering*, 7(5), 482–493.

Boomer, J. (2012). Are you ready for BYOD, *CPA Practice Advisor*, May 28, available from: https://www.cpapracticeadvisor.com/directory/business-management/article/10707592/are-you-ready-for-byod [15 August 2021].

Borcherding, J. D., Samelson, N. M. & Sebastian, S. M. (1980). Improving motivation and productivity on large projects, *Journal of the Construction Division*, 106(1), 73–89.

Bradshaw, S., Millard, C. & Walden, I. (2011). Contracts for clouds: Comparison and analysis of the Terms and Conditions of cloud computing services, *International Journal of Law and Information Technology*, 19(3), 187–223.

Buyya, R., Yeo, C. S., Venugopal, S., Broberg, J. & Brandic, I. (2009). Cloud computing and emerging IT platforms: Vision, hype, and reality for delivering computing as the 5th utility, *Future Generation Computer Systems*, 25(6), 599–616.

Carnall, C. A. (1986). Managing strategic change: An integrated approach, *Long Range Planning*, 19(6), 105–115.

Cervone, H. F. (2006). Project risk management, *OCLC Systems & Services: International Digital Library Perspectives*, 22(4), 256–262.

Chapman, C. & Ward, S. (2003). *Project Risk Management: Processes, Techniques and Insights*, Hoboken, NJ: John Wiley & Sons.

Chaudhry, P. (2012). Tech strategy—Needed: A corporate mobile device policy, *Magazine of Financial Executive Institute*, 28(5), 69.

Christ, M. H., Mintchik, N., Chen, L. & Bierstaker, J. L. (2014). Outsourcing the information system: Determinants, risks, and implications for management control systems, *Journal of Management Accounting Research*, 27(2), 77–120.

Church, K. S., Schmidt, P. J. & Ajayi, K. (2020). Forecast cloudy—Fair or stormy weather: Cloud computing insights and issues, *Journal of Information Systems*, 34(2), 23–46.

Contractor, F. J., Kumar, V., Kundu, S. K. & Pedersen, T. (2010). Reconceptualizing the firm in a world of outsourcing and offshoring: The organizational and geographical relocation of high-value company functions, *Journal of Management Studies*, 47(8), 1417–1433.

Coss, D. L. & Dhillon, G. (2020). A framework for auditing and strategizing to ensure cloud privacy, *Journal of Information Systems*, 34(2), 47–63.

Crossler, R. E., Long, J. H., Loraas, T. M. & Trinkle, B. S. (2014). Understanding compliance with bring your own device policies utilizing protection motivation theory: Bridging the intention-behavior gap, *Journal of Information Systems*, 28(1), 209–226.

Das, T. & Teng, B. S. (1996). Risk types and inter-firm alliance structures, *Journal of Management Studies*, 33(6), 827–843.

Davenport, T. H. (1998). Putting the enterprise into the enterprise system, *Harvard Business Review*, 76(4). 1–11.

Davison, R. (2002). Cultural complications of ERP, *Communications of the ACM*, 45(7), 109–111.

Dechow, N. & Mouritsen, J. (2005). On enterprise wide resource planning systems-the quest for integration and management control, *Accounting, Organizations and Society*, 30(7), 691–733.

Dechow, P. M., Sloan, R. G. & Sweeney, A. P. (1996). Causes and consequences of earnings manipulation: An analysis of firms subject to enforcement actions by the SEC, *Contemporary Accounting Research*, 13(1), 1–36.

Elliott, B. (2007). Anything is possible: Managing feature creep in an innovation rich environment, *Proceedings of the Engineering Management Conference*, Singapore, 304–307.

Ewusi-Mensah, K. (1997). Critical issues in abandoned information systems development projects, *Communications of the ACM*, 40(9), 74–80.

Fan, J., Han, F. & Liu, H. (2014). Challenges of big data analysis. *National Science Review*, 1(2), 293–314.

Fhom, H. S. (2015). Big Data: Opportunities and privacy challenges, in Richter, P., ed., *Privatheit, Öffentlichkeit und demokratische Willensbildung in Zeiten von Big Data*, 13–44. Baden-Baden: Nomos Verlagsgesellschaft mbH & Co. KG.

Fitoussi, D. & Gurbaxani, V. (2012). IT outsourcing contracts and performance measurement, *Information Systems Research,* 23(1), 129–143.

Fraser, S. D., Brooks Jr, F. P., Fowler, M., Lopez, R., Namioka, A., Northrop, L., Parnas, D. L. & Thomas, D. (2007). No silver bullet reloaded: retrospective on essence and accidents of software engineering, *Companion to the 22nd ACM SIGPLAN Conference on Object-oriented Programming Systems and Applications Companion*, 1026–1030, Montreal.

Fui-Hoon Nah, F., Lee-Shang Lau, J. & Kuang, J. (2001). Critical factors for successful implementation of enterprise systems, *Business Process Management Journal*, 7(3), 285–296.

Furnell, S. & Shah, J. N. (2020). Home working and cyber security–an outbreak of unpreparedness?, *Computer Fraud & Security, 8,* 6–12.

Gattiker, T. F. & Goodhue, D. L. (2005). What happens after ERP implementation: Undersanding the impact of interdependence and differentiation on plant-level outcomes, *MIS Quarterly*, 29(3), 559–585.

Gauld, R. (2007). Public sector information system project failures: Lessons from a New Zealand hospital organization, *Government Information Quarterly*, 24(1), 102–114.

George, B. (2012). Best practices in outsourcing: The procter & gamble experience, *IAOPs Global Excellence in Outsourcing Award*, available from: https://www.iaop.org/Download/Download.aspx?ID=1920 [15 August 2021].

Grabski, S. V., Leech, S. A. & Schmidt, P. J. (2011). A review of ERP research: A future agenda for accounting information systems, *Journal of Information Systems*, 25(1), 37–78.

Han, H.-S., Lee, J.-N. & Seo, Y.-W. (2008). Analyzing the impact of a firms capability on outsourcing success: A process perspective, *Information & Management*, 45(1), 31–42.

Han, K. & Mithas, S. (2013). Information technology outsourcing and non-it operating costs: An empirical investigation, *MIS Quarterly*, 37(1), 315–331.

Harris, M. & Patten, K. (2014). Mobile device security considerations for small- and medium-sized enterprise business mobility, *Information Management & Computer Security*, 22(1), 97–114.

Heeks, R. (2002). Information systems and developing countries: Failure, success, and local improvisations, *The Information Society*, 18(2), 101–112.

Henderson, J. C. & Venkatraman, N. (1993). Strategic alignment: Leveraging information technology for transforming organizations, *IBM Systems Journal*, 32(1), 4–16.

Heric, M. & Singh, B. (2010). Outsourcing can do much more than just cut costs, *Forbes*, 15 June, available from: http://www.forbes.com/2010/06/15/outsourcing-capability-sourcing-leadership-managing-bain.html [Accessed 15 August 2021].

Hogan, M., Liu, F., Sokol, A. & Tong, J. (2011). Nist cloud computing standards roadmap, *NIST Special Publication*, 35.

Huerta, E. & Jensen, S. (2017). An accounting information systems perspective on data analytics and Big Data. *Journal of Information Systems*, 31(3), 101–114.

Introna, L. (1997). *Management, Information and Power: A Narrative of the Involved Manager*, London: Macmillan.

Jay, J. (2009). Pricing and valuation services: The search for transparency. AITE Group, *LLC*, 11 November, available from: http://aitegroup.com/report/pricing-and-valuation-services-search-transparency [15 August 2021].

Jones, S. (2008). Social dimension of IT/IS evaluation: Views from the public sector, in Irani, Z. & Love, P. E. D., eds., *Evaluating Information Systems: Public and Private Sector*, 236–256. London: Routledge.

Joseph, R. C. (2005). To adopt or not to adopt - That is the question, *Proceedings of Americas Conference on Information Systems (AMCIS)*, Omaha, 1219–1224.

Kandukuri, B. R. & Rakshit, A. (2009). Cloud security issues, *Proceedings of the 2009 IEEE International Conference on Services Computing*, 517–520, Bangalore.

Keen, P. G. (1981). Information systems and organizational change, *Communications of the ACM*, 24(1), 24–33.

Khurana, A. & Rosenthal, S. R. (1997). Integrating the fuzzy front end of new product development, *MIT Sloan Management Review*, 38(2), 103–120.

Kim, W. (2009). Cloud computing: Today and tomorrow, *Journal of Object Technology*, 8(1), 65–72.

Klaus, T. & Blanton, J. E. (2010). User resistance determinants and the psychological contract in enterprise system implementations, *European Journal of Information Systems*, 19(6), 625–636.

Krasner, H. (2000). Ensuring e-business success by learning from ERP failures, *IT Professional*, 2(1), 22–27.

Lakhanpal, B. (1993). Understanding the factors influencing the performance of software development groups: An exploratory group-level analysis, *Information and Software Technology*, 35(8), 468–473.

Lambert, R. & Peppard, J. (2013). The information technology–organizational design relationship, in Galliers, R. D. & Leidner, D. E., eds., *Strategic Information Management*, 427–459, London: Routledge.

Laney, D. (2001). 3D data management: controlling data volume, velocity and variety. META Group Research Note, 6, 70.

Landis, L., Waligora, S., Mcgarry, F., Pajerski, R., Stark, M., Johnson, K. O. & Cover, D. (1992). Recommended approach to software development, revision 3, National Aeronautics and Space Administration (NASA), June, available from: http://ntrs.nasa.gov/archive/nasa/casi.ntrs.nasa.gov/19930009672.pdf [15 August 2021].

Larson, C. E. & LaFasto, F. M. (1989). *Teamwork: What Must Go Right, What Can Go Wrong.* Newberry Park, CA: Sage.

Laumer, S. & Eckhardt, A. (2012). Why do people reject technologies: A review of user resistance theories, in Dwivedi, Y. K., Wade, M. R., & Schneberger, S. L., eds., *Information Systems Theory*, 63–86. New York: Springer.

LaValle, S., Lesser, E., Shockley, R., Hopkins, M. S. & Kruschwitz, N. (2011). Big data, analytics and the path from insights to value, *MIT Sloan Management Review*, 52(2), 21–32.

Lee, J.-N. (2001). The impact of knowledge sharing, organizational capability and partnership quality on IS outsourcing success, *Information & Management*, 38(5), 323–335.

Lee, J.-N. & Kim, Y.-G. (1999). Effect of partnership quality on IS outsourcing success: conceptual framework and empirical validation, *Journal of Management Information Systems*, 15(4), 29–61.

Lei, D. & Hitt, M. A. (1995). Strategic restructuring and outsourcing: The effect of mergers and acquisitions and LBOs on building firm skills and capabilities, *Journal of Management*, 21(5), 835–859.

Leimbach, T., Hallinan, D., Bachlechner, D., Weber, A., Jaglo, M., Hennen, L., Nielsen, R. Ø., Nentwich, M., Strauß, S., Lynn, T. & Hunt, G. (2014). Potential and impacts of cloud computing services and social network websites, science and technology options assessment (STOA), available from: http://www.europarl.europa.eu/RegData/etudes/etudes/join/2014/513546/IPOL-JOIN_ET(2014)513546_EN.pdf [15 August 2021].

Leonardi, P. M. & Bailey, D. E. (2008). Transformational technologies and the creation of new work practices: Making implicit knowledge explicit in task-based offshoring, *MIS Quarterly*, 411–436.

Levy, D. L. (2005). Offshoring in the new global political economy, *Journal of Management Studies*, 42(3), 685–693.

Lian, K.-Y., Hsiao, S.-J. & Sung, W.-T. (2013). Intelligent multi-sensor control system based on innovative technology integration via ZigBee and Wi-Fi networks, *Journal of Network and Computer Applications*, 36(2), 756–767.

Low, C., Chen, Y. & Wu, M. (2011). Understanding the determinants of cloud computing adoption, *Industrial Management & Data Systems*, 111(7), 1006–1023.

Lynn, T. (2021). Dear cloud, I think we have trust issues: Cloud computing contracts and trust, in Lynn, T., Mooney, J. G., van der Werff, L., & Fox, G., eds., *Data Privacy and Trust in Cloud Computing*, 21–42. Cham: Palgrave Macmillan.

Lynn, T., Healy, P., Kilroy, S., Hunt, G., Van Der Werff, L., Venkatagiri, S. & Morrison, J. (2015). Towards a general research framework for social media research using big data, in *IEEE International Professional Communication Conference (IPCC)* (1–8). IEEE.

Lyytinen, K. & Robey, D. (1999). Learning failure in information systems development, *Information Systems Journal*, 9(2), 85–101.

Maier, C., Laumer, S., Eckhardt, A. & Weitzel, T. (2013). Analyzing the impact of HRIS implementations on HR personnels job satisfaction and turnover intention, *The Journal of Strategic Information Systems*, 22(3), 193–207.

Malhotra, N., Bhardwaj, M. & Kaur, R. (2012). Estimating the effects of gold plating using fuzzy cognitive maps, *International Journal of Computer Science and Information Technologies*, 3(4), 4806–4808.

Manyika, J., Chui, M., Brown, B., Bughin, J., Dobbs, R., Roxburgh, C. & Byers, A. H. (2011). Big data: The next frontier for innovation, competition, and productivity, Mckinsey Global Institute, May, available from: http://www.mckinsey.com/business-functions/business-technology/our-insights/big-data-the-next-frontier-for-innovation [15 August 2021].

Marakas, G. M. & Hornik, S. (1996). Passive resistance misuse: Overt support and covert recalcitrance in IS implementation, *European Journal of Information Systems*, 5(3), 208–219.

Markus, M. L. (1983). Power, politics, and MIS implementation, *Communications of the ACM*, 26(6), 430–444.

Markus, M. L. (2000). Paradigm shifts-e-business and business/systems integration, *Communications of the Association for Information Systems*, 4(1), Article 10.

Markus, M. L. (2004). Technochange management: Using IT to drive organizational change, *Journal of Information Technology*, 19(1), 4–20.

Martinsons, M. G. (2004). ERP in China: One package, two profiles, *Communications of the ACM*, 47(7), 65–68.

McConnell, S. (1996). *Rapid Development: Taming Wild Software Schedules*. London: Pearson Education.

McConnell, S. (2006). *Software Estimation: Demystifying the Black Art*. Redmond: Microsoft Press.

Mell, P. & Grance, T. (2011). The NIST definition of cloud computing, *National Institute of Standards and Technology (NIST)*, September, available from: http://faculty.winthrop.edu/domanm/csci411/Handouts/NIST.pdf [15 August 2021].

Michell, V. & Fitzgerald, G. (1997). The IT outsourcing market-place: Vendors and their selection, *Journal of Information Technology*, 12(3), 223–237.

Miller, K. W., Voas, J. M. & Hurlburt, G. F. (2012). BYOD: Security and privacy considerations, *IT Professional*, 14(5), 53–55.

Moffitt, K. C. & Vasarhelyi, M. A. (2013). AIS in an age of big data, *Journal of Information Systems*, 27(-2), 1–19.

Morgan, R. E. (2004). Teleworking: an assessment of the benefits and challenges, *European Business Review*, 16(4), 344–357.

Morrow, B. (2012). BYOD security challenges: Control and protect your most sensitive data. *Network Security*, 12, 5–8.

Murray, J. P. (2001). Reducing IT project complexity, in Tinnirello, P. C., ed., *New Directions in Project Management*, 435, Boca Raton, FL: CRC Press.

Nelson, R. R. (2007). IT project management: Infamous failures, classic mistakes, and best practices, *MIS Quarterly Executive*, 6(2), 67–78.

Nguyen, D. K., Lelli, F., Papazoglou, M. P. & Van Den Heuvel, W.-J. (2012). Blueprinting approach in support of cloud computing, *Future Internet*, 4(1), 322–346.

Oliveira, T., Thomas, M. & Espadanal, M. (2014). Assessing the determinants of cloud computing adoption: An analysis of the manufacturing and services sectors, *Information & Management*, 51(5), 497–510.

Opara-Martins, J., Sahandi, R. & Tian, F. (2014). Critical review of vendor lock-in and its impact on adoption of cloud computing, *Proceedings of the International Conference on Information Society (i-Society)*, 92–97. London.

Osei-Bryson, K.-M. & Ngwenyama, O. K. (2006). Managing risks in information systems outsourcing: An approach to analyzing outsourcing risks and structuring incentive contracts, *European Journal of Operational Research*, 174(1), 245–264.

Pahl, C., Zhang, L. & Fowley, F. (2013). Interoperability standards for cloud architecture, *Proceedings of the 3rd International Conference on Cloud Computing and Services Science*, Aachen, available from: http://doras.dcu.ie/17824/1/closer13-sp.pdf [15 August 2021].

Parker, M. M. & Benson, R. J. (1989) Enterprisewide information management: State-of-the-art strategic planning, *Information System Management*, 6(3), 14–23.

Peffers, K., Gengler, C. E. & Tuunanen, T. (2003). Extending critical success factors methodology to facilitate broadly participative information systems planning, *Journal of Management Information Systems*, 20(1), 51–85.

Pranggono, B. & Arabo, A. (2021). COVID-19 pandemic cybersecurity issues. *Internet Technology Letters*, 4(2), e247.

Pulakanam, V. & Suraweera, T. (2010). Implementing accounting software in small business in New Zealand: An exploratory investigation, *Accountancy Business and the Public Interest*, 9, 98–124.

Quattrone, P. & Hopper, T. (2005). A time–space odyssey: Management control systems in two multinational organisations, *Accounting, Organizations and Society*, 30(7), 735–764.

Reese, G. (2009). *Cloud Application Architectures: Building Applications and Infrastructure in the Cloud*. Sebastopol, CA: OReilly Media, Inc.

Reid, S. E. & De Brentani, U. (2004). The fuzzy front end of new product development for discontinuous innovations: A theoretical model, *Journal of Product Innovation Management*, 21(3), 170–184.

Romer, H. (2014). Best practices for BYOD security, *Computer Fraud & Security*, 1, 13–15.

Saunders, C., Gebelt, M. & Hu, Q. (1997). Achieving success in information systems outsourcing, *California Management Review*, 39(2), 63–79.

Schad, J., Dittrich, J. & Quiané-Ruiz, J.-A. (2010). Runtime measurements in the cloud: Observing, analyzing, and reducing variance, *Proceedings of the VLDB Endowment*, 3(1), 460–471.

Sclater, N. (2009). *Cloudworks, eLearning in the Cloud*. Cambridge: The Free Press.

Singh, N. (2012). BYOD genie is out of the bottle–"Devil or angel", *Journal of Business Management & Social Sciences Research*, 1(3), 1–12.

Singleton, T. W. (2010). IT audit basics: IT audits of cloud and SaaS, *ISACA Journal*, 3, 1–3.

Smith, A. L., Zhang, Y. & Kipp, P. C. (2019). Cloud-computing risk disclosure and ICFR material weakness: The moderating role of accounting reporting complexity, *Journal of Information Systems*, 33(3), 1–17.

Smith, P. G. & Reinertsen, D. G. (1998). *Developing Products in Half the Time: New Rules, New Tools*. Hoboken, NJ: John Wiley & Sons.

Smits, M., van der Poel, K. & Ribbers, P. (2003). Assessment of information strategies in insurance companies, in Galliers, R. D. & Leidner, D. E., eds., *Strategic Information Management*, 64–88, New York: Routledge.

Soh, C., Kien, S. S. & Tay-Yap, J. (2000). Enterprise resource planning: Cultural fits and misfits: Is ERP a universal solution?, *Communications of the ACM*, 43(4), 47–51.

Sonnenberg, F. K. (1992). Partnering: Entering the age of cooperation, *Journal of Business Strategy*, 13(3), 49–52.

Stratman, J. K. (2008). Facilitating offshoring with enterprise technologies: Reducing operational friction in the governance and production of services, *Journal of Operations Management*, 26(2), 275–287.

Strong, D. M. & Volkoff, O. (2010). Understanding organization—Enterprise system fit: A path to theorizing the information technology artifact, *MIS Quarterly*, *34*(4), 731–756.

Subashini, S. & Kavitha, V. (2011). A survey on security issues in service delivery models of cloud computing, *Journal of Network and Computer Applications*, 34(1), 1–11.

Sultan, N. (2010). Cloud computing for education: A new dawn?, *International Journal of Information Management*, 30(2), 109–116.

Sumner, M. (1999) Critical success factors in enterprise wide information management systems projects, *Proceedings of the 1999 ACM SIGCPR Conference on Computer Personnel Research*, 297–303, New Orleans.

Tan, B. C., Wei, K.-K., Watson, R. T., Clapper, D. L. & Mclean, E. R. (1998). Computer-mediated communication and majority influence: Assessing the impact in an individualistic and a collectivistic culture, *Management Science*, 44(1), 1263–1278.

The Standish Group (2020). *CHAOS 2020 Beyond Infinity*. Boston, MA: The Standig Group.

Umble, E. & Umble, M. (2001). Enterprise resource planning systems: A review of implementation issues and critical success factors, *Proceedings of the 32nd Annual Meeting of the Decision Sciences Institute*, 1109–1111. San Francisco.

Vasarhelyi, M. A., Kogan, A. & Tuttle, B. M. (2015). Big data in accounting: An overview, *Accounting Horizons*, 29(2), 381–396.

Vatanasakdakul, S., Aoun, C. & Li, Y. (2010) AIS in Australia: UTAUT application and cultural implication, *Proceedings of the 21st Australasian Conference on Information Systems*, 1–11, Gardens Point.

Volkoff, O., Strong, D. M. & Elmes, M. B. (2005). Understanding enterprise systems-enabled integration, *European Journal of Information Systems*, 14(2), 110–120.

Wailgum, T. (2009). 10 Famous ERP disasters, dustups and disappointments. *CIO Magazine*, 24 March, available from: http://www.cio.com/article/2429865/enterprise-resource-planning/10-famous-erp-disasters--dustups-and-disappointments.html [15 August 2021].

Ward, J. S. & Barker, A. (2013). Undefined by data: A survey of big data definitions, arXiv preprint arXiv:1309.5821.

Willcocks, L. P. & Lacity, M. C. (1999). IT outsourcing in insurance services: Risk, creative contracting and business advantage, *Information Systems Journal*, 9(3), 163–180.

Willcocks, L. P. & Lester, S. (2000). Information technology and organizational performance: Beyond the IT productivity paradox, in Galliers, R. D. & Leidner, D. E., eds., *Strategic Information Management: Challenges and Strategies in Managing Information Systems*, 588–608. Oxford:Butterworth-Heinemann.

22

NEW DEVELOPMENTS IN INFORMATION TECHNOLOGY

A further call for action

Joan Ballantine and Robert D. Galliers

Introduction

Much has been claimed about the strategic promise of, and issues relating to, new information technologies (IT) over the years, increasingly so in the so-called age of digitalisation
(e.g. Shollo & Galliers, 2015; Warren et al., 2015; Galliers et al., 2017; Günther et al., 2017;
Vial, 2018; Grover et al., 2020; Hirschheim, 2021).[1] Back in the 1980s, McFarlan (1984) argued that *Information Technology Changes the Way You Compete*, while Porter & Millar (1985)
provided guidance as to *How Information Gives You Competitive Advantage*. In the following
decade, Business Process Reengineering (BPR) was all the rage with, for example, Davenport & Short (1990) promoting *The New Industrial Engineering* and Hammer (1990) calling for
the 'obliteration' of existing business processes, rather than mere 'automation', to deliver order of magnitude improvements in business performance on the back of BPR and associated
enterprise systems (e.g. Davenport, 2000; Kalling, 2003). More recently, similar hyperbole
has been associated with so-called business intelligence systems with, for example, a recent
Gartner research report indicating that the business intelligence software market was forecast
to be worth $27.4 billion in 2020 (Gartner, 2020), representing a significant increase over
the last decade. Big data has also taken centre stage (e.g. Chen et al., 2012; McAfee & Brynjolfsson, 2012; Bhimani &Willcocks, 2014; Batistic & van der Laken, 2019), and artificial
intelligence (AI), blockchain technology and algorithmic decision-making are becoming
increasingly prevalent in business and management practice (e.g. Akerker, 2019) and research
(e.g. Zhang et al., 2020; Loureiro et al., 2021).

Having said all this, there have been more critical stances taken over the years. For example, Clemons (1986) questioned the sustainability of the competitive advantage to be
gained from IT, while others have critically reflected on business process reengineering (e.g.
Davenport, 1996; Land, 1996; Galliers, 1997; Galliers & Swan, 1999). Indeed, Galliers (2006)
confronts "some of the common myths of IS strategy discourse" in his reflection on strategic
alignment, competitive advantage and knowledge management, while Robey & Boudreau
(1999) consider some of the contradictory consequences associated with IT implementations. Additionally, focus has shifted from strategy to strategising (e.g. Galliers, 2004, 2011;
Whittington, 2006; Jarzabkowski & Spee, 2009), with emphasis being placed on the actual
practices and capabilities of organisational actors (e.g. Peppard & Ward, 2004; Whittington

DOI: 10.4324/9781003132943-27

et al., 2006; Karpovsky & Galliers, 2015; Marabelli & Galliers, 2016), and the impacts of social media in this regard (Huang et al., 2013; Baptista et al., 2016). The ethical dimension of business automation is also becoming more prevalent in the literature (e.g. Wright & Schultz, 2018). Thus, the potential benefits of, and issues associated with various aspects of, 'digitalisation' are now well-rehearsed (e.g. Newell & Marabelli, 2015; Markus, 2017).

In this chapter, we consider the major investments that have taken place in established IT such as Enterprise Resource Planning (ERP) systems and the more recent hyperbole surrounding big data, AI and digitalisation more generally. Importantly, we also consider the implications of such investments, in terms of organisational capabilities (cf. Peppard & Ward, 2004) and the very nature of digital work (e.g. Baptista et al., 2020), with particular reference to the accounting and finance professions. We commence with a reflection on ERP systems as a potential strategic asset and then consider such digitalisation phenomena as big data in a similar light. Implications for accounting practice and for accounting and finance professionals are then considered.

Information as a strategic asset: enterprise resource planning systems

ERP systems are typically the largest and most complex information systems implemented by organisations. Furthermore, ERP systems often represent one of the most significant capital investments that an organisation will make in building its IT infrastructure. While complex and costly, research has indicated that ERP systems have the potential to be used as a strategic asset and thereby enhance an organisation's competitive advantage (e.g. Poston & Grabski, 2001; Hunton et al., 2003). Additionally, a growing body of research has also reported that ERP systems have the potential to transform the accounting profession and the role of the management accountant in particular from one of controller or scorekeeper to that of a strategic business advisor (also referred to as information or methodology experts and gatekeepers) (e.g. Burns & Vaivio, 2001; Granlund & Malmi, 2002; Caglio, 2003; Scapens & Jazayeri, 2003; Burns & Baldvinsdottir, 2005; Sayed, 2006; Byrne & Pierce, 2007; Rom & Rhode, 2007; Grabski et al., 2011; Schaltegger & Zvezdov, 2015). The strategic role that ERP systems have played within organisations has undoubtedly been instrumental in changing the role of the management accountant function, leading to the rise of the 'hybrid' professional who is less engaged with traditional accounting tasks and more involved in "understanding products and processes, business operations, information systems, marketing and strategy" (Caglio, 2003, p. 145).

Given their scale, it is therefore hardly surprising that ERP systems have dominated much academic and practitioner research activity in the accounting information systems space over recent decades. Reflecting this, in a widely cited literature review, Grabski et al. (2011) identified a significant body of research which investigated three major ERP research areas: the critical success factors of ERP, the organisational impact of ERP and the economic impact of ERP. From their review, Grabski et al. (2011) summarise what is known about ERP systems in the context of accounting. First, the literature has identified several critical success factors of ERP systems implementation. Second, ERP systems have the capability to provide a competitive advantage; however, this is short-lived. Third, the success of ERP is dependent on the extent to which the system is aligned with an organisation's culture, both internal and external to the organisation. Fourth, employees have an impact on ERP systems in sometimes unpredictable ways. Fifth, ERP systems evolve over time with extensions taking "the form of business intelligence (BI) applications, inter-organisational value–chain integration enhancements, or focus on security, auditability, and reporting, among other functions" (Grabski et al., 2011, p. 64). More recent literature reviews (e.g. Ali & Miller, 2017) reinforce the earlier findings of Grabski et al. (2011) in addition to providing new insights into the factors impacting on the successful adoption and implementation of ERP system, including those related to top management support, good project management teams and communications.

While both Grabski et al. (2011) and Ali & Miller (2017) acknowledge that more research is still needed concerning the impacts of ERP systems, more recently, there is evidence from both the practitioner and academic literatures that research efforts are shifting their focus from ERP systems to issues related to big data and digitalisation more generally, including machine learning (Andreassen, 2020), given its potential for use as a strategic asset and the significant opportunities and challenges it poses to the accounting and finance professions, and more widely, for example, in terms of the societal and ethical issues involved (e.g. Galliers et al., 2015, 2017).

Information as a strategic asset: big data and digitalisation

Big data refers to "datasets that are too large and complex to manipulate or interrogate with standard methods or tools" (Cao et al., 2015, p. 423). According to Warren et al. (2015), big data consists of both structured and unstructured data, with the latter including data derived from sources such as social media postings, email messages, customer loyalty cards, website traffic, Wi-Fi sensors, electronic tags and video streams. Five characteristics of big data have been identified in the literature (e.g. McAfee & Brynjolfsson, 2012; Elragal, 2014; Gandomi & Haider, 2015; Zhang et al., 2015):

- 'volume' refers to the enormous volumes of data associated with big data;
- 'velocity' represents the speed of data creation;
- 'variety' refers to the variety of data sources;
- 'veracity' is concerned with the accuracy and credibility of the underlying data sources; and
- 'value' refers to the value associated with big data sources when aligned with organisational objectives.

The scale of big data applications and their importance as a source of competitive advantage have been reported in several studies. For example, in an early survey conducted in China, France, Germany, India, South Africa, the United Kingdom and the United States of America (Accenture, 2014), 73% of the companies taking part indicated that they were already investing more than 20% of their total technology budget on big data analytics, some three-quarters of the executives surveyed expected spending to increase on big data in the year following the study and 80%–90% of the companies taking part in the study indicated that big data was either their organisation's top priority or in its top three priorities. Fast forward to 2021: the big data market had an estimated value of $162.6 billion in 2021[2] and is expected to grow to $273.4 billion by 2026 (McKinsey & Company, 2019). Evidence is also building that big data analytics have fundamentally changed the nature of competition and taken its rightful place in business strategy (McKinsey & Company, 2019; Accenture, 2020). Reflecting this, 58% of respondents to a recent data and analytics survey (Belissent, 2019) have already appointed a chief data officer, while another 26% are planning to do so. And it is not just the large companies who are investing in big data; small and medium-sized enterprises are investing in it too.

Research on big data and digitalisation more generally is now prevalent, and numerous examples exist where organisations have embraced the opportunities afforded by these technologies. For example, Schneider (2013) provides examples of organisations in the financial services industry (Morgan Stanley); the automotive industry (Ford); supply chain, logistics and industrial engineering (Union Pacific Railroad); retail (Walmart, Sears and Kmart, Amazon); and entertainment (Time Warner, Cablevision) sectors which are using big data to gain competitive advantage. More recently, Bloom (2015) provides examples of companies who are 'moving beyond the hype' and are reaping the benefits of their investment in big data. Examples include Southwest and Delta who are using big data to understand customer behaviours to enable customers to better track their luggage. Other success stories exist in the media sector where the Huffington Post and FT.com have successfully used big data to improve the user experience and to increase the relevance of their communications, respectively. Elsewhere, some of the most successful start-up companies of the 2000s, including Spotify, Deliveroo, Strava and Twitter, have harnessed big data to create value and develop a strong brand (Trabucchi et al., 2017).

As illustrated above, many examples are provided in the popular media and the professional press regarding the strategic benefits of big data and digitalisation. However, research regarding the implications of big data and digitalisation for business and management and for accounting practice and the role of accounting and finance professionals more specifically is still at a relatively early stage. For example, Suddaby et al. (2015) had explored big data and social media, but, as has often been the case, much of the literature had tended to treat the technology as a 'black box'. More recently, our understanding of digitalisation has evolved so that the impacts of workplace digital technologies on, for example, new patterns of work, new work practices and skills, new leadership styles and the like – the very future of organising in other words – are better understood (Baptista et al., 2020). In the next section of this chapter, the academic and practitioner research that has investigated the role of big data and digitalisation and its impact on accounting will be summarised.

Implications of big data and digitalisation for accounting practice

Given the increasing importance and use of big data – and digitalisation more generally – within organisations, a number of relatively recent academic articles and professional reports have addressed its implications for various aspects of accounting practice. For example, in a commentary for a special issue dedicated to the importance of big data for accounting and auditing, Griffin & Wright (2015) argue that it represents a significant challenge to the accounting profession. They further suggest that big data "by its very nature ... cannot avoid running head-on into the traditional systems of accounting and auditing that have served our profession so well in the past" (p. 377). Supporting this view, Vasarhelyi et al. (2015) suggest that "although changes in accounting practices and standards in response to big data have yet to happen, big data has the potential to cause a paradigm shift allowing economic transactions to be traced and measured earlier and deeper" (p. 384).

Reflecting its potential impact on accounting practice, several studies have considered the implications of big data on the audit function and the auditing profession in particular. For example, Cao et al. (2015) recognise the need for auditors to make a paradigm shift away from a focus on the use of small and clean databases to large messy datasets and the computational challenges of using big data. Cao et al. (2015) also identify a number of other issues which auditors will have to address in a big data context. These include the need for auditors to develop expertise in data analytics and the difficulties associated with access to suitable hardware and software to conduct data analytics. In another study, Yoon et al. (2015) argue that big data has the potential to enrich the audit function in terms of complementing traditional data and enhancing the reliability and relevance of audit evidence. However, that said, the authors also identify a number of critical challenges which potentially face the audit function. These include issues around the integration of big data with traditional audit evidence, the need for auditors to consider how big data might be weighted when compared to traditional data sources and difficulties associated with big data privacy issues. In yet another study conducted by Brown-Liburd et al. (2015), the behavioural implications of big data on the auditing profession are identified. These include the potential for information overload to occur when dealing with big data, the difficulties associated with identifying relevant, as opposed to irrelevant, information and the potential for the characteristics of big data to create ambiguity for the auditor. In addition, Brown-Liburd et al. (2015) argue that, historically, auditors have not been particularly skilful in terms of identifying patterns in financial and non-financial data (e.g. Bedard & Biggs, 1991; Asare et al., 2000). This deficiency in skills has obvious implications for the analyses of big data.

While earlier studies have generally adopted the perspective that the auditing function will embrace big data, Alles (2015) suggests two alternative scenarios in this regard. First, in line with their clients, auditors will fully embrace the big data revolution. Alternatively, based on historical evidence, auditors will lag in their analysis of big data. Drawing on the analogy of ERP systems and the subsequent need for computerised auditing which accompanied them, Alles (2015) goes on to posit that the most likely driver for use of big data within the auditing function will be that of client use where auditors will have no choice but to incorporate the analysis of big data into their practices. However, Alles (2015) points out that history suggests that the auditing profession has been slow in terms of adapting to technological changes. As a result, Alles (2015) argues that the use of big data in audit is unlikely to happen until the audit profession perceives it as a serious threat. Interestingly, Alles's (2015) perspective on the future of big data in auditing is in contrast to that of the Federation of European Accountants,[3] which, in a discussion document on the future of audit and assurance, suggest that the impact of big data technologies is likely to be revolutionary within the audit profession (Federation of European Accountants, February 2014). However, despite the hype around the potential for big data, a recent review by Gepp et al. (2018) suggests that auditing still lags behind in terms of the use of big data techniques.

In addition to the research summarised above, some limited research has also considered how big data is likely to influence management accounting practices. For example, Warren et al. (2015) suggest that big data can play a significant role in the operation of management control systems (MCSs) (Chenhall, 2003) and budgeting processes. With respect to the former, Warren et al. (2015) suggest that the analysis of big data has the potential to assist organisations identify which performance measures should be incorporated into MCSs and how these will motivate employees to behave in a manner which is consistent with the achievement of an organisation's strategic objectives. However, Warren et al. (2015) argue that management accountants will only be able to use big data effectively where they are supported by those with the expertise to understand, mine, transform and analyse big data. More recently, there has been growing recognition that big data and digitalisation more generally have the potential to substantially transform the field of management accounting and control (Möller et al., 2020). Despite this, Bhimani (2020) argues that while research into the impact of digitalisation on management accounting is growing, conceptional discussions around big data and its impact on management accounting are still limited.

A growing body of research has also more recently considered big data in the context of the accounting curriculum – see Chapters 13 and 14 for some skills accountants need. Recognising that accountants have had a long history of handling high volumes of data and expanding their expertise to do so, Janvrin & Watson (2017) argue that big data is increasingly important in the accounting curriculum. In their paper, Janvrin & Watson (2017) identify a range of resources that could support accounting academics, including free datasets and software, in addition to numerous big data resources provided by the Big 4 accounting firms. In addition, a number of recent academic papers have provided academics with guidance regarding the integration of big data into accounting courses such as financial accounting, managerial accounting, taxation and auditing (Sledgianowski et al., 2017). A number of case studies also address big data in the context of governance, journal entry testing for fraud and the application of data analytics software (Enget et al., 2017; Fay & Negangard, 2017; Kokina et al., 2017; Riggins & Klamm, 2017). Finally, Blix et al. (2021) investigate the extent to which audit textbooks integrate data analytics and are therefore fit for purpose. Their research reports that while some textbooks provide adequate coverage of both data analytics and associated skills, others are insufficient in this regard. Based on findings, Blix et al. (2021) recommend that all audit textbooks include a separate chapter on data analytics to provide a strong foundation.

The role and impact of other forms of digitalisation, including AI and blockchain technology, on accounting and the accounting profession have also been investigated, albeit to a less extent than big data (Carlin, 2019; Karajovic et al., 2019; Schmitz & Leoni, 2019; Tan & Low, 2019). Recent literature reviews conducted by Zhang et al. (2020) and Hasan (2022) illustrate the extent to which AI is already a key influence on the accounting and auditing profession. For example, Zhang et al. (2020) report on the widespread application of AI technologies within the Big 4 accounting firms for a number of purposes: to improve the speed and quality of decision making, to monitor voice interactions, to read and identify relevant information from multiple documents, to improve audit quality, to detect fraud and assess risks and to support tax analysis and compliance tasks. More recently, Hasan (2022), drawing on a substantial literature (e.g. Kokina & Davenport, 2017; Lee & Tajudeen, 2020; Mohammad et al., 2020; Zhang et al., 2020), identifies a number of areas (expert systems, continuous auditing, decision support systems, neural networks, deep learning and machine learning, natural language processing, fuzzy logic, genetic algorithms, robotic process automation and hybrid systems) where AI is having a significant impact on accounting and auditing. While Hasan (2022) points to the benefits of using AI in accounting, he also recognises the risks involved including the potential extinction of conventional accounting tasks, the significant cost commitment required, a lack of expertise among accountants' expertise and resistance from the accounting workforce.

As a form of digitalisation, blockchain technology is also widely recognised as having a role to play in the automation of accounting and auditing processes. While blockchain technology has the potential to enhance the trustworthiness of accounting information, it is in itself a double-edged sword in that it is viewed as a potential threat to the 'status quo' of the accounting and auditing profession and their practices (Schmitz & Leoni, 2019). Consistent with a lack of skills reported for other technologies, Schmitz & Leoni (2019) also argue that if accountants and auditors are to meet the demands of industry, they must broaden both their skillset and knowledge of blockchain technology. Additional insights into the role of blockchain technology in the accounting profession are also provided by Tan & Low (2019). While recognising that the role of the accountant will evolve in that they will no longer be the central or only authority of a blockchain-based accounting information system, and that audit is likely to become more efficient and effective, Tan & Low (2019) argue that accountants will nevertheless remain very relevant and much needed in the audit process.

Implications of big data and digitalisation on the role of the accounting and finance professions

While the extant academic literature has tended to focus on the implications of big data for specific accounting functions (e.g., auditing, managerial accounting), and more recently, the accounting curriculum, a growing body of literature (mainly professional), has also investigated how big data and other forms of digitalisation are shaping the future of the accounting and finance professions. In particular, the Association of Certified Accountants (ACCA) and the Institute of Management Accountants (IMA) appear to be taking a lead in this regard. For example, an ACCA & IMA (2013a) report investigated the ten top technology trends which have the potential to fundamentally alter the accounting and finance professions. Drawing on data collected from interviews, email consultations, a series of events and a survey of over 2,100 ACCA and IMA members worldwide, the report identified big data and AI as the second- and third-most important technologies. According to the ACCA & IMA (2013a) report,

> accountants and finance professionals have a significant role to play in the increasingly connected and interconnected ecosystem that will emerge as the top 10 technologies [e.g. mobile, big data, artificial intelligence and robotics, cybersecurity] come together to create the 'new normal'.
>
> *(p. 12)*[4]

In another ground-breaking report, ACCA & IMA (2013b) argue that the role of accounting and finance professionals will change as businesses are transformed by the big data 'revolution' in particular. According to the authors, accounting and finance professionals can respond to big data in one of two ways: they can "do nothing and watch as advances in technology commoditise their skills and downgrade their role" (p. 25), or they can "adapt to the new environment and increase their influence and the value they add to organisations" (p. 25). However, to do this, accounting and finance professionals will need to reinvent themselves.

The authors of the ACCA & IMA (2013b) report also argue that the increasing use of big data within organisations presents both opportunities and challenges for accounting and finance professionals. In terms of the former, it is argued that big data presents an opportunity for finance professionals to adopt a more strategic decision-making role within businesses. With respect to the challenges, big data will also present new problems for accounting and finance professionals over the next decade. For example, new standards for measuring and valuing big data will need to be developed, and issues around ethics and privacy of data in the context of big data will need to be addressed. Such concerns are echoed in the information systems literature. For example, Newell & Marabelli (2015) raised several major concerns regarding society's increasing reliance on what they term "algorithmic decision-making". As a result, "they made an urgent call for action for research by IS scholars that would critically assess society's apparent taken-for-granted and unknowing acquiescence to this increasingly prevalent phenomenon" (Galliers et al., 2015, p. I).

Taken together, the opportunities and challenges identified by ACCA & IMA (2013b) suggest a new professional agenda for accounting and finance professionals – one that comprises three imperatives, which should be addressed over the next five to ten years. The first of these is concerned with the need to develop new metrics and standards to understand and derive the financial value of big data and other forms of digitalisation as intangible assets. This would include, for example, a consideration of the rate of obsolescence of big data and how this can be reflected through appropriate depreciation of the intangible asset. Accounting and finance professionals will also need to develop new metrics through the collection of unstructured data to be combined and integrated with other datasets for the purposes of assessing organisational performance. The second imperative identified by ACCA and IMA is the need for accounting and finance professionals to develop analytical skills to bridge the gap between "data science and data art, combining analytical skills and sophisticated models developed by mathematicians and statisticians with the skills of data art and data 'storytelling'" (p. 7). The final imperative is the requirement for accounting and finance professionals to engage in creating a visual language of data 'art' whereby 'telling the story' of big data will be increasingly important. To that end, ACCA & IMA (2013b) suggest that there will be a growing need for accounting and finance professions to have the capability to integrate statistical and analytical skills with storytelling which can be used in performance management dashboards. However, despite the challenges and imperatives of engaging with big data, ACCA argue that "accountants and finance professionals are well placed to take an active role in big data by providing a new and critical service: 'distilling' vast amounts of information into actionable insights" (p. 5).

The implications of big data and other technologies, as a driver of change within the accounting and finance professions, are given further consideration in a more recent report published by ACCA (2016). Using data collected from over 2,000 professional accountants and C-suite executives[5] employed worldwide, the authors argue that its findings provide a "fresh perspective on the outlook for professional accountants and their role in society in 2025" (p. 18). To that end, it specifically discusses the technical, ethical and interpersonal skills and the competencies which will be required of professional accountants in the future. In particular, the report identifies that digitalisation, including big data, will impact the skills of the accountant in a number of areas: namely, audit and assurance, corporate reporting, strategic planning and performance management and tax. For example, accountants will need to develop a range of skills to effectively deal with big data and other forms of digitalisation: IT knowledge; the ability to find, analyse and present data in an accessible and meaningful way; and the ability to use analytics to unlock value in both financial and non-financial data to provide insights and future predictions. The ACCA (2016) report concludes by stating that

> vital knowledge of and skills with digital technologies appear to be lacking, but all accountants need to be aware of and able to apply a range of emerging technologies; many will need to be expert users of predictive analytics, big data and smart software.
>
> *(p. 62)*

The need for accountants to be aware of the ethical implications of digitalisation, and the role that they can play in driving ethical AI, is also highlighted in a recent ACCA & IMA (2020) report: "managing the transition to mass adoption of AI in an ethical, responsible manner is essential if we are to derive sustainable long-term value from it" (p. 11). ACCA & IMA (2020) also make the point that data and technology will continue to have a strong influence on the Chief Financial Officers (CFO) of the future. Furthermore, it is essential that the CFO has an understanding of the impact of digital transformation and the skills that will be needed by accountants to address the challenges presented.

Concluding remarks

In this chapter, we have primarily considered the potential impact of big data – and digitalisation more generally – for accounting practice and accounting and finance professions. We acknowledge the clear potential that digital technologies have had – and are continuing to have – on organisations and on work practices, but we have also tried to take a balanced approach in that we avoid much of the hyperbole that often goes hand-in-hand with the IT industry. History is replete with examples of so-called IT 'solutions' that are purveyed as 'the' answer to the question of the strategic use of information. What we have tried to do here is to demonstrate that it is the skilled use and understanding of these technologies that are paramount.

Thus, we argue that the accounting and finance professions should be very much aware of the impacts, risks, challenges and opportunities arising from the use of new technologies in organisations, such as big data, drawing on lessons that should have been learned from the impacts – expected and unexpected (cf. Robey & Boudreau, 1999) – of prior technological developments, such as ERP systems. In particular, the accounting and finance professions need to urgently consider how best to address the numerous challenges associated with big data and other forms of digitalisation identified in this chapter: the need to develop new standards and metrics, issues around ethics and privacy, the need to develop appropriate expertise towards more effective big data analyses and storytelling, the need to understand how big data complements traditional accounting data and an understanding of how to deal with information overload and ambiguity associated with big data usage. Although not specifically covered in this chapter, accounting and finance professionals should also be cognisant of recent arguments which question "commonly held, and often implicit, assumptions about the nature of data" that "do not necessarily represent the world transparently" (Jones, 2019, p. 13). Such arguments challenge assumptions about data, and big data in particular, including that related to its objectivity, neutrality, infallibility, usability and provenance.

We recognise, too, that much research is required to be done in this sphere. We would advocate trans-disciplinary (cf. Galliers, 1995, 2003; Whittington, 2014) and *in situ* qualitative research that takes a practice perspective (cf. Jarzabkowski & Spee, 2009; Peppard et al., 2014) – this, with a view to uncovering the actual practices of individuals in decision making that create impact and create strategy. To support such practice, consideration also needs to be given to whether academics are appropriately trained to conduct such research in academia, not just in the area of accounting but more widely (Galliers & Huang, 2012). In the context of accounting practice, a range of skills and competencies will be required, which will require accounting and finance professionals (academics and practitioners) to develop new competencies and partner with colleagues in the strategic management and IS/IT communities in order to avoid being left behind but, more importantly, to contribute actively in understanding the multifaceted and complex nature of these emerging phenomena. After all, big data is just one in a long line of new technologies that have – and will continue to have – profound effects on work life, organisations and society. A proactive, forward-looking stance on the part of the accounting and finance professions is therefore called for. In other words, this chapter is a call for further action in this regard.

Notes

1 'Digitalisation' (see, e.g. Parviainen et al. (2017)) is preferrable to the term 'digitisation' as it captures business processes, not just the conversion of data to a digital form.
2 https://www.marketsandmarkets.com/Market-Reports/big-data-market-1068.html.

3 The Federation of European Accountants is the voice of the European accounting professions. It has a membership of approximately 800,000 professional accountants who are employed in private practice (small, medium and large accountancy firms), government and education.

4 Similar views have been expressed in a report published by the Chartered Institute of Management Accountants (CIMA) (2013).

5 'C-suite executive' is a widely used 'slang' term' which is used to collectively refer to an organisation's most senior executives.

References

ACCA (2016). Professional accountants – the future: Drivers of change and future skills (June), accessed at https://www.accaglobal.com/an/en/technical-activities/technical-resources-search/2016/june/professional-accountants-the-future-report.html, 21st June 2021.

ACCA & IMA (2013a). Digital Darwinism: Thriving in the face of technology change (October), accessed at https://www.accaglobal.com/uk/en/technical-activities/technical-resources-search/2013/october/digital-darwinism.html, 21st June 2021.

ACCA & IMA. (2013b). Big data: Its power and peril, accessed at https://www.accaglobal.com/uk/en/technical-activities/technical-resources-search/2013/december/big-data-its-power-and-perils.html, 22nd June 2021.

ACCA & IMA (2020). The CFO of the future (September), accessed at https://www.accaglobal.com/pk/en/professional-insights/pro-accountants-the-future/cfo_future.html, 26th July 2021.

Accenture. (2014). Industrial internet insights report for 2015, accessed at https://www.accenture.com/gb-en/_acnmedia/Accenture/next-gen/reassembling-industry/pdf/Accenture-Industrial-Internet-Changing-Competitive-Landscape-Industries.pdf, 29th July 2016.

Accenture. (2020). Data 2020: 3 big trends powering the data agenda, available at: https://www.accenture.com/us-en/blogs/software-engineering-blog/shail-jain-data-trends-2020, 26th July 2021.

Akerker, R. (2019). *Artificial Intelligence for Business*. Cham, Switzerland: Springer International Publishing.

Ali, M., & Miller, L. (2017). ERP system implementation in large enterprises - A systematic literature review. *Journal of Enterprise Information Management*, 30(4), 666–692.

Alles, M. G. (2015). Drivers of the use and facilitators and obstacles of the evolution of big data by the audit profession. *Accounting Horizons*, 29(2), 439–449.

Andreassen, R. I. (2020). Digital technology and changing roles: A management accountant's dream or nightmare? *Journal of Management Control*, 31, 209–238.

Asare, S., Trompeter, G., & Wright, A. (2000). The effect of accountability and time budgets on auditors' testing strategies judgments. *Contemporary Accounting Research*, 17(4), 539–560.

Baptista, J., Wilson, A., Galliers, R. D., & Bynghall, S. (2016). Social media and the emergence of *Reflexiveness* as a new capability for open strategy. *Long Range Planning*, 50, 322–336.

Baptista, J., Stein, M-K., Klein, S., Watson-Manheim, M. B., & Lee, J. (2020). Digital work and organisational transformation: Emergent Digital/Human work configurations in modern organisations. *The Journal of Strategic Information Systems*, 29(2), 101618.

Batistic, S., & van der Laken, P. (2019). History, evolution and future of big data and analytics: A bibliometric analysis of its relationship to performance in organizations. *British Journal of Management*, 30, 229–251.

Bedard, J. C., & Biggs, S. R. (1991). Pattern recognition, hypotheses generation, and auditor performance in an analytical task. *The Accounting Review*, 66(3), 622–642.

Belissent, J. (2019). Chief data officers rule and deliver results, accessed at https://go.forrester.com/blogs/chief-data-officers-rule-and-deliver-results/, 26th July 2021.

Bhimani, A. (2020). Digital data and management accounting: Why we need to rethink research methods. *Journal of Management Control*, 31, 9–23.

Bhimani, A., & Willcocks, L. (2014). Digitisation, 'Big Data' and the transformation of accounting information. *Accounting and Business Research*, 44(4), 469–490.

Blix, L. H., Edmonds, M. A., & Sorensen, K. B. (2021). How well do audit textbooks currently integrate data analytics. *Journal of Accounting Education*, 55, 1–11.

Bloom, A., (2015). 20 Examples of ROI and results with Big Data, accessed at https://tanzu.vmware.com/content/blog/20-examples-of-roi-and-results-with-big-data, 26th July 2021.

Brown-Liburd, H., Issa, H., & Lombardi, D. (2015). Behavioural implications of Big Data's impact on audit judgment and decision making and future research directions. *Accounting Horizons*, 29(2), 451–468.

Burns, J., & Baldvinsdottir, G. (2005). An institutional perspective of and praxis. *European Accounting Review*, 14, 725–757.

Burns, J., & Vaivio, J. (2001). Management accounting change. *Management Accounting Research*, 12, 389–402.

Byrne, S., & Pierce, B. (2007). Towards a more comprehensive understanding of the roles of management accountants. *European Accounting Review*, 16(3), 469–498.

Caglio, A. (2003). Enterprise resource planning systems and accountants: Towards hybridization? *The European Account Review*, 12(1), 123–153.

Cao, M., Chychyla, R., & Stewart, T. (2015). Big Data analytics in financial statement audits. *Accounting Horizons*, 29(2), 423–429.

Carlin, T. (2019). Blockchain and the journey beyond double entry. *Australian Accounting Review*, 29, 305–311.

Chartered Institute of Management Accountant (CIMA). (2013), *From Insight to Impact: Unlocking Opportunities in Big Data*. London: Chartered Institute of Management Accountants.

Chen, H., Chiang, R. H. L., & Storey, V. (2012). Business intelligence and analytics: From big data to big impact. *MIS Quarterly*, 36(4), 1165–1188.

Chenhall, R. H. (2003). Management control systems design within its organizational context; findings from contingency-based research and directions for the future. *Accounting, Organizations and Society*, 28(2–3), 127–168.

Clemons, E. K. (1986). Information systems for sustainable competitive advantage. *Information & Management*, 11(3), 131–136.

Davenport, T. H. (1996). Why re-engineering failed: The fad that forgot people. *Fast Company*, Premier Issue, 70–74.

Davenport, T. H. (2000). *Mission Critical: Realizing the Promise of Enterprise Systems*. Boston, MA: Harvard Business School Press.

Davenport, T. H., & Short, J. E. (1990). The new industrial engineering: Information technology and business process redesign. *MIT Sloan Management Review*, 3(4), 11–27.

Elragal, A. (2014). ERP and big data: The inept couple. *Procedia Technology*, 16, 242–249.

Enget, K., Saucedo, G., & Wright, N. (2017). Mystery, Inc. A Big Data case. *Journal of Accounting Education*, 38, 9–22.

Fay, R., & Negangard, E. M. (2017). Manual journal entry testing: Data analytics and the risk of fraud. *Journal of Accounting Education*, 38, 37–49.

Federation of European Accountants (2014), *Opening a Discussion: The Future of Audit and Assurance*. February, Brussels: FEE.

Galliers, R. D. (1995). A manifesto for information management research in the late 1990s. *British Journal of Management*, 6(December), Special Edition, S45-S52.

Galliers, R. D. (1997). Against obliteration: Reducing the risk in business process change, in C. Sauer & P. Yetton & Associates, (eds.), *Steps to the Future - Fresh Thinking on the Dynamics of Organisational Transformation*, San Francisco, CA: Jossey-Bass Inc., 161–180.

Galliers, R. D. (2003). Change as crisis or growth? Toward a trans-disciplinary view of Information Systems as a field of study – a response to Benbasat and Zmud's call for returning to the IT artefact. *Journal of the Association for Information Systems*, 4(1), 337–351.

Galliers, R. D. (2004). Reflections on information systems strategizing, in C. Avgerou, C. Ciborra & F. Land, (eds.), *The Social Study of Information and Communication Technology: Innovation, Actors, and Contexts*, Oxford: Oxford University Press, 231–262.

Galliers, R. D. (2006). On confronting some of the common myths of Information Systems strategy discourse, in R. Mansell, C. Avgerou, D. Quah & R. Silverstone (eds.), *The Oxford Handbook of Information and Communication Technologies*, Oxford: Oxford University Press, 225–243.

Galliers, R. D. (2011). Further developments in information systems strategising: Unpacking the concept, in R. D. Galliers & W. L. Currie (eds.). *The Oxford Handbook of Management Information Systems: Critical Perspectives and New Directions*, Oxford: Oxford University Press, 329–345.

Galliers, R. D., & Huang, J. (2012). The teaching of qualitative research methods in Information Systems: An explorative study utilising learning theory, *European Journal of Information Systems*, 21(2), 119–134.

Galliers, R. D., Newell, S., Shanks, G., & Topi, H. (2015). Call for papers: The challenges and opportunities of 'datification'. Strategic impacts of 'big' (and 'small') and real time data – for society and for organizational decision makers. *The Journal of Strategic Information Systems*, 24(1), I–II.

Galliers, R. D., Newell, S., Shanks, G., & Topi, H, (2017). Datification and its human, organizational and societal effects: The strategic opportunities and challenges of algorithmic decision-making. *The Journal of Strategic Information Systems*, 26, 185–190.

Galliers, R. D., & Swan, J. A. (1999). Information systems and strategic change: A critical review of business process re-engineering. In W. L. Currie & R. D. Galliers (eds.) *Rethinking Management Information Systems*, Oxford: Oxford University Press, 361–387.

Gandomi, A., & Haider, M. (2015). Beyond the hype: Big data concepts, methods, and analytics. *International Journal of Information Management*, 35, 137–144.

Gartner (2020). Forecast analysis: Analytics and business intelligence software, worldwide, accessed at https://www.gartner.com/en/documents/3990149-forecast-analysis-analytics-and-business-intelligence-so, 28th July 2021.

Gepp, A., Linnenluecke, M. K., O'Neill, J. T., & Smith, T. (2018). Big data techniques in auditing research and practice: Current trends and future opportunities. *Journal of Accounting Literature*, 40, 102–115.

Grabski, S. V., Leech, S. A., & Schmidt, P. J. (2011). A review of ERP research: A future agenda for accounting information systems. *Journal of Information Systems*, 25(1), 37–78.

Granlund, M., & Malmi, T. (2002). Moderate impact of ERPS on management accounting: A lag or permanent outcome? *Management Accounting Research*, 13, 299–321.

Griffin, P. A., & Wright, A. M. (2015). Commentaries on Big Data's importance for accounting and auditing. *Accounting Horizons*, 29(2), 377–379.

Grover, V., Lindberg, A., Benbasat, I., & Lyytinen, K. (2020). The perils and promises of Big Data research in Information Systems. *Journal of the Association for Information Systems*, 21(2), 268–291.

Günther, W. A., Mehrizi, M. H. R., Feldberg, F., & Huysman, M. H. (2017). Debating big data: A literature review on realizing value from big data. *The Journal of Strategic Information Systems*, 26(3), 191–209.

Hammer, M. (1990). Don't automate, obliterate. *Harvard Business Review*, 68(4), 104–112.

Hasan, A. R. (2022). Artificial intelligence in accounting & auditing: A literature review, *Open Journal of Business and Management*, 10, 440–465.

Hirschheim, R. (2021). The attack on understanding: How big data and theory have led us Astray: A comment on Gary Smith's data mining fool's gold. *Journal of Information Technology*, 36(2), 176–183.

Huang, J., Baptista, J., & Galliers, R. D. (2013). Reconceptualizing rhetorical practices in organizations: The impact of social media on internal communications. *Information & Management*, 50(2–3), 112–124.

Hunton, J. E., Lippincott, B., & Reck, J. L. (2003). Enterprise resource planning systems: Comparing firm performance of adopters and nonadopters. *International Journal of Accounting Information Systems*, 4, 165–184.

Janvrin, D. J., & Watson, M. W. (2017). "Big Data": A new twist to accounting. *Journal of Accounting Education*, 38, 3–8.

Jarzabkowski, P., & Spee, A. P. (2009). Strategy-as-practice: A review and future directions for the field. *International Journal of Management Reviews*, 11(1), 69–95.

Jones, M. (2019). What we talk about when we talk about (big) data. *The Journal of Strategic Information Systems*, 28(1), 3–16.

Kalling, T. (2003). ERP systems and the strategic management processes that lead to competitive advantage. *Information Resources Management Journal*, 16(4), 46–67.

Karajovic, M., Kim, H. M., & Laskowski, M. (2019). Thinking outside the block: Projected phases of blockchain integration in the accounting industry, *Australian Accounting Review*, 29, 319–330.

Karpovsky, A., & Galliers, R. D. (2015). Aligning in practice: From current cases to a new agenda. *Journal of Information Technology*, 30(2), 136–160.

Kokina, J., & Davenport, T. H. (2017). The emergence of artificial intelligence: How automation is changing auditing. *Journal of Emerging Technologies in Accounting*, 14, 115–122.

Kokina, J., Panamanova, D., & Corbett, A. (2017). The role of data visualization and analytics in performance management: Guiding entrepreneurial growth decision. *Journal of Accounting Education*, 38, 50–62.

Land, F. (1996). The new alchemist: Or how to transmute base organisations into corporations of gleaming gold. *The Journal of Strategic Information Systems*, 5(1), 5–17.

Lee, C. S., & Tajudeen, F. P. (2020). Usage and impact of artificial intelligence on accounting: 213 evidence from Malaysian organisations. *Asian Journal of Business and Accounting*, 13, 213–240.

Loureiro, S. M. C., Guerreiro, J. & Tussyadiah, I. (2021). Artificial intelligence in business: State of the art and future research agenda. *Journal of Business Research*, 129, 911–926.

Marabelli, M., & Galliers, R. D. (2016). A reflection on information systems strategizing: The role of power and everyday practices. *Information Systems Journal*, 27(3), 347–366.

Markus, M. L. (2017). Datification, organizational strategy, and IS research: What's the score? *The Journal of Strategic Information Systems*, 26(3), 233–241.

McAfee, A., & Brynjolfsson, E. (2012). Big data: The management revolution. *Harvard Business Review*, 90, 60–66.

McFarlan, F. W. (1984). Information technology changes the way you compete. *Harvard Business Review*, 62(3), 98–102.

McKinsey & Company. (2019). Catch then if you can: How leaders in data and analytics have pulled ahead, accessed at: https://www.mckinsey.com/~/media/McKinsey/Business%20Functions/McKinsey%20Analytics/Our%20Insights/Catch%20them%20if%20you%20can%20How%20leaders%20in%20data%20and%20analytics%20have%20pulled%20ahead/Catch-them-if-you-can-How-leaders-in-data-and-analytics-have-pulled-ahead.ashx, 28th July 2021.

Mohammad, S. J., et al. (2020). How artificial intelligence changes the future of accounting industry. *International Journal of Economics and Business Administration*, 8, 478–488.

Möller, K., Schäffer, U., & Verbeeten, F. (2020) Digitalization in management accounting and control: An editorial. *Journal of Management Control*, 31, 1–8.

Newell, S., & Marabelli, M. (2015). Strategic opportunities (and challenges) of algorithmic decision-making: A call for action on the long-term societal effects of 'datification'. *The Journal of Strategic Information Systems*, 24(1), 3–14.

Parviainen, P., Tihinen, M., Kääriäinen, J. & Teppola, S. (2017). Tackling the digitalization challenge: How to benefit from digitalization in practice. *International Journal of Information Systems and Project Management*, 5(1), 63–77.

Peppard, J., & Ward, J. (2004). Beyond strategic information systems: Towards an IS capability. *The Journal of Strategic Information Systems*, 13(2), 167–194.

Peppard, J., Galliers, R. D., & Thorogood, A. (2014). Information systems strategy as practice: Micro strategy and strategizing for IS. *The Journal of Strategic Information Systems*, 23(1), 1–10.

Porter, M. E., & Millar, V. E. (1985). How information gives you competitive advantage. *Harvard Business Review*, 63(4), 149–160.

Poston, R., & Grabski, S. (2001). Financial impacts of enterprise resource planning implementations. *International Journal of Accounting Information Systems*, 2, 271–294.

Riggins, F. J., & Klamm, B. K. (2017). Data governance case at KrauseMcMahon LLP in an era of self-service BI and Big Data. *Journal of Accounting Education*, 38, 23–36.

Robey, D., & Boudreau, M. C. (1999). Accounting for the contradictory organizational consequences of information technology: Theoretical directions and methodological implications. *Information Systems Research*, 10(2), 167–185.

Rom, A., & Rohde, C. (2007). Management accounting and integrated information systems: A literature review. *International Journal of Accounting Information Systems*, 8, 40–68.

Sayed, H. E. (2006). ERPs and accountants' expertise: The construction of relevance. *Journal of Enterprise Information Management*, 19(1), 83–96.

Scapens, W. R., & Jazayeri, M. (2003). ERP systems and management accounting change: Opportunities or impacts? A research note. *European Accounting Review*, 12(1), 201–233.

Schaltegger, S., & Zvezdov, D. (2015). Gatekeepers of sustainability information: Exploring the roles of accountants. *Journal of Accounting & Organizational Change*, 11, 333–361.

Schmitz, J., & Leoni, G. (2019). Accounting and auditing at the time of blockchain technology: A research agenda. *Australian Accounting Review*, 29, 331–342.

Schneider, S. (2013). 20+ Examples of getting results with big data, May 15th, accessed at https://blog.pivotal.io/pivotal/news/20-examples-of-getting-results-with-big-data, 29th July 2021.

Shollo, A., & Galliers, R. D. (2015). Towards an understanding of the role of business intelligence systems in organisational knowing. *Information Systems Journal*, 26(4), 339–367.

Sledgianowski, D., Gomaa, M., & Tan, C. (2017). Toward integration of Big Data, technology and information system competencies into the accounting curriculum. *Journal of Accounting Education*, 38, 81–93.

Suddaby, R., Saxton, G. D., & Gunz, S. (2015). Twittering change: The institutional work of domain change in accounting expertise. *Accounting, Organizations and Society*, 45, 52–68.

Tan, B. S., & Low, K. Y. (2019). Blockchain as the database engine in the accounting system. *Australian Accounting Review*, 29, 312–318.

Trabucchi, D., Buganza, T., Dell'Era, C., & Pellizzoni, E. (2017). Exploring the inbound and outbound strategies enabled by user generated big data: Evidence from leading smartphone applications. *Creativity and Innovation Management*, 27, 42–55.

Vasarhelyi, M. A., Kogan, A., & Tuttle, B. M. (2015). Big data in accounting: An overview. *Accounting Horizons*, 29(2), 381–396.

Vial, G. (2018). Understanding digital transformation: A review and a research agenda. *The Journal of Strategic Information Systems*, 28(2), 118–144.

Warren, J. D., Moffitt, K. C., & Byrnes, P. (2015). How big data will change accounting. *Accounting Horizons*, 29(2), 397–407.

Whittington, R. (2006). Completing the practice turn in strategy research. *Organization Studies*, 27(5), 613–634.

Whittington, R. (2014). Information systems strategy and strategy-as-practice: A joint agenda. *The Journal of Strategic Information Systems*, 23(1), 87–91.

Whittington, R., Molloy, M., Mayer, M., & Smith, A. (2006). Practices of strategising/organising: Broadening strategy work and skills. *Long Range Planning*, 39(6), 615–629.

Wright, S. A., & Schultz, A. E. (2018). The rising tide of artificial intelligence and business automation: Developing an ethical framework. *Business Horizons*, 61(6), 823–832.

Yoon, K., Hoogduin, L., & Zhang, L. (2015). Big data as complementary audit evidence. *Accounting Horizons*, 29(2), 431–438.

Zhang, J., Yang, X., & Appelbaum, D. (2015). Toward effective analysis in continuous auditing. *Accounting Horizons*, 29(2), 469–476.

Zhang, Y., Feng, X., Xie, Y., & Xu, A. H. (2020). The impact of artificial intelligence and blockchain on the accounting profession. *IEEE Access*, 8, 110461–11047, accessed at https://ieeexplore.ieee.org/stamp/stamp.jsp?arnumber=9110603, 27th February 2022.

INDEX

Note: **Bold** page numbers refer to tables; *italic* page numbers refer to figures and page numbers followed by "n" denote endnotes.

dashboarding 211–212; temporal data analysis 227–231; traditional reporting 210
V-model 52
Volkoff, O. 331
volume 195
voluntary disclosure users 175–176

Wang, R.Y. 242
Warren, J.D. 351, 353
waterfall model 52
Watson, M.W. 354
Weber, K. 249
Weller, A. 181
wide area networks (WANs) 37, *37*
Wiegmann, L. 175

Willcocks, L. 56, 163
Windsperger, J. 79
Wing, J.M. 191
wired networking 86
wireless networks 35
work-centred analysis 68
WorldCom 10
Worrell, J.L. 123
Wright, A.M. 57, 352
Wu, L.Y. 78

Yazdifar, H. 16
Yoon, K. 57, 261, 353

Zhang, Y. 354